Vauxhall Cavalier Owners Workshop Manual

Steve Rendle

Models covered

Vauxhall Cavalier front-wheel-drive models with four-cylinder petrol engines, including special/limited editions; Saloon and Hatchback
1398 cc, 1598 cc, 1796 cc & 1998 cc (inc. dohc)

Covers most features of Opel Vectra
Does not not cover Diesel engine, V6 engine, air conditioning or four-wheel-drive models

THE BOOK ®

(1570-1W6)

ABCDE
FGHIJ
KLMNO
PQSRT
2

Haynes Publishing
Sparkford Nr Yeovil
Somerset BA22 7JJ England

Haynes Publications, Inc
861 Lawrence Drive
Newbury Park
California 91320 USA

Acknowledgements
Thanks are due to Champion Spark Plug who supplied the illustrations showing spark plug conditions, to Holt Lloyd Limited who supplied the illustrations showing bodywork repair, and to Duckhams Oils who provided lubrication data. Certain other illustrations are the copyright of Vauxhall Motors Ltd, and are used with their permission. Thanks are also due to Sykes-Pickavant Limited, who provided some of the workshop tools, and all those people at Sparkford who helped in the production of this manual.

© **Haynes Publishing 1994**

A book in the **Haynes Owners Workshop Manual Series**

Printed by J. H. Haynes & Co. Ltd., Sparkford, Nr Yeovil, Somerset BA22 7JJ, England

ISBN 1 85010 967 2

British Library Cataloguing in Publication Data
A catalogue record for this book is available from the British Library

We take great pride in the accuracy of information given in this manual, but vehicle manufacturers make alterations and design changes during the production run of a particular vehicle of which they do not inform us. No liability can be accepted by the authors or publishers for loss, damage or injury caused by any errors in, or omissions from, the information given.

Restoring and Preserving our Motoring Heritage

Few people can have had the luck to realise their dreams to quite the same extent and in such a remarkable fashion as John Haynes, Founder and Chairman of the Haynes Publishing Group.

Since 1965 his unique approach to workshop manual publishing has proved so successful that millions of Haynes Manuals are now sold every year throughout the world, covering literally thousands of different makes and models of cars, vans and motorcycles.

A continuing passion for cars and motoring led to the founding in 1985 of a Charitable Trust dedicated to the restoration and preservation of our motoring heritage. To inaugurate the new Museum, John Haynes donated virtually his entire private collection of 52 cars.

Now with an unrivalled international collection of over 210 veteran, vintage and classic cars and motorcycles, the Haynes Motor Museum in Somerset is well on the way to becoming one of the most interesting Motor Museums in the world.

A 70 seat video cinema, a cafe and an extensive motoring bookshop, together with a specially constructed one kilometre motor circuit, make a visit to the Haynes Motor Museum a truly unforgettable experience.

Every vehicle in the museum is preserved in as near as possible mint condition and each car is run every six months on the motor circuit.

Enjoy the picnic area set amongst the rolling Somerset hills. Peer through the William Morris workshop windows at cars being restored, and browse through the extensive displays of fascinating motoring memorabilia.

From the 1903 Oldsmobile through such classics as an MG Midget to the mighty 'E' Type Jaguar, Lamborghini, Ferrari Berlinetta Boxer, and Graham Hill's Lola Cosworth, there is something for everyone, young and old alike, at this Somerset Museum.

Haynes Motor Museum

Situated mid-way between London and Penzance, the Haynes Motor Museum is located just off the A303 at Sparkford, Somerset (home of the Haynes Manual) and is open to the public 7 days a week all year round, except Christmas Day and Boxing Day.

Contents

Spark plug condition and bodywork colour section between pages 32 and 33

Vauxhall Cavalier 1.6 L Saloon

About this manual

Its aim

The aim of this manual is to help you get the best value from your vehicle. It can do so in several ways. It can help you decide what work must be done (even should you choose to get it done by a garage), provide information on routine maintenance and servicing, and give a logical course of action and diagnosis when random faults occur. However, it is hoped that you will use the manual by tackling the work yourself. On simpler jobs it may even be quicker than booking the car into a garage and going there twice, to leave and collect it. Perhaps most important, a lot of money can be saved by avoiding the costs a garage must charge to cover its labour and overheads.

The manual has drawings and descriptions to show the function of the various components so that their layout can be understood. Then the tasks are described and photographed in a step-by-step sequence so that even a novice can do the work.

Its arrangement

The manual is divided into eleven Chapters, each covering a logical sub-division of the vehicle. The Chapters are each divided into Sections, numbered with single figures, eg 5; and the Sections into paragraphs (or sub-sections), with decimal numbers following on from the Section they are in, eg 5.1, 5.2, 5.3 etc.

It is freely illustrated, especially in those parts where there is a detailed sequence of operations to be carried out. There are two forms of illustration: figures and photographs. The figures are numbered in sequence with decimal numbers, according to their position in the Chapter – eg Fig. 6.4 is the fourth drawing/illustration in Chapter 6. Photographs carry the same number (either individually or in related groups) as the Section or sub-section to which they relate.

There is an alphabetical index at the back of the manual as well as a contents list at the front. Each Chapter is also preceded by its own individual contents list.

References to the 'left' or 'right' of the vehicle are in the sense of a person in the driver's seat facing forwards.

Unless otherwise stated, nuts and bolts are removed by turning anti-clockwise, and tightened by turning clockwise.

Vehicle manufacturers continually make changes to specifications and recommendations, and these, when notified, are incorporated into our manuals at the earliest opportunity.

We take great pride in the accuracy of information given in this manual, but vehicle manufacturers make alterations and design changes during the production run of a particular vehicle of which they do not inform us. No liability can be accepted by the authors or publishers for loss, damage or injury caused by any errors in, or omissions from, the information given.

Project vehicles

The vehicles used in the preparation of this manual, and which appear in many of the photographic sequences, were; a 1989 1.6 L Hatchback, a 1989 2.0 SRi Hatchback, and a 1990 GSi 2000 Saloon.

Introduction to the Vauxhall Cavalier

The Cavalier covered by this manual was first introduced to the UK market in October 1988. Although there is a fundamental similarity to its predecessor, the later version is much improved in all respects. This manual covers models with petrol engines and front-wheel-drive, but other models in the range are fitted with diesel engines, and four-wheel drive is available on certain models.

Five petrol engines are available: 1.4, 1.6, 1.8 and 2.0 litre single overhead camshaft (sohc) versions, and a 2.0 litre double overhead camshaft (dohc) version, which is fitted to the performance-orientated GSi 2000 model. All the engines are of well-proven design and, provided regular maintenance is carried out, are unlikely to give trouble.

Saloon and Hatchback body styles are available, although the GSi model is only available in Saloon form.

The GSi 2000 model utilises the floorpan layout of the four-wheel-drive models, in order to accommodate fully-independent rear suspension. Other models in the range have semi-independent torsion beam rear suspension.

A five-speed manual gearbox is fitted as standard to all models, and four-speed automatic transmission is available as an option on certain models, although automatic transmission is not covered by this manual.

A wide range of standard and optional equipment is available within the Cavalier range to suit most tastes, including an anti-lock braking system.

For the home mechanic, the Cavalier is a straightforward vehicle to maintain, and most of the items requiring frequent attention are easily accessible.

Vauxhall Cavalier 1.8 GL Hatchback

General dimensions, weights and capacities

For modifications, and information applicable to later models, see Supplement at end of manual

Dimensions
Overall length:
    Saloon models.. 4430.0 mm (174.4 in)
    Hatchback models .... 4350.0 mm (171.3 in)
Overall width .... 1700.0 mm (66.9 in)
Overall height (unladen) .... 1400.0 mm (55.1 in)
Wheelbase .... 2600.0 mm (102.4 in)
Track:
    Front:
        1.4 and 1.6 litre models .... 1420.0 mm (55.9 in)
        1.8 and 2.0 litre models .... 1426.0 mm (56.1 in)
    Rear:
        Rear drum brake models.. 1423.0 mm (56.0 in)
        Rear disc brake models (except GSi 2000) .... 1426.0 mm (56.1 in)
        GSi 2000 models .... 1444.0 mm (56.9 in)
Ground clearance.. 149.0 mm (5.9 in)

Weights
Kerb weight*:
    Saloon models:
        1.4 litre models .... 997.0 to 1005.0 kg (2198.0 to 2216.0 lbs)
        1.6 litre models .... 1012.0 to 1031.0 kg (2231.0 to 2273.0 lbs)
        1.8 litre models .... 1060.0 to 1086.0 kg (2337.0 to 2395.0 lbs)
        2.0 litre models .... 1100.0 to 1199.0 kg (2426.0 to 2644.0 lbs)
    Hatchback models:
        1.4 litre models .... 1027.0 to 1035.0 kg (2265.0 to 2282.0 lbs)
        1.6 litre models .... 1042.0 to 1066.0 kg (2298.0 to 2351.0 lbs)
        1.8 litre models .... 1075.0 to 1101.0 kg (2370.0 to 2428.0 lbs)
        2.0 litre models .... 1130.0 to 1178.0 kg (2492.0 to 2597.0 lbs)
Maximum gross vehicle weight .... Refer to VIN plate
Maximum roof rack load .... 100.0 kg (221.0 lbs)
Maximum towing hitch downward load.. 75 kg (165.0 lbs)
Maximum towing weight:
    Trailer with brakes:
        1.4 litre models .... 1000.0 kg (2205.0 lbs)
        1.6 and 1.8 litre models .... 1200.0 kg (2646.0 lbs)
        2.0 litre models (except GSi 2000) .... 1350.0 kg (2977.0 lbs)
        GSi 2000 models.. 1250.0 kg (2756.0 lbs)
    Trailer without brakes:
        1.4, 1.6 and 1.8 litre models... 500.0 kg (1103.0 lbs)
        2.0 litre models (except GSi 2000) .... 580.0 kg (1279.0 lbs)
        GSi 2000 models.. 600.0 kg (1323.0 lbs)

Exact kerb weights depend upon model and specification

Capacities
Engine oil (drain and refill including filter):
    1.4 litre models... 3.00 litres (5.3 pints)
    1.6 litre models... 3.50 litres (6.2 pints)
    1.8 litre models... 4.00 litres (7.0 pints)
    2.0 litre models (except GSi 2000) .... 4.00 litres (7.0 pints)
    GSi 2000 models .... 4.50 litres (7.9 pints)
Cooling system:
    1.4 litre models... 5.6 litres (9.9 pints)
    1.6 litre models... 5.8 litres (10.2 pints)
    1.8 litre models... 6.7 litres (11.8 pints)
    2.0 litre models... 7.2 litres (12.7 pints)
Manual gearbox:
    F10/5 and F13/5 type gearbox .... 1.6 litres (2.8 pints)
    F16/5 and F20/5 type gearbox .... 1.9 litres (3.3 pints)
Power steering.. 1.0 litre (1.8 pints)

Vauxhall Cavalier 2.0 SRi Saloon

Vauxhall Cavalier GSi 2000 Saloon

Jacking, towing and wheel changing

Jacking, towing and wheel changing

The jack supplied with the vehicle tool kit should only be used for changing roadwheels. When carrying out any other kind of work, raise the vehicle using a hydraulic jack, and always supplement the jack with axle stands positioned under the vehicle jacking points.

To change a roadwheel, first remove the spare wheel, jack and wheel brace from their stowage positions under the carpet in the luggage compartment. Firmly apply the handbrake and engage first gear. Place chocks at the front and rear of the wheel diagonally opposite the one to be changed.

Where applicable, remove the wheel trim and slacken the wheel bolts using the wheel brace provided in the tool kit. Position the jack

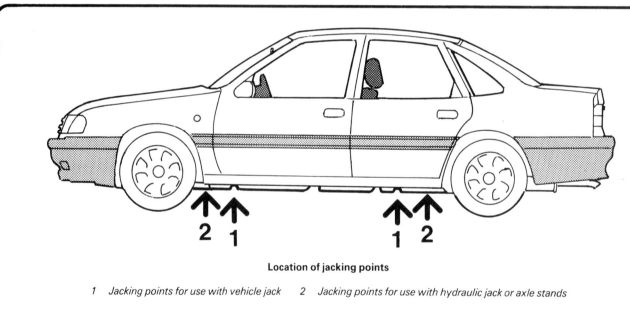

Location of jacking points

1   Jacking points for use with vehicle jack   *2   Jacking points for use with hydraulic jack or axle stands*

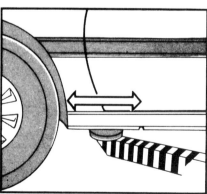

Front jacking point for hydraulic jack or axle stands

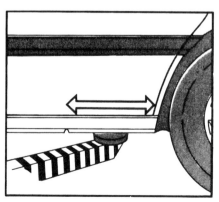

Rear jacking point for hydraulic jack or axle stands

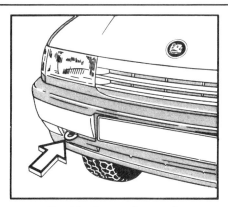

Front towing eye (arrowed)

Rear towing eye (arrowed)

head under the jacking point nearest the wheel to be changed. Raise the jack until the wheel is clear of the ground, then remove the wheel bolts and the wheel. Fit the spare wheel, and secure it with the wheel bolts. Lower the jack until the tyre is just touching the ground, and tighten the wheel nuts moderately tight. Now lower the jack fully and tighten the wheel bolts securely in a diagonal sequence. Where applicable, refit the wheel trim, then withdraw the jack and stow the wheel, jack and wheel brace in their respective locations.

When jacking up the vehicle with a trolley jack, position the jack head under one of the relevant jacking points (note that the jacking points for use with a hydraulic jack are different to those for use with the vehicle jack). **Do not** jack the vehicle under the sump or any of the steering or suspension components. Supplement the jack using axle stands. The jacking points and axle stand positions are shown in the accompanying

illustrations. **Never** *work under, around, or near a raised vehicle, unless it is adequately supported in at least two places.*

Towing

Towing eyes are fitted to the front and rear of the vehicle for attachment of a tow rope. Always turn the ignition key to position 'II' when the vehicle is being towed, so that the steering lock is released and the direction indicator and brake lamps are operational.

Before being towed, release the handbrake and place the gear lever in neutral. Note that greater than usual pedal pressure will be required to operate the brakes, since the vacuum servo unit is only operational with the engine running. Similarly, on models with power steering, greater than usual steering effort will be required.

Buying spare parts
and vehicle identification numbers

Buying spare parts

Spare parts are available from many sources, for example: Vauxhall garages, other garages and accessory shops, and motor factors. Our advice regarding spare part sources is as follows.

Officially appointed Vauxhall garages – This is the best source of parts which are peculiar to your car and are otherwise not generally available (eg complete cylinder heads, transmission components, badges, interior trim etc). It is also the only place at which you should buy parts if your vehicle is still under warranty – use of non-Vauxhall components may invalidate the warranty. To be sure of obtaining the correct parts it will always be necessary to give the storeman your car's vehicle identification number, and if possible, to take the 'old' parts along for positive identification. Remember that many parts are available on a factory exchange scheme – any parts returned should always be clean! It obviously makes good sense to go straight to the specialists on your car for this type of part for they are best equipped to supply you.

Other garages and accessory shops – These are often very good places to buy materials and components needed for the maintenance of your car (eg oil filters, spark plugs, bulbs, drivebelts, oils and greases, touch-up paint, filler paste, etc). They also sell general accessories, usually have convenient opening hours, charge lower prices and can often be found not far from home.

Motor factors – Good factors will stock all of the more important components which wear out relatively quickly (eg clutch components, pistons, valves, exhaust systems, brake cylinders/pipes/hoses/seals/shoes and pads etc). Motor factors will often provide new or reconditioned components on a part exchange basis – this can save considerable amount of money.

Vehicle identification numbers

Modifications are a continuing and unpublished process in vehicle manufacture, quite apart from major model changes. Spare parts manuals and lists are compiled upon a numerical basis, the individual vehicle numbers being essential to correct identification of the component required.

When ordering spare parts, always give as much information as possible. Quote the car model, year of manufacture and vehicle identification and/or engine numbers as appropriate.

The *vehicle identification plate* is riveted on top of the front body panel and includes the Vehicle Identification Number (VIN), vehicle weight information and paint and trim colour codes.

The *Vehicle Identification Number (VIN)* is given on the vehicle identification plate and is also stamped into the body floor panel between the driver's seat and the door sill panel; lift the flap in the carpet to see it.

The engine number is stamped on a horizontal flat located on the exhaust manifold side of the cylinder block, at the distributor end.

Location of vehicle identification plate (1) and engine number (2)

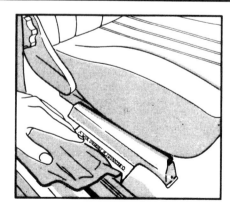

Alternative location of Vehicle Identification Number (VIN)

General repair procedures

Whenever servicing, repair or overhaul work is carried out on the car or its components, it is necessary to observe the following procedures and instructions. This will assist in carrying out the operation efficiently and to a professional standard of workmanship.

Joint mating faces and gaskets

Where a gasket is used between the mating faces of two components, ensure that it is renewed on reassembly, and fit it dry unless otherwise stated in the repair procedure. Make sure that the mating faces are clean and dry with all traces of old gasket removed. When cleaning a joint face, use a tool which is not likely to score or damage the face, and remove any burrs or nicks with an oilstone or fine file.

Make sure that tapped holes are cleaned with a pipe cleaner, and keep them free of jointing compound if this is being used unless specifically instructed otherwise.

Ensure that all orifices, channels or pipes are clear and blow through them, preferably using compressed air.

Oil seals

Whenever an oil seal is removed from its working location, either individually or as part of an assembly, it should be renewed.

The very fine sealing lip of the seal is easily damaged and will not seal if the surface it contacts is not completely clean and free from scratches, nicks or grooves. If the original sealing surface of the component cannot be restored, the component should be renewed.

Protect the lips of the seal from any surface which may damage them in the course of fitting. Use tape or a conical sleeve where possible. Lubricate the seal lips with oil before fitting and, on dual lipped seals, fill the space between the lips with grease.

Unless otherwise stated, oil seals must be fitted with their sealing lips toward the lubricant to be sealed.

Use a tubular drift or block of wood of the appropriate size to install the seal and, if the seal housing is shouldered, drive the seal down to the shoulder. If the seal housing is unshouldered, the seal should be fitted with its face flush with the housing top face.

Screw threads and fastenings

Always ensure that a blind tapped hole is completely free from oil, grease, water or other fluid before installing the bolt or stud. Failure to do this could cause the housing to crack due to the hydraulic action of the bolt or stud as it is screwed in.

When tightening a castellated nut to accept a split pin, tighten the nut to the specified torque, where applicable, and then tighten further to the next split pin hole. Never slacken the nut to align a split pin hole unless stated in the repair procedure.

When checking or retightening a nut or bolt to a specified torque setting, slacken the nut or bolt by a quarter of a turn, and then retighten to the specified setting.

Locknuts, locktabs and washers

Any fastening which will rotate against a component or housing in the course of tightening should always have a washer between it and the relevant component or housing.

Spring or split washers should always be renewed when they are used to lock a critical component such as a big-end bearing retaining nut or bolt.

Locktabs which are folded over to retain a nut or bolt should always be renewed.

Self-locking nuts can be reused in non-critical areas, providing resistance can be felt when the locking portion passes over the bolt or stud thread.

Split pins must always be replaced with new ones of the correct size for the hole.

Special tools

Some repair procedures in this manual entail the use of special tools such as a press, two or three-legged pullers, spring compressors etc. Wherever possible, suitable readily available alternatives to the manufacturer's special tools are described, and are shown in use. In some instances, where no alternative is possible, it has been necessary to resort to the use of a manufacturer's tool and this has been done for reasons of safety as well as the efficient completion of the repair operation. Unless you are highly skilled and have a thorough understanding of the procedure described, never attempt to bypass the use of any special tool when the procedure described specifies its use. Not only is there a very great risk of personal injury, but expensive damage could be caused to the components involved.

Tools and working facilities

Introduction

A selection of good tools is a fundamental requirement for anyone contemplating the maintenance and repair of a motor vehicle. For the owner who does not possess any, their purchase will prove a considerable expense, offsetting some of the savings made by doing-it-yourself. However, provided that the tools purchased meet the relevant national safety standards and are of good quality, they will last for many years and prove an extremely worthwhile investment.

To help the average owner to decide which tools are needed to carry out the various tasks detailed in this manual, we have compiled three lists of tools under the following headings: *Maintenance and minor repair, Repair and overhaul,* and *Special.* The newcomer to practical mechanics should start off with the *Maintenance and minor repair* tool kit and confine himself to the simpler jobs around the vehicle. Then, as his confidence and experience grow, he can undertake more difficult tasks, buying extra tools as, and when, they are needed. In this way, a *Maintenance and minor repair* tool kit can be built-up into a *Repair and overhaul* tool kit over a considerable period of time without any major cash outlays. The experienced do-it-yourselfer will have a tool kit good enough for most repair and overhaul procedures and will add tools from the *Special* category when he feels the expense is justified by the amount of use to which these tools will be put.

Maintenance and minor repair tool kit

The tools given in this list should be considered as a minimum requirement if routine maintenance, servicing and minor repair operations are to be undertaken. We recommend the purchase of combination spanners (ring one end, open-ended the other); although more expensive than open-ended ones, they do give the advantages of both types of spanner.

Combination spanners - 10, 11, 12, 13, 14 & 17 mm
Adjustable spanner - 9 inch
Spark plug spanner (with rubber insert)
Spark plug gap adjustment tool
Set of feeler gauges
Brake bleed nipple spanner
Screwdriver - 4 in long x $\frac{1}{4}$ in dia (flat blade)
Screwdriver - 4 in long x $\frac{1}{4}$ in dia (cross blade)
Combination pliers - 6 inch
Hacksaw (junior)
Tyre pump
Tyre pressure gauge
Oil can
Fine emery cloth (1 sheet)
Wire brush (small)
Funnel (medium size)

Repair and overhaul tool kit

These tools are virtually essential for anyone undertaking any major repairs to a motor vehicle, and are additional to those given in the *Maintenance and minor repair* list. Included in this list is a comprehensive set of sockets. Although these are expensive they will be found invaluable as they are so versatile - particularly if various drives are included in the set. We recommend the $\frac{1}{2}$ in square-drive type, as this can be used with most proprietary torque wrenches. If you cannot afford a socket set, even bought piecemeal, then inexpensive tubular box spanners are a useful alternative.

The tools in this list will occasionally need to be supplemented by tools from the *Special* list.

Sockets (or box spanners) to cover range in previous list
Reversible ratchet drive (for use with sockets)
Extension piece, 10 inch (for use with sockets)
Universal joint (for use with sockets)
Torque wrench (for use with sockets)
'Mole' wrench - 8 inch
Ball pein hammer
Soft-faced hammer, plastic or rubber
Screwdriver - 6 in long x $\frac{5}{16}$ in dia (flat blade)
Screwdriver - 2 in long x $\frac{5}{16}$ in square (flat blade)
Screwdriver - 1$\frac{1}{2}$ in long x $\frac{1}{4}$ in dia (cross blade)
Screwdriver - 3 in long x $\frac{1}{8}$ in dia (electricians)
Pliers - electricians side cutters
Pliers - needle nosed
Pliers - circlip (internal and external)
Cold chisel - $\frac{1}{2}$ inch
Scriber
Scraper
Centre punch
Pin punch
Hacksaw
Valve grinding tool
Steel rule/straight-edge
Allen keys (inc. splined/Torx type if necessary)
Selection of files
Wire brush (large)
Axle-stands
Jack (strong trolley or hydraulic type)

Special tools

The tools in this list are those which are not used regularly, are expensive to buy, or which need to be used in accordance with their manufacturers' instructions. Unless relatively difficult mechanical jobs are undertaken frequently, it will not be economic to buy many of these tools. Where this is the case, you could consider clubbing together with friends (or joining a motorists' club) to make a joint purchase, or borrowing the tools against a deposit from a local garage or tool hire specialist.

The following list contains only those tools and instruments freely available to the public, and not those special tools produced by the vehicle manufacturer specifically for its dealer network. You will find occasional references to these manufacturers' special tools in the text of this manual. Generally, an alternative method of doing the job without the vehicle manufacturers' special tool is given. However, sometimes, there is no alternative to using them. Where this is the case and the relevant tool cannot be bought or borrowed, you will have to entrust the work to a franchised garage.

> Valve spring compressor (where applicable)
> Piston ring compressor
> Balljoint separator
> Universal hub/bearing puller
> Impact screwdriver
> Micrometer and/or vernier gauge
> Dial gauge
> Stroboscopic timing light
> Dwell angle meter/tachometer
> Universal electrical multi-meter
> Cylinder compression gauge
> Lifting tackle
> Trolley jack
> Light with extension lead
> Splined sockets
> Torx sockets

Buying tools

For practically all tools, a tool factor is the best source since he will have a very comprehensive range compared with the average garage or accessory shop. Having said that, accessory shops often offer excellent quality tools at discount prices, so it pays to shop around.

There are plenty of good tools around at reasonable prices, but always aim to purchase items which meet the relevant national safety standards. If in doubt, ask the proprietor or manager of the shop for advice before making a purchase.

Care and maintenance of tools

Having purchased a reasonable tool kit, it is necessary to keep the tools in a clean serviceable condition. After use, always wipe off any dirt, grease and metal particles using a clean, dry cloth, before putting the tools away. Never leave them lying around after they have been used. A simple tool rack on the garage or workshop wall, for items such as screwdrivers and pliers is a good idea. Store all normal wrenches and sockets in a metal box. Any measuring instruments, gauges, meters, etc, must be carefully stored where they cannot be damaged or become rusty.

Take a little care when tools are used. Hammer heads inevitably become marked and screwdrivers lose the keen edge on their blades from time to time. A little timely attention with emery cloth or a file will soon restore items like this to a good serviceable finish.

Working facilities

Not to be forgotten when discussing tools, is the workshop itself. If anything more than routine maintenance is to be carried out, some form of suitable working area becomes essential.

It is appreciated that many an owner mechanic is forced by circumstances to remove an engine or similar item, without the benefit of a garage or workshop. Having done this, any repairs should always be done under the cover of a roof.

Wherever possible, any dismantling should be done on a clean, flat workbench or table at a suitable working height.

Any workbench needs a vice: one with a jaw opening of 4 in (100 mm) is suitable for most jobs. As mentioned previously, some clean dry storage space is also required for tools, as well as for lubricants, cleaning fluids, touch-up paints and so on, which become necessary.

Another item which may be required, and which has a much more general usage, is an electric drill with a chuck capacity of at least $\frac{5}{16}$ in (8 mm). This, together with a good range of twist drills, is virtually essential for fitting accessories such as mirrors and reversing lights.

Last, but not least, always keep a supply of old newspapers and clean, lint-free rags available, and try to keep any working area as clean as possible.

Spanner jaw gap comparison table

Jaw gap (in)	Spanner size
0.250	$\frac{1}{4}$ in AF
0.276	7 mm
0.313	$\frac{5}{16}$ in AF
0.315	8 mm
0.344	$\frac{11}{32}$ in AF; $\frac{1}{8}$ in Whitworth
0.354	9 mm
0.375	$\frac{3}{8}$ in AF
0.394	10 mm
0.433	11 mm
0.438	$\frac{7}{16}$ in AF
0.445	$\frac{3}{16}$ in Whitworth; $\frac{1}{4}$ in BSF
0.472	12 mm
0.500	$\frac{1}{2}$ in AF
0.512	13 mm
0.525	$\frac{1}{4}$ in Whitworth; $\frac{5}{16}$ in BSF
0.551	14 mm
0.563	$\frac{9}{16}$ in AF
0.591	15 mm
0.600	$\frac{5}{16}$ in Whitworth; $\frac{3}{8}$ in BSF
0.625	$\frac{5}{8}$ in AF
0.630	16 mm
0.669	17 mm
0.686	$\frac{11}{16}$ in AF
0.709	18 mm
0.710	$\frac{3}{8}$ in Whitworth; $\frac{7}{16}$ in BSF
0.748	19 mm
0.750	$\frac{3}{4}$ in AF
0.813	$\frac{13}{16}$ in AF
0.820	$\frac{7}{16}$ in Whitworth; $\frac{1}{2}$ in BSF
0.866	22 mm
0.875	$\frac{7}{8}$ in AF
0.920	$\frac{1}{2}$ in Whitworth; $\frac{9}{16}$ in BSF
0.938	$\frac{15}{16}$ in AF
0.945	24 mm
1.000	1 in AF
1.010	$\frac{9}{16}$ in Whitworth; $\frac{5}{8}$ in BSF
1.024	26 mm
1.063	$1\frac{1}{16}$ in AF; 27 mm
1.100	$\frac{5}{8}$ in Whitworth; $\frac{11}{16}$ in BSF
1.125	$1\frac{1}{8}$ in AF
1.181	30 mm
1.200	$\frac{11}{16}$ in Whitworth; $\frac{3}{4}$ in BSF
1.250	$1\frac{1}{4}$ in AF
1.260	32 mm
1.300	$\frac{3}{4}$ in Whitworth; $\frac{7}{8}$ in BSF
1.313	$1\frac{5}{16}$ in AF
1.390	$\frac{13}{16}$ in Whitworth; $\frac{15}{16}$ in BSF
1.417	36 mm
1.438	$1\frac{7}{16}$ in AF
1.480	$\frac{7}{8}$ in Whitworth; 1 in BSF
1.500	$1\frac{1}{2}$ in AF
1.575	40 mm; $\frac{15}{16}$ in Whitworth
1.614	41 mm
1.625	$1\frac{5}{8}$ in AF
1.670	1 in Whitworth; $1\frac{1}{8}$ in BSF
1.688	$1\frac{11}{16}$ in AF
1.811	46 mm
1.813	$1\frac{13}{16}$ in AF
1.860	$1\frac{1}{8}$ in Whitworth; $1\frac{1}{4}$ in BSF
1.875	$1\frac{7}{8}$ in AF
1.969	50 mm
2.000	2 in AF
2.050	$1\frac{1}{4}$ in Whitworth; $1\frac{3}{8}$ in BSF
2.165	55 mm
2.362	60 mm

Safety first!

Professional motor mechanics are trained in safe working procedures. However enthusiastic you may be about getting on with the job in hand, do take the time to ensure that your safety is not put at risk. A moment's lack of attention can result in an accident, as can failure to observe certain elementary precautions.

There will always be new ways of having accidents, and the following points do not pretend to be a comprehensive list of all dangers; they are intended rather to make you aware of the risks and to encourage a safety-conscious approach to all work you carry out on your vehicle.

Essential DOs and DON'Ts

DON'T rely on a single jack when working underneath the vehicle. Always use reliable additional means of support, such as axle stands, securely placed under a part of the vehicle that you know will not give way.

DON'T attempt to loosen or tighten high-torque nuts (e.g. wheel hub nuts) while the vehicle is on a jack; it may be pulled off.

DON'T start the engine without first ascertaining that the transmission is in neutral (or 'Park' where applicable) and the parking brake applied.

DON'T suddenly remove the filler cap from a hot cooling system – cover it with a cloth and release the pressure gradually first, or you may get scalded by escaping coolant.

DON'T attempt to drain oil until you are sure it has cooled sufficiently to avoid scalding you.

DON'T grasp any part of the engine, exhaust or catalytic converter without first ascertaining that it is sufficiently cool to avoid burning you.

DON'T allow brake fluid or antifreeze to contact vehicle paintwork.

DON'T syphon toxic liquids such as fuel, brake fluid or antifreeze by mouth, or allow them to remain on your skin.

DON'T inhale dust – it may be injurious to health (see *Asbestos* below).

DON'T allow any spilt oil or grease to remain on the floor – wipe it up straight away, before someone slips on it.

DON'T use ill-fitting spanners or other tools which may slip and cause injury.

DON'T attempt to lift a heavy component which may be beyond your capability – get assistance.

DON'T rush to finish a job, or take unverified short cuts.

DON'T allow children or animals in or around an unattended vehicle.

DO wear eye protection when using power tools such as drill, sander, bench grinder etc, and when working under the vehicle.

DO use a barrier cream on your hands prior to undertaking dirty jobs – it will protect your skin from infection as well as making the dirt easier to remove afterwards; but make sure your hands aren't left slippery. Note that long-term contact with used engine oil can be a health hazard.

DO keep loose clothing (cuffs, tie etc) and long hair well out of the way of moving mechanical parts.

DO remove rings, wristwatch etc, before working on the vehicle – especially the electrical system.

DO ensure that any lifting tackle used has a safe working load rating adequate for the job.

DO keep your work area tidy – it is only too easy to fall over articles left lying around.

DO get someone to check periodically that all is well, when working alone on the vehicle.

DO carry out work in a logical sequence and check that everything is correctly assembled and tightened afterwards.

DO remember that your vehicle's safety affects that of yourself and others. If in doubt on any point, get specialist advice.

IF, in spite of following these precautions, you are unfortunate enough to injure yourself, seek medical attention as soon as possible.

Asbestos

Certain friction, insulating, sealing, and other products – such as brake linings, brake bands, clutch linings, torque converters, gaskets, etc – contain asbestos. *Extreme care must be taken to avoid inhalation of dust from such products since it is hazardous to health.* If in doubt, assume that they *do* contain asbestos.

Fire

Remember at all times that petrol (gasoline) is highly flammable. Never smoke, or have any kind of naked flame around, when working on the vehicle. But the risk does not end there – a spark caused by an electrical short-circuit, by two metal surfaces contacting each other, by careless use of tools, or even by static electricity built up in your body under certain conditions, can ignite petrol vapour, which in a confined space is highly explosive.

Always disconnect the battery earth (ground) terminal before working on any part of the fuel or electrical system, and never risk spilling fuel on to a hot engine or exhaust.

It is recommended that a fire extinguisher of a type suitable for fuel and electrical fires is kept handy in the garage or workplace at all times. Never try to extinguish a fuel or electrical fire with water.

Note: *Any reference to a 'torch' appearing in this manual should always be taken to mean a hand-held battery-operated electric lamp or flashlight. It does NOT mean a welding/gas torch or blowlamp.*

Fumes

Certain fumes are highly toxic and can quickly cause unconsciousness and even death if inhaled to any extent. Petrol (gasoline) vapour comes into this category, as do the vapours from certain solvents such as trichloroethylene. Any draining or pouring of such volatile fluids should be done in a well ventilated area.

When using cleaning fluids and solvents, read the instructions carefully. Never use materials from unmarked containers – they may give off poisonous vapours.

Never run the engine of a motor vehicle in an enclosed space such as a garage. Exhaust fumes contain carbon monoxide which is extremely poisonous; if you need to run the engine, always do so in the open air or at least have the rear of the vehicle outside the workplace.

If you are fortunate enough to have the use of an inspection pit, never drain or pour petrol, and never run the engine, while the vehicle is standing over it; the fumes, being heavier than air, will concentrate in the pit with possibly lethal results.

The battery

Never cause a spark, or allow a naked light, near the vehicle's battery. It will normally be giving off a certain amount of hydrogen gas, which is highly explosive.

Always disconnect the battery earth (ground) terminal before working on the fuel or electrical systems.

If possible, loosen the filler plugs or cover when charging the battery from an external source. Do not charge at an excessive rate or the battery may burst.

Take care when topping up and when carrying the battery. The acid electrolyte, even when diluted, is very corrosive and should not be allowed to contact the eyes or skin.

If you ever need to prepare electrolyte yourself, always add the acid slowly to the water, and never the other way round. Protect against splashes by wearing rubber gloves and goggles.

When jump starting a car using a booster battery, for negative earth (ground) vehicles, connect the jump leads in the following sequence: First connect one jump lead between the positive (+) terminals of the two batteries. Then connect the other jump lead first to the negative (–) terminal of the booster battery, and then to a good earthing (ground) point on the vehicle to be started, at least 18 in (45 cm) from the battery if possible. Ensure that hands and jump leads are clear of any moving parts, and that the two vehicles do not touch. Disconnect the leads in the reverse order.

Mains electricity and electrical equipment

When using an electric power tool, inspection light etc, always ensure that the appliance is correctly connected to its plug and that, where necessary, it is properly earthed (grounded). Do not use such appliances in damp conditions and, again, beware of creating a spark or applying excessive heat in the vicinity of fuel or fuel vapour. Also ensure that the appliances meet the relevant national safety standards.

Ignition HT voltage

A severe electric shock can result from touching certain parts of the ignition system, such as the HT leads, when the engine is running or being cranked, particularly if components are damp or the insulation is defective. Where an electronic ignition system is fitted, the HT voltage is much higher and could prove fatal.

Routine maintenance

For modifications, and information applicable to later models, see Supplement at end of manual

Maintenance is essential for ensuring safety, and desirable for the purpose of getting the best in terms of performance and economy from your vehicle. Over the years, the need for periodic lubrication – oiling, greasing, and so on – has been drastically reduced, if not totally eliminated. This has unfortunately tended to lead some owners to think that because no action is required, components either no longer exist, or will last for ever. This is certainly not the case; it is essential to carry out regular visual examination as comprehensively as possible in order to spot any possible defects at an early stage before they develop into major expensive repairs.

The following service schedules are a list of the maintenance requirements, and the intervals at which they should be carried out, as recommended by the manufacturers. Where applicable, these procedures are covered in greater detail near the beginning of each relevant Chapter.

Weekly, or before a long journey

Engine, cooling system, brakes and steering
Check the engine oil level and top up if necessary (Chapter 1)
Check the coolant level, and top up if necessary (Chapter 2)
Check the brake fluid level, and top up if necessary (Chapter 8)
Check the power steering fluid level, and top up if necessary (where applicable) (Chapter 9)

Lamps and wipers
Check the operation of all interior and exterior lamps, and the wiper and washers (Chapter 11)
Check the washer fluid level(s) and top up if necessary (Chapter 11), using a screen wash such as Turtle Wax High Tech Screen Wash

Tyres
Check the tyre pressures (Chapter 9)
Visually examine the tyres for wear or damage (Chapter 9)

Every 9000 miles (15 000 km) or 12 months – whichever occurs first

---

Engine (Chapter 1)
Change the engine oil and renew the oil filter
Inspect the crankcase ventilation system for condition and security

Cooling system (Chapter 2)
Check the coolant level, and top up if necessary
Check for coolant leaks, and rectify as necessary
Inspect the radiator matrix for blockage (eg dead insects) and clean as necessary

Fuel and exhaust systems (Chapter 3)
Check for fuel leaks and rectify as necessary
Check and if necessary adjust the idle speed (where applicable) and mixture (where applicable)
Check the operation of the throttle linkage, and lubricate if necessary
Check the exhaust system for corrosion, leaks and security
Check all vacuum hoses for condition and security

Ignition and engine management systems (Chapter 4)
Check all wiring and vacuum hoses for condition and security
Check and if necessary adjust the ignition timing (1.4 and 1.6 litre models only)

Clutch (Chapter 5)
Check the clutch cable adjustment

Manual gearbox (Chapter 6)
Check for oil leaks, and rectify as necessary

Driveshafts (Chapter 7)
Check the driveshaft gaiters for condition and security

Braking system (Chapter 8)
Check the brake disc pad friction material for wear, and renew if necessary
Renew the brake fluid
Check for brake fluid leaks, and rectify as necessary
Check the handbrake linkage operation, and lubricate and adjust as necessary

Suspension and steering (Chapter 9)
Check all components for wear and damage
Check the power steering fluid level, and top up if necessary (where applicable)
Check for power steering fluid leaks, and rectify as necessary (where applicable)
Check the tension of the power steering fluid pump drivebelt, and adjust if necessary (where applicable)
Check the torque of the roadwheel bolts
Check the tyre pressures
Visually examine the tyres for wear or damage

Bodywork and fittings (Chapter 10)
Check all panels and structural members for corrosion and damage
Lubricate all locks and hinges

Electrical system (Chapter 11)
Check the operation of all interior and exterior lamps, and the wipers and washers
Check the washer fluid level, and top up if necessary
Check the condition and tension of the alternator drivebelt, and adjust or renew if necessary
Check the charge condition of the battery
Check and if necessary adjust the headlamp alignment, and where applicable, the front foglamp alignment

---

Every 18 000 miles (30 000 km) or 24 months – whichever occurs first

---

In addition to the items in the 12-monthly service, carry out the following:

Cooling system (Chapter 2)
Renew the coolant (optional, no change intervals specified by manufacturers)

Underbonnet view of a 1989 1.6 L model

1 VIN plate
2 Air cleaner casing*
3 Suspension strut top
4 Coolant expansion tank

5 Brake fluid reservoir
6 Fuel pump
7 Steering rack
8 Octane rating plug

9 Washer fluid reservoir
10 Battery
11 Ignition coil
12 Distributor (Bosch type)

13 Cooling fan motor
14 Engine oil level dipstick
15 Oil filter
16 Oil filler cap

*Refer to Chapter 3 for alternative type

Underbonnet view of a 1989 2.0 SRi model

1	VIN plate	6	Brake fluid reservoir
2	Air cleaner casing	7	Throttle body
3	Airflow meter	8	Relay box
4	Suspension strut top	9	Octane rating plug
5	Coolant expansion tank	10	Washer fluid reservoir

11	Battery
12	Power steering fluid reservoir
13	Power steering fluid hoses
14	Distributor cap

15	Engine oil level dipstick
16	Idle speed adjuster
17	Fuel pressure regulator
18	Oil filler cap
19	Thermostat housing

Underbonnet view of a 1990 GSi 2000 model

1 VIN plate	5 Brake fluid reservoir	9 Anti-theft alarm horn	13 Battery
2 Air cleaner casing	6 Air mass meter	10 ABS hydraulic modulator	14 Distributor
3 Suspension strut top	7 Fuel pressure regulator	11 Washer fluid reservoir	15 Engine oil level dipstick
4 Coolant expansion tank	8 Relay box	12 Power steering fluid reservoir	16 Oil filler cap

Front underbody view of a 1989 1.6 L model

1	Brake caliper	4	Clutch cover plate	7	Engine oil drain plug	9	Exhaust pipe
2	Subframe	5	Suspension lower arm	8	Driveshaft gaiter	10	Anti-roll bar securing nut
3	Oil filter	6	Differential cover plate				

Rear underbody view of a 1989 2.0 SRi model

1	Torsion beam	4	Shock absorber	7	Fuel flow damper	9	Fuel tank securing strap
2	Trailing arm	5	Coil spring	8	Fuel filter	10	Handbrake cable
3	Anti-roll bar	6	Exhaust expansion box				

Rear underbody view of a 1990 GSi 2000 model

1 Fuel tank securing strap	4 Semi-trailing arm	6 Handbrake cable	8 Exhaust expansion box
2 Shock absorber	5 Suspension crossmember mounting bracing bracket	7 Suspension crossmember	9 Fuel pump
3 ABS wheel sensor			

Fuel system (Chapter 3)
Renew the air cleaner element
Check the operation of the air cleaner air intake temperature control
(carburettor models only)
Renew the fuel filter

Ignition system (Chapter 4)
Inspect the condition of the spark plugs and renew as necessary
Inspect and clean the distributor cap and HT leads

Manual gearbox (Chapter 6)
Check and if necessary top up the gearbox oil level

Braking system (Chapter 8)
Check the brake drum shoe friction material for wear, and renew if
necessary

**Every 36 000 miles (60 000 km) or 48 months – whichever occurs
first**

*In addition to the items in the 12 and 24-month services, carry out the
following:*

Engine (Chapter 1)
Check the tension and condition of the timing belt, and adjust or
renew as necessary (sohc engines only)

Every 63 000 miles (105 000 km) or 7 years – whichever occurs first

*In addition to the items in the 12, 24 and 48-month services, carry out the
following:*

Engine (Chapter 1)
Renew the timing belt (dohc engine only)

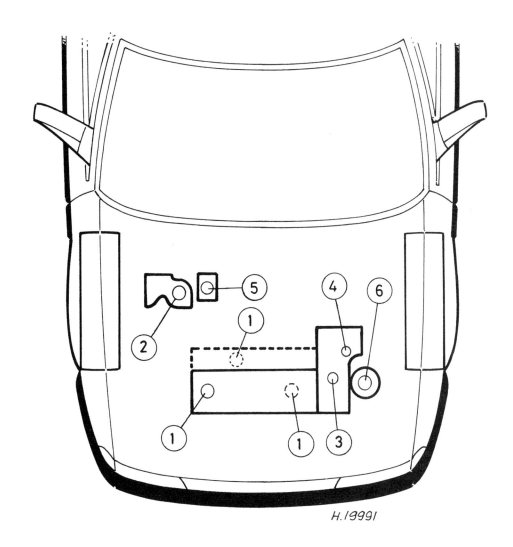

H.19991

Recommended lubricants and fluids

Component or system	Lubricant type/specification	Duckhams recommendation
1 Engine	Multigrade engine oil, viscosity range SAE 10W/40 to 20W/50, to API SG/CD	Duckhams QXR, QS, Hypergrade Plus, or Hypergrade
2 Cooling system	Ethylene glycol based antifreeze	Duckhams Universal Antifreeze and Summer Coolant
3 Manual gearbox	Gear oil, viscosity SAE 80 EP, or GM gear oil 90 188 G29	Duckhams Hypoid 80, or Hypoid 75W/90S
4 Automatic transmission	Dexron II type ATF	Duckhams Uni-Matic
5 Braking system	Hydraulic fluid to SAE J1703F or DOT 4	Duckhams Universal Brake and Clutch Fluid
6 Power steering	Dexron II type ATF	Duckhams Uni-Matic

Conversion factors

Length (distance)

Inches (in)	X	25.4	=	Millimetres (mm)	X	0.0394	= Inches (in)
Feet (ft)	X	0.305	=	Metres (m)	X	3.281	= Feet (ft)
Miles	X	1.609	=	Kilometres (km)	X	0.621	= Miles

Volume (capacity)

Cubic inches (cu in; in³)	X	16.387	=	Cubic centimetres (cc; cm³)	X	0.061	= Cubic inches (cu in; in³)
Imperial pints (Imp pt)	X	0.568	=	Litres (l)	X	1.76	= Imperial pints (Imp pt)
Imperial quarts (Imp qt)	X	1.137	=	Litres (l)	X	0.88	= Imperial quarts (Imp qt)
Imperial quarts (Imp qt)	X	1.201	=	US quarts (US qt)	X	0.833	= Imperial quarts (Imp qt)
US quarts (US qt)	X	0.946	=	Litres (l)	X	1.057	= US quarts (US qt)
Imperial gallons (Imp gal)	X	4.546	=	Litres (l)	X	0.22	= Imperial gallons (Imp gal)
Imperial gallons (Imp gal)	X	1.201	=	US gallons (US gal)	X	0.833	= Imperial gallons (Imp gal)
US gallons (US gal)	X	3.785	=	Litres (l)	X	0.264	= US gallons (US gal)

Mass (weight)

Ounces (oz)	X	28.35	=	Grams (g)	X	0.035	= Ounces (oz)
Pounds (lb)	X	0.454	=	Kilograms (kg)	X	2.205	= Pounds (lb)

Force

Ounces-force (ozf; oz)	X	0.278	=	Newtons (N)	X	3.6	= Ounces-force (ozf; oz)
Pounds-force (lbf; lb)	X	4.448	=	Newtons (N)	X	0.225	= Pounds-force (lbf; lb)
Newtons (N)	X	0.1	=	Kilograms-force (kgf; kg)	X	9.81	= Newtons (N)

Pressure

Pounds-force per square inch (psi; lbf/in²; lb/in²)	X	0.070	=	Kilograms-force per square centimetre (kgf/cm²; kg/cm²)	X	14.223	= Pounds-force per square inch (psi; lbf/in²; lb/in²)
Pounds-force per square inch (psi; lbf/in²; lb/in²)	X	0.068	=	Atmospheres (atm)	X	14.696	= Pounds-force per square inch (psi; lbf/in²; lb/in²)
Pounds-force per square inch (psi; lbf/in²; lb/in²)	X	0.069	=	Bars	X	14.5	= Pounds-force per square inch (psi; lbf/in²; lb/in²)
Pounds-force per square inch (psi; lbf/in²; lb/in²)	X	6.895	=	Kilopascals (kPa)	X	0.145	= Pounds-force per square inch (psi; lbf/in²; lb/in²)
Kilopascals (kPa)	X	0.01	=	Kilograms-force per square centimetre (kgf/cm²; kg/cm²)	X	98.1	= Kilopascals (kPa)
Millibar (mbar)	X	100	=	Pascals (Pa)	X	0.01	= Millibar (mbar)
Millibar (mbar)	X	0.0145	=	Pounds-force per square inch (psi; lbf/in²; lb/in²)	X	68.947	= Millibar (mbar)
Millibar (mbar)	X	0.75	=	Millimetres of mercury (mmHg)	X	1.333	= Millibar (mbar)
Millibar (mbar)	X	0.401	=	Inches of water (inH₂O)	X	2.491	= Millibar (mbar)
Millimetres of mercury (mmHg)	X	0.535	=	Inches of water (inH₂O)	X	1.868	= Millimetres of mercury (mmHg)
Inches of water (inH₂O)	X	0.036	=	Pounds-force per square inch (psi; lbf/in²; lb/in²)	X	27.68	= Inches of water (inH₂O)

Torque (moment of force)

Pounds-force inches (lbf in; lb in)	X	1.152	=	Kilograms-force centimetre (kgf cm; kg cm)	X	0.868	= Pounds-force inches (lbf in; lb in)
Pounds-force inches (lbf in; lb in)	X	0.113	=	Newton metres (Nm)	X	8.85	= Pounds-force inches (lbf in; lb in)
Pounds-force inches (lbf in; lb in)	X	0.083	=	Pounds-force feet (lbf ft; lb ft)	X	12	= Pounds-force inches (lbf in; lb in)
Pounds-force feet (lbf ft; lb ft)	X	0.138	=	Kilograms-force metres (kgf m; kg m)	X	7.233	= Pounds-force feet (lbf ft; lb ft)
Pounds-force feet (lbf ft; lb ft)	X	1.356	=	Newton metres (Nm)	X	0.738	= Pounds-force feet (lbf ft; lb ft)
Newton metres (Nm)	X	0.102	=	Kilograms-force metres (kgf m; kg m)	X	9.804	= Newton metres (Nm)

Power

Horsepower (hp)	X	745.7	=	Watts (W)	X	0.0013	= Horsepower (hp)

Velocity (speed)

Miles per hour (miles/hr; mph)	X	1.609	=	Kilometres per hour (km/hr; kph)	X	0.621	= Miles per hour (miles/hr; mph)

Fuel consumption*

Miles per gallon, Imperial (mpg)	X	0.354	=	Kilometres per litre (km/l)	X	2.825	= Miles per gallon, Imperial (mpg)
Miles per gallon, US (mpg)	X	0.425	=	Kilometres per litre (km/l)	X	2.352	= Miles per gallon, US (mpg)

Temperature

Degrees Fahrenheit = (°C x 1.8) + 32

Degrees Celsius (Degrees Centigrade; °C) = (°F - 32) x 0.56

*It is common practice to convert from miles per gallon (mpg) to litres/100 kilometres (l/100km),
where mpg (Imperial) x l/100 km = 282 and mpg (US) x l/100 km = 235

Fault diagnosis

Introduction

The vehicle owner who does his or her own maintenance according to the recommended schedules should not have to use this section of the manual very often. Modern component reliability is such that, provided those items subject to wear or deterioration are inspected or renewed at the specified intervals, sudden failure is comparatively rare. Faults do not usually just happen as a result of sudden failure, but develop over a period of time. Major mechanical failures in particular are usually preceded by characteristic symptoms over hundreds or even thousands of miles. Those components which do occasionally fail without warning are often small and easily carried in the vehicle.

With any fault finding, the first step is to decide where to begin investigations. Sometimes this is obvious, but on other occasions a little detective work will be necessary. The owner who makes half a dozen haphazard adjustments or replacements may be successful in curing a fault (or its symptoms), but he will be none the wiser if the fault recurs and he may well have spent more time and money than was necessary. A calm and logical approach will be found to be more satisfactory in the long run. Always take into account any warning signs or abnormalities that may have been noticed in the period preceding the fault – power loss, high or low gauge readings, unusual noises or smells, etc – and remember that failure of components such as fuses or spark plugs may only be pointers to some underlying fault.

The pages which follow here are intended to help in cases of failure to start or breakdown on the road. There is also a Fault Diagnosis Section at the end of each Chapter which should be consulted if the preliminary checks prove unfruitful. Whatever the fault, certain basic principles apply. These are as follows:

Verify the fault. This is simply a matter of being sure that you know what the symptoms are before starting work. This is particularly important if you are investigating a fault for someone else who may not have described it very accurately.

Don't overlook the obvious. For example, if the vehicle won't start, is there petrol in the tank? (Don't take anyone else's word on this particular point, and don't trust the fuel gauge either!) If an electrical fault is indicated, look for loose or broken wires before digging out the test gear.

Cure the disease, not the symptom. Substituting a flat battery with a fully charged one will get you off the hard shoulder, but if the underlying cause is not attended to, the new battery will go the same way. Similarly, changing oil-fouled spark plugs for a new set will get you moving again, but remember that the reason for the fouling (if it wasn't simply an incorrect grade of plug) will have to be established and corrected.

Don't take anything for granted. Particularly, don't forget that a 'new' component may itself be defective (especially if it's been rattling round in the boot for months), and don't leave components out of a fault diagnosis sequence just because they are new or recently fitted. When you do finally diagnose a difficult fault, you'll probably realise that all the evidence was there from the start.

Electrical faults

Electrical faults can be more puzzling than straightforward mechanical failures, but they are no less susceptible to logical analysis if the basic principles of operation are understood. Vehicle electrical wiring exists in extremely unfavourable conditions – heat, vibration and chemical attack – and the first things to look for are loose or corroded connections and broken or chafed wires, especially where the wires pass through holes in the bodywork or are subject to vibration.

All metal-bodied vehicles in current production have one pole of the battery 'earthed', ie connected to the vehicle bodywork, and in nearly all modern vehicles it is the negative (–) terminal. The various electrical components – motors, bulb holders etc – are also connected to earth, either by means of a lead or directly by their mountings. Electric current flows through the component and then back to the battery via the bodywork. If the component mounting is loose or corroded, or if a good path back to the battery is not available, the circuit will be incomplete and malfunction will result. The engine and/or gearbox are also earthed by means of flexible metal straps to the body or subframe; if these straps are loose or missing, starter motor, generator and ignition trouble may result.

Assuming the earth return to be satisfactory, electrical faults will be due either to component malfunction or to defects in the current supply. Individual components are dealt with in Chapter 11. If supply wires are

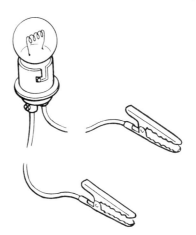

A simple test lamp is useful for tracing electrical faults

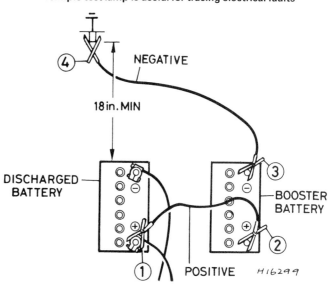

Jump start lead connections for negative earth – connect leads in order shown

Carrying a few spares can save you a long walk!

broken or cracked internally this results in an open-circuit, and the easiest way to check for this is to bypass the suspect wire temporarily with a length of wire having a crocodile clip or suitable connector at each end. Alternatively, a 12V test lamp can be used to verify the presence of supply voltage at various points along the wire and the break can be thus isolated.

If a bare portion of a live wire touches the bodywork or other earthed metal part, the electricity will take the low-resistance path thus formed back to the battery: this is known as a short-circuit. Hopefully a short-circuit will blow a fuse, but otherwise it may cause burning of the insulation (and possibly further short-circuits) or even a fire. This is why it is inadvisable to bypass persistently blowing fuses with silver foil or wire.

Spares and tool kit

Most vehicles are supplied only with sufficient tools for wheel changing; the *Maintenance and minor repair* tool kit detailed in *Tools and working facilities,* with the addition of a hammer, is probably sufficient for those repairs that most motorists would consider attempting at the roadside. In addition a few items which can be fitted without too much trouble in the event of a breakdown should be carried. Experience and available space will modify the list below, but the following may save having to call on professional assistance:

Spark plugs, clean and correctly gapped
HT lead and plug cap – long enough to reach the plug furthest from the distributor
Distributor rotor
Drivebelt(s) – emergency type may suffice
Spare fuses
Set of principal light bulbs
Tin of radiator sealer and hose bandage
Exhaust bandage
Roll of insulating tape
Length of soft iron wire
Length of electrical flex
Torch or inspection lamp (can double as test lamp)
Battery jump leads
Tow-rope
Ignition water dispersant aerosol
Litre of engine oil
Sealed can of hydraulic fluid
Emergency windscreen
Worm drive clips

If spare fuel is carried, a can designed for the purpose should be used to minimise risks of leakage and collision damage. A first aid kit and a warning triangle, whilst not at present compulsory in the UK, are obviously sensible items to carry in addition to the above.

When touring abroad it may be advisable to carry additional spares which, even if you cannot fit them yourself, could save having to wait while parts are obtained. The items below may be worth considering:

Clutch and throttle cables
Cylinder head gasket
Alternator brushes
Tyre valve core

One of the motoring organisations will be able to advise on availability of fuel etc in foreign countries.

Engine will not start

Engine fails to turn when starter operated
Flat battery (recharge, use jump leads, or push start)
Battery terminals loose or corroded
Battery earth to body defective
Engine earth strap loose or broken
Starter motor (or solenoid) wiring loose or broken
Ignition/starter switch faulty
Major mechanical failure (seizure)
Starter or solenoid internal fault (see Chapter 11)

Starter motor turns engine slowly
Partially discharged battery (recharge, use jump leads, or push start)
Battery terminals loose or corroded
Battery earth to body defective
Engine earth strap loose
Starter motor (or solenoid) wiring loose
Starter motor internal fault (see Chapter 11)

Starter motor spins without turning engine
Flat battery
Flywheel gear teeth damaged or worn
Starter motor mounting bolts loose

Engine turns normally but fails to start

Damp or dirty HT leads and distributor cap (crank engine and check for spark) – try moisture dispersant such as Holts Wet Start
No fuel in tank
Faulty automatic choke (carburettor models)
Fouled or incorrectly gapped spark plugs (remove and regap, or renew)
Other ignition system fault (see Chapter 4)
Other fuel system fault (see Chapter 3)
Poor compression (see Chapter 1)
Major mechanical failure (eg camshaft drive)

Engine fires but will not run

Faulty automatic choke (carburettor models)
Air leaks at carburettor/throttle body or inlet manifold
Fuel starvation (see Chapter 3)
Other ignition fault (see Chapter 4)

Engine cuts out and will not restart

Engine cuts out suddenly – ignition fault

Loose or disconnected LT wires
Wet HT leads or distributor cap (after traversing water splash)
Coil failure (check for spark)
Other ignition fault (see Chapter 4)

Engine misfires before cutting out – fuel fault

Fuel tank empty
Fuel pump defective or filter blocked (check for delivery)
Fuel tank filler vent blocked (suction will be evident on releasing cap)
Carburettor needle valve sticking (where applicable)
Blockage due to fuel contamination
Other fuel system fault (see Chapter 3)

Engine cuts out – other causes

Serious overheating
Major mechanical failure (eg camshaft drive)

Engine overheats

Coolant loss due to internal or external leakage (see Chapter 2)
Thermostat defective
Low oil level
Brakes binding
Radiator clogged externally or internally
Cooling fan not operating correctly
Engine waterways clogged
Ignition timing incorrect or automatic advance malfunctioning
Mixture too weak

Note: *Do not add cold water to an overheated engine or damage may result*

Low engine oil pressure

Gauge reads low or warning light illuminated with engine running

Oil level low or incorrect grade
Defective gauge or sender unit
Wire to sender unit earthed
Engine overheating
Oil filter clogged or bypass valve defective
Oil pressure relief valve defective
Oil pick-up strainer clogged
Oil pump worn or mountings loose
Worn main or big-end bearings

Note: *Low oil pressure in a high-mileage engine at tickover is not necessarily a cause for concern. Sudden pressure loss at speed is far more significant. In any event, check the gauge or warning light sender before condemning the engine.*

Engine noises

Pre-ignition (pinking) on acceleration

Incorrect grade of fuel
Ignition timing incorrect
Distributor faulty or worn
Worn or maladjusted carburettor (where applicable)
Excessive carbon build-up in engine
Engine management system fault (Chapter 4)

Whistling or wheezing noises

Leaking vacuum hose
Leaking carburettor/throttle body or manifold gasket
Blowing head gasket

Tapping or rattling

Faulty hydraulic valve lifter
Worn valve gear
Worn timing belt
Broken piston ring (ticking noise)

Knocking or thumping

Unintentional mechanical contact (eg fan blades)
Worn drivebelt
Peripheral component fault (alternator, water pump etc)
Worn big-end bearings (regular heavy knocking, perhaps less under load)
Worn main bearings (rumbling and knocking, perhaps worsening under load)
Piston slap (most noticeable when cold)

Chapter 1 Engine

For modifications, and information applicable to later models, see Supplement at end of manual

Contents

Specifications

Single overhead camshaft (sohc) engines

General

Type	Four-cylinder, in-line, water-cooled, transversely mounted at front of vehicle. Single belt-driven overhead camshaft, acting on hydraulic valve lifters

Manufacturer's engine codes:

1.4 litre	14 NV
1.6 litre	16 SV
1.8 litre	18 SV
2.0 litre	20 NE, C20 NE (catalyst models), or 20 SEH (SRi models)

Bore:

1.4 litre	77.6 mm
1.6 litre	79.0 mm
1.8 litre	84.8 mm
2.0 litre	86.0 mm

Stroke:
    1.4 litre .... 73.4 mm
    1.6 litre .... 81.5 mm
    1.8 litre .... 79.5 mm
    2.0 litre .... 86.0 mm
Cubic capacity:
    1.4 litre .... 1389 cc (84.73 cu in)
    1.6 litre .... 1598 cc (97.48 cu in)
    1.8 litre .... 1796 cc (109.56 cu in)
    2.0 litre .... 1998 cc (121.88 cu in)
Compression ratio:
    1.4 litre 9.4:1
    1.6 litre 10.0:1
    1.8 litre 10.0:1
    2.0 litre:
        20 NE and C20 NE 9.2:1
        20 SEH 10.0:1
Maximum power:
    1.4 litre .... 55 kW (75 bhp) at 5600 rpm
    1.6 litre .... 60 kW (82 bhp) at 5400 rpm
    1.8 litre .... 66 kW (90 bhp) at 5400 rpm
    2.0 litre:
        20 NE and C20 NE .... 85 kW (116 bhp) at 5200 rpm
        20 SEH .... 95 kW (129 bhp) at 5600 rpm
Maximum torque:
    1.4 litre .... 108 Nm (80 lbf ft) at 3000 rpm
    1.6 litre .... 130 Nm (96 lbf ft) at 2600 rpm
    1.8 litre .... 148 Nm (109 lbf ft) at 2800 rpm
    2.0 litre:
        20 NE .... 175 Nm (129 lbf ft) at 2600 rpm
        C20 NE .... 170 Nm (125 lbf ft) at 2600 rpm
        20 SEH .... 180 Nm (133 lbf ft) at 4600 rpm
Firing order .... 1-3-4-2 (No 1 cylinder at timing belt end)

Cylinder block

Material .... Cast iron
Maximum permissible bore out-of round .... 0.013 mm
Maximum permissible bore taper .... 0.013 mm
Maximum permissible rebore oversize .... 0.5 mm

Crankshaft and bearings

Number of main bearings.. 5

	1.4 and 1.6 litre	1.8 and 2.0 litre
Main bearing journal diameter:		
Standard	54.972 to 54.985 mm	57.982 to 57.995 mm
0.25 mm undersize	54.722 to 54.735 mm	57.732 to 57.745 mm
0.50 mm undersize	54.472 to 54.485 mm	57.482 to 57.495 mm
Main bearing shell colour codes (all models):	Bearing cap shells	Cylinder block shells
Standard	Brown	Green
0.25 mm undersize	Brown/blue	Green/blue
0.50 mm undersize	Brown/white	Green/white
Centre (thrust) main bearing journal width:	1.4 and 1.6 litre	1.8 and 2.0 litre
Standard	26.000 to 26.052 mm	25.850 to 25.900 mm
0.25 mm undersize	26.200 to 26.252 mm	26.050 to 26.100 mm
0.50 mm undersize	26.400 to 26.452 mm	26.250 to 26.300 mm
Big-end bearing journal diameter:	1.4 and 1.6 litre	1.8 and 2.0 litre
Standard	42.971 to 42.987 mm	48.970 to 48.988 mm
0.25 mm undersize	42.271 to 42.737 mm	48.720 to 48.738 mm
0.50 mm undersize	42.471 to 42.487 mm	48.470 to 48.488 mm

Big-end bearing shell colour codes (all models):
    Standard .... None
    0.25 mm undersize .... Blue
    0.50 mm undersize .... White
Main and big-end bearing journal out-of-round (all engines) .... 0.04 mm maximum
Main bearing journal clearance:
    1.4 and 1.6 litre .... 0.025 to 0.050 mm
    1.8 and 2.0 litre.. 0.015 to 0.040 mm
Big-end bearing running clearance
    1.4 and 1.6 litre .... 0.019 to 0.071 mm
    1.8 and 2.0 litre.. 0.006 to 0.031 mm
Crankshaft endfloat:
    1.4 and 1.6 litre .... 0.1 to 0.2 mm
    1.8 and 2.0 litre.. 0.050 to 0.152 mm
Connecting rod endfloat:
    1.4 and 1.6 litre .... 0.11 to 0.24 mm
    1.8 and 2.0 litre.. 0.07 to 0.24 mm

Piston and cylinder bores

	Bore diameter	Piston diameter	Identification mark
1.4 litre:			
Production size 1	77.56 mm	77.54 mm	6
	77.57 mm	77.55 mm	7
	77.58 mm	77.56 mm	8
Production size 2	77.59 mm	77.57 mm	99
	77.60 mm	77.58 mm	00
	77.61 mm	77.59 mm	01
	77.62 mm	77.60 mm	02
0.5 mm oversize	78.07 mm	78.05 mm	7 + 0.5
1.6 litre:			
Production size 1	78.95 mm	78.93 mm	5
	78.96 mm	78.94 mm	6
	78.97 mm	78.95 mm	7
	78.98 mm	78.96 mm	8
Production size 2	78.99 mm	78.97 mm	99
	79.00 mm	78.98 mm	00
	79.01 mm	78.99 mm	01
	79.02 mm	79.00 mm	02
Production size 3	79.03 mm	79.01 mm	03
	79.04 mm	79.02 mm	04
	79.05 mm	79.03 mm	05
	79.06 mm	79.04 mm	06
Production size 4	79.07 mm	79.05 mm	07
	79.08 mm	79.06 mm	08
	79.09 mm	79.07 mm	09
	79.10 mm	79.08 mm	1
0.5 mm oversize	79.48 mm	79.45 mm	8 + 0.5
1.8 litre:			
Production size 2	84.78 mm	84.76 mm	8
	84.79 mm	84.77 mm	99
	84.80 mm	84.78 mm	00
	84.81 mm	84.79 mm	01
	84.82 mm	84.80 mm	02
0.5 mm oversize	85.27 mm	85.28 mm	7 + 0.5
2.0 litre:			
Production size 2	85.98 mm	85.96 mm	8
	85.99 mm	85.97 mm	99
	86.00 mm	85.98 mm	00
	86.01 mm	85.99 mm	01
	86.02 mm	86.00 mm	02
0.5 mm oversize	86.47 mm	86.45 mm	7 + 0.5

Piston clearance in bore:
New:
    1.4 and 1.6 litre ....   0.02 mm
    1.8 and 2.0 litre ....   0.01 to 0.03 mm
After rebore (oversize):
    1.4, 1.8 and 2.0 litre ....   0.01 to 0.03 mm
    1.6 litre ....   0.02 to 0.04 mm

Piston rings

Number (per piston) ....   2 compression, 1 oil control
Ring end gap:
    Compression ....   0.3 to 0.5 mm
    Oil control (top and bottom sections) ....   0.4 to 1.4 mm
    Ring gap offset (to gap of adjacent ring)* ....   180°

See Section 40 for oil control ring sections

Cylinder head

Material ....   Light alloy
Maximum permissible distortion of sealing face ....   0.025 mm
Overall height of cylinder head (sealing surface to sealing surface) ....   96.00 ± 0.25 mm

	1.4 and 1.6 litre	**1.8 and 2.0 litre**
Valve seat width:		
Inlet	1.3 to 1.4 mm	1.0 to 1.5 mm
Exhaust	1.7 to 1.8 mm	1.7 to 2.2 mm

Camshaft

Camshaft bearing journal diameter:
1.4 and 1.6 litre:
    No 1 ....   39.435 to 39.455 mm
    No 2 ....   39.685 to 39.705 mm
    No 3 ....   39.935 to 39.955 mm
    No 4 ....   40.185 to 40.205 mm
    No 5 ....   40.435 to 40.455 mm

Are your plugs trying to tell you something?

Normal.
Grey-brown deposits, lightly coated core nose. Plugs ideally suited to engine, and engine in good condition.

Heavy Deposits.
A build up of crusty deposits, light-grey sandy colour in appearance.
Fault: Often caused by worn valve guides, excessive use of upper cylinder lubricant, or idling for long periods.

Lead Glazing.
Plug insulator firing tip appears yellow or green/yellow and shiny in appearance.
Fault: Often caused by incorrect carburation, excessive idling followed by sharp acceleration. Also check ignition timing.

Carbon fouling.
Dry, black, sooty deposits.
Fault: over-rich fuel mixture.
Check: carburettor mixture settings, float level, choke operation, air filter.

Oil fouling.
Wet, oily deposits. Fault: worn bores/piston rings or valve guides; sometimes occurs (temporarily) during running-in period.

Overheating.
Electrodes have glazed appearance, core nose very white – few deposits. Fault: plug overheating. Check: plug value, ignition timing, fuel octane rating (too low) and fuel mixture (too weak).

Electrode damage.
Electrodes burned away; core nose has burned, glazed appearance. Fault: pre-ignition. Check: for correct heat range and as for 'overheating'.

Split core nose.
(May appear initially as a crack). Fault: detonation or wrong gap-setting technique. Check: ignition timing, cooling system, fuel mixture (too weak).

WHY DOUBLE COPPER IS BETTER FOR YOUR ENGINE.

Unique Trapezoidal Copper Cored Earth Electrode — 50% Larger Spark Area — Copper Cored Centre Electrode

Champion Double Copper plugs are the first in the world to have copper core in both centre <u>and</u> earth electrode. This innovative design means that they run cooler by up to 100°C – giving greater efficiency and longer life. These double copper cores transfer heat away from the tip of the plug faster and more efficiently. Therefore, Double Copper runs at cooler temperatures than conventional plugs giving improved acceleration response and high speed performance with no fear of pre-ignition.

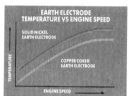

Champion Double Copper plugs also feature a unique trapezoidal earth electrode giving a 50% increase in spark area. This, together with the double copper cores, offers greatly reduced electrode wear, so the spark stays stronger for longer.

 FASTER COLD STARTING

 FOR UNLEADED OR LEADED FUEL

 ELECTRODES UP TO 100°C COOLER

 BETTER ACCELERATION RESPONSE

 LOWER EMISSIONS

 50% BIGGER SPARK AREA

 THE LONGER LIFE PLUG

Plug Tips/Hot and Cold.
Spark plugs must operate within well-defined temperature limits to avoid cold fouling at one extreme and overheating at the other.
Champion and the car manufacturers work out the best plugs for an engine to give optimum performance under all conditions, from freezing cold starts to sustained high speed motorway cruising.
Plugs are often referred to as hot or cold. With Champion, the higher the number on its body, the hotter the plug, and the lower the number the cooler the plug.

Plug Cleaning
Modern plug design and materials mean that Champion no longer recommends periodic plug cleaning. Certainly don't clean your plugs with a wire brush as this can cause metal conductive paths across the nose of the insulator so impairing its performance and resulting in loss of acceleration and reduced m.p.g.
However, if plugs are removed, always carefully clean the area where the plug seats in the cylinder head as grit and dirt can sometimes cause gas leakage.
Also wipe any traces of oil or grease from plug leads as this may lead to arcing.

DOUBLE ⊂⊂ COPPER

This photographic sequence shows the steps taken to repair the dent and paintwork damage shown above. In general, the procedure for repairing a hole will be similar; where there are substantial differences, the procedure is clearly described and shown in a separate photograph.

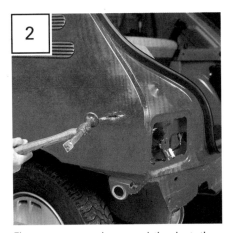

First remove any trim around the dent, then hammer out the dent where access is possible. This will minimise filling. Here, after the large dent has been hammered out, the damaged area is being made slightly concave.

Next, remove all paint from the damaged area by rubbing with coarse abrasive paper or using a power drill fitted with a wire brush or abrasive pad. 'Feather' the edge of the boundary with good paintwork using a finer grade of abrasive paper.

Where there are holes or other damage, the sheet metal should be cut away before proceeding further. The damaged area and any signs of rust should be treated with Turtle Wax Hi-Tech Rust Eater, which will also inhibit further rust formation.

For a large dent or hole mix Holts Body Plus Resin and Hardener according to the manufacturer's instructions and apply around the edge of the repair. Press Glass Fibre Matting over the repair area and leave for 20-30 minutes to harden. Then ...

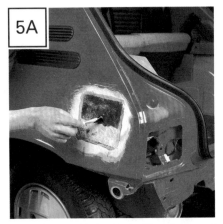

... brush more Holts Body Plus Resin and Hardener onto the matting and leave to harden. Repeat the sequence with two or three layers of matting, checking that the final layer is lower than the surrounding area. Apply Holts Body Plus Filler Paste as shown in Step 5B.

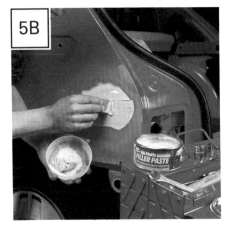

For a medium dent, mix Holts Body Plus Filler Paste and Hardener according to the manufacturer's instructions and apply it with a flexible applicator. Apply thin layers of filler at 20-minute intervals, until the filler surface is slightly proud of the surrounding bodywork.

For small dents and scratches use Holts No Mix Filler Paste straight from the tube. Apply it according to the instructions in thin layers, using the spatula provided. It will harden in minutes if applied outdoors and may then be used as its own knifing putty.

Use a plane or file for initial shaping. Then, using progressively finer grades of wet-and-dry paper, wrapped round a sanding block, and copious amounts of clean water, rub down the filler until glass smooth. 'Feather' the edges of adjoining paintwork.

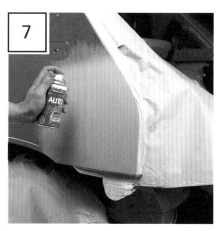

Protect adjoining areas before spraying the whole repair area and at least one inch of the surrounding sound paintwork with Holts Dupli-Color primer.

Fill any imperfections in the filler surface with a small amount of Holts Body Plus Knifing Putty. Using plenty of clean water, rub down the surface with a fine grade wet-and-dry paper – 400 grade is recommended – until it is really smooth.

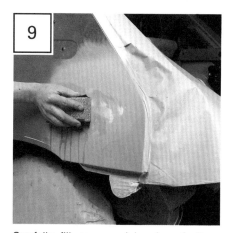

Carefully fill any remaining imperfections with knifing putty before applying the last coat of primer. Then rub down the surface with Holts Body Plus Rubbing Compound to ensure a really smooth surface.

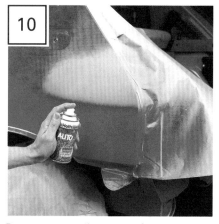

Protect surrounding areas from overspray before applying the topcoat in several thin layers. Agitate Holts Dupli-Color aerosol thoroughly. Start at the repair centre, spraying outwards with a side-to-side motion.

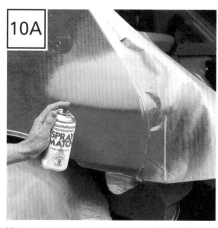

If the exact colour is not available off the shelf, local Holts Professional Spraymatch Centres will custom fill an aerosol to match perfectly.

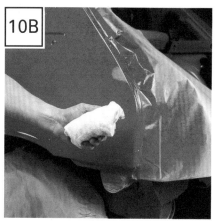

To identify whether a lacquer finish is required, rub a painted unrepaired part of the body with wax and a clean cloth.

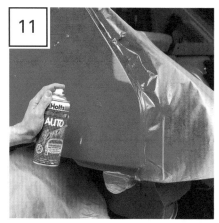

If *no* traces of paint appear on the cloth, spray Holts Dupli-Color clear lacquer over the repaired area to achieve the correct gloss level.

The paint will take about two weeks to harden fully. After this time it can be 'cut' with a mild cutting compound such as Turtle Wax Minute Cut prior to polishing with a final coating of Turtle Wax Extra.

When carrying out bodywork repairs, remember that the quality of the finished job is proportional to the time and effort expended.

HAYNES No1 for DIY

Haynes publish a wide variety of books besides the world famous range of *Haynes Owners Workshop Manuals*. They cover all sorts of DIY jobs. Specialist books such as the *Improve and Modify* series and the *Purchase and DIY Restoration Guides* give you all the information you require to carry out everything from minor modifications to complete restoration on a number of popular cars. In addition there are the publications dealing with specific tasks, such as the *Car Bodywork Repair Manual* and the *In-Car Entertainment Manual*. The *Household DIY* series gives clear step-by-step instructions on how to repair everyday household objects ranging from toasters to washing machines.

Whether it is under the bonnet or around the home there is a Haynes Manual that can help you save money. Available from motor accessory stores and bookshops or direct from the publisher.

Camshaft (continued)

	Normal	0.1 mm undersize
1.8 and 2.0 litre:		
No 1	42.455 to 42.470 mm	42.355 to 42.370 mm
No 2	42.705 to 42.720 mm	42.605 to 42.620 mm
No 3	42.955 to 42.970 mm	42.855 to 42.870 mm
No 4	43.205 to 43.220 mm	43.105 to 43.120 mm
No 5	43.455 to 43.470 mm	43.355 to 43.370 mm

Camshaft bearing diameter in housing:

	Normal	0.1 mm undersize
1.4 and 1.6 litre		
No 1	39.500 to 39.525 mm	
No 2	39.750 to 39.775 mm	
No 3	40.000 to 40.025 mm	
No 4	40.250 to 40.275 mm	
No 5	40.500 to 40.525 mm	
1.8 and 2.0 litre	**Normal**	**0.1 mm undersize**
No 1	42.500 to 42.525 mm	42.400 to 42.425 mm
No 2	42.750 to 42.775 mm	42.650 to 42.675 mm
No 3	43.000 to 43.025 mm	42.900 to 42.925 mm
No 4	43.250 to 43.275 mm	43.150 to 43.175 mm
No 5	43.500 to 43.525 mm	43.400 to 43.425 mm

Cam lift:
- 1.4 litre (inlet and exhaust) .... 6.12 mm
- 1.6 litre:
  - Inlet .... 5.61 mm
  - Exhaust .... 6.12 mm
- 1.8 litre:
  - Inlet .... 6.01 mm
  - Exhaust .... 6.39 mm
- 2.0 litre (inlet and exhaust):
  - 20 NE and C20 NE .... 6.67 mm
  - 20 SEH .... 6.70 mm

Maximum permissible radial run-out .... 0.03 mm
Endfloat .... 0.09 to 0.21 mm

Timing belt

Tension using Vauxhall gauge KM-510-A (see Section 16):

	1.4 and 1.6 litre	1.8 and 2.0 litre
New belt, cold	5.5	4.5
New belt, warm	8.0	7.5
Used belt, cold	4.0	2.5
Used belt, warm	7.0	7.0

Valves and guides

	Inlet	Exhaust
Overall length – production:		
1.4 litre	105.0 mm	105.0 mm
1.6 litre	101.5 mm	101.5 mm
1.8 and 2.0 litre	104.2 mm	104.0 mm
Overall length – service:		
1.4 litre	104.6 mm	104.6 mm
1.6 litre	101.1 mm	101.1 mm
1.8 and 2.0 litre	103.8 mm	103.6 mm
Head diameter:		
1.4 litre	33.0 mm	29.0 mm
1.6 litre	38.0 mm	31.0 mm
1.8 and 2.0 litre	41.8 mm	36.5 mm
Stem diameter (all engines):		
Standard	6.998 to 7.012 mm	6.978 to 6.992 mm
0.075 mm oversize	7.037 to 7.087 mm	7.053 to 7.067 mm
0.150 mm oversize	7.148 to 7.162 mm	7.128 to 7.142 mm
0.250 mm oversize	7.248 to 7.262 mm	7.228 to 7.242 mm
Valve guide bore (all engines):		
Standard	7.030 to 7.050 mm	
0.075 mm oversize	7.105 to 7.125 mm	
0.150 mm oversize	7.180 to 7.200 mm	
0.250 mm oversize	7.280 to 7.300 mm	
Valve clearance in guide (all engines):		
Inlet	0.018 to 0.052 mm	
Exhaust	0.038 to 0.072 mm	
Valve seat angle (all engines)	44°	
Valve clearances	Automatic adjustment by hydraulic lifters	

Flywheel

Maximum permissible lateral run-out of starter ring gear .... 0.5 mm
Refinishing limit – maximum depth of material which may be removed from clutch friction surface .... 0.3 mm

Lubrication system

Lubricant type/specification .... Multigrade engine oil, viscosity range SAE 10W/40 to 20W/50, to API SG/CD or better (Duckhams QXR, QS, Hypergrade Plus, or Hypergrade)

Lubricant capacity (drain and refill, including filter):

    1.4 litre.. 3.00 litres (5.3 pints)
    1.6 litre.. 3.50 litres (6.2 pints)
    1.8 and 2.0 litre... 4.00 litres (7.0 pints)

Quantity of oil required to raise level on dipstick from 'MIN' to 'MAX':

    1.4 and 1.6 litre .... 0.75 litre (1.3 pints)
    1.8 and 2.0 litre .... 1.00 litre (1.8 pints)

Oil pump clearances:

    Inner-to-outer gear teeth clearance (backlash) – all engines .... 0.1 to 0.2 mm
    Gear-to-housing clearance (endfloat):
        1.4 and 1.6 litre.. 0.08 to 0.15 mm
        1.8 and 2.0 litre.. 0.03 to 0.10 mm

Oil pressure at idle (engine warm).. 1.5 bar (21.8 lbf/in^2)
Oil filter element .... Champion G102

Torque wrench settings

	Nm	lbf ft
Main bearing cap bolts*:		
1.4 and 1.6 litre:		
Stage 1	50	37
Stage 2	Angle-tighten a further 45° to 60°	Angle-tighten a further 45° to 60°
1.8 and 2.0 litre:		
Stage 1	60	44
Stage 2	Angle-tighten a further 40° to 50°	Angle-tighten a further 40° to 50°
Big-end bearing cap bolts*:		
1.4 and 1.6 litre:		
Stage 1	25	18
Stage 2	Angle-tighten a further 30° to 45°	Angle-tighten a further 30° to 45°
1.8 and 2.0 litre:		
Stage 1	35	26
Stage 2	Angle-tighten a further 45°	Angle-tighten a further 45°
Camshaft sprocket bolt	45	33
Crankshaft pulley/sprocket bolt (1.4 and 1.6 litre)	55	41
Crankshaft sprocket bolt (1.8 and 2.0 litre)*:		
Stage 1	130	96
Stage 2	Angle-tighten a further 40° to 50°	Angle-tighten a further 40° to 50°
Crankshaft pulley-to-sprocket bolts (1.8 and 2.0 litre)	20	15
Cylinder head bolts*:		
1.4 and 1.6 litre:		
Stage 1	25	18
Stage 2	Angle-tighten a further 60°	Angle-tighten a further 60°
Stage 3	Angle-tighten a further 60°	Angle-tighten a further 60°
Stage 4	Angle-tighten a further 30°	Angle-tighten a further 30°
Stage 5 (engine warm)	Angle-tighten a further 30°	Angle-tighten a further 30°
1.8 and 2.0 litre:		
Stage 1	25	18
Stage 2	Angle-tighten a further 60°	Angle-tighten a further 60°
Stage 3	Angle-tighten a further 60°	Angle-tighten a further 60°
Stage 4	Angle-tighten a further 60°	Angle-tighten a further 60°
Stage 5 (engine warm)	Angle-tighten a further 30°	Angle-tighten a further 30°
Flywheel bolts*:		
1.4 and 1.6 litre:		
Stage 1	35	26
Stage 2	Angle-tighten a further 30° to 45°	Angle-tighten a further 30° to 45°
1.8 and 2.0 litre:		
Stage 1	65	48
Stage 2	Angle-tighten a further 30° to 45°	Angle-tighten a further 30° to 45°
Sump drain plug	45	33
Engine-to-gearbox bolts	75	55
Alternator bracket-to-cylinder black bolts	40	30
Engine/gearbox mounting-to-gearbox bolts*	60	44
Engine mounting-to-cylinder block bolts	60	44
Engine/gearbox mounting-to-front subframe bolts	40	30
Engine/gearbox mounting-to-body bolts*	65	48
Power steering pump bracket-to-cylinder block bolts	40	30
Exhaust manifold nuts	22	16
Inlet manifold nuts	22	16
Coolant pump bolts:		
1.4 and 1.6 litre	8	6
1.8 and 2.0 litre	25	18
Power steering pump bolts (1.6 litre)	30	22

Torque wrench settings (continued)

	Nm	lbf ft
Thermostat housing bolts:		
1.4 and 1.6 litre	10	7
1.8 and 2.0 litre	15	11
Sump bolts:		
1.4 and 1.6 litre	8	6
1.8 and 2.0 litre	5	4
Oil pump bolts	6	4
Oil pick-up pipe-to-oil pump bolts	8	6
Oil pressure relief valve plug-to-oil pump	30	22
Fuel pump-to-camshaft housing bolts (1.4, 1.6 and 1.8 litre)	18	13
Camshaft thrust plate bolts	8	6
Starter motor bolts:		
1.4 and 1.6 litre	25	18
1.8 and 2.0 litre:		
Engine side	45	33
Gearbox side	75	55

Use new bolts

Double overhead camshaft (dohc) engine

General

Type	Four-cylinder, in-line, water-cooled, transversely mounted at front of vehicle. Double belt-driven overhead camshafts, acting on hydraulic valve lifters
Manufacturer's engine codes	20 XE or C20 XE (catalyst models)
Bore	86.0 mm
Stroke	86.0 mm
Cubic capacity	1998 cc
Compression ratio	10.5 : 1
Maximum power	110 kW (150 bhp) at 6000 rpm
Firing order	1-3-4-2 (No 1 cylinder at timing belt end)

Cylinder block
All specifications as for sohc engines

Crankshaft and bearings
All specifications as for 1.8 and 2.0 litre sohc engines

Pistons and cylinder bores

	Bore diameter	Piston diameter	Identification mark
Production size 1	85.98 mm	85.95 mm	8
	85.99 mm	85.96 mm	99
	86.00 mm	85.97 mm	00
	86.01 mm	85.98 mm	01
	86.02 mm	85.99 mm	02
Production size 2			
0.5 mm oversize	86.47 mm	86.44 mm	7 + 0.5
	86.48 mm	86.45 mm	8 + 0.5
	86.49 mm	86.46 mm	9 + 0.5
	86.50 mm	86.47 mm	0 + 0.5
Piston clearance in bore (new and after rebore - oversize)	0.02 to 0.04 mm		

Piston rings
All specifications as for sohc engines

Cylinder head

Material	Light alloy
Maximum permissible distortion of sealing face	0.025 mm
Overall height of cylinder head (sealing surface to sealing surface)	135.63 mm
Valve seat width:	
Inlet	1.0 to 1.4 mm
Exhaust	1.4 to 1.8 mm

Camshaft

Camshaft bearing journal diameter	27.939 to 27.960 mm
Camshaft bearing diameter in cylinder head and bearing caps	28.000 to 28.021 mm
Cam lift (inlet and exhaust)	9.5 mm
Maximum permissible radial run-out	0.04 mm
Endfloat	0.04 to 0.144 mm

Valves and guides

	Inlet	Exhaust
Overall length - production	105.0 mm	105.0 mm
Overall length - service	104.6 mm	104.6 mm
Head diameter	33.0 ± 0.1 mm	29.0 ± 0.1 mm

Valves and guides (continued)

	Inlet	Exhaust
Stem diameter:		
Standard	6.955 to 6.970 mm	6.945 to 6.960 mm
0.075 mm oversize	7.030 to 7.045 mm	7.020 to 7.035 mm
0.150 mm oversize	7.105 to 7.120 mm	7.095 to 7.110 mm
Valve guide bore:		
Standard	7.000 to 7.015 mm	
0.075 mm oversize	7.075 to 7.090 mm	
0.150 mm oversize	7.150 to 7.165 mm	
Valve clearance in guide (all engines):		
Inlet	0.03 to 0.06 mm	
Exhaust	0.04 to 0.07 mm	
Valve seat angle	44° 40′	
Valve clearances	Automatic adjustment by hydraulic lifters	

Flywheel
All specifications as for sohc engines

Lubrication system
All specifications as for 1.8 and 2.0 litre sohc engines, except for the following:

Lubricant capacity (drain and refill, including filter) .... 4.50 litres (7.9 pints)

Torque wrench settings
All specifications as for 2.0 litre sohc engine, except for the following:

	Nm	lbf ft
Main bearing cap bolts *:		
Stage 1	60	44
Stage 2	Angle-tighten a further 40° to 50°	Angle-tighten a further 40° to 50°
Big-end bearing cap bolts*:		
Stage 1	35	26
Stage 2	Angle-tighten a further 45° to 60°	Angle-tighten a further 45° to 60°
Camshaft bearing cap nuts (main, M8)	20	15
Camshaft bearing cap nuts (rear, M6)	10	7
Camshaft sprocket bolt:		
Stage 1	50	37
Stage 2	Angle-tighten a further 40° to 50°	Angle-tighten a further 40° to 50°
Crankshaft sprocket bolt*:		
Stage 1	250	185
Stage 2	Angle-tighten a further 40° to 50°	Angle-tighten a further 40° to 50°
Crankshaft pulley-to-sprocket bolts	20	15
Cylinder head bolts*:		
Stage 1	25	18
Stage 2	Angle-tighten a further 65°	Angle-tighten a further 65°
Stage 3	Angle-tighten a further 65°	Angle-tighten a further 65°
Stage 4	Angle-tighten a further 65°	Angle-tighten a further 65°
Stage 5 (engine warm)	Angle-tighten a further 40° to 45°	Angle-tighten a further 40° to 45°
Flywheel bolts*:		
Stage 1	65	48
Stage 2	Angle-tighten a further 40° to 50°	Angle-tighten a further 40° to 50°
Inlet manifold nuts	20	15
Exhaust manifold nuts	20	15
Crankcase breather tube-to-cylinder block bolts	25	18
Timing belt tensioner pulley bolt:		
Stage 1	25	18
Stage 2	Angle-tighten a further 45° to 60°	Angle-tighten a further 45° to 60°
Timing belt idler pulley bolt:		
Stage 1	25	18
Stage 2	Angle-tighten a further 45° to 60°	Angle-tighten a further 45° to 60°
Camshaft cover bolts	8	6

* Use new bolts

---

1 General description

The engine is of four-cylinder, in-line single or double overhead camshaft type (depending on model), mounted transversely at the front of the vehicle.

The crankshaft runs in five shell-type bearings, and the centre bearing incorporates a thrust bearing shell to control crankshaft end-float.

The connecting rods are attached to the crankshaft by horizontally-split shell-type big-end bearings. On single overhead camshaft (sohc) models, the pistons are attached to the connecting rods by gudgeon pins, which are an interference fit in the connecting rod small-end bore. On double overhead camshaft (dohc) models, the gudgeon pins are fully-floating, and are secured by circlips. The aluminium alloy pistons are fitted with three piston rings: two compression rings and an oil control ring.

The camshaft on single overhead camshaft (sohc) engines is driven from the crankshaft by a toothed composite rubber belt. Each cylinder has two valves (one inlet and one exhaust), operated via rocker arms which are supported at their pivot ends by hydraulic self-adjusting valve lifters (tappets).

Fig. 1.1 Front sectional view of 1.6 litre (16 SV) engine (Sec 1)

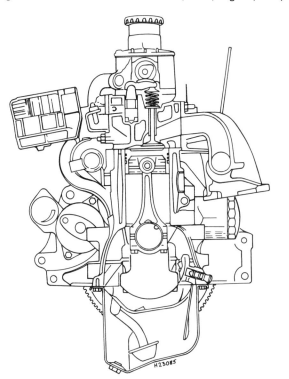

Both camshafts on double overhead camshaft (dohc) engines are driven from the crankshaft by one toothed composite rubber belt. Each cylinder has four valves (two inlet and two exhaust), operated directly from the camshafts via hydraulic self-adjusting valve lifters. One camshaft operates the inlet valves, and the other operates the exhaust valves.

The inlet and exhaust valves are each closed by a single valve spring, and operate in guides pressed into the cylinder head.

A gear-type oil pump is located in a housing attached to the front of the cylinder block, and is driven directly from the crankshaft. A full-flow type oil filter is fitted, and dohc models are fitted with a remotely-mounted oil cooler.

The distributor is driven directly from the end of the camshaft (the exhaust camshaft in the case of dohc models), and on carburettor models, the mechanical fuel pump is operated from the front end of the camshaft. The coolant pump is located at the front of the cylinder block, and is driven by the timing belt.

2   Routine maintenance

1   At the intervals specified in the *'Routine maintenance'* Section at the beginning of this manual, carry out the following tasks.

2   Check the engine oil level with the vehicle parked on level ground. Ideally, the oil level should be checked with the engine cold. The level should be maintained between the 'MAX' and 'MIN' marks on the dipstick, which is located at the distributor end of the engine, next to the exhaust manifold. Withdraw the dipstick, wipe it clean, then fully reinsert it. Withdraw the dipstick, and read off the oil level. If necessary,

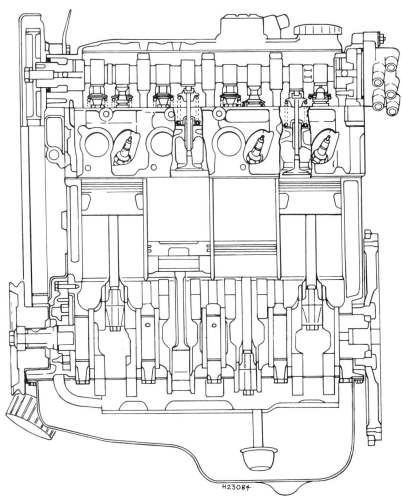

Fig. 1.2 Side sectional view of 1.6 litre (16 SV) engine (Sec 1)

2.2 Topping-up the engine oil level – 2.0 litre sohc model

top up the oil level through the filler on the camshaft cover (photo). Note that, on 1.4 and 1.6 litre models, 0.75 litre (1.3 pints) of oil is required to raise the level on the dipstick from the 'MIN' to the 'MAX' mark, and on 1.8 and 2.0 litre models 1.0 litre (1.8 pints) of oil is required. Do not overfill. The constant need for topping-up indicates a leak, which should be located and rectified without delay.

3   Renew the engine oil and filter, as described in Section 3.
4   On sohc models, check and if necessary adjust the timing belt tension, as described in Section 16.
5   Renew the timing belt as described in Section 17 (dohc models).
6   Periodically, check the engine and associated components for signs of oil, coolant or fuel leaks, and rectify any problems as necessary. Also check the crankcase ventilation system hoses for deterioration or damage, with reference to Section 4.

3 Engine oil and filter – renewal

1   Ideally, the oil should be drained with the engine hot, just after the vehicle has been driven.
2   On 2.0 litre dohc models, remove the access hatches from the engine undershield to expose the sump drain plug and the oil filter.

3.4 Sump drain plug location – 2.0 litre dohc model (engine undershield removed)

3   Place a container of suitable capacity beneath the oil drain plug at the rear of the sump.
4   Remove the oil filler cap from the camshaft cover, then using a suitable socket or spanner, unscrew the oil drain plug, and allow the oil to drain (photo). Take care to avoid scalding if the oil is hot.
5   Allow ten to fifteen minutes for the oil to drain completely, then move the container and position it under the oil filter.
6   On 1.8 and 2.0 litre models, improved access to the oil filter can be gained by jacking up the front of the vehicle and removing the right-hand roadwheel (photo). Ensure that the handbrake is applied, and that the vehicle is securely supported on axle stands. Note that further oil may drain from the sump as the vehicle is raised.
7   Using a strap wrench or a filter removal tool if necessary, slacken the filter and unscrew it from the mounting. Alternatively, if the filter is very tight, a screwdriver can be driven through the filter casing and used as a lever. Discard the filter.
8   Wipe the mating face on the filter mounting with a lint-free rag, then smear the sealing ring of the new filter with clean engine oil of the specified grade.
9   Screw the new filter into position and tighten it by hand only, **do not** use any tools.
10   Where applicable, refit the roadwheel and lower the vehicle to the ground. Fully tighten the roadwheel bolts with the vehicle resting on its wheels.
11   Examine the condition of the oil drain plug sealing ring and renew if necessary, then refit the drain plug and tighten it to the specified torque.
12   Refill the engine through the filler on the camshaft cover, using the specified grade and quantity of oil. Fill until the level reaches the 'MAX' mark on the dipstick, allowing time for the oil to drain through the engine to the sump.
13   Refit the oil filler cap, then start the engine and check for leaks. Note that the oil pressure warning lamp may stay illuminated for a few seconds when the engine is started as the oil filter fills with oil.
14   Stop the engine and recheck the oil level, topping-up if necessary.
15   On 2.0 litre dohc models, refit the access hatches to the engine undershield.
16   Dispose of the old engine oil safely; **do not** pour it down a drain.

4 Crankcase ventilation system – description and maintenance

1   A crankcase ventilation system is fitted to all models, but the systems differ in detail depending on the model concerned.
2   Oil fumes and blow-by gases (combustion gases which have passed by the piston rings) are drawn from the crankcase into the area of the cylinder head above the camshaft(s) via a hose. From here the gases are drawn into the inlet manifold/throttle body (as applicable)

3.6 Oil filter viewed through right-hand wheel arch – 2.0 litre model

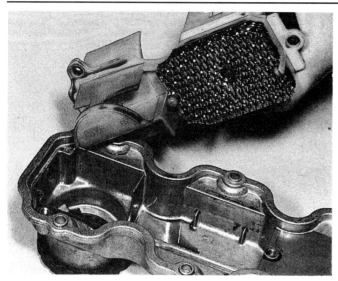

4.3 Crankcase ventilation filter removed from camshaft cover – 1.6 litre engine

and/or the air box on the carburettor (where applicable), where they are re-burnt with fresh air/fuel mixture, hence reducing harmful exhaust emissions.

3   Certain models have a mesh filter inside the camshaft cover, which should be cleaned in paraffin if clogging is evident (photo).

4   On high mileage vehicles, particularly when regularly used for short journeys, a jelly-like deposit may be evident inside the crankcase ventilation system hoses. If excessive deposits are present, the relevant hose(s) should be removed and cleaned.

5   Periodically inspect the system hoses for security and damage, and renew as necessary. Note that damaged or loose hoses can cause various engine running problems which can be difficult to trace.

6   The crankcase breather/dipstick tube can be unbolted from the cylinder block after disconnecting the hose. Use a new gasket when refitting.

5   Compression test – description and interpretation

1   If engine performance is poor, or if misfiring occurs which cannot be attributed to the ignition or fuel system, a compression test can provide diagnostic clues. If the test is performed regularly, it can give warning of trouble on a high mileage engine before any other symptoms become apparent.

2   The engine must be at operating temperature, the battery must be fully charged, and the spark plugs must be removed. The help of an assistant will also be required.

3   Disable the ignition system by disconnecting the coil LT (' + 15 ') wire. Fit the compression tester to No 1 cylinder spark plug hole.

4   Have the assistant hold the throttle wide open and crank the engine on the starter. Record the highest reading obtained on the compression tester.

5   Repeat the test on the remaining cylinders, recording the pressure developed in each.

6   The difference in pressure between any two cylinders should be no more than 1.0 bar (14.5 lbf/in^2). If the pressure in any cylinder is low, introduce a teaspoonful of clean engine oil into the spark plug hole, and repeat the test.

7   If the addition of oil temporarily improves the compression pressure, this indicates that cylinder bore or piston ring wear was responsible for the pressure loss. No improvement suggests that leaking or burnt valves, or a blown head gasket may be to blame.

8   A low reading from two adjacent cylinders is almost certainly due to the head gasket leaking between them.

9   On completion of the test, refit the spark plugs and reconnect the coil LT wire.

6   Major operations possible with the engine in the vehicle

The following operations may be carried out without removing the engine from the vehicle:

(a)   Removal and refitting of oil pressure relief valve (see Section 37)
(b)   Removal and refitting of timing belt and sprockets
(c)   Removal and refitting of camshaft housing (sohc engines)
(d)   Removal and refitting of camshaft(s)
(e)   Removal and refitting of cylinder head
(f)   Removal and refitting of sump
(g)   Removal and refitting of oil pump
(h)   Removal and refitting of piston/connecting rod assemblies
(i)   Removal and refitting of flywheel
(j)   Renewal of crankshaft front oil seal
(k)   Removal and refitting of engine/gearbox mountings

Note: *It is possible to renew the crankshaft rear oil seal with the engine in the vehicle, but this requires the use of special tools, and is a difficult operation, due to the lack of working space. For this reason, this operation is described with the engine removed from the vehicle.*

7   Major operations requiring engine removal

The engine must be removed from the vehicle to carry out the following operations:

(a)   Renewal of the crankshaft main bearings
(b)   Removal and refitting of the crankshaft
(c)   Renewal of crankshaft rear oil seal

8   Method of engine removal

The engine may be removed either on its own, or together with the gearbox. Unless work is also necessary on the gearbox, it is recommended that the engine is removed on its own. In either case, the engine or engine/gearbox assembly must be lifted out through the top of the engine compartment, using a suitable hoist and lifting tackle.

9   Engine – removal leaving manual gearbox in vehicle

Note: *A suitable hoist and lifting tackle will be required for this operation*

1   Disconnect the battery negative lead.

2   Remove the bonnet as described in Chapter 10, and on 2.0 litre dohc models, remove the engine undershield.

3   Drain the cooling system and remove the radiator, as described in Chapter 2.

4   Drain the engine oil as described in Section 3, and on 1.8 and 2.0 litre models, remove the oil filter.

5   Remove the air cleaner (or air cleaner cover), the air cleaner trunking, and the air box from the carburettor or throttle body (as applicable), with reference to Chapter 3 if necessary. On carburettor models, disconnect the hot air hose from the exhaust manifold hot air shroud and the air cleaner, and remove the hose.

6   Remove the alternator, as described in Chapter 11.

7   On 1.8 and 2.0 litre models, remove the power steering pump, as described in Chapter 9.

8   Disconnect the brake servo vacuum hose from the inlet manifold.

9   Disconnect the throttle cable from the throttle lever and the bracket on the carburettor or inlet manifold, as applicable.

10   On carburettor models, disconnect the coolant hoses from the automatic choke housing, and disconnect the wiring from the automatic choke heater and the choke pull-down solenoid (photos). Also disconnect the air box vacuum pipe from the carburettor.

11   On 1.6 and 1.8 litre models, disconnect the pressure sensor vacuum pipe from the carburettor (photo).

9.10A Disconnect the coolant hoses from the automatic choke housing ...

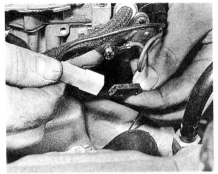

9.10B ... and disconnect the choke heater/pull-down solenoid wiring plug – 1.6 litre model

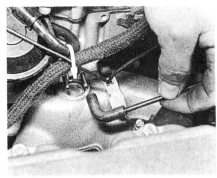

9.11 Disconnect the pressure sensor vacuum pipe from the carburettor – 1.6 litre model

9.13A Disconnecting a fuel hose from the fuel pump – 1.6 litre model

9.13B Fuel hose-to-pipe connections at right-hand side of engine compartment – 2.0 litre sohc model

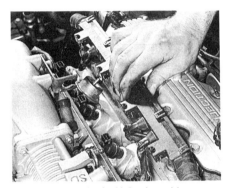

9.14 Removing the fuel injection wiring harness – 2.0 litre sohc model

12   Disconnect the coolant hose(s) from the inlet manifold and/or throttle body, as applicable.

13   Disconnect the fuel hoses from the fuel pump and vapour separator on carburettor models, from the fuel pipes at the right-hand side of the engine compartment on 2.0 litre sohc models, or from the fuel rail on 2.0 litre dohc models. Be prepared for fuel spillage, and take adequate fire precautions. Plug the open ends of the pipes and hoses, to prevent dirt ingress and further fuel leakage (photos).

14   On 2.0 litre models, disconnect all relevant wiring connections and plugs, and remove the fuel injection wiring harness. Pull up on the wiring harness housing, and compress the wiring plug retaining clips to release the harness housing from the fuel injectors (photo).

15   Disconnect the heater coolant hoses from the coolant gallery at the rear of the cylinder block, and from the cylinder head on 2.0 litre dohc models. Also, on 2.0 litre dohc models, disconnect the oil cooler pipe unions from the oil pump.

16   Disconnect the wiring from the following components

(a)   Starter motor
(b)   Distributor (note HT lead positions)
(c)   Oil pressure switch
(d)   Oil temperature switch (where applicable)
(e)   TDC sensor (where applicable)
(f)   Oil level sensor (where applicable)
(g)   Knock sensor (2.0 litre dohc models)
(h)   Coolant temperature sensor (where applicable)
(i)   Temperature gauge sender

17   Make a final check to ensure that all relevant hoses, pipes and wires have been disconnected, and that they are positioned clear of the engine.

18   Unscrew and remove the three upper engine-to-gearbox bolts, accessible from the engine compartment.

19   If not already done, apply the handbrake, then jack up the front of the vehicle, and support securely on axle stands.

20   Remove the crankshaft pulley. On 1.4 and 1.6 litre engines, the pulley is secured by four bolts, which must be unscrewed using a suitable Allen key or hexagon bit. On 1.8 and 2.0 litre engines, the pulley

is secured by a single bolt, which also secures the crankshaft sprocket. On manual gearbox models, if the engine is in the vehicle, the crankshaft can be prevented from turning by having an assistant engage first gear and depress the brake pedal. Alternatively, the flywheel ring gear teeth can be jammed using a suitable tool. Access to the crankshaft pulley is most easily obtained through the right-hand wheel arch, after removing the roadwheel.

21   Remove the front section of the exhaust system, as described in Chapter 3.

22   Remove the clutch, as described in Chapter 5.

23   On 2.0 litre dohc models, unbolt the right-hand driveshaft centre bearing support bracket from the rear of the cylinder block.

24   Unbolt and remove the gearbox bellhousing cover plate (photo).

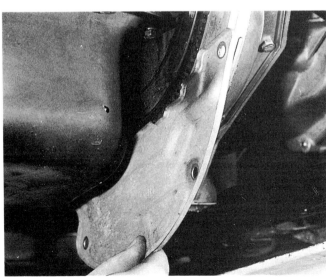

9.24 Removing the gearbox bellhousing cover plate

25   Attach a hoist and suitable lifting gear to the engine lifting brackets on the cylinder head, and support the weight of the engine.
26   Support the gearbox using a trolley jack and interposed block of wood.
27   Unbolt the right-hand engine mounting from the body and from the cylinder block, and withdraw the mounting bracket.
28   Unscrew and remove the four lower engine-to-gearbox bolts, then manipulate the engine as necessary to separate it from the gearbox. Note that the gearbox locates on dowels in the cylinder block.
29   Carefully raise the hoist, and lift the engine from the vehicle, taking care not to damage any of the surrounding components in the engine compartment.
30   With the engine removed, the gearbox can be supported by placing a suitable length of wood between the bellhousing and the front suspension subframe. Once the wooden support is in place, remove the trolley jack from under the gearbox.

10   Engine/manual gearbox – removal and separation

Note: *A suitable hoist and lifting tackle will be required for this operation.*

1   Proceed as described in Section 9, paragraphs 1 to 16 inclusive.
2   Working in the engine compartment, remove the gear selector linkage, as described in Chapter 6, Section 4.
3   Remove the retaining clip, then slide the clutch cable from the release lever, pushing the release lever back towards the bulkhead if necessary to allow the cable to be disconnected. Pull the cable support from the bracket on the gearbox casing, then move the cable to one side out of the way, taking note of its routing.
4   Disconnect the wiring from the reversing lamp switch, which is located at the front of the gearbox casing, above the left-hand mounting bracket.
5   Unscrew the securing sleeve, and disconnect the speedometer cable from the gearbox.
6   Unscrew the retaining nut, and disconnect the earth strap from the gearbox endplate.
7   Make a final check to ensure that all relevant hoses, pipes, wires etc have been disconnected, and that they are positioned clear of the engine and gearbox.
8   Proceed as described in Section 9, paragraphs 19 to 21 inclusive.
9   Disconnect the inboard ends of the driveshafts from the differential, with reference to the relevant paragraphs of Chapter 7, Section 3. Be prepared for oil spillage as the driveshafts are withdrawn, and plug the apertures in the differential, to prevent further loss of oil and dirt ingress. Support the driveshafts by suspending them with wire or string – **do not** allow them to hang down under their own weight.
10   On 2.0 litre dohc models, unbolt the right-hand driveshaft centre bearing support bracket from the rear of the cylinder block.
11   Attach a hoist and suitable lifting gear to the engine lifting brackets on the cylinder head, and support the weight of the engine.
12   Remove the left-hand gearbox mounting completely by unscrewing the two bolts securing the rubber mounting to the vehicle, body, and the three bolts securing the mounting bracket to the gearbox (photo).
13   Unbolt the right-hand engine mounting from the body and from

the cylinder block, and withdraw the mounting bracket.
14   Working under the vehicle, unscrew and remove the two nuts securing the engine/gearbox rear mounting to the front subframe, and the three bolts securing the mounting bracket to the gearbox, then withdraw the mounting bracket (photos).
15   Carefully swing the engine/gearbox assembly across the engine compartment as necessary, to allow the assembly to be lifted vertically from the vehicle by raising the hoist. Take care not to damage any of the surrounding components in the engine compartment.
16   With the engine/gearbox assembly removed, support the assembly on suitable blocks of wood positioned on a workbench, or failing that, on a clean area of the workshop floor.
17   Clean away any external dirt using paraffin or a water-soluble solvent and a stiff brush.
18   Unbolt and remove the gearbox bellhousing cover plate.
19   Ensure that both engine and gearbox are adequately supported, then unscrew and remove the engine-to-gearbox bolts.
20   Carefully withdraw the gearbox from the engine, ensuring that the weight of the gearbox is not allowed to hang on the input shaft while it is engaged with the clutch friction disc. Note that the gearbox locates on dowels positioned in the cylinder block.

11   Engine – refitting (manual gearbox in vehicle)

Note: *A suitable hoist and lifting tackle will be required for this operation. The right-hand engine mounting-to-body bolts must be renewed on refitting*

1   With the front of the vehicle raised and supported on axle stands, support the gearbox with a trolley jack and interposed block of wood, and remove the previously-positioned support from between the gearbox bellhousing and the subframe.
2   Support the engine with the hoist and lifting tackle, and gently lower it into position in the engine compartment.
3   Mate the engine and gearbox together, ensuring that the gearbox locates on the dowels in the cylinder block, then refit the three upper engine-to-gearbox bolts, but do not fully tighten them at this stage.
4   Refit the four lower engine-to-gearbox bolts, but again do not fully tighten them at this stage.
5   Fit the right-hand engine mounting bracket to the cylinder block, and tighten the securing bolts to the specified torque.
6   Manipulate the engine and gearbox as necessary to enable the right-hand engine mounting-to-body bolts to be fitted, then fit new bolts and tighten them to the specified torque.
7   Tighten all the engine-to-gearbox bolts to the specified torque, then disconnect the lifting tackle and hoist from the engine, and remove the trolley jack from beneath the gearbox.
8   On 2.0 litre dohc models, refit the right-hand driveshaft centre bearing support bracket to the rear of the cylinder block, and tighten the securing bolts.
9   Refit the gearbox bellhousing cover plate.
10   Refit the clutch, as described in Chapter 5.
11   Refit the front section of the exhaust system, as described in Chapter 3.

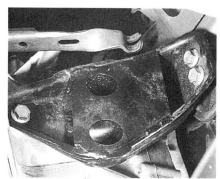

10.12 Left-hand gearbox mounting viewed from underside of vehicle

10.14A Rear engine/gearbox mounting-to-front subframe nuts

10.14B Rear engine/gearbox mounting-to-gearbox bolts (arrowed)

12   Refit the crankshaft pulley using a reversal of the removal procedure described in Section 9, paragraph 20, and tighten the securing
bolt(s) to the specified torque.
13   Lower the vehicle to the ground.
14   Refit all relevant wires, pipes and hoses, etc, using a reversal of the
removal procedure described in Section 9, paragraphs 8 to 16 inclusive.
15   On 1.8 and 2.0 litre models, refit the power steering pump, tension
the pump drivebelt, and bleed the hydraulic fluid circuit, as described in
Chapter 9.
16   Refit the alternator and tension the drivebelt, as described in
Chapter 11.
17   Refit the air cleaner components, with reference to Chapter 3 if
necessary, and on carburettor models reconnect the hot air hose to the
exhaust manifold hot air shroud.
18   Fill the engine with oil, and where applicable fit a new oil filter, as
described in Section 3.
19   Refit the radiator and refill the cooling system, as described in
Chapter 2.
20   Refit the bonnet as described in Chapter 10, and on 2.0 litre dohc
models, refit the engine undershield.
21   Reconnect the battery negative lead.

---

12   Engine/manual gearbox – reconnection and refitting

Note: *A suitable hoist and lifting tackle will be required for this operation.
New left and right-hand engine/gearbox mounting-to-body bolts must be
used on refitting*

1   Before commencing the refitting operations, check that the two
original bolts which secured the left-hand gearbox rubber mounting to
the vehicle body rotate freely in their threaded bores in the body. If
necessary, re-cut the threaded bores using on M10 x 1.25 mm tap.
2   If the clutch assembly has been removed from the flywheel, it will
prove easier to refit after the gearbox has been refitted.
3   Carefully offer the gearbox to the engine until the bellhousing is
located on the dowels in the cylinder block, then refit the engine-to-
gearbox bolts, and tighten them to the specified torque. if the clutch is
still bolted to the flywheel, ensure that the weight of the gearbox is not
allowed to hang on the input shaft as it is engaged with the clutch
friction disc.
4   Refit the gearbox bellhousing cover plate.
5   With the front of the vehicle raised and supported on axle stands,
support the engine/gearbox assembly with the hoist and lifting tackle,
then gently lower it into position in the engine compartment.
6   Working under the vehicle, refit the rear engine/gearbox mounting
to the gearbox, using new locking plates under the bolt heads, and
tighten the bolts to the specified torque.
7   Fit the two bolts securing the engine/gearbox rear mounting to the
front subframe, but do not fully tighten them at this stage.
8   Fit the right-hand engine mounting bracket to the cylinder block,
and tighten the securing bolts to the specified torque.
9   Fit new right-hand engine mounting-to-body bolts, but do not fully
tighten them at this stage.
10   Fit the left-hand gearbox mounting bracket to the gearbox, and
tighten the securing bolts to the specified torque.
11   Fit new left-hand gearbox mounting-to-body bolts, and tighten
them to the specified torque.
12   Tighten the right-hand engine mounting-to-body bolts and the
engine/gearbox rear mounting-to-front subframe bolts to their specified
torques, then remove the lifting tackle and hoist from the engine.
13   Where applicable, the clutch can now be fitted, and the gearbox
input shaft can be pressed into engagement with the splined hub of the
clutch friction disc, as described in Chapter 5, Section 9.
14   Reconnect the inboard ends of the driveshafts to the differential,
with reference to the relevant paragraphs of Chapter 7, Section 3, and
using new snap rings.
15   On 2.0 litre dohc models, refit the right-hand driveshaft centre
bearing support bracket to the rear of the cylinder block, and tighten the
securing bolts.
16   Refit the front section of the exhaust system, as described in
Chapter 3.
17   Refit the crankshaft pulley, using a reversal of the removal procedure described in Section 9, paragraph 20, and tighten the securing

bolt(s) to the specified torque.
18   Reconnect the gearbox earth strap, and tighten the securing nut.
19   Lower the vehicle to the ground.
20   Reconnect the speedometer cable to the gearbox, and tighten the
securing sleeve.
21   Reconnect the reversing lamp wiring.
22   Refit the clutch cable to the bracket on the gearbox casing, then
reconnect the cable to the release lever, and adjust the cable as
described in Chapter 5, Section 4. Ensure that the cable is routed as
noted during removal.
23   Refit the gear selector linkage, as described in Chapter 6, Section 4.
24   Proceed as described in Section 11, paragraphs 13 to 18 inclusive.
25   Top up the gearbox oil level, as described in Chapter 6.
26   Refit the bonnet as described in Chapter 10, and on 2.0 litre dohc
models, refit the engine undershield.
27   Reconnect the battery negative lead.

---

13   Engine/gearbox mountings – renewal

Note: *New left and right-hand engine/gearbox mounting-to-body bolts
must be used on refitting*

1   The engine/gearbox assembly is suspended in the engine compartment on three mountings, two of which are attached to the gearbox,
and one to the engine.

Right-hand mounting

2   On 2.0 litre dohc models, remove the engine undershield, with
reference to Chapter 10 if necessary.
3   If not already done, apply the handbrake, then raise the front of the
vehicle, and support securely on axle stands.
4   Attach suitable lifting tackle and a hoist to the engine lifting brackets
on the cylinder head, and support the weight of the engine.
5   Working under the vehicle, unbolt the engine mounting bracket
from the cylinder block, and unbolt the mounting block from the body,
then withdraw the bracket/mounting assembly.
6   Unbolt the mounting block from the bracket.
7   Fit the new mounting block to the bracket, and tighten the securing
bolts to the specified torque.
8   Refit the mounting bracket to the cylinder block, and tighten the
securing bolts to the specified torque.
9   Fit new mounting block-to-body bolts, and tighten them to the
specified torque.
10   Disconnect the lifting tackle and hoist from the engine.
11   On 2.0 litre dohc models, refit the engine undershield.
12   Lower the vehicle to the ground.

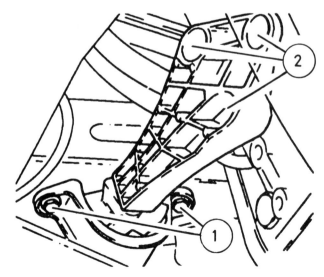

Fig. 1.3 Right-hand engine mounting (Sec 13)

1   Mounting block-to-body   *2   Mounting bracket-to-cylinder*
    bolts   *block bolts*

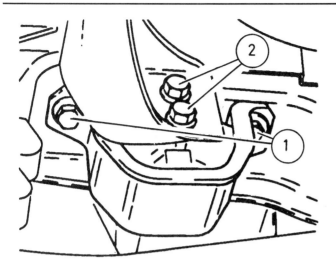

Fig. 1.4 Left-hand engine/gearbox mounting (Sec 13)

1   *Mounting block-to-body*   2   *Mounting block-to-mounting*
    bolts   *bracket bolts*

Left-hand mounting

13   Proceed as described in paragraphs 2 to 4 inclusive.
14   Working under the vehicle, unbolt the mounting block from the mounting bracket and the body.
15   Before fitting the new mounting block, check that the original engine bolts which secured the mounting block to the body rotate freely in their threaded bores in the body. If necessary, re-cut the threaded bores using an M10 x 1.25 mm tap.
16   Fit the new mounting block to the bracket, and tighten the securing bolts to the specified torque.
17   Fit new mounting block-to-body bolts, and tighten them to the specified torque.
18   Proceed as described in paragraphs 10 to 12 inclusive.

Rear mounting

19   Proceed as described in paragraphs 2 to 4 inclusive.
20   Working under the vehicle, unbolt the mounting block from the front subframe and the mounting bracket.
21   Fit the new mounting block to the subframe and mounting bracket, and tighten the securing bolts to the specified torque.
22   Proceed as described in paragraphs 10 to 12 inclusive.

---

14   Engine dismantling – general

---

1   Ideally, the engine should be mounted on a dismantling stand, but if this is not available, stand the engine on a strong bench, at a comfortable working height. Failing this, the engine will have to be stripped down on the floor.
2   Cleanliness is most important, and if the engine is dirty, it should be cleaned with paraffin in an upright position.
3   Avoid working with the engine directly on a concrete floor, as grit presents a real source of trouble.
4   If the engine oil appears extremely dirty or contaminated, avoid inverting the engine until the sump has been removed. This will prevent any contaminated 'sludge' from entering the oilways.
5   As parts are removed, clean them in a paraffin bath. Do not immerse parts with internal oilways in paraffin, as it is difficult to remove, usually requiring a high pressure hose. Clean oilways with nylon pipe cleaners.
6   It is advisable to have suitable containers available to hold small items, to prevent loss and confusion when refitting.
7   Always obtain complete sets of gaskets when the engine is being dismantled. Retain the old gaskets, with a view to using them as patterns to make replacements should new gaskets not be available.

8   Where possible, refit nuts, bolts and washers to their locations after removal of the relevant components, as this helps protect the threads, and will also prove helpful during reassembly.
9   Retain unserviceable components, in order to compare them with the new components supplied.
10   Many of the engine components are secured using socket-headed 'Torx' or 'Allen' bolts, and suitable tools will be required to remove and refit such bolts.
11   Read through each relevant Section of this Chapter carefully *before commencing work,* to ensure that any special tools which may be required are available. Many components (gaskets, oil seals, and certain bolts) must be renewed on reassembly; where applicable, obtain the required new components before starting work.
12   Before commencing a complete strip of the engine, the following ancillary components can be removed once the engine has been removed from the vehicle:

(a)   *Inlet and exhaust manifolds (where applicable)*
(b)   *Starter motor*
(c)   *Rear coolant gallery and hoses*
(d)   *Oil pressure switch*
(e)   *Oil temperature switch (where applicable)*
(f)   *Oil level sensor (where applicable)*
(g)   *Knock sensor (where applicable)*
(h)   *TDC sensor (where applicable)*
(i)   *Distributor components*
(j)   *Fuel pump (where applicable)*
(k)   *Thermostat (1.8 and 2.0 litre models)*
(l)   *Power steering pump mounting bracket (1.8 and 2.0 litre models)*
(m) *Alternator mounting bracket*
(n)   *Engine lifting brackets*
(o)   *Dipstick/crankcase breather tube*
(p)   *Inlet manifold mounting bracket (dohc models)*
(q)   *Power steering pump (where applicable on 1.6 litre models)*

---

15   Timing belt and sprockets (sohc engines) – removal and refitting

---

Note: *A suitable two-legged puller may be required to remove the crankshaft sprocket on 1.8 and 2.0 litre models*

1   Disconnect the battery negative lead.
2   On 1.8 and 2.0 litre models with power steering, remove the power steering pump drivebelt, as described in Chapter 9, Section 42.
3   Remove the alternator drivebelt, as described in Chapter 11, Section 7.
4   On 1.8 and 2.0 litre models, disconnect the wiring from the temperature gauge sender.
5   Release the securing clips and remove the main outer timing belt cover, then unclip the smaller outer timing belt cover from the coolant pump (photos).
6   On 1.6 litre models with power steering, remove the power steering pump, as described in Chapter 9, Section 43.
7   Turn the crankshaft using a suitable socket or spanner on the crankshaft sprocket bolt, until the timing mark on the camshaft sprocket is aligned with the notch in the rear timing belt cover, and the notch in the crankshaft pulley is aligned with the pointer on the rear timing belt cover (photos). Note that on 1.4 litre engine there are two notches in the crankshaft pulley, representing 5° and 10° BTDC, and the 10° BTDC notch should be aligned with the pointer – see Fig. 1.5.

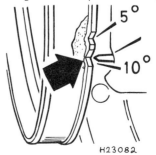

H23082

Fig. 1.5 Crankshaft pulley 10° BTDC notch aligned with pointer on rear timing belt cover – 1.4 litre engine (Sec 15)

15.5A Remove the main outer timing belt cover ...

15.5B ... and the smaller cover from the coolant pump – 2.0 litre engine

15.7A Camshaft sprocket TDC mark aligned with notch in rear timing belt cover ...

15.7B ... and notch in crankshaft pulley aligned with pointer on rear timing belt cover – 2.0 litre engine

15.8 Loosening a coolant pump securing bolt – 2.0 litre engine

8   Loosen the three coolant pump securing bolts (photo), and turn the pump to relieve the tension in the timing belt, then slide the belt from the camshaft sprocket.

9   The crankshaft pulley must now be removed. On 1.4 and 1.6 litre engines, the pulley is secured by a single bolt, which also secures the crankshaft sprocket. On 1.8 and 2.0 litre engines, the pulley is secured by four bolts, which must be unscrewed using an Allen key or hexagon bit. On manual gearbox models, if the engine is in the vehicle, the crankshaft can be prevented from turning by having an assistant engage first gear and depress the brake pedal. Alternatively, the flywheel ring gear teeth can be jammed using a suitable tool.

10   With the crankshaft pulley removed, the timing belt can be withdrawn.

11   If desired, the sprockets and the rear timing belt cover can be removed as follows, otherwise proceed to paragraph 23.

12   To remove the camshaft sprocket, first disconnect the breather hose(s) from the camshaft cover, then unscrew the securing bolts, noting the locations of the HT lead brackets and any other wiring brackets, and remove the camshaft cover.

13   Recover the gasket. Prevent the camshaft from turning by holding

it with a spanner on the flats provided between Nos 3 and 4 camshaft lobes, and unscrew the camshaft sprocket bolt.

14   Withdraw the sprocket from the end of the camshaft.

15   To remove the crankshaft sprocket on 1.4 and 1.6 litre engines, if necessary, remove the lower securing bolt from the main rear timing belt cover, and use two large screwdrivers behind the cover to lever off the sprocket. Remove the Woodruff key if it is loose.

16   To remove the crankshaft sprocket on 1,.8 and 2.0 litre engines, it will be necessary to prevent the crankshaft from turning, as described in paragraph 9. Take care when unscrewing the sprocket bolt, as it is very tight. If necessary, use a suitable two-legged puller to remove the sprocket. Recover the Woodruff key and the thrustwasher from the end of the crankshaft.

17   To remove the main rear timing belt cover, on 1.8 and 2.0 litre models disconnect the TDC sensor wiring plug, and unclip the wiring from the belt cover, then unscrew the two upper securing bolts and the lower securing bolt(s) (one in the case of 1.8 and 2.0 litre engines, two on 1.4 and 1.6 litre engines), and withdraw the cover, manipulating it from the smaller rear belt cover on the coolant pump (photos).

18   If desired, the smaller rear belt cover can be removed from the

15.17A Loosening the main rear timing belt cover lower securing bolt – 2.0 litre engine

15.17B Main rear timing belt cover lower securing bolts (arrowed) – 1.6 litre engine

15.18 Unscrewing the coolant pump rear belt cover securing bolt – 2.0 litre engine

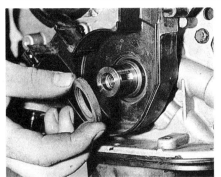

15.20A Refit the thrust washer ...

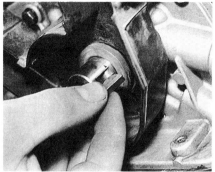

15.20B ... the Woodruff key ...

15.20C ... the crankshaft sprocket ...

15.20D ... and the washer and bolt

15.20E Tighten the bolt to the specified torque ...

15.20F ... then through the specified angle – 2.0 litre engine

15.21 Crankshaft sprocket fits with flange and pulley locating lug outermost – 1.6 litre engine

15.22A Refit the camshaft sprocket ...

15.22B ... and tighten the securing bolt to the specified torque – 2.0 litre engine

15.22C Fit the camshaft cover gasket ...

15.22D ... then fit the cover and tighten the securing bolts. Note position of HT lead brackets – 2.0 litre engine

15.23 Refitting the timing belt – 2.0 litre engine

15.24A Refitting the crankshaft pulley – 1.6 litre engine

15.24B Tightening a crankshaft pulley securing bolt – 2.0 litre engine

coolant pump, after unscrewing the securing bolt (photo), by rotating it to disengage it from the retaining flange on the pump.

19   Refit the rear timing belt cover(s) using a reversal of the removal procedure, and ensuring that the main cover engages correctly with the smaller cover on the coolant pump.

20   On 1.8 and 2.0 litre engines, refit the thrustwasher and the Woodruff key to the end of the crankshaft, then refit the crankshaft sprocket, and tighten the securing bolt to the specified torque in the two stages given in the Specifications. Ensure that the washer is in place under the bolt head, and prevent the crankshaft from turning as during removal (photos).

21   On 1.4 and 1.6 litre engines, refit the Woodruff key to the end of the crankshaft where applicable, and refit the crankshaft sprocket with the flange and locating lug for the crankshaft pulley outermost (photo).

22   Refit the camshaft sprocket, ensuring that the locating pin on the end of the camshaft engages with the hole in the sprocket, and tighten the securing bolt to the specified torque. Prevent the camshaft from turning as during removal. Check the condition of the camshaft cover gasket and renew if necessary, then refit the camshaft cover, ensuring that the HT lead brackets and any other wiring bracket are correctly located, and reconnect the breather hose(s) (photos).

23   Temporarily refit the crankshaft pulley and ensure that the crankshaft pulley and camshaft sprocket timing marks are still aligned as described in paragraph 7, then refit the timing belt around the sprockets (photo), starting at the crankshaft sprocket.

24   Refit the crankshaft pulley, and tighten the securing bolt(s) to the specified torque (photos). If necessary, prevent the crankshaft from turning as during removal.

25   Adjust the timing belt tension, as described in Section 16.

26   On 1.6 litre models with power steering, refit the power steering

pump, as described in Chapter 9, Section 43.

27   Refit the outer timing belt covers, and on 1.8 and 2.0 litre models, reconnect the temperature gauge sender wiring.

28   Refit the alternator drivebelt and adjust the drivebelt tension, as described in Chapter 11, Section 7.

29   On 1.8 and 2.0 litre models with power steering, refit the power steering pump drivebelt and adjust the drivebelt tension, as described in Chapter 9, Section 42.

30   Reconnect the battery negative lead.

16   Timing belt tension (sohc engines) – checking and adjustment

Note: *The manufacturers specify the use of a special gauge, Vauxhall tool No KM-510-A, for checking the timing belt tension. If access to a suitable gauge cannot be obtained, it is strongly recommended that the vehicle is taken to a Vauxhall dealer to have the belt tension checked at the earliest opportunity*

1   The tension of a used timing belt should be checked with the engine at normal operating temperature. The tension of a new timing belt should be checked with the engine cold.

2   Release the securing clips and remove the main outer timing belt cover, then unclip the smaller outer timing belt cover from the coolant pump.

3   Turn the crankshaft through at least quarter of a turn clockwise, using a suitable socket or spanner on the crankshaft sprocket bolt.

4   If the special gauge is available, place the locked gauge at the centre of the belt run between the coolant pump and the camshaft sprocket. The gauge should locate on the timing belt as shown in Fig. 1.6.

5   Slowly release the operating lever on the gauge, then lightly tap the

Fig. 1.6 Tension gauge KM-510-A correctly positioned on timing belt. Belt must pass through points A, B and C – sohc engines (Sec 16)

16.5 Note the reading on the scale of the tension gauge – 1.6 litre engine

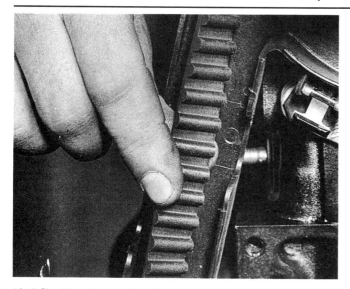

16.12 Checking timing belt tension by twisting belt through 90° between thumb and forefinger

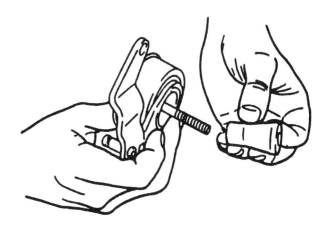

Fig. 1.7 Belt tensioner pulley and spacer sleeve. Note that smaller diameter of spacer sleeve fits against pulley – dohc engine (Sec 17)

gauge two or three times, and note the reading on the scale (photo).

6 If the reading is not as specified, loosen the three coolant pump securing bolts, and rotate the pump in the required direction to achieve the desired reading on the gauge. Rotate the pump clockwise to increase the belt tension, or anti-clockwise to decrease the tension.

7 Lightly tighten the coolant pump securing bolts.

8 Remove the tensioning gauge, and turn the crankshaft through one full turn clockwise.

9 Re-check the belt tension as described in paragraphs 4 and 5.

10 If the tension is not as specified, repeat paragraphs 6 to 9 inclusive until the desired, consistent, reading is obtained.

11 On completion of adjustment, remove the checking gauge, tighten the coolant pump bolts to the specified torque, and refit the outer timing belt covers.

12 If the special checking gauge is not available, the timing belt tension can be checked approximately by twisting the belt between the thumb and forefinger, at the centre of the run between the coolant pump and the camshaft sprocket. It should just be possible to twist the belt through 90° using moderate pressure (photo). If adjustment is necessary, proceed as described previously in this Section, but have the belt tension checked by a Vauxhall dealer using the special gauge at the earliest opportunity. If in doubt, err on the tight side when adjusting the tension, as if the belt is too slack, it may jump on the sprockets, which could result in serious engine damage.

17 Timing belt, sprockets and belt tensioner and idler pulleys (dohc engine) – removal and refitting

Note: *The timing belt must be renewed on refitting; never refit a used belt. A suitable two-legged puller may be required to remove the crankshaft sprocket*

1 Disconnect the battery negative lead.

2 Disconnect the air cleaner trunking from the airflow meter, then remove the cover and the air cleaner element from the air cleaner. If desired, for improved access, the complete air cleaner assembly can be removed, as described in Chapter 3, Section 31.

3 Remove the power steering pump drivebelt, as described in Chapter 9, Section 42.

4 Remove the alternator drivebelt, as described in Chapter 11, Section 7.

5 Remove the three securing screws, and withdraw the outer timing belt cover. Recover the rubber grommets from the screw holes in the cover if they are loose.

6 Turn the crankshaft using a suitable Torx socket on the crankshaft sprocket bolt, until the timing marks on the camshaft sprockets are aligned with the notches in the camshaft cover, and the notch in the crankshaft pulley is aligned with the pointer on the rear timing belt cover (photos).

17.6A Camshaft sprocket TDC mark aligned with notch in camshaft cover

17.6B ... and notch in crankshaft pulley aligned with pointer on rear timing belt cover (circled) – dohc engine

17.7 Crankshaft pulley and securing bolts viewed through right-hand wheel arch (wheel removed) – dohc engine

17.8 Timing belt tensioner pulley securing bolt (arrowed) – dohc engine

17.10 Disconnecting a breather hose from the rear of the camshaft cover – dohc engine

17.11 Removing the spark plug cover – dohc engine

17.12 Unscrewing a camshaft cover securing bolt – dohc engine

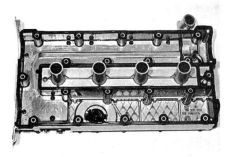

17.13 Camshaft cover removed to show one-piece rubber gasket – dohc engine

7   Extract the six securing bolts using a suitable splined bit, and withdraw the crankshaft pulley (photo). If necessary, counterhold the crankshaft using a suitable socket on the crankshaft sprocket bolt. If the engine is in the vehicle, the crankshaft can be prevented from turning by having an assistant engage first gear and depress the brake pedal. Alternatively, the flywheel ring gear teeth can be jammed using a suitable tool. Before removing the pulley, check that the timing marks are still aligned.

8   Loosen the securing bolt and release the timing belt tensioner pulley, then slide the belt from the sprockets and pulleys (photo).

9   If desired, the sprockets, tensioner and idler pulleys, and the rear timing belt cover can be removed as follows, otherwise proceed to paragraph 27.

10   To remove the camshaft sprockets, first disconnect the breather hoses from the camshaft cover (photo).

11   Extract the two securing bolts and remove the spark plug cover (photo), then disconnect the HT leads from the spark plugs, and unclip them from the end of the camshaft cover. If necessary, mark the HT leads for position, to avoid confusion when refitting.

12   Unscrew the twenty securing bolts and withdraw the camshaft cover (photo).

13   Recover the one-piece rubber gasket (photo).

14   Prevent the relevant camshaft from turning by holding it with a spanner on the flats provided in front of No 1 cam lobe, and unscrew the camshaft sprocket bolt (photo).

15   Withdraw the sprocket from the end of the camshaft, then repeat the procedure for the remaining camshaft sprocket.

16   To remove the crankshaft sprocket, it will be necessary to prevent the crankshaft from turning by bolting a suitable metal bar to the sprocket using two of the crankshaft pulley bolts, or by jamming the flywheel ring gear teeth. A suitable Torx socket will be required to unscrew the sprocket bolt – take care, as the bolt is very tight. If necessary, use a suitable two-legged puller to remove the sprocket. Recover the thrustwashers from the end of the crankshaft, and from under the bolt head.

17   To remove the belt tensioner pulley, simply unscrew the securing bolt from the centre of the pulley, then withdraw the pulley complete with mounting plate (photo). Recover the spacer sleeve from the pulley bolt.

18   To remove the belt idler pulley, unscrew the securing bolt from the centre of the pulley, then withdraw the pulley and recover the spacer sleeve from the pulley bolt.

19   The rear timing belt cover can now be removed after unscrewing the upper and middle studs for the timing belt outer cover screws. Note that the upper stud simply unscrews from the cylinder head, but the middle stud is secured by a bolt. Unscrew the two upper and single lower right-hand rear belt cover securing bolts, and withdraw the rear belt cover (photos).

20   Refit the rear timing belt cover using a reversal of the removal procedure.

21   Refit the belt idler and tensioner pulleys, noting that the spacer sleeves should be fitted with their smaller diameters against the pulleys. Do not fully tighten the tensioner pulley bolt at this stage.

22   Refit the thrustwasher to the end of the crankshaft, then refit the crankshaft sprocket. Apply a little grease to the threads of the securing bolt, and tighten it to the specified torque in the two stages given in the Specifications. Ensure that the thrustwasher is in place under the bolt head, and prevent the crankshaft from turning as during removal.

23   Refit the camshaft sprockets, ensuring that the locating pins on the ends of the camshafts engage with the holes in the sprockets, with the sprocket timing marks facing forwards, then tighten the securing bolts to the specified torque in the two stages given in the Specifications. Prevent the camshafts from turning as during removal.

24   Check the condition of the camshaft cover rubber gasket and renew if necessary, then refit the camshaft cover and tighten the securing bolts (photo).

25   Refit the HT leads to the spark plugs (ensuring that they are refitted to their correct cylinders), then clip the leads to the end of the camshaft cover, refit the spark plug cover and tighten the securing bolts.

26   Reconnect the breather hose to the camshaft cover.

27   Temporarily refit the crankshaft pulley, and ensure that the crankshaft pulley and camshaft sprocket timing marks are still aligned as described in paragraph 6, then fit a **new** timing belt around the sprockets and pulleys, starting at the crankshaft sprocket.

17.14 Spanner positioned to counterhold exhaust camshaft – dohc engine

17.17 Timing belt pulley components – dohc engine

1 Tensioner pulley securing bolt
2 Tensioner pulley mounting plate
3 Idler pulley securing bolt

17.19A Timing belt outer cover screw upper stud (1) and rear belt cover upper securing bolts (2) – dohc engine

17.19B Rear timing belt cover lower right-hand securing bolt – dohc engine

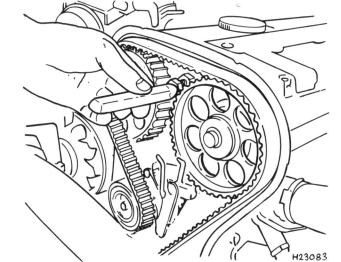

17.24 Tightening a camshaft cover securing bolt – dohc engine

28 Refit the crankshaft pulley, and tighten the securing bolts to the specified torque. If necessary, prevent the crankshaft from turning as during removal.
29 Adjust the timing belt tension, as described in Section 18.
30 Refit the outer timing belt cover, ensuring that the rubber grommets are in place in the screw holes, and tighten the securing screws.
31 Refit the alternator drivebelt and adjust the drivebelt tension, as described in Chapter 11, Section 7.
32 Refit the power steering pump drivebelt and adjust the drivebelt tension, as described in Chapter 9, Section 42.
33 Refit the air cleaner components as applicable, with reference to Chapter 3, Section 31 if necessary.
34 Reconnect the battery negative lead.

---

18 Timing belt tension (dohc engine) – adjustment

Note: *The manufacturers specify the use of special adjustment wrench, Vauxhall tool No KM-666, for adjusting the timing belt tension. If access to this tool cannot be obtained, an approximate adjustment can be achieved using the method described in this Section, however, it is emphasised that the vehicle should be taken to a dealer at the earliest possible opportunity to have the tension adjusted using the special tool. Do not drive the vehicle over any long distance until the belt tension has been adjusted by a dealer*

Approximate adjustment
1 No checking of timing belt adjustment is specified, and the following adjustment procedure applies to a newly-fitted belt. The adjustment must be carried out with the engine cold.

2 With the timing belt cover removed and the tensioner pulley bolt slackened, ensure that the TDC marks on the camshaft sprockets and the crankshaft pulley are aligned as described in Section 17, paragraph 6. If necessary, turn the crankshaft to achieve alignment.
3 Have an assistant press the tensioner pulley against the belt until the belt can just be twisted through 45°, using moderate pressure with the thumb and forefinger, on the longest belt run between the exhaust camshaft sprocket and the belt idler pulley.

Fig. 1.8 Working anti-clockwise from the TDC mark on the exhaust camshaft sprocket, mark the seventh tooth on the sprocket (Sec 18)

4   Have the assistant hold the tensioner pulley in position, and tighten the tensioner pulley bolt to the specified torque in the two stages given in the Specifications.
5   Turn the crankshaft clockwise through two complete revolutions, and check that, with the crankshaft pulley TDC mark aligned with the pointer on the rear timing belt cover, the TDC marks on the camshaft sprockets are still aligned with the notches in the camshaft cover.
6   Proceed as described in Section 17, paragraph 30 onwards.
7   Have the belt tension adjusted by a Vauxhall dealer using the manufacturer's special tool at the earliest opportunity.

Adjustment using Vauxhall special tool
8   Proceed as described in paragraphs 1 and 2.
9   Fit the special tool KM-666 to the belt tensioner pulley mounting plate, in accordance with the tool manufacturer's instructions.
10   Working anti-clockwise from the TDC mark on the exhaust camshaft sprocket, mark the seventh tooth on the sprocket – see Fig. 1.8.
11   Turn the crankshaft clockwise until this tooth is aligned with the TDC notch in the camshaft cover. The crankshaft must be turned evenly and without jerking, to prevent the timing belt from jumping off the sprockets and pulleys.
12   Tighten the tensioner pulley bolt to the specified torque in the two stages given in the Specifications.
13   Remove special tool KM-666.
14   Turn the crankshaft clockwise until the TDC marks on the camshaft sprockets are aligned with the notches in the camshaft cover, and check that the crankshaft pulley TDC mark is aligned with the pointer on the rear timing belt cover.
15   Proceed as described in Section 17, paragraph 30 onwards.

---

19 Camshaft front oil seal (sohc engines) – renewal

1   The camshaft front oil seal may be renewed with the engine in the vehicle without removing the camshaft as follows.
2   Remove the timing belt and the camshaft sprocket, as described in Section 15.
3   Punch or drill a small hole in the centre of the now-exposed oil seal. Screw in a self-tapping screw, and pull on the screw with pliers to extract the seal.
4   Clean the oil seal seat with a wooden or plastic scraper.
5   Grease the lips of the new seal, and drive it into position until it is flush with the housing, using a suitable socket or tube. Take care not to damage the seal lips during fitting.
6   Refit the camshaft sprocket and the timing belt, as described in Section 15, and tension the timing belt as described in Section 16.

---

20 Camshaft rear oil seal (sohc engines) – renewal

1   The camshaft rear oil seal may be renewed with the engine in the vehicle without removing the camshaft as follows.
2   On 1.4 and 1.6 litre models, remove the distributor as described in Chapter 4, Section 8, and on 1.8 and 2.0 litre models, remove the distributor components as described in Chapter 4, Section 8.

3   On 1.4 and 1.6 litre models, the seal takes the form of an O-ring on the rear of the distributor body. Prise off the old O-ring using a screwdriver, then fit the new O-ring, and refit the distributor as described in Chapter 4, Section 8.
4   On 1.8 and 2.0 litre models, prise the seal from the camshaft housing, fit the new seal so that it is flush with the end of the housing, then refit the distributor components as described in Chapter 4, Section 8.

---

21 Camshaft housing and camshaft (sohc engines) – removal and refitting

Note: *The engine must be cold when removing the camshaft housing.* **Do not** *remove the camshaft housing from a hot engine. New cylinder head bolts must be used on refitting, and suitable sealer will be required when refitting the camshaft housing. Also see paragraph 3 before starting work.*

1   The camshaft can only be removed without disturbing the housing if a special tool is available to depress the cam followers whilst the camshaft is withdrawn.
2   If such a tool is available, the camshaft can be removed with reference to Section 22, after removing the timing belt and camshaft sprocket as described in Section 15.
3   Assuming that the special tool is not available, the camshaft housing must be removed. Since the cylinder head bolts must be removed, it is strongly recommended that a new cylinder head gasket is fitted. If the gasket is not renewed, and it 'blows' on reassembly, the cylinder head will have to be removed in order to renew the gasket, and another new set of bolts will have to be obtained for refitting. *You have been warned!*
4   Removal and refitting of the camshaft housing is described in Section 23 or 24 (as applicable) along with cylinder head removal and refitting. If it is decided not to disturb the cylinder head, the relevant paragraphs referring specifically to cylinder head removal and refitting can be ignored.
5   Removal of the camshaft from the housing is described in Section 22.

---

22 Camshaft housing and camshaft (sohc engines) – dismantling, inspection and reassembly

1   With the camshaft housing removed from the cylinder head as described in Section 21, proceed as follows.
2   On 1.4 and 1.6 litre models, remove the distributor as described in Chapter 4, Section 8, and on 1.8 and 2.0 litre models, remove the distributor components as described in Chapter 4, Section 8, and prise out the camshaft rear oil seal.
3   On carburettor models, remove the fuel pump, with reference to Chapter 3 if necessary.
4   Working at the distributor end of the camshaft, unscrew the two camshaft thrustplate securing bolts, using a suitable Allen key or hexagon bit (photo).
5   Withdraw the thrustplate, noting which way round it is fitted (photo).

22.4 Camshaft thrustplate and securing bolts – 1.6 litre engine

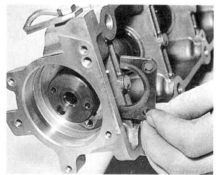

22.5 Removing the camshaft thrustplate – 2.0 litre engine

22.6 Withdrawing the camshaft from the housing – 2.0 litre engine

22.10A Prising out the camshaft front oil seal – 2.0 litre engine

22.10B Fitting a new camshaft front oil seal using a suitable diameter tool – 2.0 litre engine

22.13 Tightening a camshaft thrustplate securing bolt – 2.0 litre engine

22.14 Fitting a new camshaft rear oil seal – 2.0 litre engine

6   Carefully withdraw the camshaft from the distributor end of the camshaft housing, taking care not to damage the bearing journals (photo).
7   With the camshaft removed, examine the bearings in the camshaft housing for signs of obvious wear or pitting. If evident, a new camshaft housing will probably be required.
8   The camshaft itself should show no marks or scoring on the journal or cam lobe surfaces. If evident, renew the camshaft. Note that if the camshaft is renewed, all the rocker arms should also be renewed.
9   Check the camshaft thrustplate for signs of wear or grooves, and renew if evident.
10   It is advisable to renew the camshaft front oil seal as a matter of course if the camshaft has been removed. Prise out the old seal using a screwdriver, and drive in the new seal until it is flush with the housing, using a suitable socket or tube (photos).
11   Commence reassembly by liberally oiling the bearings in the housing and the oil seal lip.
12   Carefully insert the camshaft into the housing from the distributor end, taking care to avoid damage to the bearings.
13   Refit the thrustplate, and tighten the securing bolts (photo). Check the camshaft endfloat by inserting a feeler blade between the thrustplate and the camshaft end flange. If the endfloat exceeds that specified, renew the thrustplate.
14   On 1.8 and 2.0 litre models, fit a new camshaft rear oil seal (photo).
15   Where applicable, refit the fuel pump, with reference to Chapter 3 if necessary.
16   On 1.4 and 1.6 litre models, refit the distributor as described in Chapter 4, Section 8, and on 1.8 and 2.0 litre models, refit the distributor as described in Chapter 4, Section 8.
17   Refit the camshaft housing, as described in Section 23 or 24, as applicable.

18   If a new camshaft has been fitted, it is important to observe the following running-in schedule (unless otherwise specified by the manufacturer) immediately after initially starting the engine:

One minute at 2000 rpm
One minute at 1500 rpm
One minute at 3000 rpm
One minute at 2000 rpm

19   Change the engine oil (but not the filter, unless due in any case) approximately 600 miles (1000 km) after fitting a new camshaft.

23   Cylinder head (sohc engines) – removal and refitting (engine in vehicle)

Note: *The engine must be cold when the cylinder head is removed.* **Do not** *remove the cylinder head from a hot engine. New cylinder head bolts and a new cylinder head gasket must be used on refitting, and suitable sealer will be required when refitting the camshaft housing.*

1   Disconnect the battery negative lead.
2   Drain the cooling system, as described in Chapter 2, Section 3.
3   Disconnect the exhaust downpipe from the manifold, with reference to Chapter 3, Section 26 or 52, as applicable.
4   The cylinder head can be removed complete with the manifolds, or the manifolds can be detached from the cylinder head prior to removal, with reference to the relevant Sections of Chapter 3. If no work is to be carried out on the inlet manifold, it can be unbolted from the cylinder head and supported to one side out of the way, thus avoiding the need

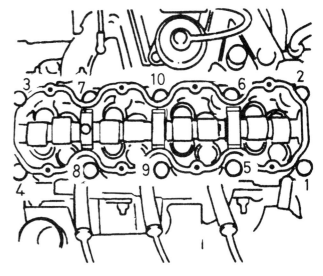

Fig. 1.9 Cylinder head bolt loosening sequence – sohc engines (Sec 23)

23.7 Disconnecting a camshaft cover breather hose – 2.0 litre engine

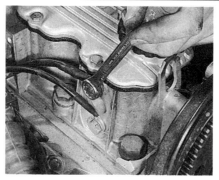

23.10 Unbolting the fuel injection wiring harness earth leads from the camshaft housing – 2.0 litre engine

23.11 Disconnecting the crankcase breather tube stub hose – 1.6 litre engine

23.19A Disconnecting the crankcase breather tube stub hose – 2.0 litre engine

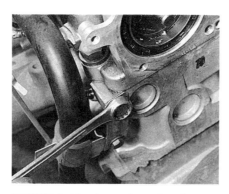

23.19B Unbolting the crankcase breather tube bracket from the cylinder head – 2.0 litre model

23.24 Lifting the camshaft housing from the cylinder head – 1.6 litre engine

to disconnect the relevant hoses, pipes and wiring.

5　If the cylinder head is to be removed complete with the manifolds, disconnect all relevant hoses, pipes and wiring from the inlet manifold and associated components, with reference to Chapter 3, Section 24 or 50 as applicable. On carburettor models, disconnect the hot air hose from the shroud on the exhaust manifold. Loosen the alternator mountings, with reference to Chapter 11, Section 8, then unbolt the upper alternator mounting from the inlet manifold.

6　If the inlet manifold is to be left in the engine compartment, proceed as follows, otherwise proceed to paragraph 15.

7　Disconnect the air cleaner trunking from the air box on the carburettor or throttle body, or directly from the throttle body (as applicable), and disconnect the camshaft cover breather hose which runs to the carburettor or throttle body (as applicable) (photo).

8　On 1.8 and 2.0 litre models, disconnect the smaller coolant hose form the top of the thermostat housing.

9　On 1.6 litre models, disconnect the breather hose (which runs from the camshaft cover to the inlet manifold) at the camshaft cover.

10　On fuel injection models, unbolt the two wiring harnesses earth leads from the camshaft housing (photo).

11　On 1.4 and 1.6 litre models, disconnect the stub hose which connects the crankcase breather tube to the rear of the camshaft housing (photo).

12　Loosen the alternator mountings with reference to Chapter 11, Section 8, then unbolt the upper alternator mounting from the inlet manifold.

13　Make a final check to ensure that all necessary hoses, pipes and wires have been disconnected, then unscrew the securing nuts, noting the location of the engine lifting bracket, and lift the inlet manifold from the cylinder head. Ensure that the manifold is properly supported, taking care not to strain any of the hoses, pipes and wires, etc, which are still connected.

14　Recover the manifold gasket from the cylinder head.

15　If desired, remove the exhaust manifold, with reference to Chapter 3, Section 25 or 51, as applicable.

16　Remove the timing belt and the camshaft sprocket, as described in Section 15.

17　Unscrew the two upper rear timing belt cover securing bolts from the camshaft housing.

18　Disconnect the HT leads from the spark plugs and the coil, labelling them if necessary to aid refitting, and remove the distributor cap with reference to Chapter 4, Section 7. Where applicable, disconnect the distributor wiring plug.

19　If not already done, disconnect the stub hose which connects the crankcase breather tube to the camshaft housing. On 1.8 and 2.0 litre models, unscrew the bolt securing the crankcase breather tube bracket to the end of the cylinder head (photo).

20　Disconnect the coolant hoses from the thermostat housing.

21　On carburettor models, disconnect the fuel hoses from the fuel pump. Be prepared for fuel spillage, and plug the open ends of the hoses, to prevent further fuel loss and dirt ingress.

22　Make a final check to ensure that all relevant hoses, pipes and wires, etc, have been disconnected.

23　Working from the outside inwards in a spiral pattern as shown in Fig. 1.9, loosen all the cylinder head bolts by a quarter of a turn, then loosen all the bolts by half a turn, and finally loosen and remove the bolts. Recover the washers.

24　Lift the camshaft housing from the cylinder head (photo). If necessary, tap the housing gently with a soft-faced mallet to free it from the cylinder head, but **do not** lever at the mating faces. Note that the camshaft housing is located on dowels.

25　Lift the rocker arms and their thrust pads from the cylinder head, keeping them in order so that they can be refitted in their original positions (photos).

26　Lift the hydraulic valve lifters from the cylinder head, and place them upright in an oil bath until they are to be refitted (photo). Ensure that the depth of oil is sufficient to fully cover the valve lifters, and keep the lifters in order, so that they can be refitted in their original positions.

27　Lift the cylinder head from the cylinder block (photo). If necessary, tap the cylinder head gently with a soft-faced mallet to free it from the block, but **do not** lever at the mating faces. Note that the cylinder head is located on dowels.

28　Recover the cylinder head gasket and discard it.

29　Clean the cylinder head and block mating faces, and the camshaft

23.25A Lift the rocker arms ...

23.25B ... and their thrust pads from the cylinder head – 1.6 litre engine

23.26 Lift the hydraulic valve lifters from the cylinder head – 1.6 litre engine

23.27 Lifting the cylinder head from the cylinder block – 1.6 litre engine

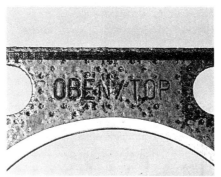
23.31A Cylinder head gasket 'OBEN/TOP' markings

23.31B Cylinder head gasket correctly located over dowel in cylinder block

housing and cylinder head mating faces by careful scraping. Take care not to damage the cylinder head and camshaft housing, which are made of light alloy and are easily scored. Cover the coolant passages and other openings with masking tape or rag to prevent dirt and carbon falling in. Mop out all the oil from the bolt holes; if oil is left in the holes, hydraulic pressure could crack the block when the bolts are refitted.

30 If desired, the cylinder head can be dismantled and inspected as described in Section 25 and 26, and the camshaft housing can be dismantled as described in Section 22.

31 Commence refitting by locating a new gasket on the block so that the word 'OBEN' or 'TOP' can be read from above (photos).

32 With the mating faces scrupulously clean, locate the cylinder head

on the block so that the positioning dowels engage in their holes.

33 Refit the hydraulic valve lifters, thrust pads and rocker arms to the cylinder head in their original positions. Liberally oil the valve lifter bores, and if new lifters are being fitted, initially immerse each one in a container of clean engine oil and compress it (by hand) several times to charge it. Lubricate the contact faces of the valve lifters, thrust pads and rocker arms with a little molybdenum disulphide grease (photo).

34 Temporarily refit the crankshaft sprocket, and ensure that the timing marks are still positioned as they were before the timing belt was removed (see Section 15).

35 Apply sealing compound (Vauxhall part No 15 03 166, or equivalent) to the cylinder head top mating face (photo), then refit the camshaft housing to the cylinder head.

36 Fit the **new** cylinder head bolts, ensuring that the washers are in place under their heads, and screw the bolts in *by hand* as far as possible (photo).

37 Tighten the bolts working from the inside outwards in a spiral pattern as shown in Fig. 1.10. Tighten the bolts in the four stages given in the Specifications – ie tighten all bolts to the Stage 1 torque, then tighten all bolts to Stage 2 and so on (photos).

38 Further refitting is a reversal of the removal procedure, bearing in mind the following points.

39 Ensure that the HT leads are refitted to their correct cylinders.

40 Refit the camshaft sprocket and the timing belt as described in Section 15, and tension the timing belt as described in Section 16.

41 Where applicable, refit the manifolds to the cylinder head, with reference to the relevant Sections of Chapter 3, using new gaskets.

42 Reconnect the exhaust downpipe to the manifold, using a new gasket, with reference to Chapter 3, Section 26 or 52, if necessary.

43 Refit the upper alternator mounting to the inlet manifold, then adjust the alternator drivebelt tension, as described in Chapter 11, Section 7.

44 Refill the cooling system, as described in Chapter 2, Section 5.

45 On completion, check that all relevant hoses, pipes and wires, etc, have been reconnected.

46 When the engine is started, check for signs of leaks.

47 Once the engine has reached normal operating temperature, check and if necessary adjust the idle speed (where applicable) and the

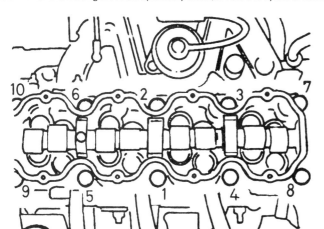
Fig. 1.10 Cylinder head bolt tightening sequence – sohc engines (Sec 23)

23.33 Lubricate the valve lifter contact faces with molybdenum disulphide grease

23.35 Apply sealing compound to the cylinder head top mating face

23.36 Fit new cylinder head bolts, ensuring that the washers are in place

23.37A Tighten the cylinder head bolts to the specified torque ...

23.37B ... then through the specified angle – 2.0 litre engine

mixture (where applicable), with reference to the relevant Sections of Chapter 3, and finally tighten the cylinder head bolts to the Stage 5 setting.

24 Cylinder head (sohc engines) – removal and refitting (engine removed)

Note: *New cylinder head bolts and a new cylinder head gasket must be used on refitting, and suitable sealer will be required when refitting the camshaft housing*

24.3 Upper rear timing belt cover securing bolts (arrowed) – 1.6 litre engine

1   The cylinder head can be removed complete with the manifolds, or the manifolds can be detached from the cylinder head prior to removal, with reference to the relevant Sections of Chapter 3.
2   Remove the timing belt and the camshaft sprocket, as described in Section 15.
3   Unscrew the two upper rear timing belt cover securing bolts from the camshaft housing (photo).
4   Disconnect the HT leads from the spark plugs, labelling them if necessary to aid refitting, and remove the distributor cap with reference to Chapter 4, Section 7.
5   If not already done, disconnect the stub hose which connects the crankcase breather tube to the camshaft housing. On 1.8 and 2.0 litre models, unscrew the bolt securing the crankcase breather tube bracket to the end of the cylinder head.
6   Make a final check to ensure that all relevant hoses, pipes and wires have been disconnected.
7   Proceed as described in Section 23, paragraphs 23 to 41 inclusive, but in addition note the following.
8   On completion check that all relevant hoses, pipes and wires, etc, have been reconnected.
9   Note that after the engine has been refitted and run to normal operating temperature, the cylinder head bolts must be finally tightened to the Stage 5 setting.

25 Cylinder head (sohc engines) – dismantling and reassembly

Note: *A valve spring compressor tool will be required for this operation. New valve stem oil seals must be used on reassembly*

1   With the cylinder head removed as described in Section 23 or 24 (as applicable), clean away all external dirt.
2   If not already done, remove the thermostat housing, and on 1.4 and 1.6 litre models, the thermostat, as described in Chapter 2. Remove the manifolds as described in Chapter 3 (photo). Remove the spark plugs if not already done.
3   To remove a valve, fit a valve spring compressor tool. Ensure that the arms of the compressor tool are securely positioned on the head of

25.2 Removing the thermostat housing – 2.0 litre engine

25.3 Valve spring compressor tool fitted to No 1 exhaust valve – 2.0 litre engine

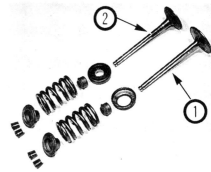

25.7 Inlet (1) and exhaust (2) valve components

25.11 Inserting an exhaust valve into its guide

25.12 Fit the valve seat (exhaust valve shown)

25.13 Slide the oil seal fitting sleeve down the valve stem ...

25.14A ... then fit the valve stem oil seal ...

25.14B ... and push onto the spring seat using a suitable socket

25.15A Fit the valve spring ...

25.15B ... and the spring cap

25.17 Retain the split collets with a little grease

the valve and the spring cap (photo).

4   Compress the valve spring to relieve the pressure of the spring cap acting on the collets. If the spring cap sticks on the valve stem, support the compressor tool and give the end a light tap with a hammer to help free the spring cap.

5   Extract the two split collets, then slowly release the compressor tool.

6   Remove the spring cap, spring, valve stem oil seal, and the spring seat, then withdraw the valve.

7   Repeat the procedure for the remaining valves, keeping all components in strict order, so that they can be refitted in their original positions (photo).

8   The cylinder head and valves can be inspected for wear and damage as described in Section 26.

9   With all components cleaned, commence reassembly as follows.

10   Starting at one end of the cylinder head, fit the valve components as follows.

11   Insert the appropriate valve into its guide, ensuring that the valve stem is well lubricated with clean engine oil (photo). Note that if the original components are being refitted, all components must be refitted in their original positions.

12   Fit the spring seat (photo).

13   New valve stem oil seals should be supplied with a fitting sleeve, which fits over the collet groove in the valve stem, to prevent damage to the oil seal as it is slid down the valve stem (photo). If no sleeve is supplied, wind a short length of tape round the top of the valve stem to cover the collet groove.

14   Push the valve stem oil seal down the valve stem using a suitable tube until the seal is fully engaged with the spring seat (photos). Remove the fitting sleeve or tape, as applicable, from the valve stem.

15   Fit the valve spring and the spring cap (photos).

16   Fit the spring compressor tool, and compress the valve spring until the spring cap passes beyond the collet groove in the valve stem.

17   Apply a little grease to the collet groove, then fit the split collets into the groove, with the narrow ends nearest the spring (photos). The grease should hold them in the groove.

18   Slowly release the compressor tool, ensuring that the collets are not dislodged from the groove. When the compressor is fully released, give the top of the valve assembly a sharp tap with a soft-faced mallet to settle the components.

19   Repeat the procedure for the remaining valves, ensuring that all components are refitted in their original positions, where applicable.

20   Where applicable, refit the manifolds as described in Chapter 3, and/or the thermostat and thermostat housing as described in Chapter 2. Refit the spark plugs if desired.

21   Refit the cylinder head as described in Section 23 or 24, as applicable.

26 Cylinder head – inspection and renovation

Note: *Refer to a dealer for advice before attempting to carry out valve grinding or valve seat recutting operations, as these operations may not be possible for the DIY mechanic, due to the fitment of hardened valve seats for use with unleaded petrol*

1   Bearing in mind that the cylinder head is of light alloy construction and is easily damaged, use a blunt scraper or rotary wire brush to clean all traces of carbon deposits from the combustion spaces and the ports. The valve stems and valve guides should also be freed from any carbon deposits. Wash the combustion spaces and ports down with paraffin, and scrape the cylinder head surface free of any foreign matter with the side of a steel rule, or a similar article.

2   If the engine is installed in the car, clean the pistons and the top of the cylinder bores. If the pistons are still in the block, then it is essential that great care is taken to ensure that no carbon gets into the cylinder bores, as this could scratch the cylinder walls or cause damage to the pistons and rings. To ensure this does not happen, first turn the crankshaft so that two of the pistons are at the top of their bores. Stuff rag into the other two bores or seal them off with paper and masking tape. The waterways should also be covered with small pieces of masking tape, to prevent particles of carbon entering the cooling system and damaging the coolant pump.

3   Press a little grease into the gap between the cylinder walls and the

two pistons which are to be worked on. With a blunt scraper, carefully scrape away the carbon from the piston crown, taking great care not to scratch the aluminium. Also scrape away the carbon from the surrounding lip of the cylinder wall. When all carbon has been removed, scrape away the grease which will now be contaminated with carbon particles, taking care not to press any into the bores. To assist prevention of carbon build-up, the piston crown can be polished with a metal polish. Remove the rags or masking tape from the other two cylinders, and turn the crankshaft so that the two pistons which were at the bottom are now at the top. Place rag or masking tape in the cylinders which have been decarbonised, and proceed as just described.

4   Examine the heads of the valves for pitting and burning, especially the heads of the exhaust valves. The valve seatings should be examined at the same time. If the pitting on the valve and seat is very slight, the marks can be removed by grinding the seats and valves togethers with coarse, and then fine, valve grinding paste.

5   Where bad pitting has occurred to the valve seats, it will be necessary to recut them and fit new valves. This latter job should be entrusted to the local dealer or engineering works. In practice it is very seldom that the seats are so badly worn. Normally it is the valve that is too badly worn for refitting, and the owner can easily purchase a new set of valves and match them to the seats by valve grinding.

6   Valve grinding is carried out as follows. Smear a trace of coarse carborundum paste on the seat face and apply a suction grinder tool to the valve head. With a semi-rotary motion, grind the valve head to its seat, lifting the valve occasionally to redistribute the grinding paste. When a dull matt even surface is produced on both the valve seat and the valve, wipe off the paste and repeat the process with fine carborundum paste, lifting and turning the valve to redistribute the paste as before. A light spring placed under the valve head will greatly ease this operation. When a smooth unbroken ring of light grey matt finish is produced, on both valve and valve seat faces, the grinding operation is complete. Carefully clean away every trace of grinding compound, taking great care to leave none in the ports or in the valve guides. Clean the valves and valve seats with a paraffin-soaked rag, then with a clean rag, and finally, if an air line is available, blow the valves, valve guides and valve ports clean.

7   Check that all valve springs are intact. If any one is broken, all should be renewed. Check the free height of the springs against new ones. If some springs are not long enough, replace them all. Springs suffer from fatigue and it is a good idea to renew them even if they look serviceable.

8   The cylinder head can be checked for warping either by placing it on a piece of plate glass or using a straight-edge and feeler blades. If there is any doubt or if its block face is corroded, have it re-faced by your dealer or motor engineering works.

9   On 1.8 and 2.0 litre sohc models, always renew the sealing ring between the cylinder head and the thermostat housing when the head is removed for overhaul (photo). Reference to Chapter 2 will show that a considerable amount of work is involved if it is wished to renew the sealing ring with the cylinder head installed.

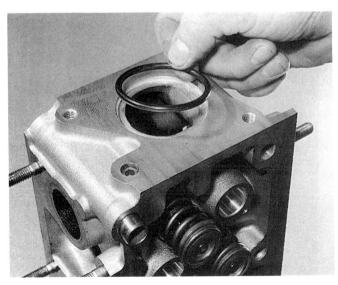

26.9 Renewing the thermostat housing sealing ring – 2.0 litre engine

26.10 Oil pressure regulating valve (1) and plug (2) – 2.0 litre engine

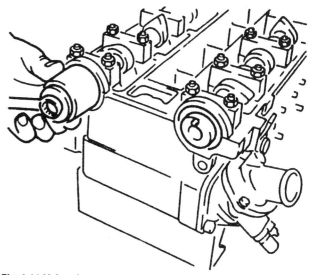

Fig. 1.11 Using the camshaft sprocket bolt, washer, and a suitable tube to fit a new camshaft front oil seal – dohc engine (Sec 27)

10 On sohc models, if the oil pressure regulating valve in the cylinder head is to be renewed, access is gained via the circular plug covering the end of the valve (photo). The old valve must be crushed, then its remains extracted, and a thread (M10) cut in the valve seat to allow removal using a suitable bolt. A new valve and plug can then be driven into position. In view of the intricacies of this operation, it is probably best to have the valve renewed by a Vauxhall dealer if necessary.

diameter with a washer and the camshaft sprocket bolt. Screw the camshaft sprocket bolt into the end of the camshaft to draw the oil seal into position on its shoulder – see Fig. 1.11.
6 Where applicable, repeat the procedure on the remaining camshaft oil seal.
7 Refit the camshaft sprocket(s) and a new timing belt as described in Section 17, and tension the timing belt as described in Section 18.

27 Camshaft front oil seal (dohc engine) – renewal

Note: A new timing belt must be used on refitting

1 The camshaft front oil seals may be renewed with the engine in the vehicle without removing the camshafts as follows.
2 Remove the timing belt and the relevant camshaft sprocket(s), as described in Section 17.
3 Punch or drill a small hole in the centre of the now-exposed oil seal. Screw in a self-tapping screw, and pull on the screw with pliers to extract the seal.
4 Clean the oil seal seat with a wooden or plastic scraper.
5 Turn the camshaft until the locating peg for the camshaft sprocket is uppermost, then lubricate the lips of a new camshaft front oil seal with a little grease, and fit the oil seal, using a tube or socket of suitable

28 Camshafts (dohc engine) – removal, inspection and refitting

Note: A new timing belt must be used on refitting

1 Remove the timing belt and the relevant camshaft sprocket(s), as described in Section 17.
2 If the exhaust camshaft is to be removed, unscrew the two securing bolts and remove the distributor from the end of the cylinder head, with reference to Chapter 4, Section 8 if necessary.
3 Check the camshaft bearing caps for identification marks, and if none are present, make corresponding marks on the bearing caps and the top surface of the cylinder head using a centre punch. Note the orientation of the bearing caps before removal, as they must be refitted in exactly the same positions from which they are removed (photo).
4 Loosen the relevant camshaft bearing cap nuts in half-turn stages –

28.3 Camshaft bearing cap. Note position of identification mark (arrowed) – dohc engine

28.4 Exhaust camshaft rear bearing cap securing nuts (arrowed) – dohc engine

ie loosen all the nuts by half a turn, then loosen all the nuts by a further half turn and so on (this is necessary to slowly relieve the tension in the valve springs). Note that the exhaust camshaft rear bearing cap which also supports the distributor is secured by four nuts (photo).

5   Remove the bearing cap nuts and the bearing caps, then carefully lift the relevant camshaft from the cylinder head without jerking.

6   Repeat the procedure for the remaining camshaft if desired.

7   With the camshaft(s) removed, examine the bearing surfaces in the cylinder head and bearing caps for signs of obvious wear or pitting. If evident, the cylinder head and all bearing caps must be renewed as a matched set, as there is no provision for refacing if the bearing caps cannot be renewed individually.

8   The camshaft(s) should show no marks or scoring on the journal or cam lobe surfaces. if evident, renew the camshaft(s).

9   It is advisable to renew the camshaft front oil seal(s) as a matter of course. Prise the old seal(s) from the front of the camshaft(s) and discard them.

10 . Commence refitting by liberally coating the contact faces of the hydraulic valve lifters and the camshaft(s) with molybdenum disulphide paste.

11   Coat the mating faces of the front and rear bearing caps with sealing compound (Vauxhall part No 15 04 200, or equivalent) and refit the bearing caps in their original positions as noted during removal.

12   Tighten the camshaft bearing cap nuts to the specified torque in half-turn stages, as when loosening the nuts. Note that when refitting the exhaust camshaft, the two smaller rear bearing cap securing nuts should be tightened after all the main camshaft bearing cap nuts have been tightened. Note also that the two smaller nuts should be tightened to a lower torque wrench setting than the main nuts.

13   Turn the camshaft until the locating peg for the camshaft sprocket is uppermost, then lubricate the lips of a rear camshaft front oil seal with a little grease, and fit the oil seal, using a tube or socket of suitable diameter with a washer and the camshaft sprocket bolt. Screw the camshaft sprocket bolt into the end of the camshaft to draw the oil seal into position on its shoulder – see Fig. 1.11.

14   Where applicable, repeat the procedure for the remaining camshaft.

15   Where applicable, refit the distributor with reference to Chapter 4, Section 8. Fit a new timing belt and the camshaft sprocket(s) as described in Section 17, then tension the timing belt as described in Section 18.

---

29 Cylinder head (dohc engine) – removal and refitting (engine in vehicle)

Note: *The engine must be cold when the cylinder head is removed. Do not remove the cylinder head from a hot engine. New cylinder head bolts, a new cylinder head gasket and a new timing belt must be used on refitting*

1   Disconnect the battery negative lead.

2   Drain the cooling system, as described in Chapter 2, Section 3.

3   Remove the front section of the exhaust system, as described in Chapter 3, Section 52.

4   The cylinder head can be removed complete with the inlet manifold, or the inlet manifold can be detached from the cylinder head prior to removal, with reference to Chapter 3, Section 50. If no work is to be carried out on the inlet manifold, it can be unbolted from the cylinder head and supported to one side out of the way, thus avoiding the need to disconnect the relevant hoses, pipes and wiring.

5   If the cylinder head is to be removed complete with the inlet manifold, disconnect all relevant hoses, pipes and wiring from the inlet manifold and associated components, with reference to Chapter 3, Section 50, and unbolt the manifold support bracket from the manifold. Loosen the alternator mountings with reference to Chapter 11, Section 8, then unbolt the upper alternator mounting from the inlet manifold.

6   If the inlet manifold is to be left in the engine compartment, proceed as follows, otherwise proceed to paragraph 17.

7   Disconnect the wiring plug from the airflow meter, and the breather hose from the air box on the throttle body, then disconnect the air cleaner trunking and remove the airflow meter/air box assembly from the throttle body. Refer to Chapter 3 if necessary.

8   Disconnect the end of the throttle cable from the throttle valve lever, then unbolt the throttle cable support bracket and remove it from the inlet manifold.

9   Unscrew the two earth lead securing nuts from the fuel rail (one at each end of the rail) and disconnect the three earth leads.

10   Disconnect the wiring plug from the throttle position switch.

11   Pull up on the wiring harness housing, and disconnect the wiring plugs from the fuel injectors by compressing the retaining clips. Move the wiring harness housing to one side.

12   Disconnect the two breather hoses from the rear of the camshaft cover.

13   Loosen the alternator mountings, with reference to Chapter 11, Section 8, then unbolt the upper alternator mounting from the inlet manifold.

14   Unbolt the manifold support bracket from the manifold.

15   Make a final check to ensure that all necessary hoses, pipes and wires have been disconnected, then unscrew the securing nuts and lift the inlet manifold from the cylinder head. Ensure that the manifold is properly supported, taking care not to strain any of the hoses, pipes and wires, etc, which are still connected.

16   Recover the manifold gasket from the cylinder head.

17   Remove the timing belt, camshaft sprockets, and timing belt tensioner and idler pulleys, as described in Section 17.

18   Unscrew the upper and middle studs for the timing belt outer cover screws. Note that the upper stud simply unscrews from the cylinder head, but the middle stud is secured by a bolt.

19   Unscrew the two upper rear timing belt cover securing bolts from the cylinder head.

20   Remove the distributor cap and HT leads with reference to Chapter 4, Section 7.

21   Disconnect the distributor wiring plug.

22   Disconnect the coolant hose from the left-hand end of the cylinder head.

23   Unscrew the bolt securing the crankcase breather tube bracket to the end of the cylinder head.

24   Disconnect the radiator top hose from the thermostat housing, and disconnect the wiring plugs from the temperature gauge sender and the coolant temperature sensor (both situated in the thermostat housing).

25   Make a final check to ensure that all relevant hoses, pipes and wires have been disconnected.

26   Using a suitable Torx socket, and working in the order shown in Fig. 1.12, loosen all the cylinder head bolts by a quarter of a turn, then loosen all the bolts by half a turn, and finally loosen and remove the bolts. Recover the washers.

27   Lift the cylinder head from the cylinder block. If necessary, tap the cylinder head gently with a soft-faced mallet to free it from the block, but **do not** lever at the mating faces. Note that the cylinder head is located on dowels.

28   Recover the cylinder head gasket and discard it.

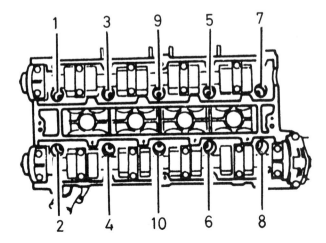

Fig. 1.12 Cylinder head bolt loosening sequence – dohc engine (Sec 29)

29.35A Tighten the cylinder head bolts to the specified torque ...

29.35B ... and then through the specified angle – dohc engine

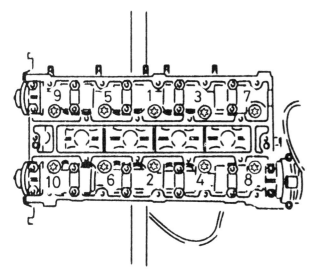

Fig. 1.13 Cylinder head bolt tightening sequence – dohc engine
(Sec 29)

mind the following points.

37   Refit the timing belt tensioner and idler pulleys, camshaft sprockets and a new timing belt as described in Section 17, and tension the timing belt as described in Section 18.

38   Where applicable, refit the inlet manifold to the cylinder head with reference to Chapter 3, Section 50, using a new gasket.

39   Refit the front section of the exhaust system as described in Chapter 3, Section 52, using a new gasket.

40   Refit the upper alternator mounting to the inlet manifold (where applicable), then adjust the alternator drivebelt tension, as described in Chapter 11, Section 7.

41   Refill the cooling system, as described in Chapter 2, Section 5.

42   On completion, check that all relevant hoses, pipes and wires, etc, have been reconnected.

43   When the engine is started, check for signs of leaks.

44   Once the engine has reached normal operating temperature, check and if necessary adjust the mixture (where applicable) with reference to Chapter 3, Section 40, and finally tighten the cylinder head bolts to the Stage 5 setting.

29   Clean the cylinder head and block mating faces by careful scraping. Take care not to damage the cylinder head, which is made of light alloy and is easily scored. Cover the coolant passages and other openings with masking tape or rag, to prevent dirt and carbon falling in. Mop out all the oil from the bolt holes; if oil is left in the holes, hydraulic pressure could crack the block when the bolts are refitted.

30   If desired, the cylinder head can be dismantled and inspected as described in Section 31 and 26 respectively.

31   Commence refitting by locating a new gasket on the block so that the word 'OBEN' or 'TOP' is uppermost at the timing belt end of the engine.

32   With the mating faces scrupulously clean, locate the cylinder head on the block so that the positioning dowels engage in their holes.

33   Temporarily refit the crankshaft pulley and the camshaft sprockets, and ensure that the timing marks are still positioned as they were before the timing belt was removed (see Section 17).

34   Fit the **new** cylinder head bolts, ensuring that the washers are in place under their heads, and screw the bolts in *by hand* as far as possible.

35   Tighten the bolts in the order shown in Fig. 1.13. Tighten the bolts in the four stages given in the Specification – ie tighten all bolts to the Stage 1 torque, then tighten all bolts to Stage 2 and so on (photos).

36   Further refitting is a reversal of the removal procedure, bearing in

30   Cylinder head (dohc engine) – removal and refitting (engine removed)

Note: *New cylinder head bolts, a new cylinder head gasket, and a new timing belt must be used on refitting*

1   The gasket head can be removed complete with the inlet manifold, or the inlet manifold can be detached from the cylinder head prior to removal, with reference to Chapter 3, Section 50.

2   Proceed as described in Section 29, paragraphs 17 to 19 inclusive.

3   If not already done, remove the distributor cap and HT leads with reference to Chapter 4, Section 7.

4   Unscrew the bolt securing the crankcase breather tube bracket to the end of the cylinder head.

5   Make a final check to ensure that all relevant hoses, pipes and wires have been disconnected.

6   Proceed as described in Section 29, paragraphs 26 to 38 inclusive, but in addition note the following.

7   On completion, check that all relevant hoses, pipes and wires, etc, have been reconnected.

8   Note that after the engine has been refitted and run to normal operating temperature, the cylinder head bolts must be finally tightened to the Stage 5 setting.

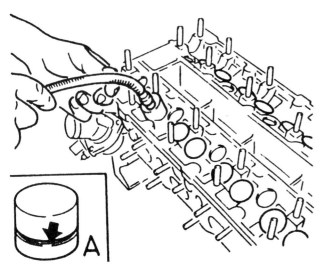

Fig. 1.14 Remove the hydraulic valve lifters using a rubber plunger. Inset (A) shows valve lifter upright, with oil groove (arrowed) at bottom – dohc engine (Sec 31)

32.5 Removing the flywheel – 1.6 litre engine

12 Where applicable, refit the manifolds and/or the thermostat and housing.
13 Refit the cylinder head, as described in Section 29 or 30, as applicable.

31 Cylinder head (dohc engine) – dismantling and reassembly

1 With the cylinder head removed as described in Section 29 or 30 (as applicable), clean away all external dirt.
2 If not already done, remove the thermostat housing and thermostat as described in Chapter 2, and remove the manifolds as described in Chapter 3.
3 Remove the spark plugs (if not already done), and remove the distributor with reference to Chapter 4, Section 8.
4 Remove the camshafts as described in Section 28.
5 Remove the hydraulic valve lifters from their bores using a rubber suction plunger tool – do not invert the cylinder head in order to remove the valve lifters. Keep the valve lifters upright at all times (oil groove at bottom – see Fig. 1.14), and immerse them in order of removal in a container of clean engine oil until they are to be refitted.
6 To remove the valve components, proceed as described in Section 25, paragraphs 3 to 7 inclusive.
7 The cylinder head and valves can be inspected for wear and damage as described in Section 26.
8 With all components cleaned, refit the valve components as described in Section 25, paragraphs 10 to 19 inclusive.
9 Refit the hydraulic valve lifters to the cylinder head in their original positions. Liberally oil the valve lifter bores, and if new lifters are being fitted, initially immerse each one in a container of clean engine oil and compress it (by hand) several times to charge it.
10 Refit the camshafts, as described in Section 28.
11 Refit the spark plugs if desired, and refit the distributor with reference to Chapter 4, Section 8.

32 Flywheel – removal, inspection and refitting

Note: *New flywheel securing bolts must be used on refitting*

1 If not already done, remove the clutch, as described in Chapter 5, and the starter motor, as described in Chapter 11.
2 If the engine is in the vehicle, remove the clutch release bearing and its guide sleeve, as described in Chapter 5.
3 Although the flywheel bolt holes are offset so that the flywheel can only be fitted in one position, it will make refitting easier if alignment marks are made between the flywheel and the end of the crankshaft.
4 Prevent the flywheel from turning by jamming the ring gear teeth using a suitable tool. Access is most easily obtained through the starter motor aperture if the engine is in the vehicle.
5 Unscrew the securing bolts, and remove the flywheel (photo). *Take care, as the flywheel is heavy!*
6 With the flywheel removed, it can be inspected as follows.
7 If the teeth on the flywheel starter ring are badly worn, or if some are missing, then it will be necessary to remove the ring and fit a new one.
8 The old ring can be split with a cold chisel, after making a cut with a hacksaw blade between two gear teeth. Take great care not to damage the flywheel during this operation, and use eye protectors at all times. Once the ring has been split, it will spread apart and can be lifted from the flywheel.

32.13A Tool for locking flywheel fitted to engine-to-gearbox bolt hole – 1.6 litre engine

32.13B Tighten the flywheel securing bolts to the specified torque ...

32.13C ... and then through the specified angle – 1.6 litre engine

9   The new ring gear must be heated to 180 to 230°C (356° to 446°F) and unless facilities for heating by oven or flame are available, leave the fitting to a dealer or motor engineering works. The new ring gear must not be overheated during this work, or the temper of the metal will be altered.

10   The ring should be tapped gently down onto its register, and left to cool naturally – the contraction of the metal on cooling will ensure that it is a secure and permanent fit.

11   If the clutch friction disc contact surface of the flywheel is scored, or on close inspection, shows evidence of small hair cracks (caused by overheating), it may be possible to have the flywheel surface ground, provided the overall thickness of the flywheel is not reduced too much. Consult a specialist engine repairer and if it is not possible, renew the flywheel complete.

12   Refitting is a reversal of removal, bearing in mind the following points.

13   Align the previously-made marks on the flywheel and crankshaft, and fit new flywheel securing bolts. Tighten them to the specified torque in the two stages given in the Specifications, whilst preventing the flywheel from turning, as during removal (photos).

14   Where applicable, refit the clutch release bearing, guide sleeve, and the clutch, as described in Chapter 5.

34.4 Fitting a new crankshaft rear oil seal – 2.0 litre engine

---

33   Crankshaft front oil seal – renewal

Note: *On 2.0 litre dohc models, the timing belt must be renewed on refitting*

1   Remove the timing belt and the rear timing belt cover, as described in Section 15 or 17, as applicable. Ensure that the Woodruff key is removed from the end of the crankshaft.

2   On 2.0 litre dohc engines, remove the spacer ring from the end of the crankshaft.

3   Punch or drill a small hole in the centre of the now-exposed oil seal. Screw in a self-tapping screw, and pull on the screw with pliers to extract the seal. Several attempts may be necessary. Be careful not to damage the sealing face of the crankshaft.

4   Clean the oil seal seat with a wooden or plastic scraper.

5   Before fitting the new oil seal, steps must be taken to protect the oil seal lips from damage, and from turning back on the shoulder at the front end of the crankshaft. Grease the seal lips, and then wind tape around the end of the crankshaft to form a gentle taper.

6   Tap the seal into position using a suitable socket or tube, until the seal is flush with the outer face of the oil pump housing.

7   On 2.0 litre dohc engines, coat the oil pump mating face of the spacer ring with sealing compound (Vauxhall part No 15 04 200, or equivalent), then push the spacer ring onto the end of the crankshaft, until it is seated against the oil pump.

8   Refit the rear timing belt cover and the timing belt (a new belt in the case of 2.0 litre dohc models), as described in Section 15 or 17, as applicable. Tension the timing belt as described in Section 16 or 18, as applicable.

---

34   Crankshaft rear oil seal – renewal

1   With the engine removed from the vehicle, remove the flywheel, as described in Section 32.

2   Punch or drill a small hole in the centre of the now-exposed oil seal. Screw in a self-tapping screw, and pull on the screw with pliers to extract the seal. Several attempts may be necessary. Be careful not to damage the sealing face of the crankshaft.

3   Clean the oil seal seat with a wooden or plastic scraper.

4   Grease the lips of the new seal, then tap the seal into position using a suitable tube, until flush with the outer faces of the cylinder block and rear main bearing cap (photo).

5   Refit the flywheel, as described in Section 32.

---

35   Sump – removal and refitting

Note: *The sump gasket(s) must be renewed on refitting and suitable sealer will be required for use on the oil pump and rear main bearing cap-to-cylinder block joints*

1   If the engine is in the vehicle, proceed as follows, otherwise proceed to paragraph 9.

2   Disconnect the battery negative lead.

3   On dohc models, remove the engine undershield, with reference to Chapter 10, Section 32.

4   Drain the engine oil, with reference to Section 3 if necessary, then refit and tighten the drain plug.

5   Apply the handbrake, then jack up the front of the vehicle, and support securely on axle stands.

6   Remove the front section of the exhaust system, as described in Chapter 3, Section 26 or 52, as applicable.

7   Where applicable, disconnect the wiring from the oil level sensor.

8   Unscrew the securing bolts and remove the engine-to-gearbox blanking plate from the bellhousing.

9   Remove the securing bolts, and withdraw the sump. Note that on 1.6, 1.8 and 2.0 litre models, the sump baffle will probably be pulled away from the cylinder block with the sump, but cannot be removed until the oil pick-up pipe has been removed.

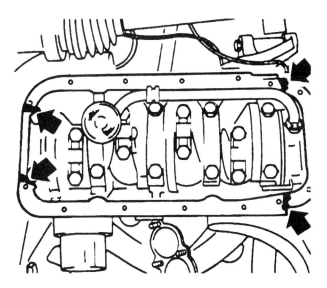

Fig. 1.15 Apply sealing compound (arrows) to oil pump and rear main bearing cap joints before refitting sump (Sec 35)

35.14 Applying sealing compound to the joint between the oil pump and cylinder block – 2.0 litre engine

35.15 Locating a new cork gasket on the cylinder block – 1.6 litre engine

10　On 1.4, 1.6 and 2.0 litre dohc models, recover the cork gasket.
11　On 1.6, 1.8 and 2.0 litre models, in order to remove the sump baffle, it is necessary to unbolt the bracket securing the oil pick-up pipe to the cylinder block. The baffle can then be manipulated over the oil pick-up pipe. On 1.6 and 2.0 litre dohc models, recover the second cork gasket, and on 1.8 and 2.0 litre sohc models, prise the rubber gasket from the sump baffle.
12　If desired, the oil pick-up pipe can be removed by unscrewing the single bolt securing the support bracket to the cylinder block (if not already done), and the two bolts securing the end of the pipe to the oil pump. Recover the O-ring.

13　Clean all traces of old gasket and sealing compound from the mating faces of the cylinder block, sump baffle (where applicable), and sump.
14　Commence refitting by applying sealing compound (Vauxhall part No 15 03 294 or equivalent) to the joints between the oil pump and cylinder block, and the rear main bearing cap and cylinder block – see Fig. 1.15 (photo).
15　On 1.4, 1.6 and 2.0 litre dohc models, locate a new cork gasket on the cylinder block, if necessary applying a little sealing compound to hold it in place (photo).
16　On 1.8 and 2.0 litre sohc models, locate a new rubber gasket over the sump baffle flange, ensuring that it is seated correctly (photo).

35.16 Locate a new rubber gasket over the sump baffle flange – 2.0 litre engine

35.17A Manipulate the sump baffle over the oil pick-up pipe ...

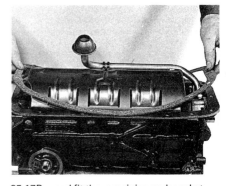

35.17B ... and fit the remaining cork gasket – 1.6 litre engine

35.18A Fit a new O-ring to the oil pick-up pipe ...

35.18B ... and tighten the securing bolts to the specified torque – 2.0 litre engine

35.19 Refitting the oil pick-up pipe bracket –
2.0 litre engine

35.20A Refitting the sump – 2.0 litre engine

35.20B Coat the sump securing bolts with
thread-locking compound before fitting

17   On 1.6, 1.8 and 2.0 litre models, offer the sump baffle up to the
cylinder block, manipulating it over the oil pick-up pipe where applicable. On 1.6 and 2.0 litre dohc models, locate the remaining new cork
gasket on the sump baffle, but **do not** use sealing compound (photos).
18   If the oil pick-up pipe has been removed, refit it to the oil pump
using a new O-ring (photos).
19   Where applicable, refit the bracket securing the oil pick-up pipe to
the cylinder block, ensuring that it passes through the relevant hole in
the sump baffle on 1.6, 1.8 and 2.0 litre models (photo).
20   Coat the sump securing bolts with thread-locking compound, then
refit the sump, and tighten the bolts to the specified torque (photos).
21   If the engine is in the vehicle, further refitting is a reversal of the
removal procedure, but refit the front section of the exhaust system
with reference to Chapter 3, Section 26 or 52, as applicable. On completion, refill the engine with oil, as described in Section 3 of this
Chapter.

36   Oil pump – removal and refitting

Note: *On 2.0 litre dohc models, the timing belt must be renewed on
refitting*

1   Remove the timing belt, sprockets and the rear timing belt cover, as
described in Section 15 or 17, as applicable.
2   Remove the sump, oil pick-up pipe and sump baffle (where applicable), as described in Section 35.
3   On 1.8 and 2.0 litre engines, unscrew the oil filter from its mounting
on the oil pump, with reference to Section 3 if necessary.
4   On 2.0 litre dohc engine if the engine is still in the vehicle, disconnect
the oil cooler pipe unions from the oil pump, and move the pipes to one
side out of the way (photo).

36.4 Oil cooler pipe unions at oil pump – dohc
engine

36.9 Fit a new oil pump gasket to the cylinder
block – 2.0 litre engine

36.11A Oil pump inner gear must engage
with hexagon flats on crankshaft (arrowed)
on 1.4 and 1.6 litre engines ...

36.11B ... and with two flats (arrowed) on 1.8
and 2.0 litre engines

36.11C Tighten the oil pump securing bolts to
the specified torque – 2.0 litre sohc engine

Fig. 1.16 Oil pump securing bolts (arrowed) and crankshaft spacer
ring (A) – dohc engine (Sec 36)

5   Disconnect the wiring from the oil pressure switch mounted on the
oil pump.
6   On 2.0 litre dohc engines, remove the spacer ring from the end of
the crankshaft – see Fig. 1.16.
7   Remove the securing bolts, and withdraw the oil pump from the
cylinder block. Recover the gasket.
8   The oil pump can be dismantled for inspection, as described in
Section 37.
9   Thoroughly clean the mating faces of the oil pump and cylinder
block, then locate a new gasket on the block (photo).

10   Before refitting the oil pump, steps must be taken to protect the oil
seal lips from damage, and from turning back on the shoulder at the
front end of the crankshaft. Grease the seal lips, and then wind tape
around the crankshaft to form a gentle taper.
11   Refit the oil pump, ensuring that the inner gear engages with the
flats on the crankshaft, and tighten the securing bolts to the specified
torque, then remove the tape from the end of the crankshaft (photos).
12   On 2.0 litre dohc engines, coat the oil pump mating face of the
spacer ring with sealing compound (Vauxhall part No 15 04 200, or
equivalent), then push the spacer ring onto the end of the crankshaft
until it is seated against the oil pump.
13   Reconnect the wiring to the oil pressure switch.
14   On 2.0 litre dohc models, reconnect the oil cooler pipes to the oil
pump, and tighten the unions.
15   On 1.8 and 2.0 litre engines, fit a new oil filter, with reference to
Section 3.
16   Refit the sump baffle (where applicable), oil pick-up tube and
sump, as described in Section 35.
17   Refit the rear timing belt cover and the timing belt (a new belt in the
case of 2.0 litre dohc models), as described in Section 15 or 17 as
applicable, and tension the timing belt as described in Section 16 or 18,
as applicable.

37 Oil pump – dismantling, inspection and reassembly

Note: A new crankshaft front oil seal must be used on reassembly

1   With the oil pump removed as described in Section 36, proceed as
follows.
2   Remove the securing screws and withdraw the rear cover (photo).
The screws may be very tight, in which case it may be necessary to use
an impact driver to remove them.
3   Check the clearance between the inner and outer gear teeth (back-
lash) using a feeler gauge (photo).
4   Check the clearance between the edges of the gears and the

37.2 Removing an oil pump rear cover
securing screw – 2.0 litre sohc engine

37.3 Check the clearance between the inner
and outer gear teeth ...

37.4 ... and between the edges of the gears
and the housing – 2.0 litre sohc engine

37.7 Oil pressure relief valve components –
2.0 litre sohc engine

37.8A Prise out the old crankshaft front oil
seal ...

37.8B ... and fit the new seal using a suitable
socket – 2.0 litre sohc engine

38.1 Oil cooler viewed through front spoiler. Securing nuts arrowed – dohc model

39.3 Big-end cap centre punch identification marks (circled). Note that lug on bearing cap faces flywheel end of engine – 2.0 litre sohc engine

housing (endfloat) using a straight edge and a feeler gauge (photo).

5   If any of the clearances are outside the specified limits, renew the components as necessary.

6   Ensure that the gears and the interior of the pump body are scrupulously clean before reassembly, and note that the outer gear is marked with a punch dot to indicate the gear outer face.

7   The oil pressure relief valve components can be removed from the pump by unscrewing the cap (photo). Examine the spring and plunger, and renew if necessary. Thoroughly clean the components before refitting.

8   Always renew the crankshaft front oil seal at the front of the oil pump housing. Prise out the old seal using a screwdriver, and fit the new seal using a suitable socket or tube, so that it is flush with the outer face of the housing (photos).

9   Ensure that the mating faces of the rear cover and the pump housing are clean, then coat the pump housing mating face with sealing compound (Vauxhall part No 15 03 166, or equivalent) and refit the rear cover. Refit and tighten the securing screws.

10   Refit the oil pump, as described in Section 36.

38   Oil cooler (dohc engine) – removal and refitting

1   To gain sufficient access to enable the oil cooler to be removed, the radiator must be removed, as described in Chapter 2, or alternatively, the front bumper must be removed, as described in Chapter 10 (photo).

2   With the appropriate component(s) removed for access, unscrew the oil cooler pipe unions from the oil cooler. Be prepared for oil spillage, and plug the open ends of the pipes, to prevent further oil leakage and dirt ingress.

3   Unscrew the two securing nuts, and withdraw the oil cooler from its

mounting brackets.

4   Refitting is a reversal of removal, but on completion, check and if necessary top up the engine oil level, as described in Section 3.

39   Pistons and connecting rods – removal and refitting

Note: *New big-end cap bolts must be used on refitting*

1   Remove the cylinder head, as described previously in this Chapter.

2   Remove the sump, oil pick-up pipe and sump baffle (where applicable), as described in Section 35.

3   If the connecting rods and big-end caps are not marked to indicate their positions in the cylinder block (ie cylinder numbers), centre-punch them at adjacent points either side of the cap/rod joint. Note to which side of the engine the marks face (photo).

4   Unscrew the big-end cap bolts from the first connecting rod, and remove the cap. If the bearing shells are to be re-used, tape the cap and shell together.

5   Check the top of the piston bore for a wear ridge. If evident, carefully scrape it away with a ridge reaming tool, otherwise as the piston is pushed out of the block, the piston rings may jam against the ridge.

6   Place the wooden handle of a hammer against the bottom of the connecting rod, and push the piston/rod assembly up and out of the cylinder bore. Recover the bearing shell, and tape it to the connecting rod if it is to be re-used.

7   Remove the remaining three assemblies in a similar way. Rotate the crankshaft as necessary to bring the big-end bolts to the most accessible position.

8   The piston can be separated from the connecting rod by removing the circlips which secure the fully-floating gudgeon pin. Note the

39.14A Piston crown arrow must point towards timing belt end of engine – 1.6 litre engine ...

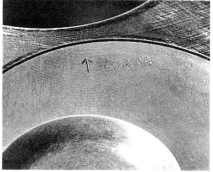

39.14B ... and similarly for the 2.0 litre sohc engine

39.14C Lugs (arrowed) on connecting rod and big-end cap must point towards flywheel end of engine – 1.6 litre engine

39.15 Tapping a piston into its bore – 2.0 litre sohc engine

11   Ensure that the seats for the bearing shells are absolutely clean, and then fit the shells into the seats.
12   Wipe out the cylinder bores and oil them. Oil the piston rings liberally, and ensure that the ring gaps are positioned as described in Section 40.
13   Fit a piston ring compressor tool to the first assembly to be installed.
14   Insert the rod and piston into the top of the cylinder bore, so that the base of the compressor stands on the block. Check that the connecting rod markings are towards the side of the engine noted during removal. Note that the arrow or notch, as applicable, on the piston crown should point towards the timing belt end of the engine, and the lugs on the connecting rods should point towards the flywheel end of the engine (photos).
15   Apply the wooden handle of a hammer to the piston crown and tap the assembly into the bore, at the same time releasing the compressor (photo).
16   Oil the relevant crankpin, then guide the big-end of the connecting rod near to the crankpin, and pull it firmly onto the crankpin. Ensure that the bearing shell remains in position in the connecting rod.
17   Fit the big-end cap, with the markings towards the side of the engine noted during removal (photo). Note that the lug should point towards the flywheel end of the engine.
18   Fit new big-end cap bolts, and tighten them to the specified torque in the two stages given in the Specifications (photos).
19   Repeat the procedure on the remaining three assemblies.
20   Refit the sump baffle (where applicable), oil pick-up pipe and sump, as described in Section 35.
21   Refit the cylinder head, as described previously in this Chapter.

orientation of the piston and connecting rod before separation, and if necessary, make alignment marks. Reassembly is a reversal of dismantling ensuring that the piston and connecting rod are correctly orientated.
9   The pistons and connecting rods can be examined for wear and damage, as described in Section 40, and the bearings can be examined as described in Section 42.
10   Commence reassembly by laying the piston/connecting rod assemblies out in their correct order, complete with bearing shells, ready for refitting into their respective bores in the cylinder block.

40   Pistons and connecting rods – examination and renovation

1   Examine the mating faces of the big-end caps to see if they have ever been filed, in a mistaken attempt to take up bearing wear. This is

39.17 Fitting a big-end bearing cap – 2.0 litre sohc engine

39.18A Tighten the big-end cap bolts to the specified torque ...

39.18B ... then through the specified angle – 2.0 litre sohc engine

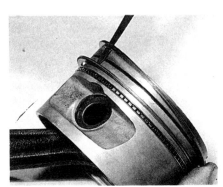
40.5A Using a feeler gauge to aid removal of a piston ring – 2.0 litre sohc engine

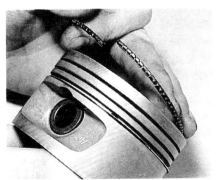
40.5B Removing the centre section of the oil control ring – 2.0 litre sohc engine

40.6 Measuring a piston ring end gap using a feeler gauge

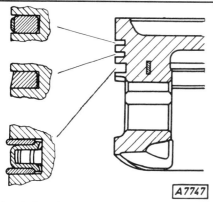

Fig. 1.17 Sectional view showing correct orientation of piston rings – all engines (Sec 40)

extremely unlikely, but if evident, the offending connecting rods and caps must be renewed.

2   Check the alignment of the rods visually, and if all is not well, take the rods to a Vauxhall dealer for a more detailed check.

3   The gudgeon pins are an interference (shrink) fit in the connecting rod small ends. Separation of the pistons and rods is a job for a dealer due to the special tools required, as is any remedial action required if the gudgeon pin is no longer an interference fit in the rod.

4   Examine the pistons for ovality, scoring and scratches.

5   If new rings are to be fitted to the existing pistons, expand the old rings over the tops of the pistons. The use of two or three old feeler gauges will be helpful in preventing the rings dropping into empty grooves. Note that the oil control ring is in three sections, and note which way up each ring is fitted, for use when refitting (photos).

6   Before fitting the new rings to the pistons, insert them into their relevant cylinder bores, and check that the ring end gaps are within the specified limits using a feeler gauge (photo). Check the ring gaps at the upper and lower limits of the piston travel in the bores.

7   If any of the ring end gaps exceed the specified tolerance, the relevant rings will have to be renewed, and if the ring grooves in the pistons are worn, new pistons may be required.

8   Clean out the piston ring grooves using a piece of old piston ring as a scraper. Take care not to scratch the surface of the pistons. Protect your fingers – piston ring edges are sharp. Also probe the groove oil return holes, to ensure that they are not blocked.

9   Check the cylinder bores for signs of wear ridges towards the top of the bores. If wear ridges are evident, and new piston rings are being fitted, the top ring must be stepped to clear the wear ridge, or the bore must be de-ridged using a suitable scraper.

10   Fit the oil control ring sections with the lower steel ring gap offset 25.0 to 50.0 mm (1.0 to 2.0 in) to the right of the spreader ring gap, and the upper steel ring gap offset by the same distance to the left of the spreader ring gap.

11   Fit the lower compression ring, noting that the ring is tapered or stepped. The ring should be fitted with the word 'TOP' uppermost.

12   Fit the upper compression ring, and offset the ring gap by 180° to the lower compression ring gap. If a stepped ring is being fitted, fit the ring with the smaller diameter of the step uppermost.

13   If new pistons are to be fitted, they must be selected from the grades available, after measuring the cylinder bores as described in Section 43.

14   Normally the appropriate oversize pistons are supplied by the dealer when the block is rebored.

15   Whenever new piston rings are being installed, the glaze on the original cylinder bores should be 'broken', using either abrasive paper or a glaze-removing tool in an electric drill. If abrasive paper is used, use strokes at 60° to the bore centre line, to create a cross-hatching effect.

---

41   Crankshaft and main bearings – removal and refitting

Note: *New main bearing cap bolts must be used on refitting*

1   With the engine removed from the vehicle, proceed as follows.

2   Remove the cylinder head, as described previously in this Chapter.

3   Remove the sump, oil pick-up pipe and sump baffle (where applicable), as described in Section 35.

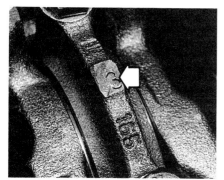

41.8 Main bearing cap identification mark (arrowed) – 1.6 litre engine

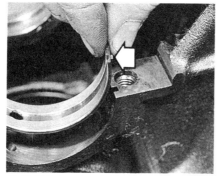

41.16 Main bearing shell tag (arrowed) engages with groove in cylinder block – 2.0 litre sohc engine

41.18 Fitting a central main bearing shell. Note thrust flanges – 2.0 litre sohc engine

41.21 Lowering the crankshaft into the crankcase – 2.0 litre sohc engine

41.23 Lubricate the main bearing shells before fitting the caps – 2.0 litre sohc engine

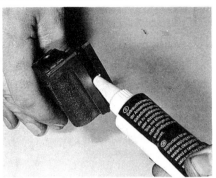

41.24A Fill the side grooves of the rear main bearing cap with RTV jointing compound ...

41.24B ... and the lower surfaces with sealing compound – 2.0 litre sohc engine

41.26A Tighten the main bearing cap bolts to the specified torque ...

41.26B ... then through the specified angle – 2.0 litre sohc engine

41.29A Check crankshaft endfloat using a dial gauge ...

41.29B ... or a feeler gauge – 2.0 litre sohc engine

4   Remove the oil pump, as described in Section 36.
5   Remove the flywheel, as described in Section 32.
6   Remove the pistons and connecting rods, as described in Section 39.
7   Invert the engine so that it is standing on the top face of the cylinder block.
8   The main bearing caps are numbered 1 to 4 from the timing belt end of the engine. The rear (flywheel end) cap is not marked. To ensure that the caps are refitted the correct way round, note that the numbers are read from the coolant pump side of the engine with the engine inverted (photo).
9   Unscrew and remove the main bearing cap bolts, and tap off the bearing caps. If the bearing shells are to be re-used, tape them to their respective caps.
10   Note that the centre bearing shell incorporates thrust flanges to control crankshaft endfloat.
11   Lift the crankshaft from the crankcase.
12   Extract the upper bearing shells, and identify them for position if they are to be re-used.
13   The crankshaft and bearings can be examined for wear and damage, as described in Section 42, and the cylinder block and bores can be examined as described in Section 43.
14   Commence refitting by ensuring that the crankcase and crankshaft are thoroughly clean, and that all oilways are clear. If possible, blow through the oil drillings with compressed air, and inject clean engine oil into them.
15   Wipe clean the bearing shell seats in the crankcase and the bearing caps, then fit the upper bearing shells to their seats.
16   Note that there is a tag on the back of each bearing shell, which engages with a groove in the relevant seat in the crankcase or bearing cap (photo).
17   If new bearing shells are being fitted, wipe away all traces of protective grease.
18   Note that the central bearing shells have thrust flanges which control crankshaft endfloat (photo). Note also that the shells fitted to the crankcase all have oil duct holes, while only the centre main bearing cap shell has an oil duct hole.
19   When the shells are firmly located in the crankcase and the bearing

caps, lubricate them with clean engine oil.
20   Fill the lips of a new crankshaft rear oil seal with grease, and fit it to the end of the crankshaft.
21   Carefully lower the crankshaft into position in the crankcase (photo).
22   If necessary, seat the crankshaft using light blows with a rubber hammer on the crankshaft balance webs.
23   Lubricate the main bearing journals and shells (photo), and then fit numbers 2, 3 and 4 main bearing caps, and tighten the new bolts as far as possible by hand.
24   Fill the side grooves of the rear main bearing cap with RTV jointing compound (Vauxhall part No 15 03 294, or equivalent), and coat the lower surfaces of the bearing cap with sealing compound (Vauxhall part No 15 04 200, or equivalent) (photos). Fit the bearing cap, and tighten the new bolts as far as possible by hand.
25   Fit the front (No 1) main bearing cap, and tighten the new bolts as far as possible by hand, ensuring that the bearing cap is exactly flush with the end face of the cylinder block.
26   Working from the centre bearing cap outwards, tighten the bearing cap securing bolts to the specified torque in the two stages given in the Specifications; ie tighten all bolts to Stage 1, then tighten all bolts to Stage 2 (photos).
27   When all bolts have been fully tightened, inject further RTV jointing compound into the side grooves of the rear main bearing cap, until it is certain that they are full.
28   Now rotate the crankshaft, and check that it turns freely, with no signs of binding or tight spots.
29   Check that the crankshaft endfloat is within the specified limits, using a dial gauge, or by inserting a feeler gauge between the thrust flange of the centre main bearing shell and the machined surface of the crankshaft (photos). Before measuring, ensure that the crankshaft is fully forced towards one end of the crankcase, to give the widest possible gap at the measuring location. Incorrect endfloat will most likely be due to crankshaft wear or to incorrect regrinding, assuming that the correct bearing shells have been fitted.
30   Refit the previously-removed components, with reference to the relevant Sections of this Chapter.

42.9 Check the condition of the TDC sensor wheel teeth at the front of the crankshaft – 2.0 litre sohc engine

42.10 Check the condition of the pins (arrowed) in the front crankshaft balance weight – 2.0 litre sohc engine

10   Similarly, check the condition of the pins in the front crankshaft balance weight, which serve as detent points for the plug-in diagnostic sensor used by Vauxhall dealers (photo).

42   Crankshaft and bearings – examination and renovation

Crankshaft
1   Examine the crankpin and main journal surfaces for signs of scoring or scratches, and check the ovality and taper of the crankpins and main journals. If the bearing surface dimensions do not fall within the tolerance ranges given in the Specifications at the beginning of this Chapter, the crankpins and/or main journals will have to be reground.
2   Big-end and crankpin wear is accompanied by distinct metallic knocking, particularly noticeable when the engine is pulling from low revs, and some loss of oil pressure.
3   Main bearing and main journal wear is accompanied by severe engine vibration rumble – getting progressively worse as engine revs increase – and again by loss of oil pressure.
4   If the crankshaft requires regrinding, take it to an engine reconditioning specialist, who will machine it for you and supply the correct undersize bearing shells.

Big-end and main bearing shells
5   Inspect the big-end and main bearing shells for signs of general wear, scoring, pitting and scratches. The bearings should be matt grey in colour. With lead-indium bearings, should a trace of copper colour be noticed, the bearings are badly worn, as the lead bearing material has worn away to expose the indium underlay. Renew the bearings if they are in this condition, or if there are any signs of scoring or pitting. **You are strongly advised to renew the bearings – regardless of their condition at time of major overhaul. Refitting used bearings is a false economy.**
6   The undersizes available are designed to correspond with crankshaft regrind sizes. The bearings are in fact, slightly more than the stated undersize, as running clearances have been allowed for during their manufacture.
7   Main and big-end bearing shells can be identified as to size by the marking on the back of the shell. Standard size shell bearings are marked STD or .00, undersize shells are marked with the undersize such as 0.020 u/s. This marking method applies only to replacement bearing shells, and not to those used during production.
8   An accurate method of determining bearing wear is by the use of Plastigage. The crankshaft is located in the main bearings (and, if necessary, the big-end bearings), and the Plastigage filament is located across the journal. Vauxhall recommend that the crankshaft journal and bearing shells are lightly lubricated, to prevent the Plastigage from tearing as the bearing cap is removed. The bearing cap should be fitted, and the bolts tightened to the specified torque. The cap is then removed, and the width of the filament is checked against a scale which shows the bearing running clearance. The clearance should be compared with that given in the Specifications.
9   Where applicable, check the teeth of the TDC sensor wheel for damage (photo). If evident, the crankshaft must be renewed.

43   Cylinder block and bores – examination and renovation

1   Examine the cylinder bores for taper, ovality, scoring and scratches. Start by carefully examining the top of the cylinder bores. If they are at all worn, a very slight ridge will be found on the thrust side. This marks the top of the piston ring travel. The owner will have a good indication of the bore wear prior to dismantling the engine, or removing the cylinder head. Excessive oil consumption, accompanied by blue smoke from the exhaust, is a sure sign of worn cylinder bores and piston rings.
2   Measure the bore diameter across the block, and just below any ridge. This can be done with an internal micrometer or a dial gauge. Compare this with the diameter of the bottom of the bore, which is not subject to wear. If no measuring instruments are available, use a piston from which the rings have been removed, and measure the gap between it and the cylinder wall with a feeler gauge. Refer to the Specifications. If the cylinder wear exceeds the permitted tolerances, then the cylinders will need reboring, in which case note the following points:

(a)   *Piston and cylinder bores are closely matched in production. The actual diameter of the piston is indicated by numbers on its crown; the same numbers stamped on the crankcase indicate the bore diameter*
(b)   *After reboring has taken place, the cylinder bores should be measured accurately and oversize pistons selected from the grades available to give the specified piston-to-bore clearance*
(c)   *For grading purposes, the piston diameter is measured across the bottom of the skirt*

3   If the wear is marginal and within the tolerances given, new special piston rings can be fitted to offset the wear.
4   Thoroughly examine the crankcase and cylinder block for cracks and damage, and use a piece of wire to probe all oilways and waterways to ensure that they are unobstructed.
5   Note that the rubber plug located adjacent to the bellhousing flange on the cylinder block covers the aperture for the installation of a diagnostic TDC sensor. The sensor, when connected to a suitable monitoring unit, indicates TDC from the position of the pins set into the crankshaft balance weight.

44   Examination and renovation – general

With the engine completely stripped, clean all components and examine them for wear. Each component should be checked, and where necessary renewed or renovated, as described in the relevant

Sections of this Chapter.

Renew main and big-end bearing shells as a matter of course, unless it is known that they have had little wear, and are in perfect condition.

If in doubt as to whether to renew a component which is still just serviceable, consider the time and effort which will be incurred should the component fail at an early date after rebuild. Obviously, the age and expected life of the vehicle must influence the standards applied.

Gaskets, oil seals and O-rings must all be renewed as a matter of routine. Flywheel, cylinder head, and main and big-end bearing cap bolts must be renewed, because of the high stress to which they are subjected.

Take the opportunity to renew the engine core plugs while they are easily accessible. Knock out the old plugs with a hammer and chisel or punch. Clean the plug seats, smear the new plugs with sealing compound, and tap them squarely into position.

45   Engine reassembly – general

1   To ensure maximum life, with minimum trouble, from a rebuilt engine, not only must everything be correctly assembled, but it must also be spotlessly clean. All oilways and coolant passages must be clear, and all washers must be fitted in their original positions. Oil all bearings and other moving surfaces thoroughly with clean engine oil during assembly.

2   Before assembly begins, renew any bolts or studs with damaged threads.

3   Gather together a torque wrench, an angle-torque gauge, suitable sockets and bits, an oil can, clean line-free rag, and a set of engine gaskets and oil seals, together with a new oil filter.

4   If they have been removed, new cylinder head bolts, flywheel bolts, big-end bearing cap bolts and main bearing cap bolts will also be required.

5   On completion of reassembly, refit the applicable ancillary components listed in Section 14.

46   Initial start-up after major overhaul or repair

1   Make a final check to ensure that everything has been reconnected to the engine, and that no rags or tools have been left in the engine compartment.

2   Check that oil and coolant levels are correct.

3   Start the engine. This may take a little longer than usual, as fuel is pumped to the engine.

4   Check that the oil pressure warning lamp goes out when the engine starts. This may take a few seconds as the new oil filter fills with oil.

5   Run the engine at a fast tickover, and check for leaks of oil, fuel and coolant. If a new camshaft has been fitted to sohc models, pay careful attention to the running-in procedure given in Section 22. Where applicable, check the power steering and/or automatic transmission fluid cooler unions for leakage. Some smoke and odd smells may be experienced, as assembly lubricants and sealers burn off the various components.

6   Bring the engine to normal operating temperature. Check the ignition timing (where applicable) and if necessary adjust the idle speed (where applicable) and the mixture (where applicable), as described in Chapter 3.

7   Stop the engine, and if the cylinder head has been removed, tighten the bolts to the Stage 5 setting.

8   Allow the engine to cool, then recheck the oil and coolant levels. Top up if necessary.

9   If new bearings, pistons, etc, have been fitted, the engine should be run-in at reduced speeds and loads for the first 500 miles (800 km) or so. It is beneficial to change the engine oil and filter after this mileage.

47   Fault diagnosis – engine

Symptom	Reason(s)
Engine fails to start	Discharged battery
	Loose battery connection
	Loose or broken ignition leads
	Moisture on spark plugs, distributor cap, or HT leads
	Incorrect spark plug gaps
	Cracked distributor cap or rotor
	Other ignition system fault
	Dirt or water in fuel
	Empty fuel tank
	Faulty fuel pump
	Other fuel system fault
	Faulty starter motor
	Low cylinder compressions
Engine idles erratically	Inlet manifold air leak
	Leaking cylinder head gasket
	Worn rocker arms (where applicable)
	Faulty hydraulic tappets
	Worn camshaft lobes
	Faulty fuel pump
	Loose crankcase ventilation hose(s)
	Idle adjustment incorrect (where applicable)
	Uneven cylinder compressions
	Fuel injection system fault (where applicable)

Symptom	Reason(s)
Engine misfires	Spark plugs worn or incorrectly gapped
	Dirt or water in fuel
	Carburettor adjustment incorrect (where applicable)
	Burnt out valve
	Leaking cylinder head gasket
	Distributor cap cracked
	Uneven cylinder compressions
	Worn carburettor (where applicable)
	Other ignition system fault
	Faulty hydraulic tappets
	Fuel injection system fault (where applicable)
Engine stalls	Idle adjustment incorrect (where applicable)
	Inlet manifold air leak
	Ignition timing incorrect (where applicable)
	Ignition system fault
	Fuel injection system fault (where applicable)
	Loose crankcase ventilation hose(s)
Excessive oil consumption	Worn pistons, cylinder bores or piston rings
	Valve guides and valve stem seals worn
	Oil leaks
Engine backfires	Carburettor adjustment incorrect (where applicable)
	Ignition timing incorrect (where applicable)
	Inlet manifold air leak
	Sticking valve
	Fuel injection system fault (where applicable)

Note: *This Section is not intended as an exhaustive guide to fault diagnosis, but summarises the more common faults which may be encountered during a vehicle's life. Consult a dealer for more detailed advice*

Chapter 2 Cooling system

For modifications, and information applicable to later models, see Supplement at end of manual

Contents

Specifications

System type
Pressurised, with remote expansion tank. Coolant pump driven by timing belt

Coolant
Type/specification .... Ethylene glycol based antifreeze (Duckhams Universal Antifreeze and Summer Coolant)

Capacity:
1.4 litre models	5.6 litres (9.9 pints)
1.6 litre models	5.8 litres (10.2 pints)
1.8 litre models	6.7 litres (11.8 pints)
2.0 litre models	7.2 litres (12.7 pints)

Thermostat
Starts to open at (all models)	92°C (198°F)
Fully open at (all models)	107°C (225°F)

Expansion tank cap
Opening pressure (all models)	1.20 to 1.35 bar (17.4 to 19.6 lbf/in^2)

Cooling fan switch
Switches on at (all models)	100°C (212°F)
Switches off at (all models)	95°C (203°F)

Torque wrench settings

	Nm	lbf ft
Coolant pump bolts:		
1.4 and 1.6 litre models (M6 bolts)	8	6
1.8 and 2.0 litre models (M8 bolts)	25	18
Thermostat cover bolts:		
1.4 and 1.6 litre models	10	7
1.8 and 2.0 litre models	8	6

1 General description

Engine cooling is achieved by a conventional pump-assisted system, in which the coolant is pressurised. The system consists of a radiator, a coolant pump driven by the engine timing belt, an electric cooling fan, a thermostat, an expansion tank, and connecting hoses. Hoses also carry coolant to and from the heater matrix, which provides heat for the ventilation and heating system.

The system works in the following way. Cold coolant from one side of the radiator, which is mounted at the front of the engine compartment, passes to the coolant pump, which forces the coolant through the coolant passages in the cylinder block and cylinder head. The coolant absorbs heat from the engine, and then returns to the radiator via the heater matrix. As the coolant flows across the radiator it is cooled, and the cycle is repeated.

Air flows through the radiator, to cool the coolant as a result of the vehicle's forward motion. However, if the coolant temperature exceeds a given figure, a temperature-sensitive switch in the radiator switches on the electric fan, to increase the airflow through the radiator. The fan only operates when necessary, with a consequent reduction in noise and energy consumption.

To reduce the time taken for the engine to warm up when starting from cold, the thermostat, located in the cylinder head outlet, prevents coolant flowing to the radiator until the temperature has risen sufficiently. Instead, the outflow from the cylinder head bypasses the radiator, and is redirected around the engine. When the temperature reaches a given figure, the thermostat opens, to allow coolant to flow to the radiator. The thermostat is operated by the expansion of a temperature-sensitive wax capsule.

An expansion tank is incorporated in the system, to allow for coolant expansion. The system is topped up through a filler cap on the expansion tank.

2 Routine maintenance

1 At the intervals specified in the *'Routine maintenance'* Section at the beginning of this manual, carry out the following tasks.
2 Check the coolant level in the expansion tank. The level should be checked with the engine cold. If necessary, remove the filler cap from the tank, and top up with a coolant mixture of the same strength as the original coolant (photo). If the engine is warm, cover the filler cap with a thick cloth, and unscrew the cap slowly, to gradually relieve the system pressure. Take care to avoid scalding by steam or coolant escaping from the pressurised system. If frequent topping-up is required, suspect a leak in the system, or a blowing cylinder head gasket, and rectify accordingly.

2.2 Topping-up the coolant – 2.0 litre sohc model

3 Renew the coolant at the specified intervals, with reference to Sections 3, 4 and 5, and check the antifreeze strength at the beginning of each winter.
4 Check the cooling system hoses and connections for condition and security, and rectify any faults as necessary.
5 Periodically, it is advisable to clean the radiator matrix, using a soft brush or compressed air to remove dead insects and other debris which may impair cooling efficiency. Take care not to damage the radiator fins.

3 Cooling system – draining

1 With the vehicle parked on level ground, remove the expansion tank filler cap. If the engine is warm, cover the filler cap with a thick cloth, and unscrew the cap slowly, to gradually relieve the system pressure. Take care to avoid scalding by steam or coolant escaping from the pressurised system.
2 On GSi 2000 models, remove the engine undershield, with reference to Chapter 10.
3 Position a suitable container beneath the radiator bottom hose connection, then slacken the hose clip and ease the hose from the radiator stub. If the hose joint has not been disturbed for some time, it will be necessary to manipulate the hose to break the joint. Allow the coolant to drain into the container.
4 As no cylinder block drain plug is fitted, and the radiator bottom hose may be situated halfway up the radiator, the system cannot be drained completely. Care should therefore be taken when refilling the system to maintain antifreeze strength.
5 If the coolant has been drained for a reason other than renewal, then provided it is clean and less than two years old, it can be re-used.
6 If the coolant has been drained for renewal, and is badly contaminated, the coolant system should be flushed as described in Section 4. As the system cannot be drained completely, it is advisable to flush the system whenever the coolant is renewed, to minimise the impurities remaining in the system.

4 Cooling system – flushing

1 If coolant renewal has been neglected, or if the antifreeze mixture has become diluted, then in time the cooling system will gradually lose efficiency, as the coolant passages become restricted due to rust, scale deposits and other sediment. To restore coolant system efficiency, it is necessary to flush the system clean.
2 The radiator should be flushed independently of the engine, to avoid unnecessary contamination.
3 To flush the radiator, disconnect the top hose at the radiator, then insert a garden hose into the radiator top inlet. Direct a flow of clean water through the radiator, and continue flushing until clean water emerges from the radiator bottom outlet (the bottom hose should have been disconnected to drain the system). If after a reasonable period, the water still does not run clear, the radiator can be flushed with a good proprietary cleaning agent such as Holts Radflush or Holts Speedflush. It is important that the manufacturer's instructions are followed carefully. If the contamination is particularly bad, insert the hose in the radiator bottom outlet, and flush the radiator in reverse.
4 To flush the engine, proceed as follows.

1.4 and 1.6 litre models

5 Remove the thermostat as described in Section 9, then temporarily refit the thermostat cover.
6 With the radiator top and bottom hoses disconnected from the radiator, insert a garden hose into the radiator bottom hose. Direct a flow of clean water through the engine, and continue flushing until clean water emerges from the radiator top hose.
7 On completion of flushing, refit the thermostat, and reconnect the hoses.

1.8 and 2.0 litre models

8 Remove the thermostat and cover assembly, as described in Section 9.
9 With the radiator bottom hose disconnected from the radiator, insert a garden hose into the radiator bottom hose. Direct a flow of clean water through the engine, and continue flushing until clean water

emerges from the thermostat housing. It is advisable to place a sheet of plastic under the thermostat housing to deflect water away from the engine and surrounding components during the flushing process.
10   On completion of flushing, refit the thermostat and cover assembly, reconnect the hoses and remove the sheet of plastic.

5   Cooling system – filling

1   Before attempting to fill the cooling system, make sure that all hoses and clips are in good condition, and that the clips are tight. Note that an antifreeze mixture must be used all year round, to prevent corrosion of the alloy engine components – refer to Section 6.
2   On 1.4 and 1.6 litre models, disconnect the wire and unscrew the coolant temperature sender from the inlet manifold.
3   Remove the expansion tank cap, and fill the system by slowly pouring the coolant into the expansion tank to prevent air locks from forming.
4   If the coolant is being renewed, begin by pouring in a couple of pints of water, followed by the correct quantity of antifreeze (see Section 6), then top up with more water.
5   On 1.4 and 1.6 litre models, refit the coolant temperature sender when coolant free of air bubbles emerges from the orifice in the inlet manifold.
6   Top up the coolant level to the 'KALT' (or 'COLD') mark on the expansion tank, then refit the expansion tank cap.
7   Start the engine and run it until it reaches normal operating temperature, then stop the engine and allow it to cool.
8   Check for leaks, particularly around disturbed components. Check the coolant level in the expansion tank, and top up if necessary. Note that the system must be cold before an accurate level is indicated in the expansion tank. If the expansion tank cap is removed while the engine is still warm, cover the cap with a thick cloth and unscrew the cap slowly, to gradually relieve the system pressure. Take care to avoid scalding by steam or coolant escaping from the pressurised system.
9   On GSi 2000 models, refit the engine undershield on completion.

6   Coolant mixture – general

1   It is important to use an antifreeze mixture in the cooling system all year round, to prevent corrosion of the alloy engine components. The coolant mixture should be made up from clean, preferably soft, tap water, and a good quality antifreeze containing corrosion inhibitor. Ensure that the antifreeze is ethylene glycol based, as the cheaper methanol based types evaporate over a period of time.
2   The proportions of water and antifreeze used will depend on the degree of protection required. A coolant mixture containing 25% antifreeze should be regarded as the minimum strength required to

maintain good anti-corrosion properties. Details of the degree of protection provided against freezing will be supplied with the antifreeze by the manufacturers. For absolute protection, use a 50% antifreeze mixture.
3   The coolant mixture should be renewed every two years, as the corrosion inhibitors will deteriorate with time.
4   Before filling the system with fresh coolant, drain and flush the system, as described in Sections 3 and 4, and check that all hoses are secure and that the clips are tight. Antifreeze has a searching action, and will leak more rapidly than plain water.
5   Refill the system as described in Section 5. All future topping-up should be carried out using a coolant mixture of the same proportions as that used to initially fill the system.
6   Do not use antifreeze in the windscreen wash system, as it will attack the vehicle paintwork. Note that antifreeze is poisonous, and must be handled with due care.

7   Radiator – removal and refitting

1   The radiator can be removed complete with the coolant fan and shroud if there is no need to disturb the fan. If desired, the fan and its shroud can be removed from the radiator, with reference to Section 12.
2   Drain the cooling system, as described in Section 3.
3   Disconnect the radiator top hose and the expansion tank at the radiator.
4   Disconnect the battery negative lead, then disconnect the wiring from the cooling fan switch, located at the bottom right-hand side of the radiator.
5   Disconnect the cooling fan wiring connector, noting its location for use when refitting.
6   Compress and remove the two radiator securing clips, located at the top corners of the radiator (photo).
7   Pull the top of the radiator back towards the engine to free it from the top mountings, then lift the radiator to disengage the lower securing lugs. Move the radiator clear of the vehicle, taking care not to damage the cooling fins (photos).
8   The radiator can be inspected and cleaned as described in Section 8.
9   Refitting is a reversal of removal, bearing in mind the following points.
10   Ensure that the radiator rubber mountings are in good condition and renew if necessary, and ensure that the lower securing lugs engage correctly as the radiator is refitted.
11   Refill the cooling system, as described in Section 5.

8   Radiator – inspection and cleaning

1   If the radiator has been removed due to suspected blockage, reverse-flush it as described in Section 4.
2   Clean dirt and debris from the radiator fins, using an air jet or a soft brush. Take care, as the fins are easily damaged and are sharp.

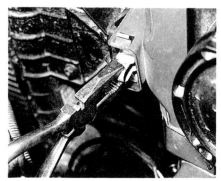
7.6 Compressing a radiator securing clip – 2.0 litre sohc model

7.7A Radiator freed from top right-hand mounting – 1.6 litre model

7.7B Withdrawing the radiator – 2.0 litre sohc model

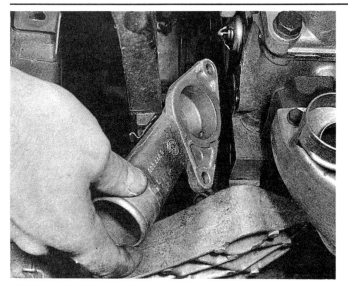

9.6 Remove the thermostat housing ...

7 Withdraw the thermostat from the cylinder head, noting that coolant may be released from the radiator bottom outlet as the thermostat is withdrawn, even though the cooling system has been partially drained (photo).

8 Remove the sealing ring from the edge of the thermostat.

9 If desired, the thermostat can be tested, as described in Section 10.

10 Refitting is a reversal of removal, using a new sealing ring, and bearing in mind the following points.

11 Refit the camshaft sprocket and timing belt, and tension the timing belt, as described in Chapter 1, Sections 15 and 16 respectively.

12 Refill the cooling system, as described in Section 5.

1.8 and 2.0 litre models

13 Partially drain the cooling system, as described in Section 3.

14 Disconnect the radiator top hose from the thermostat cover.

15 Unscrew and remove the three thermostat cover securing bolts, and withdraw the cover complete with thermostat. Recover the O-ring (photos).

16 If desired, the thermostat can be tested, as described in Section 10.

17 Note that if it is necessary to renew the thermostat, the complete cover and thermostat must be renewed as an assembly, as the two cannot be separated.

18 Refitting is a reversal of removal, but use a new O-ring, and on completion refill the cooling system, as described in Section 5.

3 If necessary, a radiator specialist can perform a 'flow test' on the radiator, to establish whether an internal blockage exists.

4 A leaking radiator must be referred to a specialist for permanent repair. Do not attempt to weld or solder a leaking radiator, as damage to the plastic components may result.

5 In an emergency, minor leaks from the radiator can be cured by using a radiator sealant such as Holts Radweld with the radiator *in situ*.

---

10 Thermostat – testing

1 A rough test of the thermostat may be made by suspending it with a piece of string in a container full of water. Heat the water to bring it to the boil – the thermostat must open by the time the water boils. If not, renew it.

2 If a thermometer is available, the precise opening temperature of the thermostat may be determined, and compared with the figures given in the Specifications. The opening temperature is also marked on the thermostat (photo).

3 A thermostat which fails to close as the water cools must also be renewed.

---

9 Thermostat – removal and refitting

Note: *A new O-ring should be used when refitting the thermostat*

1.4 and 1.6 litre models

1 Partially drain the cooling system, as described in Section 3.

2 Remove the timing belt and the camshaft sprocket, as described in Chapter 1, Section 15.

3 Unscrew and remove the two upper bolts securing the rear timing belt cover to the cylinder head, and the lower right-hand bolt securing the cover to the cylinder block.

4 Disconnect the coolant hose from the thermostat housing.

5 Pull the rear timing belt cover forwards, away from the cylinder head, for access to the two thermostat housing securing bolts.

6 Unscrew and remove the two thermostat housing securing bolts, and lift off the thermostat housing (photo).

---

11 Coolant pump – removal and refitting

Models with sohc engines

1 If the engine is in the vehicle, drain the cooling system, as described in Section 3.

2 Remove the timing belt, as described in Chapter 1, Section 15.

3 Unscrew and remove the bolt securing the smaller rear timing belt cover on the coolant pump to the cylinder block (photo).

9.7 ... and withdraw the thermostat – 1.6 litre model

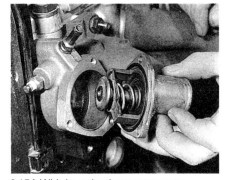

9.15A Withdraw the thermostat cover complete with thermostat ...

9.15B ... and recover the O-ring – 2.0 litre sohc model

10.2 View of thermostat showing opening temperature markings –
1.6 litre model

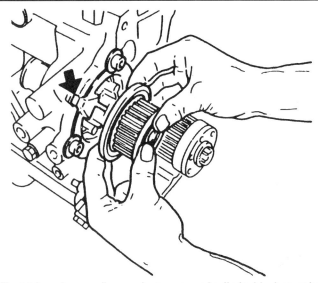

**Fig. 2.1 Lugs (arrowed) on coolant pump and cylinder block must be
aligned – dohc models (Sec 11)**

4   Unscrew and remove the three coolant pump securing bolts (photo).
5   Withdraw the coolant pump from the cylinder block, and recover
the O-ring (photos). It may be necessary to tap the pump lightly with a
plastic-faced hammer to free it from the cylinder block.
6   If desired, the rear timing belt cover can be removed from the pump
by rotating the cover to release it from the flange on the pump.
7   No overhaul of the coolant pump is possible, and if faulty, the unit
must be renewed.
8   Refitting is a reversal of removal, bearing in mind the following
points.
9   Before refitting the pump, smear the pump mounting face in the
cylinder block with a waterproof grease.
10   Use a new O-ring when refitting the pump. Do not fully tighten the
pump securing bolts until the timing belt has been fitted and tensioned.
11   Refit and tension the timing belt, as described in Chapter 1,
Sections 15 and 16 respectively.
12   If the engine is in the vehicle, refill the cooling system, as described
in Section 5.

Models with dohc engine
13   If the engine is in the vehicle, drain the cooling system, as
described in Section 3.
14   Remove the timing belt, camshaft sprockets, crankshaft sprocket,
timing belt tensioner and idler rollers, and the timing belt rear cover, as
described in Chapter 1, Section 17.
15   Proceed as described in paragraphs 4 and 5.

11.3 Unscrewing the bolt securing the coolant pump rear timing belt
cover to the cylinder block – 2.0 litre sohc model

11.4 Coolant pump securing bolt (arrowed) –
2.0 litre sohc model

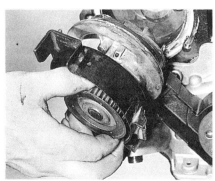

11.5A Withdraw the coolant pump ...

11.5B ... and recover the O-ring – 2.0 litre
sohc model

12.3 Withdrawing the fan shroud assembly – 2.0 litre sohc model

16   No overhaul of the coolant pump is possible, and if faulty, the unit must be renewed.
17   Refitting is a reversal of removal, bearing in mind the following points.
18   Before fitting the pump, smear the pump mating face in the cylinder block with a waterproof grease.
19   Refit the pump using a new O-ring, and ensure that the lugs on the pump and the cylinder block are aligned before tightening the pump securing bolts – see Fig. 2.1.
20   Refit the remaining components, and tension the timing belt, as described in Chapter 1, Sections 17 and 18 respectively.
21   If the engine is in the vehicle, refill the cooling system, as described in Section 5.

12   Cooling fan – removal and refitting

1   Disconnect the battery negative lead.
2   Disconnect the wiring from the cooling fan, noting the location of the wiring connector for use when refitting.
3   Unscrew the two upper fan shroud securing bolts from the top corners of the shroud, then tilt the assembly back slightly towards the engine, and withdraw it upwards away from the radiator (photo).
4   To separate the fan motor from the shroud, unscrew the three securing nuts. If desired, the fan blades can be separated from the motor by removing the securing spring clip from the end of the motor shaft.
5   No spare parts are available for the motor, and if the unit is faulty, it must be renewed.

6   Reassembly (where applicable), and refitting are reversals of the dismantling and removal procedures, but ensure that the lower end of the fan shroud locates correctly on the radiator.
7   On completion, start the engine and run it until it reaches normal operating temperature, then continue to run the engine and check that the cooling fan cuts in and functions correctly.

13   Expansion tank and coolant level sensor – removal and refitting

Expansion tank
1   The expansion tank is secured by a single screw at its front edge. If the tank is to be moved for access purposes, it should be possible to move it sufficiently within the confines of the hoses once the securing screw has been removed. If the tank is to be removed completely, proceed as follows.
2   Disconnect the two hoses from the top of the expansion tank, and suspend them above the height of the engine to prevent coolant loss.
3   Remove the tank securing screw, then manipulate the tank from its location, holding it as high as possible above the engine.
4   Position a suitable container beneath the tank, then disconnect the bottom hose and allow the contents of the tank to drain into the container. Suspend the bottom hose as high as possible above the engine to prevent coolant loss.
5   Refitting is a reversal of removal, but on completion check and if necessary top up the coolant level, as described in Section 2. The coolant drained from the expansion tank during removal can be re-used, provided it has not been contaminated.

Coolant level sensor
6   The coolant level sensor, where fitted, is an integral part of the expansion tank cap. If the level sensor is faulty, the complete cap assembly must be renewed.

14   Temperature gauge sender – removal and refitting

1   The sender is screwed into the inlet manifold on 1.4 and 1.6 litre models, and into the thermostat housing on 1.8 and 2.0 litre models (photos).
2   Partially drain the cooling system, as described in Section 3 to minimise coolant spillage.
3   Disconnect the battery negative lead.
4   Disconnect the wiring from the switch, then unscrew the switch from its location.
5   Refitting is a reversal of removal, bearing in mind the following points.
6   Coat the sender threads with sealant before fitting.
7   Top up the cooling system, as described in Section 5.
8   On completion, start the engine and check the operation of the temperature gauge. Also check for coolant leaks.

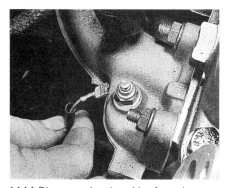

14.1A Disconnecting the wiring from the temperature gauge sender – 1.6 litre model

14.1B Temperature gauge sender location (arrowed) – 2.0 litre sohc model

14.1C Temperature gauge sender location (arrowed) – 2.0 litre dohc model

15.1 Cooling fan switch location (2.0 litre sohc model viewed from below)

15 Cooling fan switch – removal and refitting

Note: *A new sealing ring should be used when refitting the switch*

1   The cooling fan switch is located at the bottom right-hand corner of the radiator (photo).
2   If a faulty switch is suspected, the circuit to the fan motor can be tested by temporarily bridging the terminals in the switch wiring plug, and switching the ignition on. If the cooling fan now operates, the switch is faulty and should be renewed. To remove the switch, proceed as follows.
3   Disconnect the battery negative lead, then disconnect the switch wiring plug if not already done.
4   Drain the cooling system, as described in Section 3.
5   Unscrew the switch from the radiator and recover the sealing ring.
6   Refitting is a reversal of removal, but use a new sealing ring, and refill the cooling system as described in Section 5.
7   On completion, start the engine and run it until it reaches normal operating temperature, then continue to run the engine and check that the cooling fan cuts in and functions correctly.

16 Fault diagnosis – cooling system

Symptom	Reason(s)
Overheating	Coolant level low
	Cooling fan inoperative
	Radiator blocked either internally or externally
	Kinked or collapsed hose, causing coolant flow restriction
	Thermostat stuck shut
	Ignition timing incorrect
	Fuel system fault (weak mixture)
	Exhaust system restricted
	Engine oil level low
	Cylinder head gasket blown
	Brakes binding
	New or rebuilt engine not yet run-in
Overcooling	Thermostat missing, stuck open or incorrect rating
Loss of coolant	Loose hose clip(s)
	Leaking hose(s)
	Leaking radiator
	Expansion tank cap defective
	Cylinder head gasket blown
	Cracked cylinder head or block
Oil and/or combustion gases in coolant	Cylinder head gasket blown
	Cracked cylinder head or block

Note: *This Section is not intended as an exhaustive guide to fault diagnosis, but summarises the more common faults which may be encountered during a vehicle's life. Consult a dealer for more detailed advice*

Chapter 3 Fuel and exhaust systems

For modifications, and information applicable to later models, see Supplement at end of manual

Contents

Specifications

Part A: Carburettor fuel system

General

Fuel tank capacity	61.0 litres (13.4 gallons)
Fuel octane rating:	
Leaded	98 RON (4-star)
Unleaded (see Chapter 4, Section 11)	95 RON (Premium)
Carburettor type	Pierburg 2E3

Air cleaner element

Application:	
1396 cc and 1598 cc	Champion W103
1796 cc	Champion U512

Pierburg 2E3 carburettor – 1.4 litre (14 NV) engine

Idle speed	900 to 950 rpm
Idle mixture (CO content)	0.5 to 1.5%
Fast idle speed	2200 to 2600 rpm
Choke valve gap	1.5 to 3.5 mm
Choke pull-down gap:	
'Small'	1.7 to 2.1 mm
'Large'	2.5 to 2.9 mm
Idle fuel jet	45
Idle air bleed	130

Pierburg 2E3 carburettor

	Primary	Secondary
Venturi diameter	20.0 mm	24.0 mm
Main jet	X95	X110

Pierburg 2E3 carburettor – 1.6 litre (16 SV) engine

Idle speed	900 to 950 rpm	
Idle mixture (CO content)	0.5 to 1.5%	
Fast idle speed	2000 to 2400 rpm	
Choke valve gap	1.5 to 3.5 mm	
Choke pull-down gap:		
Up to 1990:		
'Small'	1.3 to 1.7 mm	
'Large'	1.9 to 2.3 mm	
From 1990:		
'Small'	1.5 to 1.7 mm	
'Large'	2.0 to 2.2 mm	
Idle fuel jet	45	
Idle air bleed	132.5	

	Primary	Secondary
Venturi diameter	20.0 mm	24.0 mm
Main jet:		
Up to 1990	X95	X105
From 1990	X92.5	X105

Pierburg 2E3 carburettor – 1.8 litre (18 SV) engine

Idle speed	900 to 950 rpm	
Idle mixture (CO content)	0.5 to 1.5%	
Fast idle speed	1900 to 2300 rpm	
Choke valve gap	1.5 to 3.5 mm	
Choke pull-down gap:		
'Small'	2.2 mm	
'Large'	3.3 mm	
Idle fuel jet	42.5	
Idle air bleed	137.5	

	Primary	Secondary
Main jet	107.5	125

Torque wrench settings

	Nm	lbf ft
Inlet manifold nuts	22	16
Exhaust manifold nuts	22	16
Exhaust downpipe-to-manifold bolts	25	18
Exhaust fixings except flexible joint bolts	25	18
Exhaust flexible joint bolts	12	9
Fuel pump bolts	18	13
Fuel tank mounting strap bolts	20	15

Part B : Fuel injection system

General

System type:	
All models except GSi 2000, up to 1990	Motronic M4.1
All models except GSi 2000, from 1990	Motronic M1.5
GSi 2000 models	Motronic M2.5
Fuel tank capacity:	
All models except GSi 2000	61.0 litres (13.4 gallons)
GSi 2000 models	65.0 litres (14.3 gallons)
Fuel octane rating*:	
Leaded	98 RON (4-star)
Unleaded (see Chapter 4, Section 11)	95 RON (Premium)

Note: *Models fitted with a catalytic converter must only be operated on unleaded fuel*

Air filter element

Type	Champion U554

Fuel filter element

Type	Champion L201

Idle adjustments

Idle speed (dependent on idle speed adjuster – no adjustment possible):	
All models except GSi 2000	720 to 880 rpm
GSi 2000 models	890 to 990 rpm
Idle mixture (CO content) – models without catalytic converter:	
All models except GSi 2000	0 to 1.0%
GSi 2000 models	0.7 to 1.2%

Torque wrench settings

All specifications as for carburettor models except for the following:

	Nm	lbf ft
Fuel pump clamp bolt	4	3
Fuel flow damper securing nut	20	15
Oxygen sensor	30	22

PART A : CARBURETTOR FUEL SYSTEM

1 General description

The fuel system on all carburettor models comprises a fuel tank, a fuel pump, a vapour separator (1.6 and 1.8 litre models only), a down-draught carburettor, and a thermostatically-controlled air cleaner.

The fuel tank is mounted under the rear of the vehicle, forward of the rear suspension. The tank is ventilated to the atmosphere, and has a simple filler pipe and a fuel gauge sender unit.

The fuel pump is a mechanical diaphragm type, actuated by a pushrod bearing on the camshaft.

The fuel vapour separator is used to stabilise the fuel supply to the carburettor. Vapour is purged from the carburettor fuel supply, thus improving hot starting qualities.

The carburettor is a Pierburg 2E3 type, a full description of which is given in Section 14.

The air cleaner has a wax or vacuum-controlled air intake supplying a blend of hot and cold air to suit the prevailing engine operating conditions. A fuller description is given in Section 6.

All engines available within the Cavalier range can be operated on unleaded petrol – see Chapter 4, Section 11.

2 Fuel system – precautions

Warning: *Many of the procedures given in this Chapter involve the disconnection of fuel pipes and system components, which may result in some fuel spillage. Before carrying out any operation on the fuel system, refer to the precautions given in the 'Safety first!' Section at the beginning of this manual, and follow them implicitly. Petrol is a highly dangerous and volatile substance, and the precautions necessary when handling it cannot be overstressed.*

Certain adjustment points in the fuel system are protected by tamperproof caps, plugs or seals. In some territories, it is an offence to drive a vehicle with broken or missing tamperproof seals. Before disturbing a tamperproof seal, check that no local or national laws will be broken by doing so, and fit a new tamperproof seal after adjustment is complete, where required by law. Do not break tamperproof seals on a vehicle which is still under warranty.

When working on fuel system components, scrupulous cleanliness must be observed, and care must be taken not to introduce any foreign matter into fuel lines or components. Carburettors in particular are delicate instruments, and care should be taken not to disturb any components unnecessarily. Before attempting work on a carburettor, ensure that the relevant spares are available. Full overhaul procedures for carburettors have not been given in this Chapter, as complete stripdown of a carburettor is unlikely to cure a fault which is not immediately obvious, without introducing new problems. If persistent problems are encountered, it is recommended that the advice of a Vauxhall dealer or carburettor specialist is sought. Most dealers will be able to provide carburettor re-setting and servicing facilities, and if necessary it should be possible to purchase a reconditioned carburettor.

Refer to Chapter 4, Section 2 for precautions to be observed when working on vehicles fitted with an engine management system.

3 Routine maintenance

1   At the intervals specified in the *'Routine maintenance'* Section at the beginning of this manual, carry out the following tasks.
2   Renew the air cleaner element, as described in Section 4.
3   Check and if necessary adjust the idle speed and mixture, as described in Section 16.
4   Check all fuel lines and hoses for damage and security, including those located under the underbody.
5   Lubricate the throttle control mechanism, and check the throttle pedal and cable for free movement and correct adjustment.
6   Examine the exhaust system for security, damage and any signs of leaks, and rectify as necessary.
7   Examine the fuel tank for leaks, particularly around the fuel gauge sender unit, and check for signs of corrosion or damage.
8   Check the operation of the air cleaner intake air temperature control mechanism, as described in Section 6.

4 Air cleaner element – renewal

Early round type

1   Release the spring clips from the perimeter of the air cleaner cover.
2   Unscrew and remove the small cross-head screw securing the cover extension to the main body near the inlet duct
3   Unscrew and remove the three central cross-head cap nuts securing the air cleaner to the carburettor, taking care not to drop the washers and seals (photo).
4   Separate the cover from the main body, then lift out the element (photo).
5   Wipe clean the inside surfaces of the cover and main body.
6   Locate the new element in the air cleaner body, and refit the cover using a reversal of the removal procedure.

Square type with air box

7   If desired, to improve access, unclip the coolant expansion tank hose from the air cleaner cover.
8   Release the two clips from the left-hand side of the cover, and unscrew the two screws from the right-hand side, then lift the cover sufficiently to remove the element.
9   Wipe clean the inside surfaces of the cover and main body.
10   Refitting is a reversal of removal, noting that the element fits with the rubber locating flange uppermost.

5 Air cleaner – removal and refitting

Early round type

1   Remove the air cleaner element, as described in the previous Section.
2   Release the crankcase ventilation hose from the plastic clip on the left-hand side of the air cleaner body (see photo 4.4).

4.3 Air cleaner-to-carburettor mounting cap nuts

4.4 Removing the air cleaner element – note clip for crankcase ventilation hose (arrowed)

5.3 The air cleaner body locates over the hot air hose

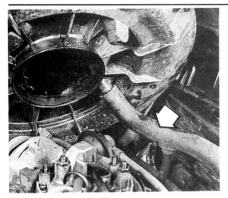

5.4 Disconnecting the crankcase ventilation hose (arrowed)

5.16A Air cleaner casing front ...

5.16B ... and rear securing nuts

3   Disconnect the inlet duct from the hot air hose on the exhaust manifold (photo), and lift the air cleaner body from the carburettor.
4   With the body tilted to the rear, disconnect the crankcase ventilation hose from the stub on the underside of the body (photo), and where applicable, disconnect the vacuum hose from the air temperature control flap thermostat.
5   Remove the seal from under the air cleaner body.
6   Check the hot air hose for condition, and renew it if necessary.
7   Fit a new air cleaner body-to-carburettor seal.
8   Connect the crankcase ventilation hose to the stub on the underside of the body, and also connect the vacuum hose for the air temperature control flap.
9   Locate the body on the carburettor, and at the same time locate the inlet duct on the hot air hose on the exhaust manifold.
10   Engage the crankshaft ventilation hose in the plastic clip.
11   Refit the air cleaner element, with reference to Section 4.

Square type with air box
12   Remove the air cleaner element, as described in the previous Section.
13   Loosen the clamp screw and disconnect the air trunking from the end of the cover.
14   Loosen the clamp screw and disconnect the hot air hose from the air cleaner casing (the hose which connects to the exhaust manifold hot air shroud).
15   Disconnect the air temperature control vacuum pipe from the air box on the carburettor.
16   The lower casing is secured to the wing by three nuts and bolts, one located at the front, and two at the rear (photos). One of the rear fixings is located underneath the casing, which makes access difficult.
17   The air intake tube must now be disconnected from the front body panel, or the casing must be disconnected from the air intake tube.
18   In the workshop it was found easier to disconnect the casing from the air intake tube, although this is a difficult task, and some patience may be required. The two components are most easily separated by levering with two screwdrivers inserted between the air cleaner casing and the tube, one at the top, and one underneath. Push the screwdrivers into the joint, and lever until the retaining lugs are released, then pull the casing from the tube. The aid of an assistant will prove helpful, and care must be taken not to use excessive force, which may damage the plastic components.
19   If desired, the air intake tube can be removed by manipulating it to release the securing lugs from the front body panel. Again, this is a tricky operation, and patience will be required. For improved access, the headlamp can be removed, as described in Chapter 11.,
20   Refitting is a reversal of removal.

6   Air cleaner intake air temperature control – description and testing

1   The air cleaner is thermostatically-controlled, to provide air at the most suitable temperature for combustion with minimum exhaust emission levels.

2   The optimum air temperature is achieved by drawing in cold air from an intake at the front of the vehicle, and blending it with hot air drawn from a shroud on the exhaust manifold. The proportion of hot and cold air is varied by the position of a flap valve in the air cleaner intake spout, which is controlled by either a vacuum diaphragm or wax-type unit. The vacuum diaphragm type is regulated by a heat sensor located within the air cleaner body (photo).
3   To check the operation of the air temperature control, the engine must be cold. First check the position of the flap valve. On the vacuum type, remove the air cleaner cover and check that the flap is open to admit only cold air from outside the car, then start the engine and check that the flap now moves to admit only hot air from the exhaust manifold. On the wax type, the flap should already be positioned to admit only hot air from the exhaust manifold.
4   Temporarily refit the cover on the vacuum type.
5   Run the engine until it reaches its normal operating temperature.
6   On the vacuum type, remove the air cleaner cover and check that the flap is now positioned to admit only cold air from outside the car, or in cold weather, a mixture of hot and cold air. Refit the cover after making the check. On the wax type, use a mirror to check that the flap is positioned in the same way as given for the vacuum type.
7   If the flap does not function correctly, the air cleaner casing must be renewed. Note that the vacuum type thermostat can be renewed separately if necessary.

7   Fuel pump – testing

Note: *Refer to Section 2 before proceeding*

1   Disconnect the ignition coil LT lead.
2   Place a clean wad of rag under the pump outlet, then disconnect the pump outlet hose. Be prepared for fuel spillage, and take adequate fire precautions.
3   Have an assistant crank the engine on the starter. Well-defined spurts of fuel must be ejected from the pump outlet – if not, the pump is probably faulty (or the tank is empty). Dispose of the fuel-soaked rag safely.
4   No spare parts are available for the pump, and if faulty, the unit must be renewed.

8   Fuel pump – removal and refitting

Note: *Refer to Section 2 before proceeding*

1   The fuel pump is located at the rear right-hand end of the camshaft housing.
2   Disconnect the battery negative lead.
3   Disconnect the fuel hoses from the pump (photo). If necessary, label the hoses so that they can be reconnected to their correct locations. Be prepared for fuel spillage, and take adequate fire precautions. Plug the

6.2 Air cleaner flap valve operating mechanism

8.3 Disconnecting a fuel hose from the fuel pump – 1.6 litre model

8.4 Withdrawing the fuel pump and plastic insulating block – 1.6 litre model

1 Flap valve   2 Operating rod

open ends of the hoses to prevent dirt ingress and further fuel spillage.

4   Unscrew the two securing bolts, and withdraw the pump from the camshaft housing (photo).

5   Recover the plastic insulating block.

6   Refitting is a reversal of removal, but ensure that the fuel hoses are reconnected to their correct locations as noted during removal, and tighten the securing bolts to the specified torque.

7   Run the engine and check for leaks on completion. If leakage is evident, stop the engine immediately and rectify the problem without delay. Note that the engine may take a longer time than usual to start when the pump has been removed, as the pump refills with fuel.

9   Fuel tank – removal and refitting

Note: *Refer to Section 2 before proceeding*

1   Disconnect the battery negative lead.

2   Siphon out any remaining fuel in the tank through the filler pipe. Siphon the fuel into a clean metal container which can be sealed.

3   Chock the front wheels, then jack up the rear of the vehicle, and support securely on axle stands placed under the body side members.

4   Disconnect the exhaust system front flexible joint. Suspend the front section of the exhaust system with wire or string from the underbody.

5   Disconnect the rear section of the exhaust system from its rubber mountings, and allow it to rest on the rear suspension torsion beam. It is advisable to support the rear section of the exhaust at its front end, with wire or string from the underbody, to avoid straining the system.

6   Unclip the handbrake cable from the bracket on the left-hand fuel tank securing strap.

7   Disconnect the fuel hoses from the fuel level sender unit located in the right-hand side of the fuel tank. Make a note of the hose positions for use when refitting. Be prepared for fuel spillage, and take adequate fire precautions. Plug the open ends of the hoses, to prevent dirt ingress and further fuel loss.

8   Disconnect the wiring plug from the fuel level sender unit.

9   Disconnect the filler and vent hoses from the rear of the fuel tank.

10   Support the weight of the fuel tank on a jack with interposed block of wood.

11   Unscrew the securing bolts from the tank mounting straps, then remove the straps and lower the tank sufficiently to enable the discon-nection of the remaining vent hose.

12   With the aid of an assistant, withdraw the tank sideways from the right-hand side of the vehicle. Note that as the tank is withdrawn, some residual fuel may be released.

13   If the tank contains sediment or water, it may be cleaned out using two or three rinses with clean fuel. Shake vigorously using several changes of fuel, but before doing so, remove the fuel level sender unit, as described in Section 10. *This procedure should be carried out in a well-ventilated area, and it is vital to take adequate fire precautions – refer to the* 'Safety first!' *Section at the beginning of this manual for further details.*

14   Any repairs to the fuel tank should be carried out by a professional. **Do not** under any circumstances attempt to weld or solder a fuel tank.

Removal of all residual fuel vapour requires several hours of specialist cleaning.

15   Refitting is a reversal of removal, ensuring that all hoses are reconnected to their correct locations as noted during removal.

16   On completion, fill the fuel tank, then run the engine and check for leaks. If leakage is evident, stop the engine immediately and rectify the problem without delay. Note that the engine may take a longer time than usual to start when the fuel tank has been removed, as the pump refills with fuel.

10   Fuel level sender unit – removal and refitting

Note: *Refer to Section 2 before proceeding*

1   Disconnect the battery negative lead.

2   Siphon out any remaining fuel in the tank through the filler pipe. Siphon the fuel into a clear metal container which can be sealed.

3   Chock the front wheels, then jack up the rear of the vehicle, and support securely on axle stands placed under the body side members.

4   The sender unit is located in the right-hand side at the fuel tank.

5   Make alignment marks on the sender unit and the fuel tank, so that the sender unit can be refitted in its original position.

6   Disconnect the fuel hoses from the sender unit. Be prepared for fuel spillage, and take adequate fire precautions. Plug the open ends of the hoses, to prevent dirt ingress and further fuel loss.

7   Disconnect the wiring plug from the fuel level sender unit.

8   To remove the sender unit, engage a flat piece of metal as a lever between two of the slots on the sender unit rim, and turn it anti-clockwise.

9   Withdraw the unit carefully, to avoid bending the float arm.

10   Recover the sealing ring.

11   Refitting is a reversal of removal, bearing in mind the following points.

12   Examine the condition of the sealing ring, and renew if necessary.

13   Ensure that the marks made on the sender unit and fuel tank before removal are aligned.

14   Ensure that the hoses are reconnected to their correct locations as noted during removal.

15   On completion, fill the fuel tank, then run the engine and check for leaks. Also check that the fuel gauge reads correctly. If leakage is evident, stop the engine immediately and rectify the problem without delay. Note that the engine may take a longer time than usual to start when the sender unit has been removed, as the fuel pump refills with fuel.

11   Fuel vapour separator (1.6 and 1.8 litre models) – removal and refitting

Note: *Refer to Section 2 before proceeding*

1   The fuel vapour separator is located on a bracket attached to the side of the carburettor.

2   Note the locations of the three fuel hoses, labelling them if necessary for use when refitting, then disconnect the hoses from the vapour separator. Be prepared for fuel spillage, and take adequate fire precautions. Plug the open ends of the hoses, to prevent dirt ingress and further fuel spillage.

3   Remove the two securing screws, and lift the vapour separator from its bracket.

4   Check the body of the separator for cracks or leaks before refitting, and renew if necessary.

5   Refitting is a reversal of removal, but ensure that the three fuel hoses are connected to their correct locations as noted during removal.

6   Run the engine and check the hose connections for leaks on completion. If leakage is evident, stop the engine immediately and rectify the problem without delay.

12   Throttle pedal – removal and refitting

1   Working inside the vehicle, remove the lower trim panel from the driver's footwell.

2   Slide the cable retainer from the bracket on the top of the pedal, and disconnect the cable end from the pedal.

3   Extract the circlip from the right-hand end of the pedal pivot shaft, then slide out the pivot shaft from the left-hand side of the pivot bracket (photo). Recover the pivot bushes and the pedal return spring.

4   Examine the pivot bushes for wear, and renew if necessary.

5   Refitting is a reversal of removal, but on completion check the throttle mechanism for satisfactory operation, and check the throttle cable adjustment, as described in Section 13.

13   Throttle cable – removal, refitting and adjustment

Removal and refitting

1   Remove the air cleaner, on early models. On later models, disconnect the air trunking from the air cleaner, then disconnect the vacuum

pipe and breather hose from the air box. Extract the three securing screws and lift off the air box, complete with air trunking (photo).

2   Extract the clip from the cable end fitting at the bracket on the carburettor, then slide the cable end grommet from the bracket (photos).

3   Slide the cable end from the throttle valve lever on the carburettor.

4   Working inside the vehicle, remove the lower trim panel from the driver's footwell.

5   Slide the cable retainer from the bracket on the top of the pedal, and disconnect the cable end from the pedal.

6   Make a careful note of the cable routing, then withdraw the cable through the bulkhead into the engine compartment.

7   Refitting is a reversal of removal, bearing in mind the following points.

8   Ensure that the cable is correctly routed, as noted before removal.

9   Ensure that the bulkhead grommet is correctly seated in its hole.

10   On completion, check the throttle mechanism for satisfactory operation, and if necessary adjust the cable, as described in the following paragraphs.

Adjustment

11   Two points of cable adjustment are provided. A stop screw is located on the pedal arm to control the fully-released position of the pedal stop (photo), and a clip is located on a threaded section of the cable sheath at the bracket on the carburettor, to adjust the cable free play.

12   The cable should be adjusted so that when the throttle pedal is released, there is very slight free play in the cable at the carburettor end.

13   Check that when the throttle pedal is fully depressed, the throttle valve is fully open. Adjust the position of the clip on the cable sheath, and the pedal stop screw, to achieve the desired results.

14   Carburettor – description

The Pierburg 2E3 carburettor is of twin-venturi, fixed-jet sequential-throttle type. The primary throttle valve operates alone except at high

12.3 Throttle pedal pivot assembly. Circlip arrowed

13.1 Removing an air box securing screw

13.2A Extract the throttle cable end clip ...

13.2B ... and slide the grommet from the bracket

13.11 Throttle pedal stop screw

14.1A Side view of carburettor, showing accelerator pump (1) and main choke pull-down diaphragm unit (2)

14.1B Side view of carburettor, showing automatic choke housing (1), vapour separator (2) and secondary throttle valve vacuum diaphragm (3)

14.1C Side view of carburettor, showing secondary choke pull-down solenoid (1) and power valve (2)

engine speeds and loads, when the secondary throttle valve is operated, until at full-throttle, both are fully open. This arrangement allows good fuel economy during light acceleration and cruising, but also gives maximum power at full-throttle. The secondary throttle valve is vacuum-operated, according to the vacuum produced in the primary venturi. The primary throttle barrel and venturi diameters are smaller than their secondary counterparts. The carburettor is a complicated instrument, with various refinements and sub-systems added to achieve improved driveability, economy and exhaust emission levels (photos).

A separate idle system operates independently from the main jet system, supplying fuel via the mixture control screw.

The main jets are calibrated to suit engine requirements at mid-range throttle openings. To provide the necessary fuel enrichment at full throttle, a vacuum-operated power valve is used. The valve provides extra fuel under the low vacuum conditions associated with wide throttle openings.

To provide an enriched mixture during acceleration, an accelerator pump delivers extra fuel to the primary main venturi. The accelerator pump is operated mechanically by a cam on the throttle linkage.

A fully-automatic choke is fitted, operated by a coolant and electrically-heated bi-metal coil. When the engine is cold, the bi-metal coil is fully wound up, holding the choke plate (fitted to the primary barrel) closed. As the engine warms up, the bi-metal coil is heated and therefore unwinds, progressively opening the choke plate. A vacuum-operated pull-down system is employed, whereby, if the engine is under choke but is only cruising (ie not under heavy load) the choke plate is opened against the action of the bi-metal coil. The pull-down system prevents an over-rich mixture, which reduces fuel economy and may cause unnecessary engine wear when the engine is cold. A secondary pull-down solenoid is fitted, which operates in conjunction with the main diaphragm unit to modify the pull-down characteristics, improving fuel economy.

1.8 litre models are fitted with an idle cut-off solenoid. This is an electrically-operated valve, which interrupts the idle mixture circuit when the ignition is switched off, this preventing dieselling or engine 'run-on'.

15 Carburettor – removal and refitting

Note: *Refer to Section 2 before proceeding. New gasket(s) must be used when refitting the carburettor. A tachometer and an exhaust gas analyser will be required to check the idle speed and mixture on completion*

1 Disconnect the battery negative lead.
2 Remove the air cleaner, on early models. On later models, disconnect the air trunking from the air cleaner, then disconnect the vacuum pipe and breather hose from the air box. Extract the three securing screws and lift off the air box, complete with air trunking.

15.6 Disconnecting the air box vacuum pipe from the carburettor – 1.6 litre model

3 On 1.4 litre models, disconnect the fuel supply hose from the carburettor, and on 1.6 and 1.8 litre models, disconnect the fuel supply and return hoses from the vapour separator. Be prepared for fuel spillage, and take adequate fire precautions. Plug the ends of the hoses, to prevent dirt ingress and further fuel spillage.
4 Extract the clip from the throttle cable end fitting at the bracket on the carburettor, then slide the cable end grommet from the bracket, and slide the cable end from the throttle valve lever.
5 Disconnect the coolant hoses from the automatic choke housing, noting their locations, as an aid to refitting. Be prepared for coolant spillage, and plug the hoses, or secure them with their ends facing upwards, to prevent further coolant loss.
6 Disconnect the two vacuum pipes from the front of the carburettor, noting their locations and routing for use when refitting (photo).
7 Disconnect the choke heater wiring plug.
8 Unscrew the three securing nuts, and withdraw the carburettor from the inlet manifold studs.
9 Recover the gasket(s) and insulator block which fit between the carburettor and the inlet manifold.
10 Refitting is a reversal of removal, but renew the gasket(s).
11 On completion, carry out the following checks and adjustments.
12 Check the throttle cable free play and adjust if necessary, as described in Section 13.
13 Check and if necessary top up the coolant level, as described in Chapter 2.
14 Check and if necessary adjust the idle speed and mixture, as described in Section 16.

16.3 Carburettor idle speed adjustment (throttle stop) screw (arrowed)

16.4 Tamperproof plug (arrowed) covering idle mixture adjustment screw

17.8 Carburettor top cover securing screws (arrowed)

16   Carburettor – idle speed and mixture adjustment

Note: *Refer to Section 2 before proceeding. To carry out the adjustments, an accurate tachometer and an exhaust gas analyser (CO meter) will be required*

1   In order to check the idle speed and mixture adjustment, the following conditions must be met:

(a)   The engine must be at normal operating temperature
(b)   All electrical consumers (cooling fan, heater blower, headlamps etc) must be switched off
(c)   The ignition timing and spark plug gaps must be correctly adjusted – see Chapter 4
(d)   The throttle cable free play must be correctly adjusted – see Section 13
(e)   The air intake trunking must be free from leaks, and the air filter must be clean

2   Connect a tachometer and an exhaust gas analyser to the vehicle, in accordance with the equipment manufacturer's instructions.
3   Start the engine, and run it at 2000 rpm for approximately 30 seconds, then allow it to idle. If the idle speed is outside the specified limits, adjust by means of the throttle stop screw (photo).
4   When the idle speed is correct, check the CO level in the exhaust gas. If it is outside the specified limits, adjust by means of the idle mixture adjustment screw. In production, the screw is covered by a tamperproof plug; ensure that no local or national laws are being broken before removing the plug (photo).
5   With the idle mixture correct, readjust the idle speed if necessary.
6   If the cooling fan cuts in during the adjustment procedure, stop the adjustments, and proceed when the cooling fan stops.
7   When both idle speed and mixture are correctly set, stop the engine and disconnect the test equipment.
8   Fit a new tamperproof plug to the idle mixture adjustment screw, where this is required by law.

17   Carburettor needle valve and float – removal and refitting

Note: *Refer to Section 2 before proceeding. A new carburettor top cover gasket must be used on reassembly. A tachometer and an exhaust gas analyser will be required to check the idle speed and mixture on completion*

1   Disconnect the battery negative lead.
2   Remove the air cleaner, on early model. On later models, disconnect the air trunking from the air cleaner, then disconnect the vacuum pipe and breather hose from the air box. Extract the three securing screws and lift off the air box, complete with air trunking.
3   Thoroughly clean all external dirt from the carburettor.
4   Disconnect the fuel supply hose at the carburettor. Be prepared for fuel spillage, and take adequate fire precautions. Plug the end of the hose, to prevent dirt ingress and further fuel spillage.

5   Identify the automatic choke coolant hose locations as an aid to refitting, then disconnect the hoses. Be prepared for coolant spillage, and either plug the hoses, or secure them with their ends facing upwards, to prevent further coolant loss.
6   Disconnect the choke heater wiring plug.
7   Disconnect the lower vacuum hoses from the choke pull-down unit.
8   Remove the four carburettor top cover securing screws, noting their locations, as two different lengths of screw are used (photo).
9   Lift off the top cover and recover the gasket.
10   Using a suitable pin punch, tap the float retaining pin from the base of the top cover, and lift out the float and needle valve.
11   Inspect the components for damage, and renew as necessary. Check the needle valve for wear, and check the float for leaks by shaking it to see if it contains petrol.
12   Clean the mating faces of the carburettor body and top cover.
13   Refitting is a reversal of removal, bearing in mind the following points.
14   After refitting, check the float and needle valve for full and free movement. Refer to Chapter 12 for details of float level adjustment.
15   Use a new gasket between the top cover and the carburettor body.
16   Ensure that all hoses, pipes and wires are correctly reconnected.
17   On completion, check and if necessary top up the coolant level, as described in Chapter 2, and check and if necessary adjust the idle speed and mixture, as described in Section 16.

18   Carburettor secondary throttle valve vacuum diaphragm – renewal

Note: *The diaphragm unit must be renewed in its entirety, as no spares are available*

1   Remove the air cleaner, on early models. On later models, disconnect the air trunking from the air cleaner, then disconnect the vacuum pipe and breather hose from the air box. Extract the three securing screws and lift off the air box, complete with air trunking.
2   Disconnect the vacuum pipe from the diaphragm unit.
3   Prise the diaphragm operating rod balljoint from the secondary throttle valve linkage.
4   On 1.6 and 1.8 litre models, remove the two securing screws and lift the vapour separator from the bracket. Move the vapour separator to one side, taking care not to strain the fuel hoses.
5   Remove the three securing screws, and withdraw the diaphragm unit complete with its bracket from the carburettor body.
6   Refitting is a reversal of removal.

19   Carburettor power valve diaphragm – renewal

Note: *Refer to Section 2 before proceeding*

1   Disconnect the battery negative lead.

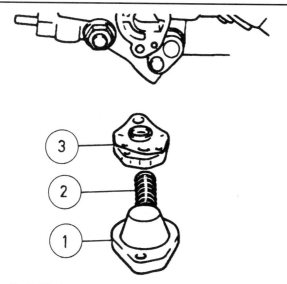

Fig. 3.1 Carburettor power valve components (Sec 19)

1 *Cover*   3 *Diaphragm assembly*
2 *Spring*

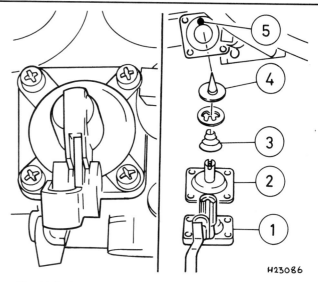

Fig. 3.2 Carburettor accelerator pump components (Sec 20)

1 *Cover with operating lever*   4 *Valve*
2 *Diaphragm*   5 *Air passage*
3 *Spring*

2   Remove the air cleaner, on early models. On later models, disconnect the air trunking from the air cleaner, then disconnect the vacuum pipe and breather hose from the air box. Extract the three securing screws and lift off the air box, complete with air trunking.
3   Thoroughly clean all external dirt from the area around the power valve housing.
4   Remove the two securing screws, and lift off the power valve cover, spring, and diaphragm assembly.
5   Clean the mating faces of the cover and housing.
6   Locate the spring on the cover and diaphragm assembly, ensuring that it is correctly seated, then press the diaphragm assembly and cover together. Note that the vacuum hole in the diaphragm must align with the corresponding holes in the housing flange and cover.
7   Further refitting is a reversal of removal, but ensure that the diaphragm is correctly seated.

---

20   Carburettor accelerator pump diaphragm – renewal

Note: *Refer to Section 2 before proceeding*

1   Proceed as described in Section 19, paragraphs 1 and 2.
2   Thoroughly clean all external dirt from the area around the accelerator pump housing.
3   Remove the four securing screws and lift off the accelerator pump cover. Recover the diaphragm, spring, valve retainer and valve. Note the orientation of the valve retainer.
4   Clean the mating faces of the cover and housing.
5   Check the condition of the valve, and renew if necessary.
6   Commence refitting by locating the valve, valve retainer and spring in the housing. Note that the valve retainer can only be fitted in one position. The larger diameter of the spring should rest against the valve retainer.
7   Locate the diaphragm on the housing, ensuring that the spring is correctly seated, and refit the cover. Tighten the cover securing screws progressively to avoid distorting the diaphragm.
8   Further refitting is a reversal of removal.

---

21   Carburettor automatic choke unit – removal, refitting and adjustment

Removal and refitting

Note: *Refer to Section 2 before proceeding. A tachometer and an exhaust*

gas analyser will be required to check the idle speed and mixture on completion. If the coolant housing is removed, new O-rings will be required for refitting

1   Proceed as described in Section 19, paragraphs 1 and 2.
2   Note the position of the bi-metal housing alignment marks as an aid to refitting, if necessary making additional marks for clarity, then remove the three securing screws and lift off the bi-metal housing. Place the housing to one side, taking care not to strain the coolant hoses or electric choke wiring.
3   Remove the three screws securing the choke housing to the carburettor body, and withdraw the choke assembly, taking care not to bend the choke operating rod.
4   If it is necessary to remove the bi-metal housing for renewal, proceed as follows; otherwise proceed to paragraph 8.
5   Identify the automatic choke coolant hose locations as an aid to refitting, then disconnect the hoses. Be prepared for coolant spillage, and either plug the hoses, or secure then with their ends facing upwards, to prevent further loss of coolant.
6   Disconnect the wiring from the electric choke heater, and withdraw the bi-metal housing.
7   The coolant housing can be separated from the bi-metal housing by unscrewing the central securing bolt. Recover the O-rings from under the bolt head, and from the rim of the coolant housing.
8   Commence refitting by locating the choke assembly on the carburettor body, ensuring that the lever on the choke assembly engages with the choke operating rod. Tighten the three securing screws.
9   Check and if necessary adjust the choke valve gap and the fast idle cam position, as described elsewhere in this Section.
10   Connect the bi-metal spring to the choke lever, position the bi-metal housing on the choke housing, and loosely fit the securing screws. Align the marks on the bi-metal housing and the choke housing as noted during removal, then tighten the securing screws.
11   Where applicable, refit the coolant housing to the bi-metal housing, using new O-rings if necessary, and reconnect the coolant hoses and electric choke heater wiring.
12   Further refitting is a reversal of removal, bearing in mind the following points.
13   If the coolant hoses have been disconnected, check the coolant level, as described in Chapter 2.
14   Check and if necessary adjust the fast idle speed, as described elsewhere in this Section.

Choke valve gap – adjustment
15   With the bi-metal housing removed as described previously in this Section, proceed as follows.

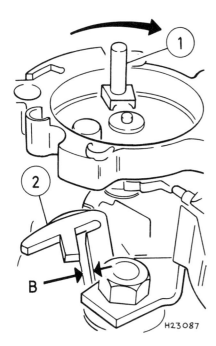

Fig. 3.3 Choke valve gap adjustment (Sec 21)

1   *Choke operating lever*   *B   See text*
2   *Adjuster segment*

16   Press the choke operating lever fully clockwise, and retain it in position with a rubber band – see Fig. 3.3.
17   Move the throttle lever to the fully-open position, and measure the choke valve gap between the lower side of the choke plate and the wall of the primary barrel. Check that the gap is as given in the Specifications.
18   If necessary, adjust the choke valve gap by bending the segment (2) in Fig. 3.3. If the gap is too small, enlarge gap (B) in Fig. 3.3 by levering with a screwdriver. If the gap is too large, decrease gap (B) using a pair of pliers.
19   If no further adjustments are to be carried out, refit the bi-metal housing, as described previously in this Section.

Fast idle cam position – adjustment

20   With the bi-metal housing removed, and the choke valve gap ('B' in Fig. 3.3) correctly set as described previously in this Section, proceed as follows.
21   Open the throttle valve, then close the choke valve using light finger pressure on the choke drive lever – see Fig. 3.4. Close the throttle valve.
22   Check that the fast idle speed adjustment screw is resting against the stop on the second highest step of the fast idle cam.
23   If adjustment is required, first check that the choke return spring is correctly positioned, then adjust by bending the lever (2) in Fig. 3.4.
24   Refit the bi-metal housing, as described previously in this Section.

Fast idle speed adjustment

Note: *To carry out the adjustment, an accurate tachometer and an exhaust gas analyser (CO meter) will be required*

25   Check the idle speed and mixture, as described in Section 16. The idle speed **must** be correct before attempting to check or adjust the fast idle speed.
26   With the engine at normal operating temperature, and a tachometer connected in accordance with the equipment manufacturer's instructions, proceed as follows.
27   Position the fast idle speed adjustment screw on the second highest step of the fast idle cam – see Fig. 3.5.

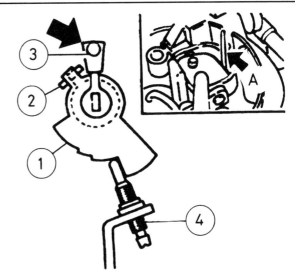

Fig. 3.4 Fast idle cam adjustment (Sec 21)

1   *Fast idle cam*   4   *Fast idle speed adjustment screw*
2   *Adjustment lever*   A   *See text*
3   *Choke drive lever*

28   Start the engine without touching the throttle pedal, and check that the fast idle speed is as specified. If adjustment is required, stop the engine and proceed as follows.
29   Remove the tamperproof cap from the fast idle speed adjustment screw, ensure that no local or national laws are being broken by doing so (photo).
30   Ensure that the adjustment screw is still resting on the second highest step of the fast idle cam, then start the engine, again without touching the throttle pedal.
31   Turn the adjustment screw using a suitable screwdriver, until the specified fast idle speed is obtained.
32   If the cooling fan cuts in during the adjustment procedure, stop the adjustments, and proceed when the cooling fan stops.
33   On completion of adjustment, stop the engine and disconnect the tachometer.
34   Fit a new tamperproof cap to the fast idle speed adjustment screw, where this is required by law.

---

22   Carburettor automatic choke vacuum pull-down units – removal, refitting and adjustment

Main diaphragm unit – removal and refitting

Note: *Refer to Section 2 before proceeding. A new star clip must be used when refitting the diaphragm unit*

1   Proceed as described in Section 19, paragraphs 1 and 2.
2   Disconnect the diaphragm unit vacuum pipes.
3   Using a suitable pin punch, tap out the roll pin securing the diaphragm unit to the carburettor top cover.
4   Note the position of the bi-metal housing alignment marks as an aid to refitting, if necessary making additional marks for clarity, then remove the three securing screws, and lift off the bi-metal housing. Place the housing to one side, taking care not to strain the coolant hoses or electric choke heater wiring.
5   Remove the three screws securing the choke assembly to the carburettor body. Allow the choke assembly to drop down, but do not disconnect the choke linkage.
6   Remove the star clip which secures the diaphragm unit to the

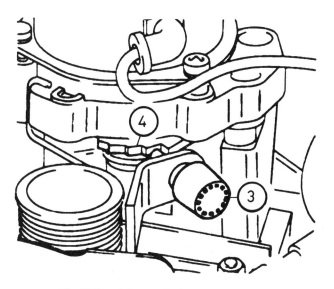

Fig. 3.5 Fast idle speed adjustment (Sec 21)

3   Fast idle speed
    adjustment screw

4   Screw positioned on
    second highest step of cam

21.29 Tamperproof cap (arrowed) covering fast idle speed adjustment screw

carburettor top cover, and withdraw the diaphragm unit.
7   Refitting is a reversal of removal, but use a new star clip to secure the diaphragm unit to the carburettor top cover. Before refitting the air box to the top of the carburettor, check and if necessary adjust the choke pull-down, as follows.

Vacuum pull-down adjustment

8   With the air cleaner or air box removed from the top of the carburettor, as described in Section 19, paragraph 2, proceed as follows.
9   Note the position of the bi-metal housing alignment marks as an aid to refitting, if necessary making additional marks for clarity, then re-

move the three securing screws, and lift off the bi-metal housing. Place the housing to one side, taking care not to strain the coolant hoses or electric choke heater wiring.
10   Position the fast idle speed adjustment screw on the highest step of the fast idle cam, and check that the choke valve is closed.
11   Move the pull-down arm towards the diaphragm unit by pushing on the adjustment screw until resistance is felt. Hold the arm in this position.
12   Using a drill shank of appropriate diameter, or a similar item, measure the clearance between the lower side of the choke plate and the wall of the primary barrel (photo). Check that the clearance is as given for the 'small' choke pull-down gap in the Specifications.
13   If adjustment is necessary, turn the adjustment screw in the appropriate direction, using a suitable Allen key, until the clearance is correct.
14   Now push the pull-down arm towards the diaphragm unit as far as its stop, and hold the arm in this position.
15   As before measure the clearance between the lower side of the choke plate and the wall of the primary barrel. Check that the clearance is as given for the 'large' choke pull-down gap in the Specifications.
16   If adjustment is necessary, turn the adjustment screw in the appropriate direction until the clearance is correct.
17   Connect the bi-metal spring to the choke lever, position the bi-metal housing on the choke housing and loosely fit the securing screws. Align the marks on the bi-metal housing and the choke housing as noted during removal, then tighten the securing screws.
18   Refit the air box to the top of the carburettor on completion.

Secondary pull-down solenoid – removal and refitting

19   This unit operates in conjunction with the main diaphragm unit.
20   To remove the solenoid unit, first proceed as described in Section 19, paragraphs 1 and 2.
21   Disconnect the diaphragm unit vacuum pipe.
22   Disconnect the wiring plug, then unscrew the securing screw, and withdraw the solenoid unit and its mounting bracket from the carburettor. Note that the securing screw also secures the wiring plug earth lead (photo).
23   Refitting is a reversal of removal, but ensure that the wiring plug earth lead is in place under the solenoid bracket securing screw.

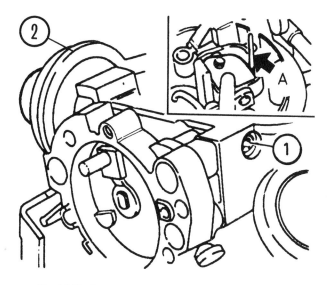

Fig. 3.6 Choke vacuum pull-down adjustment (Sec 22)

1   Adjustment screw   2   Diaphragm unit
A   Twist drill

22.12 Checking the vacuum pull-down gap using a twist drill

22.22 Secondary choke pull-down solenoid securing screw and earth lead

23 Carburettor idle cut-off solenoid (1.8 litre models) – description and testing

Note: *Refer to Section 2 before proceeding*

1   On 1.8 litre models, the carburettor is fitted with an idle cut-off solenoid. This is an electrically-operated valve, which interrupts the idle mixture circuit when the ignition is switched off, thus preventing the engine from running-on.

2   The idle cut-off solenoid is energised all the time that the ignition is switched on. A defective solenoid, or a break in its power supply, will cause the engine to stall or idle roughly, although it will run normally at speed.

3   If the operation of the solenoid is suspect, first check that battery voltage is present at the solenoid terminal when the ignition is switched on (using a 12 volt test lamp or similar suitable test device).

4   If no voltage is present, then the fault lies in the wiring to the solenoid. If voltage is present, the solenoid can be tested as follows.

5   With the solenoid unscrewed from the carburettor, connect the body of the solenoid to the negative terminal of a 12 volt battery. When the battery positive terminal is connected to the solenoid centre ter-

minal, there should be an audible click, and the needle at the tip of the solenoid should retract.

6   A defective idle cut-off solenoid must be renewed.

24 Inlet manifold – removal and refitting

Note: *Refer to Section 2 before proceeding. A new manifold gasket must be used on refitting*

1   Disconnect the battery negative lead.

2   Drain the cooling system, as described in Chapter 2.

3   Proceed as described in Section 15, paragraphs 2 to 7 inclusive, ignoring the reference to coolant spillage in paragraph 5.

4   Disconnect the coolant hose from the rear of the manifold (photo).

5   Where applicable, disconnect the camshaft cover breather hose from the rear of the manifold (photo).

6   Unscrew the union and disconnect the brake servo vacuum hose from the manifold.

7   On 1.4 and 1.6 litre models, disconnect the wiring from the temperature gauge sender.

8   Unscrew and remove the top alternator mounting nut and bolt.

9   On 1.4 and 1.6 litre models, disconnect and remove the stub hose which connects the crankcase breather tube to the rear of the camshaft housing.

10   Make a final check to ensure that all relevant hoses, pipes and wires have been disconnected.

11   Unscrew the securing nuts, and withdraw the manifold from the cylinder head (photo). Note the position of the rear engine lifting bracket, which is secured by one of the manifold nuts, and recover the manifold gasket.

12   It is possible that some of the manifold studs may be unscrewed from the cylinder head when the manifold securing nuts are unscrewed. In this event, the studs should be screwed back into the cylinder head once the manifold has been removed, using two manifold nuts locked together.

13   If desired, the carburettor can be removed from the manifold, with reference to Section 15.

14   Refitting is a reversal of removal, bearing in mind the following points.

15   If the carburettor has been removed from the manifold, refit it, using a new gasket.

16   If the alternator mounting bracket has been unbolted from the manifold, refit it before refitting the manifold, as access to the securing bolt is extremely limited once the manifold is in place.

17   Refit the manifold using a new gasket, and ensure that the engine

Fig. 3.7 Carburettor idle cut-off solenoid (arrowed) – 1.8 litre models (Sec 23)

24.4 Disconnecting the coolant hose ...

24.5 ... and the camshaft cover breather hose (arrowed) from the inlet manifold – 1.6 litre model

24.11 Withdrawing the inlet manifold – 1.6 litre model

lifting bracket is in place under the relevant manifold nut. Tighten the nuts to the specified torque.

18   Ensure that all relevant hoses, pipes and wires are correctly reconnected.

19   Refill the cooling system, as described in Chapter 2.

20   Check the throttle cable free play and adjust if necessary, as described in Section 13.

21   If the carburettor has been disturbed, check and if necessary adjust the idle speed and mixture, as described in Section 16.

25   Exhaust manifold – removal and refitting

Note: *New manifold-to-cylinder head and manifold-to-downpipe gaskets must be used on refitting*

1   Disconnect the battery negative lead.

2   Disconnect the HT leads from the spark plugs, if necessary labelling to ensure refitting to the correct cylinders.

3   Loosen the clamp screw and disconnect the air cleaner hot air tube from the shroud on the manifold.

4   Remove the securing screws and withdraw the hub air shroud from the manifold (photos).

5   Working under the manifold, unscrew and remove the four bolts securing the exhaust downpipe to the manifold.

6   Separate the downpipe from the manifold, and support with wire or string. Do not allow the front section of the exhaust system to hang under its own weight. Recover the gasket.

7   Unscrew the securing nuts, and withdraw the manifold from the cylinder head. Note the position of the front engine lifting bracket, which is secured by one of the manifold nuts, and recover the manifold gasket (photos).

8   It is possible that some of the manifold studs may be unscrewed from the cylinder head when the manifold securing nuts are unscrewed. In this event, the studs should be screwed back into the cylinder head once the manifold has been removed, using two manifold nuts locked together.

9   Refit the manifold using a new gasket, and ensure that the engine lifting bracket is in place under the relevant manifold nut. Tighten the nuts to the specified torque.

10   Reconnect the exhaust downpipe to the manifold, using a new gasket, and tighten the securing bolts to the specified torque.

11   Further refitting is a reversal of removal.

26   Exhaust system – checking, removal and refitting

Note: *All relevant gaskets and/or sealing rings should be renewed on refitting*

1   Periodically, the exhaust system should be checked for signs of leaks or damage. Also inspect the exhaust system rubber mountings and renew if necessary.

2   Small holes or cracks can be repaired using proprietary exhaust

25.4A Remove the securing screws ...

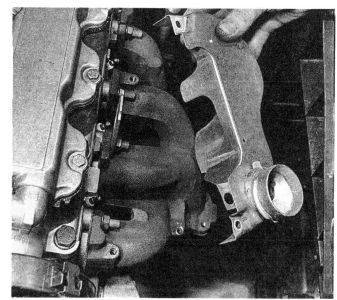

25.4B ... and withdraw the exhaust manifold hot air shroud – 1.6 litre model

25.7A Unscrew the exhaust manifold securing nuts, noting the location of the engine lifting bracket

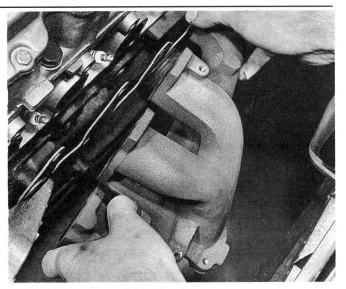

25.7B Withdraw the manifold and gasket

repair products. Holts Flexiwrap and Holts Gun Gum exhaust repair systems ca be used for effective repairs to exhaust pipes and silencer boxes, including ends and bends. Holts Flexiwrap is an MOT approved permanent exhaust repair.
3   The original factory-fitted exhaust system consists of three separate sections, all of which can be renewed individually.
4   Before renewing an individual section of the exhaust system, it is wise to inspect the remaining sections. If corrosion or damage is evident on more than one section of the system, it may prove more economical to renew the entire system.
5   Individual sections of the exhaust system can be removed as follows.

Front section
6   Raise the vehicle, and support securely on axle stands placed under the body side members.
7   Unscrew the two securing bolts, and disconnect the exhaust front section from the centre section at the flexible joint. Recover the sealing ring and the springs.
8   Unbolt the exhaust front section from the bracket on the cylinder block.
9   Unscrew and remove the four bolts securing the downpipe to the exhaust manifold, and withdraw the exhaust front section. Recover the downpipe-to-manifold gasket.
10   Refitting is a reversal of removal, but use a new gasket when reconnecting the downpipe to the manifold, and a new sealing ring when connecting the flexible joint. Tighten all fixings to the specified torque.

Centre section
11   Raise the vehicle, and support securely on axle stands placed under the body side members.
12   Unscrew the clamp bolt, and disconnect the exhaust centre section from the rear section. If necessary, tap round the joint with a hammer to break the seal, and gently prise the two sections apart. Note that the end of the centre section fits inside the rear section, to form a sleeve joint.
13   Unscrew the two securing bolts, and disconnect the exhaust centre section from the front section at the flexible joint. Recover the sealing ring and the springs.
14   Release the exhaust centre section from its rubber mountings on the underbody, and withdraw it from the vehicle.
15   Refitting is a reversal of removal, but use a new sealing ring when connecting the flexible joint, and lubricate the pipes with exhaust assembly paste when connecting the centre section to the rear section. Tighten all fixings to the specified torque.

Rear section
16   Proceed as described in paragraphs 11 and 12.

17   Release the exhaust rear section from its rubber mountings on the underbody, and withdraw it from the vehicle.
18   Refitting is a reversal of removal, but lubricate the pipes with exhaust assembly paste when connecting the rear section to the centre section. Tighten the clamp bolt to the specified torque while counterholding the nut.

PART B : FUEL INJECTION SYSTEM

27   General description

The fuel injection system is of the Bosch Motronic type, which is available in several different versions, depending on model. The system is under the overall control of the Motronic engine management system (see Chapter 4), which also controls the ignition timing.
Fuel is supplied from the rear-mounted fuel tank by an electric fuel pump mounted under the rear of the vehicle, via a pressure regulator, to the fuel rail. The fuel rail acts as a reservoir for the four fuel injectors, which inject fuel into the cylinder inlet tracts, upstream of the inlet valves. On sohc engines, the fuel injectors receive an electrical pulse once per crankshaft revolution, which operates all four injectors simultaneously. On dohc engines, sequential fuel injection is used, whereby each injector receives an individual electrical pulse allowing the four injectors to operate independently, which enables finer control of the fuel supply to each cylinder. The duration of the electrical pulse determines the quantity of fuel injected, and pulse duration is computed by the Motronic module, on the basis of information received from the various sensors.
On sohc engines, inlet air passes from the air cleaner through a vane type airflow meter, before passing to the cylinder inlet tracts via the throttle valve. A flap in the vane airflow meter is deflected in proportion to the airflow; this deflection is converted into an electrical signal, and passed to the Motronic module. A potentiometer screw located on the airflow meter provides the means of idle mixture adjustment, by altering the reference voltage supplied to the Motronic module.
On dohc engines, inlet air passes from the air cleaner through a hot wire type air mass meter, before passing to the cylinder inlet tracts via a two-stage throttle body assembly. The electrical current required to maintain the temperature of the hot wire in the air mass meter is directly proportional to the mass flow rate of the air trying to cool it. The current is converted into a signal, which is passed to the Motronic module. The throttle body contains two throttle valves which open progressively,

allowing high torque at part throttle, and full-throttle, high-speed 'breathing' capacity. A potentiometer screw located on the air mass meter provides the means of idle mixture adjustment, by altering the reference voltage supplied to the Motronic module.

A throttle position sensor enables the Motronic module to compute the throttle position, and on certain models, its rate of change. Extra fuel can thus be provided for acceleration when the throttle is opened suddenly. Information from the throttle position sensor is also used to cut off the fuel supply on the overrun, thus improving fuel economy and reducing exhaust gas emissions.

Idle speed is controlled by a variable-orifice solenoid valve, which regulates the amount of air bypassing the throttle valve. The valve is controlled by the Motronic module; there is no provision for direct adjustment of the idle speed.

Additional sensors inform the Motronic module of engine coolant temperature, air temperature, and on models fitted with a catalytic converter, exhaust gas oxygen content.

A fuel filter is incorporated in the fuel supply line, to ensure that the fuel supplied to the injectors is clean.

A fuel pump cut-off relay is controlled by the Motronic module, which cuts the power to the fuel pump should the engine stop with the ignition switched on, in the event of an accident.

Certain models are fitted with a catalytic converter, to reduce harmful exhaust emissions.

All engines available within the Cavalier range can be operated on unleaded petrol – see Chapter 4, Section 11. Note that models fitted with a catalytic converter must only be operated on unleaded petrol, and leaded petrol **must not** be used.

28   Fuel injection system – precautions

Refer to Section 2 in Part A of this Chapter, but note that the fuel injection system is pressurised, therefore extra care must be taken when disconnecting fuel lines. When disconnecting a fuel line union, loosen the union slowly, to avoid a sudden release of pressure which may cause fuel to spray out.

29   Routine maintenance

1   At the intervals specified in the *'Routine maintenance'* Section at the beginning of this manual, carry out the following tasks.
2   Renew the air cleaner element, as described in Section 30.
3   Renew the fuel filter, as described in Section 32.
4   On all models except those fitted with a catalytic converter, check and if necessary adjust the idle mixture, as described in Section 40.
5   Check all fuel lines and hoses for damage and security, including those located under the underbody.
6   Lubricate the throttle control mechanism, and check the throttle pedal and cable for free movement and correct adjustment.
7   Examine the exhaust system for security, damage and any signs of leaks, and rectify as necessary.
8   Examine the fuel tank for leaks, particularly around the fuel gauge sender unit, and check for signs of corrosion or damage.

30   Air cleaner element – renewal

Refer to Section 4 in Part A of this Chapter, but on all except GSi 2000 models, take care not to strain the airflow meter wiring (photo).

31   Air cleaner – removal and refitting

1   Unclip the coolant expansion tank hose from the air cleaner cover, and move it to one side out of the way.

30.0 Removing the air cleaner element

2   Loosen the clamp screw and disconnect the air trunking from the airflow meter on all except GSi 2000 models, or from the end of the air cleaner cover on GSi 2000 models (photo).
3   On all except GSi 2000 models, disconnect the battery negative lead, then disconnect the wiring plug from the airflow meter.
4   Release the two securing clips from the left-hand side of the air cleaner cover, and unscrew the two captive securing screws from the right-hand side, then lift off the cover.
5   Lift out the filter element.
6   Proceed as described in paragraphs 8 and 9 of Section 5 in Part A of this Chapter, but note that the casing must be disconnected from the air intake tube, as the air intake tube cannot be disconnected from the front body panel with the casing attached.
7   All fuel-injected models are fitted with an intake air resonance box, to reduce induction noise. This box is located under the wheel arch, and connects to a pipe on the air intake tube.
8   To remove the resonance box, which must be removed before the air intake tube can be removed, first apply the handbrake, then jack up the front of the vehicle, and support securely on axle stands placed under the body side members.
9   Remove the securing screws, and withdraw the lower splash shield from the wing to expose the resonance box.
10   Unscrew the single securing screw, and pull the resonance box from the connector tube (photo).
11   If desired, the air intake tube can be removed after pulling off the connector tube from under the wing (photo).

31.2 Loosening the air trunking clamp screw at the airflow meter

31.10A Remove the securing screw ...

31.10B ... and withdraw the resonance box

31.11 Removing the resonance box connector tube

12   Manipulate the air intake tube to release the securing lugs from the front body panel. This is a tricky operation, and patience will be required. For improved access, the headlamp can be removed, as described in Chapter 11.

13   Refitting of all components is a reversal of removal, noting that the air cleaner element fits with the rubber locating flange uppermost.

32   Fuel filter – renewal

Note: *Refer to Section 28 before proceeding*

1   The fuel filter is located on the fuel pump bracket under the rear of the vehicle, on the right-hand side of the spare wheel well on all except GSi 2000 models, or in front of the fuel tank on GSi 2000 models (photos).

2   Disconnect the battery negative lead.

3   Have a suitable container to hand, to catch the fuel which will be released as the filter is removed.

4   Clamp the fuel hoses on either side of the filter, to minimise fuel loss when the hoses are disconnected.

5   Loosen the clamp screws, and disconnect the fuel hoses from the filter. Be prepared for fuel spillage, and take adequate fire precautions.

6   Loosen the clamp bolt(s), and withdraw the fuel filter from its bracket. Note the orientation of the flow direction arrow on the body of the filter, and the position of the 'AUS' (out) marking on the filter end face.

7   Refitting is a reversal of removal, ensuring that the flow direction markings are correctly orientated.

8   Run the engine and check for leaks on completion. If leakage is

evident, stop the engine immediately, and rectify the problem without delay.

33   Fuel pump – testing

1   If the fuel pump is functioning, it should be possible to hear it 'buzzing' by listening under the rear of the vehicle when the ignition is switched on. Unless the engine is started, the fuel pump should switch off after approximately one second. If the noise produced is excessive, this may be due to a faulty fuel flow damper. The damper can be renewed with reference to Section 37.

2   If the pump appears to have failed completely, check the appropriate fuse and relay.

3   To test the fuel pump, special equipment is required, and it is recommended that any suspected faults are referred to a Vauxhall dealer.

34   Fuel pump – removal and refitting

Note: *Refer to Section 28 before proceeding*

1   The fuel pump is located on a bracket under the rear of the vehicle, on the right-hand side of the spare wheel well on all except GSi 2000 models, or in front of the fuel tank on GSi 2000 models.

2   Disconnect the battery negative lead.

32.1A Fuel filter (arrowed) – all models except GSi 2000

32.1B Fuel filter (1), fuel flow damper (2) and fuel pump (3) – GSi 2000 models

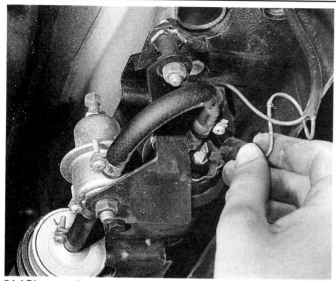

34.4 Disconnecting a fuel pump wiring plug – all models except GSi 2000

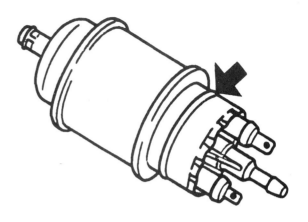

Fig. 3.8 Fuel pump clamping sleeve should rest against rim (arrowed) on pump body (Sec 34)

3   Have a suitable container to hand, to catch the fuel which will be released as the damper is removed.
4   Disconnect the wiring plug(s) from the fuel pump (photo).
5   Clamp the fuel hoses on either side of the damper, to minimise fuel loss when the hoses are disconnected.
6   Loosen the clamp screws, and disconnect the fuel hoses from the pump. Be prepared for fuel spillage, and take adequate fire precautions.
7   Loosen the clamp bolt, and slide the pump from its bracket.
8   Refitting is a reversal of removal, ensuring that the pump is fitted the correct way round in its bracket. Push the pump into the rubber clamping sleeve as far as the rim on the pump body – see Fig. 3.8.
9   Run the engine and check for leaks on completion. If leakage is evident, stop the engine immediately, and rectify the problem without delay.

---

35   Fuel tank – removal and refitting

Note: *Refer to Section 28 before proceeding*

All models except GSi 2000
1   Refer to Section 9 in Part A of this Chapter, but note that one of the fuel hoses connects to a pipe in the side of the tank.

GSi 2000 models
2   Disconnect the battery negative lead.
3   Siphon out any remaining fuel in the tank through the filler pipe. Siphon the fuel into a clean metal container which can be sealed.
4   Chock the front wheels, then jack up the rear of the vehicle, and support on axle stands placed under the body side members.
5   Open the fuel filler flap, then pull back the rubber seal to expose the fuel filler pipe securing screw – see Fig. 3.9. Remove the screw.
6   Release the fuel tank vent hoses from the clips on the underbody.
7   Support the weight of the fuel tank on a jack, with interposed block of wood.
8   Unscrew the securing bolts from the tank mounting straps, then remove the straps and lower the tank sufficiently to enable the fuel hoses, vent hoses and fuel level sender unit wiring to be disconnected (photo).
9   Disconnect the vent hoses and the fuel level sender unit wiring. Note the positions of the vent hoses as an aid to refitting.
10   Disconnect the fuel hoses from the tank and the fuel level sender unit, making a note of the hose positions for use when refitting. Be prepared for fuel spillage, and take adequate fire precautions. Plug the open ends of the hoses, to prevent dirt ingress and further fuel loss.
11   Lower the fuel tank, and withdraw it from under the vehicle.
12   If the tank contains sediment or water, it may be cleaned out using

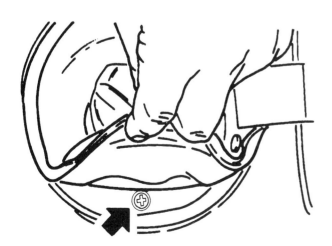

Fig. 3.9 Fuel filler pipe securing screw (arrowed) – GSi 2000 models (Sec 35)

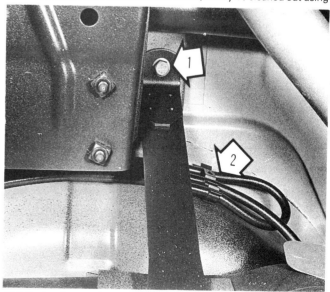

35.8 Fuel tank mounting strap securing bolt (1) and vent hose securing clips (2) – GSi 2000 models

Fig. 3.10 Vauxhall special tool KM-673 for removing fuel level sender unit on GSi 2000 models (Sec 36)

36.1 Fuel level sender unit – all models except GSi 2000

two or three rinses with clean fuel. Shake vigorously using several changes of fuel, but before doing so, remove the fuel level sender unit, as described in Section 36. *This procedure should be carried out in a well-ventilated area, and it is vital to take adequate fire precautions – refer to the 'Safety first!' Section at the beginning of this manual for further details.*

13   Any repairs to the fuel tank should be carried out by a professional, as the tank is made of plastic.

14   Refitting is a reversal of removal, ensuring that all hoses are reconnected to their correct locations as noted during removal.

15   On completion, fill the fuel tank, then run the engine and check for leaks. If leakage is evident, stop the engine immediately, and rectify the problem without delay.

---

36 Fuel level sender unit – removal and refitting

Note: *Refer to Section 28 before proceeding*

All models except GSi 2000
1   Refer to Section 10, noting that there is only one hose connected to the sender unit, and that this must also be disconnected from the union on the inside of the unit before it can be withdrawn completely from the tank (photo).

GSi 2000 models
2   Remove the fuel tank, as described in Section 35.

3   Make alignment marks on the sender unit and the fuel tank so that the sender unit can be refitted in its original position.

4   To remove the sender unit, a suitable improvised tool must be used which engages with the cut-outs in the sender unit retaining ring. The Vauxhall special tool KM-673 for this purpose is shown in Fig. 3.10.

5   Withdraw the unit carefully, to avoid bending the float arm.

6   Recover the sealing ring.

7   Refitting is a reversal of removal, bearing in mind the following points.

8   Examine the sealing ring, and renew if necessary.

9   Ensure that the marks made on sender unit and fuel tank before removal are aligned.

10   Refit the fuel tank, as described in Section 35.

---

37 Fuel flow damper – removal and refitting

Note: *Refer to Section 28 before proceeding*

1   The fuel flow damper is located on the fuel pump bracket under the

rear of the vehicle, on the right-hand side of the spare wheel well on all except GSi 2000 models, or in front of the fuel tank on GSi 2000 models (photo). The damper is positioned in the fuel feed line between the fuel pump and the fuel filter, and its purpose is to reduce pressure fluctuations in the fuel return line, thus reducing noise levels.

2   Disconnect the battery negative lead.

3   Have a suitable container to hand, to catch the fuel which will be released as the damper is removed.

4   Clamp the fuel hoses on either side of the damper, to minimise fuel loss when the hoses are disconnected.

5   Loosen the clamp screws, and disconnect the fuel hoses from the damper. Be prepared for fuel spillage, and take adequate fire precautions.

6   Unscrew the securing nut, and withdraw the damper from the bracket.

7   Refitting is a reversal of removal.

8   Run the engine and check for leaks on completion. If leakage is evident; stop the engine immediately, and rectify the problem without delay.

37.1 Fuel flow damper – all models except GSi 2000

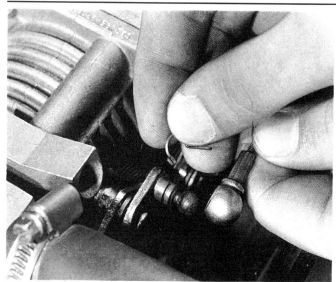

39.4A Disconnecting the throttle cable end from the throttle valve lever – all models except GSi 2000

39.4B Throttle cable end grommet in bracket on inlet manifold

38 Throttle pedal – removal and refitting

Refer to Section 12 in Part A of this Chapter.

39 Throttle cable – removal, refitting and adjustment

Removal and refitting

1 Refer to Section 13 in Part A of this Chapter, but note the following.
2 Ignore the reference to removing the air box on all except GSi 2000 models.
3 For 'carburettor' substitute 'throttle body', and note that the cable bracket is bolted to the inlet manifold.
4 On all except GSi 2000 models, the throttle cable end connects to a balljoint on the throttle valve lever, and is retained by a clip (photos).

Adjustment

5 Refer to Section 13 in Part A of this Chapter, but for 'carburettor' substitute 'throttle body'.

40 Idle mixture – adjustment

Note: *No adjustment of idle mixture is possible on models fitted with a catalytic converter, and no adjustment of idle speed is possible with the Motronic system. Refer to Section 28 before proceeding. A tachometer and an exhaust gas analyser (CO meter) will be required to carry out adjustment.*

1 In order to check the idle mixture adjustment, the following conditions must be met:

(a) The engine must be at normal operating temperature
(b) All electrical consumers (cooling fan, heater blower, headlamps etc) must be switched off
(c) The spark plug gaps must be correctly adjusted – see Chapter 4
(d) The throttle cable free play must be correctly adjusted – see Section 39
(e) The air intake trunking must be free from leaks, and the air filter must be clean

2 Connect a tachometer and an exhaust gas analyser to the vehicle in accordance with the equipment manufacturer's instructions.
3 Start the engine and turn it at 2000 rpm for approximately 30 seconds, then allow it to idle. Check that the idle speed is within the specified limits. No adjustment of idle speed is possible, and if outside

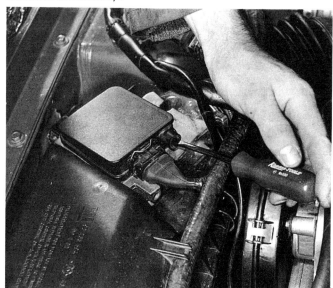

40.4A Adjusting the idle mixture – all models except GSi 2000

40.4B Tamperproof plug (arrowed) covering idle mixture adjustment screw – GSi 2000 models

41.14 Fuel pressure regulator (arrowed) – GSi 2000 models

the specified limits, the problem should be referred to a dealer.

4   With the idle speed correct, check the CO level in the exhaust gas. If it is outside the specified limits, adjust by means of the idle mixture adjustment screw in the airflow meter or air mass meter, as applicable. In production, the screw is covered by a tamperproof plug; ensure that no local or national laws are being broken before removing the plug (photos).

5   If the cooling fan cuts in during the adjustment procedure, stop the adjustments, and proceed when the cooling fan stops.

6   When the idle mixture is correctly set, stop the engine and disconnect the test equipment.

7   Fit a new tamperproof plug to the idle mixture adjustment screw, where this is required by law.

---

41   Fuel pressure regulator – removal and refitting

Note: *Refer to Section 28 before proceeding*

All models except GSi 2000

1   Disconnect the battery negative lead.

2   For improved access, remove the idle speed adjuster as described in Section 42, and disconnect the wiring harness housing from the fuel injectors and move it to one side, taking care not to strain the wiring. Pull up on the wiring harness housing, and compress the wiring plug retaining clips to release the harness housing from the injectors.

3   Position a wad of rag beneath the pressure regulator, to absorb the fuel which will be released as the regulator is removed.

4   Loosen the clamp screws and disconnect the fuel hoses from the regulator. Be prepared for fuel spillage, and take adequate fire precautions.

5   Disconnect the vacuum pipe from the top of the pressure regulator and withdraw the regulator.

6   Refitting is a reversal of removal.

7   On completion, check the fuel line connections for leaks, pressurising the system by switching the ignition on and off several times.

GSi 2000 models

8   Disconnect the battery negative lead.

9   Disconnect the wiring plug from the air mass meter. Recover the sealing ring.

10   Loosen the clamp screw securing the air trunking to the right-hand end of the air mass meter.

11   Using a suitable Allen key or hexagon bit, unscrew the four bolts securing the air box to the throttle body. Lift the air box from the throttle body and disconnect the hose from the base of the air box, then withdraw the air box/air mass meter assembly.

12   Disconnect the two breather hoses from the rear of the camshaft cover, and move them to one side.

13   Disconnect the wiring plug from the throttle position sensor.

14   Disconnect the vacuum pipe from the top of the pressure regulator (photo).

15   Position a wad of rag beneath the regulator, to absorb the fuel which will be released as the regulator is removed.

16   Using a suitable spanner or socket, and working underneath the regulator, unscrew the four Torx type securing bolts, then withdraw the regulator. Be prepared for fuel spillage, and take adequate fire precautions.

17   Refitting is a reversal of removal, ensuring that all wires, pipes and hoses are correctly reconnected. Note that the regulator vacuum pipe should be routed over the top of the camshaft cover breather hoses.

18   On completion, check the regulator for leaks, pressurising the system by switching the ignition on and off several times.

---

42   Idle speed adjuster – removal and refitting

All models (except GSi 2000)

1   Disconnect the battery negative lead.

2   Disconnect the wiring plug from the idle speed adjuster (photo).

3   The adjuster can be removed complete with its connecting hoses, or separately, leaving the hoses in place.

4   Loosen the relevant clamp screws, then disconnect the hoses, and withdraw the idle speed adjuster (photo).

5   Refitting is a reversal of removal.

GSi 2000 models

6   Disconnect the battery negative lead.

7   Loosen the clamp screw, and disconnect the hose from underneath the air box on the throttle body. Remove the clamp from the hose.

8   Apply the handbrake, then jack up the front of the vehicle, and support securely on axle stands placed under the body side members.

42.2 Disconnecting the idle speed adjuster wiring plug – all models except GSi 2000

42.4 Withdrawing the idle speed adjuster complete with hoses – all models except GSi 2000

42.7 Disconnecting the hose from the air box – GSi 2000 models

42.10 Idle speed adjuster (arrowed) viewed from underneath vehicle – GSi 2000 models

9　Remove the engine undershield, as described in Chapter 10.
10　Working underneath the vehicle, disconnect the wiring plug from the idle speed adjuster, which is located underneath the inlet manifold above the starter motor (photo).
11　Loosen the clamp screw and disconnect the remaining idle speed adjuster hose from the inlet manifold, then withdraw the adjuster downwards complete with the hoses.
12　If the hoses are to be removed from the adjuster, mark their locations before removal so that they can be correctly reconnected. Once the adjuster has been refitted, it is impossible to swap the hose positions.
13　Refitting is a reversal of removal, but ensure that the idle speed adjuster rests horizontally, with the wiring routed over the top of the coolant hose. If the wiring is routed under the coolant hose, this may cause the idle speed adjuster to be bent downwards, resulting in a restriction or fracture in the air hose to the inlet manifold.

43　Throttle position sensor – removal and refitting

All models except GSi 2000

Models up to 1990 (Motronic M4.1 system)
1　Disconnect the battery negative lead.
2　Disconnect the wiring plug from the throttle position sensor (photo).
3　Remove the two securing screws and withdraw the sensor from the throttle body (photo).

4　Refitting is a reversal of removal, but before tightening the securing screws, adjust the position of the sensor as follows.
5　Turn the sensor body anti-clockwise until resistance is felt, then tighten the securing screws.
6　When the throttle valve is opened, an audible click should be noticeable from the sensor, and similarly, this should be repeated as the throttle valve is closed.
7　If necessary, adjust the position of the sensor until a click is heard just as the throttle valve begins to open.

Models from 1990 (Motronic M1.5 system)
8　The procedure is as described previously for models up to 1990, except that no adjustment is required when refitting, as the sensor can only be fitted in one position.

GSi 2000 models
9　Disconnect the battery negative lead.
10　Disconnect the wiring plug from the air mass meter. Recover the sealing ring.
11　Loosen the clamp screw securing the air trunking to the right-hand end of the air mass meter.
12　Using a suitable Allen key or hexagon bit, unscrew the four bolts securing the air box to the throttle body. Lift the air box from the throttle body, and disconnect the hose from the base of the air box, then withdraw the air box/air mass meter assembly.
13　Proceed as described in paragraphs 2 to 7 inclusive (photo).

44　Airflow meter (all models except GSi 2000) – removal and refitting

Note: *If the air funnel is removed, a new gasket must be used on refitting. The airflow meter securing bolts must be coated with thread-locking compound on refitting*

1　Proceed as described in Section 31, paragraphs 1 to 4 inclusive.
2　Unscrew the single bolt securing the airflow meter to the front of the air cleaner cover (photo).
3　Unscrew the four securing bolts from inside the air cleaner cover, recover the two reinforcing plates, and withdraw the airflow meter (photo).
4　If desired, the air funnel can be unclipped from inside the air cleaner cover.
5　Refitting is a reversal of removal, bearing in mind the following points.
6　If the air funnel has been removed, refit it using a new gasket.
7　Coat the threads of the four airflow meter securing bolts which fit inside the air cleaner cover with thread-locking compound.

43.2 Disconnecting the throttle position sensor wiring plug (models up to 1990) – all models except GSi 2000

43.3 Removing a throttle position sensor securing screw (models up to 1990) – all models except GSi 2000

43.13 Disconnecting the throttle position sensor wiring plug – GSi 2000 model

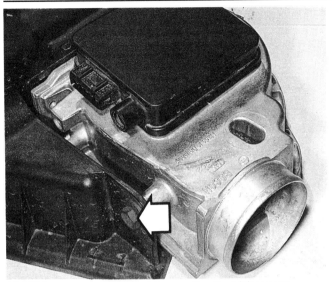

44.2 Airflow meter securing bolt (arrowed) – all models except GSi 2000

44.3 Airflow meter securing bolts and reinforcing plates, and air funnel – all models except GSi 2000

45.2 Recover the sealing ring from the air mass meter wiring plug – GSi 2000 model

45   Air mass meter (GSi 2000 models) – removal and refitting

1   Disconnect the battery negative lead.
2   Disconnect the wiring plug from the air mass meter. Recover the sealing ring (photo).

3   Loosen the clamp screws from the air trunking on either side of the air mass meter, then disconnect the air trunking and withdraw the meter.
4   Refitting is a reversal of removal, but inspect the air mass meter wiring plug sealing ring and renew if necessary.

46   Fuel injectors – removal and refitting

Note: *Refer to Section 28 before proceeding. New O-rings must be used when refitting the injectors. Where applicable, a tachometer and an exhaust gas analyser will be required to check the idle mixture on completion*

All except GSi 2000 models

1   Disconnect the battery negative lead.
2   Unscrew the union nut, and disconnect the brake servo vacuum hose from the inlet manifold.
3   Remove the idle speed adjuster, complete with hoses, with reference to Section 42 if necessary.
4   Disconnect the vacuum pipe from the top of the fuel pressure regulator.
5   Disconnect the wiring harness housing from the fuel injectors, and move it to one side, taking care not to strain the wiring, Pull up on the wiring harness housing, and compress the wiring plug retaining clips to release the harness housing from the injectors.
6   Remove the four bolts from the brackets securing the fuel rail to the inlet manifold, then lift the fuel rail complete with fuel injectors suf-

46.6A Remove the outer ...

46.6B ... and inner fuel rail securing bolts ...

46.6C ... and lift the fuel rail from the inlet manifold (inlet manifold removed for clarity) – all models except GSi 2000

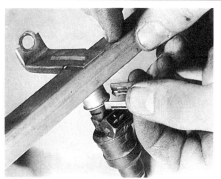

46.7A Withdraw the securing clip ...

46.7B ... then pull the injector from the fuel rail – all models except GSi 2000

46.9 Fit new seals to the injectors

46.22 Throttle cable bracket securing bolts (arrowed) – GSi 2000 model

46.24 Earth leads secured to fuel rail stud (arrowed) – GSi 2000 model

ficiently to enable the injector(s) to be removed (photos). Take care not to strain the fuel hoses.

7   To remove an injector from the fuel rail, prise out the metal securing clip using a screwdriver, then pull the injector from the fuel rail (photos).

8   Overhaul of the fuel injectors is not possible, as no spares are available. If faulty, an injector must be renewed.

9   Commence refitting by fitting new seals to both ends of each fuel injector (photo). Even if only one injector has been removed, new seals should be fitted to all four injectors.

10   Refitting is a reversal of removal, ensuring that all hoses, pipes and wires are correctly reconnected.

11   On completion, where applicable, check and if necessary adjust the idle mixture, as described in Section 40.

GSi 2000 models

12   Disconnect the battery negative lead.

13   Loosen the clamp screw securing the air trunking to the left-hand end of the air mass meter.

14   Using a suitable Allen key or hexagon bit, unscrew the four bolts securing the air box to the throttle body. Lift the air box from the throttle body, and disconnect the hose from the base of the air box, then withdraw the air box.

15   Position a wad of rag beneath one of the fuel hose unions on the fuel rail, to absorb the fuel which will be released as the union is disconnected.

16   Slowly loosen the fuel hose union to relieve the pressure in the fuel line, then disconnect the hose from the fuel rail. Be prepared for fuel spillage, and take adequate fire precautions. Plug the end of the fuel hose, to prevent dirt ingress and further fuel leakage.

17   Repeat paragraphs 15 and 16 for the remaining fuel hose-to-fuel rail union.

18   Disconnect the two breather hoses from the rear of the camshaft cover. Disconnect the larger hose from the throttle body, and remove the hose completely.

19   Disconnect the vacuum pipe from the top of the fuel pressure regulator.

20   Disconnect the wiring plug from the air mass meter. Recover the sealing ring.

21   Disconnect the wiring plug from the throttle position sensor.

22   Slide the end of the throttle cable from the throttle valve lever on the throttle body, then unbolt the cable bracket from the inlet manifold, and move it to one side (photo).

23   Disconnect the wiring harness housing from the fuel injectors, and move it to one side, taking care not to strain the wiring. Pull up on the wiring harness housing, and compress the wiring plug retaining clips to release the housing from the injectors.

24   Unscrew and remove the two fuel rail securing nuts, and withdraw the fuel rail complete with fuel injectors from the inlet manifold. Note the position of the earth leads on the fuel rail securing studs (photo).

25   Proceed as described in paragraphs 7 to 11 inclusive.

---

47 Throttle body – removal and refitting

Note: *Refer to Section 28 before proceeding. A new throttle body gasket must be used on refitting*

All except GSi 2000 models

1   Disconnect the battery negative lead.

2   Loosen the clamp screws securing the air trunking to the throttle body and the airflow meter, then withdraw the air trunking.

3   Loosen the clamp screw, and disconnect the idle speed adjuster hose from the throttle body.

4   Disconnect the camshaft cover breather hose from the throttle body.

5   Disconnect the coolant hoses from the throttle body. Be prepared for coolant spillage, and clamp or plug the open ends of the hoses, to prevent further coolant loss.

6   Disconnect the wiring plug from the throttle position sensor.

7   Release the securing clip, then disconnect the throttle cable end balljoint from the throttle valve lever.

8   Slide the throttle cable grommet from the bracket on the inlet

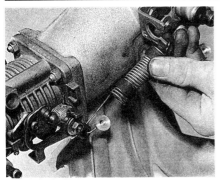

47.8 Unhook the throttle return spring from the bracket on the inlet manifold (inlet manifold removed for clarity) – all models except GSi 2000

47.10A Unscrew the securing nuts ...

47.10B ... and withdraw the throttle body (inlet manifold removed for clarity) – all models except GSi 2000

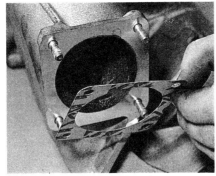

47.15 Refit the throttle body, using a new gasket

47.23 Remove the fuel hose bracket (arrowed) from the throttle body – GSi 2000 model

manifold, then unhook the throttle return spring from the bracket (photo).

9   Make a final check to ensure that all relevant hoses and wires have been disconnected and moved clear of the throttle body.

10   Unscrew the four securing nuts, and withdraw the throttle body from the inlet manifold (photos). Access to the lower nuts is difficult and it may be necessary to move the two fuel hoses to one side for improved access. Take care not to strain the hoses.

11   Recover the gasket.

12   If desired, the throttle position sensor can be removed from the throttle body, with reference to Section 43.

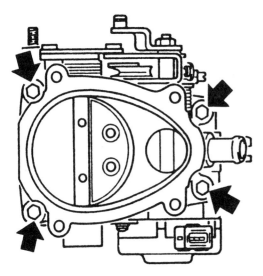

Fig. 3.11 Throttle body securing nuts (arrowed) – GSi 2000 models
(Sec 47)

13   Refitting is a reversal of removal, bearing in mind the following points.

14   Where applicable, refit the throttle position sensor, as described in Section 43.

15   Refit the throttle body, using a new gasket (photo).

16   Ensure that all hoses and wires are correctly reconnected and routed.

17   Check and if necessary top up the coolant level, as described in Chapter 2.

18   Check and if necessary adjust the throttle cable free play, as described in Section 39.

GSi 2000 models

19   Disconnect the battery negative lead.

20   Loosen the clamp screw securing the air trunking to the left-hand side of the air mass meter.

21   Using a suitable Allen key or hexagon bit, unscrew the four bolts securing the air box to the throttle body. Lift the air box from the throttle body, and disconnect the hose from the base of the air box, then withdraw the air box.

22   Disconnect the wiring plug from the throttle position sensor.

23   Unscrew the retaining nut, and remove the fuel hose bracket from the left-hand side of the throttle body (photo).

24   Slide the throttle cable end from the throttle valve lever.

25   Disconnect the breather hose from the front of the throttle body.

26   Disconnect the vacuum pipe from the top of the fuel pressure regulator.

27   Make a final check to ensure that all relevant hoses, pipes and wires have been disconnected and moved clear of the throttle body.

28   Unscrew the four securing nuts, and withdraw the throttle body from the inlet manifold. Recover the gasket.

29   If desired, the throttle position sensor can be removed from the throttle body, with reference to Section 43.

30   **Do not** under any circumstances attempt to adjust the throttle valve linkage. If the throttle valve linkage is faulty, refer the problem to a Vauxhall dealer.

31   Refitting is a reversal of removal, bearing in mind the following points.

32   Where applicable, refit the throttle position sensor, as described in Section 43.
33   Refit the throttle body, using a new gasket.
34   Ensure that all hoses, pipes and wires are correctly reconnected and routed.
35   On completion, check and if necessary adjust the throttle cable free play, as described in Section 39.

48   Catalytic converter   description

Certain models are available with a catalytic converter, to reduce exhaust emissions.

The purpose of the catalytic converter is to change potentially harmful hydrocarbon and carbon monoxide exhaust gases into harmless gases and water vapour. The converter consists of a stainless steel canister containing a catalyst-coated honeycomb ceramic. The catalyst is a mixture of three precious metals, platinum, palladium and rhodium.

The exhaust gases pass freely through the honeycomb, where the catalyst speeds up the chemical change of the exhaust gases, without being permanently altered itself.

To avoid damage to the catalyst, the engine must be kept properly tuned, and unleaded petrol must **always** be used. Normal leaded petrol will 'poison' the catalyst, and **must not** be used.

To enable the Motronic engine management system to achieve complete combustion of the fuel mixture, and thus to minimise exhaust emissions, an oxygen sensor is fitted in the exhaust gas stream. The sensor monitors the oxygen level in the exhaust gas, and sends a signal to the Motronic module. The module constantly alters the fuel/air mixture within a narrow band to reduce emissions, and to allow the catalytic converter to operate at maximum efficiency. No adjustment of idle mixture is therefore possible on models fitted with a catalytic converter.

49   Oxygen sensor (catalytic converter models)   removal and refitting

Note: *If the original sensor is to be refitted, Vauxhall special grease Part No 19 48 602 will be required   see text*

1   Start the engine, and run it until it reaches normal operating temperature. Stop the engine.
2   Disconnect the battery negative lead, then disconnect the oxygen sensor wiring plug, which is located behind the coolant expansion tank.
3   Apply the handbrake, then jack up the front of the vehicle, and support securely on axle stands placed under the body side members.

49.5 Oxygen sensor location in front section of exhaust system GSi 2000 model

4   On GSi 2000 models, remove the engine undershield, as described in Chapter 10.
5   Using a suitable spanner, unscrew the oxygen sensor from the front section of the exhaust system (photo). It is advisable to wear suitable gloves, as the exhaust system will be extremely hot.
6   Withdraw the oxygen sensor and its wiring, taking care not to burn the wiring on the exhaust system. If the sensor is to be re-used, take care that the sealing ring is not lost, and that the sensor is not dropped.
7   If a new sensor is being fitted, it will be supplied with the threads coated in a special grease to prevent it seizing in the exhaust system.
8   If the original sensor is being refitted, ensure that the screw thread is clean. If possibe, coat the thread with Vauxhall grease Part No. 19 48 062; alternatively use a lithium based copper grease.
9   Refitting is a reversal of removal. Check the exhaust system for leakage as soon as the engine is re-started.

50   Inlet manifold   removal and refitting

Note: *Refer to Section 28 before proceeding. A new manifold gasket must be used on refitting*

All models except GSi 2000
1   Disconnect the battery negative lead.
2   Remove the idle speed adjuster and its hoses, with reference to Section 42 if necessary.
3   Release the securing clip, then disconnect the throttle cable and balljoint from the throttle valve lever. Slide the throttle cable grommet from the bracket on the inlet manifold, and move the throttle cable to one side out of the way.
4   Loosen the clamp screw and disconnect the air trunking from the throttle body.
5   Unscrew the union nut and disconnect the brake servo vacuum hose from the inlet manifold (photo).
6   Disconnect the camshaft cover breather hose from the throttle body.
7   Disconnect the coolant hoses from the throttle body. Be prepared for coolant spillage, and clamp or plug the open ends of the hoses, to prevent further coolant loss.
8   Disconnect the wiring plug from the throttle position sensor.
9   Disconnect the vacuum pipe from the top of the fuel pressure regulator.
10   Disconnect the wiring harness housing from the fuel injectors and move it to one side, taking care not to strain the wiring. Pull up on the wiring harness housing, and compress the wiring plug retaining clips to release the harness housing from the injectors.

50.5 Disconnecting the brake servo vacuum hose   all models except GSi 2000

50.14A Unscrew the securing nuts ...

50.14B ... and withdraw the inlet manifold – all models except GSi 2000

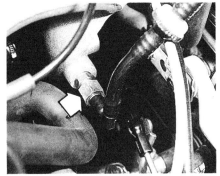

50.37 Brake servo vacuum hose connection at inlet manifold (arrowed) – GSi 2000 models

11   Disconnect the fuel hoses from the fuel rail. Be prepared for fuel spillage, and take adequate fire precautions. Clamp or plug the open ends of the hoses, to prevent dirt ingress and further fuel leakage.

12   Unscrew and remove the top alternator mounting nut and bolt.

13   Make a final check to ensure that all relevant hoses, pipes and wires have been disconnected.

14   Unscrew the securing nuts, and withdraw the manifold from the cylinder head (photos). Recover the gasket.

15   It is possible that some of the manifold studs may be unscrewed from the cylinder head when the manifold securing nuts are unscrewed. In this event, the studs should be screwed back into the cylinder head once the manifold has been removed, using two manifold nuts locked together.

16   If desired, the ancillary components can be removed from the manifold, with reference to the relevant Sections of this Chapter.

17   Refitting is a reversal of removal, bearing in mind the following points.

18   Where applicable refit any ancillary components to the manifold, with reference to relevant Sections of this Chapter.

19   If the alternator mounting bracket has been unbolted from the manifold, refit it before refitting the manifold, as access to the securing bolt is extremely limited once the manifold is in place.

20   Refit the manifold using a new gasket, and tighten the securing nuts to the specified torque.

21   Ensure that all relevant hoses, pipes and wires are correctly reconnected.

22   On completion, check and if necessary top up the coolant level, as described in Chapter 2.

23   Check and if necessary adjust the throttle cable free play, as described in Section 39.

24   If any of the fuel injection system components have been disturbed or renewed, where applicable check and if necessary adjust the idle mixture, as described in Section 40.

GSi 2000 models

25   Disconnect the battery negative lead.

26   Disconnect the wiring plug from the air mass meter. Recover the sealing ring.

27   Loosen the clamp screw securing the air trunking to the right-hand end of the air mass meter.

28   Using a suitable Allen key or hexagon bit, unscrew the four bolts securing the air box to the throttle body. Lift the air box from the throttle body, and disconnect the hose from the base of the air box then withdraw the air box/air mass meter assembly.

29   Disconnect the wiring plug from the throttle position sensor.

30   Slide the throttle cable end from the throttle valve lever, then pull the cable end grommet from the bracket on the inlet manifold, and move the throttle cable to one side out of the way.

31   Disconnect the two breather hoses from the rear of the camshaft cover. Disconnect the larger hose from the throttle body, and remove the hose completely.

32   Position a wad of rag beneath one of the fuel hose unions on the fuel rail, to absorb the fuel which will be released as the union is disconnected.

33   Slowly loosen the fuel hose union, to gradually relieve the pressure in the fuel feed line, then disconnect the hose from the fuel rail. Be prepared for fuel spillage, and take adequate fire precautions. Plug the

end of the fuel hose, to prevent dirt ingress and further fuel leakage.

34   Repeat paragraphs 32 and 33 for the remaining fuel hose-to-fuel rail union.

35   Disconnect the vacuum pipe from the top of the fuel pressure regulator.

36   Disconnect the wiring harness housing from the fuel injectors and move it to one side, taking care not to strain the wiring. Pull up on the wiring harness housing, and compress the wiring plug retaining clips to release the housing from the injectors.

37   Unscrew the union nut, and disconnect the brake servo vacuum hose from the left-hand side of the inlet manifold (photo).

38   Unscrew the retaining nut, and remove the fuel hose bracket from the left-hand side of the throttle body.

39   Unscrew the securing nuts, and disconnect the earth leads from the fuel rail securing studs at either end of the fuel rail.

40   Unscrew the securing bolt, and remove the cable/hose bracket from the left-hand end of the inlet manifold.

41   Remove the idle speed adjuster, as described in Section 42.

42   Unscrew and remove the top alternator mounting nut and bolt.

43   Make a final check to ensure that all relevant hoses, pipes and wires have been disconnected.

44   Proceed as described in paragraphs 14 to 24 inclusive, ignoring the reference to checking the coolant level.

---

51 Exhaust manifold – removal and refitting

Note: *New manifold-to-cylinder head, and manifold-to-downpipe, gaskets must be used on refitting*

All models except GSi 2000

1   Disconnect the battery negative lead.

2   Disconnect the HT leads from the spark plugs, if necessary labelling them to ensure refitting to the correct cylinders.

3   Working under the manifold, unscrew and remove the four bolts securing the exhaust downpipe to the manifold.

4   Separate the downpipe from the manifold, and support with wire or string. Do not allow the front section of the exhaust system to hang under its own weight. Recover the gasket.

5   Unscrew the securing nuts, and withdraw the manifold from the cylinder head (photo). Recover the gasket.

6   It is possible that some of the manifold studs may be unscrewed from the cylinder head when the manifold securing nuts are unscrewed. In this event, the studs should be screwed back into the cylinder head once the manifold has been removed, using two manifold nuts locked together.

7   Refit the manifold using a new gasket, and tighten the securing nuts to the specified torque.

8   Reconnect the exhaust downpipe to the manifold, using a new gasket and tighten the securing bolts to the specified torque.

9   Further refitting is a reversal of removal.

GSi 2000 models

10   A tubular exhaust manifold is fitted, which incorporates the front section of the exhaust system.

11   Refer to Section 52 for details of removal and refitting.

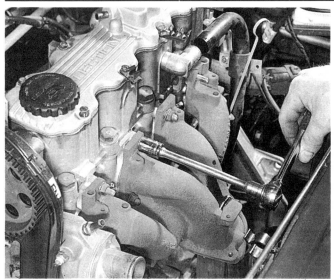

51.5 Unscrewing an exhaust manifold securing nut – all models except GSi 2000

---

52 Exhaust system – checking, removal and refitting

Note: *All relevant gaskets and/or sealing rings should be renewed on refitting*

1 Periodically, the exhaust system should be checked for signs of leaks or damage. Also inspect the exhaust system rubber mountings, and renew if necessary.

2 Small holes or cracks can be repaired using proprietary exhaust repair products, but where more serious corrosion or damage is evident, renewal will be necessary.
3 The original factory-fitted exhaust system consists of four separate sections, all of which can be renewed individually.
4 On models fitted with a catalytic converter, an oxygen sensor is fitted to the front section of the exhaust, and the catalytic converter is fitted in place of the front expansion box in the conventional exhaust system. The manufacturers do not specify any renewal intervals for the catalytic converter.
5 Before renewing an individual section of the exhaust system, it is wise to inspect the remaining sections. If corrosion or damage is evident on more than one section of the system, it may prove more economical to renew the entire system.
6 Individual sections of the exhaust system can be removed as follows.

Front section – all models except GSi 2000
7 On models with a catalytic converter, disconnect the battery negative lead, and disconnect the oxygen sensor wiring plug, which is located behind the coolant expansion tank.
8 Raise the vehicle, and support securely on axle stands placed under the body side members.
9 Unscrew the two securing bolts, and disconnect the exhaust front section from the front expansion box or catalytic converter (as applicable) at the flexible joint. Recover the sealing ring and the springs (photo).
10 Unbolt the exhaust front section from the bracket on the cylinder block (photo).
11 Unscrew and remove the four bolts securing the downpipe to the exhaust manifold, and withdraw the exhaust front section (photo). Recover the downpipe-to-manifold gasket.
12 Refitting is a reversal of removal, but use a new gasket when reconnecting the downpipe to the manifold, and a new sealing ring when connecting the flexible joint. Tighten all fixings to the specified torque.

52.9 Exhaust front section flexible joint – non-GSi 2000 models

52.10 Exhaust front section support bracket – non-GSi 2000 models

52.11 Unscrewing a downpipe-to-exhaust manifold bolt – all models except GSi 2000

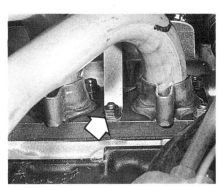

52.17 Exhaust manifold nut (arrowed) securing exhaust heat shield – GSi 2000 models

52.26 Exhaust centre section-to-rear section clamp (arrowed) – non-GSi 2000 model

52.28 Exhaust centre section forward rubber mountings – GSi 2000 models

Front section – GSi 2000 models

13 Proceed as described in paragraphs 7 and 8.

14 Remove the engine undershield, as described in Chapter 10.

15 Proceed as described in paragraphs 9 and 10.

16 Working in the engine compartment, remove the bolts securing the exhaust manifold heat shield to the cylinder head.

17 Unscrew the two lower exhaust manifold securing nuts which also secure the heat shield brackets, and withdraw the heat shield (photo).

18 Unscrew the remaining manifold securing nuts, then withdraw the manifold/exhaust front section from the vehicle. Recover the manifold gasket.

19 It is possible that some of the manifold studs may be unscrewed from the cylinder head when the manifold securing nuts are unscrewed. In this event, the studs should be screwed back into the cylinder head once the manifold has been removed, using two manifold nuts locked together.

20 Refitting is a reversal of removal, but use a new manifold gasket, and use a new sealing ring when reconnecting the flexible joint. Tighten all fixings to the specified torque.

Front expansion box/catalytic converter

21 Proceed as described in paragraphs 8 and 9.

22 Unscrew the three securing nuts and bolts, and disconnect the expansion box/catalytic converter from the exhaust centre section flanged joint. Recover the gasket.

23 Withdraw the expansion box/catalytic converter from the vehicle.

24 Refitting is a reversal of removal, but use a new sealing ring when reconnecting the flexible joint, and a new gasket when reconnecting the flanged joint. Tighten all fixings to the specified torque.

Centre section

25 Raise the vehicle, and support securely on axle stands placed under the body side members.

26 Unscrew the clamp bolt, and disconnect the exhaust centre section from the rear section (photo). If necessary, tap around the joint with a hammer to break the seal, and gently prise the two sections apart. Note that the end of the centre section fits inside the rear section, to form a sleeve joint.

27 Proceed as described in paragraph 22.

28 Release the exhaust centre section from its rubber mountings on the underbody, and withdraw it from the vehicle (photo).

29 Refitting is a reversal of removal, but use a new gasket when reconnecting the flanged joint, and lubricate the pipes with exhaust assembly paste when connecting the centre section to the rear section. Tighten all fixings to the specified torque.

Rear section

30 Proceed as described in paragraphs 25 and 26.

31 Release the exhaust rear section from its rubber mountings on the underbody, and withdraw it from the vehicle.

32 Refitting is a reversal of removal, but lubricate the pipes with exhaust assembly paste when connecting the rear section to the centre section. Tighten the clamp bolt to the specified torque while counter-holding the nut.

PART C : FAULT DIAGNOSIS

53 Fault diagnosis – carburettor fuel system

Note: *High fuel consumption and poor performance are not necessarily due to carburettor faults. Make sure that the ignition system is properly adjusted, and that the engine itself is in good mechanical condition. Items such as binding brakes or under-inflated tyres should not be overlooked*

Symptom	Reason(s)
Engine will not start	Fuel tank empty
	Fault in fuel line
	Fuel pump faulty
	Faulty or maladjusted automatic choke
	Air leak at inlet manifold
	Ignition system fault
Fuel consumption excessive	Leak in fuel system
	Air cleaner element choked, giving rich mixture
	Carburettor worn
	Carburettor float chamber flooding due to incorrect float level, or worn needle valve
	Carburettor idle adjustments incorrect
	Faulty or maladjusted automatic choke
	Unsympathetic driving style
Lack of power	Fault in fuel line
	Fuel pump faulty
	Air leak at inlet manifold
	Faulty or maladjusted automatic choke
	Ignition system fault
Poor or erratic idling	Carburettor idle adjustments incorrect
	Air leak at inlet manifold
	Leak in ignition system vacuum hose
	Leak in brake servo vacuum hose
	Ignition system fault
	Faulty carburettor idle cut-off solenoid (1.8 litre models)
Backfiring in exhaust	Air leak in exhaust system
	Ignition system fault
	Mixture grossly incorrect
	Exhaust valve(s) burnt or sticking, or faulty hydraulic lifter

Symptom	Reason(s)
Spitting back in inlet manifold or carburettor	Mixture very weak Ignition system fault Inlet valve(s) burnt or sticking or faulty hydraulic lifter

Note: *This Section is not intended as an exhaustive guide to fault diagnosis, but summarises the more common faults which may be encountered during a vehicle's life. Consult a dealer for more detailed advice.*

54   Fault diagnosis – fuel injection system

Note: *High fuel consumption and poor performance are not necessarily due to fuel injection system faults. Make sure that the ignition system is properly adjusted, and that the engine itself is in good mechanical condition. Items such as binding brakes or under-inflated tyres should not be overlooked*

Symptom	Reason(s)
Engine will not start	Fuel tank empty Fault in fuel line Fuel pump faulty Faulty fuel pump relay or blown fuse Air leak at inlet manifold Fuel filter blocked Faulty fuel pressure regulator Faulty idle speed adjuster Faulty fuel injector(s) Motronic system fault
Fuel consumption excessive	Leak in fuel system Faulty fuel pressure regulator Mixture incorrect Air cleaner element choked Faulty airflow or air mass meter (as applicable) Faulty throttle position sensor Faulty idle speed adjuster Motronic system fault Unsympathetic driving style
Lack of power	Fault in fuel line Faulty fuel pressure regulator Faulty fuel injector(s) Fuel pump faulty Air leak at inlet manifold Air cleaner element choked Motronic system fault
Poor or erratic idling	Faulty idle speed adjuster Air leak at inlet manifold Faulty fuel pressure regulator Faulty airflow meter or air mass meter (as applicable) Leak in brake servo vacuum hose Motronic system fault
Backfiring in exhaust	Air leak in exhaust system Mixture grossly incorrect Exhaust valve(s) burnt or sticking, or faulty hydraulic lifter Motronic system fault
Spitting back in inlet manifold or throttle body	Mixture very weak Inlet valve(s) burnt or sticking, or faulty hydraulic lifter Motronic system fault

Note: *This Section is not intended as an exhaustive guide to fault diagnosis, but summarises the more common faults which may be encountered during a vehicle's life. In-depth fault diagnosis of the Motronic system requires the use of specialist dedicated test equipment, to analyse the fault codes stored in the Motronic module memory. Consult a dealer for more detailed advice*

Chapter 4
Ignition and engine management systems

For modifications, and information applicable to later models, see Supplement at end of manual

Contents

Specifications

System type
1.4 litre models	Bosch HEI inductive discharge system
1.6 litre models	MSTS, with Lucas or Bosch 'Hall-effect' distributor
1.8 litre models	MSTS with crankshaft speed/position sensor
2.0 litre models (except GSi 2000):	
Up to 1990	Motronic M4.1 with crankshaft speed/position sensor
From 1990	Motronic M1.5 with crankshaft speed/position sensor
GSi 2000 models	Motronic M2.5 with 'Hall-effect' distributor

Coil
Output	16.0 to 20.0 kilovolts
Primary winding resistance (GSi 2000 models only)*	0.2 to 0.34 ohms
Secondary winding resistance (GSi 2000 models only)*	7.2 to 8.2 ohms

No figures were available for other models at the time of writing

Distributor
Direction of rotor arm rotation	Anti-clockwise (viewed from cap)
Firing order	1-3-4-2 (No 1 cylinder at timing belt end of engine)
Dwell angle	Automatically controlled by electronic module (not adjustable)

Ignition timing*
1.4 litre models	5° BTDC
1.6 litre models	10° BTDC
1.8 and 2.0 litre models†	8 to 12° BTDC

For details of ignition timing adjustment required in order to operate vehicles on unleaded petrol, refer to Section 11
†Ignition timing electronically controlled – no adjustment possible

Spark plugs*
Champion recommendation for plug type:	
GSi 2000 models	RC9MCC
All other models	RN7YCC or RN7YC
Champion recommendation for plug gap:	
RN7YCC and RC9MCC	0.8 mm (0.032 in)
RN7YC	0.7 mm (0.028 in)

Information on spark plug types and electrode gaps is as recommended by Champion Spark Plug. Where alternative types are used, refer to the manufacturer's recommendations

Ignition HT leads (boxed set)
1.4 litre models (1988/89)	Champion LS-18
1.4 litre models (1989 on)	Champion LS-36
1.6 litre models (male distributor)	Champion LS-16
1.6 litre models (except male distributor)	Champion LS-36
1.8 & 2.0 litre models (except 20SEH)	Champion LS-37
2.0 litre models (SEH)	Champion LS-39

Torque wrench setting
	Nm	lbf ft
Spark plugs	25	18

1 General description

The ignition system is responsible for igniting the air/fuel mixture in each cylinder at the correct moment, in relation to engine speed and load. A number of different types of ignition systems are fitted to models within the Cavalier range, ranging from a basic breakerless electronic system, to a fully-integrated engine management system controlling both ignition and fuel injection systems. Each system is described in further detail later in this Section.

The ignition system is based on feeding low tension voltage from the battery to the coil, where it is converted to high tension voltage. The high tension voltage is powerful enough to jump the spark plug gap in the cylinders many times a second under high compression pressures, providing that the system is in good condition. The low tension (or primary) circuit consists of the battery, the lead to the ignition switch, the lead from the ignition switch to the low tension coil windings, and also to the supply terminal on the electronic module, and the lead from the low tension coil windings to the control terminal on the electronic module. The high tension (or secondary) circuit consists of the high tension coil windings, the HT (high tension) lead from the coil to the distributor cap, the rotor arm, the HT leads to the spark plugs, and the spark plugs.

The system functions in the following manner. Current flowing through the low tension coil windings produces a magnetic field around the high tension windings. As the engine rotates, a sensor produces an electrical impulse which is amplified in the electronic module and used to switch off the low tension circuit.

The subsequent collapse of the magnetic field over the high tension windings produces a high tension voltage, which is then fed to the relevant spark plug via the distributor cap and rotor arm. The low tension circuit is automatically switched on again by the electronic module, to allow the magnetic field to build up again before the firing of the next spark plug. The ignition is advanced and retarded automatically, to ensure that the spark occurs at the correct instant in relation to the engine speed and load.

HEI (High Energy Ignition) system – 1.4 litre models

This is the least sophisticated system fitted to the model range, and comprises a breakerless distributor and an electronic switching/amplifier module in addition to the coil and spark plugs.

The electrical impulse which is required to switch off the low tension circuit is generated by a magnetic trigger coil in the distributor. A trigger wheel rotates within a magnetic stator, the magnetic field being provided by a permanent magnet. The magnetic field across the two poles (stator arm and trigger wheel) is dependent on the air gap between the two poles. When the air gap is at its minimum, the trigger wheel arm is directly opposite the stator arm, and this is the trigger point. As the magnetic flux between the stator arm and trigger wheel varies, a voltage is induced in the trigger coil mounted below the trigger wheel. This voltage is sensed and then amplified by the electronic module, and used to switch off the low tension circuit. There is one trigger arm and one stator arm for each cylinder.

The ignition advance is a function of the distributor, and is controlled both mechanically and by a vacuum-operated system. The mechanical governor mechanism consists of two weights which move out from the distributor shaft due to centrifugal force as the engine speed rises. As the weights move outwards, they rotate the trigger wheel relative to the distributor shaft and so advance the spark. The weights are held in position by two light springs, and it is the tension of the springs which is largely responsible for correct spark advancement.

The vacuum control consists of a diaphragm, one side of which is connected via a small-bore hose to the carburettor, and the other side to the distributor. Depression in the inlet manifold and carburettor, which varies with engine speed and throttle position, causes the diaphragm to move, so moving the baseplate and advancing or retarding the spark. A fine degree of control is achieved by a spring in the diaphragm assembly.

MSTS (Microprocessor-controlled Spark Timing System) – 1.6 and 1.8 litre models

This system comprises a 'Hall-effect' distributor (1.6 litre models) or a crankshaft speed/position sensor (1.8 litre models), a manifold pressure sensor, an oil temperature sensor, and an MSTS module, in addition to the coil and spark plugs.

On 1.6 litre models, the electrical impulse which is required to switch

off the low tension circuit is generated by a sensor in the distributor. A trigger vane rotates in the gap between a permanent magnet and the sensor. The trigger vane has four cut-outs, one for each cylinder. When one of the trigger vane cut-outs is in line with the sensor, magnetic flux can pass between the magnet and the sensor. When a trigger vane segment is in line with the sensor, the magnetic flux is diverted through the trigger vane away from the sensor. The sensor senses the change in magnetic flux, and sends an impulse to the MSTS module, which switches off the low tension circuit.

On 1.8 litre models, the electrical impulse which is required to switch off the low tension circuit is generated by a crankshaft speed/position sensor, which is activated by a toothed wheel on the crankshaft. The toothed wheel has 35 equally-spaced teeth, with a gap in the 36th position. The gap is used by the sensor to determine the crankshaft position relative to TDC (top dead centre) of No 1 piston.

Engine load information is supplied to the MSTS module by a pressure sensor, which is connected to the carburettor by a vacuum pipe. Additional information is supplied by an oil temperature sensor. The module selects the optimum ignition advance setting based on the information received from the sensors. The degree of advance can thus be constantly varied to suit the prevailing engine conditions.

Motronic system – all 2.0 litre models except GSi 2000

This system controls both the ignition and the fuel injection systems.

The Motronic module receives information from a crankshaft speed/position sensor (similar to that described previously in this Section for 1.8 litre models with the MSTS system), an engine coolant temperature sensor mounted in the thermostat housing, a throttle position sensor, an airflow meter, and on models fitted with a catalytic converter, an oxygen sensor mounted in the exhaust system (see Chapter 3).

The module provides outputs to control the fuel pump, fuel injectors, idle speed and ignition circuit. Using the inputs from the various sensors, the module computes the optimum ignition advance, and fuel injector pulse duration, to suit the prevailing engine conditions. This system gives very accurate control of the engine under all conditions, improving fuel consumption and driveability, and reducing exhaust gas emissions.

Further details of the fuel injection system components are given in Chapter 3.

Motronic system – GSi 2000 models

The system is similar to that described for other 2.0 litre models, with the following differences.

In addition to the crankshaft speed/position sensor, a 'Hall-effect' distributor is used (similar to that described previously in this Section for 1.6 litre models with the MSTS system).

Additionally, the Motronic module receives information from a cylinder block-mounted knock sensor, which senses 'knocking' (or pre-ignition) just as it begins to occur, enabling the module to retard the ignition timing, thus preventing engine damage.

2 Ignition and engine management systems – precautions

Warning: *The HT voltage generated by an electronic ignition system is extremely high and, in certain circumstances, could prove fatal. Take care to avoid receiving electric shocks from the HT side of the ignition system. Do not handle HT leads, or touch the distributor or coil, when the engine is running. If tracing faults in the HT circuit, use well-insulated tools to manipulate live leads*

Engine management modules are very sensitive components, and certain precautions must be taken, to avoid damage to the module when working on a vehicle equipped with an engine management system, as follows.

When carrying out welding operations on the vehicle using electric welding equipment, the battery and alternator should be disconnected.

Although underbonnet-mounted modules will tolerate normal underbonnet conditions, they can be adversely affected by excess heat or moisture. If using welding equipment or pressure washing equipment in the vicinity of the module, take care not to direct heat, or jets of water or steam, at the module. If this cannot be avoided, remove the module from the vehicle, and protect its wiring plug with a plastic bag.

Before disconnecting any wiring, or removing components, always ensure that the ignition is switched off.

Do not attempt to improvise fault diagnosis procedures using a test lamp or multimeter, as irreparable damage could be caused to the module.

After working on ignition/engine management system components, ensure that all wiring is correctly reconnected before reconnecting the battery or switching on the ignition.

3 Routine maintenance

Note: *Refer to Section 2 before proceeding*

1   At the intervals specified in the *'Routine maintenance'* Section at the beginning of this manual, carry out the following tasks.
2   Check the spark plugs as described in Section 4.
3   Renew the spark plugs, as described in Section 4.
4   On 1.4 and 1.6 litre models, check and if necessary adjust the ignition timing, as described in Section 10.
5   Remove the distributor cap and HT leads, and wipe them clean. Also wipe clean the coil connections. Remove the rotor arm, then visually check the distributor cap, rotor arm and HT leads for hairline cracks, and signs of arcing. When refitting the distributor cap, check that the ends of the HT leads are fitted securely to the cap, plugs and coil. Also make sure that the spring-tensioned carbon brush in the centre of the distributor cap moves freely, and that the HT segments are not worn excessively.
6   Inspect the electrical and vacuum connections of the ignition/ engine management systems, and make sure that they are clean and secure.

4 Spark plugs and HT leads – inspection and renewal

Note: *Refer to Section 2 before proceeding*

1   The correct functioning of the spark plugs is vital for the correct running and efficiency of the engine. It is essential that the plugs fitted are appropriate for the engine, and the suitable type is specified at the beginning of this chapter. If this type is used and the engine is in good condition, the spark plugs should not need attention between scheduled service replacement intervals. Spark plug cleaning is rarely necessary and should not be attempted unless specialised equipment is available, as damage can easily be caused to the firing ends.
2   On GSi 2000 models, unscrew the two securing bolts and withdraw the spark plug cover from the camshaft cover.
3   If necessary, identify each HT lead for position, so that the leads can be refitted to their correct cylinders, then disconnect the leads from the plugs by pulling on the connectors, not the leads.
4   Clean the area around each spark plug using a small paintbrush, then using a plug spanner (preferably with a rubber insert), unscrew and remove the plugs (photo). Cover the spark plug holes with a clean rag to prevent the ingress of any foreign matter.
5   The condition of the spark plugs will tell much about the overall condition of the engine.
6   If the insulator nose of the spark plug is clean and white, with no deposits, this is indicative of a weak mixture, or too hot a plug (a hot plug transfers heat away from the electrode slowly – a cold plug transfers heat away quickly).
7   If the tip and insulator nose is covered with hard black-looking deposits, then this is indicative that the mixture is too rich. Should the plug be black and oily, then it is likely that the engine is fairly worn, as well as the mixture being too rich.
8   If the insulator nose is covered with light tan to greyish brown deposits, then the mixture is correct, and it is likely that the engine is in good condition.
9   The spark plug gap is of considerable importance, because if it is either too large or too small, the size of the spark and its efficiency will be seriously impaired. The spark plug gap should be set to the figure given in the Specifications.
10   To set it, measure the gap with a feeler gauge and then bend open, or close, the outer plug electrode until the correct gap is achieved. The centre electrode should never be bent, as this may crack the insulation and cause plug failure, if nothing worse.

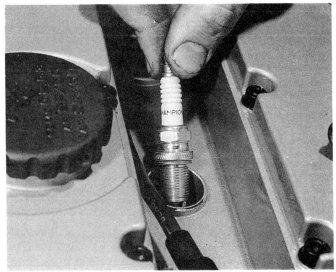

4.4 Removing a spark plug – GSi 2000 model

11   Before fitting new spark plugs check that their threaded connector sleeves are tight.
12   Screw in the plugs by hand, then tighten them to the specified torque. **Do not** exceed the torque figure.
13   Push the HT leads firmly onto the spark plugs, ensuring that they are connected to their correct cylinders.
14   On GSi 2000 models, refit the spark plug cover.
15   The HT leads and distributor cap should be cleaned and checked at regular intervals.

5 Coil – description and testing

Note: *Refer to Section 2 before proceeding. An ohmmeter will be required to test the coil.*

1   The ignition coil is either a cylindrical metal canister or a moulded plastic unit. It is clamped or bolted to the left-hand inner wing panel, near the suspension strut top mounting (under the power steering fluid reservoir, on models so equipped). On all except 2.0 litre sohc models, the ignition amplifier module is mounted on the coil's bracket or baseplate (photo).
2   When removing and refitting the coil, note carefully the LT wiring connections before disconnecting them; usually they are physically different to prevent incorrect refitting, but if not, use the terminal marks or numbers in conjunction with the relevant wiring diagram at the back of this manual to ensure that the connections are correctly remade. If the connections are reversed, so will the coil's polarity be; while the engine may still run, spark plug life will be reduced and poor starting and/or misfiring may ensue.
3   To test the coil, first disconnect the LT wiring and the HT lead. Test the coil's primary windings by connecting a multi-meter across the LT terminals ('+' or '15' and '–' or '1') and the secondary windings by testing across the HT terminal ('4') and one of the LT terminals (usually the '–/1' terminal, although in some cases, either terminal may serve). On GSi 2000 models, results should closely approximate the specified values; on all other models, typical primary resistances are less than 1 ohm, while secondary resistances can be expected to be in the 4000 to 12 000 ohms range.
4   If the results obtained differ significantly from those given, showing windings that are shorted or open circuit, the coil must be renewed.

6 Coil – removal and refitting

Note: *Refer to Section 2 before proceeding*

1   Disconnect the battery negative lead.

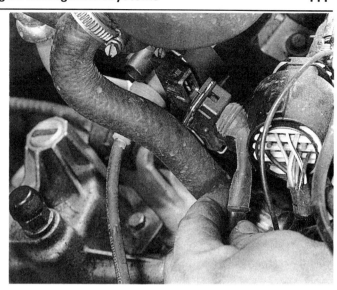

5.1 Ignition coil – 1.6 litre model – note ignition timing basic adjustment coding plug (arrow)

6.2 Disconnecting the coil LT wiring plug – 2.0 litre model

2   Disconnect the wiring from the coil (photo).
3   Note that on models with power steering, one of the coil securing bolts also secures the power steering fluid reservoir bracket.
4   Withdraw the ignition coil.
5   On models with a cylindrical type coil, the mounting clamp can be removed from the coil by loosening the clamp nut.
6   Refitting is a reversal of removal, but where applicable, ensure that the coil suppressor is in position before refitting the coil securing bolts, and ensure that all leads are securely reconnected.

7 Distributor cap and rotor arm – removal and refitting

Note: *Refer to Section 2 before proceeding*

1.4 and 1.6 litre models
1   Disconnect the battery negative lead.
2   If necessary, identify each HT lead for position, so that the leads can be refitted to their correct cylinders, then disconnect the leads from the spark plugs by pulling on the connectors, not the leads. Similarly, disconnect the HT lead from the coil. Pull the leads from the clips on the camshaft cover.
3   On the Bosch distributor, prise away the two spring clips with a screwdriver, and lift off the distributor cap. On the Lucas distributor,

unscrew the two small bolts and lift off the cap (photos).
4   The rotor arm is a push fit on the end of the distributor shaft.
5   If desired, on the Bosch distributor, the plastic shield can be pulled from the end of the distributor, to allow examination of the distributor components (photo).
6   Refitting is a reversal of removal, noting that the rotor arm can only be fitted in one position. Ensure that the HT leads are correctly reconnected.

1.8 and 2.0 litre models (except GSi 2000)
7   Proceed as described in paragraphs 1 and 2.
8   Using a suitable Torx socket, unscrew the three captive securing screws and withdraw the distributor cap (photo).
9   Withdraw the plastic shield from the rotor arm housing. The shield is an interference fit in the housing, via an O-ring seal located in a groove in its periphery. Ease out the shield, taking care not to damage the rotor arm (photo).
10   Using a suitable Allen key or hexagon bit, extract the two securing screws and withdraw the rotor arm, leaving the metal rotor hub in the housing (photos).
11   Examine the O-ring on the plastic shield, and renew if necessary.
12   Refitting is a reversal of removal, noting that the rotor arm can only be fitted in one position. If necessary, turn the metal rotor hub so that the screw holes align with those in the rotor arm and the end of the camshaft. Ensure that the HT leads are correctly reconnected.

7.3A Removing the distributor cap – 1.6 litre model (Bosch distributor)...

7.3B ... and 1.6 litre model (Lucas distributor)

7.5 Removing the rotor arm and plastic shield – 1.6 litre model (Bosch distributor)

7.8 Unscrewing a distributor cap securing screw – 2.0 litre model

7.9 Removing the plastic shield from the rotor arm housing – 2.0 litre model

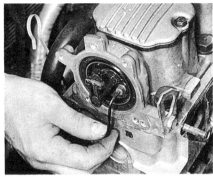

7.10A Extract the two securing screws ...

7.10B ... and withdraw the rotor arm – 2.0 litre model

8.3 Disconnecting the distributor wiring plug – 1.6 litre model (Bosch distributor)

8.6 TDC arrow on the Lucas distributor body

GSi 2000 models

13   Disconnect the battery negative lead.
14   Unscrew the two securing bolts and withdraw the spark plug cover from the camshaft cover.
15   If necessary, identify each HT lead for position, so that the leads can be refitted to their correct cylinders, then disconnect the leads from the spark plugs by pulling on the connectors, not the leads. Similarly, disconnect the HT lead from the coil. Pull the leads from the clips on the camshaft cover.
16   Using a suitable Torx socket, unscrew the three captive securing screws and withdraw the distributor cap.
17   Proceed as described in paragraphs 4 to 6 inclusive.

---

8   Distributor – removal and refitting

Note: *Refer to Section 2 before proceeding. A tachometer and a timing light will be required to check the ignition timing on completion*

1.4 and 1.6 litre models

1   Disconnect the battery negative lead.
2   Remove the distributor cap, as described in Section 7.
3   Disconnect the distributor wiring plug (photo).
4   On 1.4 litre models, disconnect the vacuum pipe from the diaphragm unit on the side of the distributor.
5   If the original distributor is to be refitted, make alignment marks between the distributor body and the camshaft housing, so that the distributor can be refitted in its original position.
6   Using a suitable socket or spanner on the crankshaft pulley bolt, or by engaging top gear and pushing the vehicle backwards or forwards as necessary (with the handbrake released!), turn the crankshaft to bring No 1 cylinder to the firing point. No 1 cylinder is at the firing point when:

(a)   *The relevant timing marks are aligned. On 1.4 litre models, the pointer on the rear timing belt cover should be aligned halfway between the two notches in the crankshaft pulley. On 1.6 litre models, the pointer on the rear timing belt cover should be aligned with the notch in the crankshaft pulley*

(b)   *The tip of the rotor arm is pointing to the position occupied by the No 1 cylinder HT lead terminal in the distributor cap*

8.7A Unscrew the clamp nut ...

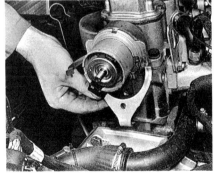

8.7B ... remove the clamp plate ...

8.7C ... and withdraw the distributor

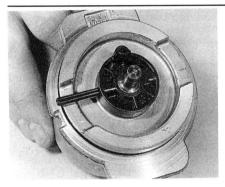

9.13 Removing the drive collar roll pin –
1.6 litre model (Bosch distributor)

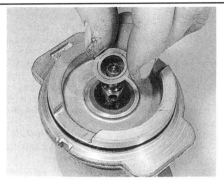

9.14 Removing the thrustwashers

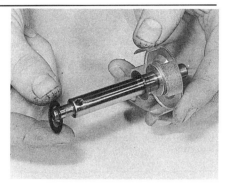

9.15 Recovering the thrustwashers from the
shaft– 1.6 litre model (Bosch distributor)

9.16A Removing the spring clip ...

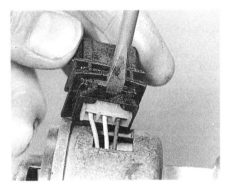

9.16B ... and disconnecting the small wiring
plug – 1.6 litre model (Lucas distributor)

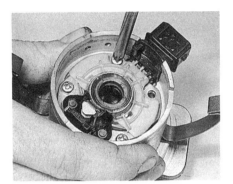

9.17A Remove the securing screws ...

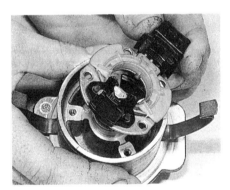

9.17B ... and withdraw the sensor plate – 1.6
litre model (Bosch distributor)

9.17C Sensor plate screw (arrowed) – 1.6 litre
model (Lucas distributor)

(c)   *On the Bosch distributor, the rotor arm is aligned with the notch
in the distributor body (remove the rotor arm and plastic shield,
then refit the rotor arm to check the alignment with the notch).
On the Lucas distributor, the rotor arm is approximately aligned
with the **TDC** arrow stamped in the distributor body (photo)*

7   Unscrew the clamp nut and remove the clamp plate, then withdraw
the distributor from the camshaft housing (photos).
8   If desired, the distributor can be dismantled, as described in Section 9.
9   Check the condition of the O-ring on the rear of the distributor body,
and renew if necessary.
10   Commence refitting by checking that No 1 cylinder is still at the
firing point. The relevant timing marks should be aligned. If the engine
has been turned whilst the distributor has been removed, check that No
1 cylinder is on its firing stroke by removing No 1 cylinder spark plug and
placing a finger over the plug hole. Turn the crankshaft until compression can be felt, which indicates that No 1 piston is rising on its

compression stroke. Continue turning the crankshaft until the relevant
timing marks are in alignment.
11   Turn the rotor arm to the position noted in paragraph 6 (c), and hold
the rotor arm in this position as the distributor is fitted, noting that the
distributor driveshaft will only engage with the camshaft in one position. If the original distributor is being refitted, align the marks made on
the distributor body and camshaft housing before removal.
12   Refit the clamp plate and nut, but do not fully tighten the nut at this
stage.
13   On the Bosch distributor, remove the rotor arm, then refit the
plastic shield and the rotor arm.
14   On 1.4 litre models, reconnect the vacuum pipe to the diaphragm
unit.
15   Reconnect the distributor wiring plug.
16   Refit the distributor cap as described in Section 7.
17   Reconnect the battery negative lead.
18   Check and if necessary adjust the ignition timing, as described in
Section 10.

GSi 2000 models

19   Disconnect the battery negative lead.
20   Remove the distributor cap, as described in Section 7.
21   Disconnect the distributor wiring plug.
22   Unscrew the two securing bolts, and remove the distributor from the cylinder head.
23   Examine the O-ring on the rear of the distributor, and renew if necessary.
24   Refitting is a reversal of removal, but note that the distributor should be fitted so that the wiring plug is positioned on the upper left-hand side of the distributor body, when viewed from the distributor cap end.

---

9   Distributor – dismantling, inspection and reassembly

Note: *Before contemplating dismantling of a distributor, check the cost and availability of replacement parts. It may prove more economical to renew the complete distributor assembly.*

1.4 litre models

1   With the distributor removed as described in Section 8, proceed as follows.
2   Pull off the rotor arm, and remove the plastic shield.
3   Although the top bearing plate can be removed after unscrewing the two securing screws, this is of academic interest, as other than the vacuum diaphragm unit, no spares are available for the distributor, and no adjustments are required.
4   If desired, the vacuum diaphragm unit can be removed by extracting the two securing screws and unhooking the operating arm from the distributor baseplate. Note that the screws are of differing lengths; the longer screw also secures one of the distributor cap clips.
5   The vacuum unit can be tested by applying suction to the vacuum port, and checking that the operating rod moves into the unit as suction is applied. Remove the suction, and check that the operating rod returns to its original position. If the operating rod does not move as described, renew the vacuum unit.
6   Check the distributor cap for corrosion of the segments, and for signs of tracking, indicated by a thin black line between the segments. Make sure that the carbon brush in the centre of the cap moves freely, and stands proud of the surface of the cap. Renew the cap if necessary.

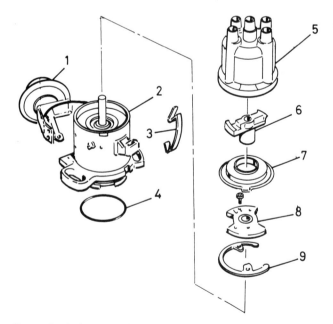

Fig. 4.1 Exploded view of distributor fitted to 1.4 litre models (Sec 9)

1 Vacuum diaphragm unit	*6 Rotor arm*
2 Body	*7 Plastic shield*
3 Cap retaining clip	*8 Top bearing plate*
4 Seal ring	*9 Abutment ring*
5 Distributor cap	

7   If the metal portion of the rotor arm is badly burnt or loose, renew it. If slightly burnt or corroded; it may be cleaned with a fine file.
8   Examine the seal ring at the rear of the distributor body, and renew if necessary.
9   Reassembly is a reversal of dismantling, ensuring that the vacuum unit operating arm is correctly engaged with the peg on the baseplate – several attempts may be required to reconnect it.
10   Refit the distributor as described in Section 8, and then check and if necessary adjust the ignition timing, as described in Section 10.

1.6 litre models

11   Before attempting dismantling, check that spare parts can be obtained.
12   With the distributor removed as described in Section 8, pull off the rotor arm and, on the Bosch distributor, remove the plastic shield.
13   Using a suitable pin punch, carefully drive out the roll pin securing the plastic drive collar to the rear of the distributor shaft (photo).
14   Lift off the drive collar, and recover the thrustwashers from the end of the shaft (photo).
15   Withdraw the shaft, complete with the trigger vane, from the distributor body, and recover the thrustwashers from the shaft (photo).
16   On the Lucas distributor, extract the spring clip from inside the body, then withdraw the terminal block. Pull the small wiring plug from inside the terminal block (photos).
17   Remove the screws, and lift the sensor plate from the distributor body (photos)..
18   Examine the distributor cap and rotor arm, as described in paragraphs 6 and 7. Examine the O-rings at the rear of the distributor body, and on the rear of the shaft, and renew if necessary.
19   Reassembly is a reversal of dismantling, ensuring that the thrustwashers are correctly located. Note that the drive collar should be refitted so that the drive peg on the collar is aligned with the groove in the top of the distributor shaft (it is possible to fit the drive collar 180° out of position).
20   Refit the distributor as described in Section 8, and then check and if necessary adjust the ignition timing, as described in Section 10.

GSi 2000 models

21   The distributor cap and rotor arm can be examined as described in paragraphs 6 and 7.

---

10   Ignition timing – checking and adjustment

Note: *Refer to Section 2 before proceeding. A tachometer and a timing light will be required during this procedure. For details of ignition timing adjustment required in order to operate vehicles on unleaded petrol, refer to Section 11*

1.4 and 1989 1.6 litre models

1   Start the engine and run it until it reaches normal operating temperature, then switch off.
2   On 1.4 litre models, disconnect the vacuum pipe from the distributor vacuum diaphragm unit.
3   On all models use a spanner applied to the crankshaft pulley bolt to rotate the crankshaft clockwise until the notch in the pulley's inboard rim aligns with the pointer protruding from the oil pump housing. On 1.4 litre models, where two notches (indicating 10° and 5° BTDC respectively) are found, rotate the crankshaft until the **second** notch (in the direction of rotation – ie 5° BTDC) aligns. Use white paint or similar to emphasise the pointer and notch, to make them easier to see.
4   Connect a timing light to No 1 cylinder (nearest the timing belt end of the engine) HT lead, also a tachometer; follow the equipment manufacturer's instructions for connection.
5   Start the engine and allow it to idle – the speed should be between 700 and 1000 rpm.
6   On 1.4 litre models, aim the timing light at the pointer and check that it is aligned with the crankshaft pulley notch.
7   On 1.6 litre models, disconnect the ignition timing basic adjustment coding plug (which is a length of Black wire joining Brown/Red and Brown/Yellow wires in a connector plug clipped to the wiring or heater/cooling system hoses beneath the battery/ignition coil – see photo 5.1).; this causes the MSTS module to adopt its basic adjustment mode, sending a constant firing signal corresponding to 10° BTDC and eliminating any advance below 2000 rpm. Aim the timing light at the pointer and check that it is aligned with the crankshaft pulley notch.

11.3 Octane coding plug (arrowed) – 2.0 litre model

8   If the notch and pointer are not aligned, loosen the distributor clamp nut and turn the distributor body slightly in the required direction to align.
9   Tighten the distributor clamp nut, and check that the notch and pointer are still aligned.
10   Stop the engine, and disconnect the timing light and tachometer.
11   On 1.6 litre models, reconnect the basic adjustment coding plug; on 1.4 litre models, reconnect the vacuum pipe to the distributor vacuum diaphragm unit.

1.8 and 2.0 litre models
12   No adjustment of the ignition timing is possible on 1.8 and 2.0 litre models, as the adjustment is carried out automatically by the electronic control module.
13   The ignition timing can be checked by a Vauxhall dealer, using specialist dedicated test equipment, if a fault is suspected.

---

11 Ignition timing – adjustment for use with unleaded petrol

1.4 litre models
1   All models with the 1.4 litre engine have the ignition timing adjusted for use with 95 RON unleaded petrol before they leave the factory, and no further adjustment is required.
2   Leaded petrol (98 RON) can be used if desired, with no adverse effects.

1.6, 1.8 and 2.0 litre models
Note: *2.0 litre models equipped with a catalytic converter must be operated on 95 RON unleaded petrol at all times, and although an octane coding plug may be fitted, it should **not** be tampered with*

3   1.6, 1.8 and 2.0 litre models are equipped with an octane coding plug, which is located in a clip at the left-hand rear of the engine compartment (photo).

4   The plug is reversible in its connector, and is marked either 'A' or '98' on one side, which corresponds to the position for use with *98 RON leaded* petrol, and either 'B' or '95' on the other side, which corresponds to the position for use with *95 RON unleaded* petrol. All vehicles are set for use with 95 RON unleaded petrol before they leave the factory.
5   To change the coding for use with a different type of petrol, first allow the fuel tank to become practically empty.
6   Fill the fuel tank with the required type of petrol.
7   Ensure that the ignition is switched off, then remove the coding plug from its clip and disconnect the wiring connector.
8   Rotate the plug through 180°, so that the appropriate octane mark is uppermost (see paragraph 4), then reconnect the wiring connector and refit the plug to its clip.
9   Note that using petrol with a higher octane rating than that set will not cause damage, but petrol with a lower octane rating than that set **must not** be used.

---

12 Electronic modules – removal and refitting

Note: *Refer to Section 2 for precautions to be observed when working with electronic modules*

HEI module (1.4 litre models)
Note: *Suitable heat sink compound must be used when refitting the module*

1   The module is mounted on a metal plate, beneath the ignition coil, on the left-hand side of the engine compartment.
2   Remove the ignition coil as described in Section 6, and slide the coil from its clamp.
3   The module can be removed from the mounting plate by unscrewing the two securing screws.
4   Before refitting the module, heat sink compound should be applied to the mounting plate to improve heat dissipation. If a new module is being fitted, it should be supplied with suitable heat sink compound. Similar compounds can be purchased from DIY electrical shops.
5   Refitting is a reversal of removal.

MSTS module (1.6 and 1.8 litre models)
6   The module is mounted on the engine compartment bulkhead, above the steering rack (photo).
7   Disconnect the battery negative lead.
8   If desired, for improved access, remove the air box from the top of the carburettor.
9   Disconnect the wiring plug from the module.
10   Unscrew the two securing nuts, and withdraw the module from the bulkhead.
11   Refitting is a reversal of removal.

Motronic module (2.0 litre models)
12   The module is mounted in the driver's footwell, behind the side trim panel.
13   Disconnect the battery negative lead.
14   Remove the driver's footwell side trim panel, as described in Chapter 10, Section 36.
15   Unscrew the three module securing screws, two at the top of the

12.6 MSTS module location – 1.6 litre model

12.15 Lowering the Motronic module from the footwell – 2.0 litre model

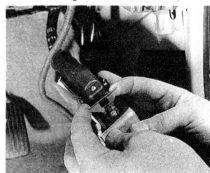

12.16 Releasing the Motronic module wiring plug clip – 2.0 litre model

13.1 MSTS manifold pressure sensor –
1.6 litre model

13.11 Unscrewing the MSTS oil temperature
sensor – 1.6 litre model (engine removed)

13.17 Unscrewing the crankshaft
speed/position sensor securing bolt – 1.8 litre
model

module, and a single screw at the bottom, and lower the module from
the footwell (photo).
16   Release the retaining clip, and disconnect the module wiring plug
(photo).
17   Withdraw the module, noting the plastic insulating sheet on its
rear face.
18   Refitting is a reversal of removal, but ensure that the insulating
sheet is in place on the rear face of the module.

13   MSTS components – removal and refitting

Note: *Refer to Section 2 before proceeding. Procedures for removal and
refitting of the ignition system components and electronic module are
given elsewhere in the relevant Sections of this Chapter*

Manifold pressure sensor
1   The sensor is located on the engine compartment bulkhead, to the
left of the MSTS module, under the edge of the windscreen cowl panel
(photo).
2   Disconnect the battery negative lead.
3   Lift up the edge of the windscreen cowl panel for access to the
sensor.
4   Disconnect the sensor wiring plug, and the vacuum pipe.
5   Pull the pressure sensor upwards to release it from its bracket, and
withdraw it from the vehicle.
6   Refitting is a reversal of removal.

Oil temperature sensor
7   The sensor is screwed into the inlet manifold side of the cylinder
block, next to the starter motor's right-hand end.
8   The sensor can be reached quite easily from above, but if it is to be
removed from beneath, ensure that the handbrake is applied, and that
the vehicle is securely supported on axle stands.
9   Disconnect the battery negative lead.
10   Disconnect the sensor wiring plug.
11   Using a suitable spanner, unscrew the sensor and remove it
(photo). Be prepared for oil spillage, and plug the hole in the cylinder
block to prevent dirt ingress and further oil loss.
12   Refitting is a reversal of removal.

Crankshaft speed/position sensor (1.8 litre models)
13   The sensor is located on the exhaust manifold side of the engine, in
the lower cylinder block behind the oil pump.
14   Disconnect the battery negative lead.
15   Release the relevant outer timing belt cover securing clips, and
unclip the sensor wiring from the timing belt cover.
16   Disconnect the sensor wiring connector, noting its location.
17   Unscrew the securing bolt, and withdraw the sensor from the
cylinder block (photo).
18   Examine the sensor sealing ring, and renew if necessary (photo).
19   Refitting is a reversal of removal, ensuring that the sensor wiring is
correctly located on the timing belt cover, and that the wiring connector
is correctly located.

13.18 Examine the crankshaft speed/position sensor sealing ring –
1.8 litre model

14   Motronic system components – removal and refitting

Note: *Refer to Section 2 before proceeding. Procedures for removal and
refitting of the ignition system components and electronic module are
given elsewhere in the relevant Sections of this Chapter. Removal and
refitting procedures for all fuel injection system components are given in
Chapter 3*

Coolant temperature sensor
1   On all except GSi 2000 models, the sensor is located in the end of
the thermostat housing, on the inlet manifold side of the engine.
2   On GSi 2000 models, the sensor is located in the thermostat
housing, on the exhaust manifold side of the engine.
3   Disconnect the battery negative lead.
4   Partially drain the cooling system, as described in Chapter 2.
5   Disconnect the sensor wiring plug (photo).
6   Using a suitable spanner, unscrew the sensor and withdraw it from
the thermostat housing.
7   Refitting is a reversal of removal.
8   On completion, top up the cooling system, as described in Chapter
2.

Crankshaft speed/position sensor
9   Proceed as described in Section 13, paragraphs 13 to 19 inclusive.

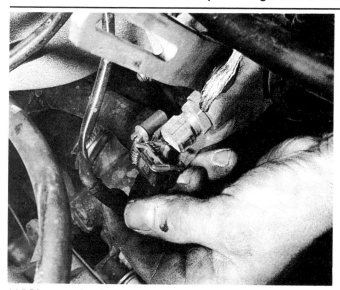

14.5 Disconnecting the coolant temperature sensor wiring plug – 2.0 litre model (alternator removed)

Knock sensor (GSi 2000 models)

10   The sensor is located at the lower inlet manifold side of the cylinder block, below the idle speed adjuster, and is only accessible from below the vehicle.

11   Disconnect the battery negative lead.

12   Apply the handbrake, then jack up the front of the vehicle, and support securely on axle stands placed under the body side members.

13   Remove the engine undershield, as described in Chapter 10.

14   Disconnect the sensor wiring plug.

15   Unscrew the securing bolt, and withdraw the sensor from the cylinder block.

16   Refitting is a reversal of removal, but note that the mating faces of the sensor and cylinder block must be cleaned thoroughly before fitting the sensor.

15   Fault diagnosis – ignition system

Note: *Refer to Section 2 before proceeding*

1   There are two main symptoms indicating ignition faults: either the engine will not start or fire, or the engine is difficult to start and misfires. If a regular misfire is present, the fault is almost certain to be in the high tension (secondary) circuit.

Engine fails to start

2   If the starter motor fails to turn the engine, check the battery and the starter motor, as described in Chapter 11.

3   Disconnect the HT lead from any spark plug, and hold the end of the cable approximately 5.0 mm (0.2 in) away from the cylinder head using *well-insulated pliers*. While an assistant spins the engine on the starter motor, check that a regular blue spark occurs. If so, remove and check the spark plugs, as described in Section 4. If the engine fails to start

due to either damp HT leads or distributor cap, a moisture dispersant, such as Holts Wet Start can be very effective. To prevent the problem recurring, Holts Damp Start can be used to provide a sealing coat, so excluding any further moisture from the ignition system. In extreme difficulty, Holts Cold Start will help to start a car when only a very poor spark occurs.

4   If no spark occurs, disconnect the coil HT lead from the distributor cap, and check for a spark as in paragraph 3. If sparks now occur, check the distributor cap, rotor arm, and HT leads as described in Sections 3 and 4, and renew the relevant component(s) as necessary.

5   If no sparks occur, check the continuity of the coil HT lead using a test meter, and renew as necessary. Should the lead be serviceable, check that all wiring and wiring plugs are secure on the distributor and electronic module.

6   Check the coil, as described in Section 5.

7   If the above checks reveal no faults, but there is still no spark, the distributor or the electronic module must be suspect. Consult a Vauxhall dealer for further testing, or test by substitution of a known good unit.

Engine misfires

8   If the engine misfires regularly, run it at a fast idling speed, then pull off each of the spark plug HT leads in turn, and listen to the note of the engine. *Hold the plug leads with a well-insulated pair of pliers.*

9   No difference in engine running will be noticed when the lead from the defective circuit is removed. Removing the lead from one of the good cylinders will accentuate the misfire.

10   Remove the plug lead from the end of the plug in the defective circuit, and hold it about 5.0 mm (0.2 in) away from the cylinder head, again using *well-insulated pliers*. While an assistant spins the engine on the starter motor, check that a regular blue spark occurs. If so, the fault must lie in the spark plug.

11   If the spark is irregular, it is likely that there is a break in the HT lead. Check the continuity of the lead using a test meter, while manipulating the lead to see if the continuity is broken. If necessary, renew the lead.

12   If the above checks reveal no faults, the distributor or the electronic module must be suspect. Consult a Vauxhall dealer for further testing, or test by substitution of a known good unit.

16   Fault diagnosis – engine management system

Note: *Refer to Section 2 before proceeding*

1   If no fault has been found in the ignition system (see Section 15), then a fault in the engine management system must be suspected.

2   Do not immediately assume that a fault is caused by a faulty electronic module. First check that all the wiring is in good condition, and that all wiring plugs are securely connected. Similarly check any vacuum pipes, where applicable.

3   Unless components are freely available for testing by substitution, further investigation should be left to a Vauxhall dealer or other competent specialist. Note that the MSTS and Motronic modules have a self-analysis function, which stores fault codes in the module memory. These fault codes can only be decoded using specialist dedicated test equipment, available to a Vauxhall dealer.

4   Note that relays, modules and other components cannot necessarily be substituted from another vehicle. The control modules in particular are dedicated to particular engine, gearbox and territory combinations.

Chapter 5 Clutch

For modifications, and information applicable to later models, see Supplement at end of manual

Contents

Specifications

System type .... Single dry plate, operated by cable

Friction disc diameter
1.4 litre models	190.5 mm (7.5 in)
1.6 and 1.8 litre models	200.0 mm (7.9 in)
2.0 litre sohc models	215.9 mm (8.5 in)
2.0 litre dohc models	228.6 mm (9.0 in)

Clutch adjustment dimension (pedal movement/stroke)
All models .... 134.0 to 141.0 mm (5.3 to 5.5 in)

Torque wrench settings

	Nm	lbf ft
Clutch cover-to-flywheel bolts	15	11
Clutch bellhousing cover plate bolts	7	5
Clutch release fork-to-pivot shaft clamp bolt	35	26
Gearbox endplate bolts:		
M7 bolts	15	11
M8 bolts	20	15
Input shaft socket-headed screw	15	11

1 General description

The clutch is of single dry plate type, and consists of five main components: friction disc, pressure plate, diaphragm spring, cover and release bearing.

The friction disc is free to slide along the splines of the gearbox input shaft, and is held in position between the flywheel and the pressure plate by the pressure exerted on the pressure plate by the diaphragm spring. Friction lining material is riveted to both sides of the friction disc, and spring cushioning between the friction linings and the hub absorbs transmission shocks, and helps to ensure a smooth take-up of power as the clutch is engaged.

The diaphragm spring is mounted on pins, and is held in place in the cover by annular fulcrum rings.

The release bearing is located on a guide sleeve at the front of the gearbox, and the bearing is free to slide on the sleeve, under the action of the release arm which pivots inside the clutch bellhousing.

The release arm is operated by the clutch pedal, via a cable. As wear

takes place on the friction disc over a period of time, the clutch pedal will rise progressively, relative to its original position. No periodic adjustment of the clutch cable is specified by the manufacturers.

When the clutch pedal is depressed, the release arm is actuated by means of the cable. The release arm pushes the release bearing forwards, to bear against the centre of the diaphragm spring, thus pushing the centre of the diaphragm spring inwards. The diaphragm spring acts against the fulcrum rings in the cover, and so as the centre of the spring is pushed in, the outside of the spring is pushed out, so allowing the pressure plate to move backwards away from the friction disc.

When the clutch pedal is released, the diaphragm spring forces the pressure plate into contact with the friction linings on the friction disc, and simultaneously pushes the friction disc forwards on its splines, forcing it against the flywheel. The friction disc is now firmly sandwiched between the pressure plate and the flywheel, and drive is taken up.

An unusual feature of this particular engine/clutch/gearbox layout is that the clutch assembly, release bearing and guide sleeve oil seal can be renewed without removing the engine or gearbox from the vehicle.

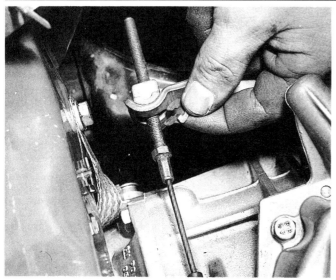

3.2 Remove the clip from the threaded rod at the clutch release arm

3.3 Clutch cable attachment to lug on bellhousing

2 Routine maintenance

1   At the intervals specified in the *'Routine maintenance'* Section at the beginning of this manual, check the clutch cable adjustment, as described in Section 4.
2   Periodically check the condition of the cable. Inspect the cable strands for fraying, and ensure that the cable is correctly routed, to avoid chafing against surrounding components. Renew the cable, as described in Section 3, if excessive wear or damage is evident.

3 Clutch cable – removal and refitting

1   Working in the engine compartment, measure the length of the threaded rod protruding through the plastic block at the release arm end of the cable. This will enable approximate presetting of the cable when refitting.
2   Remove the clip from the threaded rod at the release arm, then slide the rod from the release arm (photo). Push the release arm towards the engine, and if necessary slacken the cable adjuster, to aid removal.
3   Pull the cable assembly from the lug on the clutch bellhousing (photo).
4   Working inside the vehicle, remove the lower trim panel from the drivers footwell, then unhook the return spring from the clutch pedal, and disconnect the cable end from the pedal. Note that the end of the return spring retains the cable end in the pedal. Access is limited, and it may prove easier to remove the clutch pedal, as described in Section 5, before disconnecting the cable.
5   The cable assembly can now be withdrawn into the engine compartment, by pulling it through the bulkhead. Take care not to damage the bulkhead grommet as the cable is withdrawn.
6   Refitting is a reversal of removal. Position the threaded rod so that the length of thread protruding through the plastic block is as noted before removal, then adjust the cable as described in Section 4. Ensure that the bulkhead grommet is correctly seated.

4 Clutch cable – adjustment

1   The clutch cable will not normally require adjustment, but if the clutch assembly or the cable has been renewed, the following initial adjustment will be required.
2   Using a tape measure or similar, measure and record the distance from the centre of the clutch pedal's rubber pad to a fixed point on the steering wheel rim – the pedal must be hanging in its normal at-rest

position, neither raised to eliminate free play nor depressed – then repeat the measurement with the pedal fully depressed (photos).
3   Subtract the first measurement from the second to calculate the pedal movement/stroke, this should be within the specified range. If the pedal movement/stroke is more or less than that specified, the cable must be adjusted as follows.
4   Working in the engine compartment, remove the clip from the threaded rod at the release arm on the gearbox, then turn the adjuster as required. Turn the adjuster clockwise to increase pedal movement, or anti-clockwise to decrease pedal movement. Recheck the pedal movement, and then refit the clip to the threaded rod on completion.
5   On a vehicle in which the clutch has covered a high mileage, it may no longer be possible to adjust the cable to achieve the specified pedal movement, and this indicates that the clutch friction disc requires renewal. Note that when correctly adjusted, the clutch pedal will rest slightly higher than the brake pedal – it is incorrect for the two pedals to be in alignment. If the pedals are aligned, the cable requires adjustment. Note also that there should be no play in the clutch pedal.

Note: *During the 1989 model year, some vehicles were produced with the brake pedal height incorrectly set, resulting in the brake pedal resting approximately 15.0 mm (0.6 in) above the clutch pedal, instead of 4.0 mm (0.16 in) below. If desired, the brake pedal height can be reset by adjusting the vacuum servo operating fork dimension, as described in Chapter 8, Section 19.*

4.2A Checking clutch adjustment — measure distance from steering wheel rirm to centre of pedal rubber (pedal at rest) ...

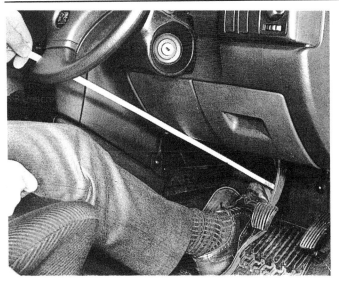

4.2B ...depress pedal fully and repeat measurement from same point on steering wheel to pedal's new position

5 Clutch pedal – removal and refitting

1 Proceed as described in Section 3, paragraphs 1 and 2.
2 Working inside the vehicle, remove the lower trim panel from the driver's footwell.
3 Remove the locking clip from the right-hand end of the pedal pivot shaft, then unscrew the pedal retaining nut and recover the washer(s) (photo).
4 Push the pivot shaft out of the pedal bracket, towards the centre of the vehicle, then lower the pedal and return spring. Note the position of

any washers and/or spacers on the pivot shaft, so that they can be refitted in their original positions.
5 Disconnect the cable end of the pedal by releasing the return spring, and withdraw the pedal and return spring from the vehicle (photos).
6 Refitting is a reversal of removal, but before inserting the pedal pivot shaft, smear the surface with a little molybdenum disulphide grease.
7 On completion, adjust the clutch cable if necessary, as described in Section 4.

6 Clutch – removal (engine and gearbox in vehicle)

Note: *The manufacturers recommend the use of special tools for this procedure, although suitable alternatives can be improvised as described in the text. It is suggested that this Section, and Section 9, are read thoroughly before work commences, in order that suitable tools can be made available as required.*

1 Where applicable, remove the left-hand front wheel trim, then loosen the roadwheel bolts. Apply the handbrake, jack up the front of the vehicle and support on axle stands. Remove the roadwheel for improved access. On GSi 2000 models, remove the engine undershield, with reference to Chapter 10.
2 Unscrew the securing bolts and remove the cover plate from the base of the clutch bellhousing.
3 Unscrew the retaining nut, and disconnect the earth strap from the gearbox endplate (photo).
4 Place a suitable container beneath the gearbox endplate, to catch the oil which will be released, then unscrew the securing bolts and remove the endplate (photo). Note the location of the studded bolt which retains the earth strap. For improved access, remove the wheel arch liner, as described in Chapter 10, Section 31.
5 Recover the gasket.
6 Extract the circlip from inside the end of the input shaft, using a pair of circlip pliers.
7 Using a twelve-point splined key, unscrew the socket-headed screw from the end of the input shaft.

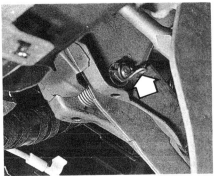

5.3 Clutch pedal pivot locking clip (arrowed)

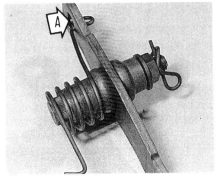

5.5A Clutch pedal components assembled as when in place in vehicle. Clutch cable is retained by return spring at 'A'

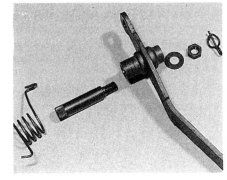

5.5B Clutch pedal pivot components

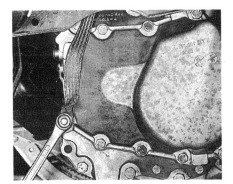

6.3 Unscrew the earth strap retaining nut

6.4 Removing the gearbox endplate (wheel arch liner removed)

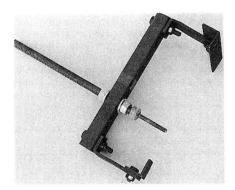

6.8 Improvised tool for disengaging gearbox input shaft from clutch

8 The input shaft can now be pulled out of engagement with the splined hub of the clutch friction disc. The manufacturers specify the use of special tools for this operation (tool Nos KM-556-1-A and KM-556-4), but an alternative can be improvised as shown (photo). The tool bolts into place on the end of the gearbox, using the endplate securing bolts (see photo 9.4). Tool dimensions will vary according to gearbox type.

9 Alternatively, screw an M7 bolt into the end of the input shaft, and use the bolt to pull the shaft out to its stop. It is likely that the input shaft will be a very tight fit, in which case it may prove difficult to withdraw, without using the special tool previously described. In certain cases, a slide hammer can be attached to the end of the shaft to enable it to be withdrawn.

10 Before the clutch assembly can be removed, the pressure plate must be compressed against the tension of the diaphragm spring, otherwise the assembly will be too thick to be withdrawn through the space between the flywheel and the edge of the bellhousing.

11 Three special clamps are available from the manufacturers for this purpose (tool No KM-526-A), but suitable alternatives can be made up from strips of metal. The clamps should be U-shaped, and conform to the dimensions given below, and in Fig. 5.1. Bevel the edges of the clamps to ease fitting, and cut a slot in one of the U-legs, to clear the pressure plate rivets.

Thickness of metal strip – 3.0 mm (0.12 in)
Distance between U-legs – 15.0 mm (0.59 in)

12 Have an assistant depress the clutch pedal fully, then fit each clamp securely over the edge of the cover/pressure plate, engaging the clamps in the apertures around the rim of the cover (photo). Turn the crankshaft using a suitable spanner on the sprocket bolt, to bring each clamp location into view.

13 Once the clamps have been fitted, have the assistant release the clutch pedal.

14 Progressively loosen and remove the six bolts and spring washers which secure the clutch cover to the flywheel. As previously, turn the crankshaft to bring each bolt into view. Note the position of the mark on the flywheel which aligns with the notch in the rim of the clutch cover.

15 The clutch assembly can now be withdrawn downwards from the bellhousing (photo). Be prepared to catch the friction disc, which may drop out of the cover as it is withdrawn, and note which way round the friction disc is fitted. The greater projecting side of the hub should face away from the flywheel.

16 The pressure plate can be compressed against the tension of the diaphragm spring, in a vice fitted with soft jaw protectors, in order to remove the clamps.

17 The clutch components can be inspected for wear and damage, as described in Section 8.

7 Clutch – removal (engine and/or gearbox removed)

1 After obtaining access to the clutch by removing the gearbox, or by removing and separating the engine/gearbox assembly, proceed as follows.

2 Note the position of the mark on the flywheel which aligns with the notch in the rim of the clutch cover, then progressively unscrew the six bolts and spring washers which secure the clutch cover to the flywheel.

3 With all the bolts removed, lift off the clutch assembly. Be prepared to catch the friction disc as the cover assembly is lifted from the flywheel, and note which way round the friction disc is fitted. The greater projecting side of the hub should face away from the flywheel.

4 The clutch components can be inspected for wear and damage, as described in Section 8.

8 Clutch – inspection

1 With the clutch assembly removed, clean off all traces of dust using a dry cloth. Although most friction discs now have asbestos-free linings, some do not, and it is wise to take suitable precautions; asbestos dust is harmful, and must not be inhaled.

2 Examine the linings of the friction disc for wear and loose rivets, distortion, cracks, broken torsion springs and worn splines. The surface of the friction linings may be highly glazed, but, as long as the friction material pattern can be clearly seen, this is satisfactory. If there is any sign of oil contamination, indicated by a continuous, or patchy, shiny black discolouration, the plate must be renewed, and the source of the contamination traced and rectified. This will be either a leaking crankshaft oil seal or gearbox input shaft oil seal – or both. Renewal procedures are given in Chapter 1 and Chapter 6 respectively. The friction disc must also be renewed if the lining thickness has worn down to, or just above, the level of the rivets heads.

3 Check the machined faces of the flywheel and pressure plate. If either is grooved, or heavily scored, renewal is necessary. The pressure plate must also be renewed if any cracks are apparent, or if the diaphragm spring is damaged or its pressure suspect.

4 With the clutch removed, it is advisable to check the condition of the release bearing, as described in Section 11.

9 Clutch – refitting (engine and gearbox in vehicle)

Note: *The circlip in the end of the input shaft, and the gearbox endplate gasket, should be renewed on reassembly*

1 Some replacement clutch assemblies are supplied with the pressure plate already compressed using the three clamps described in

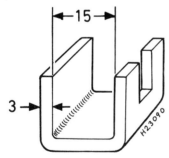

Fig. 5.1 Clutch pressure plate retaining clamp dimensions (in mm) (Sec 6)

6.12 Clamp fitted to compress clutch pressure plate prior to removal

6.15 Withdrawing the clutch assembly from the bellhousing

9.1 Clamp fitted to compress clutch pressure plate prior to installation. Note slot cut in clamp to clear pressure plate rivet

9.4 Using the improvised tool to engage the input shaft with the clutch friction disc

9.5A Stamped clutch alignment mark on flywheel – 1.6 litre model

9.5B Notch in clutch cover (A) aligned with paint mark on flywheel (B) – 2.0 litre model

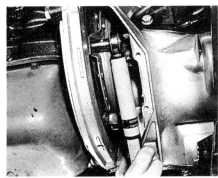

9.5C Tightening a clutch cover-to-flywheel bolt to the specified torque

paragraph 11. If this is not the case, the pressure plate should be compressed against the tension of the diaphragm spring, using a vice fitted with soft jaw protectors, and the clamps used during removal should be fitted (photo).

2   It is important to ensure that no oil or grease gets on the friction disc linings, or the pressure plate and flywheel faces. It is advisable to refit the clutch assembly with clean hands, and to wipe down the pressure plate and flywheel faces with a clean rag before assembly begins.

3   Apply a smear of molybdenum disulphide grease to the splines of the friction disc hub, then offer the disc to the flywheel, with the greater projecting side of the hub facing away from the flywheel. Hold the friction disc against the flywheel while the cover/pressure plate assembly is offered into position.

4   The input shaft must now be pushed through the hub of the friction disc, until its end engages in the spigot bearing in the end of the crankshaft. **Under no circumstances** *must the shaft be hammered home, as gearbox damage may result.* If the input shaft cannot be pushed home by hand, steady pressure should be exerted on the end of the shaft. The manufacturers specify the use of a special tool for this operation (tool No KM-564), but the improvised tool used in Section 6 to withdraw the shaft can also be used, by repositioning the nut as shown (photo).

5   With the input shaft pushed fully home, position the cover/pressure plate assembly so that the mark on the flywheel is in alignment with the notch in the rim of the clutch cover, then refit and progressively tighten the six clutch cover-to-flywheel bolts and spring washers in a diagonal sequence (photos). Turn the crankshaft, using a suitable spanner on the sprocket bolt, to gain access to each bolt in turn, and finally tighten all bolts to the specified torque.

6   Have an assistant depress the clutch pedal, then remove the three clamps from the edge of the cover/pressure plate, again turning the crankshaft for access to each clamp.

7   Once the clamps have been removed, have the assistant release the clutch pedal.

8   Screw the socket-headed screw into the end of the input shaft, then fit a new circlip.

9   Using a new gasket, refit the gearbox endplate, and tighten the securing bolts to the specified torque. Ensure that the studded bolt which retains the earth strap is fitted to its correct location, as noted during removal.

10   Reconnect the gearbox earth strap, and fit the retaining nut.

11   Refit the cover plate to the base of the clutch bellhousing, and tighten the securing bolts. Where applicable, refit the wheel arch liner, and on GSi 2000 models, refit the engine undershield.

12   Refit the roadwheel, then lower the vehicle to the ground, and finally tighten the roadwheel bolts. Refit the wheel trim, where applicable.

13   Check the clutch cable adjustment, as described in Section 4.

14   Check and if necessary top up the gearbox oil level, as described in Chapter 6, Section 2.

---

10   Clutch – refitting (engine and/or gearbox removed)

---

1   Unless the engine and gearbox are to be refitted to the vehicle as an assembly, it will prove easier to fit the clutch with the engine and gearbox in position in the vehicle, as described in Section 9, as this eliminates the need for clutch friction disc centralisation. Note that if the engine alone has been removed, leaving the gearbox in place, the clutch cannot be refitted until the engine and gearbox are mated together in the vehicle.

2   If desired, the clutch can be refitted before the engine and gearbox are mated and refitted as follows.

3   It is important to ensure that no oil or grease gets on the friction disc linings, or the pressure plate and flywheel faces. It is advisable to refit the clutch assembly with clean hands, and to wipe down the pressure plate and flywheel faces with a clean rag before assembly begins.

4   Place the friction disc against the flywheel, ensuring that it is fitted the correct way round. The greater projecting side of the hub should face away from the flywheel.

10.5 Notch (arrowed) in clutch cover must align with flywheel mark

Where possible, use a blunt instrument, but if a screwdriver is used, wrap tape around the blade to prevent damage to the bearing surface. Moving the bar sideways or up and down will move the friction disc in whichever direction is necessary to achieve centralisation. With the bar removed, view the friction disc hub, in relation to the hole in the end of the crankshaft and the circle created by the ends of the diaphragm spring fingers. When the hub appears exactly in the centre, all is correct. Alternatively, if a clutch aligning tool can be obtained, this will eliminate all the guesswork, and obviate the need for visual alignment.

8   Tighten the cover retaining bolts gradually in a diagonal sequence, to the specified torque. Remove the alignment tool.

9   The engine and gearbox can now be mated together, as described in Chapter 1 to 6 as applicable.

10   On completion, check the clutch cable adjustment, as described in Section 4.

11 Clutch release bearing and arm – removal and refitting

Note: *If the release bearing guide sleeve is removed, a new O-ring should be used on refitting*

1   Access to the release bearing can be obtained either with the engine and gearbox in the vehicle, by removing the clutch assembly as described in Section 6, or by separating the engine and gearbox, leaving the clutch assembly in place.

2   Unscrew the clamp bolt securing the release fork to the release arm pivot shaft.

3   If not already done, disconnect the clutch cable from the release arm, by removing the clip from the threaded rod, and then sliding the threaded rod from the release arm.

4   Pull the release bearing from the guide sleeve, then pull the release arm pivot shaft up and out of the bellhousing, and withdraw the release fork (photos). Where applicable, pull the bearing from the plastic collar.

5   Spin the release bearing, and check it for roughness. Hold the outer race, and attempt to move it laterally against the inner race. If any

5   Fit the clutch cover assembly, aligning the mark on the flywheel with the notch in the rim of the clutch cover (photo). Insert the six bolts and spring washers, and tighten them finger-tight, so that the friction disc is gripped, but can still be moved.

6   The friction disc must now be centralised, so that when the engine and gearbox are mated, the gearbox input shaft splines will pass through the splines in the friction disc hub.

7   Centralisation can be carried out by inserting a round bar or a long screwdriver through the hole in the centre of the friction disc, so that the end of the bar rests in the spigot bearing in the centre of the crankshaft.

11.4A Pull the release bearing from the guide sleeve ...

11.4B ... then pull out the release arm pivot shaft, and withdraw the release fork

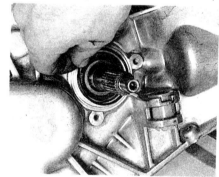

11.6A Fitting a new guide sleeve O-ring ...

11.6B ... followed by the guide sleeve

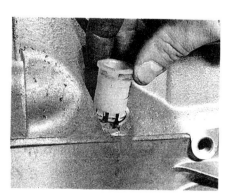

11.7 Renewing a release arm pivot shaft nylon bush

11.10 Tightening the release fork clamp bolt

excessive movement or roughness is evident, renew the bearing. If a new clutch has been fitted, it is wise to renew the release bearing as a matter of course.

6   If desired, the release bearing guide sleeve can be removed by unscrewing the three securing bolts, and then the input shaft oil seal can be renewed. Recover the O-ring which fits between the guide sleeve and the bellhousing. Prise the old oil seal from the guide sleeve, and fit a new seal using a suitable tube drift or socket. Fill the space between the lips of the oil seal with lithium-based grease, then refit the guide sleeve, using a new O-ring. The O-ring should be fitted dry (photos).

7.   The nylon bushes supporting the release arm pivot shaft can be renewed if necessary, by tapping them from their lugs in the bellhousing using a suitable drift. Drive the new bushes into position, ensuring that

their locating tabs engage with the slots in the bellhousing lugs (photo).

8   Refitting of the release bearing and arm is a reversal of the removal procedure, bearing in mind the following points.

9   Lightly smear the inner surfaces of the release arm pivot bushes, and the outer surface of the release bearing guide sleeve, with molybdenum disulphide grease.

10   Where applicable, fit the release bearing to the plastic collar, then fit the release bearing and fork together, and tighten the release fork clamp bolt to the specified torque (photo).

11   Refit the clutch assembly as described in Section 9, or reconnect the engine and gearbox as described in Chapter 1 or 6, as applicable.

12   On completion, check the clutch cable adjustment as described in Section 4.

12   Fault diagnosis – clutch

Symptom	Reason(s)
Judder when taking up drive	Loose or worn engine/gearbox mountings Friction disc linings worn, or contaminated with oil Clutch cable sticking or defective Friction disc hub sticking on input shaft splines
Clutch fails to disengage	Clutch cable sticking or defective Friction disc linings contaminated with oil Friction disc hub sticking on input shaft splines Incorrect cable adjustment
Clutch slips	Clutch cable sticking or defective Incorrect cable adjustment Faulty pressure plate, or weak or broken diaphragm spring Friction disc linings contaminated with oil
Noise when depressing clutch pedal	Worn release bearing Defective release mechanism Faulty pressure plate or diaphragm spring
Noise when releasing clutch pedal	Faulty pressure plate or diaphragm spring Broken friction disc torsion spring(s) Gearbox internal wear

Note: *This Section is not intended as an exhaustive guide to fault diagnosis, but summarises the more common faults which may be encountered during a vehicle's life. Consult a dealer for more detailed advice*

Chapter 6 Manual gearbox

For modifications, and information applicable to later models, see Supplement at end of manual

Contents

Specifications

General

Gearbox type	Five forward speeds and one reverse, synchromesh on all forward gears. Integral differential

Manufacturer's designation:

1.4 litre models	F10/5
1.6 litre models	F13/5
1.8 litre and 2.0 litre sohc models (except SRi)	F16/5W
2.0 litre SRi models	F16/5 CR
2.0 litre dohc models	F20/5

Gear ratios

	F10/5 and F13/5	F16/5W	F16/5CR and F20/5
1st	3.55:1	3.55:1	3.55:1
2nd	1.96:1	1.95:1	2.16:1
3rd	1.30:1	1.28:1	1.48:1
4th	0.89:1	0.89:1	1.13:1
5th	0.71:1	0.71:1	0.89:1
Reverse	3.31:1	3.33:1	3.33:1

Final drive ratio

F10/5	4.29:1
F13/5	3.94:1
F16/5W	3.55:1
F16/5CR	3.55:1
F20/5	3.55:1

Lubrication

Oil type/specification	Gear oil, viscosity SAE 80EP, or GM gear oil 90 188 629 (Duckhams Hypoid 80, or Hypoid 75W/90S)

Oil capacity:

F10/5 and F13/5	1.6 litres (2.9 pints)
F16/5 and F20/5	1.9 litres (3.3 pints)

Torque wrench settings

	Nm	lbf ft
Gear selector tube clamp bolt	15	11
Gearchange lever housing-to-floor pan bolts	6	4
Gear selector cover-to-gearbox bolts	15	11
Speedometer drivegear retaining plate bolt	4	3
Reversing lamp switch to gearbox	20	15
Endplate-to-gearbox bolts:		
M7 bolts	15	11
M8 bolts	20	15
Differential cover plate-to-gearbox bolts:		
Steel cover plate	30	22
Alloy cover plate	18	13
Engine-to-gearbox bolts	75	55
Clutch bellhousing cover plate bolts	7	5
Left-hand gearbox mounting-to-gearbox bolts	65	48
Left-hand gearbox mounting-to-body bolts	75	55
Rear gearbox mounting-to-front subframe bolts	40	30
Intermediate plate-to-gearbox bolts	15	11
Interlock bridge piece-to-intermediate plate screws	7	5
5th gear selector interlock pawl-to-intermediate plate screws	7	5
5th gear selector fork-to-intermediate plate bolts	22	16
Input shaft socket-headed screw	15	11

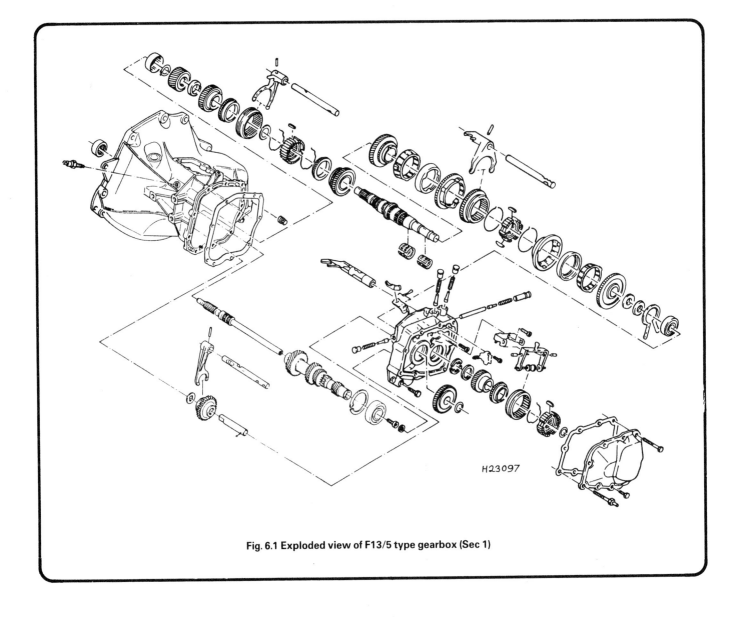

Fig. 6.1 Exploded view of F13/5 type gearbox (Sec 1)

H23097

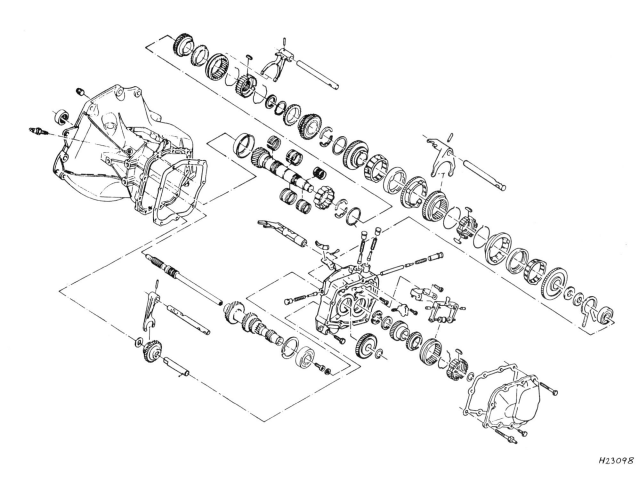

H23098

Fig. 6.2 Exploded view of F16/5 type gearbox (Sec 1)

1 General description

A five-speed gearbox is fitted to all models. Four different types of gearbox are used, depending on the power output of the engine fitted – see Specifications.

Drive from the clutch is picked up by the input shaft, which runs in parallel with the mainshaft. The input shaft and mainshaft gears are in constant mesh, and selection of gears is by sliding synchromesh hubs, which lock the appropriate mainshaft gear to the mainshaft.

The 5th speed components are located in an extension housing at the end of the gearbox, which allows some component commonality with the four-speed gearboxes used in other Vauxhall front-wheel-drive vehicles.

Reverse gear is obtained by sliding an idler gear into mesh with two straight-cut gears on the input shaft and mainshaft.

All the forward gear teeth are helically cut, to reduce noise and improve wear characteristics.

The differential is mounted in the main gearbox casing, and drive is transmitted to the differential by a pinion gear on the end of the mainshaft. The inboard ends of the driveshafts locate directly into the differential.

Gear selection is by a floor-mounted gearchange lever, via a remote control linkage.

2 Routine maintenance

1 At the intervals specified in the *'Routine maintenance'* Section at the beginning of this manual, check and if necessary top up the gearbox oil

level as follows. Note that the vehicle must be standing on a level surface.

2 Unscrew the gearbox oil level plug, which is located in the rear left of the differential housing on F10/5 and F13/5 gearboxes, and in the rear right of the differential housing on F16/5 and F20/5 gearboxes (photos). The oil level should be up to the bottom of the level plug orifice.

2.2A Gearbox oil level plug (arrowed) – F13/5 type gearbox (viewed from above)

2.2B Gearbox oil level plug (arrowed) – F16/5 type gearbox (viewed from below, with driveshaft removed)

2.3A Gearbox breather/filler plug (arrowed) – F16/5 type gearbox

3   If necessary, top up the oil level through the breather/filler orifice in the gear selector cover. Unscrew the breather/filler plug, and top up with the specified grade of oil, until oil just begins to run from the level plug orifice. Refit the level plug and the breather/filler plug on completion (photos).
4   Renewal of the gearbox oil is not specified by the manufacturers, and no drain plug is provided. If it is desired to renew the oil as a precautionary measure, the oil may be drained by removing the differential cover plate. Use a new gasket when refitting the cover plate. Fill the gearbox through the breather/filler orifice, as described previously in this Section.
5   Periodically inspect the gearbox for oil leaks, and check the gear selector linkage components for wear and smooth operation.

3   Gear selector linkage – adjustment

Note: *On completion of adjustment, a new plug must be fitted to the adjuster hole in the gear selector cover. Obtain a new plug before starting work.*

1   Working in the engine compartment, loosen the clamp bolt securing the gear selector tube to the linkage (photo).
2   Extract the plug from the adjuster hole in the gear selector cover (photo).
3   Looking towards the front of the vehicle, grip the gear selector tube, and twist it in an anti-clockwise direction until a 4.5 mm (0.18 in) diameter twist drill can be inserted through the adjuster hole in the gear selector cover, to engage with the hole in the selector lever (photo).
4   Working inside the vehicle, pull back on the front edge of the

2.3B Topping-up the gearbox oil level – F13/5 type gearbox

gearchange lever gaiter, and free its lower end from the centre console, to allow access to the base of the lever.
5   The help of an assistant will now be required, to hold the gearchange lever in neutral in the 1st/2nd gear plane. The lever should be resting against the reverse stop, and the arrow and notch should be aligned as shown (photo).

3.1 Gear selector tube-to-linkage clamp bolt (arrowed)

3.2 Extract the plug from the adjuster hole ...

3.3 ... and insert a twist drill to engage with the selector lever

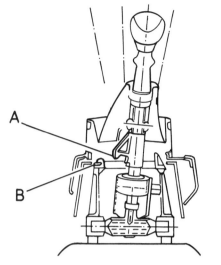

Fig. 6.3 Gearchange lever free play between hook (A) and stop (B) should be a maximum of 3.0 mm (0.12 in) (Sec 3)

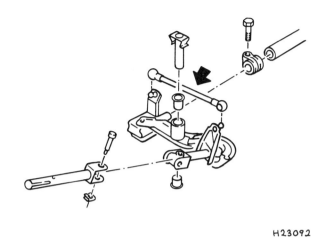

Fig. 6.4 Gear selector linkage components – link rod arrowed (Sec 4)

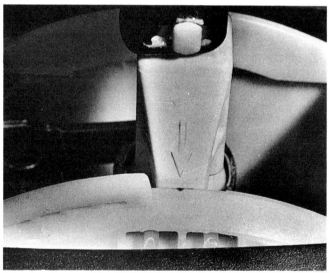

3.5 Arrow on gearchange lever aligned with notch in reverse stop

6   Without moving the gearchange lever, tighten the clamp bolt securing the gear selector tube to the linkage in the engine compartment.
7   Referring to Fig. 6.3, check that the free play between the hook (A) and the stop (B) at the base of the gearchange lever is as specified.
8   Refit the gearchange lever gaiter to the centre console.
9   Remove the twist drill from the adjuster hole in the gear selector cover, and seal the hole with a **new** plug.
10   Finally, check that all gears can be engaged easily with the vehicle at rest, engine running, and clutch pedal depressed.

---

4   Gear selector linkage – removal, overhaul and refitting

Gearchange lever housing assembly
1   Working in the engine compartment, loosen the clamp bolt securing the gear selector tube to the linkage.
2   Remove the gearchange lever as described in Section 5.

3   Remove the front section of the centre console, as described in Chapter 10, Section 38.
4   Unscrew the four bolts securing the gearchange lever housing to the floorpan.
5   The housing and selector tube can now be withdrawn. Pull the assembly towards the rear of the vehicle, to feed the selector tube through the bulkhead. As the selector tube is fed through the bulkhead, have an assistant remove the clamp from the end of the selector tube in the engine compartment, to avoid damage to the rubber boot on the bulkhead.
6   If desired, the rubber boot can be renewed by pulling the old boot from the bulkhead, and pushing the new boot into position, ensuring that it is correctly seated.
7   The selector tube bush in the gearchange lever housing can be renewed after sliding the selector tube from the housing. Prise the bush insert from the front of the housing, then prise the bush from the insert. Refitting is a reversal of removal, but lubricate the inside of the bush with a little silicone grease.
8   Refitting of the assembly is a reversal of removal, but before tightening the selector tube clamp bolt, adjust the gear selector linkage as described in Section 3.

Gear selector linkage
9   Loosen the clamp bolt securing the gear selector tube to the linkage.
10   Prise off the securing clip, then withdraw the pivot pin from the linkage universal joint.
11   Release the spring clip, then pull the bellcrank pivot pin from the bracket on the rear engine/gearbox mounting.
12   Withdraw the linkage from the vehicle.
13   Check the linkage components for wear, and renew as necessary. The pivot bushes can be renewed by prising out the old bushes and pressing in the new, and the link rod can be renewed by pulling it from the balljoints. Further dismantling is not recommended.
14   Refitting is a reversal of removal, but before tightening the selector tube clamp bolt, adjust the gear selector linkage as described in Section 3.

---

5   Gearchange lever – removal and refitting

1   Pull back on the front edge of the gearchange lever gaiter, and free its lower end from the centre console to allow access to the case of the lever (photo).
2   Release the clip from the base of the lever shaft, then withdraw the pivot pin, and lift out the lever (photo).
3   Refitting is a reversal of removal.

5.1 Free the gearchange lever gaiter from the centre console

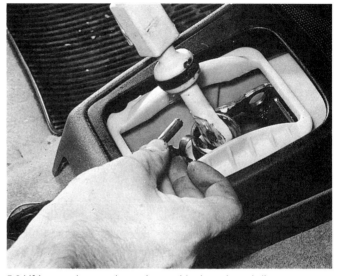

5.2 Lifting out the gearchange lever with pivot pin and clip

6   Gearchange lever gaiter – renewal

1   Remove the gearchange lever, as described in Section 5.
2   Immerse the gearchange lever knob in hot water (approximately 80°C/176°F) for a few minutes, then twist the knob and tap it from the lever. There is a strong possibility that the knob will be destroyed during removal.
3   Slide the old gaiter from the lever, and fit the new one. Use a little liquid detergent to aid fitting if necessary.
4   Refit the knob, preheating it in hot water as during removal, and driving it on with a soft-faced mallet. Ensure that the knob is fitted the correct way round.
5   Refit the gearchange lever, as described in Section 5.

7   Differential bearing oil seals – renewal

Note: *A balljoint separator tool will be required for this operation. The driveshaft snap ring(s) and lower arm-to-suspension strut balljoint locking pin(s) must be used on reassembly*

1   The differential bearing oil seals can be renewed with the gearbox *in situ* as follows.
2   Where applicable, remove the wheel trim from the relevant front roadwheel, then loosen the roadwheel bolts. Apply the handbrake, jack up the front of the vehicle, and support on axle stands positioned under the body side members. Remove the roadwheel.
3   Extract the locking pin, then unscrew the castellated nut from the lower arm-to-suspension strut balljoint.
4   Using a balljoint separator tool, disconnect the lower arm-to-suspension strut balljoint.
5   The inboard end of the driveshaft (or intermediate shaft) must now be disconnected with reference to the relevant paragraphs of Chapter 7, Section 3. Support the driveshaft by suspending it with string or wire – do not allow the driveshaft to hang under its own weight.
6   Prise the oil seal from the differential, using a screwdriver or similar instrument.
7   Smear the sealing lip of the new oil seal with gearbox oil, then using a tool of suitable diameter, drive the new seal into the differential, until it sits flush on its seat.
8   Reconnect the inboard end of the driveshaft with reference to the relevant paragraphs of Chapter 7, Section 3, using a new snap-ring.
9   Reconnect the lower arm-to-suspension strut balljoint, then fit the castellated nut and tighten to the specified torque (Chapter 9). Secure the nut with a new locking pin.
10   Refit the roadwheel, then lower the vehicle to the ground, and finally tighten the roadwheel bolts. Refit the wheel trim, where applicable.
11   Top up the gearbox oil level, as described in Section 2.

8   Gearbox – removal and refitting (leaving engine in vehicle)

Note: *This is an involved procedure, and it is suggested that the Section is read through thoroughly before commencing work. Various components must be renewed on reassembly, suitable equipment will be required to support the engine, and a special tool will be required to engage the gearbox input shaft with the clutch on refitting*

Removal
1   Disconnect the battery negative lead.
2   Working in the engine compartment, loosen the clamp bolt securing the gear selector tube to the linkage – see photo 3.1, then pull the selector tube towards the engine compartment bulkhead to separate it from the linkage.
3   Remove the retaining clip, then slide the clutch cable from the release lever, pushing the release lever back towards the bulkhead if necessary, to allow the cable to be disconnected. Pull the cable support from the bracket on the gearbox casing, then move the cable to one side out of the way, taking note of its routing.
4   Disconnect the wiring from the reversing lamp switch, which is located at the front of the gearbox casing, above the left-hand mounting bracket.

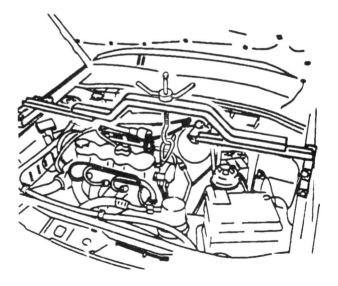

Fig. 6.5 Vauxhall special tool No KM-263 used to support engine
(Sec 8)

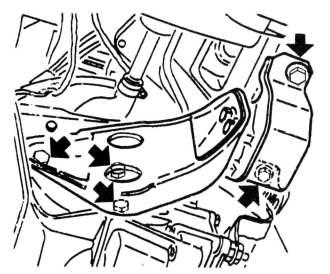

Fig. 6.6 Remove the left-hand gearbox mounting by unscrewing the five bolts (arrowed) (Sec 8)

Fig. 6.7 Driving out 3rd/4th gear selector fork roll pin. Note block of wood between selector shaft and mainshaft gears (Sec 8)

5   Unscrew the securing sleeve, and disconnect the speedometer cable from the gearbox.

6   Unscrew and remove the three upper engine-to-gearbox bolts.

7   The engine must now be supported from its left-hand lifting bracket. Ideally, the engine should be supported using a strong wooden or metal beam, resting on blocks positioned securely in the channels at the sides of the engine compartment. The Vauxhall special tool designed specifically for this purpose is shown in Fig. 6.5. Alternatively, the engine can be supported using a suitable hoist and lifting tackle, but in this case, the hoist must be of such a design to enable the engine to be supported with the vehicle raised off the ground, leaving sufficient clearance to withdraw the gearbox from under the front of the vehicle.

8   Where applicable, remove the wheel trims, then loosen the front roadwheel bolts on both sides of the vehicle. Apply the handbrake, then jack up the front of the vehicle, and support securely on axle stands positioned under the body side members. Note that the vehicle must be raised sufficiently high to enable the gearbox to be withdrawn from under the front of the vehicle. Remove the front roadwheels.

9   Ensure that the engine is adequately supported as described in paragraph 7, then remove the front subframe, as described in Chapter 9, Section 4.

10   Disconnect the inboard ends of the driveshafts with reference to the relevant paragraphs of Chapter 7, Section 3. Be prepared for oil spillage as the driveshafts are withdrawn, and plug the apertures in the differential to prevent further oil loss and dirt ingress. Support the driveshafts by suspending them with wire or string – do not allow the driveshafts to hang down under their own weight.

11   Unscrew the retaining nut, and disconnect the earth strap from the gearbox endplate.

12   Place a suitable container beneath the gearbox endplate to catch the oil which will be released, then unscrew the securing bolts and remove the endplate. Note the location of the studded bolt which retains the earth strap. For improved access, remove the wheel arch liner, as described in Chapter 10, Section 31.

13   Recover the gasket.

14   Extract the circlip from inside the end of the input shaft, using a pair of circlip pliers.

15   Using a twelve-point splined key, unscrew the socket-headed screw from the end of the input shaft.

16   The input shaft must now be pulled out of engagement from the splined hub of the clutch friction disc, as described in Chapter 5, Section 6. Note that there is no need to remove the clutch assembly, unless renewal of the clutch components is required.

17   Support the gearbox with a trolley jack, with as interposed block of wood to spread the load.

18   Remove the left-hand gearbox mounting completely, by unscrewing the two bolts securing the rubber mounting to the vehicle body, and the three bolts securing the mounting bracket to the gearbox   see Fig. 6.6.

19   Unscrew the securing bolts, and remove the cover plate from the base of the clutch bellhousing.

20   Ensure that the gearbox is adequately supported, then unscrew and remove the remaining engine-to-gearbox bolts.

21   The gearbox can now be lowered and withdrawn from under the front of the vehicle. The help of an assistant will greatly ease this operation.

Refitting

22   Before commencing the refitting operations, check that the two original bolts which secured the left-hand gearbox rubber mounting to the vehicle body rotate freely in their threaded bores in the body. If necessary, re-cut the threaded bores, using an M10 x 1.25 mm tap.

23   If the clutch assembly has been removed from the flywheel, it will prove easier to refit after the gearbox has been refitted.

24   Commence refitting by positioning the gearbox under the front of the vehicle, and support with a trolley jack and interposed block of wood, as during removal.

25   Raise the gearbox sufficiently to enable the lower engine-to-gearbox bolts to be fitted, then refit the bolts, but do not fully tighten them at this stage.

26   Refit the left-hand gearbox mounting, using two new bolts to secure the rubber mounting to the vehicle body. Tighten all bolts to the specified torque.

27   Tighten the previously-fitted lower engine-to-gearbox bolts to the specified torque, then withdraw the trolley jack from under the gearbox.

28   Where applicable, the clutch can now be fitted, and the gearbox input shaft can be pressed into engagement with the splined hub of the clutch friction disc, as described in Chapter 5, Section 9.

29   Screw the socket-headed screw into the end of the input shaft, then fit a new circlip.

30   Using a new gasket, refit the gearbox endplate, and tighten the securing bolts to the specified torque. Ensure that the studded bolt which retains the earth strap is fitted to its correct location, as noted during removal.

31   Reconnect the gearbox earth strap, and fit the retaining nut.

32   Refit the cover plate to the base of the clutch bellhousing, and tighten the securing bolts.

33   Reconnect the inboard ends of the driveshafts with reference to the relevant paragraphs of Chapter 7, Section 3, using new snap-rings.

34   Refit the front subframe, as described in Chapter 9, Section 4.

35   Refit the front roadwheels, but do not fully tighten the roadwheel bolts yet.

36   If a hoist and lifting tackle has been used to support the engine, either disconnect the lifting tackle, or lower the hoist sufficiently to enable the vehicle to be lowered to the ground.

37   Lower the vehicle to the ground, then tighten the roadwheel bolts to the specified torque, and refit the wheel trims (where applicable).

38   Disconnect and remove the equipment used to support the engine, if not already done.
39   Refit the three upper engine-to-gearbox bolts, and tighten them to the specified torque.
40   Reconnect the speedometer cable, and tighten the securing sleeve.
41   Reconnect the reversing lamp switch wiring.
42   Refit the clutch cable support to the bracket on the gearbox casing, then reconnect the cable to the release lever, and adjust the cable as described in Chapter 5, Section 4. Ensure that the cable is routed as noted during removal.
43   Reconnect the gear selector tube to the linkage, then adjust the linkage as described in Section 3 before tightening the clamp bolt.
44   Top up the gearbox oil level, as described in Section 2.
45   Reconnect the battery negative lead.

---

9   Gearbox overhaul – general

If gearbox overhaul is considered necessary, careful consideration should be given to the likely cost. It is often more economical to obtain a factory exchange or good second-hand unit, rather than to fit new components to the existing gearbox.

Overhaul of the gearbox requires the use of certain special tools, and a number of components must be renewed regardless of their condition. It is suggested that the relevant procedures are studied closely before starting work, in order to ensure that the necessary tools and new components are available.

Before starting work on the gearbox, drain the gearbox oil, by removing the differential cover plate. Prepare a clean working surface, with containers and trays handy to store the various components. Label all components as they are removed, and make a note of the orientation of fitted components if any confusion is likely to arise during reassembly.

All circlips should be renewed as a matter of course, as should bearings, unless they are known to be in perfect condition.

Before commencing reassembly, all components must be absolutely clean. Lubricate all components with clean gear oil during reassembly.

---

10   Gearbox – dismantling into major assemblies

Note: *Suitable gear pullers will be required during this procedure*

1   With the gearbox removed from the vehicle, clean away external dirt, using paraffin or another suitable solvent and a stiff brush.
2   Unscrew the four securing bolts, and lift the gear selector cover from the gearbox casing. Manipulate the selector mechanism as necessary to enable the selector cover to be withdrawn. Recover the gasket.
3   Unbolt the retaining plate, and withdraw the speedometer driven gear (photos).
4   Unscrew and remove the reversing lamp switch (photo).
5   Unscrew the securing bolts, and remove the cover plate from the clutch bellhousing, if not already done.

6   If not already done, unscrew the securing bolts, and remove the endplate from the gearbox. Place a suitable container beneath the gearbox, to catch the oil which will be released as the endplate is removed. Note the location of the studded bolt which retains the earth strap. Recover the gasket.
7   Unscrew the securing bolts and withdraw the gearbox intermediate plate, complete with the geartrains, from the main gearbox casing (photo). If necessary, *lightly* tap the end of the input shaft with a soft-faced mallet, to free the main gearbox casing from the geartrains.
8   Extract the swarf-collecting magnet from its location in the intermediate plate, and recover the thrustwasher from the reverse roller shaft.
9   Using a suitable Allen key, or hexagon bit, unscrew the two securing bolts and lift the 5th gear selector fork from the intermediate plate. Take care not to lose the two slider bars which rest in the ends of the fork, and which may drop out as the fork is withdrawn.
10   Engage two gears simultaneously by moving the relevant selector forks, eg 3rd and reverse.
11   Extract the circlip from the end of the mainshaft, then using a two-legged puller, draw the 5th gear synchro unit from the mainshaft.
12   Lift the synchro ring from the 5th driven gear, then using a two-legged puller, draw the 5th driven gear from the mainshaft.
13   Lift the split type needle roller bearing from the mainshaft, followed by the thrustwasher retaining ring, and the two thrustwasher halves.
14   Extract the circlip from the end of the input shaft, then using a two-legged puller, draw the 5th driving gear from the input shaft.
15   Using a suitable Allen key, or a hexagon bit, unscrew the two screws which secure the 5th gear selector interlock pawl to the intermediate plate, and withdraw the pawl.
16   Using a forked tool, or a slide hammer with a suitable improvised end attachment, withdraw the four detent plugs from the edge of the intermediate plate (photos). Be prepared to catch the coil springs which will be released, and withdraw the detent plungers. Keep all the components identified so that they can be refitted in their original positions.
17   Move the 5th gear selector dog to its engaged position, and move the 1st/2nd gear selector fork to engage 2nd gear.
18   Using a suitable Allen key, or a hexagon bit, unscrew the two securing screws, and withdraw the interlock pin bridge piece.
19   Return all gears to neutral.
20   Place a block of wood between the top of the 3rd/4th gear selector shaft and the mainshaft gears, then drive out the 3rd/4th gear selector fork roll pin, using a suitable punch. Withdraw the selector shaft and fork.
21   Similarly, remove the reverse selector shaft and fork. Position the block of wood between the selector shaft and the input shaft gears.
22   Slide the interlock rod from its location in the intermediate plate.
23   Pull the 5th gear selector dog from its location in the intermediate plate.
24   Proceed as follows, according to gearbox type.

F10/5 and F13/5 gearboxes
25   Using circlip pliers, compress the circlips retaining the mainshaft and input shaft bearings in the intermediate plate.
26   Withdraw the geartrains, along with the reverse idler gear, and 1st/2nd gear selector shaft and fork, from the intermediate plate. If necessary, tap the shafts and bearings with a plastic-faced hammer to release them.

10.3A Unbolt the retaining plate ...

10.3B ... and withdraw the speedometer drivegear

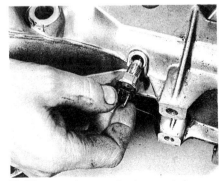
10.4 Remove the reversing lamp switch

10.7 Withdrawing the intermediate plate and geartrains

10.16A Levering out a detent plug

10.16B Detent plug extraction tool suitable for attachment to a slide hammer

10.32 Compressing the mainshaft bearing circlip – F16/5 type gearbox

10.33 Expanding the input shaft bearing circlip – F16/5 type gearbox

27 If desired, the reverse idler shaft can be removed from the intermediate plate, by mounting the shaft in a vice, and tapping the intermediate plate from it, using a soft-faced mallet.

28 If desired, the 1st/2nd gear selector fork can be removed from the selector shaft, by driving out the roll pin.

29 The clutch release components can be removed from the bellhousing, as described in Chapter 5, Section 11. For details of differential overhaul, refer to Section 15.

F16/5 and F20/5 type gearboxes

30 Drive out the 1st/2nd gear selector fork roll pin, again placing a block of wood between the selector shaft and the mainshaft gears, and withdraw the selector shaft and fork.

31 The help of an assistant will now be required, to remove the mainshaft and input shaft from the intermediate plate.

32 Using suitable pliers, squeeze together the ends of the large circlip which retains the mainshaft bearing in the intermediate plate (photo). A piece of strong, thin rod can be formed into a retaining clip to keep the circlip compressed (see photo 18.9). If this method is used, ensure that the retaining clip is securely located, as injury could result if the clip is dislodged.

33 With the mainshaft bearing circlip held compressed, expand the legs of the circlip which retains the input shaft bearing in the intermediate plate (photo).

34 With the help of an assistant, withdraw the geartrains from the intermediate plate. This is a tricky operation, and some patience will be required. The shafts and bearings may require a little gentle tapping with a plastic-faced hammer, to release them from the intermediate plate. Recover the reverse idler gear, which will be withdrawn with the geartrains.

35 If desired, the reverse idler shaft can be removed from the intermediate plate, by mounting the shaft in a vice, and tapping the intermediate plate from it, using a soft-faced mallet.

36 The clutch release components can be removed from the bellhousing, as described in Chapter 5, Section 11. For details of differential overhaul, refer to Section 15.

11 Input shaft – overhaul

1 If not already done, extract the circlip from inside the end of the input shaft using a pair of circlip pliers, then using a twelve-point splined key, unscrew the socket-headed screw from the end of the shaft.

2 Support the end of the gear cluster, then press or tap the shaft from it, using a round bar or drift of suitable diameter – see Fig. 6.8.

3 Support the bearing, then press or tap the gear cluster from it, using a metal tube of suitable diameter.

4 On F10/5 and F13/5 type gearboxes, remove the large circlip which retains the bearing in the intermediate plate from the gear cluster.

5 Examine all components for wear and damage. If any of the gears are worn or damaged, the complete gear cluster must be renewed, as must the corresponding gears on the mainshaft.

Fig. 6.8 Pressing the input shaft from the gear cluster (Sec 11)

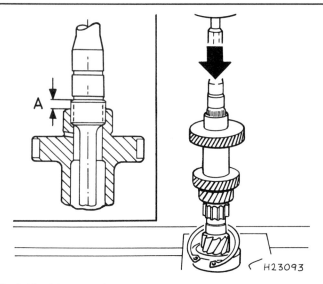

Fig. 6.9 Push input shaft into gear cluster, and measure projection of splined section of shaft (A) (Sec 11)

11.9 Fit the bearing with the circlip groove nearest the gear cluster

6   Spin the bearing, and check it for roughness. Hold the outer race, and attempt to move it laterally against the inner race. If any excessive movement or roughness is evident, renew the bearing.
7   Commence reassembly as follows.
8   On F10/5 and F13/5 type gearboxes, fit a new bearing-to-intermediate plate retaining circlip over the gear cluster.
9   Press the bearing onto the gear cluster, using a metal tube of suitable diameter. On F16/5 and F20/5 type gearboxes, the bearing should be fitted with the circlip groove nearest the gear cluster (photo).
10   Push the shaft into the gear cluster by hand, and measure dimension 'A' as shown in Fig. 6.9 (photo). Dimension 'A' should be between 0 and 5.0 mm (0 and 0.2 in). If 'A' is less than 0 mm, fit a new 'size 2' shaft – refer to a Vauxhall dealer for details of available shaft sizes. If 'A' is greater than 5.0 mm (0.2 in), fit a new gear cluster.
11   Support the gear cluster on the bearing, then press the shaft into the gear cluster, with the shorter-splined end towards the bearing.
12   If the engine and gearbox are to be mated together with the clutch assembly bolted to the flywheel, refit the socket-headed screw and the circlip to the end of the input shaft (photos). Otherwise leave refitting of the screw and circlip until the clutch has been fitted, with the engine and gearbox in the vehicle.

12   Mainshaft (F10/5 and F13/5 type gearboxes) – overhaul

Note: *A press, or suitable gear pullers, will be required during this procedure; some of the components may be a very tight fit on the shaft*

1   Support the 1st gear, then press the shaft from the bearing and gear. Alternatively, a suitable puller can be used to pull the gear and bearing

from the shaft, but if this method is used, ensure that the claws of the puller locate on the main body of the gear, **not** solely on the gear teeth.
2   Recover the large circlip which retains the bearing in the intermediate plate, the thrustwasher, and the axial needle bearing, all of which fit between the bearing and 1st gear.
3   Lift the three 1st gear synchro rings from the 1st/2nd gear synchro unit.
4   Remove the split type needle roller bearing.
5   Extract the 1st/2nd gear synchro unit retaining circlip.
6   Support the 2nd gear, then press the shaft from the 1st/2nd gear synchro unit and 2nd gear. Alternatively, a suitable puller can be used, bearing in mind the point made in paragraph 1.
7   Recover the three 2nd gear synchro rings which fit between the synchro unit and 2nd gear.
8   Attention must now be turned to the opposite end of the shaft.
9   Extract the circlip which secures the pinion gear to the end of the shaft.
10   Support the pinion gear, then press the shaft from the gear. Alternatively, a suitable puller can be used, bearing in mind the point made in paragraph 1.
11   Support the 4th gear, then press the shaft from the thrustwasher and 4th gear. There is very little clearance available to support the gear; ideally, a thin steel plate should be used to support the gear in the groove between the gear teeth and synchro teeth - see Fig. 6.10.
12   Lift the 4th gear synchro ring from the 3rd/4th synchro unit.
13   Extract the 3rd/4th synchro unit retaining circlip.
14   Support the 3rd gear, then press the shaft from the 3rd/4th synchro unit and 3rd gear. Alternatively, a suitable puller can be used, bearing in mind the point made in paragraph 1.
15   Recover the 3rd gear synchro ring which fits between the synchro unit and 3rd gear.
16   Examine all components for wear and damage. If any of the gears

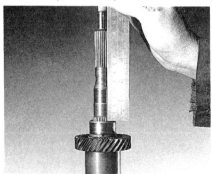

11.10 Measuring dimension 'A' – see Fig. 6.9

11.12A Fit the socket-headed screw to the end of the input shaft ...

11.12B ... then fit the circlip

12.20 Fit 3rd gear – F13/5 type gearbox

12.21 Fit the 3rd gear synchro ring

12.22 Using a tube to fit the 3rd/4th synchro unit

12.23 Fit a new 3rd/4th synchro unit retaining circlip

12.24 Fit the 4th gear synchro ring ...

12.25 ... followed by 4th gear

12.26A Fit the thrustwasher ...

12.26B ... and press home with a suitable tube

12.27 Fit the pinion gear ...

are worn or damaged, all the gears on the mainshaft must be renewed, as must the input shaft gear cluster.

17   The synchro units can be overhauled as described in Section 14.

18   Renew all circlips as a matter of course, and the bearings, unless their condition is known to be perfect.

19   With all components clean and well oiled, commence reassembly as follows.

20   Slide the 3rd gear onto the pinion gear end of the shaft (photo).

21   Fit the 3rd gear synchro ring (photo).

22   Fit the 3rd/4th synchro unit. Press or drive the synchro unit down the shaft, using a length of suitable-diameter tubing applied to the synchro hub (photo). The manufacturers recommend that the synchro unit is preheated to a temperature of 100°C (212°F) before fitting.

23   Fit a new 3rd/4th synchro unit retaining circlip (photo).

24   Fit the 4th gear synchro ring to the synchro unit, ensuring that the sliding keys in the synchro unit engage with the cut-outs in the synchro ring (photo).

25   Fit the 4th gear (photo).

26   Fit the thrustwasher, with the cut-outs against 4th gear. Press or drive the thrustwasher down the shaft, using a length of tubing. The manufacturers recommend that the thrustwasher is preheated to a temperature of 100°C (212°F) before fitting (photos).

27   Fit the pinion gear, with the collar against the thrustwasher, using the same method as used to fit the thrustwasher (photo).

28   Fit a new pinion gear securing circlip (photo).

29   Attention must now be turned to the opposite end of the shaft.

30   Slide the 2nd gear onto the shaft (photo).

31   Fit the three 2nd gear synchro rings, ensuring that the lugs and cut-outs in the three rings engage as shown in photos 13.35A, B and C.

32   Fit the 1st/2nd gear synchro unit, with the reverse gear teeth nearest the 2nd gear (photo). Press or drive the synchro unit down the shaft, using a length of suitable tubing. The manufacturers recommend that the synchro unit is preheated to a temperature of 100°C (212°F) before fitting.

12.28 ... and secure with a new circlip

12.30 Fit 2nd gear

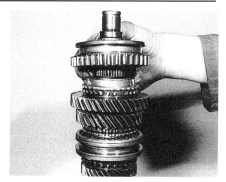

12.32 Fit the 1st/2nd gear synchro unit ...

12.33 ... and secure with a new circlip

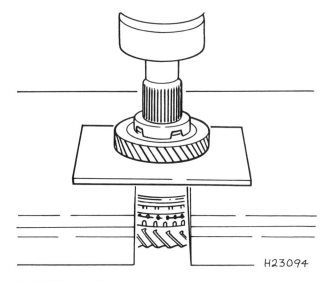

Fig. 6.10 Thin steel plated used to support 4th gear when pressing mainshaft from gear and thrustwasher – F10/5 and F13/5 type gearboxes (Sec 12)

33   Fit a new 1st/2nd gear synchro unit retaining circlip (photo).
34   Fit the split type needle roller bearing.
35   Fit the three 1st gear synchro rings, ensuring that the lugs and cut-outs in the three rings engage as shown in photos 13.35 A, B and C.
36   Fit the 1st gear.
37   Fit the axial needle bearing.
38   Fit the thrustwasher, with the larger diameter against the axial needle bearing. Press or drive the thrustwasher down the shaft, using a length of tubing. The manufacturers recommend that the thrustwasher is preheated to a temperature of 100°C (212°F) before fitting.
39   Fit a new bearing-to-intermediate plate retaining circlip.
40   Fit the bearing to the end of the shaft. Press or drive the bearing down the shaft, using a length of suitable-diameter tubing applied to the bearing inner race.
41   Check that all gears turn freely, and that the synchro sleeves slide freely.

13   Mainshaft (F16/5 and F20/5 type gearboxes) – overhaul

Note: *A press, or suitable gear pullers, will be required during this procedure; some of the components may be a very tight fit on the shaft*

1   Support the 1st gear, then press the shaft from the bearing and gear. Alternatively, a suitable puller can be used to pull the gear and bearing from the shaft, but if this method is used, ensure that the claws of the puller locate on the main body of the gear, **not** solely on the gear teeth.
2   Recover the large circlip which retains the bearing in the intermedi-

ate plate, the thrustwasher, and the axial needle bearing, all of which fit between the bearing and 1st gear.
3   Lift the three 1st gear synchro rings from the 1st/2nd gear synchro unit.
4   Remove the split type needle roller bearing.
5   Extract the 1st/2nd gear synchro unit retaining circlip, and lift off the thrustwasher.
6   Support the 2nd gear, then press the shaft from the 1st/2nd gear synchro unit and 2nd gear. Alternatively, a suitable puller can be used, bearing in mind the point made in paragraph 1.
7   Recover the three 2nd gear synchro rings which fit between the synchro unit and 2nd gear.
8   Lift off the split type needle roller bearing, followed by the thrustwasher retaining ring, and the two thrustwasher halves.
9   Lift off the 3rd gear.
10   Lift the 3rd gear synchro ring from the 3rd/4th gear synchro unit.
11   Remove the split type needle roller bearings.
12   Extract the 3rd/4th gear synchro unit retaining circlip, and remove the thrustwasher.
13   Support the 4th gear, then press the shaft from the 3rd/4th gear synchro unit and 4th gear. Alternatively, a suitable puller can be used, bearing in mind the point made in paragraph 1.
14   Recover the 4th gear synchro ring which fits between the synchro unit and 4th gear.
15   Lift off the split type needle roller bearing, followed by the thrustwasher retaining ring, and the two thrustwasher halves.
16   Lift off the roller bearing.
17   The pinion gear is an integral part of the shaft, and cannot be removed.

13.22 Sliding the roller bearing onto the mainshaft – F16/5 type gearbox

13.23A Locate the thrustwasher halves ...

13.23B ... and their retaining ring on the bearing

13.23C Thrustwasher half lug engaged with hole in shaft (arrowed)

13.24 Fit the split type needle roller bearing ...

18   Examine all components for wear and damage. If any of the gears are worn or damaged, all the gears on the mainshaft must be renewed, as must the input shaft gear cluster.

19   The synchro units can be overhauled as described in Section 14.

20   Renew all circlips as a matter of course, and the bearings, unless their condition is known to be perfect.

21   With all parts clean and well oiled, commence reassembly as follows.

22   Slide the roller bearing onto the shaft, with the smaller diameter of the roller cage against the pinion gear (photo).

23   Locate the thrustwasher halves on the bearing so that their lugs engage with the hole in the shaft, and then fit the retaining ring (photos).

24   Fit the split type needle roller bearing (photo).

25   Fit the 4th gear (photo).

26   Fit the 4th gear synchro ring (photo).

27   Fit the 3rd/4th gear synchro unit, with the larger chamfered side of the sleeve furthest from the 4th gear (photo). Press or drive the synchro unit down the shaft, using a length of suitable-diameter tubing applied to the synchro hub. The manufacturers recommend that the synchro

unit is preheated to a temperature of 100°C (212°F) before fitting.

28   Fit the thrustwasher, followed by a new circlip (photos).

29   Fit the 3rd gear synchro ring to the synchro unit, ensuring that the sliding keys in the synchro unit engage with the cut-outs in the synchro ring (photo).

30   Fit the split type needle roller bearing (photo).

31   Fit the 3rd gear (photo).

32   Locate the thrustwasher halves in the shaft groove so that their lugs engage with the hole in the shaft, and then fit the retaining ring (photos).

33   Fit the split type needle roller bearing (photo).

34   Fit the 2nd gear (photo).

35   Fit the three 2nd gear synchro rings, ensuring that the lugs and cut-outs in the three rings engage as shown (photos).

36   Fit the 1st/2nd gear synchro unit, with the reverse gear teeth nearest the 2nd gear (photo). Press or drive the synchro unit down the shaft, using a length of suitable diameter tubing applied to the synchro hub. The manufacturers recommend that the synchro unit is preheated to a temperature of 100°C (212°F) before fitting.

13.25 ... 4th gear ...

13.26 ... 4th gear synchro ring ...

13.27 ... and the 3rd/4th gear synchro unit

13.28A Fit the thrustwasher ...

13.28B ... followed by a new circlip

13.29 Fit the 3rd gear synchro ring ...

13.30 ... followed by the split type needle roller bearing ...

13.31 ... and 3rd gear

13.32A Engage the thrustwasher half lugs with the hcle in the shaft ...

13.32B ... then fit the retaining ring

13.33 Fit the split type needle roller bearing ...

13.34 ... followed by 2nd gear

13.35A Fit the inner 2nd gear synchro ring ...

13.35B ... engage the lugs on the intermediate ring with the cut-outs in the inner ring ...

13.35C ... then engage the lugs on the inner ring with the cut-outs in the outer ring

13.36 Fit the 1st/2nd gear synchro unit

13.37A Fit the thrustwasher ...

13.37B ... followed by a new circlip

13.38 Fit the split type needle roller bearing

13.39A Fit the first ...

13.39B ... second ...

13.39C ... and third 1st gear synchro rings

13.40 Fit 1st gear

13.41 Fit the axial needle bearing ...

13.42 ... followed by the thrustwasher

13.43 Fit a new bearing-to-intermediate plate retaining circlip ...

13.44 ... followed by the bearing

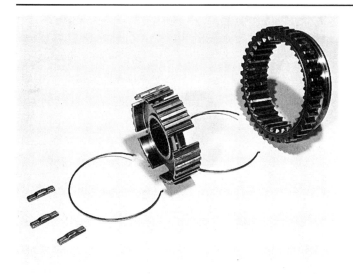

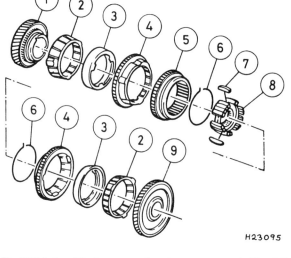

H23095

14.1 Synchroniser unit components

37 Fit the thrustwasher, followed by a new circlip (photos).
38 Fit the split type needle roller bearing (photo).
39 Fit the three 1st gear synchro rings, ensure that the lugs and cut-outs in the three rings engage as shown previously for the 2nd gear synchro rings (photos).
40 Fit the 1st gear (photo).
41 Fit the axial needle bearing (photo).
42 Fit the thrustwasher, with the larger diameter against the axial needle bearing (photo). Press or drive the thrustwasher down the shaft, using a length of tubing. The manufacturers recommend that the thrustwasher is preheated to a temperature of 100°C (212°F) before fitting.
43 Fit a new bearing-to-intermediate plate retaining circlip (photo).
44 Fit the bearing to the end of the shaft (photo). Press or drive the bearing down the shaft, using a length of suitable diameter tubing applied to the bearing inner race.
45 Check that all gears turn freely, and that the synchro sleeves slide freely.

Fig. 6.11 1st and 2nd gear synchroniser components (Sec 14)

1	2nd gear	6	Synchro springs
2	Inner synchro rings	7	Sliding key
3	Intermediate synchro rings	8	Synchro hub
4	Outer synchro rings	9	1st gear
5	Synchro sleeve		

4 Reassembly is a reversal of dismantling. Ensure that the sleeve and the hub are orientated so that the sliding keys can engage with the cut-outs in the sleeve. The hooked ends of the two synchro springs should both engage in the same sliding key, with the two springs running in opposite directions in relation to each other (photos).
5 To check the synchro rings for wear, twist them onto their relevant gear cones. The ring should 'stick' to the cone, and should show a definite clearance between the ring teeth and the synchro teeth on the gear shoulder. If these conditions are not met, renew the synchro ring(s).

14 Synchroniser units – overhaul

1 To dismantle a synchro unit, remove the two synchro springs, taking care not to allow the sliding keys to fly out, then slide the sleeve from the hub. Recover the three sliding keys (photo).
2 If either the hub or sleeve shows signs of wear in its teeth, the individual part may be renewed, but general wear is best rectified by complete renewal of the unit.
3 Renew the synchro springs if they are broken, or have become weak.

15 Differential – overhaul

1 Before considering overhaul of the differential assembly, compare the price of the new components required with the cost of a new or reconditioned unit, as it may prove more economical to fit a complete new assembly.
2 Note that if the crownwheel, or the pinion gear on the gearbox mainshaft are to be renewed, they must be renewed as a matched pair.
3 Due to the requirement for special tools to set the differential bearings preload, it is recommended that overhaul of the differential is entrusted to a Vauxhall dealer, who will have the necessary expertise to complete the task effectively.

14.4A The sliding keys should engage with the cut-outs (arrowed) in the synchro sleeve

14.4B Fit the sliding keys ...

14.4C ... and engage the hooked ends of the synchro springs

16.2 Withdraw the selector finger and selector rod from the cover

16.3 Extract the circlip from the top of the guide pin

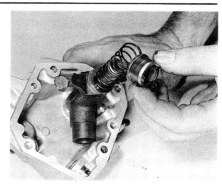

16.4A Withdraw the retainer and coil spring ...

16.4B ... the thrustwasher ...

16.4C ... and the intermediate selector lever

16.7 Correct orientation of fork smaller hole (arrowed) on reassembly

17.2 Input shaft bearing location – F16/5 type gearbox

17.4A Left-hand differential bearing oil seal location ...

17.4B ... and right-hand oil seal location – F16/5 type gearbox

17.6A Left-hand gearbox mounting – F16/5 type gearbox

17.6B Gearbox/engine mounting bolt locking plates (arrowed) must be renewed on refitting

16 Gear selector cover – overhaul

1   Unscrew and remove the oil breather/filler plug.
2   Drive out the roll pin to release the selector finger from the selector rod, and withdraw both components from the cover (photo).
3   Extract the circlip from the top of the guide pin (photo).
4   Withdraw the retainer, coil spring, thrustwasher and intermediate selector lever (photo).
5   If desired, the selector linkage can be dismantled, and any worn components can be renewed – refer to Section 4.
6   The selector rod oil seal can be renewed by prising the old seal from the selector cover, and fitting the new seal using a suitable piece of tubing, or a socket.
7   Reassembly is a reversal of the dismantling procedure, but note that when refitting the selector rod, the rod must be orientated so that the smaller hole in the fork on the end of the rod is closest to the guide pin (photo).

17 Main gearbox casing – overhaul

1   The clutch release bearing, sleeve and arm can be removed from the bellhousing, as described in Chapter 5, Section 11.
2   Inspect the input shaft bearing (photo), and renew if necessary by drifting out the old bearing, using a tube of suitable diameter on the bearing outer race. Fit a new bearing in the same way.
3   The mainshaft bearing (F10/5 and F13/5 type gearboxes) or the mainshaft bearing outer race (F16/5 and F20/5 type gearboxes) can be removed from the gearbox casing, using a suitable puller. Access is limited, and it may be necessary to remove the differential in order to use a puller, particularly on F10/5 and F13/5 type gearboxes.
4   The differential bearing oil seals can be renewed as described in Section 6 (photos).
5   Due to the requirement for special tools to set the bearing preload when refitting, it is recommended that the differential assembly is not removed from the gearbox, unless absolutely necessary.
6   If desired, the gearbox and gearbox/engine mountings can be unbolted from the gearbox casing. Note that if the gearbox/engine mounting is removed, the locking plates under the bolt heads must be renewed on refitting. Check that the condition of the mounting rubbers, and renew them if deterioration or damage is evident (photos).

18 Gearbox – reassembly

F10/5 and F13/5 type gearboxes

1   Where applicable, refit the reverse idler shaft to the intermediate plate, by tapping it into place as far as the stop, using a soft-faced mallet. Ensure that the locking ball is in position.
2   Where applicable, refit the 1st/2nd gear selector fork to the selector shaft, and secure with a new roll pin. Note that the cut-outs in the selector shaft should face away from the selector fork. The roll pin should protrude from the outer end of the selector fork by approximately 2.0 mm (0.08 in).
3   Mesh the input shaft and the mainshaft geartrains together with the reverse idler gear, and engage the 1st/2nd gear selector fork in the

groove of the 1st/2nd gear synchro unit. The reverse idler gear selector fork groove should be uppermost. The input shaft and mainshaft can be locked together with cable ties, to aid refitting.
4   Locate the assembly into the intermediate plate, with the help of an assistant if necessary.
5   Fit the circlips which retain the mainshaft and input shaft bearings in the intermediate plate. Ensure that the circlips engage positively in their grooves – some manipulation may be required to achieve this.
6   Proceed to paragraph 13.

F16/5 and F20/5 type gearboxes

7   Where applicable, refit the reverse idler shaft to the intermediate plate, by tapping it into place as far as the stop, using a soft-faced mallet. Ensure that the locking ball is in position.
8   Mesh the input shaft and the mainshaft geartrains together with the reverse idler gear. The reverse idler gear selector fork groove should be uppermost. The input shaft and mainshaft can be locked together with cable ties, to assist refitting.
9   To aid refitting, fit a retaining clip to keep the mainshaft bearing retaining circlip compressed, as described during the dismantling procedure in Section 10. Ensure that the retaining clip is securely locked, as injury could result if the clip is dislodged (photo).
10   Using circlip pliers, expand the input shaft bearing retaining circlip in the intermediate plate.
11   Locate the geartrain assembly into the intermediate plate, with the help of an assistant if necessary (photo).
12   Release the input shaft bearing retaining circlip, and remove the retaining clip from the mainshaft bearing retaining circlip. Ensure that the circlips engage positively in their grooves – some manipulation may be required to achieve this.

All gearbox types

13   Slide the interlock rod into position in the intermediate plate (photo).
14   Engage the reverse selector fork with the reverse idler gear, then refit the reverse selector shaft. Note that the cut-outs in the selector shaft should face away from the selector fork. Place a block of wood between the selector shaft and the input shaft gears, then secure the fork to the shaft using a new roll pin (photos).
15   On F16/5 and F20/5 type gearboxes, engage the 1st/2nd gear selector fork with the 1st/2nd gear synchro unit, then fit the selector shaft, and secure the fork to the shaft with a new roll pin (photo). Place a block of wood between the selector shaft and the mainshaft gears when fitting the roll pin. Note that the cut-outs in the selector shaft should face away from the selector fork.
16   Fit the 5th gear selector dog to the intermediate plate (photo).
17   Engage the 3rd/4th gear selector fork with the 3rd/4th gear synchro unit, then fit the selector shaft, and secure the fork to the shaft with a new roll pin (photo). Again, position a block of wood between the selector shaft and the mainshaft gears when fitting the roll pin. Note that the cut-outs in the selector shaft should face away from the selector fork.
18   Move the 5th gear selector dog to its engaged position, and move the 1st/2nd gear selector fork to engage 2nd gear.
19   Fit the interlock pin to the bridge piece, then fit the bridge piece, and secure with two new screws, coated with thread-locking compound (photos). Tighten the screws to the specified torque.
20   Return all gears to neutral.

18.9 Retaining clip fitted to mainshaft bearing circlip

18.11 Fitting the geartrain assembly to the intermediate plate – F16/5 type gearbox

18.13 Slide the interlock rod into the intermediate plate

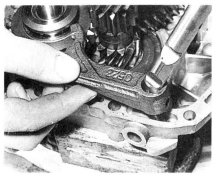

18.14A Fit the reverse selector fork and shaft ...

18.14B ... and secure with a new roll pin

18.15 Fit the 1st/2nd gear selector fork and shaft

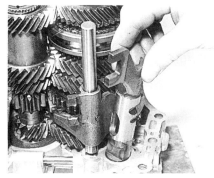

18.16 Fit the 5th gear selector dog ...

18.17 ... followed by the 3rd/4th selector fork and shaft

18.19A Fit the interlock pin to the bridge piece ...

18.19B ... then fit the bridge piece

18.21A Fit the 5th gear interlock pawl ...

18.21B ... and tighten the securing screws to the specified torque

18.22A Fit the thrustwasher halves to the end of the mainshaft ...

18.22B ... followed by the retaining ring ...

18.22C ... and the split type needle roller bearing

18.23 Fit the 5th driven gear

18.24A Fit the 5th driving gear ...

18.24B ... and secure with a new circlip

18.25 Fit the synchro ring to 5th driven gear

18.26A Fit the 5th gear synchro unit ...

18.26B ... and secure with a new circlip

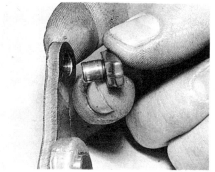

18.27A Fit the slider bars to the 5th gear selector fork ...

18.27B ... then fit the selector fork ...

18.27C ... and tighten the bolts

18.28A Fitting 5th gear detent plunger ...

18.28B ... spring ...

18.28C ... and plug

18.29A Fit the swarf-collecting magnet

18.29B Fit the reverse idler shaft thrustwasher

18.30A Fit a new gasket to the main gearbox casing ...

18.30B ... then fit the geartrains and intermediate plate

18.31 Tighten the intermediate plate securing bolts to the specified torque

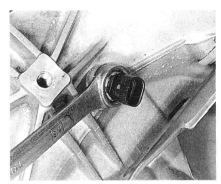

18.32 Refit the reversing lamp switch

18.33A Fit a new O-ring ...

18.33B ... and small oil seal to the speedometer driven gear

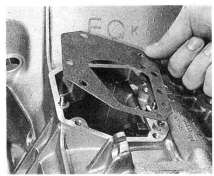

18.34A Fit a new gear selector cover gasket ...

21   Fit the 5th gear selector interlock pawl to the intermediate plate, then move the 3rd/4th gear selector shaft so that the pawl aligns with the cut-out in the shaft. Secure the interlock pawl with two new screws, coated with thread-locking compound. Tighten the screws to the specified torque (photos).
22   Fit the two thrustwasher halves to the end of the mainshaft, followed by the thrustwasher retaining ring and the split type needle roller bearing (photos).
23   Fit the 5th driven gear, with the synchro cone furthest from the intermediate plate (photo).
24   Support the intermediate plate and the lower end of the input shaft, and then press or drive the 5th driving gear onto the input shaft, using a suitable metal tube. Fit a new circlip to the end of the input shaft (photos).
25   Fit the synchro ring to the 5th driven gear (photo).
26   Support the intermediate plate and the lower end of the mainshaft, then fit the 5th gear synchro unit, so that the side where the sliding keys are visible is against the 5th driven gear. Press or drive the synchro unit down the shaft, using a length of suitable diameter tubing applied to the

synchro hub. The manufacturers recommend that the synchro unit is preheated to a temperature of 100°C (212°F) before fitting. Fit a new circlip to the end of the mainshaft (photos).
27   Ensure that the slider bars are fitted to the ends of the 5th gear selector fork, then position the selector fork so that it engages with the cut-out in the 5th gear selector dog. Secure the selector fork with two new bolts, coated with thread-locking compound, and tighten the bolts to the specified torque (photos).
28   Insert the four detent plungers and springs into the edge of the intermediate plate, and tap in new plugs (photos). Note that the 3rd/4th gear detent plug is longer than the others.
29   Fit the swarf-collecting magnet to its location in the intermediate plate, and fit the thrustwasher to the reverse idler shaft (photos). Retain both components with a small amount of grease.
30   Place a new gasket on the main gearbox casing flange, and fit the geartrains and intermediate plate into the casing (photos). Note that the mainshaft pinion gear and differential crownwheel teeth must mesh as the geartrains are installed. If necessary, gently tap the intermediate plate into position, using a soft-faced mallet.

18.34B ... then fit the selector cover

18.35A Fitting a new endplate gasket ...

18.35B ... and the endplate

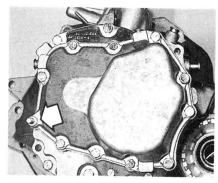

18.35C Correct location of studded bolt for earth strap (arrowed)

18.36 Fitting the clutch bellhousing cover plate

31   Fit the intermediate plate securing bolts, and tighten them to the specified torque (photo).
32   Refit the reversing lamp switch (photo).
33   Fit a new O-ring and small oil seal to the speedometer driven gear, then refit the gear to the gearbox casing, and secure with the retaining plate (photos).
34   Fit the gear selector cover to the gearbox casing, using a new gasket. Manipulate the selector mechanism as necessary to enable the selector cover to be fitted, and tighten the securing bolts to the specified torque (photos).
35   If the engine and gearbox are to be mated together with the clutch assembly bolted to the flywheel, the endplate can be refitted to the gearbox. Otherwise leave refitting of the endplate until the clutch has been fitted, with the engine and gearbox in the vehicle. Use a new gasket, and tighten the securing bolts to the specified torque, ensuring that the studded bolt which retains the earth strap is fitted to its correct location, as noted during dismantling (photos).
36   Similarly, the cover plate can be refitted to the clutch bellhousing if desired (photo).
37   Refit the differential cover plate using a new gasket, if not already done (photos).

18.37A Fitting a new differential cover plate gasket ...

18.37B ... and the cover plate

19 Fault diagnosis – manual gearbox

Symptom	Reason(s)
Gearbox noisy in neutral	Input shaft bearings worn
Gearbox noisy in all gears	Oil level low, or incorrect grade of oil Mainshaft or differential bearings worn Crownwheel and pinion worn Differential bearing adjustment incorrect
Gearbox noisy in one gear	Worn or damaged gear teeth
Ineffective synchromesh	Oil level low, or incorrect grade of oil Worn synchro units or synchro rings
Gearbox jumps out of gear	Worn synchro unit Worn selector forks Worn detent plunger or spring
Difficulty in engaging gears*	Gear selector linkage adjustment incorrect Worn selector forks or selector mechanism Clutch fault (see Chapter 5)
Noise when cornering	Wheel bearing or driveshaft fault (see Chapters 10 and 8 respectively) Differential fault

When attempting to engage reverse gear, it is normal to have to wait a couple of seconds with the clutch pedal fully depressed, the engine idling and the vehicle stationary, before it will engage. This is not a fault

Note: *This Section is not intended as an exhaustive guide to fault diagnosis, but summarises the more common faults which may be encountered during a vehicle's life. Consult a dealer for more detailed advice*

Chapter 7 Driveshafts

For modifications, and information applicable to later models, see Supplement at end of manual

Contents

Specifications

Type..	Unequal-length open shafts, with constant velocity joint at each end. Certain models have vibration damper fitted to right-hand shaft
Driveshaft joint grease specification..	GM grease 19 41 521 (Duckhams LBM 10)

Torque wrench settings

Front hub nut*

	Nm	lbf ft
Stage 1	130	96
Stage 2	Loosen nut fully	
Stage 3	20	15
Stage 4	Angle-tighten a further 90°	Angle-tighten a further 90°
Lower arm-to-suspension strut balljoint nut..............................	70	52
Roadwheel bolts	90	66

Refer to Section 3, paragraph 17

1 General description

Drive from the differential is taken to the roadwheels by two open driveshafts with a constant velocity joint at each end.

The driveshafts are splined at both ends. The inner ends fit into the differential, and are retained by snap-rings, while the outer ends fit into the front hubs, and are retained by the front hub nuts.

The right-hand driveshaft is longer than the left-hand one, due to the position of the differential. Certain models have a two-piece vibration damper fitted to the right-hand driveshaft.

Note: *On GSi 2000 models, the right-hand driveshaft consists of two parts; a driveshaft, with two constant velocity joints, and a plain intermediate shaft. The driveshaft's inboard joint fits over splines on the intermediate shaft's outboard end, the intermediate shaft being supported at this point by a bearing which is secured in a bracket bolted to the rear of the engine's cylinder block. Refer to Chapter 12, Section 10, for details.*

2 Routine maintenance

1 At the intervals specified in the *'Routine maintenance'* Section at the beginning of this manual, examine the driveshaft joint rubber gaiters for damage or leaks. Damaged or leaking gaiters should be renewed without delay, to avoid damage to the joint through dirt or water ingress.

3 Driveshaft – removal and refitting

Note: *The following components must be renewed when refitting the driveshaft: hub nut, washer and split pin, driveshaft retaining snap-ring, and lower arm-to-suspension strut balljoint nut locking pin. A balljoint separator tool will be required for this operation. Refer to the note at the end of Section 1 before proceeding.*

1 Where applicable, remove the wheel trim from the relevant front roadwheel, then loosen the roadwheel bolts. Apply the handbrake, jack up the front of the vehicle, and support on axle stands positioned under the body side members. Remove the roadwheel.

2 Extract the split pin from the castellated hub nut on the end of the driveshaft

3 The hub nut must now be loosened. The nut is extremely tight, and a suitable extension bar will be required to loosen it. To prevent the driveshaft from turning, insert two roadwheel bolts, and insert a metal bar between them to counterhold the hub (see photos 3.17A and 3.17B, which show the nut being tightened). Remove the hub nut and washer from the driveshaft (photo).

4 Extract the locking pin, then unscrew the castellated nut from the lower arm-to-suspension strut balljoint (photos).

5 Using a balljoint separator tool, disconnect the lower arm-to-suspension strut balljoint (photo).

6 A suitable tool will now be required to release the inner end of the driveshaft from the differential or, as applicable, the intermediate shaft. To release the right-hand driveshaft, a flat steel bar with a good chamfer on one end can be used. The left-hand driveshaft is more difficult to release, and a suitable square or rectangular-section bar will be required (photo).

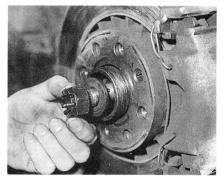

3.3 Removing the hub nut and washer from the driveshaft

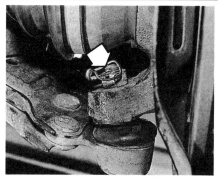

3.4A Extract the locking pin (arrowed) ...

3.4B ... then remove the balljoint castellated nut

3.5 Using a balljoint separator tool to disconnect the balljoint

3.6 Using a square-section bar to release the left-hand driveshaft – 2.0 litre model

3.7 Withdrawing the left-hand driveshaft from the differential ...

7   Lever between the driveshaft and the differential and the differential housing to release the driveshaft snap-ring from the differential. If necessary, use the bar as a drift to drive out the left-hand driveshaft. Have a suitable container available, to catch the oil which will be released as the driveshaft is withdrawn from the differential. Support the driveshaft, and do not allow it to hang under its own weight (photo).

8   Plug the opening in the differential, to prevent further oil loss and dirt ingress.

9   Withdraw the outer end of the driveshaft from the hub, and remove the driveshaft from the vehicle (photo). It should be possible to pull the driveshaft from the hub by hand, but if necessary tap the end of the shaft with a soft-faced mallet to release it. **Do not** *use heavy blows, as damage to the driveshaft joints may result.*

10   **Do not** *allow the vehicle to rest on its wheels with one or both driveshafts removed, as damage to the wheel bearings(s) may result.* If moving the vehicle is unavoidable, temporarily insert the outer end of the driveshaft(s) in the hub(s) and tighten the hub nut(s): in this case, the inner end(s) of the driveshaft(s) must be supported, for example by suspending with string from the vehicle underbody. **Do not** *allow the driveshaft to hang down under its own weight.*

11   Certain models have a two-piece vibration damper fitted to the right-hand driveshaft (photo). If the damper is removed for any reason, it is important to refit it so that the distance between the inner end of the outer joint gaiter and the outer face of the damper is as shown in Fig. 7.1.

12   Before refitting a driveshaft, make sure that the contact faces of the shaft and wheel bearing are absolutely clean – see Fig. 7.2.

13   Commence refitting by applying a little molybdenum disulphide grease to the driveshaft splines, then insert the outer end of the shaft into the hub. Fit a new washer, and screw on a new hub nut finger tight.

14   Fit a new snap-ring to the inboard end of the driveshaft, then remove the plug from the opening in the differential, and push the driveshaft into the differential as far as possible (photo).

15   Place a screwdriver or similar tool on the weld bead of the inner driveshaft joint, **not** the metal cover, and drive the shaft into the differential (or over the intermediate shaft) until the retaining snap-ring engages positively. Pull on the **outer** circumference of the joint to check the engagement.

16   Reconnect the lower arm-to-suspension strut balljoint, then fit the castellated nut, and tighten to the specified torque. Secure the nut with a new locking pin.

17   Tighten the new hub nut to the specified torque, in the stages given in the Specifications. Prevent the driveshaft from turning, as

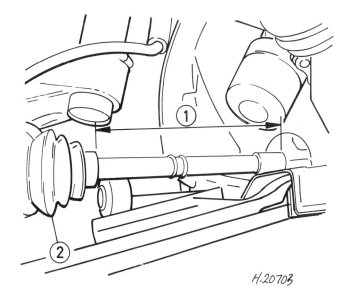

Fig. 7.1 Driveshaft damper weight distance from outer joint gaiter (2) (Sec 3)

1 = 268.0 to 270.0 mm (10.5 to 10.6 in)

3.9 ... and the hub

3.11 Vibration damper fitted to right-hand driveshaft – 2.0 litre model

3.14 Fit a new snap-ring (arrowed) to the driveshaft

3.17A Tighten the hub nut to the specified torque ...

3.17B ... then through the specified angle (see Specifications)

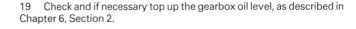

during removal (photos). If the holes for the split pin do not line up with any of the slots in the nut, loosen (**do not** tighten) the nut, until the holes line up with the nearest slots to enable the split pin to be fitted. Use a new split pin, bending over the ends of the pin to secure it.

18   Refit the roadwheel, then lower the vehicle to the ground, and finally tighten the roadwheel bolts. Refit the wheel trim, where applicable.

19   Check and if necessary top up the gearbox oil level, as described in Chapter 6, Section 2.

4   Driveshaft joint – renewal

Note: *Check to ensure that a new securing circlip is supplied when ordering a new driveshaft joint.*

1   A worn driveshaft joint must be renewed, as it cannot be over-hauled. If driveshaft joint wear is apparent on a vehicle in which the driveshaft has covered in excess of 48 000 miles (80 000 km), the manufacturers recommend that the complete driveshaft is renewed.
2   With the driveshaft removed, as described in Section 3, release the metal securing band and slide the rubber gaiter from the worn joint.
3   Using circlip pliers, expand the cirlip which secures the joint to the driveshaft – see Fig. 7.3.

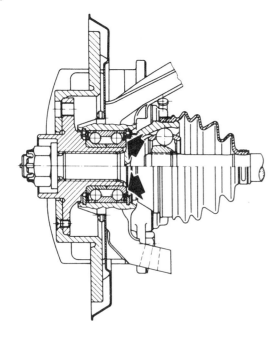

Fig. 7.2 Sectional view of front hub assembly (Sec 3)

Clean the contact faces (arrowed) of the driveshaft and wheel bearing

Fig. 7.3 Driveshaft joint retaining circlip (arrowed) (Sec 4)

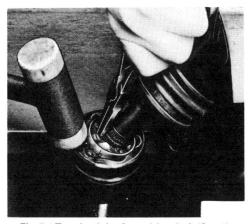

Fig. 7.4 Tapping joint from driveshaft (Sec 4)

4   Using a soft-faced mallet, tap the joint from the driveshaft – Fig. 7.4.
5   Ensure that a new circlip is fitted to the new joint, then tap the new joint onto the driveshaft until the circlip engages in its groove.
6   Pack the joint with the specified type of grease.
7   Refit the rubber gaiter to the new joint with reference to Section 5.
8   Refit the driveshaft to the vehicle, as described in Section 3.

5   Driveshaft joint gaiter – renewal

1   With the driveshaft removed as described in Section 3, remove the relevant joint as described in Section 4. Note that if both gaiters on a driveshaft are to be renewed, it is only necessary to remove one joint.
2   Release the remaining securing band and slide the gaiter from the driveshaft.
3   Clean the old grease from the joint, then repack the joint with the specified type of fresh grease. If excessively worn or damaged, the driveshaft joint should be renewed, with reference to Section 4 if necessary.
4   Slide the new gaiter onto the driveshaft so that the smaller diameter opening is located in the groove in the driveshaft.
5   Refit the joint, using a new securing circlip. Tap the joint onto the driveshaft until the circlip engages in its groove.
6   Slide the gaiter over the joint, then squeeze the gaiter to expel as much air as possible.
7   Secure the gaiter using new securing bands. To fit a securing band, wrap it around the gaiter, and while pulling on the band as tight as possible, engage the lug on the end of the band with one of the slots. Use a screwdriver if necessary to push the band as tight as possible before engaging the lug and slot. Finally tighten the band by compressing the raised square portion of the band with pliers.

6   Fault diagnosis – driveshafts

Symptom	Reason(s)
Knocking noise when accelerating with steering on lock	Worn outer constant velocity joint
Vibration	Worn constant velocity joint Damaged or distorted driveshaft Damaged or missing vibration damper (where applicable) Out-of-balance roadwheel
Knocking noise when taking up drive, or on overrun	Worn constant velocity joint Worn splines on driveshaft, hub, or differential side gears Loose hub nut Loose roadwheel bolts Worn suspension components (see Chapter 9)

Note: *This Section is not intended as an exhaustive guide to fault diagnosis, but summarises the more common faults which may be encountered during a vehicle's life. Consult a dealer for more detailed advice*

Chapter 8 Braking system

For modifications, and information applicable to later models, see Supplement at end of manual

Contents

Specifications

System type
1.4, 1.6 and 1.8 litre models:

Conventional braking system .... Front discs and rear drums, with vacuum servo assistance, dual hydraulic circuit split diagonally, pressure-proportioning valves in rear hydraulic circuit. Cable-operated handbrake on rear wheels

ABS .... Front and rear discs, with vacuum servo assistance, operated via hydraulic modulator, dual hydraulic circuit split front/rear, pressure-proportioning valves in rear hydraulic circuit. Cable-operated handbrake on rear wheels

2.0 litre models:

Conventional braking system .... Front and rear discs, with vacuum servo assistance, dual hydraulic circuit split diagonally, pressure-proportioning valves in rear hydraulic circuit. Cable-operated handbrake on rear wheels

ABS .... As for 1.4, 1.6 and 1.8 litre models with ABS

Front discs
Type:

1.4, 1.6 and 1.8 litre models .... Solid

2.0 litre models... Ventilated

Diameter:

1.4, 1.6 and 1.8 litre models .... 236.0 mm (9.3 in)

2.0 litre models... 256.0 mm (10.1 in)

Maximum disc run-out .... 0.1 mm (0.004 in)

Minimum pad friction material thickness (including backing plate).......... 7.0 mm (0.28 in)

Minimum disc thickness after machining*:

1.4, 1.6 and 1.8 litre models .... 10.7 mm (0.42 in)

2.0 litre models... 22.0 mm (0.87 in)

When this dimension is reached, only one further new set of brake pads is permissible, then renew the discs

Rear discs
Type... Solid
Diameter:
    All models except GSi 2000.. 260.0 mm (10.2 in)
    GSi 2000 models.. 270.0 mm (10.6 in)
Maximum disc run-out.. 0.1 mm (0.004 in)
Minimum pad friction material thickness (including backing plate).......... 7.0 mm (0.28 in)
Minimum disc thickness after machining*........................ 8.0 mm (0.32 in)
Minimum handbrake shoe friction material thickness (lining only)........... 1.0 mm (0.04 in)

*When this dimension is reached, only one further new set of disc pads is permissible, then renew the discs

Rear drums
Internal diameter... 200.0 mm (7.9 in)
Minimum shoe friction material thickness..................... 0.5 mm (0.02 in) above rivet heads

Brake fluid type/specification...................................
Hydraulic fluid to FMVSS 571 DOT 4, or SAE J1703 (Duckhams Universal Brake and Clutch Fluid)

Torque wrench settings

	Nm	lbf ft
Caliper and wheel cylinder bleed screws	9	7
Front brake disc securing screw	4	3
Rear brake disc securing screw	8	6
Rear drum securing screw	4	3
Rear caliper mounting bolts	80	59
Front caliper guide bolts (2.0 litre models)	30	22
Front caliper mounting bolts (1.4, 1.6 and 1.8 litre models)	95	70
Front caliper-to-mounting bracket bolts (2.0 litre models)	30	22
Front caliper bracket-to-hub carrier bolts (all models)	95	70
Master cylinder mounting nuts	22	16
Master cylinder stop screw (ATE type)	6	4
Pressure proportioning valve to master cylinder:		
ATE type	12	9
GMF type	40	30
Vacuum servo-to-support bracket nuts	20	15
Vacuum servo support bracket-to-bulkhead bolts	22	16
Handbrake lever securing bolts	20	15
Brake fluid line union nuts	16	12
Front brake fluid hose-to-caliper union bolt	40	30
Rear brake backplate/stub axle spring bolts (all models except GSi 2000):		
Stage 1	50	37
Stage 2	Angle-tighten a further 30°	Angle-tighten a further 30°
Stage 3	Angle-tighten a further 15°	Angle-tighten a further 15°
Rear wheel cylinder mounting bolts	9	7
ABS hydraulic modulator mounting bolts	8	6
ABS wheel sensor mounting bolts	8	6

1 General description

The footbrake operates on all four wheels. Solid or ventilated disc brakes are fitted at the front, and self-adjusting drum or solid disc brakes are fitted at the rear, depending on model. Actuation is hydraulic, with vacuum servo assistance. The handbrake is cable-operated, and acts on the rear wheels only.

The hydraulic system is split into two circuits. On non-ABS models, the system is split diagonally, and on ABS models, the system is split front and rear. In the event of a hydraulic fluid leak in one circuit, the remaining circuit will still function, so that some braking capability remains.

The hydraulic fluid supply to the rear brakes is regulated so that the front brakes always lock first under heavy braking. The fluid pressure to the rear brakes is controlled by two valves, one for each brake, which are either screwed into the master cylinder, or mounted on the rear under-body of the vehicle, depending on model.

The brake servo is of the direct-acting type, fitted between the pedal and the master cylinder. The servo is powered by vacuum developed in the inlet manifold. Should the servo fail, the brakes will still operate, but increased pedal pressure will be required.

ABS (Anti-lock Braking System) is available as an option for all models. The system comprises an electronic control unit, roadwheel sensors, hydraulic modulator, and the necessary valves and relays. Disc brakes are fitted to all four wheels. The purpose of the system is to prevent wheel(s) locking during heavy brake applications. This is achieved by automatic release of the brake on the locked wheel, followed by reapplication of the brake. This procedure is carried out several times a second by the hydraulic modulator. The modulator is controlled by the electronic control unit, which itself receives signals from the wheel sensors, which monitor the locked or unlocked state of the wheels. The two front brakes are modulated separately, but the two rear brakes are modulated together. The ABS unit is fitted between the brake master cylinder and the brakes, the vacuum servo and master cylinder being of similar type for both non-ABS and ABS models.

Should the ABS develop a fault, it is recommended that a complete test is carried out by a Vauxhall dealer, who will have the necessary specialist diagnostic equipment

2 Routine maintenance

1   At the intervals specified in the 'Routine maintenance' Section at the beginning of this manual, carry out the following tasks.
2   Check the brake fluid level in the reservoir, and top up if necessary.

2.2 Topping-up the brake fluid level – 2.0 litre model

4.5 Removing the dust cap from a rear caliper bleed screw – 2.0 litre model

The reservoir is translucent, so the level can be viewed without removing the filler cap. A slow fall in fluid level as the disc pads wear is normal, and provided the level stays above the 'MIN' mark, there is no need to top up to compensate for this. If topping-up is necessary, use only fresh fluid of the specified type (photo). A regular need for topping-up indicates a leak, which must be located and rectified without delay.
3   Inspect the disc pads, and where applicable, the rear brake shoes, for wear, and renew if necessary as described in Sections 5, 6 and 7, as applicable.
4   Bleed the brake hydraulic system, and renew the brake fluid as described in Section 4.
5   Inspect the handbrake linkage and cables, and lubricate and adjust as necessary.
6   Inspect all hydraulic fluid pipes and hoses for damage or leaks, and rectify as necessary. Pay particular attention to the protective anti-corrosion coating on the metal pipes.

---

3   Anti-lock braking system (ABS) – precautions

1   If the ABS develops a fault, the complete system should be tested by a Vauxhall dealer, who will have the necessary specialist equipment to make a quick and accurate diagnosis of the problem. Due to the special equipment required, it is not practical for the DIY mechanic to carry out the test procedure.
2   To prevent possible damage to the electronic control unit, always disconnect the control unit wiring plug before carrying out electrical welding work.
3   It is recommended that the control unit is removed if the vehicle is being subjected to high temperatures, as may be encountered, for instance, during certain paint-drying processes.
4   If using steam cleaning equipment, do not aim the water/steam jet directly at the control unit.
5   Do not disconnect the control unit wiring plug with the ignition switched on.
6   Do not use a battery booster to start the engine.
7   After working on the ABS components, ensure that all wiring plugs are correctly reconnected, and have the complete system tested by a Vauxhall dealer having the dedicated ABS test equipment at the earliest opportunity.

---

4   Brake hydraulic system – bleeding

Note: *If brake fluid is spilt on the paintwork, the affected area must be washed down with cold water immediately – brake fluid is an effective paint stripper!*

1   If any of the hydraulic components in the braking system have been removed or disconnected, or if the fluid level in the reservoir has been allowed to fall appreciably, it is inevitable that air will have been introduced into the system. The removal of all this air from the hydraulic system is essential if the brakes are to function correctly, and the process of removing it is known as bleeding.
2   Where an operation has only affected one circuit of the hydraulic system (the system is split diagonally on non-ABS models, and front and rear on ABS models), then it will only be necessary to bleed the relevant circuit. If the master cylinder has been disconnected and reconnected, or the fluid level has been allowed to fall appreciably, then the complete system must be bled.
3   One of three methods can be used to bleed the system, although Vauxhall recommend the use of a pressure bleeding kit.

Bleeding – two-man method
4   Gather together a clean jar, and a length of rubber or plastic bleed tubing which will fit the bleed screws tightly. The help of an assistant will be required.
5   Remove the dust cap and clean around the bleed screw on the relevant caliper of wheel cylinder (photo), then attach the bleed tube to the screw. If the complete system is being bled, start at the front of the vehicle. When bleeding the complete system on models with ABS, the front brakes **must** be bled before the rears.
6   Check that the fluid reservoir is topped up, and then destroy the vacuum in the brake servo by giving several applications of the brake pedal.
7   Immerse the open end of the bleed tube in the jar, which should contain two or three inches of hydraulic fluid. The jar should be positioned about 300 mm (12.0 in) above the bleed screw, to prevent any possibility of air entering the system down the threads of the bleed screw when it is slackened.
8   Open the bleed screw half a turn, and have the assistant depress the brake pedal slowly to the floor. With the brake pedal still depressed, retighten the bleed screw, and then have the assistant quickly release the pedal. Repeat the procedure.
9   Observe the submerged end of the tube in the jar. When air bubbles cease to appear, tighten the bleed screw when the pedal is being held fully down by the assistant.
10   Top up the fluid reservoir. It must be kept topped up throughout the bleeding operations. If the connecting holes to the master cylinder are exposed at any time due to low fluid level, the air will be drawn into the system, and work will have to start all over again.
11   Assuming that the complete system is being bled, the procedure should be repeated on the diagonally-opposite rear brake, and then on the front and rear brakes of the other circuit on non-ABS models, or on the remaining front brake and then on the rear brakes on ABS models.
12   On completion, remove the bleed tube, and discard the fluid which has been bled from the system, unless it is required to make up the level in the bleed jar. Never re-use old fluid.

5.6 Front disc pad anti-rattle springs (arrowed) – 1.4, 1.6 and 1.8 litre models

5.7 Removing an anti-rattle spring – 1.4, 1.6 and 1.8 litre models

5.8 Withdrawing the outboard disc pad – 1.4, 1.6 and 1.8 litre models

13   On completion of bleeding, top up the fluid level in the reservoir. Check the action of the brake pedal, which should be firm, and free from any 'sponginess' which would indicate that air is still present in the system.

Bleeding – with one-way valve

14   There are a number of one-man brake bleeding kits currently available from motor accessory shops. It is recommended that one of these kits should be used whenever possible, as they greatly simplify the bleeding operations, and also reduce the risk of expelled air or fluid being drawn back into the system.
15   Proceed as described in paragraphs 5 and 6.
16   Open the bleed screw half a turn, then depress the brake pedal to the floor, and slowly release it. The one-way valve in the bleeder device will prevent expelled air from returning to the system at the completion of each stroke. Repeat the operation until clear hydraulic fluid, free from air bubbles, can be seen coming through the tube. Tighten the bleed screw.
17   Proceed as described in paragraphs 11 to 13 inclusive.

Bleeding – with pressure bleeding kit

18   These too are available from motor accessory shops, and are usually operated by air pressure from the spare tyre.
19   By connecting a pressurised container to the master cylinder fluid reservoir, bleeding is then carried out by simply opening each bleed screw in turn and allowing the fluid to run out, rather like turning on a tap, until no air bubbles are visible in the fluid being expelled.
20   Using this method, the large reserve of fluid provides a safeguard against air being drawn into the master cylinder during the bleeding operations.
21   This method of bleeding is recommended by Vauxhall.
22   Begin bleeding with reference to paragraphs 5 and 6, and proceed as described in paragraphs 11 to 13 inclusive.

---

5   Disc pads – inspection and renewal

Note: *When working on the brake components, take care not to disperse brake dust into the air, or to inhale it, since it may contain asbestos, which is injurious to health.*

Front disc pads

1   Where applicable, remove the wheel trims, then loosen the front roadwheel bolts and apply the handbrake. Jack up the front of the vehicle, and support on axle stands positioned under the body side members.
2   Remove the roadwheels. Turn the steering to full right-hand lock, and check the wear of the friction material on the right-hand brake pads. Check that the thickness of the friction material (including the backing plate) is not less than the minimum given in the Specifications.
3   Turn the steering to full left-hand lock, and check the left-hand brake pads in the same way.
4   If any brake pad is worn below the specified minimum thickness, renew **all** the front pads as a set.

5   If the pads require renewal, proceed as follows according to model.

1.4, 1.6 and 1.8 litre models
6   Note how the anti-rattle springs are located (photo), then drive the upper and lower pad retaining pins out from the **inboard** side of the caliper, using a suitable pin punch.
7   Remove the anti-rattle springs (photo).
8   Push the pads away from the disc slightly, then using a pair of pliers, withdraw the outboard pad (photo).
9   Withdraw the inboard pad, and the shim which fits between the pad and the caliper piston (photo).
10   Brush the dust and dirt from the caliper, but take care not to inhale it. Carefully remove any rust from the edge of the brake disc.
11   In order to accommodate the new thicker pads, the caliper piston must be depressed fully into its cylinder bore, using a flat bar of metal such as a tyre lever. The action of depressing the piston will cause some fluid level in the reservoir to rise, so to avoid spillage, syphon out some fluid using an old hydrometer or a teat pipette. Refer to the note at the beginning of Section 4. Do not lever between the piston and disc to depress the piston.
12   Check that the cutaway recesses in the piston are positioned vertically. If necessary, carefully turn the piston to its correct position.
13   Apply a little brake grease to the top and bottom edges of the backplates on the new brake pads.
14   Locate the new pads in the caliper, ensuring that the shim is in place between the inboard pad and the piston. Ensure that the friction material faces the disc, and check that the pads are free to move slightly.
15   Locate the anti-rattle springs on the pads, then insert the pad retaining pins from the **outboard** side of the caliper, while depressing the springs. Tap the pins firmly into the caliper (photo).
16   Repeat the operations on the remaining side of the vehicle.
17   Refit the roadwheels and lower the vehicle to the ground. Do not fully tighten the roadwheel bolts until the vehicle is resting on its wheels.
18   Apply the footbrake hard several times to position the pads against the discs.
19   Check and if necessary top up the brake fluid level.
20   New brake pads should be carefully bedded in and, where possible, heavy braking should be avoided during the first 100 miles (160 km) or so after fitting new pads.

2.0 litre models
21   Where applicable, pull the pad wear sensor from the inboard pad, and disconnect the wiring at the connector under the wheel arch, next to the suspension strut (photo). Note the wire routing.
22   Using a screwdriver, prise the pad retaining clip from the outboard edge of the caliper, noting how it is located (photo).
23   Prise out the two guide bolt dust caps from the inboard edge of the caliper, then using a suitable Allen key or hexagon bit, unscrew the guide bolts, and lift the caliper and inboard pad from the bracket. Recover the outboard brake pad (photos). Suspend the caliper body with wire or string, to avoid straining the brake fluid hose.
24   Pull the inboard pad from the caliper piston, noting that it is retained by a clip attached to the pad backing plate (photo).
25   Proceed as described in paragraphs 10 to 12 inclusive (photo).
26   Apply a little brake grease to the contact surfaces of the new brake pads.

5.9 Withdrawing the inboard disc pad and shim – 1.4, 1.6 and 1.8 litre models

5.15 Fitting a disc pad retaining pin – 1.4, 1.6 and 1.8 litre models

5.21 Withdrawing the pad wear sensor from the inboard pad – GSi 2000 model

5.22 Prising out the disc pad retaining clip – 2.0 litre model

5.23A Removing a caliper guide bolt dust cap – 2.0 litre model

5.23B Withdrawing the caliper and inboard pad, and the outboard pad – 2.0 litre model

5.24 Removing the inboard pad from the caliper piston – 2.0 litre model

5.25 Caliper piston cutaway recess (arrowed) correctly positioned – 2.0 litre model

5.29 Tightening a caliper guide bolt – 2.0 litre model

27   Fit the new inboard pad to the caliper piston, ensuring that the piston is correctly located.
28   Locate the outboard pad on the caliper bracket, with the friction material facing the disc.
29   Refit the caliper to the bracket, and tighten the guide bolts to the specified torque (photo).
30   Refit the guide bolt dust caps.
31   Refit the pad retaining clip, locating it as noted before removal.
32   Where applicable, fit a new pad wear sensor to the inboard pad, and connect the wiring at the connector under the wheel arch. Route the wiring as noted during removal.
33   Repeat the operations on the remaining side of the vehicle.
34   Proceed as described in paragraphs 17 to 20 inclusive.

Rear disc pads
35   Where applicable, remove the wheel trims, then loosen the rear roadwheel bolts and chock the front wheels. Jack up the rear of the

vehicle, and support on axle stands positioned under the body side members. Remove the roadwheels.
36   Check the wear of the friction material on the brake pads, on both sides of the vehicle. Check that the thickness of the friction material (including the backing plate) is not less than the minimum given in the Specifications.
37   If any brake pad is worn below the specified minimum thickness, renew **all** the rear pads as a set as follows.
38   Note how the anti-rattle spring is located, then drive out the upper and lower pad retaining pins from the outside of the caliper using a suitable pin punch (photo).
39   Remove the anti-rattle spring (photo).
40   Push the pads away from the disc slightly, then using a pair of pliers, withdraw the outboard pad and anti-squeal shim which fits between the pad and the caliper body.
41   Withdraw the inboard pad and anti-squeal shim.
42   Proceed as described in paragraphs 10 and 11.

5.38 Driving out a rear disc pad retaining pin

5.39 Removing a rear disc pad retaining pin anti-rattle spring

5.43 Checking a rear caliper piston cut away recess angle with a card template

43   Check that the cutaway recesses in the pistons are positioned downwards, at approximately 23° to the horizontal. A template made of card may be used to check the setting (photo). If necessary, carefully turn the pistons to their correct positions.

44   Apply a little brake grease to the top and bottom edges of the backplates on the new brake pads.

45   Locate the new pads and the anti-squeal shims in the caliper. Ensure that the friction material faces the disc, and check that the pads are free to move slightly.

46   Locate the anti-rattle spring on the pads, then insert the pad retaining pins from the inside edge of the caliper, while depressing the spring. Tap the pins firmly into the caliper.

47   Repeat the operations on the remaining side of the vehicle.

48   Proceed as described in paragraphs 17 to 20 inclusive.

6   Rear brake shoes (drum brakes) – inspection and renewal

Note: *When working on the brake components, take care not to disperse brake dust into the air, or to inhale it, since it may contain asbestos, which is injurious to health*

1   It is recommended that the brake shoes are inspected when necessary by removing the drums. This will enable a proper inspection of the linings to be made, and additionally, the wheel cylinders can be inspected for leaks. If preferred, however, a provisional inspection of the state of wear of the rear shoe linings can be made by removing the plugs from the inspection holes in the brake backplates.

2   Use a torch or inspection lamp, and if necessary a mirror, to check that the friction material has not worn down to less than the specified minimum.

3   If any one of the shoes has worn below the specified limit, **all four** rear brake shoes must be renewed as a set, as follows.

4   Where applicable, remove the wheel trims, then loosen the rear roadwheel bolts and chock the front wheels. Jack up the rear of the vehicle, and support on axle stands positioned under the body side members . Remove the roadwheels.

5   Fully release the handbrake.

6   Extract the drum securing screw and remove the drum (photo). If the drum is tight, remove the plug from the inspection hole in the brake backplate, and push the handbrake operating lever towards the brake shoe to move the shoes away from the drum. If necessary, slacken the handbrake cable adjuster.

7   Note the location and orientation of all components before dismantling, as an aid to reassembly.

8   Clean the dust and dirt from the drum and shoes, but take care not to inhale it.

9   Remove the shoe hold-down pins, springs and cups by depressing the cups and turning them through 90° using a pair of pliers (photos). Note that the hold-down pins are removed through the rear of the brake backplate.

10   Disconnect the handbrake cable from the operating lever.

11   The upper and lower return springs may now be unhooked and the shoes removed separately, or the assembly of shoes, adjuster strut and springs may be removed together. The second course of action is

Fig. 8.1 Pushing the handbrake operating lever to move the brake shoes away from the drum (Sec 6)

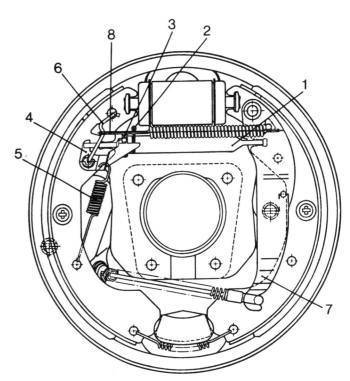
Fig. 8.2 Rear drum brake components (Sec 6)

1 Adjuster strut	5 Adjuster lever return
2 Thermoclip	spring
3 Adjuster wheel	6 Adjuster lever bracket
4 Adjuster lever	7 Handbrake operating lever
	8 Upper shoe return spring

6.6 Extracting a brake drum securing screw

6.9A Release the shoe hold-down cup ...

6.9B ... then withdraw the cup and spring

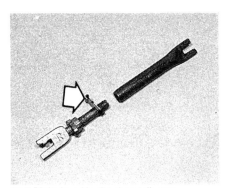

6.19 Right-hand brake shoe adjuster components – thermoclip arrowed

6.22A Right-hand adjuster strut correctly fitted to shoes

6.22B Fitting the upper return spring to the shoes

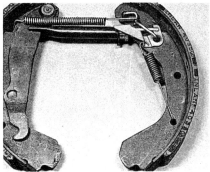

6.22C Adjuster lever spring fitted to leading shoe

6.24 Rear brake components correctly assembled. Hub removed for clarity

particularly easy if the hub is removed – see Chapter 9. Take care not to damage the wheel cylinder rubber boots. Before removing the return springs, note the position and orientation of the springs and adjuster strut.

12   If the shoes are to be removed for some time, fit a stout rubber band or a spring clip to the wheel cylinder, to prevent the pistons from being pushed out of their bores. In any event, **do not** press the brake pedal while the drum is removed.

13   Clean the dust and dirt from the brake backplate, but take care not to inhale it.

14   Apply a small amount of brake grease to the shoe rubbing areas on the backplate.

15   Investigate and rectify any source of contamination of the linings (wheel cylinder or hub bearing oil seal leaking).

16   Although linings are available separately (without shoes), renewal of the shoes complete with linings is to be preferred, unless the reader has the necessary skills and equipment to fit new linings to the old shoes.

17   If not already done, dismantle the shoes, strut and springs. Note the position and orientation of the components.

18   If both brake assemblies are dismantled at the same time, take care not to mix up the components. Note that the left-hand and right-hand adjuster components are marked; the threaded rod is marked 'L' or 'R', and the other 'handed' components are colour-coded black for the left-hand side, and silver for the right-hand side.

19   Dismantle and clean the adjuster strut. Apply a smear of silicone-based grease to the adjuster threads. If new brake linings or shoes are to be fitted, the thermoclip on the adjuster strut must also be renewed (photo).

20   Examine the return springs. If they are distorted, or if they have seen extensive service, renewal is advisable. Weak springs may cause the brakes to bind.

21   If a new handbrake operating lever was not supplied with the new shoes (where applicable), transfer the lever from the old shoes. The lever may be secured with a pin and circlip, or by a rivet, which will have to be drilled out.

7.16A Fitting the lower shoe return spring – all models except GSi 2000

7.16B Handbrake shoe components correctly assembled – all models except GSi 2000

7.26 Handbrake shoe adjuster and upper shoe return spring correctly fitted – GSi 2000 models

22 If the components are to be refitted as an assembly, assemble the new shoes, springs and adjuster components. Expand the adjuster strut to ease fitting (photos).

23 Offer the shoes to the brake backplate. Be careful not to damage the wheel cylinder boots, or to displace the pistons. Remember to remove the rubber band or spring clip from the wheel cylinder, where applicable.

24 When the shoes are in position, insert the hold-down pins and secure them with the springs and cups (photo).

25 Reconnect the handbrake cable, then refit the hub, and adjust the bearing if the hub was removed.

26 If fitting the shoes and springs together as an assembly is found too difficult, it is possible to fit the shoes and secure them with the hold-down pins, then to introduce the adjuster strut and fit the return springs and adjuster.

27 Back off the adjuster wheel to reduce the length of the strut, until the brake drum will pass over the shoes.

28 Make sure that the handbrake operating lever is correctly positioned, with the pin on the edge of the shoe web, not riding on top of it, then refit and secure the brake drum.

29 Repeat the operations on the remaining side of the vehicle.

30 Adjust the brakes by operating the footbrake at least fifteen times. A clicking noise will be heard at the drums, as the automatic adjusters operate. When the clicking stops, adjustment is complete.

31 Check the handbrake cable adjustment, as described in Section 26.

32 Refit the roadwheels, and lower the vehicle to the ground. Do not fully tighten the roadwheel bolts until the vehicle is resting on its wheels.

33 New brake linings should be carefully bedded-in and, where possible, heavy braking should be avoided during the first 100 miles (160 km) or so after fitting new linings.

7 Handbrake shoes (rear disc brakes) – inspection and renewal

Note: *When working on the brake components, take care not to disperse brake dust into the air, or to inhale it, since it may contain asbestos which is injurious to health.*

1 Although 2.0 litre models are fitted with rear disc brakes, the handbrake operates independently of the footbrake, using brake shoes on the inside of the disc in a similar manner to rear drum brake models.

2 To inspect the handbrake shoes on all except GSi 2000 models, it is necessary to remove the hub/disc, as described in Chapter 9, Section 13.

3 To inspect the handbrake shoes on GSi 2000 models it will be necessary to remove the brake disc, as described in Section 10.

4 With the hub/disc or the disc (as applicable) removed, check that the friction material has not worn down to less than the specified minimum.

5 If any one of the shoes has worn below the specified limit, all four handbrake shoes must be renewed as a set, as follows.

All models except GSi 2000

6 Clean the dust and dirt from the various components, but take care not to inhale it.

7 Disconnect the handbrake cable and the return spring from the handbrake operating lever at the brake backplate. If necessary, slacken the handbrake cable adjustment, with reference to Section 26.

8 Remove the shoe hold-down pins, springs and cups by depressing the cups and turning them through 90° using a pair of pliers. Note that the hold-down pins are removed through the rear of the brake backplate.

9 The shoes, adjuster, handbrake operating lever and return springs can now be removed together as an assembly.

10 Note the position and orientation of all components, then unhook the upper and lower return springs from the shoes, and recover the handbrake operating lever and the adjuster.

11 Apply a little brake grease to the threads of the adjuster, then screw it together to its minimum length. Also apply a little brake grease to the shoe rubbing areas on the lockplate.

12 Fit one of the new brake shoes, and secure it to the backplate with the hold-down pin, spring and cup.

13 Fit the handbrake operating lever in position.

14 Fit the remaining brake shoe, and secure with the hold-down pin, spring and cup.

15 Hook the upper return spring onto the shoes.

16 Fit the adjuster between the lower ends of the shoes, as noted before dismantling, then fit the lower return spring (photos).

17 Reconnect the handbrake cable and the return spring to the handbrake operating lever.

18 Refit the hub/disc, and adjust the wheel bearing play, as described in Chapter 9, Sections 13 and 11 respectively, but do not refit the roadwheel at this stage.

19 Repeat the operations on the remaining side of the vehicle.

20 Check the handbrake cable adjustment, as described in Section 26.

21 Refit the roadwheels and lower the vehicle to the ground. Do not fully tighten the roadwheel bolts until the vehicle is resting on its wheels.

GSi 2000 models

22 Proceed as described in paragraphs 6 and 7.

23 Remove the shoe hold-down pins, springs and cups by turning the cups through 90° using a suitable screwdriver. Note that the hold-down pins are removed through the rear of the brake backplate.

24 Proceed as described in paragraphs 10 to 14 inclusive.

25 Hook the lower return spring onto the shoes.

26 Fit the adjuster between the upper ends of the shoes, as noted before dismantling, then fit the upper return spring (photo).

27 Reconnect the handbrake cable and the return spring to the handbrake operating lever.

28 Refit the brake disc as described in Section 10, but do not refit the roadwheel at this stage.

29 Proceed as described in paragraphs 19 to 21 inclusive.

8 Front disc caliper – removal, overhaul and refitting

Note: *Refer to the note at the beginning of Section 4 before proceeding. Before dismantling a caliper, check that suitable replacement parts can be obtained, and retain the old components to compare then with the new ones. New sealing rings must be used on the fluid hose union bolt on refitting.*

8.20A Extract the nylon compression sleeve (arrowed) ...

8.20B ... then withdraw the caliper locating pin rubber – 1.4, 1.6 and 1.8 litre models

8.31 Caliper bracket securing bolts (arrowed) – 2.0 litre model

1.4, 1.6 and 1.8 litre models

1   Where applicable, remove the wheel trims, then loosen the relevant front roadwheel bolts and apply the handbrake. Jack up the front of the vehicle, and support securely on axle stands positioned under the body side members. Remove the roadwheel.

2   Remove the brake disc pads, as described in Section 5.

3   Working under the bonnet, remove the brake fluid reservoir cap, and secure a piece of polythene over the filler beck with a rubber band, or by refitting the cap. This will reduce the loss of fluid during the following procedure.

4   Unscrew the brake fluid hose union bolt from the rear of the caliper, and disconnect the hose. Recover the two sealing rings from the union bolt (one either side of the hose end fitting). Be prepared for fluid spillage, and plug the open ends to prevent dirt ingress and further fluid loss.

5   Prise out the two caliper bracket mounting bolt dust caps from the inboard edge of the caliper bracket, then using a suitable Allen key or hexagon bit, unscrew the mounting bolts, and withdraw the caliper assembly from the vehicle.

6   If desired, the caliper can be overhauled as follows. Otherwise, proceed to paragraph 24 for details of refitting.

7   Brush the dirt and dust from the caliper, but take care not to inhale it.

8   Mount the caliper bracket in a soft-jawed vice, then separate the caliper body from the mounting bracket by pressing the front face of the caliper body downwards and simultaneously sliding the caliper body from the locating pins on the bracket. Recover the guide springs from the bracket, noting their orientation.

9   Using a screwdriver, prise the dust seal retaining clip from the piston dust seal, then carefully prise off the dust seal.

10   Place a thin piece of wood in front of the piston to prevent it from falling out of its bore and sustaining damage, then apply low air pressure – eg from a foot pump – to the hydraulic fluid union hole in the rear of the caliper body, to eject the piston from its bore.

11   Remove the wood and carefully withdraw the piston.

12   Carefully prise the seal from the groove in the caliper piston bore, using a plastic or wooden instrument.

13   Inspect the surfaces of the piston and its bore in the caliper for scoring, or evidence of metal-to-metal contact. If evident, renew the complete caliper assembly.

14   If the piston and bore are in good condition, discard the seals and obtain a repair kit, which will contain all the necessary renewable items.

15   Clean the piston and cylinder bore with brake fluid or methylated spirit – nothing else!

16   Commence reassembly by fitting the seal into the caliper bore.

17   Locate the dust seal in its groove in the piston. Dip the piston in clean brake fluid and insert it squarely into the cylinder. Check that the cutaway recesses in the piston are positioned horizontally. If necessary, carefully turn the piston to its correct position.

18   When the piston has been partially depressed, engage the dust seal with the rim of the caliper bore, and fit the retaining clip.

19   Push the piston further into its bore, but not as far as the stop, ensuring that it does not jam.

20   If desired, the caliper body locating pin rubbers can be renewed. Extract the nylon compression sleeve from within each rubber, then carefully compress the rubber shoulder, and push the rubber through the hole in the caliper body to remove it from the inboard end (photos).

21   Fit the new rubbers using a reversal of the removal procedure.

22   Secure the caliper bracket in a soft-jawed vice, and refit the guide springs in the positions noted before removal.

23   Engage the caliper body with the locating pins on the bracket, then press the caliper body into position until the locating pin rubbers in the caliper body rest against the bracket.

24   Refit the caliper bracket to the hub carrier, and tighten the securing bolts to the specified torque. Refit the dust caps to the bolts.

25   Reconnect the brake fluid hose union, using new sealing rings on the union bolt.

26   Refit the disc pads, as described in Section 5.

27   Remove the polythene from the brake fluid reservoir filler neck, and bleed the relevant brake hydraulic circuit, as described in Section 4.

28   Refit the roadwheel and lower the vehicle to the ground. Do not fully tighten the roadwheel bolts until the vehicle is resting on its wheels.

2.0 litre models

29   Proceed as described in paragraphs 1 to 4 inclusive.

30   Withdraw the caliper body from the vehicle.

31   If desired, the caliper bracket can be removed from the hub carrier by unscrewing the two securing bolts (photo).

32   To overhaul the caliper, proceed as follows. Otherwise, proceed to paragraph 42 for details of refitting.

33   Brush the dirt and dust from the caliper, but take care not to inhale it.

34   Using a screwdriver, carefully prise the dust seal from the end of the piston and the caliper body, and remove it.

35   Proceed as described in paragraphs 10 to 15 inclusive.

36   Commence reassembly by fitting the seal into the caliper bore.

37   Locate the dust seal in its groove in the piston. Dip the piston in clean brake fluid and insert it squarely into the cylinder. Check that the cutaway recesses in the piston are positioned vertically. If necessary, carefully turn the piston to its correct position.

38   When the piston has been partially depressed, engage the dust seal with the rim of the caliper bore.

39   Push the piston further into its bore, but not as far as the stop, ensuring that it does not jam.

40   If desired, the guide bolt sleeves can be renewed. Extract the nylon compression sleeve from within each rubber, then carefully compress the rubber shoulder, and push the rubber through the hole in the caliper body to remove it from the inboard end.

41   Fit the new sleeves using a reversal of the removal procedure.

42   Where applicable, refit the caliper bracket to the hub carrier, and tighten the securing bolts to the specified torque.

43   Proceed as described in paragraphs 25 to 28 inclusive.

9   Rear disc caliper – removal, overhaul and refitting

Note: *Refer to the note at the beginning of Section 4 before proceeding. Before dismantling a caliper, check that suitable replacement parts can be obtained, and retain the old components to compare them with the new ones.*

1   Where applicable, remove the wheel trim, then loosen the relevant rear roadwheel bolts and check the front wheels. Jack up the rear of the

9.5A Withdrawing a rear caliper mounting bolt ...

9.5B ... which also secures the ABS sensor bracket – GSi 2000 model

vehicle, and support on axle stands positioned under the body side members. Remove the roadwheel.

2   Remove the disc pads, as described in Section 5.

3   Working under the bonnet, remove the brake fluid reservoir cap and secure a piece of polythene over the filler neck with a rubber band, or by refitting the cap. This will reduce the loss of fluid during the following procedure.

4   Unscrew the brake fluid pipe union nut from the rear of the caliper, and disconnect the pipe. Take care not to strain the pipe. Be prepared for fluid spillage, and plug the open ends to prevent dirt ingress and further fluid loss.

5   Unscrew the two mounting bolts and withdraw the caliper from the vehicle, noting that on GSi 2000 models, the caliper securing bolts also secure the ABS sensor bracket (photos). Take care not to strain the ABS sensor wiring, where applicable.

6   If desired, the caliper can be overhauled as follows. Otherwise, proceed to paragraph 20 for details of refitting.

7   Brush the dirt and dust from the caliper, but take care not to inhale it.

8   Note that no attempt must be made to separate the two halves of the caliper.

9   Using a screwdriver, prise the dust seal retaining clips from the piston dust seals, then carefully prise off the dust seals.

10   Using a suitable clamp, clamp one of the pistons in its fully retracted position, then apply low air pressure – eg from a foot pump – to the hydraulic fluid union hole in the rear of the caliper body, to eject the remaining piston from its bore. Take care not to drop the piston, which may result in damage.

11   Temporarily close off the bore of the removed piston, using a suitable flat piece of wood or similar improvised tool, then remove the clamp from the remaining piston, and again apply air pressure to the caliper union to eject the piston.

12   Carefully prise the seals from the grooves in the caliper piston bores, using a plastic or wooden instrument.

13   Inspect the surfaces of the pistons and their bores in the caliper for scoring, or evidence of metal-to-metal contact. If evident, renew the complete caliper assembly.

14   If the pistons and bores are in good condition, discard the seals and obtain a repair kit, which will contain all the necessary renewable items. Also obtain a tube of brake cylinder paste.

15   Clean the piston and cylinder bore with brake fluid or methylated spirit – nothing else!

16   Apply a little brake cylinder paste to the pistons, cylinder bores and piston seals.

17   Commence reassembly by fitting the seals to the grooves in the caliper bores.

18   Locate the dust seals in their grooves in the pistons, then insert the pistons carefully into their bores until they enter the seals. It may be necessary to rotate the pistons to prevent them from jamming in the seals.

19   When the pistons have been partially depressed, engage the dust seals with the rims of the caliper bores, and fit the retaining clips.

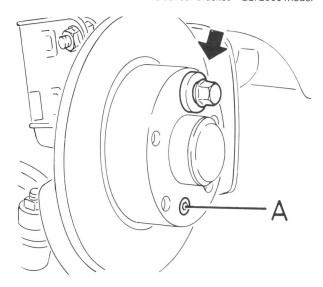

Fig. 8.3 Refit a wheel bolt and spacer (arrowed) opposite the disc securing screw (A) before checking brake disc run-out (Sec 10)

20   Refit the caliper and tighten the securing bolts to the specified torque, ensuring that the ABS sensor bracket is in position, where applicable.

21   Reconnect the brake fluid pipe to the caliper, and tighten the union nut.

22   Refit the disc pads, as described in Section 5.

23   Remove the polythene from the brake fluid reservoir filler neck, and bleed the relevant brake hydraulic circuit, as described in Section 4.

24   Refit the roadwheel and lower the vehicle to the ground. Do not fully tighten the roadwheel bolts until the vehicle is resting on its wheels.

10 Brake disc – inspection, removal and refitting

1   Where applicable, remove the wheel trim, then loosen the relevant roadwheel bolts. If checking a front disc, apply the handbrake, and if checking a rear disc, chock the front wheels, then jack up the relevant end of the vehicle and support on axle stands positioned under the body side members. Remove the roadwheel.

2   Where applicable, check that the brake disc securing screw is tight, then fit a spacer approximately 10.0 mm (0.4 in) thick to one of the roadwheel bolts, and refit and tighten the bolt in the hole opposite the disc securing screw – see Fig. 8.3.

10.12 Removing a disc securing screw – 1.6 litre model

10.18 Withdrawing the rear brake disc – GSi 2000 model

3   Rotate the brake disc, and examine it for deep scoring or grooving. Light scoring is normal, but if excessive, the disc should be removed and either renewed or machined (within the specified limits) by a suitable engineering works.
4   Using a dial gauge, or a flat metal block and feeler gauges, check that the disc run-out does not exceed the figure given in the Specifications. Measure the run-out 10.0 mm (0.4 in) in from the outer edge of the disc.
5   On all except GSi 2000 models, if the rear disc run-out is excessive, check the rear wheel bearing adjustment, as described in Chapter 9, Section 11.
6   If the front disc run-out (all models), or the rear disc run-out (GSi 2000 models), is excessive, remove the disc as described later in this Section, and check that the disc-to-hub surfaces are perfectly clean. Refit the disc and check the run-out again.
7   If the run-out is still excessive, the disc should be renewed.
8   To remove a disc, proceed as follows.

Front disc
9   Where applicable, remove the roadwheel bolt and spacer used when checking the disc.
10   Remove the disc pads, as described in Section 5.
11   On 2.0 litre models, unscrew the two securing bolts and remove the caliper bracket.
12   Remove the securing screw and withdraw the disc from the hub, where applicable tilting it to clear the brake caliper (photo).
13   Refitting is a reversal of removal, but make sure that the mating faces of the disc and hub are perfectly clean, and apply a little locking fluid to the threads of the securing screw. Refit the disc pads, as described in Section 5.

Rear disc – all models except GSi 2000
14   On these models, the disc is integral with the rear hub, and removal and refitting is described in Chapter 9, Section 13.

Rear disc – GSi 2000 models
15   Where applicable, remove the roadwheel bolt and spacer used when checking the disc.
16   Remove the disc pads, as described in Section 5.
17   Remove the brake caliper with reference to Section 9, but leave the hydraulic fluid pipe connected. Move the caliper to one side, and suspend it using wire or string to avoid straining the pipe.
18   Remove the securing screw and withdraw the disc from the hub (photo). If the disc is tight, collapse the handbrake shoes by inserting a screwdriver through the adjuster hole in the disc and turning the adjuster wheel.
19   Refitting is a reversal of removal, but make sure that the mating faces of the disc and hub are perfectly clean, and apply a little locking fluid to the threads of the securing screw. Refit the disc pads, as described in Section 5.

11   Brake drum – removal, inspection and refitting

Note: *When working on the brake components, take care not to disperse brake dust into the air, or to inhale it, since it may contain asbestos, which is injurious to health*

1   Where applicable, remove the wheel trim, then loosen the relevant rear roadwheel bolts and chock the front wheels. Jack up the rear of the vehicle, and support on axle stands positioned under the body side members. Remove the roadwheel.
2   Fully release the handbrake.
3   Extract the drum securing screw and remove the drum. If the drum is tight, remove the plug from the inspection hole in the brake backplate, and push the handbrake operating lever towards the brake shoe to move the shoes away from the drums. If necessary, slacken the handbrake cable adjuster.
4   Brush the dirt and dust from the drum, taking care not to inhale it.
5   Examine the internal friction surface of the drum. If they are deeply scored, or so worn that the drum has become ridged to the width of the shoes, then both drums must be renewed.
6   Regrinding of the friction surface is not recommended, since the internal diameter of the drum will no longer be compatible with the shoe friction material contact diameter.
7   Refit the brake drum and tighten the securing screw. If necessary, back off the adjuster wheel until the drum will pass over the shoes.
8   Adjust the brakes by operating the footbrake a number of times. A clicking noise will be heard at the drum as the automatic adjuster operates. When the clicking stops, adjustment is complete.
9   Refit the roadwheel and lower the vehicle to the ground. Do not fully tighten the roadwheel bolts until the vehicle is resting on its wheels.

12   Rear wheel cylinder (drum brakes) – removal, overhaul and refitting

Note: *Refer to the notes at the beginning of Sections 4 and 11 before proceeding. Before dismantling a wheel cylinder, check that suitable replacement parts can be obtained, and retain the old components to compare them with the new ones*

1   Where applicable, remove the wheel trim, then loosen the relevant rear roadwheel bolts and chock the front wheels. Jack up the rear of the vehicle and support on axle stands positioned under the body side members. Remove the roadwheel.
2   Fully release the handbrake.
3   Extract the drum securing screw and remove the drum. If the drum is tight, remove the plug from the inspection hole in the brake backplate,

12.4 Rear brake wheel cylinder (1). Note orientation of upper shoe return spring (2)

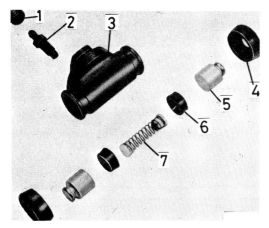

Fig. 8.5 Exploded view of a rear brake wheel cylinder (Sec 12)

1 Dust cap	5 Piston
2 Bleed screw	6 Piston seal
3 Cylinder body	7 Spring
4 Dust seal	

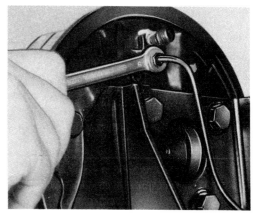

Fig. 8.4 Unscrewing rear wheel cylinder brake fluid pipe union (Sec 12)

spring, but if they are not, tap the end of the cylinder body on a piece of wood, or apply low air pressure – eg from a foot pump – to the hydraulic fluid union hole in the rear of the cylinder body, to eject the pistons from their bores.
12   Inspect the surfaces of the pistons and their bores in the cylinder body for scoring, or evidence of metal-to-metal contact. If evident, renew the complete wheel cylinder assembly.
13   If the pistons and bores are in good condition, discard the seals and obtain a repair kit, which will contain all the necessary renewable items.
14   Lubricate the piston seals with clean brake fluid, and insert them into the cylinder bores with the spring between them, using finger pressure only.
15   Dip the pistons in clean brake fluid, and insert them into the cylinder bores.
16   Fit the dust seals, and check that the pistons can move freely in their bores.
17   Refit the wheel cylinder to the backplate, and tighten the securing bolts.
18   Reconnect the brake fluid pipe to the cylinder, and tighten the union nut.
19   Push the brake shoes against the pistons, then refit the upper return spring as noted before removal.
20   Refit the brake drum and tighten the securing screw. If necessary, back off the adjuster wheel until the drum will pass over the shoes.
21   Remove the polythene from the brake fluid reservoir filler neck, and bleed the relevant brake hydraulic circuit, as described in Section 4.
22   Adjust the brakes by operating the footbrake a number of times. A clicking noise will be heard at the drum as the automatic adjuster operates. When the clicking stops, adjustment is complete.
23   Refit the roadwheel and lower the vehicle to the ground. Do not fully tighten the roadwheel bolts until the vehicle is resting on its wheels.

13   Rear brake backplate – removal and refitting

Models with rear drum brakes
1   Where applicable, remove the wheel trim, then loosen the relevant rear roadwheel bolts and chock the front wheels. Jack up the rear of the vehicle, and support on axle stands positioned under the body side members. Remove the roadwheel.
2   Remove the brake drum with reference to Section 11.
3   Remove the rear hub, as described in Chapter 9, Section 13.
4   Remove the brake shoes, as described in Section 6.
5   Remove the brake wheel cylinder, as described in Section 12.
6   Using a screwdriver, prise out the lockplate which secures the handbrake cable in the backplate.
7   Unscrew the four securing bolts, and withdraw the stub axle and backplate.
8   Refitting is a reversal of removal, bearing in mind the following points.
9   Coat the rear face of the stub axle flange with a little lithium-based grease.

and push the handbrake operating lever towards the brake shoe to move the shoes away from the drum. If necessary, slacken the handbrake cable adjuster.
4   Using a pair of pliers, unhook the upper return spring from the brake shoes, noting its orientation, then push the upper ends of the shoes apart until they are clear of the wheel cylinder (photo).
5   Working under the bonnet, remove the brake fluid reservoir cap and secure a piece of polythene over the filler neck with a rubber band, or by refitting the cap. This will reduce the loss of fluid during the following procedure.
6   Unscrew the brake fluid pipe union nut from the rear of the wheel cylinder, and disconnect the pipe. Take care not to strain the pipe. Be prepared for fluid spillage, and plug the open ends to prevent dirt ingress and further fluid loss.
7   Unscrew the two securing bolts from the rear of the brake backplate, and withdraw the wheel cylinder.
8   If desired, the wheel cylinder can be overhauled as follows. Otherwise, proceed to paragraph 17 for details of refitting.
9   Brush the dirt and dust from the wheel cylinder, but take care not to inhale it.
10   Pull the rubber dust seals from the ends of the cylinder body.
11   The pistons will normally be ejected by the pressure of the coil

10   Tighten the brake backplate/stub axle securing bolts to the specified torque, in the three stages given in the Specifications.
11   Refit the brake wheel cylinder, as described in Section 12.
12   Refit the brake shoes, as described in Section 6.
13   Refit the rear hub, as described in Chapter 9, Section 13.
14   Refit the brake drum with reference to Section 11.
15   Before refitting the roadwheel and lowering the vehicle to the ground, check and if necessary adjust the handbrake, as described in Section 26.

Models with rear disc brakes (except GSi 2000 models)
16   Proceed as described in paragraph 1.
17   Remove the rear hub/disc, as described in Chapter 9, Section 13.
18   Remove the handbrake shoes, as described in Section 7.
19   Unscrew the four securing bolts, and withdraw the stub axle and lockplate.
20   Refitting is a reversal of removal, bearing in mind the following points.
21   Coat the rear face of the stub axle flange with a little lithium-based grease.
22   Tighten the brake backplate/stub axle securing bolts to the specified torque, in the three stages given in the Specifications.
23   Refit the handbrake shoes, as described in Section 7.
24   Refit the rear hub/disc, as described in Chapter 9, Section 13.
25   Before refitting the roadwheel and lowering the vehicle to the ground, check and if necessary adjust the handbrake, as described in Section 26.

GSi 2000 models
26   Proceed as described in paragraph 1.
27   Remove the brake disc with reference to Section 10.
28   Remove the rear hub, as described in Chapter 9, Section 24.
29   Remove the handbrake shoes, as described in Section 7.
30   Using a suitable splined key, unscrew the four securing bolts and withdraw the backplate.
31   Refitting is a reversal of removal, bearing in mind the following points.
32   Refit the handbrake shoes, as described in Section 7.
33   Refit the rear hub, as described in Chapter 9, Section 24.
34   Refit the brake disc with reference to Section 10.
35   Before refitting the roadwheel and lowering the vehicle to the ground, check and if necessary adjust the handbrake, as described in Section 26.

14   Front brake disc shield – removal and refitting

1   Where applicable, remove the wheel trim, then loosen the relevant front roadwheel bolts and apply the handbrake. Jack up the front of the vehicle, and support on axle stands positioned under the body side members. Remove the roadwheel.
2   Remove the brake disc, as described in Section 10.
3   Using a screwdriver inserted through the holes in the hub flange, extract the three screws securing the disc shield to the hub carrier.
4   Using plate shears or an alternative suitable tool, cut a section of metal from the rear edge of the shield to enable the shield to be withdrawn over the hub, then remove the shield.
5   If a new shield is to be fitted, cut out a section of metal, as during removal of the old shield, to enable the shield to be fitted. Deburr the cut edges, and coat them with anti-corrosion paint.
6   Further refitting is a reversal of removal, bearing in mind the following points.
7   Refit the brake disc, as described in Section 10.
8   Do not fully tighten the roadwheel bolts until the vehicle is resting on its wheels.

15   Master cylinder – removal and refitting

Note: *Refer to the note at the beginning of Section 4 before proceeding*

1   Disconnect the battery negative lead.
2   Depress the footbrake pedal several times to dissipate the vacuum in the servo unit.
3   Disconnect the wiring plug from the brake fluid level sensor in the reservoir filler cap.

Fig. 8.6 Cutting a section of metal from a new front brake disc shield prior to fitting (Sec 14)

4   If possible, use a teat pipette or an old hydrometer to remove the brake fluid from the reservoir. This will reduce the loss of fluid later in the procedure.
5   Locate a suitable container beneath the master cylinder, to catch the brake fluid which will be released.
6   Identify the brake fluid pipes for position, then unscrew the union nuts and disconnect the pipes from the master cylinder.
7   Unscrew the two securing nuts, and withdraw the master cylinder from the studs on the vacuum servo unit (photo).
8   Clean the external surfaces of the cylinder, then using a screwdriver, carefully prise the fluid reservoir and its seals from the top of the cylinder.
9   If desired, on models with a conventional braking system, the master cylinder can be overhauled, as described in Section 16.
10   No overhaul of the master cylinder is possible on models with ABS.
11   Refitting is a reversal of removal, but use new seals when fitting the brake fluid reservoir, and on completion, bleed the complete brake hydraulic system, as described in Section 4.

16   Master cylinder (conventional braking system) – overhaul

Note: *Before dismantling the master cylinder, check that suitable replacement parts can be obtained and retain the old components to compare them with the new ones*

1   With the master cylinder removed as described in Section 15, proceed as follows, according to type.

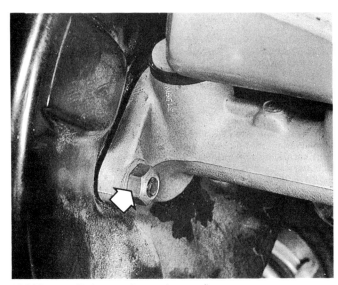

15.7 Master cylinder securing nut (arrowed)

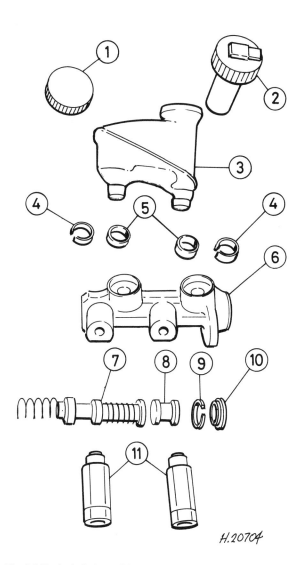

Fig. 8.7 Exploded view of GMF type master cylinder (Sec 16)

1 Filler cap (standard)
2 Filler cap (with fluid level sensor)
3 Fluid reservoir
4 Fluid reservoir retaining clips
5 Fluid reservoir seals
6 Cylinder body
7 Secondary piston and springs
8 Primary piston
9 Circlip
10 Sealing ring
11 Pressure-proportioning valves

H.20704

GMF type master cylinder

2 Clamp the master cylinder in a soft-jawed vice.
3 Where applicable, unscrew the pressure-proportioning valves from the base of the cylinder.
4 Carefully prise out the sealing ring from the end of the cylinder bore.
5 Depress the primary piston slightly using a suitable piece of wood or plastic, then hold the piston in the depressed position by inserting a smooth pin or rod of 3.0 mm (0.12 in) diameter through the primary fluid reservoir port in the cylinder.
6 Extract the circlip from the end of the cylinder bore using a screwdriver. Take care not to damage the piston or cylinder bore.
7 Withdraw the pin or rod retaining the piston.
8 Withdraw the primary piston assembly from the cylinder, if necessary tapping the cylinder on a wooden block to free the piston from the bore.
9 Apply low air pressure – eg from a foot pump – to the front fluid

Fig. 8.8 Holding the primary piston depressed while extracting the circlip from the cylinder body – GMF type master cylinder (Sec 16)

reservoir port in the cylinder, to eject the secondary piston assembly.
10 Clean all the components, in clean brake fluid or methylated spirit only, and examine them for wear and damage. In particular, check the surfaces of the pistons and cylinder bore for scoring and corrosion. If the bore shows signs of wear, renew the complete master cylinder assembly.
11 If the cylinder bore is in good condition, obtain a repair kit, which will contain all the necessary renewable items. A Vauxhall dealer will supply a preassembled kit of parts, which should be fitted as follows.
12 Lubricate the cylinder bore with clean brake fluid or brake grease, then clamp the cylinder in a soft-jawed vice, with the bore horizontal.
13 Remove the plug from the end of the assembly tube, and insert the short part of the tube into the cylinder bore as far as the shoulder on the tube.
14 Use a suitable piece of wood or plastic to push the components out of the tube and into the cylinder bore, then hold the primary piston in the depressed position by inserting the pin or rod used during dismantling through the cylinder primary fluid reservoir port.
15 Fit a new circlip to the end of the cylinder bore, ensuring that it seats correctly, and that the piston is free to move.
16 Depress the primary piston, and withdraw the pin or rod from the fluid reservoir port.
17 Fit a new sealing ring to the end of the cylinder bore.
18 Where applicable, screw the pressure-proportioning valves into the base of the cylinder.
19 Refit the master cylinder, as described in Section 15.

ATE type master cylinder
20 Clamp the master cylinder in a soft-jawed vice.
21 Where applicable, unscrew the pressure-proportioning valves from the base of the cylinder.
22 Carefully prise out the sealing ring from the end of the cylinder bore.
23 Depress the primary piston slightly using a suitable piece of wood or plastic, then extract the circlip from the end of the cylinder bore.
24 Withdraw the primary piston assembly, noting the location of the stop washers.
25 Depress the secondary piston, again using a piece of wood or plastic, and withdraw the stop screw from the cylinder body – Fig. 8.10.
26 Withdraw the secondary piston assembly from the cylinder, if necessary tapping the cylinder on a wooden block to free the piston from the bore.
27 Clean all the components, in clean brake fluid or methylated spirit only, and examine them for wear and damage. In particular, check the surfaces of the pistons and cylinder bores for scoring and corrosion. If the bore shows signs of wear, renew the complete master cylinder assembly.
28 If the cylinder bore is in good condition, obtain a repair kit, which will contain all the necessary renewable items. A Vauxhall dealer will supply a preassembled kit of parts, which should be fitted as follows.
29 Lubricate the cylinder bore with clean brake fluid or brake grease, then clamp the cylinder in a soft-jawed vice, with the bore horizontal.
30 Fit a new sealing ring to the stop screw, then screw it into the cylinder body a little way, but not so far that it protrudes into the bore.

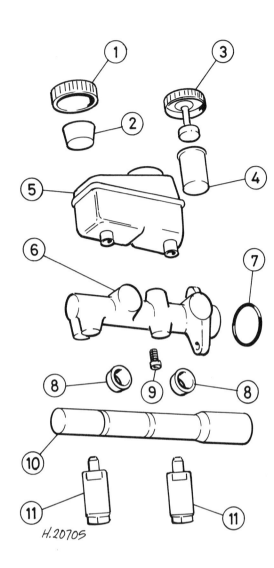

Fig. 8.9 Exploded view of ATE type master cylinder (Sec 16)

1	Filler cap (standard)
2	Strainer
3	Filler cap (with fluid level sensor)
4	Guide sleeve for float
5	Fluid reservoir
6	Cylinder body
7	Sealing ring
8	Fluid reservoir seals
9	Stop screw
10	Repair kit assembly tube
11	Pressure-proportioning valves

31   Remove the plugs from the ends of the assembly tube, then remove all the components from the short part of the tube, and push the short part into the long part until they are flush.
32   Insert the assembly tube into the cylinder bore as far as the collar on the short sleeve, then use a piece of wood or plastic to push the secondary piston assembly into the bore until it contacts the end of the cylinder.
33   Lightly tighten the stop screw, then withdraw the piece of wood or plastic and the assembly tube, and fully tighten the stop screw.
34   Reposition the master cylinder in the vice, with the bore facing upwards.
35   Smear the primary piston skirt and the seal grooves with the special grease provided in the repair kit. Fit the stop washer to the piston.
36   Adjust the assembly tube so that the end of the long part is flush with the inner shoulder of the short part.

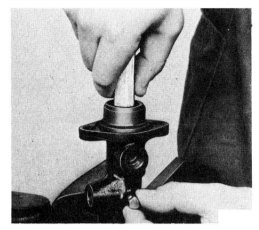

Fig. 8.10 Depressing the secondary piston while extracting the stop screw – ATE type master cylinder (Sec 16)

37   Fit the front seal to the primary piston, with the open end of the seal facing the front of the master cylinder.
38   Place the assembly tube over the cylinder to compress the seal, insert the piston and tube part way into the bore, and withdraw the tube.
39   Place the intermediate ring on the primary piston, then fit the remaining seal using the assembly tube as described previously.
40   Place the stop washer as the primary piston, then depress the piston slightly using a piece of wood or plastic, and fit a new circlip to the end of the cylinder bore. Ensure that the circlip is correctly seated, and that the piston is free to move.
41   Fit a new sealing ring to the end of the cylinder bore.
42   Where applicable, screw the pressure-proportioning valves into the base of the cylinder.
43   Refit the master cylinder, as described in Section 15.

17   Master cylinder (ABS) – overhaul

1   The master cylinder fitted to models with ABS cannot be dismantled, and no attempt should be made at overhaul.
2   If faulty, the complete unit must be renewed, as described in Section 15.

18   Vacuum servo – description and testing

1   The vacuum servo is fitted between the brake pedal and the master cylinder, and provides assistance to the driver when the pedal is depresses, reducing the effort required to operate the brakes. The unit is operated by vacuum from the inlet manifold. With the brake pedal released, vacuum is channelled to both sides of the internal diaphragm. However, when the pedal is depressed, one side of the diaphragm is opened to atmosphere, resulting in assistance to the pedal effort. Should the vacuum servo develop a fault, the hydraulic system is not affected, but greater effort will be required at the pedal.
2   The operation of the servo can be checked as follows.
3   With the engine stopped, destroy the vacuum in the servo by depressing the brake pedal several times.
4   Hold the brake pedal depressed and start the engine. The pedal should sink slightly as the engine is started.
5   If the pedal does not sink, check that the servo vacuum hose for leaks.
6   If no defects are found in the vacuum hose, the fault must lie in the servo itself.
7   No overhaul of the servo is possible, and if faulty, the complete unit must be renewed.

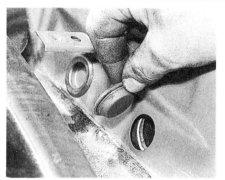

19.10A Remove the plugs ...

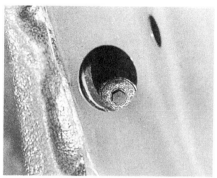

19.10B ... to expose the servo securing bolts

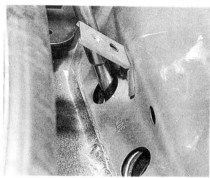

19.11A Unscrew the securing bolts ...

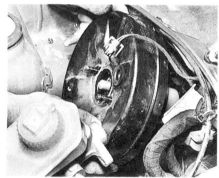

19.11B ... and withdraw the servo

19.15 Measuring the servo operating fork dimension using a bolt inserted through the pivot pin hole

19 Vacuum servo – removal and refitting

Note: *During the 1989 model year, some vehicles were produced with the brake pedal height incorrectly set, resulting in the brake pedal resting approximately 15.0 mm (0.6 in) above the clutch pedal, instead of 4.0 mm (0.16 in below). The correct pedal height can be set by adjusting the vacuum servo operating fork dimension, as described in paragraphs 15 and 16*

1   Disconnect the battery negative lead.
2   Working inside the vehicle, remove the lower trim panel from the driver's footwell.
3   Disconnect the wiring plug from the brake lamp switch, then twist the switch anti-clockwise and remove it from its bracket.
4   Pull the spring clip from the right-hand end of the servo fork-to-pedal pivot pin.
5   Using a suitable pair of pliers, pull back the end of the pedal return spring from the pedal, to enable the servo fork-to-pedal pivot pin to be removed. Withdraw the pivot pin.
6   Remove the windscreen cowl panel, as described in Chapter 10, Section 30, then remove the windscreen wiper motor and linkage as described in Chapter 11, Section 50.
7   Remove the coolant expansion tank as described in Chapter 2, Section 13.
8   Pull the vacuum pipe from the brake servo.
9   Unscrew the two securing nuts, and carefully withdraw the brake master cylinder from the studs on the servo, Move the master cylinder forwards slightly, taking care not to strain the brake pipes.
10   Remove the two plugs covering the servo securing bolts from the cowl panel (photos).
11   Using a suitable Allen key or hexagon bit, unscrew the servo securing bolts and remove them completely, then lift the servo from the bulkhead (photos).
12   If desired, the mounting bracket can be removed from the servo by unscrewing the four securing nuts. Note that the bracket will stick to the

servo, as it is fitted with sealing compound.
13   The servo cannot be overhauled, and if faulty, the complete unit must be renewed.
14   Before refitting the servo, check that the operating fork dimension is correct as follows.
15   Measure the distance from the end face of the servo casing to the centre of the pivot pin hole in the end of the operating fork. The distance should be 144.0 mm (5.6 in). To make accurate measurement easier, insert a bolt or bar of suitable diameter through the pivot pin hole, and measure to the centre of the bolt or bar (photo).
16   If adjustment is necessary, slacken the locknut, turn the fork to give the specified dimension, then tighten the locknut.
17   Where applicable, coat the contact faces of the servo and the mounting bracket with sealing compound, then refit the bracket to the servo, and tighten the securing nuts to the specified torque.
18   Coat the threads of the servo securing bolts with locking fluid, then fit the servo to the bulkhead and tighten the securing bolts.
19   Refit the securing bolt cover plugs to the cowl panel.
20   Refit the master cylinder to the servo, and tighten the securing nuts to the specified torque.
21   Reconnect the vacuum pipe to the servo.
22   Refit the coolant expansion tank, as described in Chapter 2, Section 13.
23   Refit the windscreen wiper motor and linkage as described in Chapter 11, Section 50, then refit the windscreen cowl panel.
24   Further refitting is a reversal of removal. On completion, check the operation of the servo, as described in Section 18.

20 ABS hydraulic modulator – removal and refitting

Note: *Refer to Section 3, and the note at the beginning of Section 4, before proceeding.*

1   Disconnect the battery negative lead.
2   Remove the brake fluid reservoir cap, and secure a piece of poly-

20.4 ABS hydraulic modulator cover removed to expose wiring
harness clamp screws (1), earth lead (2) and relays (3)

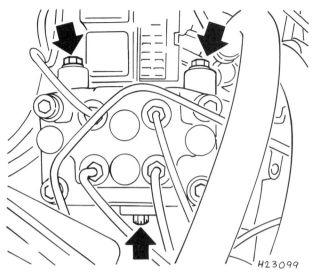

Fig. 8.11 ABS hydraulic modulator securing screws (arrowed)
(Sec 20)

thene over the filler neck with a rubber band, or by refitting the cap. This
will reduce the loss of fluid during the following procedure.
3   Remove the securing screw, and withdraw the plastic cover from
the hydraulic modulator.
4   Remove the two clamp screws, and lift off the modulator wiring
harness clamp (photo).
5   Disconnect the modulator wiring plug, levering it from the socket
with a screwdriver if necessary.
6   Unscrew the brake fluid pipe union nuts, and disconnect the pipes
from the modulator. Be prepared for fluid spillage, and plug the open
ends to prevent dirt ingress and further fluid loss. Move the pipes just
clear of the modulator, taking care not to strain them.
7   Unscrew the three modulator securing nuts (see Fig. 8.11), then tilt
the modulator slightly, and withdraw it upwards from its bracket,
sufficiently to gain access to the earth lead securing nut at the front
lower edge of the modulator.
8   Unscrew the securing nut and disconnect the earth lead, then
withdraw the modulator from the vehicle, taking care not to spill brake
fluid on the vehicle paintwork.
9   If a new modulator is to be fitted, pull the two relays from the top of
the old modulator, and transfer them to the new unit. No attempt must
be made to dismantle the modulator.
10   Before refitting the modulator, check that the bolts securing the
mounting bracket to the body panel are tight, and that the modulator
rubber mountings are in good condition. Renew the rubber mountings if
necessary.
11   Refitting is a reversal of removal, bearing in mind the following
points.
12   Make sure that the earth lead is reconnected before fitting the
modulator to its mounting bracket.
13   On completion, remove the polythene sheet from the brake fluid

reservoir filler neck, and bleed the complete brake hydraulic system, as
described in Section 4.
14   Check that the ABS warning lamp extinguishes when first starting
the engine after the modulator has been removed. At the earliest
opportunity, take the vehicle to a Vauxhall dealer, and have the complete system tested, using the dedicated ABS test equipment.

21   ABS wheel sensor – removal and refitting

Note: *Refer to Section 3 before proceeding*

Front wheel sensor

1   Disconnect the battery negative lead.
2   Where applicable, remove the wheel trim, then loosen the relevant
front roadwheel bolts and apply the handbrake. Jack up the front of the
vehicle, and support on axle stands positioned under the body side
members. Remove the roadwheel.
3   Unclip the sensor wiring connector from the retaining clip under the
wheel arch, then separate the two halves of the wiring connector,
prising them apart with a screwdriver if necessary (photo).
4   Using a suitable Allen key or hexagon bit, unscrew the bolt securing
the wheel sensor to its mounting bracket, then carefully lever the sensor
from the bracket using a screwdriver (photo). Recover the seal ring.
5   Examine the condition of the seal ring, and renew if necessary.
6   Refitting is a reversal of removal, bearing in mind the following
points.
7   Smear a little grease on the sensor casing before fitting it to the
bracket.

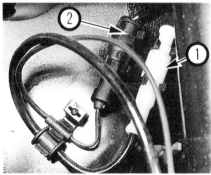

21.3 ABS front wheel sensor wiring
connector (1) and disc pad wear sensor
wiring connector (2) under wheel arch –
GSi 2000 model

21.4 ABS front wheel sensor securing bolt
(arrowed) – GSi 2000 model

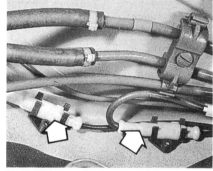

21.12 ABS rear wheel sensor wiring
connectors (arrowed) on rear underbody –
GSi 2000 model

21.14 ABS rear wheel sensor (arrowed) – GSi 2000 model

8   Do not fully tighten the roadwheel bolts until the vehicle is resting on its wheels.
9   Check that the ABS warning lamp extinguishes when first starting the engine after a wheel sensor has been removed. At the earliest opportunity, take the vehicle to a Vauxhall dealer, and have the complete system tested, using the dedicated ABS test equipment.

Rear wheel sensor
10   Disconnect the battery negative lead.
11   Where applicable, remove the wheel trim, then loosen the relevant rear roadwheel bolts and chock the front wheels. Jack up the rear of the vehicle, and support on axle stands positioned under the body side members. Remove the roadwheel.
12   Unclip the sensor wiring connector from the retaining clip on the rear underbody, then separate the two halves of the wiring connector, prising them apart with a screwdriver if necessary (photo).
13   Note the routing of the sensor wiring, and, where applicable, release it from the clips on the underbody.
14   Using a suitable Allen key or hexagon bit, unscrew the bolt securing the wheel sensor to the trailing arm (or the mounting bracket on GSi 2000 models), then carefully lever the sensor from its location using a screwdriver (photo). Recover the seal ring.
15   Proceed as described in paragraphs 5 to 9 inclusive.

22   ABS electronic control module – removal and refitting

Note: *Refer to Section 3 before proceeding*

1   Ensure that the ignition is switched off, then disconnect the battery negative lead.
2   The control module is located under a cover in the passenger sill, to the left-hand side of the seat.
3   Extract the three securing screws, and lift the cover from the control module. Note that two of the screws are covered by plastic trim plugs.
4   Lift the control module from its recess, then release the retaining clip and disconnect the module wiring plug. Withdraw the module (photos).
5   Refitting is a reversal of removal.
6   Check that the ABS warning lamp extinguishes when first starting the engine after the module has been removed. At the earliest opportunity, take the vehicle to a Vauxhall dealer, and have the complete system tested, using the dedicated ABS test equipment.

23   ABS relays – removal and refitting

Note: *Refer to Section 3 before proceeding*

Solenoid valve and pump motor relays
1   The Solenoid valve and pump motor relays are mounted on the hydraulic modulator.
2   Disconnect the battery negative lead.
3   Remove the securing screw and withdraw the plastic cover from the hydraulic modulator.
4   Pull out the appropriate relay. The small relay is for the solenoid valve, and the large relay is for the pump motor.
5   Refitting is a reversal of removal.
6   Check that the ABS warning lamp extinguishes when first starting the engine after a relay has been removed. At the earliest opportunity, take the vehicle to a Vauxhall dealer, and have the complete system tested, using the dedicated ABS test equipment.

Surge arrester relay
7   The surge arrester relay is located in the relay box at the left rear of the engine compartment.
8   Disconnect the battery negative lead.
9   Unclip the lid and open the relay box, then pull out the relay (photo).
10   Refitting is a reversal of removal, with reference to paragraph 6.

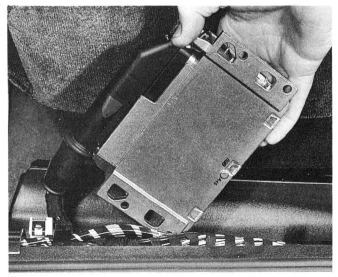

22.4A Lift out the ABS control module ...

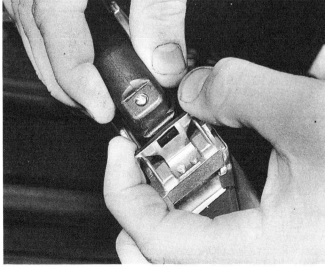

22.4B ... and release the wiring plug retaining clip

23.9 ABS surge arrester relay (arrowed)

24.10 Brake pressure-proportioning valve (1) and retaining clip (2) on rear underbody – GSi2000 model

24   Rear brake pressure-proportioning valves – removal and refitting

Note: *Refer to the note at the beginning of Section 4 before proceeding. Note also that the valve must only be renewed in pairs, and both valves must be of the same calibration*

Master cylinder-mounted valves

1   Remove the brake fluid reservoir cap, and secure a piece of polythene over the filler neck with a rubber band, or by refitting the cap. This will reduce the loss of fluid during the following procedure.
2   Locate a suitable container beneath the master cylinder, to catch the brake fluid which will be released.
3   Identify the two lower brake pipes for position, then unscrew the union nuts and disconnect the pipes from the proportioning valves in the base of the master cylinder. Plug the open ends of the pipes to prevent dirt ingress.
4   Unscrew the proportioning valves from the master cylinder, and plug the open ends of the cylinder to prevent dirt ingress.
5   Refitting is a reversal of removal, but on completion, remove the polythene from the brake fluid reservoir filler neck, and bleed the complete hydraulic system, as described in Section 4.

Rear underbody-mounted valves

6   Proceed as described in paragraph 1.
7   Chock the front wheels, then jack up the rear of the vehicle, and support securely on axle stands positioned under the body side members.
8   Working under the rear of the vehicle, unscrew the union nut and disconnect the brake pipe from one of the valves. Be prepared for fluid spillage, and plug the open end of the pipe to prevent dirt ingress and further fluid spillage.
9   Similarly, disconnect the flexible hose from the valve.
10   Pull the valve retaining clip from the bracket on the underbody, noting that on certain models, the retaining clip also secures the ABS sensor wiring, and withdraw the valve (photo).
11   Repeat the procedure for the remaining valve.
12   Proceed as described in paragraph 5.

25   Brake fluid pipes and hoses – removal and refitting

Note: *Refer to the note at the beginning of Section 4 before proceeding*

Rigid pipes

1   Some of the commonly-used brake pipes can be obtained from Vauxhall parts dealers, ready-formed and complete with unions, but other brake pipes must be prepared using 4.75 mm (0.19 in) diameter

brake pipe. Kits for making the brake pipes can be obtained from certain motor accessory shops.
2   Before removing a brake pipe, remove the brake fluid reservoir cap, and secure a piece of polythene over the filler neck with a rubber band, or by refitting the cap. This will reduce the loss of fluid when the pipe is disconnected.
3   Jack up the vehicle, and support securely on axle stands positioned under the body side members.
4   To remove a brake pipe, unscrew the unions at each end, and release the pipe from the retaining clips.
5   Refitting is a reversal of removal, taking care not to overtighten the unions.
6   On completion, remove the polythene from the brake fluid reservoir filler neck, and bleed the relevant hydraulic circuit(s), as described in Section 4.

Flexible hoses

7   Proceed as described previously for the rigid pipes, but note that a flexible pipe must never be installed twisted, although a slight 'set' is permissible to give it clearance from adjacent components.
8   When reconnecting a flexible hose to a front brake caliper, note that the sealing rings on the union bolt must be renewed.

26   Handbrake – adjustment

Models with rear drum brakes

1   The handbrake will normally be kept in correct adjustment by the self-adjusting action of the rear brake shoes. However, due to cable stretch over a period of time, the travel of the handbrake lever may become excessive, in which case the following operations should be carried out.
2   Chock the front wheels, jack up the rear of the vehicle, and support securely on axle stands positioned under the body side members.
3   Fully release the handbrake.
4   Turn the knurled nut on the cable adjuster (mounted on the torsion beam), until the brake shoes can just be heard to rub when the rear wheels are turned by hand in the normal direction of rotation (photo).
5   Loosen the adjuster nut until the wheels are just free to turn.
6   The handbrake must start to operate with the lever on the second notch of the ratchet.
7   On completion of adjustment, check the handbrake cables for free movement, and apply a little grease to the adjuster threads to prevent corrosion.
8   Lower the vehicle to the ground.

Models with rear disc brakes

9   Where applicable, remove the wheel trims, then loosen the rear roadwheel bolts and chock the front wheels. Jack up the rear of the

26.4 Handbrake cable adjuster. Knurled nut arrowed – all models except GSi 2000

vehicle, and support securely on axle stands positioned under the body side members. Remove the roadwheels.

10   Pull the handbrake lever as far as the second notch on the ratchet.

11   On GSi 2000 models fitted with a catalytic converter, unscrew the four securing nuts and withdraw the exhaust centre box heat shield by carefully sliding it round the centre box.

12   On all except GSi 2000 models, loosen the knurled nut on the cable adjuster (mounted on the torsion beam).

13   On GSi 2000 models, loosen the nut securing the cable equaliser yoke to the handbrake lever operating rod.

14   Using a screwdriver inserted through the adjuster hole in one of the discs/hubs (photo), turn the adjuster wheel until the brake shoes can just be heard to rub when the disc/hub is turned by hand in the normal direction of rotation.

15   Turn the adjuster wheel back until the disc/hub is just free to turn.

16   Repeat paragraphs 14 and 15 on the remaining side of the vehicle.

17   Tighten the nut on the cable adjuster or the equaliser, as applicable, until the brake shoes just begin to operate. Check that the shoes operate equally on both wheels.

18   Fully release the handbrake, then apply it again.

19   The discs/hubs must lock when the handbrake lever reaches the sixth notch on the ratchet. If necessary, turn the nut on the cable adjuster or equaliser, as applicable, to achieve this.

20   Where applicable, refit the exhaust heat shield.

21   Refit the roadwheels and lower the vehicle to the ground. Do not fully tighten the roadwheel bolts until the vehicle is resting on its wheels.

27   Handbrake cable – removal and refitting

Models with rear drum brakes

1   The handbrake cable is in two sections. The longer section runs from the handbrake operating rod, via the adjuster, to the right-hand brake assembly. The shorter section runs from the adjuster to the left-hand brake assembly. The two sections of the cable can be renewed independently.

2   Where applicable, remove the wheel trim(s), then loosen the relevant rear roadwheel bolts. Chock the front wheels, jack up the rear of the vehicle, and support securely on axle stands positioned under the body side members. Remove the roadwheel(s).

3   Note the routing of the handbrake cable(s), as an aid to refitting.

4   Remove the relevant brake drum(s), with reference to Section 11.

Longer cable

5   Note the length of exposed thread at the handbrake cable adjuster on the torsion beam, then unscrew the adjuster nut from the threaded rod.

6   Disconnect the cable from the handbrake lever operating rod on the vehicle underbody (photo).

7   Detach the cable from the guides on the underbody. Note that the cable can be fed through certain guides, but in some cases, the guide brackets must be bent away from the underbody to allow the cable to be withdrawn.

8   Detach the cable from the adjuster on the torsion beam.

9   Unhook the cable end from the lever on the brake shoe, then using a screwdriver, prise out the lockplate which secures the handbrake cable in the backplate.

10   Withdraw the cable from the vehicle, releasing it from the guide on the torsion beam.

11   Refitting is a reversal of removal, bearing in mind the following points.

26.14 Using a screwdriver to turn the handbrake adjuster wheel – model with rear disc brakes

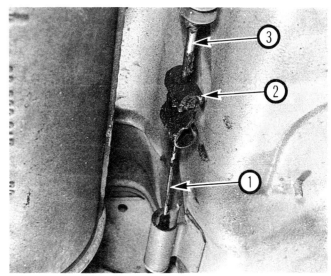

27.6 Handbrake cable connection to handbrake lever operating rod

1 Handbrake cable	3 Handbrake lever operating rod
2 Connecting link	

27.27 Handbrake cable end fitting at brake shoe operating lever (1) and cable bracket on semi-trailing arm (2) – GSi 2000 model

12   Screw the adjuster nut onto the threaded rod to the position noted before removal.
13   Ensure that the handbrake cable is routed as noted before removal.
14   Refit the brake drum, with reference to Section 11.
15   Before refitting the roadwheel(s) and lowering the vehicle to the ground, adjust the handbrake, as described in Section 26.

Shorter cable
16   Note the length of exposed thread at the handbrake cable adjuster on the torsion beam, then unscrew the adjuster nut from the threaded rod.
17   Proceed as described in paragraphs 8 to 15 inclusive.

Models with rear disc brakes (except GSi 2000)
18   The procedure is as described for models with rear drum brakes, bearing in mind the following points.

19   Ignore the references to removal and refitting of the brake drum.
20   Note that there is no lockplate securing the handbrake cable to the brake backplate, but the return spring must be unhooked from the cable end.
21   On models with a catalytic converter, when removing the longer cable, unscrew the four securing nuts and withdraw the exhaust centre box heat shield by carefully sliding it round the centre box.

GSi 2000 models
22   The left and right-hand handbrake cables, and the equaliser yoke, are removed as an assembly on GSi 2000 models.
23   Loosen the rear roadwheel bolts, then chock the front wheels, jack up the rear of the vehicle, and support securely on axle stands positioned under the body side members. Remove the roadwheels.
24   Note the routing of the handbrake cables, as an aid to refitting.
25   On models with a catalytic converter, unscrew the four securing nuts and withdraw the exhaust centre box heat shield by carefully sliding it round the centre box.
26   Note the length of exposed thread at the cable equaliser yoke, then unscrew the securing nut and disconnect the equaliser yoke from the handbrake lever operating rod.
27   Unhook the cable ends from the brake shoe operating levers and the return springs (photo).
28   Detach the cable from the guides on the underbody and the semi-trailing arms. Note that the cables can be fed through certain guides, but in some cases, the guide brackets may have to be bent away from the underbody to allow the cables to be withdrawn.
29   Withdraw the cables and equaliser assembly from the vehicle.
30   Refitting is a reversal of removal, bearing in mind the following points.
31   Use a new self-locking nut to secure the equaliser yoke to the handbrake lever operating rod, and screw the nut onto the rod to the position noted before removal.
32   Ensure that the cables are routed as noted before removal.
33   Before refitting the roadwheels and lowering the vehicle to the ground, adjust the handbrake, as described in Section 26.

28   Handbrake lever – removal and refitting

1   Disconnect the battery negative lead.
2   Jack up the vehicle, and support on axle stands positioned securely under the body side members.
3   On models with a catalytic converter, unscrew the four securing nuts and withdraw the exhaust centre box heat shield by carefully sliding it round the centre box.
4   On all except GSi 2000 models, note the length of exposed thread at the handbrake cable adjuster on the torsion beam, then slacken the adjuster to enable the cable to be disconnected from the handbrake lever operating rod. Disconnect the cable from the operating rod, and slide the rubber sealing grommet from the underbody and operating rod.

Fig. 8.12 Handbrake lever securing bolts (arrowed) (Sec 28)

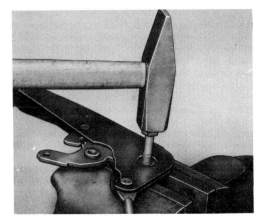

Fig. 8.13 Driving out the handbrake lever ratchet segment securing sleeve (Sec 28)

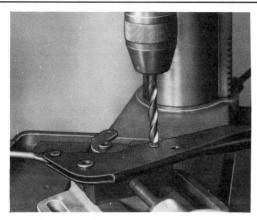

Fig. 8.14 Drilling out the handbrake lever pawl pivot pin (Sec 28)

5 On GSi 2000 models, note the length of exposed thread at the handbrake cable equaliser yoke, then unscrew the securing nut and disconnect the equaliser yoke from the handbrake lever operating rod. Slide the rubber sealing grommet from the underbody and operating rod.

6 Remove the front passenger seat, as described in Chapter 10, Section 40.

7 Remove the rear section of the centre console, as described in Chapter 10, Section 38.

8 Access to the handbrake lever-to-floor mounting bolts is provided by slits in the carpet. If no slits are provided, either carefully cut some, or release and fold back the carpet.

9 Unscrew the mounting bolts, and withdraw the handbrake lever sufficiently to disconnect the handbrake 'on' warning lamp switch wiring.

10 Disconnect the wiring and withdraw the handbrake lever and operating rod from the vehicle.

11 A worn ratchet segment can be renewed by driving the securing sleeve from the handbrake lever, using a metal rod or a bolt of suitable diameter.

12 Drive the new sleeve supplied with the new segment into the lever to permit a little play between the segment and lever.

13 If desired, a new pawl can be fitted if the original pivot rivet is drilled out.

14 Rivet the new pawl so that the pawl is still free to move.

15 The handbrake 'on' warning lamp switch can be removed from the lever assembly after unscrewing the securing bolt.

16 Refitting is a reversal of removal, bearing in mind the following points.

17 Refit the rear section of the centre console, as described in Chapter 10, Section 38.

18 Refit the front passenger seat, as described in Chapter 10, Section 40.

19 On GSi 2000 models, use a new self-locking nut to secure the equaliser yoke to the handbrake lever operating rod, and screw the nut onto the rod to the position noted before removal.

20 On all except GSi 2000 models, tighten the cable adjuster to expose the length of thread noted before removal.

21 Before lowering the vehicle to the ground, adjust the handbrake, as described in Section 26.

29 Brake pedal – removal and refitting

1 Disconnect the battery negative lead.

2 Remove the lower trim panel from the driver's footwell.

3 Disconnect the wiring plug from the brake lamp switch, then twist the switch anti-clockwise and remove it from its bracket.

4 Pull the spring clip from the right-hand end of the servo fork-to-pedal pivot pin (photo).

5 Using a suitable pair of pliers, pull back the end of the pedal return spring from the pedal, to enable the servo fork-to-pedal pivot pin to be removed. Withdraw the pivot pin (photo).

6 Pull the locking clip from the left-hand end of the pedal pivot pin.

7 Unscrew the nut from the left-hand end of the pivot pin, then slide the pivot pin from the right-hand end of the pedal mounting bracket. If necessary, tap the end of the pivot pin with a soft-faced hammer to free the splines from the mounting bracket. Recover any washers which may be positioned on the pivot pin, noting their locations.

8 Withdraw the pedal and return spring.

9 Refitting is a reversal of removal, bearing in mind the following points.

10 Ensure that the pedal return spring is correctly located on the pedal before refitting.

11 Coat the pedal pivot pin with a little molybdenum disulphide grease.

12 Ensure that any washers on the pedal pivot pin are positioned as noted before removal.

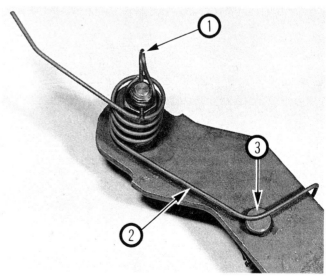

29.4 Brake servo fork-to-pedal pivot pin spring clip (arrowed)

29.5 Brake pedal assembly removed from vehicle

1 Locking clip   3 Pedal pivot pin
2 Pedal return spring

30 Fault diagnosis – braking system

Symptom	Reason(s)
Excessive pedal travel	Low fluid level Air in hydraulic system Fluid leak Faulty rear brake self-adjuster mechanism (rear drum brakes) Faulty master cylinder Faulty vacuum servo Excessive disc run-out
Brake pedal feels spongy	Air in hydraulic system Fluid leak Faulty master cylinder Faulty vacuum servo
Excessive pedal pressure required to stop vehicle	Air in hydraulic system Fluid leak Faulty vacuum servo Caliper or wheel cylinder piston seized Pad or shoe friction material worn or contaminated Incorrect grade of pads fitted New pads or shoes fitted – not yet bedded-in Faulty ABS modulator (where applicable)
Brakes pull to one side	Pad or shoe friction material worn or contaminated Caliper or wheel cylinder piston seized Faulty rear brake self-adjuster mechanism (rear drum brakes) Pads or shoes renewed on one side only Disc or drum badly worn or distorted Type, steering or suspension defect – see Chapter 9
Brakes binding	Air in hydraulic system Caliper or wheel cylinder piston seized Faulty master cylinder Faulty rear brake self-adjuster mechanism (rear drum brakes) Incorrectly adjusted handbrake cable
Judder felt through brake pedal or steering wheel when braking	Excessive disc run-out or thickness variation Pads or shoe friction material badly worn or contaminated Caliper mountings loose or worn Wear in suspension or steering components – see Chapter 9
Pedal pulsates when braking hard – models with ABS	Normal feature of ABS – no fault

Note: *This Section is not intended as an exhaustive guide to fault diagnosis, but summarises the more common faults which may be encountered during a vehicle's life. Consult a dealer for more detailed advice, particularly regarding faults with ABS.*

Chapter 9 Suspension and steering

For modifications, and information applicable to later models, see Supplement at end of manual

Contents

Specifications

General

Front suspension type	Independent, with MacPherson struts and anti-roll bar
Rear suspension type:	
All models except GSi 2000	Semi-independent torsion beam, with trailing arms, coil springs and telescopic shock absorbers. Anti-roll bar on some models. Manual level control system standard on some models, optional on others
GSi 2000 models	Fully independent, with semi-trailing arms, coil springs, telescopic shock absorbers and anti-roll bar
Steering type	Rack and pinion. Power steering standard on some models, optional on others
Vehicle condition for 'laden' measurements	70 kg (154 lb) in each front seat, fuel tank half-full

Front suspension (laden)

Camber	$-40' \pm 40'$
Castor	$+2° \pm 1°$
Toe in	$+15' \pm 10'$
Toe out on turns	$1° 30' \pm 45'$
Max deviation between wheels on toe out	$40'$

Rear suspension (laden, after depressing rear of vehicle several times)
GSi 2000 & C20 XE models
    Camber .... $-2°\ 10'\ \pm\ 40'$
    Toe in .... $+25'\ +\ 30'/-20'$
Other models
    Camber .... $-1°40'\ \pm\ 30'$
    Toe in .... $+10'\ +\ 30'/-20'$

Steering
Ratio:
    Manual steering..   22 : 1 or 24.5 : 1
    Power steering ....   18 : 1
Power steering fluid:
    Type ....   Dexron II type ATF (Duckhams Uni-Matic)
    Capacity ....   1.0 litre (1.8 pints)
Power steering drivebelt tension (1.8 and 2.0 litre models – measured
with Vauxhall special gauge):
    New belt...   250 to 300 N (56 to 68 lbf)
    Used belt...   450 N (101 lbf)

Wheels and tyres
Wheel size .... $5\frac{1}{2}$J x 13, $5\frac{1}{2}$J x 14 or 6J x 15
Tyre size:
    $5\frac{1}{2}$J x 13 wheels..   165 R13-82T
    $5\frac{1}{2}$J x 14 wheels..   175/70 R14-82T, 195/60 R14-85H, or 195/60 R14-85V
    6J x 15 wheels..   195/60 R15-87V or 205/55 R15-87V

Tyre pressures:*	**Front**	**Rear**
1.4, 1.6 and 1.8 litre models with 165 R13, 175/70 R14, or 195/60 R14 tyres	1.9 (27)	1.7 (24)
2.0 litre models (except GSi 2000) with 195/60 R14 tyres	2.2 (32)	2.0 (29)
GSi 2000 models with 195/60 R15, or 205/55 R15 tyres	2.3 (33)	2.1 (30)

The pressures quoted are for a normal load (up to 3 passengers). For full-load pressures, consult your handbook or a Vauxhall dealer

Torque wrench settings

	Nm	**lbf ft**
Front suspension – all models		
Subframe-to-underbody bolts:		
Front bolts...	115	85
Centre bolts...	170	125
Rear bolts:		
Stage 1	100	74
Stage 2	Angle-tighten a further 75°	Angle-tighten a further 75°
Stage 3	Angle-tighten a further 15°	Angle-tighten a further 15°
Lower arm-to-suspension strut balljoint nut...........................	70	52
Lower arm-to-subframe front (horizontal) pivot bolt	110	81
Lower arm damper weight bolts (where applicable)...................	20	15
Suspension strut upper mounting nut.................................	55	41
Suspension strut piston rod nut.....................................	70	52
Suspension strut ring nut...	200	148
Anti-roll bar-to-subframe bolts	20	15
Balljoint-to-lower arm nuts	60	44
Rear suspension – all models except GSi 2000		
Trailing arm-to-underbody fixings....................................	105	77
Shock absorber upper mounting nut..................................	20	15
Shock absorber lower mounting bolt..................................	70	52
Anti-roll bar fixings..	22	16
Stub axle-to-trailing arm bolts:		
Stage 1..	50	37
Stage 2..	Angle-tighten a further 30°	Angle-tighten a further 30°
Stage 3..	Angle-tighten a further 15°	Angle-tighten a further 15°
Rear hub nut (see Section 11)..	25	18
Rear suspension – GSi 2000 models		
Crossmember rear tube-to-body bolts.................................	60	44
Forward crossmember-to-body bolts...................................	125	92
Crossmember mounting bracing bracket-to-underbody bolts...........	65	48
Semi-trailing arm-to-crossmember nuts...............................	100	74
Shock absorber upper mounting nut..................................	20	15
Shock absorber lower mounting bolt..................................	110	81
Anti-roll bar fixings..	22	16
Rear hub nut...	300	221
Steering		
Steering wheel retaining nut	25	18
Steering gear mounting bolts (to bulkhead)	12	9
Tie-rod-to-steering gear bolts..	95	70

Torque wrench settings (continued)

	Nm	lbf ft
Tie-rod end clamp bolts..	20	15
Tie-rod-end-to-suspension strut balljoint nut	60	44
Steering shaft-to-flexible coupling pinch-bolt	22	16
Steering gear pinion-to-flexible coupling pinch-bolt............................	22	16
Steering gear pinion nut	40	30
Steering gear damper adjuster locknut	60	44
Fluid pipe-to-power steering gear unions	42	31
Fluid pipe-to-power steering pump union	37	27
Fluid pipe-to-pipe and pipe-to-hose unions	28	21
Power steering pump mounting bolts:		
1.6 litre models	30	22
1.8 and 2.0 litre models:		
Bolts 'A' and 'C' in Fig. 9.24	25	18
Bolts 'B' in Fig. 9.24	40	30
Power steering pump pulley bolt (1.6 litre models)............................	25	18
Steering column-to-dashboard mounting bracket bolt........................	22	16
Steering column upper right-hand mounting bolt or self-locking nut		
(as applicable)..	22	16
Roadwheels		
Roadwheel bolts..	90	66

---

1   General description

The front suspension consists of MacPherson struts, lower arms, and an anti-roll bar. The lower arms and the anti-roll bar are mounted on a detachable U-shaped front subframe, which also carried the rear engine/transmission mounting.

Each lower arm is attached to the subframe by a horizontal front bush and a vertical rear bush. In conjunction with the steering geometry, this arrangement allows the front wheels to steer themselves against any imbalance in the braking forces, thus maintaining stability when braking with one side of the vehicle on a slippery surface, and the other on dry tarmac.

The hub carriers are mounted between the lower ends of the MacPherson struts, and the lower arms, and carry the double-row ball type wheel bearings and the brake assemblies.

The rear suspension on all models except the GSi 2000 is of semi-independent type, consisting of a torsion beam and trailing arms with double-conical coil springs and telescopic shock absorbers. The front ends of the trailing arms are attached to the vehicle underbody by horizontal bushes, and the rear ends are located by the shock absorbers, which are bolted to the underbody at their upper ends. The coil springs are mounted independently of the shock absorbers, and act directly between the trailing arms and the underbody. Certain models are fitted

with an anti-roll bar, which is mounted between the torsion beam and the rear ends of the trailing arms.

A manual rear suspension level control system is available as standard equipment on some models, and as an optional extra on others. The system operates using compressed air-filled shock absorbers. The rear suspension level is adjusted by altering the air pressure in the shock absorbers, via a valve located in the luggage compartment.

The rear suspension on GSi 2000 models is of fully independent type, consisting of semi-trailing arms, with double-conical coil springs, telescopic shock absorbers and an anti-roll bar. The front end of each semi-trailing arm is attached to a suspension crossmember by two horizontal bushes, and the rear ends are located by the shock absorbers, which are bolted to the underbody at their upper ends. The coil springs are mounted independently of the shock absorbers, and act directly between the semi-trailing arms and the underbody. The anti-roll bar is located on the suspension crossmember, and is attached to each semi-trailing arm via a vertical link. The suspension crossmember is bolted directly to the vehicle underbody at its forward end.

The steering gear is of rack-and-pinion type. Movement is transmitted to the front wheels via tie-rods, which are connected to the rack through a sliding sleeve at their inner ends, and to the suspension struts via balljoints at their outer ends.

The steering column consists of an outer column which incorporates a deformable section, and a shaft connected to a flexible coupling at its lower end.

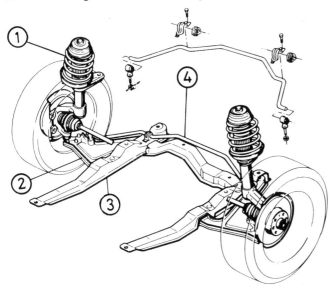

Fig. 9.1 Front suspension layout – all models (Sec 1)

1	*MacPherson strut*	3	*Subframe*
2	*Lower arm*	4	*Anti-roll bar*

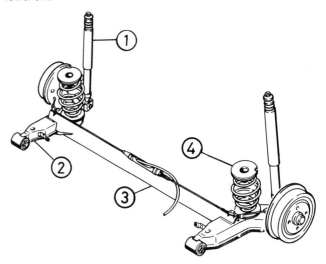

Fig. 9.2 Rear suspension layout – all models except GSi 2000 (model with rear drum brakes shown) (Sec 1)

1	*Shock absorber*	3	*Torsion beam*
2	*Trailing arm*	4	*Coil spring*

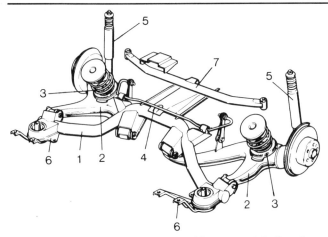

Fig. 9.3 Rear suspension layout – GSi 2000 models (Sec 1)

1 Crossmember	5 Shock absorber
2 Semi-trailing arm	6 Crossmember mounting
3 Coil springs	bracing bracket
4 Anti-roll bar	7 Crossmember rear tube

Power steering is fitted as standard to certain models, and is available as an option on others. The power steering is hydraulically-operated, and pressure is supplied by a fluid pump driven via a drivebelt from the engine crankshaft. On 1.8 and 2.0 litre models, fluid cooler pipes are mounted beneath the radiator to keep the temperature of the hydraulic fluid within operating limits.

---

2   Routine maintenance

---

1   At the intervals specified in the *'Routine maintenance'* Section at the beginning of this manual, carry out the following tasks.
2   Check the tyre pressures, and inspect the surfaces of the tyres for damage and wear.
3   Check the torque of the roadwheel bolts.
4   Where applicable, check the power steering fluid level in the reservoir and top up if necessary (photo). To check the fluid level, the engine must be stopped. Read off the level on the dipstick attached to the reservoir filler cap. With the fluid at operating temperature (80°C/176°F), the level should be on the 'MAX' mark, and with the fluid cold (20°C/68°F), the level should be on the 'MIN' mark. A regular need for topping-up indicates a leak, which should be located and rectified without delay.
5   Where applicable, check the tension of the power steering fluid pump drivebelt, and adjust if necessary, as described in Section 42.

2.4 Topping-up the power steering fluid level – 2.0 litre model

6   Check the condition of the tie-rod end balljoint rubber seals, and renew if signs of wear or damage are evident.
7   Check the condition of the steering rack rubber bellows, and renew if signs of wear or damage are evident, as described in Section 36.
8   Periodically inspect all suspension and steering components for wear and damage, using the following as a guide, and take corrective action as necessary.

Front suspension
9   Apply the handbrake, jack up the front of the vehicle, and support on axle stands positioned securely under the body side members.
10   Visually inspect the lower arm balljoint dust covers for splits or deterioration, and renew the balljoint assembly as described in Section 8 if any damage is apparent.
11   Grasp the roadwheel at the 12 o'clock and 6 o'clock positions, and try to rock it. Very slight free play may be evident, but if the movement is excessive, further investigation is necessary to determine the source. Continue rocking the wheel while an assistant depresses the brake pedal. If the movement is now eliminated, or significantly reduced, it is likely that the wheel bearing is at fault. If the free play is still evident with the footbrake depressed, then this indicates wear in the suspension joints or mountings. Pay particular attention to the lower arm balljoint and mountings. Renew any worn components as described in the relevant Sections of this Chapter.
12   Using a large screwdriver or a flat bar, check for wear in the anti-roll bar mountings and the lower arm mounting by carefully levering against these components. Some movement is to be expected, as the mountings are made of rubber, but excessive wear should be obvious. Renew any worn bushes.

Rear suspension
13   Chock the front wheels, jack up the rear of the vehicle, and support on axle stands positioned securely under the body side members.
14   Visually inspect the rear suspension components for any obvious signs of wear or damage. Pay particular attention to the rubber mounting bushes and renew as necessary.
15   Grasp the roadwheel at the 12 o'clock and 6 o'clock positions, and try to rock it. Any excess movement indicates incorrect adjustment or wear in the wheel bearings. Wear may also be accompanied by a rumbling sound when the wheel is spun, or a noticeable roughness if the wheel is turned slowly. Adjustment (where applicable) and renewal procedures are described in Sections 11, 12 or 23, as applicable.

Shock absorber
16   Check for any signs of fluid leakage around the front suspension strut and rear shock absorber body. If any leaks are apparent, the shock absorber is defective internally, and renewal is necessary.
17   The efficiency of the shock absorbers may be checked by bouncing the vehicle at each corner. The body should return to its normal position and stop after being depressed. If the body rises and returns on a rebound, the shock absorber is probably faulty. Also examine the upper and lower mountings for signs of wear. Renew worn components as necessary.

Steering
18   Observe the tie-rod end balljoints while an assistant turns the steering wheel back and forth through an arc of about 20°. If there is any side-to-side movement of the balljoints as the steering is turned, renewal will be necessary, as described in Section 46. Renewal is also necessary if the rubber seals around the balljoints are split, damaged, or show any signs of deterioration.
19   Inspect the flexible rubber coupling at the base of the steering column, and renew if the rubber shows any signs of deterioration or damage – see Section 32.
20   It is advisable to have the front wheel alignment checked periodically, particularly if abnormal tyre wear is noticed.

---

3   Front wheel bearing – renewal

Note: *The bearing will probably be destroyed during the removal operation. The use of a suitable puller will greatly ease the procedure.*

1   Remove the relevant suspension strut/hub carrier assembly, as described in Section 5.
2   Unscrew the securing screw, and remove the brake disc from the hub.

3.4 Removing the half inner bearing race from the hub

3.5 Removing a brake disc shield securing screw

3.6 Extracting the outer bearing retaining circlip

3.9 Fitting a new front wheel bearing using a socket, nut, bolt, washers, and length of bar

3.12 Drawing the hub into the bearing using improvised tools

3   Support the hub carrier on two metal bars positioned as shown in Fig. 9.4, then using a metal bar or tube of suitable diameter, press or drive the hub from the wheel bearing. Alternatively, screw two road-wheel bolts into the hub and, using progressively thicker packing pieces, tighten the bolts to force the hub from the bearing. Note that one half of the inner bearing race will remain on the hub.

4   Using a suitable puller, pull the half inner bearing race from the hub. Alternatively, support the bearing race on suitably thin metal bars, and press or drive the hub from the bearing race (photo).

5   Remove the three securing screws, and lift the brake disc shield from the hub carrier (photo).

6   Extract the inner and outer bearing retaining circlips (photo).

7   Using a suitable puller, pull the bearing from the hub carrier, applying pressure to the outer race. Alternatively, support the hub carrier, and press or drive out the bearing.

8   Before installing the new bearing, thoroughly clean the bearing location in the hub carrier, and fit the outer bearing retaining circlip ('A' in Fig. 9.5). Note that the circlip tabs should be positioned towards the bottom of the hub carrier.

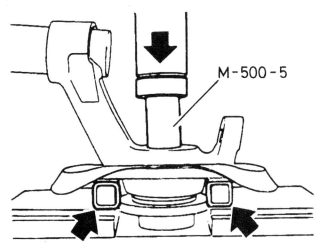

Fig. 9.4 Pressing the front hub from the wheel bearing (Sec 3)

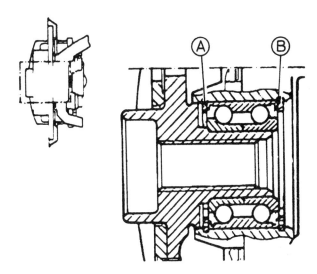

Fig. 9.5 Cross-sectional view of front wheel bearing/hub assembly (Sec 3)

A   *Outer bearing retaining circlip*   B   *Inner bearing retaining circlip*

4.10A Front subframe front securing bolt

4.10B Front subframe rear securing bolt which also secures rear end of lower arm

9   Press or drive the new bearing into position until it contacts the outer circlip, applying pressure to the outer race (photo).
10   Fit the inner bearing retaining circlip, with the tabs positioned towards the bottom of the hub carrier.
11   Fit the brake disc shield.
12   Press or draw the hub into the bearing. The bearing inner track **must** be supported during this operation. This can be achieved using a suitable socket, long bolt, washers and a length of bar as shown (photo).
13   Refit the brake disc.
14   Refit the suspension strut/hub carrier assembly, as described in Section 5.

4   Front subframe – removal and refitting

Note: *Suitable equipment will be required to support the engine during this procedure. A balljoint separator tool will be required. The lower arm-to-suspension strut balljoint nut locking pins must be renewed on refitting.*

1   The subframe is removed complete with the lower arms and the anti-roll bar as an assembly.
2   Before removing the subframe, the engine must be supported from its left-hand lifting bracket. Ideally, the engine should be supported using a strong wooden or metal beam resting on blocks positioned securely in the channels at the sides of the engine compartment. The Vauxhall special tool designed specifically for this purpose is shown in Fig. 6.5 in Chapter 6. Alternatively, the engine can be supported using a suitable hoist and lifting tackle, but in this case, the hoist must be of such a design as to enable the engine to be supported with the vehicle raised off the ground, leaving sufficient clearance to withdraw the subframe from under the front of the vehicle.
3   Where applicable, remove the wheel trims, then loosen the front roadwheel bolts on both sides of the vehicle. Apply the handbrake, then jack up the front of the vehicle, and support securely on axle stands positioned under the body side members. Remove the front road-wheels.
4   Remove the front section of the exhaust system, with reference to Chapter 3, Section 26 or 52, as applicable. On GSi 2000 models, unbolt the oil cooler hose bracket from the right-hand side of the subframe.
5   Working on one side of the vehicle, extract the locking pin, then unscrew the castellated nut from the lower arm-to-suspension strut balljoint.
6   Using a balljoint separator tool, disconnect the lower arm-to-suspension strut balljoint.
7   Repeat paragraphs 5 and 6 for remaining lower arm.
8   Ensure that the engine is adequately supported, then unscrew and remove the two nuts and washers securing the rear engine/gearbox mounting to the subframe.

9   Support the subframe on a trolley jack, with an interposed wooden beam to prevent the subframe from tipping as it is withdrawn.
10   Unscrew and remove the six bolts securing the subframe to the vehicle underbody. Note that the rear bolts also secure the lower arms to the subframe (photos). The bolts are very tight, and a suitable extension bar will probably be required to loosen them.
11   Lower the jack supporting the subframe, and withdraw the assembly from under the front of the vehicle.
12   If desired, the anti-roll bar and/or the lower arms can be removed from the subframe, with reference to Sections 9 and 6 respectively.
13   Refitting is a reversal of removal, bearing in mind the following points.
14   If the anti-roll bar and/or the lower arms have been removed from the subframe, refit them with reference to Section 9 and/or 6, as applicable.
15   Tighten all nuts and bolts to the specified torques, noting that the rear subframe-to-underbody bolts must be tightened in three stages – see Specifications.
16   Secure the lower arm-to-suspension strut balljoint nuts with new locking pins.
17   Refit the front section of the exhaust system, with reference to Chapter 3, Section 26 or 52, as applicable. On GSi 2000 models, refit the oil cooler hose bracket to the right-hand side of the subframe.
18   Finally tighten the roadwheel bolts when the vehicle has been lowered to the ground, and where applicable, refit the wheel trims.

5   Front suspension strut – removal, overhaul and refitting

Note: *A balljoint separator tool will be required during this procedure, and a spring compressor tool will be required if the strut is to be overhauled. The tie-rod end balljoint self-locking nut, the driveshaft retaining snap-ring, and the hub nut must be renewed on refitting*

1   Where applicable, remove the wheels trim, then loosen the relevant front roadwheel bolts. Apply the handbrake, then jack up the front of the vehicle, and support securely on axle stands positioned under the body side members. Remove the relevant front roadwheel.
2   Where applicable, remove the ABS wheel sensor from the hub carrier, with reference to Chapter 8, Section 21 if necessary, and disconnect the wiring from the strut.
3   Remove the brake caliper from the hub carrier, as described in Chapter 8, Section 8. The caliper can be suspended out of the way, using wire or string, to avoid the need to disconnect the hydraulic fluid hose.
4   Unscrew and remove the self-locking nut from the tie-rod end-to-suspension strut balljoint.
5   Using a balljoint separator, disconnect the tie-rod end-to-suspension strut balljoint.
6   Disconnect the outboard end of the driveshaft from the hub carrier,

5.7 Unscrewing the suspension strut top mounting nut

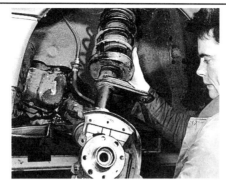

5.8 Withdrawing a suspension strut

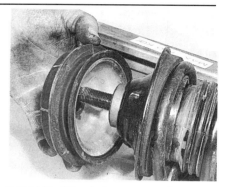

5.13A Lift off the strut upper mounting rubber ...

5.13B ... and the bearing

5.14 Lift off the upper spring seat and damper ring

as described in Chapter 7, Section 3. Support the driveshaft by suspending with wire or string – **do not** allow the driveshaft to hang down under its own weight.

7   Working in the engine compartment, unscrew the nut securing the suspension strut to the suspension turret. In order to unscrew the nut, it will be necessary to counterhold the suspension strut piston rod using a suitable splined key (photo). Support the suspension strut as the nut is unscrewed, as once the nut has been removed, the strut is free to drop from the vehicle.

8   Withdraw the suspension strut/hub carrier assembly from the vehicle (photo).

9   If desired, the suspension strut can be overhauled as follows, otherwise proceed to paragraph 30 for details of the refitting procedure.

10   The hub, wheel bearing and brake disc shield can be removed, as described in Section 3.

11   With the suspension strut resting on a bench or clamped in a vice, fit a spring compressor tool, and compress the coil spring to relieve the pressure on the upper spring seat. Ensure that the compressor tool is securely located on the spring, in accordance with the tool manufacturer's instructions.

12   Hold the strut piston rod with the splined key used during strut removal, and unscrew the piston rod nut.

13   Lift off the strut upper mounting rubber and the bearing (photos).

14   Lift off the upper spring seat and damper ring, then carefully release the spring compressor and remove the spring (photo). Note which way up the spring is fitted.

15   Slide the bellows and the rubber buffer which fits inside the bellows from the strut (photo).

16   To remove the shock absorber cartridge, the ring nut must be unscrewed from the top of the strut tube. This nut is extremely tight. One method which can be used to unscrew the nut is to invert the strut and clamp the nut in a vice, then lever the strut round using a long bar and a bolt passed through the tie-rod bracket.

17   With the ring nut removed, the shock absorber cartridge can be withdrawn (photos).

18   The shock absorber can be tested by clamping the lower end in a vice, then fully extending and contracting the shock absorber several times. Any evidence of jerky movement or lack of resistance indicates

the need for renewal.

19   Examine all components for wear or damage and renew as necessary. Pay particular attention to the mounting rubber and the bearing.

20   Commence reassembly by sliding the shock absorber cartridge into the strut, and refitting the ring nut.

21   Clamp the strut in a vice, and tighten the ring nut to the specified torque, using a suitably large long-reach socket.

22   Refit and compress the coil spring, ensuring that the lower end of the spring rests against the lug on the lower spring seat (photo).

23   Refit the rubber buffer and the bellows.

24   Refit the upper spring seat and the damper ring, ensuring that the mark on the damper ring is aligned with the hole in the spring seat, as shown in Fig. 9.6. The spring seat should be positioned with the hole at right angles to (ie 90° away from) the end of the spring.

25   Lubricate the bearing with a little grease, then refit it with the visible part of the bearing race uppermost.

26   Refit the strut upper mounting rubber.

27   Counterhold the strut piston rod, and tighten the piston rod nut to the specified torque. This can be achieved by holding the piston rod using the splined key fitted to a torque wrench, and tightening the nut using a spanner until the specified torque is reached (photo).

28   Carefully release and remove the spring compressor tool, ensuring that the spring seats correctly at top and bottom. Ensure that the lower end of the spring still rests against the lug on the lower spring seat.

29   The strut can now be refitted to the vehicle as follows.

30   Locate the top end of the strut in the suspension turret, then refit the securing nut and tighten it to the specified torque using the method described in paragraph 27.

31   Reconnect the outboard end of the driveshaft to the hub carrier, as described in Chapter 7, Section 3.

32   Reconnect the tie-rod end balljoint to the suspension strut, and tighten a new self-locking nut to the specified torque.

33   Refit the brake caliper to the hub carrier, as described in Chapter 8, Section 8.

34   Where applicable, refit the ABS wheel sensor to the hub carrier, with reference to Chapter 8, Section 21, and reconnect the wiring to the strut.

35   Refit the roadwheel, and lower the vehicle to the ground. Finally

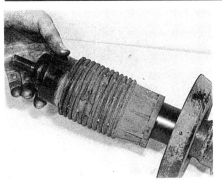

5.15 Slide off the bellows and the rubber buffer

5.17A Remove the ring nut ...

5.17B ... and withdraw the shock absorber cartridge

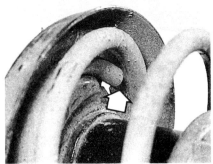

5.22 Lower end of spring rests against lug (arrowed) on lower spring seat

5.27 Tightening the piston rod nut

tighten the roadwheel bolts with the vehicle resting on its wheels, and where applicable, refit the wheel trim.

36   Check and if necessary adjust the front wheel alignment, as described in Section 48.

---

6   Front suspension lower arm – removal and refitting

Note: *A new lower arm-to-suspension strut balljoint nut locking pin, and (where applicable) a new anti-roll bar-to-lower arm nylock nut must be used on refitting*

1   Where applicable, remove the wheel trim, then loosen the relevant front roadwheel bolts. Apply the handbrake, then jack up the front of the vehicle, and support securely on axle stands positioned under the body side members. Remove the relevant front roadwheel.

2   Unscrew and remove the nut securing the end of the anti-roll bar to the lower arm. Recover the dished washers and mounting rubbers.

3   Extract the locking pin, then unscrew the castellated nut from the lower arm-to-suspension strut balljoint.

4   Using a balljoint separator tool, disconnect the lower arm-to-suspension strut balljoint.

5   Unscrew and remove the two pivot bolts securing the lower arm to the subframe (photo). Note that the rear pivot bolt also secures the

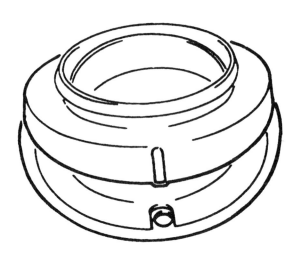

Fig. 9.6 Mark on suspension strut damper ring aligned with hole in spring seat (Sec 5)

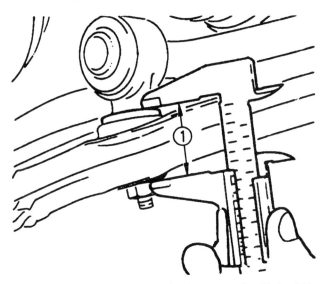

Fig. 9.7 Front anti-roll bar rubber bush compression (1) should be 38.0 to 39.0 mm (1.49 to 1.53 in) (Sec 6)

6.5 Lower arm front pivot bolt

subframe to the underbody. Both bolts are very tight, and a suitable extension bar will probably be required to loosen them.
6   Pull the lower arm from the subframe, and withdraw it from the vehicle.
7   Note that certain 2.0 litre models have a damper weight bolted to the right-hand lower arm. If the right-hand lower arm is to be renewed on such a vehicle, it is important to ensure that the damper weight is transferred to the new arm.
8   Note that the metal sleeves in the rear mounting bush can be discarded when refitting the lower arm.
9   Commence refitting by pushing the lower arm into position in the subframe.
10   Fit the two pivot bolts, then hold the lower arm in a horizontal position, and tighten the bolts to the specified torque. Note that the rear bolt must be tightened in three stages – see Specifications.
11   Reconnect the lower arm-to-suspension strut balljoint, and tighten the castellated nut to the specified torque. Secure the nut with a new locking pin.
12   Reconnect the end of the anti-roll bar to the lower arm, noting that the dished washer which retain the mounting rubbers should be fitted with their concave sides facing towards the lower arm. Note that on certain models, nylock type nuts are used to secure the anti-roll bar to the lower arms – these nuts should be renewed on refitting.
13   Tighten the anti-roll bar-to-lower arm nuts to give the specified rubber bush compression shown in Fig. 9.7. If necessary, renew the rubber bushes.
14   Refit the roadwheel and lower the vehicle to the ground. Finally tighten the roadwheel bolts with the vehicle resting on its wheels, and where applicable, refit the wheel trim.
15   Check and if necessary adjust the front wheel alignment, as described in Section 48.

7   Front suspension lower arm bushes – renewal

1   Remove the lower arm, as described in Section 6.
2   The bushes are a tight fit in the lower arm, and must be pressed out.
3   If a press is not available, the bushes can be drawn out using a long bolt, nut, washers and a suitable diameter socket or length of metal tubing.
4   The vertical bush should be pressed out through the top of the lower arm, from below, and the horizontal bush should be pressed out towards the front of the lower arm, from the rear.
5   Lubricate the new bushes using soapy water, then fit them to the lower arm, using the method described in paragraph 3.
6   The new vertical bush should be pressed into the lower arm from below, and the new horizontal bush should be pressed into the lower arm from front to rear. The horizontal bush should project from the lower arm equally at both ends.
7   Refit the lower arm, as described in Section 6.

8   Front suspension lower arm balljoint – renewal

1   Remove the lower arm, as described in Section 6.
2   Mount the lower arm in a vice, then drill the heads from the three rivets which secure the balljoint to the lower arm, using a 12.0 mm (0.47 in) diameter drill.
3   If necessary, tap the rivets from the lower arm, then remove the balljoint.
4   The new balljoint should be fitted using three special bolts, spring washers and nuts, available from a Vauxhall parts centre.
5   Ensure that the balljoint is fitted the correct way up, noting that the securing nuts should be positioned on the underside of the lower arm.
6   Tighten the balljoint-to-lower arm nuts to the specified torque.
7   Refit the lower arm, as described in Section 6.

9   Front anti-roll bar – removal and refitting

Note: *Where applicable, the nylock type nuts securing the anti-roll bar to the lower arms must be renewed on refitting*

1   Support the engine, and raise the vehicle as described in Section 4, paragraphs 2 and 3.
2   If desired, remove the front section of the exhaust system, with reference to Chapter 3, Section 26 or 52, as applicable.
3   Working under the vehicle, unscrew and remove the locknuts securing the ends of the anti-roll bar to the lower arms. Recover the dished washers and mounting rubbers.
4   Ensure that the engine is adequately supported, then unscrew and remove the two nuts and washers securing the engine/transmission rear mounting to the subframe.
5   Support the subframe on a trolley jack, with an interposed wooden beam to spread the load.
6   Unscrew and remove the two rear and two centre bolts securing the subframe to the vehicle underbody. Note that the rear bolts also secure the lower arms to the subframe. The bolts are very tight, and a suitable extension bar will probably be required to loosen them.
7   Loosen, but do not remove the two front subframe-to-underbody securing bolts.
8   Carefully lower the subframe until the anti-roll bar-to-subframe bolts are accessible, then unscrew and remove the bolts.
9   Lift the anti-roll bar from the subframe and the lower arms, and withdraw it from the vehicle.
10   Note that on certain models, a damper weight is fitted to the centre of the anti-roll bar (photo). If the anti-roll bar is to be renewed, the damper weight (where applicable) must be transferred to the new component, and positioned as shown in Fig. 9.8.

9.10 Front anti-roll bar damper weight

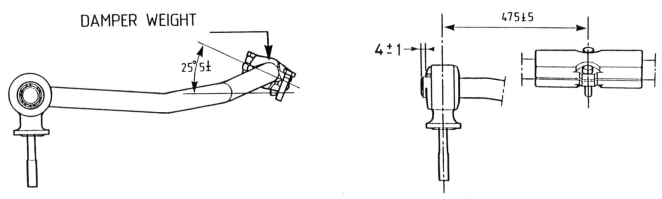

Fig. 9.8 Correct position of front anti-roll bar damper weight (Sec 9)

All dimensions in mm

11   If desired, the anti-roll bar mounting bushes can be renewed, as described in Section 10.
12   Refitting is a reversal of removal, bearing in mind the following points.
13   Reconnect the ends of the anti-roll bar to the lower arm, noting that the dished washers which retain the mounting rubbers should be fitted with their concave sides facing towards the lower arm. Note that on certain models, nylock type nuts are used to secure the anti-roll bar to the lower arms – these nut should be renewed on refitting.
14   Tighten the anti-roll bar-to-lower arm nuts to give the specified rubber bush compression shown in Fig. 9.7. If necessary, renew the rubber bushes.
15   Tighten all nuts and bolts to the specified torques, noting that the rear subframe-to-underbody bolts must be tightened in three stages – see Specifications.
16   Where applicable, refit the front section of the exhaust system, with reference to Chapter 3, Section 26 or 52, as applicable.
17   Finally tighten the roadwheel bolts when the vehicle is resting on its wheels, and where applicable, refit the wheel trims.

10   Front anti-roll bar bushes – renewal

1   Remove the anti-roll bar, as described in Section 9.
2   To renew an anti-roll bar end mounting bush, mount the anti-roll bar in a vice, then light hammer blows on a suitable drift, drive the end link from the anti-roll bar.

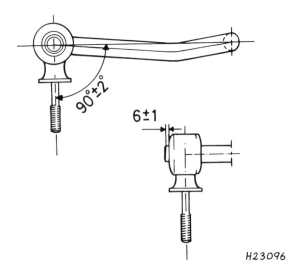

Fig. 9.9 Correct position of end link on front anti-roll bar (Sec 10)

Dimensions in mm

3   The bush can now be prised from the end link, using a screwdriver or similar tool.
4   Lubricate the new bush with a little soapy water to aid fitting, then press it into place in the end link.
5   If necessary, repeat the procedure on the remaining end link.
6   With either end link removed, the anti-roll bar-to-subframe mounting bushes can be renewed if desired, by sliding the bushes along the bar and manipulating them until they can be withdrawn from the end of the bar. Fit the new bushes in the same way.
7   Press or drive the end link(s) onto the anti-roll bar to the position shown in Fig. 9.9.
8   Before refitting the anti-roll bar, examine the anti-roll bar-to-lower arm bushes, and renew if necessary.
9   Refit the anti-roll bar, as described in Section 9.

11   Rear wheel bearing (all models except GSi 2000) – adjustment

Note: *A new split pin must be used to secure the hub nut on completion of adjustment*

1   Where applicable, remove the wheel trim, then loosen the rear roadwheel bolts on the relevant side of the vehicle. Chock the front wheels, then jack up the rear of the vehicle, and support securely on axle stands positioned under the body side members. Remove the roadwheel.
2   Prise the dust cover from the centre of the hub (photo).
3   Extract the split pin from the end of the stub axle, then loosen the hub nut.

11.2 Removing the dust cover from the rear hub – model with rear disc brakes

11.5 Loosen rear hub nut until spacer washer can be moved with a screwdriver – model with rear disc brakes

4   Tighten the hub nut to a torque of 25 Nm (18 lbf ft), whilst simultaneously turning the hub.
5   Gradually loosen the hub nut until the spacer washer under the nut can just be moved with a screwdriver, without levering on the hub (photo).
6   If the split pin hole in the stub axle is not aligned with any of the slots in the hub nut, **tighten** the nut until the nearest slots align, then check that the spacer washer can still be moved as described in paragraph 5. If the washer cannot be moved, **slacken** the nut until the nearest slots in the nut align with the split pin hole.
7   Secure the hub nut using a new split pin, then refit the dust cover to the centre of the hub.
8   Refit the roadwheel and lower the vehicle to the ground. Finally tighten the roadwheel bolts with the vehicle resting on its wheels, and where applicable, refit the wheel trim.

12   Rear wheel bearing (all models except GSi 2000) – renewal

Note: *The rear hub oil seal must be renewed on reassembly*

1   If wear in the bearings is evident, indicated by a rumbling sound when the wheel is spun, or a noticeable roughness if the wheel is turned slowly, then the bearings should be renewed as follows. Note that each hub runs on two taper-roller bearings, and both the inner and outer bearing should be renewed if wear is evident.
2   Remove the hub, as described in Section 13.
3   If the outer bearing inner race is still in the hub, prise it out using a screwdriver.
4   Prise the oil seal from the inner end of the hub, and extract the inner bearing inner race (photo).
5   Support the hub on blocks or in a vice, then press or drive out the bearing outer races.
6   Thoroughly clean the internal bore of the hub with paraffin or a suitable solvent.
7   Before fitting the new bearings, remove any burrs which may be present in the bore of the hub, using a fine file or scraper.
8   Fit the new bearing outer races, with the larger internal diameters of the races facing outwards from the centre of the hub. Press or tap the races into position, using a metal tube of suitable diameter. Take care to keep the races square in the hub bore as they are installed, otherwise they may jam and crack.
9   Pack the bearing races with lithium-based grease, and apply a liberal quantity of grease to the space in the hub between the bearing races.
10   Place the inner bearing inner race in position, lubricate the lip of a new oil seal, and tap the seal squarely into place, using a suitable tube or a piece of wood.

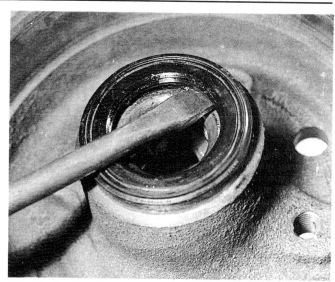

12.4 Prise the oil seal from the inner end of the hub – model with rear disc brakes

11   Refit the hub, and adjust the wheel bearing play, as described in Sections 13 and 11 respectively.

13   Rear hub (all models except GSi 2000) – removal and refitting

Note: *A new split pin must be used to secure the hub nut on refitting*

Models with rear drum brakes

1   Where applicable, remove the wheel trim, then loosen the rear roadwheel bolts on the relevant side of the vehicle. Chock the front wheels, then jack up the rear of the vehicle, and support securely on axle stands positioned under the body side members. Remove the roadwheel.
2   Remove the brake drum, with reference to Chapter 8, Section 11.
3   Prise the dust cover from the centre of the hub.
4   Extract the split pin from the end of the stub axle, then unscrew the hub nut. If the hub nut is tight, counterhold the hub by refitting two roadwheel bolts and inserting a long screwdriver or similar tool between them, although this should not prove necessary unless the nut has been overtightened.
5   Remove the hub nut and the thrustwasher from the stub axle, then withdraw the hub. Be prepared to catch the outer wheel bearing inner race, which may drop out of the hub as it is removed.
6   Commence refitting by placing the hub and the outer wheel bearing inner race on the stub axle. Take care not to damage the oil seal at the inner end of the hub.
7   Fit the thrustwasher and the hub nut, then adjust the wheel bearing play, as described in Section 11, paragraphs 4 to 6 inclusive.
8   Secure the hub nut using a new split pin, then refit the dust cover to the centre of the hub.
9   Refit the brake drum, with reference to Chapter 8, Section 11, and check the handbrake adjustment, as described in Chapter 8, Section 26.
10   Finally tighten the roadwheel bolts when the vehicle has been lowered to the ground, and where applicable, refit the wheel trim.

Models with rear disc brakes

11   On models with rear disc brakes, the hub is integral with the brake disc.
12   Proceed as described in paragraph 1.
13   Remove the brake caliper, as described in Chapter 8, Section 9, but leave the hydraulic fluid pipe connected. Move the caliper to one side, and suspend it using wire or string to avoid straining the pipe.
14   Proceed as described in paragraphs 3 and 4.
15   Remove the hub nut and the spacer washer from the stub axle, then withdraw the hub/disc. If the hub/disc is tight, collapse the handbrake shoes, by inserting a screwdriver through the adjuster hole in the hub/disc and turning the adjuster wheel. Be prepared to catch the outer wheel bearing inner race, which may drop out of the hub/disc as it is removed.

13.16 Refit the hub/disc ...

13.17A ... the thrustwasher ...

13.17B ... and the hub nut – model with rear disc brakes

16   Commence refitting by placing the hub/disc and the outer wheel bearing inner race on the stub axle (photo). Take care not to damage the oil seal at the inner end of the hub/disc. If necessary, slacken off the brake shoe adjuster wheel, to allow the hub/disc to pass over the brake shoes.

17   Proceed as described in paragraphs 7 and 8 (photos).

18   Check the handbrake adjustment, as described in Chapter 8, Section 26, then refit the brake caliper, as described in Chapter 8, Section 9.

19   Finally tighten the roadwheel bolts when the vehicle has been lowered to the ground, and where applicable, refit the wheel trim.

14   Rear shock absorber – removal and refitting

1   On all models except the GSi 2000, it is important to note that only one shock absorber should be removed at a time. Note that shock absorbers should be renewed in pairs.

2   On models with manual rear suspension level control, depressurise the system, by releasing the air through the valve in the luggage compartment.

3   Working in the luggage compartment, prise off the cap which covers the shock absorber top mounting. On Hatchback models, pull back the flap covering the first-aid kit and warning triangle storage compartment for access to the right-hand shock absorber.

4   Counterhold the shock absorber piston rod, and unscrew the shock absorber top mounting nut (photo). Remove the washer and the upper mounting rubber.

5   Drive the rear wheels up onto ramps, and chock the front wheels. Alternatively, chock the front wheels, then jack up the rear of the vehicle, and support securely on axle stands placed under the body side members. If the vehicle is jacked up, the relevant trailing arm (semi-trailing arm on GSi 2000 models) must be supported with a jack as the vehicle is raised.

6   Working under the rear of the vehicle, where applicable, disconnected the manual suspension level control air line from the shock absorber.

7   Unscrew and remove the bolt and washer securing the lower end of the shock absorber to the trailing arm (semi-trailing arm on GSi 2000 models) (photo).

8   On all models except the GSi 2000, compress the shock absorber by hand, if necessary prising the lower end to free it from the trailing arm.

9   Withdraw the shock absorber from under the vehicle, and recover the lower mounting rubber and cup from the top of the shock absorber.

10   The shock absorber can be tested by clamping the lower mounting eye in a vice, then fully extracting and contracting the shock absorber several times. Any evidence of jerky movement or lack of resistance indicates the need for renewal.

11   Before refitting the shock absorber, examine the mounting rubbers for wear or damage, and renew if necessary.

12   Refitting is a reversal of removal, bearing in mind the following points.

13   Where applicable, ensure that the shock absorber is fitted with the air line union facing the correct way round.

14   Tighten the shock absorber lower mounting bolt to the specified torque.

15   On models with manual rear suspension level control, pressurise the system to 0.8 bar (12.0 lbf in^2), and check for air leaks.

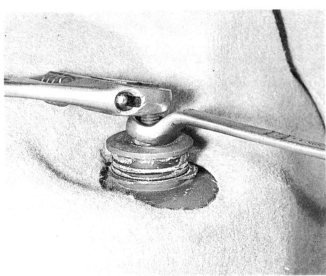

14.4 Unscrewing a rear shock absorber top mounting nut – Hatchback model

14.7 Unscrewing a rear shock absorber lower mounting bolt – non-GSi 2000 model

15 Rear shock absorber mounting rubbers – renewal

1 The shock absorber top mounting rubbers can be renewed without removing the shock absorber as follows. On all models except the GSi 2000, it is important to note that, due to the design of the rear suspension, only one shock absorber should be disconnected at a time.

2 Proceed as described in Section 14, paragraphs 2 to 4 inclusive.

3 Keeping the roadwheels resting on the ground, jack up the rear of the vehicle slightly, to enable the shock absorber to be compressed sufficiently by hand to release the top mounting from the body.

4 Remove the lower mounting rubber from the top of the shock absorber.

5 Fit the new mounting rubbers using a reversal of the removal procedure.

6 On models with manual rear suspension level control, pressurise the system to 0.8 bar (12.0 lbf/ft^2) on completion.

16 Rear suspension coil spring (all models except GSi 2000) – removal and refitting

1 Due to the design of the rear suspension, it is important to note that only one coil spring should be removed at a time. Note that rear springs should be renewed in pairs, and if the springs are to be renewed, it is advisable to renew the spring damping rubbers at the same time.

2 On models with manual rear suspension level control, depressurise the system by releasing the air through the valve in the luggage compartment.

3 Chock the front wheels, then jack up the rear of the vehicle, and support securely on axle stands placed under the body side members.

4 Raise the relevant trailing arm slightly using a jack.

5 Unscrew and remove the bolt and washer securing the lower end of the shock absorbers to the trailing arm, and free the lower end of the shock absorber.

6 Carefully lower the jack supporting the trailing arm, and remove the coil spring and its damping rubbers. Lever the trailing arm downwards slightly if necessary to remove the spring.

7 Refitting is a reversal of removal, ensuring that the spring locates correctly on the trailing arm and the underbody.

8 Tighten the shock absorber lower mounting bolt to the specified torque.

9 If the springs are being renewed, repeat the procedure on the remaining side of the vehicle.

10 On models with manual rear suspension level control, pressurise the system to 0.8 bar (12.0 lbf/in^2) on completion.

17 Rear suspension torsion beam/trailing arms assembly (all models except GSi 2000) – removal and refitting

1 Where applicable, remove the wheel trims, then loosen the rear roadwheel bolts on both sides of the vehicle. Chock the front wheels, then jack up the rear of the vehicle, and support securely on axle stands positioned under the body side members. Remove the rear roadwheels.

2 On models with manual rear suspension level control, depressurise the system by releasing the air through the valve in the luggage compartment.

3 On models with a catalytic converter, unbolt and remove the exhaust heat shield.

4 Measure the length of the thread projecting from the handbrake cable adjuster on the torsion beam, then loosen the adjuster nut to slacken the cable.

5 Disconnect the rear section of the handbrake cable from the underbody cable joiner bracket, and unclip the cable from the underbody.

6 Working in the engine compartment, remove the filler cap from the brake hydraulic fluid reservoir, then place a piece of polythene across the top of the reservoir filler hole, and refit the filler cap. This will minimise fluid loss when the brake lines are disconnected.

7 Disconnect the flexible hoses from the rigid brake pipes at the front edge of each trailing arm. Be prepared for fluid loss, and plug the open ends of the pipes and hoses, to prevent ingress of dirt and further fluid loss.

17.9 Trailing arm securing bolt (arrowed)

8 Where applicable, unbolt the ABS sensor brackets, and release the wiring from the brackets on the trailing arms. Support the sensor bracket by suspending with wire or string from the vehicle underbody.

9 Loosen, but **do not** remove, the nuts and bolts securing the front ends of the trailing arms to the vehicle underbody (photo).

10 Support the torsion beam with a trolley jack and interposed block of wood. Position the jack securely under the centre of the torsion beam.

11 Unscrew and remove the bolts securing the lower ends of the shock absorbers to the trailing arms, then gently lower the jack supporting the torsion beam.

12 Remove the coil springs, with reference to Section 16 if necessary.

13 Ensure that the torsion beam is adequately supported, then remove the nuts and bolts securing the front ends of the trailing arms to the vehicle underbody. The help of an assistant will greatly ease this task – ensure that the torsion beam does not slip off the jack.

14 Withdraw the torsion beam/trailing arms assembly from under the rear of the vehicle.

15 If desired, the brake components can be removed from the trailing arms, with reference to the relevant Sections of Chapter 8. The stub axles can be removed with reference to Section 20, and where applicable, the anti-roll bar car be removed with reference to Section 18.

16 If necessary, the trailing arm bushes can be renewed, with reference to Section 19.

17 Commence reassembly by refitting any components which were removed from the torsion beam/trailing arms assembly, with reference to the relevant Sections of this Chapter and/or Chapter 8, as applicable.

18 Support the torsion beam/trailing arms assembly on the trolley jack, and position the assembly under the rear of the vehicle.

19 Raise the jack, and fit the bolts and nuts which secure the front ends of the trailing arms to the underbody. Do not fully tighten the fixings at this stage.

20 Refit the coil springs, with reference to Section 16 if necessary.

21 Raise the rear ends of the trailing arms, and refit the bolts securing the lower ends of the shock absorbers. Tighten the bolts to the specified torque. Withdraw the jack from under the rear of the vehicle.

22 Where applicable, refit the ABS sensor brackets, and refit the wiring to the brackets on the trailing arms.

23 Remove the plugs from the brake pipes and hoses, and reconnect the unions.

24 Reconnect the handbrake cable to the underbody cable joiner bracket, and refit the cable to the underbody clip(s).

25 Tighten the handbrake cable adjuster nut to expose the length of thread measured during removal, then adjust the handbrake cable, as described in Chapter 8, Section 26.

26 On models with a catalytic converter, refit the exhaust heat shield.

27 Refit the rear roadwheels, then lower the vehicle to the ground and finally tighten the roadwheel bolts. Where applicable, refit the wheel trims, and remove the chocks from the front wheels.

28 On models with manual rear suspension level control, pressurise the system to 0.8 bar (12.0 lbf/in^2).

18.2 Rear anti-roll bar-to-trailing arm securing bolt (arrowed)

18.3 Rear anti-roll bar clamp

29   Ensure that the vehicle is parked on level ground, then with the equivalent of a load of 70.0 kg (154.0 lbs) in each front seat, 'bounce' the vehicle to settle the suspension.
30   Without disturbing the position of the vehicle, place chocks at the front and rear edges of the front wheels, to prevent the vehicle from moving.
31   Working under the rear of the vehicle, tighten the fixings securing the front ends of the trailing arms to the underbody to the specified torque.
32   Finally, recheck the handbrake cable adjustment, then remove the polythene from beneath the brake hydraulic fluid reservoir cap, and bleed the brake hydraulic system, as described in Chapter 8, Section 4.

6   Refitting is a reversal of removal.
7   Tighten all fixings to the specified torque.

19   Rear suspension trailing arm bushes (all models except GSi 2000) – renewal

1   The trailing arm bushes can be renewed without removing the torsion beam/trailing arms assembly from the vehicle, as follows.
2   Proceed as described in Section 17, paragraphs 1 and 2.
3   Unclip the flexible hoses and the rear ends of the rigid brake pipes from the vehicle underbody.
4   Support the torsion beam with a trolley jack and interposed block of wood. Position the jack under the centre of the torsion beam.
5   Unscrew and remove the nuts and bolts securing the trailing arms to the underbody.
6   Gently lower the jack until the trailing arm bushes are accessible, then support the torsion beam on axle stands. Take care not to strain the brake pipes.
7   A special Vauxhall tool is available for removal and fitting of the bushes, but a suitable alternative can be improvised using a long bolt, nut, washers, and a length of suitable diameter metal tubing or a socket.
8   Prior to removing a bush, cut the flange from the inner end of the bush using a sharp knife – see Fig. 9.10.
9   Removal of the bush will be made easier if the bush housing in the trailing arm is heated to approximately 70°C (158°F) using a heat gun or a hair dryer. **Do not** use a naked flame, due to the close proximity of the fuel tank.
10   Draw the bush from the trailing arm, using the tool described in paragraph 7.
11   Lubricate the new bush with a little soapy water, then draw it into position, ensuring that the mouldings in the end of the bush are positioned as shown in Fig. 9.11.

18   Rear anti-roll bar (all models except GSi 2000) – removal and refitting

1   Chock the front wheels, then jack up the rear of the vehicle, and support securely on axle stands placed under the body side members.
2   Unscrew and remove the nuts and bolts securing the ends of the anti-roll bar to the trailing arms (photo).
3   Unscrew and remove the nuts and bolts securing the anti-roll bar clamps to the torsion beam, and withdraw the anti-roll bar from the vehicle (photo).
4   Examine the anti-roll bar mounting bushes for wear or damage, and renew as necessary.
5   To renew the bushes, slide them from the ends of the anti-roll bar.

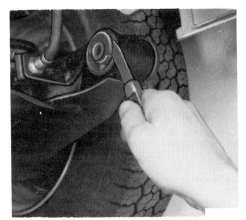

Fig. 9.10 Cutting inner flange from trailing arm bush – all models except GSi 2000 (Sec 19)

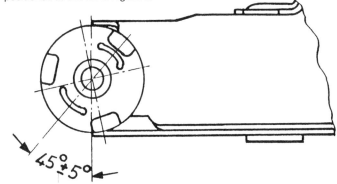

Fig. 9.11 Trailing arm bush positioning – all models except GSi 2000 (Sec 19)

20.2 Three of the four stub axle-to-trailing arm securing bolts (arrowed)

12   Repeat the procedure on the remaining trailing arm – the bushes should always be renewed in pairs.
13   Raise the torsion beam using the jack, and fit the bolts and nuts which secure the front ends of the trailing arms to the underbody. Do not fully tighten the fixings at this stage. Withdraw the axle stands.
14   Clip the rigid brake pipes and the flexible hoses to the vehicle underbody.
15   Proceed as described in Section 17, paragraphs 27 to 31 inclusive.

20   Rear stub axle (all models except GSi 2000) – removal and refitting

1   Remove the relevant rear hub, as described in Section 13.
2   Working behind the brake backplate, unscrew and remove the four bolts securing the stub axle and the brake backplate to the trailing arm (photo). Support the backplate as the bolts are removed, and once the stub axle is free, refit the bolts in order to locate the backplate, thus avoiding unnecessary strain on the brake fluid pipe.
3   Refitting is a reversal of removal, but coat the rear face of the stub axle flange where it contacts the brake backplate with a little lithium-based grease, and refit the rear hub as described in Section 13.
4   Tighten the stub axle/brake backplate securing bolts to the specified torque in the three stages given in the Specifications.

21   Rear suspension level control system – adjustment

1   With the vehicle unladen, use a tyre pressure gauge on the air valve to check that the system pressure is 0.8 bar (12.0 lbf/in²). Adjust if necessary.
2   With the vehicle standing on a level surface, measure the distance from the centre of the rear bumper to the ground. Subtract 50.0 mm (2.0 in) from the distance measured, and note the new value.
3   Load the vehicle, and if necessary the pressure in the system until the noted value for the bumper height is reached. **Do not** exceed a pressure of 5.0 bar (72.5 lbf/in²).
4   After unloading the vehicle, depressurise the system to restore the originally-measured bumper height, observing the minimum permissible pressure of 0.8 bar (12.0 lbf/in²).
5   Do not drive an unladen vehicle with the system fully inflated.

22   Rear suspension level control system components – removal and refitting

Air valve
1   Working in the luggage compartment, pull back the floor covering for access to the air valve.

2   Fully depressurise the system.
3   Remove the cap and the retaining sleeve from the valve, then compress the retaining lugs and push the valve downwards, taking care not to damage the air lines.
4   Unscrew the air line unions from the valve, and then withdraw the valve from the vehicle.
5   Refitting is a reversal of removal, but on completion, pressurise the system and check for air leaks.

Air lines
6   To remove an air line, first fully depressurise the system.
7   Unscrew the unions at the shock absorber and air valve, then release the air line from the clips on the vehicle underbody.
8   Refitting is a reversal of removal, but on completion, pressurise the system and check for air leaks.

Shock absorber
9   Removal and refitting of the shock absorbers is covered in Section 14.

23   Rear wheel bearing (GSi 2000 models) – renewal

Note: *This is a difficult operation, and it is suggested that this Section is read carefully before commencing work. A torque wrench capable of measuring the high torque of the rear hub nut and a suitable puller will be required. A new hub nut and locking collar must be used on reassembly*

1   Loosen the relevant rear roadwheel bolts, chock the front wheels, then jack up the rear of the vehicle, and support securely on axle stands positioned under the body side members. Remove the roadwheels.
2   Remove the locking clip and release the brake fluid line from the bracket on the semi-trailing arm. Note that the locking clip also supports the ABS sensor wire.
3   Unscrew the securing bolts, and withdraw the brake caliper and the ABS sensor bracket from the brake backplate. Support the caliper and the ABS sensor bracket out of the way, by suspending with string or wire from the vehicle underbody.
4   Remove the securing screw and withdraw the brake disc. If necessary, retract the handbrake shoes to enable the disc to be removed, by turning the adjuster with a screwdriver inserted through one of the unthreaded holes in the disc – see Chapter 8, Section 26.
5   Using a splined key inserted through one of the unthreaded holes in the hub flange, unscrew the four brake backplate securing bolts. Note that the upper bolts are shorter than the lower bolts, and are fitted with locking plates.
6   Prise out the plastic cover from the rear of the ABS toothed sensor wheel, to expose the rear hub nut (photos).

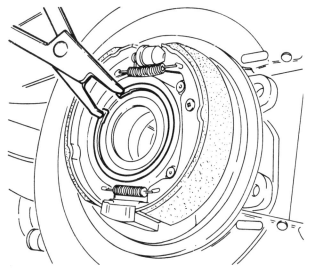

Fig. 9.12 Extracting the rear hub bearing retaining circlip – GSi 2000 models (Sec 23)

23.6A Prise out the plastic cover (arrowed) ...

23.6B ... for access to the rear hub nut – GSi 2000 model

7   Relieve the staking on the hub nut locking collar, then prise the locking collar from the ABS sensor wheel.
8   Screw two wheel bolts into the hub flange, and use a long metal bar between the bolts to hold the hub stationary, then unscrew the hub nut using a suitable socket and extension bar. Note that the hub nut is extremely tight.
9   Pull the ABS sensor wheel from the hub, if necessary using a suitable three-legged puller.
10   Press the rear hub outwards from the bearing, using a suitable puller attached to the semi-trailing arm. Note that the inner bearing track may stay on the hub as it is removed.
11   Extract the bearing retaining circlip from the outer edge of the semi-trailing arm, then press or drive out the bearing, applying pressure to the bearing outer race. If desired, the bearing can be removed in the same way as the rear hub using a suitable puller, again noting that pressure must be applied to the bearing outer race.
12   If the inner bearing race has remained on the hub, remove it using a suitable puller.
13   Clean all components, and examine them for wear and damage.
14   Commence reassembly by pressing the new bearing into the semi-trailing arm, using pressure on the bearing outer track. If necessary, a suitable tube or socket with a long bolt, nut and washers may be used to draw the bearing into position. Press the bearing into the semi-trailing arm until it rests against the shoulder.
15   Fit the bearing retaining circlip, ensuring that it seats correctly in its groove.
16   Have an assistant support the bearing inner track at the inner end of the semi-trailing arm using a suitable metal tube, then carefully drive in the rear hub from outside. Do not use excessively sharp blows, as the bearing is easily damaged.
17   Fit the ABS sensor wheel to the inner end of the hub. If necessary, have an assistant support the outer end of the hub, and drive the sensor wheel fully home from the inside. Take care not to damage the teeth on the sensor wheel.
18   Fit a new hub nut and tighten it to the specified torque, holding the hub stationary as during removal.
19   Fit a new locking collar to the hub nut, and stake it to the ABS sensor wheel.
20   Refit the plastic cover to the rear of the ABS sensor wheel.
21   Refit the brake backplate securing bolts, and tighten them to the specified torque. Ensure that the shorter bolts are fitted to the top of the plate, and make sure that the locking plates are fitted.
22   Refit the brake disc and tighten its securing screw, then operate the handbrake several times to operate the adjuster mechanism and bring the shoes to their correct seat position.
23   Refit the brake caliper and the ABS sensor bracket to the brake backplate, and tighten the securing bolts to the specified torque.
24   Reconnect the brake fluid line to its bracket on the semi-trailing arm, and secure with the locking clip.
25   Refit the roadwheel, then lower the vehicle to the ground. Finally tighten the roadwheel bolts with the vehicle resting on its wheels.

24 Rear hub (GSi 2000 models) – removal and refitting

1   Removal and refitting of the rear hub is described in Section 23, as part of the wheel bearing renewal procedure.
2   Note that the wheel bearing will almost certainly be destroyed during removal of the hub, and must therefore be renewed.
3   Refer to the note at the beginning of Section 23 before proceeding.

25 Rear suspension coil spring (GSi 2000 models) – removal and refitting

1   Note that the rear springs should be renewed in pairs, and if the springs are to be renewed, it is advisable to renew the spring damping rubbers at the same time.
2   Chock the front wheels, jack up the rear of the vehicle, and support securely on axle stands positioned under the body side members.
3   Working under the rear of the vehicle, remove the locking clips and release the brake fluid lines from their brackets on either side of the vehicle underbody. Note that the locking clips also support the ABS sensor wires.
4   Working on each side of the vehicle in turn, support the semi-trailing arm with a trolley jack, then unscrew and remove the bolt and washer securing the lower end of the shock absorber to the semi-trailing arm. Carefully lower the trolley jack, and withdraw it once the shock absorber has been disconnected from the semi-trailing arm.
5   Disconnect the fuel outlet hose from the fuel filter, located on the right-hand side of the underbody in front of the fuel tank. Be prepared for fuel spillage, and take adequate fire precautions. Plug the open ends of the filter and hose, to prevent further fuel spillage and dirt ingress.
6   Support the rear plate of the rear suspension crossmember with a trolley jack, then unscrew and remove the two securing bolts from the crossmember rear tube.
7   Carefully lower the trolley jack supporting the crossmember rear plate, taking care not to strain any of the hoses, pipes or wires, until the coil springs and their rubber dampers can be withdrawn. Note the orientation of the springs as they are removed.
8   Commence refitting by positioning the springs and their seats between the semi-trailing arms and the underbody as noted during removed.
9   Carefully raise the jack supporting the crossmember rear plate, then refit the crossmember rear tube-to-underbody bolts, and tighten them to the specified torque.
10   Reconnect the fuel outlet hose to the fuel filter, and tighten the clamp screw.
11   Reconnect the shock absorbers to the semi-trailing arms, supporting the semi-trailing arms with a trolley jack as during removal. Tighten the securing bolts to the specified torque.

26.5 Brake fluid line/ABS sensor wire bracket and locking clip on semi-trailing arm – GSi 2000 model

26.9 Rear suspension crossmember rear tube securing bolt – GSi 2000 model

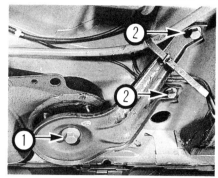

26.13 Forward crossmember securing bolt (1) and crossmember mounting bracing bracket bolts (2) – GSi 2000 model

12   Refit the brake lines to the brackets on the underbody, and secure with the locking clips.
13   Lower the vehicle to the ground.

26   Rear suspension assembly (GSi 2000 models) – removal and refitting

1   Loosen the rear roadwheel bolts, chock the front wheels, then jack up the rear of the vehicle, and support securely on axle stands positioned under the body side members. Remove the roadwheels.
2   Remove the rear half of the exhaust system (from the front expansion box rearwards), as described in Chapter 3.
3   Disconnect the handbrake cables and their return springs from the handbrake operating levers, with reference to Chapter 8, Section 27.
4   Withdraw the handbrake cables from the brackets on the semi-trailing arms.
5   Remove the locking clips and release the brake fluid lines from their brackets on the semi-trailing arms. Note that the locking clips also support the ABS sensor wires (photo).
6   Unscrew the securing bolts, and withdraw the brake calipers and the ABS sensor brackets from the brake backplates. Support the calipers and the ABS sensor brackets out of the way by suspending with string or wire from the vehicle underbody.
7   Working on each side of the vehicle in turn, support the semi-trailing arm with a trolley jack, then unscrew and remove the bolt and washer securing the lower end of the shock absorber to the semi-trailing arm. Carefully lower the trolley jack, and withdraw it once the shock absorber has been disconnected from the semi-trailing arm.
8   Disconnect the fuel outlet hose from the fuel filter, located on the right-hand side of the underbody in front of the fuel tank. Be prepared for fuel spillage, and take adequate fire precautions. Plug the open ends of the filter and hose, to prevent further fuel spillage and dirt ingress.
9   Support the rear plate of the rear suspension crossmember with a trolley jack, then unscrew and remove the two securing bolts from the crossmember rear tube (photo).
10   Carefully lower the trolley jack supporting the crossmember rear plate, until the coil springs and their rubber dampers can be withdrawn. Note the orientation of the springs as they are removed.
11   Make a check to ensure that all relevant hoses, pipes, cables and wires are clear of the rear suspension assembly.
12   With the weight of the rear suspension assembly supported on the trolley jack positioned under the crossmember rear plate, unscrew and remove the two forward crossmember securing bolts, noting that the bolts also pass through the crossmember mounting bracing brackets.
13   Unscrew and remove the two bolts in each case securing the crossmember mounting bracing brackets to the underbody, then with the help of an assistant, carefully lower the rear suspension assembly and withdraw it from under the vehicle (photo).
14   If desired, the assembly can be dismantled with reference to the relevant Sections of this Chapter.

15   If desired, the crossmember front mounting bushes can be renewed using a suitable diameter tube or socket, nut, bolt, washers and distance pieces as necessary to draw out the old bushes and fit the new ones. Lubricate the rear bushes with a little soapy water to aid fitting.
16   Commence refitting by positioning the rear suspension assembly under the rear of the vehicle, and raising it (with the aid of an assistant) using a trolley jack positioned under the crossmember rear plate as during removal.
17   Refit the two forward crossmember securing bolts, ensuring that they also pass through the crossmember mounting bracing brackets, but do not fully tighten them at this stage.
18   Refit the crossmember mounting bracing bracket-to-underbody bolts and tighten them to the specified torque, then tighten the two forward crossmember securing bolts to the specified torque.
19   If necessary, lower the trolley jack supporting the crossmember rear plate, and refit the coil springs and their dampers between the semi-trailing arms and the underbody, as noted during removal.
20   Carefully raise the trolley jack supporting the crossmember rear plate, then fit the two crossmember rear tube securing bolts, and tighten them to the specified torque. Withdraw the trolley jack.
21   Reconnect the fuel outlet hose to the fuel filter, and tighten the clamp screw.
22   Working on each side of the vehicle in turn, raise the semi-trailing arm with a trolley jack to allow the lower shock absorber securing bolt and washer to be fitted. Tighten the bolts to the specified torque, then withdraw the trolley jack.
23   Refit the brake calipers and the ABS sensor brackets to the brake backplates, and tighten the securing bolts to the specified torque.
24   Reconnect the brake fluid lines to their brackets on the semi-trailing arms, and secure with the locking clips.
25   Refit the handbrake cables to their brackets on the semi-trailing arms, and reconnect the cable ends and return springs to the handbrake operating levers, then check the handbrake cable adjustment, as described in Chapter 8, Section 26.
26   Refit the rear half of the exhaust system, with reference to Chapter 3.
27   Refit the roadwheels and lower the vehicle to the ground. Finally tighten the roadwheel bolts with the vehicle resting on its wheels.

27   Rear suspension semi-trailing arm (GSi 2000 models) – removal and refitting

1   Loosen the relevant rear roadwheel bolts, chock the front wheels, then jack up the rear of the vehicle, and support securely on axle stands positioned under the body side members. Remove the roadwheel.
2   Working under the rear of the vehicle, remove the locking clip and release the brake fluid line from its bracket on the semi-trailing arm. Note that the locking clip also supports the ABS sensor wire.
3   Unscrew the two securing bolts, and withdraw the brake caliper and the ABS sensor bracket from the brake backplate. Support the caliper

and the ABS sensor bracket out of the way by suspending with string or wire from the vehicle underbody.

4   Disconnect the handbrake cable and its return spring from the handbrake operating lever, with reference to Chapter 8, Section 27.

5   Withdraw the handbrake cable from the bracket on the semi-trailing arm.

6   Disconnect the anti-roll bar end link from the semi-trailing arm, by unscrewing the single securing nut and bolt. Recover the rubber bush and the spacer sleeve.

7   Support the semi-trailing arm with a trolley jack, then unscrew and remove the bolt and washer securing the lower end of the shock absorber to the semi-trailing arm.

8   Carefully lower the trolley jack sufficiently to enable the coil spring and its rubber dampers to be withdrawn. Note the orientation of the spring as it is removed. Once the spring has been removed, withdraw the jack.

9   Check that all relevant hoses, pipes, cables and wires have been positioned clear of the semi-trailing arm.

10   Unscrew and remove the two self-locking nuts and bolts securing the forward end of the semi-trailing arm to the suspension crossmember, then withdraw the semi-trailing arm from under the vehicle.

11   Refer to Section 23 for details of removal and refitting of the rear hub components.

12   If desired, the semi-trailing arm mounting bushes can be renewed using a suitable diameter tube or socket, nut, bolt, washers and distance pieces as necessary to draw out the old bushes and fit the new ones. To aid removal of the old bushes, the protruding ends of the bushes can be cut off using a sharp knife. Lubricate the new bushes with a little soapy water to aid fitting.

13   Commence refitting by manipulating the forward end of the semi-trailing arm into position in the suspension crossmember brackets.

14   Fit the semi-trailing arm securing bolts, with new self-locking nuts, but do not fully tighten them at this stage. Note that the bolt heads must face each other.

15   Support the semi-trailing arm with a trolley jack, then refit the coil spring and its rubber dampers as noted during removal.

16   Carefully raise the trolley jack to allow the lower shock absorber securing bolt and washer to be fitted. Tighten the bolt to the specified torque then withdraw the trolley jack.

17   Refit the rubber bush and the spacer sleeve, and reconnect the anti-roll bar end link to the semi-trailing arm. Tighten the securing nut to the specified torque while counterholding the bolt using a suitable spanner.

18   Refit the handbrake cable to the bracket on the semi-trailing arm, and reconnect the cable end and return spring to the handbrake operating lever, then check the handbrake cable adjustment, as described in Chapter 8, Section 26.

19   Refit the brake caliper and the ABS sensor bracket to the brake backplate, and tighten the securing bolts to the specified torque.

20   Reconnect the brake fluid line to its bracket on the semi-trailing arm, and secure with the locking clip.

21   Refit the roadwheel, then lower the vehicle to the ground. Finally tighten the roadwheel bolts with the vehicle resting on its wheels.

22   With the vehicle resting on its wheels, release the handbrake, and 'bounce' the rear of the car to settle the suspension components.

23   Chock the front wheels, and load each front seat with the equivalent of 70 kg (154 lbs). Working under the rear of the vehicle, tighten the semi-trailing arm securing nuts (self-locking) to the specified torque, while counterholding the bolts using a suitable spanner.

28   Rear suspension crossmember (GSi 2000 models) – removal and refitting

1   Removal and refitting of the rear suspension crossmember is described in Section 26, where the crossmember is removed as part of the complete rear suspension assembly. The relevant components can then be removed from the crossmember, with reference to the relevant Sections of this Chapter.

29   Rear anti-roll bar (GSi 2000 models) – removal and refitting

1   Chock the front wheels, then jack up the rear of the vehicle, and

support securely on axle stands positioned under the body side members.

2   Working under the rear of the vehicle, remove the locking clips and release the brake fluid lines from their brackets on either side of the vehicle underbody. Note that the locking clips also support the ABS sensor wires.

3   Disconnect the fuel outlet hose from the fuel filter, located on the right-hand side of the underbody is front of the fuel tank. Be prepared for fuel spillage, and take adequate fire precautions. Plug the open ends of the filter and hose, to prevent further fuel loss and dirt ingress.

4   Support the rear plate of the rear suspension crossmember using a trolley jack, then unscrew and remove the two securing bolts from the crossmember rear tube.

5   Carefully lower the trolley jack, taking care not to strain any of the hoses, pipes or wires, to allow access to the anti-roll bar-to-crossmember securing brackets.

6   Disconnect the anti-roll bar end links from the semi-trailing arms by unscrewing the single securing nut and bolt in each case. Recover the rubber bushes and the spacer sleeves.

7   Unscrew and remove the two bolts securing the anti-roll bar clamp brackets to the suspension crossmember, and withdraw the anti-roll bar from the vehicle (photo).

8   With the anti-roll bar removed from the vehicle, the end links can be removed by sliding them from the ends of the bar.

9   Examine the anti-roll bar mounting bushes for wear or damage, and renew as necessary.

10   If desired, the rubber bushes can be removed from the end links for renewal by pressing them out using a suitable diameter length of bar, or a suitable tube, nut, bolt and washers.

11   The mounting bushes which locate in the clamp brackets can be slid from the end of the anti-roll bar, after removal of one of the end links.

12   Lubricate the new bushes with soapy water to aid fitting.

13   Where applicable, refit the end links to the anti-roll bar.

14   Commence refitting by positioning the anti-roll bar under the rear of the vehicle, and securing the end links. Use new rubber bushes and spacer sleeves, and tighten the nuts to the specified torque while counterholding the bolts using a suitable spanner.

15   Refit the clamps securing the anti-roll bar to the suspension crossmember, and tighten the securing bolts to the specified torque.

16   Carefully raise the jack supporting the crossmember, then refit the bolts securing the crossmember rear tube to the underbody, and tighten them to the specified torque.

17   Reconnect the fuel outlet hose to the fuel filter, and tighten the clamp screw.

18   Reconnect the brake lines to their brackets on the underbody, and secure with the locking clips.

19   Lower the vehicle to the ground.

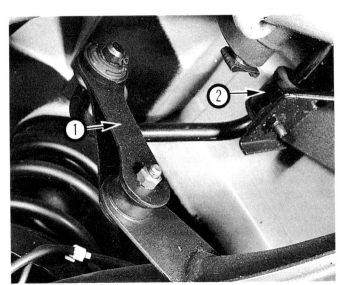

29.7 Rear anti-roll bar end link (1) and clamp bracket (2) – GSi 2000 model

30.3 Disconnecting the horn push pad wiring

30.4 Prising back the tabs on the steering wheel retaining nut lockwasher

30.7 Two-legged puller fitted to remove steering wheel

30 Steering wheel – removal and refitting

Note: *A suitable two-legged puller will be required for this operation*

1   Disconnect the battery negative lead.
2   Set the front wheels in the straight-ahead position, and unless unavoidable, do not move them until the steering wheel has been refitted.
3   Prise the horn push pad from the centre of the steering wheel, and disconnect the wiring (photo).
4   Using a screwdriver, prise back the tabs on the lockwasher securing the steering wheel retaining nut (photo).
5   Unscrew and remove the steering wheel retaining nut and the lockwasher.
6   Make alignment marks between the steering wheel and the end of the column shaft.
7   A suitably small two-legged puller must now be fitted to the steering wheel in order to pull it from the column shaft (photo). Note that the steering wheel is a very tight fit on the shaft.
8   Commence refitting by gently tapping the steering wheel into position on the column shaft, using a suitable metal tube or socket, and ensuring that the marks made during removal are aligned. Before tapping the wheel fully home, check the centralisation, as described in Section 31.
9   Refit the lockwasher and the steering wheel retaining nut, and tighten the nut to the specified torque. Bend up the lockwasher tabs to secure the nut.

10   Refit the horn push pad, ensuring that the wiring is securely connected, and reconnect the battery negative lead.

31 Steering wheel – centralising

1   The steering straight-ahead position is achieved when the reference dimension between the centre of the tie-rod-to-steering gear bolt locking plate(s), and the centre of the rib on the right-hand steering gear mounting clamp, is as shown in Fig. 9.13. In this position, the flexible rubber coupling upper pinch-bolt should lie horizontally on top of the steering shaft – see Fig. 9.14.
2   Check that the steering wheel is centralised.
3   If the steering wheel is off-centre by more than 5°, it should be removed, then moved the required number of splines on the column shaft to achieve centralisation, and refitted as described in Section 30.

32 Steering shaft flexible rubber coupling – renewal

1   Position the front roadwheels in the straight-ahead position.
2   Working in the engine compartment, loosen the steering gear mounting bolts.
3   Working in the driver's footwell, remove the lower trim panel by releasing the retaining clips.
4   Unscrew and remove the two pinch-bolts from the flexible coupling (photo).

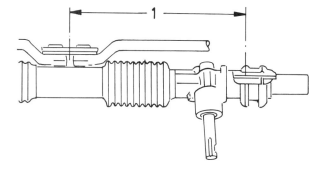

H. 20707

Fig. 9.13 Steering centralised for setting of steering wheel straight-ahead position (Sec 31)

1 = 325.0 mm (12.8 in)

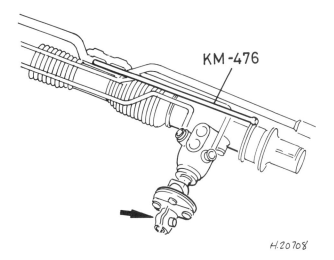

H.20708

Fig. 9.14 Flexible coupling upper pinch-bolt alignment (arrowed) with steering gear centralised (Sec 31)

32.4 Steering shaft flexible rubber coupling. Upper pinch-bolt arrowed

5   Push the coupling upwards, remove it from the steering gear pinion shaft, then tilt it and withdraw it from the steering shaft.
6   Before refitting, ensure that the steering gear and the steering wheel are centralised, with reference to Section 31.
7   Fit the coupling, and refit the pinch-bolts, but do not tighten them at this stage.
8   Push downwards on the coupling, and tighten the lower pinch-bolt.
9   Tighten the steering gear mounting bolts to the specified torque.
10   Pull the steering shaft upwards until it contacts the bearing stop, then tighten the coupling upper pinch-bolt.
11   Refit the driver's footwell lower trim panel.

33 Steering column – removal and refitting

Note: *A bolt extractor will be required during this operation. A new shear-head bolt and (where applicable) a new self-locking nut must be used to secure the column on refitting*

1   Disconnect the battery negative lead.
2   Set the front wheels in the straight-ahead position.
3   Working in the driver's footwell, remove the lower trim panel by releasing the retaining clips.
4   On models with an adjustable tilt steering column, move the column to its fully raised position, then unscrew the adjuster lever.
5   Remove the steering wheel, as described in Section 30, for improved access.
6   Prise out the screw covers from the front face of the steering column shrouds, then remove the two column shroud securing screws.
7   Remove the three securing screws from the underside of the lower column shroud, then remove both the upper and lower shrouds.
8   Disconnect the wiring plugs from the ignition switch and the indicator and wiper switches, and where applicable, disconnect the

horn push wires from the switch housing.
9   On models with a fixed steering column, depress the indicator switch and wiper switch retaining clips and withdraw the switches. On models with an adjustable tilt steering column, unscrew the two Torx screws securing the indicator/wiper switch assembly to the steering column, and remove the switch assembly.
10   Insert the ignition key into the ignition switch, and turn it to position '11'.
11   Insert a thin rod into the hole in the lock housing, then press the rod to release the detent spring, and pull out the lock cylinder using the key (photo).
12   Working at the lower end of the steering shaft, unscrew and remove the upper pinch-bolt securing the steering shaft to the flexible rubber coupling.
13   Unscrew and remove the bolt securing the column to the dashboard mounting bracket (photo).
14   Two fixings must now be extracted from the column upper mounting bracket. The right-hand bolt is of the shear-head type, and must be centre-punched, drilled and removed using a bolt extractor (photo). A conventional bolt, or a self-locking nut, is used on the left-hand side.
15   Withdraw the column assembly into the vehicle interior, and then remove it from the vehicle. Handle the column carefully, avoiding knocks or impact of any kind, which may damage the collapsible section of the column.
16   If desired, the column can be overhauled, as described in Section 34.
17   Commence refitting by ensuring that the roadwheels are still in the straight-ahead position, and that the flexible coupling is positioned so that the upper pinch-bolt will be horizontal on top of the steering shaft.
18   If a new column assembly is to be fitted, a large plastic washer will be found at the base of column tube. This washer is used to centre the shaft in the tube, and should be removed when fitting is complete.
19   Offer the column into position, and reconnect the flexible coupling. Refit the pinch-bolt, but do not fully tighten it at this stage.
20   Loosely fit the upper mounting fixings, using a new shear-head bolt, and (where applicable) a new self-locking nut.
21   Refit the bolt securing the column to the dashboard mounting bracket, and tighten the bolt to the specified torque.
22   Tighten the upper mounting fixings. The shear-head bolt should be tightened until the head breaks off, and the conventional bolt or self-locking nut, as applicable, should be tightened to the specified torque.
23   Pull upwards on the steering shaft until the shaft contacts the bearing stop, then tighten the flexible coupling upper pinch-bolt.
24   Prise the plastic centring washer from the base of the column tube, and remove it from the steering shaft.
25   Further refitting is a reversal of the removal procedure. Refit the steering wheel, as described in Section 30.
26   On completion, carry out a test drive along a route with several corners, and check that the steering mechanism operates smoothly.

34 Steering column – overhaul

Fixed steering column
1   If the steering column is in position in the vehicle, proceed as described in Section 33, paragraphs 1 to 11 inclusive.

33.11 Removing the lock cylinder – adjustable tilt steering column

33.13 Steering column-to-dashboard mounting bracket bolt (arrowed) viewed through instrument panel aperture

33.14 Column upper mounting shear-head bolt (arrowed)

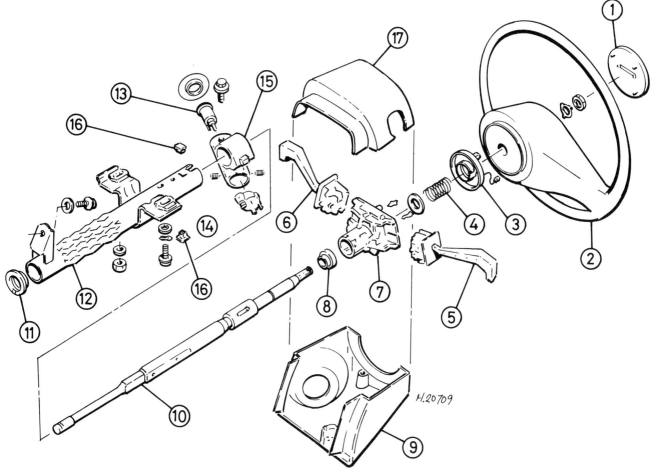

Fig. 9.15 Exploded view of fixed type steering column and associated components (Sec 34)

1	Horn push pad	6	Wash/wipe switch
2	Steering wheel	7	Switch housing
3	Cam assembly	8	Bearing
4	Spring	9	Lower column shroud
5	Lighting switch	10	Steering shaft

11	Centralising plastic discs
12	Column tube
13	Lock barrel
14	Ignition switch
15	Lock housing

16	Switch housing safety plugs
17	Upper column shroud

2   Prise out the ignition switch housing safety plugs (see Fig. 9.15), then turn the housing anti-clockwise, and pull it from the steering column.

3   The bearing can be removed from the ignition switch housing by prising apart the two bearing fixing catches, and pressing or driving out the bearing with a piece of suitable diameter tubing on the bearing outer race. When pressing in the new bearing, make sure that the thrust-washer and contact springs are correctly located – see Fig. 9.16.

4   The ignition switch is secured to the steering lock housing by two grub screws. Remove the screws to extract the switch. It is recommended that the switch and the lock cylinder are not both removed at the same time, so that their mutual alignment is not lost.

5   If the steering column is in position in the vehicle, unscrew and remove the upper pinch-bolt from the steering shaft flexible rubber coupling in the driver's footwell.

6   Withdraw the steering shaft from the steering column tube.

7   Commence reassembly by fitting the temporary plastic centring washer, which will be supplied with a new column or steering shaft, into the base of the column tube.

8   Insert the shaft into the column tube, and if the column is in position in the vehicle, engage the bottom end of the shaft with the flexible coupling and refit the upper pinch-bolt, but do not tighten it at this stage.

9   Where applicable, refit the ignition switch, and tighten the grub screws.

10   Refit the ignition switch housing, using new safety plugs.

11   If the column is in position in the vehicle, pull upwards on the steering shaft until the shaft contacts the bearing stop, then tighten the

flexible coupling upper pinch-bolt. Ensure that the roadwheels are still in the straight-ahead position, and that the flexible coupling is positioned so that the upper pinch-bolt is horizontal on top of the steering shaft.

Fig. 9.16 Sectional view of ignition switch housing (Sec 34)

A   Thrustwasher   B   Contact springs

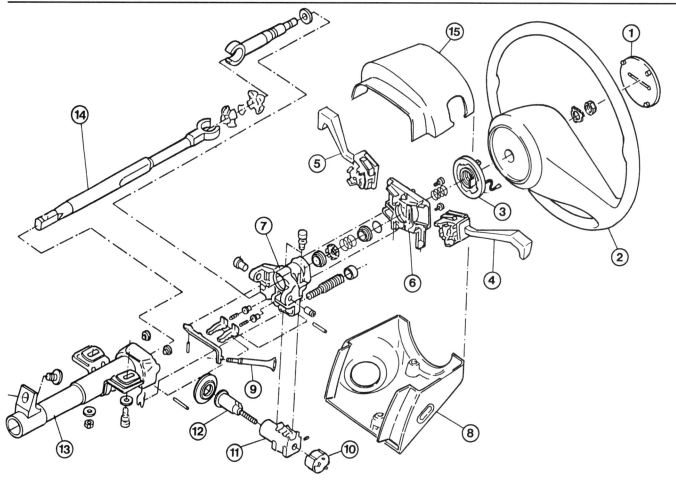

Fig. 9.17 Exploded view of adjustable tilt type steering column and associated components (Sec 34)

1	Horn push pad	5	Wash/wipe switch
2	Steering wheel	6	Switch housing
3	Cam assembly	7	Bearing housing
4	Lighting switch	8	Lower column shroud
9	Tilt adjuster lever	13	Column tube
10	Ignition switch	14	Steering shaft
11	Lock housing	15	Upper column shroud
12	Lock barrel		

12   Where applicable, further reassembly is a reversal of dismantling. Refit the steering wheel, as described in Section 30.
13   On completion, carry out a test drive along a route with several corners, and check that the steering mechanism operates smoothly.

Adjustable tilt steering column
Note: *New shear-head bolts must be used to secure the lock housing on reassembly*

14   If the steering column is in position in the vehicle, proceed as described in Section 33, paragraphs 1 to 11 inclusive.
15   The tilt adjuster spring can be removed by simply prising it free using a screwdriver. Be careful, as the spring may fly out.
16   The ignition switch is secured to the lock housing by two grub screws. Access to the 'hidden' grub screw is virtually impossible with the steering column installed. For this, and further dismantling, the column must therefore be removed, as described in Section 33.
17   The lock housing is secured to the bearing housing by two shear-head bolts, which must be centre-punched, drilled and removed using a bolt extractor, if the two housings are to be separated (photo).
18   The column bearing upper race can be renewed after removing the retaining ring, pressure rings and spring. Note that it may be necessary to compress the spring in order to remove the retaining ring. Take care, as the spring may fly out as the retaining ring is removed.
19   To remove the bearing housing from the column, the fulcrum pins must be extracted, using a suitable nut and bolt to draw them out. Vauxhall special tool KM-585 is available for this purpose – see Fig. 9.18.
20   The column bearing lower race can be driven from the upper shaft using a hammer and a suitable drift or chisel. Press or drive the new race onto the shaft.

21   The column bearings themselves can only be renewed complete with the housing.

34.17 Lock housing shear-head bolt location (arrowed) – adjustable tilt steering column

Fig. 9.18 Extracting the bearing housing fulcrum pins using special tool KM-585 – adjustable tilt type steering column (Sec 34)

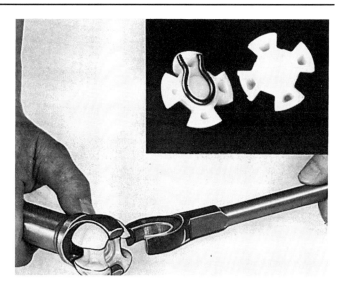

Fig. 9.19 Steering shaft universal joint. Spring clip location inset – adjustable tilt type steering column (Sec 34)

22   The shaft universal joint and the tilt mechanism detent components can be dismantled for component renewal if necessary.
23   Reassembly is a reversal of dismantling, noting the following points.
24   When reconnecting the steering shaft universal joint, note that the spring clips should be located in the recesses of each half of the joint – see Fig. 9.19.
25   If the lock housing and bearing housing have been separated, clean out the securing bolt holes with a tap. Apply thread-locking compound to new shear-head bolts, and tighten the bolts until their heads break off.
26   After fitting the bearing housing fulcrum pins, stake them both in three equidistant places.
27   If the bearings have been renewed, the gaps between the bearing housing and the buffers which limit the movement in the upper position should be checked to ensure that they are equal. Check the gap with a feeler gauge. A kit containing different thicknesses of buffer, with instructions, is available if required.

35   Steering damper – removal and refitting

1   Certain models are equipped with a steering damper, which is fitted between the rack and the rack housing.
2   Remove the securing nut from the moving end of the damper, and recover the washer.
3   Unbolt the clamp assembly from the rack housing, and withdraw the damper from its tube. Take care not to lose the rubbers and washer from the end of the damper.
4   When refitting, secure the clamp assembly to the rack housing first, then tighten the securing nut at the moving end of the damper, to obtain a dimension 'A', as shown in Fig. 9.20.

36   Steering gear bellows – renewal

Note: *New bellows securing clips will be required for refitting*

1   Remove the steering gear, as described in Section 37 or 39, as applicable.
2   Remove the mounting clamp and rubber from the left-hand end of the steering gear.
3   On power steering gear, disconnect the fluid pipe unions from the left-hand end of the steering gear.
4   Remove the outer bellows securing clips from each end of the steering gear, then slide off the bellows/tube assembly.
5   Remove the inner bellows securing clips, and separate the bellows from the tube.
6   Fit the new bellows to the tube, using new clips. The clips should be positioned so that when the steering gear is fitted to the vehicle, the ends of the clips point upwards.
7   Fit the bellows/tube assembly to the steering gear, and secure with new clips, again positioned with the ends of the clips pointing upwards. Ensure that the bellows are not twisted.
8   On power steering gear, reconnect the fluid pipe unions, using new O-rings.
9   Refit the mounting clamp and rubber, then refit the steering gear, as described in Section 37 or 39, as applicable.

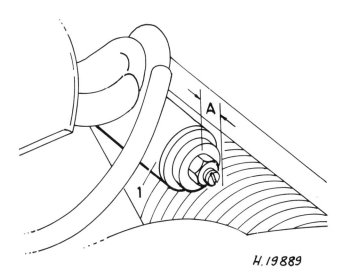

H.19889

Fig. 9.20 Steering damper securing nut setting (Sec 35)

1   *Damper tube   A = 12.5 to 13.5 mm (0.49 to 0.53 in)*

37   Manual steering gear – removal and refitting

Note: *New steering gear clamp-to-bulkhead bolts, and new tie-rod-to-steering gear bolt locking plates, must be used on refitting*

1   Disconnect the battery negative lead.

37.4A Prise off the locking plate ...

37.4B ... then unscrew and remove the tie-rod-to-steering gear bolts

37.9 Removing the steering gear

37.11 Tightening a steering gear mounting bolt

2   On carburettor models, for improved access, remove the air cleaner casing from the top of the carburettor. On certain models, it may be necessary to unbolt the coolant expansion tank and/or the brake master cylinder for access to the right-hand steering gear mounting clamp.
3   Set the front wheels in the straight-ahead position.
4   Prise the locking plate(s) from the tie-rod-to-steering gear bolts, then unscrew and remove the bolts and recover the washers and spacer plate (photos).
5   If a steering damper is fitted, unbolt the clamp assembly from the steering gear, and remove the damper.
6   Working in the driver's footwell, remove the lower trim panel by releasing the retaining clips.
7   On models with an adjustable tilt steering column, move the column to its fully raised position.
8   Unscrew and remove the upper pinch-bolt securing the steering shaft to the flexible rubber coupling.
9   Working in the engine compartment, unbolt the two clamps securing the steering gear to the bulkhead, then manipulate the steering gear out from the left-hand side of the engine compartment (photo). The help of an assistant may be required to release the flexible rubber coupling from the steering shaft as the steering gear is withdrawn. Note that on some models, various wires and hoses may be secured to the steering gear with cable ties – ensure that, where applicable, all wires and hoses are free before the steering gear is removed.
10   Refitting is a reversal of removal, bearing in mind the following points.
11   Use new mounting bolts to secure the steering gear clamps to the bulkhead (photo).
12   The tie-rod-to-steering gear bolt locking plate(s) must be renewed on refitting.
13   On completion, check the steering wheel centralisation, as described in Section 31.

38   Manual steering gear – overhaul

Note: *A new pinion nut locking ring, damper slipper seal, and rack housing sealing cap, must be used on reassembly*

1   Remove the steering gear, as described in Section 37, and remove the mounting rubbers and clamps.
2   Clean away all external dirt.
3   Release the outer bellows securing clips from each end of the steering gear, then slide off the bellows/tube assembly.
4   Extract the sliding bar and the guide plate from the rack.
5   Release the locknut from the rack adjuster screw.
6   Unscrew and remove the adjuster screw, and extract the coil spring, seal and damper slipper.
7   Unscrew and remove the lower pinch-bolt from the flexible rubber coupling, then remove the coupling and the rubber boot from the pinion.
8   Extract the pinion nut locking ring, then unscrew the pinion nut and extract the seal.
9   Withdraw the rack and the pinion.
10   Drive the metal sealing cap from the end of the rack housing, using a long rod.
11   Further dismantling is not possible. If the rack bushes or pinion needle bearing are worm, the complete rack housing must be renewed. The pinion can only be renewed complete with the ball bearing.
12   Note that two different ratios of steering gear may be fitted, and components are not interchangeable between the two. The pinion shaft for steering gear with a ratio of 22 : 1 has no identification groove, and the corresponding rack has 28 teeth. The pinion shaft for steering gear with a ratio of 24.5 : 1 has a single identification groove, and the corresponding rack has 32 teeth.
13   Clean away old lubricant, then apply grease (Vauxhall grease 19 48 588, or equivalent) to all moving components. Insert an amount 50.0 g (1.8 oz) of the grease between the rack bushes inside the housing.
14   Insert the rack into the housing, and locate it so that the end furthest from the pinion is positioned as shown in Fig. 9.22.
15   Fit the pinion so that, when meshed with the rack, its cut-out is positioned at right-angles to the rack housing, facing towards the right-hand end of the housing – see Fig. 9.22.
16   Apply grease to the pinion ball bearing, then screw in the pinion nut and tighten it to the specified torque.
17   Fit a new pinion nut locking ring, driving it into place using a piece of metal tubing or a suitable socket.
18   The damper slipper adjustment must now be set. Make up two tubular distance pieces to the dimensions shown in Fig. 9.23.
19   Using the tie-rod-to-steering gear bolts, secure the sliding bar, guide plate and distance pieces to the rack.
20   Fit a new damper slipper seal, then fit the damper slipper and the coil spring into their hole. Screw in the adjuster screw until some resistance is felt – a target turning torque of 5 Nm (3.7 lbf ft) is specified.
21   From this position, back off the adjuster screw by between 20° and 40°. Check that the rack moves freely throughout its entire travel.
22   Without disturbing the adjuster screw, fit the locknut and tighten it to the specified torque. This can be achieved by counterholding the adjuster screw using a suitable socket fitted to a torque wrench, and turning the locknut with a spanner until the specified torque is reached. Take care not to move the adjuster screw.

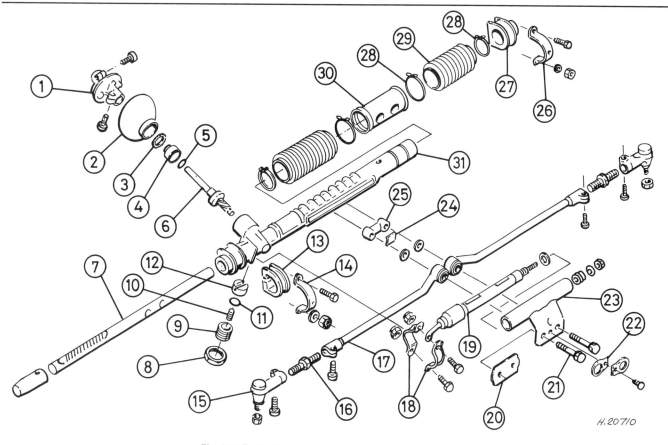

Fig. 9.21 Exploded view of manual steering gear (Sec 38)

1	Flexible coupling	9	Adjuster screw
2	Rubber cover	10	Spring
3	Locking ring	11	O-ring
4	Pinion nut	12	Damper slipper
5	O-ring	13	Mounting rubber
6	Pinion	14	Mounting clamp
7	Rack	15	Tie-rod end
8	Locknut	16	Tie-rod adjuster pin

17	Tie-rod	25	Sliding bar
18	Steering damper clamp	26	Mounting clamp
19	Steering damper	27	Mounting rubber
20	Spacer plate	28	Bellows securing clip
21	Tie-rod-to-steering gear bolt	29	Bellows
22	Locking plate	30	Tube
23	Steering damper tube	31	Rack housing
24	Guide plate		

23   Tap a new sealing cap into the end of the rack housing.
24   Remove the tie-rod-to-steering gear bolts, and the distance pieces.
25   Refit the bellows/tube assembly, and secure the bellows with new clips. Position the clips so that when the steering gear is installed in the vehicle, the ends of the clips point upwards, and ensure that the bellows are not twisted.

26   Refit the steering gear mounting rubbers and clamps, noting that the right-hand mounting clamp fits with the concave end of the clamp pointing downwards with the steering gear installed in the vehicle.
27   Refit the rubber boot and the flexible rubber coupling to the pinion, and tighten the pinch-bolt.
28   Refit the steering gear, as described in Section 37, but before

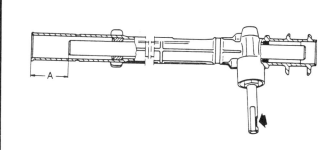

Fig. 9.22 Correct position of pinion cut-out (arrowed) (Sec 38)

A = 61.0 mm (2.4 in)

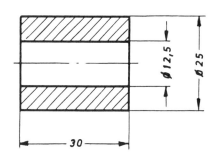

Fig. 9.23 Distance piece for damper slipper adjustment (Sec 38)

All dimensions in mm

finally tightening the mounting bolts and reconnecting the tie-rods, check the steering wheel centralisation, as described in Section 31. If the pinion position is incorrect (ie the upper flexible rubber coupling pinch-bolt position is not as specified), then the pinion will have to be withdrawn from the steering gear and moved as necessary to correct the setting.

29   After refitting the steering gear, carry out a test drive along a route with several corners. The steering should show a well-defined self-centring action. If not, the rack damper slipper has been over-adjusted, and must be reset. The steering gear must be removed again to enable adjustment to be carried out.

39   Power steering gear – removal and refitting

Note: *New steering gear mounting bolts, and new tie-rod-to-steering gear bolt locking plates, must be used on refitting. New O-rings should be used when reconnecting fluid pipe unions*

1   Proceed as described in Section 37, paragraphs 1 to 3 inclusive.
2   Disconnect the fluid hoses from the pipes at the left-hand end of the steering gear. Be prepared for fluid spillage, and plug the open ends of the pipes and hoses, to prevent dirt ingress and further fluid loss.
3   Where applicable, to provide space for the steering gear to be withdrawn, remove the relay box from the left-hand side of the engine compartment, with reference to Chapter 11, Section 16 if necessary.
4   Proceed as described in Section 37, paragraph 4 to 9 inclusive.
5   If fluid has been leaking from the fluid pipe union(s) on the steering gear, the relevant union(s) should be disconnected in order to renew the O-ring(s). Note that the O-rings should always be renewed whenever the unions are disconnected. A suitable hexagon bit or Allen key may be required to unscrew some unions. Tighten the union(s) to the specified torque after fitting new O-rings.
6   Refitting is a reversal of removal, bearing in mind the following points.
7   Before refitting, centralise the steering gear by counting the number of turns of the pinion shaft required to move the rack from lock to lock, then set the rack by turning the pinion shaft from the full lock position through half the number of turns counted. Note that fluid may be ejected from the steering gear pipes as the rack is turned, and it may be necessary to remove the plugs from the ends of the pipes to allow the rack to turn.
8   Use new mounting bolts to secure the steering gear clamps to the bulkhead.
9   The tie-rod-to-steering gear bolt locking plate(s) must be renewed on refitting.
10   Reconnect the flexible rubber coupling to the steering shaft (with the rack and steering wheel centralised) so that the upper pinch-bolt lies horizontally on top of the steering shaft – see Fig. 9.14.
11   Renew the O-ring when reconnecting the fluid hose-to-pipe union.
12   On completion, top up the fluid level, and bleed the fluid circuit as described in Section 41.

40   Power steering gear – overhaul

1   Overhaul of the power steering gear is not recommended by the manufacturers.
2   Fluid leaks from the hydraulic fluid pipe unions can normally be corrected by renewing the unions seals with the rack installed.
3   Bellows renewal is covered in Section 36.
4   Adjustment of the power steering gear should not be attempted.
5   Any faults with the steering gear should be referred to a Vauxhall dealer, although renewal of the complete assembly will probably be the only course of action available.

41   Power steering fluid circuit – bleeding

1   With the engine stopped, initially fill the reservoir to the level of 'MAX' mark on the dipstick attached to the reservoir filler cap.
2   Start the engine, and immediately top up the fluid level to the 'MIN' mark on the dipstick. **Do not** allow the reservoir to run dry at any time. The help of an assistant will ease this operation.

42.4 Adjusting the length of the power steering pump threaded rod – 2.0 litre model

3   With the engine running at idle speed, turn the steering wheel slowly two or three times approximately 45° left and right of the centre, then turn the wheel twice from lock to lock. Do not hold the wheel on either lock, as this imposes strain on the hydraulic system.
4   Stop the engine, and check the fluid level. With the fluid at operating temperature (80°/176°F), the level should be on the 'MAX' mark, and with the fluid cold (20°C/68°F), the level should be on the 'MIN' mark. Top up if necessary.

42   Power steering pump drivebelt – removal, refitting and adjustment

1.6 litre models
1   The power steering pump is driven by the alternator drivebelt.
2   Drivebelt removal, refitting and adjustment procedures are given in Chapter 11, Section 7.

1.8 and 2.0 litre models
3   Slacken the adjuster and mounting bolts shown in Fig. 9.24.
4   Slacken the adjuster nuts, and adjust the length of the threaded rod in order to remove or tension the belt as desired (photo).

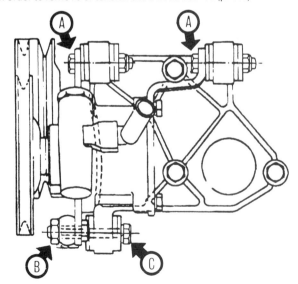

Fig. 9.24 Mounting and adjuster bolts (arrowed) must be loosened to adjust drivebelt tension – 1.8 and 2.0 litre models (Sec 42)

For A, B and C see 'Torque wrench settings' in Specifications

5   To tension the belt, Vauxhall specify the use of a special gauge, and checking values for use with this gauge are given in the Specifications for reference purposes. The correct belt tension can be approximated by adjusting the length of the threaded rod to give a belt deflection of approximately 10.0 mm (0.4 in) under moderate thumb pressure at the midpoint of the belt run between the pulleys. If in doubt, err on the slack side, as an excessively tight belt may cause pump damage.

6   Tighten the adjuster nuts, and tighten the adjuster and mounting bolts to the specified torque on completion.

7   If a new drivebelt has been fitted, recheck the tension after a few hundred miles.

43 Power steering pump – removal and refitting

Note: *A new fluid pipe union O-ring must be used on refitting*

1.6 litre models

1   Remove the air cleaner casing from the right-hand front wing, as described in Chapter 3, Section 5, for improved access.

2   Remove the alternator/power steering pump drivebelt, with reference to Chapter 11, Section 7.

3   Unscrew the three securing bolts, and remove the power steering pump pulley.

4   Unclip and remove the outer timing belt cover.

5   Disconnect the fluid pipe union and the hose from the pump. Be prepared for fluid spillage, and plug the open ends of the pump and the pipes, to prevent dirt ingress and further fluid spillage.

6   Unscrew the two pump securing bolts, and withdraw the pump from the cylinder block towards the alternator.

7   No overhaul of the pump is possible, and if faulty, a new unit must be fitted.

8   Refitting is a reversal of removal, but renew the O-ring when reconnecting the fluid pipe union, and tension the alternator/power steering pump drivebelt, as described in Chapter 11, Section 7.

9   On completion, top up the fluid level, and bleed the fluid circuit as described in Section 41.

1.8 and 2.0 litre models

10   Remove the power steering pump drivebelt, as described in Section 42.

11   Disconnect the fluid pipe union and the flexible fluid hose from the pump (photo). Be prepared for fluid spillage, and plug the open ends of the pump, pipe and hose, to prevent dirt ingress and further fluid loss.

12   Unscrew and remove the four mounting bolts shown in Fig. 9.26. Recover the nuts, and take care not to lose the rubber insulators which fit into the mounting bracket.

13   Withdraw the pump from the vehicle.

43.11 Fluid pipe union (1) and flexible hose connection (2) at power steering pump – 2.0 litre model

14   No overhaul of the pump is possible, and if faulty, a new unit must be fitted.

15   Refitting is a reversal of removal, but renew the O-ring when reconnecting the fluid pipe union, and before finally tightening the pump mounting bolts, tension the drivebelt, as described in Section 42.

16   On completion, top up the fluid level, and bleed the fluid circuit as described in Section 41.

44 Power steering fluid reservoir – removal and refitting

1   The reservoir can be removed for the mounting bracket by unscrewing the clamp screw and removing the clamp.

2   Have a suitable container ready to catch the fluid, then disconnect the fluid hoses from the reservoir and drain the fluid. Plug the open ends of the hoses, to prevent dirt ingress and further fluid loss.

3   If desired, the mounting bracket can be unbolted from the body panel, but note that on certain models, the bolts securing the bracket also secure the ignition coil and suppressor – refer to Chapter 4, Section 6 if necessary. Where applicable, unclip the brake fluid pipes and any wiring from the bracket before removal.

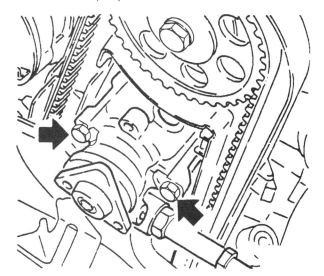

Fig. 9.25 Power steering pump mounting bolts (arrowed) – 1.6 litre models (Sec 43)

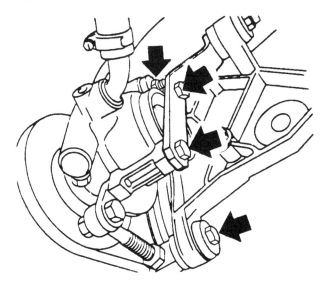

Fig. 9.26 Power steering pump mounting bolts (arrowed) – 1.8 and 2.0 litre models (Sec 43)

45.2 Power steering fluid cooler pipe unions at left-hand side of engine compartment (radiator removed) – 2.0 litre model

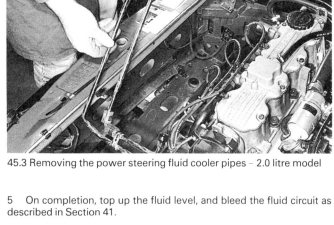

45.3 Removing the power steering fluid cooler pipes – 2.0 litre model

4   Refitting is a reversal of removal, but on completion, bleed the fluid circuit as described in Section 41.

5   On completion, top up the fluid level, and bleed the fluid circuit as described in Section 41.

---

45   Power steering fluid cooler pipes (1.8 and 2.0 litre models) – removal and refitting

Note: *New fluid pipe union O-rings must be used on refitting*

1   Remove the radiator, as described in Chapter 2, Section 7.
2   Working at the left-hand side of the engine compartment, disconnect the fluid cooler pipe unions (photo). Be prepared for fluid spillage, and plug the open ends of the pipes to prevent dirt ingress and further fluid loss.
3   Release the three plastic clips securing the pipes to the lower body panel, then manipulate the pipes from the engine compartment (photo).
4   Refitting is a reversal of removal, but renew the O-rings when reconnecting the fluid pipe unions, and refit the radiator as described in Chapter 2, Section 7.

---

46   Tie-rod end – removal and refitting

Note: *A balljoint separator tool will be required for this operation. A new tie-rod end balljoint self-locking nut must be used on refitting*

1   Where applicable, remove the wheel trim, then loosen the relevant front roadwheel bolts. Apply the handbrake, then jack up the front of the vehicle, and support securely on axle stands positioned under the body side members. Remove the relevant front roadwheel.
2   Loosen the tie-rod end clamp bolt, which secures the tie-rod end to the threaded adjuster pin on the tie-rod (photo).
3   Unscrew the self-locking nut from the tie-rod end-to-suspension strut balljoint.
4   Using a balljoint separator, disconnect the tie-rod end-to-suspension strut balljoint (photo).
5   Note the position of the tie-rod end on the adjuster pin, either by

46.2 Tie-rod end viewed from underneath

1   Tie-rod end clamp bolt   3   Tie-rod clamp bolt
2   Threaded adjuster pin

46.4 Disconnecting the tie-rod end-to-suspension strut balljoint

marking the pin with paint or tape, or by counting the number of threads exposed, then unscrew the tie-rod end from the tie-rod.

6   Note that the tie-rod ends are handed. The right-hand tie-rod end is marked 'R', but the left-hand tie-rod end has no marking.

7   Commence refitting by screwing the tie-rod end onto the adjuster pin to approximately the same position as was noted during removal.

8   Reconnect the tie-rod end balljoint to the suspension strut, and tighten a new self-locking nut to the specified torque.

9   Tighten the tie-rod end clamp bolt.

10   Refit the roadwheel, and lower the vehicle to the ground. Finally tighten the roadwheel bolts with the vehicle resting on its wheels, and where applicable, refit the wheel trim.

11   Check the front wheel alignment, as described in Section 48, and adjust if necessary. No harm will result from driving the vehicle a short distance to have the alignment checked.

47   Tie-rod – removal and refitting

Note: *A new tie-rod-to-steering gear bolt locking plate, and where applicable, a new tie-rod end balljoint self-locking nut, must be used on refitting. If the tie-rod is to be removed complete with the tie-rod end, a balljoint separator tool will be required*

1   The tie-rod can either be removed leaving the tie-rod end in place, or as an assembly with the tie-rod end.

2   Proceed as described in Section 46, paragraph 1.

3   If the tie-rod is to be removed complete with the tie-rod end, proceed as described in Section 46, paragraphs 3 and 4.

4   If the tie-rod is to be removed independently of the tie-rod end, loosen the tie-rod clamp bolt, which secures the tie-rod to the threaded adjuster pin on the tie-rod end.

5   Prise the locking plate(s) from the tie-rod-to-steering gear bolts, then unscrew and remove the bolts, and recover the washers and spacer plate (photo).

6   If the tie-rod is being removed complete with the tie-rod end, the assembly can now be withdrawn from the vehicle.

7   If the tie-rod is to be removed independently of the tie-rod end, note the position of the tie-rod end on the adjuster pin, either by marking the pin with paint or tape, or by counting the number of threads exposed, then unscrew the tie-rod from the tie-rod end and withdraw it from the vehicle.

8   Refitting is a reversal of removal, bearing in mind the following points.

9   The tie-rod-to-steering gear bolt locking plate(s) must be renewed on refitting.

10   If the tie-rod is being refitted complete with the tie-rod end, reconnect the tie-rod end balljoint to the suspension strut, and tighten a new self-locking nut to the specified torque.

11   If the tie-rod is being refitted with the tie-rod end already in place

on the vehicle, screw the tie-rod onto the adjuster pin to approximately the same position as noted during removal, and tighten the clamp bolt.

12   Finally tighten the roadwheel bolts with the vehicle resting on its wheels, and where applicable, refit the wheel trim.

13   On completion, check the front wheel alignment, as described in Section 48 and adjust if necessary. No harm will result from driving the vehicle a short distance to have the alignment checked.

48   Front wheel alignment – checking and adjustment

1   Accurate front wheel alignment is essential for precise steering and handling, and for even tyre wear. Before carrying out any checking or adjusting operations, make sure that the tyres are correctly inflated, that all steering and suspension joints and linkages are in sound condition and that the wheels are not buckled or distorted, particularly around the rims. It will also be necessary to have the car positioned on flat level ground, with enough space to push the car backwards and forwards through about half its length.

2   Front wheel alignment consists of four factors:

Camber is the angle at which the roadwheels are set from the vertical when viewed from the front or rear of the vehicle. Positive camber is the angle (in degrees) that the wheels are tilted outwards at the top from the vertical.

Castor is the angle between the steering axis and a vertical line when viewed from each side of the vehicle. Positive castor is indicated when the steering axis is inclined towards the rear of the vehicle at its upper end.

Steering axis inclination is the angle, when viewed from the front or rear of the vehicle, between the vertical and an imaginary line drawn between the upper and lower front suspension strut mountings.

Toe setting is the amount by which the distance between the front inside edges of the roadwheels differs from that between the rear inside edges, when measured at hub height. If the distance between the front edges is less than that at the rear, the wheels are said to 'toe-in'. If it is greater than at the rear, the wheels 'toe-out.'

3   Camber, castor and steering axis inclination are set during manufacture, and are not adjustable. Unless the vehicle has suffered accident damage, or there is gross wear in the suspension mountings or joints, it can be assumed that these settings are correct. If for any reason it is believed that they are not correct, the task of checking them should be left to a Vauxhall dealer, who will have the necessary special equipment needed to measure the small angles involved.

4   It is, however, within the scope of the home mechanic to check and adjust the front wheel toe setting. To do this, a tracking gauge must first be obtained. Two types are gauges are available, and can be obtained from motor accessory shops. The first type measures the distance between the front and rear inside edges of the roadwheels, as previously described, with the car stationary. The second type, known as a scuff plate, measures the actual position of the contact surface of the tyre, in relation to the road surface, with the vehicle in motion. This is achieved by pushing or driving the front tyre over a plate, which then moves slightly according to the scuff of the tyre, and shows this movement on a scale. Both types have their advantages and disadvantages, but either can give satisfactory results if used correctly and carefully. Alternatively, a tracking gauge can be fabricated from a length of steel tubing, suitably cranked to clear the sump and clutch bellhousing, with a setscrew and a locknut at one end.

5   Many tyre specialists will also check toe settings free, or for a nominal charge.

6   Make sure that the steering is in the straight-ahead position when making measurements.

7   If adjustment is found to be necessary, clean the ends of the tie-rods in the area of the adjustment pin and clamp bolts.

8   Slacken the clamp bolts (one on each tie-rod balljoint and one on each tie-rod), and turn the adjustment pin on each tie-rod by the same amount in the same direction. Only turn each pin by a quarter turn at a time before rechecking.

9   When adjustment is correct, tighten the clamp bolts to the specified torque. Check that the tie-rod lengths are equal to within 5 mm (0.2 in), and that the steering wheel spokes are in the correct straight-ahead position.

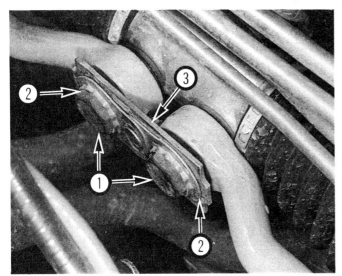

47.5 Tie-rod-to-steering gear bolts (1), locking plates (2) and spacer plate (3)

49   Wheels and tyres – general care and maintenance

Wheels and tyres should give no real problems in use provided that a close eye is kept on them with regard to excessive wear or damage. To this end, the following points should be noted.

Ensure that tyre pressures are checked regularly and maintained correctly. Checking should be carried out with the tyres cold and not immediately after the vehicle has been in use. If the pressures are checked with the tyres hot, an apparently high reading will be obtained owing to heat expansion. Under no circumstances should an attempt be made to reduce the pressures to the quoted cold reading in this instance, or effective underinflation will result.

Underinflation will cause overheating of the tyre owing to excessively flexing of the casing, and the tread will not sit correctly on the road surface. This will cause a consequent loss of adhesion and excessive wear, not to mention the danger of sudden tyre failure due to heat build-up.

Overinflation will cause rapid wear of the centre part of the tyre tread coupled with reduced adhesion, harsher ride, and the danger of shock damage occurring in the tyre casing.

Regularly check the tyres for damage in the form of cuts or bulges, especially in the sidewalls. Remove any nails or stoned embedded in the tread before they penetrate the tyre to cause deflation. If removal of a nail *does* reveal that the tyre has been punctured, refit the nail so that its point of penetration is marked. Then immediately change the wheel and have the tyre repaired by a tyre dealer. Do *not* drive on a tyre in such a condition. In many cases a puncture can be simply repaired by the use of an inner tube of the correct size and type. If in any doubt as to the possible consequences of any damage found, consult your local tyre dealer for advice.

Periodically remove the wheels and clean any dirt or mud from the inside and outside surfaces. Examine the wheels rims for signs of rusting, corrosion or other damage. Light alloy wheels are easily damaged by 'kerbing' whilst parking, and similarly steel wheels may become dented or buckled. Renewal of the wheel is very often the only course of remedial action possible.

The balance of each wheel and tyre assembly should be maintained to avoid excessive wear, not only to the tyres but also to the steering and suspension components. Wheel imbalance is normally signified by vibration through the vehicle's bodyshell, although in many cases it is particularly noticeable through the steering wheel. Conversely, it should be noted that wear or damage in suspension or steering components may cause excessive tyre wear. Out-of-round or out-of-true tyres, damaged wheels and wheel bearing wear/maladjustment also fall into this category. Balancing will not usually cure vibration caused by such wear.

Wheel balancing may be carried out with the wheel either on or off the vehicle. If balanced on the vehicle, ensure that the wheel-to-hub relationship is marked in some way prior to subsequent wheel removal so that it may be refitted in its original position.

General tyre wear is influenced to a large degree by driving style – harsh braking and acceleration or fast cornering will all produce more rapid tyre wear. Interchanging of tyres may result in more even wear, but this should only be carried out where there is no mix of tyre types on the vehicle. However, it is worth bearing in mind that if this is completely effective, the added expense of replacing a complete set of tyres simultaneously is incurred, which may prove financially restrictive for many owners.

Front tyres may wear unevenly as a result of wheel misalignment. The front wheels should always be correctly aligned according to the settings specified by the vehicle manufacturer.

Legal restrictions apply to the mixing of tyre types on a vehicle. Basically this means that a vehicle must not have tyres of differing construction on the same axle. Although it is not recommended to mix tyre types between front axle and rear axle, the only legally permissible combination is crossply at the front and radial at the rear. When mixing radial ply tyres, textile braced radials must always go on the front axle, with steel braced radials at the rear. An obvious disadvantage of such mixing is the necessity to carry two spare tyres to avoid contravening the law in the event of a puncture.

In the UK, the Motor Vehicles Construction and Use Regulations apply to many aspects of tyre fitting and usage. It is suggested that a copy of these regulations is obtained from your local police if in doubt as to the current legal requirements with regard to tyre condition, minimum tread depth, etc.

50   Fault diagnosis – suspension and steering

Symptom	Reason(s)
Vehicle pulls to one side	Incorrect front or rear wheel alignment Accident damage to steering and/or suspension components Binding brake on one side of vehicle (see Chapter 8) Incorrect tyre pressures
Vehicle wanders	Incorrect front or rear wheel alignment Excessive wear in suspension mountings, joints or components Excessive wear in steering joints or components Incorrect tyre pressures
Wheel wobble or vibration	Roadwheels out of balance Roadwheel or tyre damage Excessive wear in steering joints or components Faulty shock absorber or front strut Worn or damaged driveshaft joint (see Chapter 7) Worn wheel bearings
Excessive pitching or rolling on corners, or during braking	Faulty shock absorber or front strut Worn anti-roll bar rubber bushes or loose mounting clamps
Stiff or heavy steering	Low tyre pressures Incorrect front or rear wheel alignment Damaged or unlubricated steering rack or balljoints Lack of power assistance (where applicable)
Excessive play at steering wheel	Wear in rack-and-pinion components Wear in tie-rod end balljoints Worn steering shaft flexible coupling Worn steering shaft universal joint (where applicable)

Symptom	Reason(s)
Lack of power assistance (where applicable)	Low fluid level (check for leaks) Pump drivebelt slack or broken Faulty pump Faulty steering gear
Noisy operation of power steering	Air in system Low fluid level (check for leaks) Pump drivebelt slack Worn pump or steering gear

Note: *This Section is not intended as an exhaustive guide to fault diagnosis, but summarises the more common faults which may be encountered during a vehicle's life. Consult a dealer for more detailed advice.*

Chapter 10 Bodywork and fittings

For modifications, and information applicable to later models, see Supplement at end of manual

Contents

1 General description

The bodyshell and floorpan are of pressed steel, and form an integral part of the vehicle's structure, without the need for a separate chassis.

Various areas are strengthened, to provide for suspension, steering and engine mounting points, and load distribution.

Extensive corrosion protection is applied to all new vehicles. Various anti-corrosion preparations are used, including galvanising, zinc phosphatisation and pvc underseal. Protective wax is injected into the box sections and other hollow cavities.

Extensive use is made of plastic for peripheral components, such as the radiator grille, bumpers and wheel trims, and for much of the interior trim.

Interior fittings are to a high standard on all models, and a wide range of optional equipment is available throughout the range.

With the exception of the rear quarter windows, all fixed glass is bonded in position, using a special adhesive. Any work in this area should be entrusted to a Vauxhall dealer or glass replacement specialist.

2 Maintenance – bodywork and underframe

The general condition of a vehicle's bodywork is the one thing that significantly affects its value. Maintenance is easy but needs to be regular. Neglect, particularly after minor damage, can lead quickly to further deterioration and costly repair bills. It is important also to keep watch on those parts of the vehicle not immediately visible, for instance the underside, inside all the wheel arches and the lower part of the engine compartment.

The basic maintenance routine for the bodywork is washing – preferably with a lot of water, from a hose. This will remove all the loose solids which may have stuck to the vehicle. It is important to flush these off in such a way as to prevent grit from scratching the finish. The wheel arches and underframe need washing in the same way to remove any accumulated mud which will retain moisture and tend to encourage rust. Paradoxically enough, the best time to clean the underframe and wheel arches is in wet weather when the mud is thoroughly wet and soft. In very wet weather the underframe is usually cleaned of large accumulations automatically and this is a good time for inspection.

Periodically, except on vehicles with a wax-based underbody protective coating, it is a good idea to have the whole of the underframe of the vehicle steam cleaned, engine compartment included, so that a thorough inspection can be carried out to see what minor repairs and renovations are necessary. Steam cleaning is available at many garages and is necessary for removal of the accumulation of oily grime which sometimes is allowed to become thick in certain areas. If steam cleaning facilities are not available, there are some excellent grease solvents available, such as Holts Engine Degreasant, which can be brush applied. The dirt can then be simply hosed off. Note that these methods should not be used on vehicles with wax-based underbody protective coating or the coating will be removed. Such vehicles should be inspected annually, preferably just prior to winter, when the underbody should be washed down and any damage to the wax coating repaired using Holts Undershield. Ideally, a completely fresh coat should be applied. It would also be worth considering the use of such wax-based protection for injection into door panels, sills, box sections, etc, as an additional safeguard against rust damage where such protection is not provided by the vehicle manufacturer.

After washing paintwork, wipe off with a chamois leather to give an unspotted clear finish. A coat of clear protective wax polish, like the many excellent Turtle Wax polishes, will give added protection against chemical pollutants in the air. If the paintwork sheen has dulled or oxidised, use a cleaner/polisher combination such as Turtle Wax Hard Shell to restore the brilliance of the shine. This requires a little effort, but such dulling is usually caused because regular washing has been neglected. Care needs to be taken with metallic paintwork, as special non-abrasive cleaner/polisher is required to avoid damage to the finish.

Always check that the door and ventilator opening drain holes and pipes are completely clear so that water can be drained out. Bright work should be treated in the same way as paint work. Windscreens and windows can be kept clear of the smeary film which often appears by the use of a proprietary glass cleaner like Holts Mixra. Never use any form of wax or other body or chromium polish on glass.

3 Maintenance – upholstery and carpets

Mats and carpets should be brushed or vacuum cleaned regularly to keep them free of grit. If they are badly stained remove them from the vehicle for scrubbing or sponging and make quite sure they are dry before refitting. Seats and interior trim panels can be kept clean by wiping with a damp cloth and Turtle Wax Carisma. If they do become stained (which can be more apparent on light coloured upholstery) use a little liquid detergent and a soft nail brush to scour the grime out of the grain of the material. Do not forget to keep the headlining clean in the same way as the upholstery. When using liquid cleaners inside the vehicle do not over-wet the surfaces being cleaned. Excessive damp could get into the seams and padded interior causing stains, offensive odours or even rot. If the inside of the vehicle gets wet accidentally it is worthwhile taking some trouble to dry it out properly, particularly where carpets are involved. *Do not leave oil or electric heaters inside the vehicle for this purpose.*

4 Minor body damage – repair

The colour bodywork repair photographic sequences between pages 32 and 33 illustrate the operations detailed in the following sub-sections.

Note: *For more detailed information about bodywork repair, Haynes Publishing produces a book by Lindsay Porter called The Car Bodywork Repair Manual. This incorporates information on such aspects as rust treatment, painting and glass fibre repairs, as well as details on more ambitious repairs involving welding and panel beating.*

Repair of minor scratches in bodywork

If the scratch is very superficial, and does not penetrate to the metal of the bodywork, repair is very simple. Lightly rub the area of the scratch with a paintwork renovator like Turtle Wax Color Back, or a very fine cutting paste like Holts Body + Plus Rubbing Compound, to remove loose paint from the scratch and to clear the surrounding bodywork of wax polish. Rinse the area with clean water.

Apply touch-up paint to the scratch using a fine paint brush; continue to apply fine layers of paint until the surface of the paint in the scratch is level with the surrounding paintwork. Allow the new paint at least two weeks to harden; then blend it into the surrounding paintwork by rubbing the scratch area with a paintwork renovator or a very fine cutting paste, such as Holts Body + Plus Rubbing Compound or Turtle Wax Color Back. Finally, apply wax polish from one of the Turtle Wax range of wax polishes.

Where the scratch has penetrated right through to the metal of the bodywork, causing the metal to rust, a different repair technique is required. Remove any loose rust from the bottom of the scratch with a penknife, then apply rust inhibiting paint, such as Turtle Wax Rust Master, to prevent the formation of rust in the future. Using a rubber or nylon applicator fill the scratch with bodystopper paste like Holts Body + Plus Knifing Putty. If required, this paste can be mixed with cellulose thinners, such as Holts Body + Plus Cellulose Thinners, to provide a very thin paste which is ideal for filling narrow scratches. Before the stopper-paste in the scratch hardens, wrap a piece of smooth cotton rag around the top of a finger. Dip the finger in cellulose thinners, such as Holts Body + Plus Cellulose Thinners, and then quickly sweep it across the surface of the stopper-paste in the scratch; this will ensure that the surface of the stopper-paste is slightly hollowed. The scratch can now be painted over as described earlier in this Section.

Repair of dents in bodywork

When deep denting of the vehicle's bodywork has taken place, the first task is to pull the dent out, until the affected bodywork almost attains its original shape. There is little point in trying to restore the original shape completely, as the metal in the damaged area will have stretched on impact and cannot be reshaped fully to its original contour. It is better to bring the level of the dent up to a point which is about $\frac{1}{8}$ in (3 mm) below the level of the surrounding bodywork. In cases where the dent is very shallow anyway, it is not worth trying to pull it out at all. If the underside of the dent is accessible, it can be hammered out gently from behind, using a mallet with a wooden or plastic head. Whilst doing this, hold a suitable block of wood firmly against the outside of the panel to absorb the impact from the hammer blows and thus prevent a large area of the bodywork from being 'belled-out'.

Should the dent be in a section of the bodywork which has a double skin or some other factor making it inaccessible from behind, a different technique is called for. Drill several small holes through the metal inside the area – particularly in the deeper section. Then screw long self-tapping screws into the holes just sufficiently for them to gain a good purchase in the metal. Now the dent can be pulled out by pulling on the protruding heads of the screws with a pair of pliers.

The next stage of the repair is the removal of the paint from the damaged area, and from an inch or so of the surrounding 'sound' bodywork. This is accomplished most easily by using a wire brush or abrasive pad on a power drill, although it can be done just as effectively by hand using sheets of abrasive paper. To complete the preparation for filling, score the surface of the bare metal with a screwdriver or the tang of a file, or alternatively, drill small holes in the affected area. This will provide a really good 'key' for the filler paste.

To complete the repair see the Section on filling and re-spraying.

Repair of rust holes or gashes in bodywork

Remove all paint from the affected area and from an inch or so of the surrounding 'sound' bodywork, using an abrasive pad or a wire brush on a power drill. If these are not available a few sheets of abrasive paper will do the job just as effectively. With the paint removed you will be able to gauge the severity of the corrosion and therefore decide whether to renew the whole panel (if this is possible) or to repair the affected area. New body panels are not as expensive as most people think and it is often quicker and more satisfactory to fit a new panel than to attempt to repair large areas of corrosion.

Remove all fittings from the affected area except those which will act as a guide to the original shape of the damaged bodywork (eg headlamp shells etc). Then, using tin snips or a hacksaw blade, remove all loose metal and any other metal badly affected by corrosion. Hammer the edges of the hole inwards in order to create a slight depression for the filler paste.

Wire brush the affected area to remove the powdery rust from the surface of the remaining metal. Paint the affected area with rust inhibiting paint like Turtle Wax Rust Master; if the back of the rusted area is accessible treat this also.

Before filling can take place it will be necessary to block the hole in some way. This can be achieved by the use of aluminium or plastic mesh, or aluminium tape.

Aluminium or plastic mesh, or glass fibre matting, is probably the best material to use for a large hole. Cut a piece to the approximate size and shape of the hole to be filled, then position it in the hole so that its edges are below the level of the surrounding bodywork. It can be retained in position by several blobs of filler paste around its periphery.

Aluminium tape should be used for small or very narrow holes. Pull a piece off the roll and trim it to the approximate size and shape required, then pull off the backing paper (if used) and stick the tape over the hole; it can be overlapped if the thickness of one piece is insufficient. Burnish down the edges of the tape with the handle of a screwdriver or similar, to ensure that the tape is securely attached to the metal underneath.

Bodywork repairs – filling and re-spraying

Before using this Section, see the Sections on dent, deep scratch, rust holes and gash repairs.

Many types of bodyfiller are available, but generally speaking those proprietary kits which contain a tin of filler paste and a tube of resin hardener are best for this type of repair, like Holts Body + Plus or Holts No Mix which can be used directly from the tube. A wide, flexible plastic or nylon applicator will be found invaluable for imparting a smooth and well contoured finish to the surface of the filler.

Mix up a little filler on a clean piece of card or board – measure the hardener carefully (follow the maker's instructions on the pack) otherwise the filler will set too rapidly or too slowly. Alternatively, Holts No Mix can be used straight from the tube without mixing, but daylight is required to cure it. Using the applicator apply the filler paste to the prepared area; draw the applicator across the surface of the filler to achieve the correct contour and to level the filler surface. As soon as a contour that approximates to the correct one is achieved, stop working the paste – if you carry on too long the paste will become sticky and begin to 'pick up' on the applicator. Continue to add thin layers of filler paste at twenty-minute intervals until the level of the filler is just proud of the surrounding bodywork.

Once the filler has hardened, excess can be removed using a metal plane or file. From then on, progressively finer grades of abrasive paper should be used, starting with a 40 grade production paper and finishing with 400 grade wet-and-dry paper. Always wrap the abrasive paper around a flat rubber, cork, or wooden block – otherwise the surface of the filler will not be completely flat. During the smoothing of the filler surface the wet-and-dry paper should be periodically rinsed in water. This will ensure that a very smooth finish is imparted to the filler at the final stage.

At this stage the 'dent' should be surrounded by a ring of bare metal, which in turn should be encircled by the finely 'feathered' edge of the good paintwork. Rinse the repair area with clean water, until all of the dust produced by the rubbing-down operation has gone.

Spray the whole repair area with a light coat of primer, either Holts Body + Plus Grey or Red Oxide Primer - this will show up any imperfections in the surface of the filler. Repair these imperfections with fresh filler paste or bodystopper, and once more smooth the surface with abrasive paper. If bodystopper is used, it can be mixed with cellulose thinners to form a really thin paste which is ideal for filling small holes. Repeat this spray and repair procedure until you are satisfied that the surface of the filler, and the feathered edge of the paintwork are perfect. Clean the repair area with clean water and allow to dry fully.

The repair area is now ready for final spraying. Paint spraying must be carried out in a warm, dry, windless and dust free atmosphere. This condition can be created artificially if you have access to a large indoor working area, but if you are forced to work in the open, you will have to pick your day very carefully. If you are working indoors, dousing the floor in the work area with water will help to settle the dust which would otherwise be in the atmosphere. If the repair area is confined to one body panel, mask off the surrounding panels; this will help to minimise the effects of a slight mis-match in paint colours. Bodywork fittings (eg chrome strips, door handles etc) will also need to be masked off. Use genuine masking tape and several thicknesses of newspaper for the masking operations.

Before commencing to spray, agitate the aerosol can thoroughly, then spray a test area (an old tin, or similar) until the technique is mastered. Cover the repair area with a thick coat of primer; the thickness should be built up using several thin layers of paint rather than one thick one. Using 400 grade wet-and-dry paper, rub down the surface of the primer until it is really smooth. While doing this, the work area should be thoroughly doused with water, and the wet-and-dry paper periodically rinsed in water. Allow to dry before spraying on more paint.

Spray on the top coat using Holts Dupli-Colour Autospray, again building up the thickness by using several thin layers of paint. Start spraying in the centre of the repair area and then work outwards, with a side-to-side motion, until the whole repair area and about 2 inches of the surrounding original paintwork is covered. Remove all masking material 10 to 15 minutes after spraying on the final coat of paint.

Allow the new paint at least two weeks to harden, then, using a paintwork renovator or a very fine cutting paste such as Turtle Wax Color Back or Holts Body + Plus Rubbing Compound, blend the edges of the paint into the existing paintwork. Finally, apply wax polish.

Plastic components

With the use of more and more plastic body components by the vehicle manufacturers (eg bumpers, spoilers, and in some cases major body panels), rectification of more serious damage to such items has become a matter of either entrusting repair work to a specialist in this field, or renewing complete components. Repair of such damage by the DIY owner is not really feasible owing to the cost of the equipment and materials required for effecting such repairs. The basic technique involves making a groove along the line of the crack in the plastic using a rotary burr in a power drill. The damaged part is then welded back together by using a hot air gun to heat up and fuse a plastic filler rod into the groove. Any excess plastic is then removed and the area rubbed down to a smooth finish. It is important that a filler rod of the correct plastic is used, as body components can be made of a variety of different types (eg polycarbonate, ABS, polypropylene).

Damage of a less serious nature (abrasions, minor cracks etc) can be repaired by the DIY owner using a two-part epoxy filler repair material like Holts Body + Plus or Holts No Mix which can be used directly from the tube. Once mixed in equal proportions (or applied direct from the tube in the case of Holts No Mix), this is used in similar fashion to the bodywork filler used on metal panels. The filler is usually cured in twenty to thirty minutes, ready for sanding and painting.

If the owner is renewing a complete component himself, or if he has repaired it with epoxy filler, he will be left with the problem of finding a suitable paint for finishing which is compatible with the type of plastic used. At one time the use of a universal paint was not possible owing to the complex range of plastics encountered in body component applications. Standard paints, generally speaking, will not bond to plastic or rubber satisfactorily, but Holts Professional Spraymatch maints to match any plastic or rubber finish can be obtained from dealers. However, it is now possible to obtain a plastic body parts finishing kit which consists of a pre-primer treatment, a primer and coloured top coat. Full instructions are normally supplied with a kit, but basically the method of use is to first apply the pre-primer to the component concerned and allow it to dry for up to 30 minutes. Then the primer is applied and left to dry for about an hour before finally applying the special coloured top coat. The result is a correctly coloured component where the paint will flex with the plastic or rubber, a property that standard paint does not normally possess.

5 Major body damage   repair

Major impact or rust damage should only be repaired by a Vauxhall dealer or other competent specialist. Alignment jigs are needed for successful completion of such work, superficially effective repairs may leave dangerous weaknesses in the structure. Unrectified distortion can also impose severe stresses on steering and suspension components with consequent premature failure.

6 Bonnet – removal and refitting

1 Open the bonnet, and support it in the fully-open position.
2 On models fitted with an underbonnet lamp, disconnect the battery negative lead, then prise the lamp from the bonnet and disconnect the wiring. If the bonnet is to be refitted, to aid routing of the wiring on refitting, tie a length of string to the end of the wiring, then withdraw the wiring through the bonnet and untie the string, leaving it in position in the bonnet.
3 Similarly, disconnect the windscreen washer fluid hose from the connector in the bonnet, but tie the string to the connector, to prevent it from slipping into an inaccessible position in the bonnet.
4 Mark the position of the hinges on the bonnet.
5 With the help of an assistant, support the weight of the bonnet, then

6.5 Lifting the bonnet from the vehicle

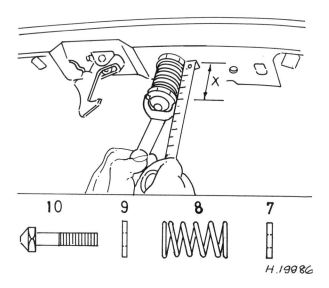

Fig. 10.1 Bonnet lock striker adjustment (Sec 6)

7 Locknut 9 Washer
8 Spring 10 Striker pin
X = 40.0 to 45.0 mm (1.57 to 1.77 in)
measured from bonnet panel to washer (9)

unscrew the securing bolts from the hinges, and lift the bonnet from the vehicle (photo). If the bonnet is to be refitted, rest it carefully on rags or cardboard, to avoid damaging the paint.
6   If a new bonnet is to be fitted, transfer all the serviceable fittings (rubber buffers, lock striker etc) to it.
7   If desired, the bonnet hinges can be removed from the vehicle, after unscrewing the three bolts in each case securing them to the upper flanges of the front wings.
8   Refitting is a reversal of removal, bearing in mind the following points.
9   Align the hinges with the previously-made marks on the bonnet.
10   If the original bonnet is being refitted, draw the windscreen washer fluid hose, and where applicable, the underbonnet lamp wiring, through the bonnet using the string.
11   If the lock striker has been disturbed, adjust it to the dimension shown in Fig. 10.1, then tighten the locknut.
12   If necessary, adjust the hinge bolts and the front rubber buffers until a good fit is obtained with the bonnet shut.

7 Bonnet lock components – removal and refitting

1   Open the bonnet, and support it in the fully-open position.
2   The bonnet lock hook is riveted to the bonnet, and removal involves drilling out the rivet. Secure the hook assembly with a new rivet when refitting.
3   To remove the bonnet lock striker from the bonnet, loosen the locknut, then unscrew the striker and recover the washers and spring. When refitting, adjust the striker dimension as shown in Fig. 10.1 before tightening the locknut.
4   To remove the locking spring, disconnect the end of the bonnet release cable from the spring, then unhook the end of the spring from the slot in the front body panel, and manipulate the spring out through the top of the panel, taking care not to damage the paint. Refitting is a reversal of removal.
5   On completion, close the bonnet, and check that the lock and the bonnet release mechanism operate satisfactorily.

8 Bonnet lock release cable – removal and refitting

1   Open the bonnet, and support it in the fully-open position.
2   Unscrew the release cable clip from the front body panel.
3   Disconnect the end of the release cable from the locking spring under the front body panel.
4   Disconnect the release cable from the release handle in the driver's footwell. If necessary, remove the release handle from its retainer for access to the cable end.
5   Pull the cable assembly through the grommet in the engine compartment bulkhead into the engine compartment.
6   Release the cable from any remaining clips and cable ties, and withdraw it from the engine compartment.
7   Refitting is a reversal of removal, but ensure that the cable is correctly routed, and on completion check the release mechanism for satisfactory operation.

9 Boot lid (Saloon models) – removal and refitting

1   Open the bonnet lid fully.
2   On models with central locking, disconnect the battery negative lead, then disconnect the wiring from the lock solenoid. If the boot lid is to be refitted, tie a length of string to the end of the wiring, then feed the wiring through the boot lid and untie the string, leaving it in position in the boot lid to assist refitting.
3   Mark the position of the hinges on the boot lid.
4   With the help of an assistant, support the weight of the boot lid, then unscrew the securing bolts from the hinges, and lift the boot lid from the vehicle. If the boot lid is to be refitted, rest it carefully on rags or cardboard, to avoid damaging the paint.
5   If a new boot lid is to be fitted, transfer all the serviceable fittings (rubber buffers, lock mechanism etc) to it.
6   If desired, the boot lid hinge counterbalance springs can be removed, but before unhooking them from the vehicle body, note their position so that they can be refitted in their original positions – see Fig. 10.2. Use a suitable lever to unhook the springs.
7   Refitting is a reversal of removal, bearing in mind the following points.
8   Align the hinges with the precisely-made marks on the boot lid.
9   Where applicable, draw the central locking solenoid wiring through the boot lid, using the string.
10   If necessary, adjust the hinge bolts and the rubber buffer until a good fit is obtained with the boot lid shut.
11   If necessary, adjust the position of the lock striker on the body, to achieve satisfactory lock operation.

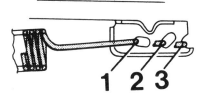

Fig. 10.2 Boot lid hinge counterbalance spring locations – Saloon models (Sec 9)

1   Position for basic boot lid
2   Position for boot lid with outer plastic trim panel or spoiler
3   Position for boot lid with outer plastic trim panel and spoiler

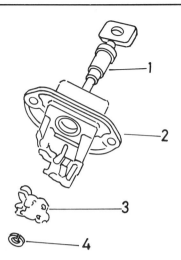

Fig. 10.3 Boot lid/tailgate lock cylinder components (Sec 11)

| 1 | Lock cylinder | 3 | Operating lever assembly |
| 2 | Housing | 4 | Circlip |

10   Boot lid lock (Saloon models) – removal and refitting

1   Open the boot lid fully.
2   Unscrew the two securing screws, then withdraw the lock and disconnect the operating rod.
3   Refitting is a reversal of removal, but if necessary adjust the position of the lock striker on the body, to achieve satisfactory lock operation.

11   Boot lid lock cylinder (Saloon models) – removal and refitting

1   Open the boot lid fully.
2   Unscrew the two securing nuts, then withdraw the lock cylinder complete with the housing, and disconnect the operating rods(s).
3   To remove the lock cylinder from the housing, insert the key into the

lock, then extract the circlip and the operating lever assembly from the end of the lock cylinder, and withdraw the cylinder from the housing.
4   Refitting is a reversal of removal, but check the operations of the lock on completion.

12   Tailgate (Hatchback models) – removal and refitting

1   Open the tailgate fully.
2   Disconnect the battery negative lead.
3   Remove the securing screws, and withdraw the tailgate trim panels.
4   Disconnect all the relevant wiring now exposed, and disconnect the washer fluid hose.
5   If the original tailgate is to be refitted, tie string to the ends of all the relevant wires, and if necessary the washer fluid hose, then feed the wiring and the hose through the top edge of the tailgate. Untie the string, leaving it in position in the tailgate to assist refitting.
6   Prise off the rear roof trim panel, taking care not to break the securing clips, and lower the rear of the headlining slightly for access to the tailgate hinge securing screws (photos). Mark the hinge positions on the body.
7   Have an assistant support the weight of the tailgate, then disconnect the tailgate struts from their mounting balljoints, with reference to Section 15.
8   Ensure that the tailgate is adequately supported, then remove the hinge securing screws and withdraw the tailgate from the vehicle. If the tailgate is to be refitted, rest it carefully on rags or cardboard, to avoid damaging the paint.
9   If desired, the hinges can be removed from the tailgate by driving out the hinge pins.
10   If the tailgate can be moved up and down on its hinges due to wear in the hinge pins or their holes, it may be possible to drill out the holes and fit slightly oversize pins. Consult a Vauxhall dealer for further advice.
11   If a new tailgate is to be fitted, transfer all serviceable components to it.
12   Refitting is a reversal of removal, bearing in mind the following points.
13   Align the hinges with the previously-made marks on the body.
14   If the original tailgate is being refitted, draw the wiring and washer fluid hose (where applicable) through the tailgate, using the string.
15   If necessary, adjust the hinge bolts and the rubber buffers, to obtain a good fit when the tailgate is shut.
16   If necessary, adjust the position of the lock striker on the body, to achieve satisfactory lock operation.

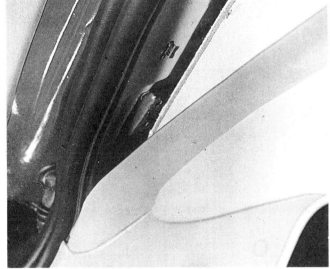

12.6A Prise off the rear roof trim panel ...

12.6B ... for access to the tailgate hinge screws

13.1 Tailgate lock (trim panel removed)

14.1 Tailgate lock cylinder housing – model with central locking (trim panel removed)

13   Tailgate lock (Hatchback models) – removal and refitting

1   Proceed as described in Section 10, but note that for access to the lock, the rear tailgate trim panel must be removed, after unscrewing the securing screws. Note also that the lock is secured by three screws (photo).

14   Tailgate lock cylinder (Hatchback models) – removal and refitting

1   Proceed as described in Section 11, but note that for access to the lock cylinder, the rear tailgate trim panel must be removed after un-screwing the securing screws (photo).

15   Tailgate strut (Hatchback models) – removal and refitting

1   Open the tailgate fully, and have an assistant support it.
2   Release the strut from its mounting balljoints by prising the spring clips a little way out (photo), and pulling the strut off the balljoints. If the

strut is to be re-used, do not remove the spring clips completely, and do not prise them out further than 6.0 mm (0.24 in).
3   Refitting is a reversal of removal.

16   Door – removal and refitting

Front door
1   The door hinges are welded onto the door frame and the body pillar, so that there is no provision for adjustment or alignment.
2   To remove a door, open it fully and support it under its lower edge on blocks covered with pads of rag.
3   Where applicable, disconnect the battery negative lead, and discon-nect the wiring connector from the front edge of the door. To release the connector, twist the locking collar, then pull the connector from the socket in the door (photo).
4   Using a suitable punch, drive the large roll pin from the door check arm pivot.
5   Remove the plastic covers from the hinge pins, then drive out the pins using a suitable punch. Have an assistant support the door as the pins are driven out, then withdraw the door from the vehicle.
6   Refitting is a reversal of removal, using a new check link roll pin.
7   If the door can be moved up and down on its hinges due to wear in

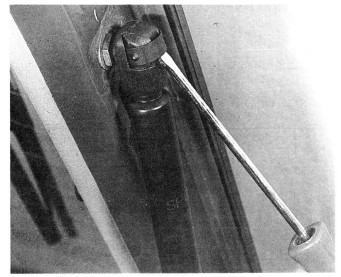

15.2 Prising the spring clip from a tailgate strut balljoint

16.3 Disconnect the wiring connector from the front edge of the door

17.2 Window regulator handle securing clip

17.3 Remove the plastic surround from the door interior handle

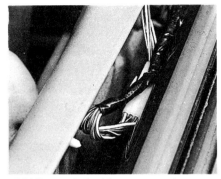

17.7 Mirror switch wiring connector in bracket at top of door

the hinge pins or their holes, it may be possible to drill out the holes and fit slightly oversize pins. Consult a Vauxhall dealer for further advice.

8   Door closure may be adjusted by altering the position of the lock striker on the body pillar, using an Allen key or suitable hexagon bit.

Rear door

9   The removal and refitting procedure for rear doors is as described for front doors, but note that on models with central locking or electric windows, it will be necessary to remove the door inner trim panel, as described in Section 17, in order to disconnect the wiring harness and feed it through the front edge of the door.

---

17   Door inner trim panel – removal and refitting

Front door

1   Prise the trim plate from the door lock button in the top rear edge of the door, then pull the lock button from the lock operating rod.

2   On models with manually-operated windows, release the securing clip and remove the window regulator handle. To release the securing clip, insert a length of wire with a hooked end between the handle and the trim bezel on the door trim panel, and manipulate it to free the securing clip from the handle (photo). Take care not to damage the door trim panel.

3   Prise the plastic surround from the door interior handle (photo).

4   Remove the seven trim panel securing screws which are located along the bottom edge of the door, and around the bottom edge of the armrest/hand grip.

5   The plastic clips securing the trim panel to the door must now be released. This can be done using a screwdriver, but it is preferable to use a forked tool, to minimise the possibility of damage to the trim panel and the clips. The clips are located around the outer edge of the trim panel.

6   Once the clips have been released, pull the trim panel away from the door, and push the large clip at the rear of the door pocket rearwards to allow the trim panel to be withdrawn.

7   When working on the driver's door of models with electric door mirrors, it will be necessary to disconnect the mirror switch wiring connectors as the trim panel is withdrawn. Disconnect the battery negative lead before disconnecting the connector, and note the position of the connector in the bracket at the top of the door (photo).

8   Similarly on models with door-mounted kerb lights, prise out the lamp and disconnect the wiring.

9   If desired, the plastic insulating sheet can be removed from the door after removing the loudspeaker (with reference to Chapter 11 if necessary) and the door trim panel rear securing clip, which is attached to the door by a single screw. Take care not to damage the sheet.

10   The door pocket can be removed from the door trim panel by the three securing screws which are accessible from the rear of the trim panel, and releasing the single clip.

11   If desired, the door assist handle can be prised free from the door trim panel. Take care not to damage the securing clips.

12   Refitting is a reversal of removal, bearing in mind the following points.

13   If the plastic insulating sheet has been removed from the door, make sure that it is refitted intact, and securely glued to the door. If the sheet is damaged or detached, rainwater may leak into the vehicle or damage the door trim.

14   Where applicable, ensure that the door mirror switch wiring connector is correctly positioned in its bracket before refitting the trim panel.

15   Ensure that all the trim panel securing clips engage as the panel is refitted, and if any of the clips were broken during removal, renew them on refitting.

Rear door

16   Proceed as described in paragraphs 1 to 3 inclusive.

17   On models with a door-mounted electric window operating switch, disconnect the battery negative lead, then carefully prise the switch from the door trim panel and disconnect the wiring plug.

18   Remove the three trim panel securing screws. Two are located under the interior handle surround, and the third is situated at the base of the door assist handle.

19   Proceed as described in paragraph 5.

20   Once the securing clips have been released, pull the trim panel away from the door (photo).

21   If desired, the plastic insulating sheet can be removed from the door by peeling it back from the door skin. Take care not to damage the sheet.

22   If desired, the door assist handle can be prised free from the door trim panel. Take care not to damage the securing clips.

23   Refitting is a reversal of removal, bearing in mind the following points.

24   If the plastic insulating sheet has been removed from the door, make sure that it is refitted intact, and securely glued to the door. If the sheet is damaged or detached, rainwater may leak into the vehicle or damage the door trim.

25   Where applicable, ensure that the electric window switch wiring is routed so that it does not foul the window regulator mechanism.

26   Ensure that all the trim panel securing clips engage as the panel is refitted, and if any of the clips were broken during removal, renew them on refitting.

17.20 Removing a rear door inner trim panel

20.2 Extract the circlip from the end of the lock cylinder ...

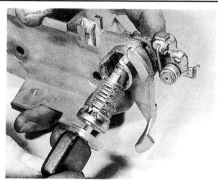

20.3A ... then withdraw the lock cylinder using the key ...

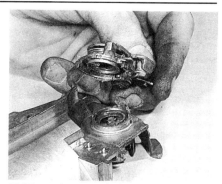

20.3B ... and recover the lever assembly

18 Door interior handle – removal and refitting

1   Remove the door inner trim panel, as described in Section 17.
2   Slide the handle assembly rearwards to free it from the door, then unhook the operating rod, and withdraw the assembly.
3   Refitting is a reversal of removal, but check the mechanism for satisfactory operation before refitting the door inner trim panel, then refit the trim panel with reference to Section 17.

19 Door exterior handle – removal and refitting

Front door
1   Remove the door inner trim panel, as described in Section 17.
2   Peel back the plastic insulating sheet sufficiently to gain access to the exterior handle.
3   Unscrew the two nuts securing the exterior handle to the door.
4   When working on the driver's door of models with central locking, unclip the microswitch from the rear edge of the exterior handle assembly.
5   Release the two lower retaining clips, then manipulate the exterior handle assembly through the outside of the door, and disconnect the operating rods.
6   Refitting is a reversal of removal, but check the operation of the mechanism before refitting the door inner trim panel, and refit the trim panel with reference to Section 17.

Rear door
7   Fully lower the window, then proceed as described in paragraphs 1 and 2.
8   Pull the weatherstrip from the rear edge of the window aperture, then unscrew the now exposed window rear guide rail securing screw. Note that the screw is of the Torx type.
9   Unscrew the remaining window rear guide rail securing screw (Torx type), which is accessible through the inner door skin, then withdraw the guide rail from the door. The weatherstrip can be left attached to the guide rail, in which case position the guide rail to one side out of the way, taking care not to damage the vehicle paintwork.
10   Reach in through the aperture in the rear of the door, and unclip the plastic shield from the door lock.
11   Unscrew the three Torx type lock securing bolts from the rear edge of the door, and lower the lock assembly inside the door.
12   Unscrew the two nuts securing the exterior handle to the door.
13   Release the two lower retaining clips, then manipulate the exterior handle through the outside of the door, and disconnect the operating rods.
14   Refitting is a reversal of removal, but check the operation of the door lock, handle and window regulator mechanisms before refitting the door trim panel, and refit the trim panel with reference to Section 17.

20 Door lock barrel – removal and refitting

1   Remove the door exterior handle, as described in Section 19.

2   Insert the key into the lock, then extract the circlip from the end of the lock cylinder (photo).
3   Withdraw the lock cylinder using the key, and recover the lever assembly (photos).
4   Refitting is a reversal of removal, but check the operation of the door lock, handle and window regulator mechanisms before refitting the door trim panel, and refit the trim panel with reference to Section 17.

21 Door lock – removal and refitting

Front door
1   Remove the door inner trim panel, as described in Section 17.
2   Unscrew the door trim panel rear securing clip, and peel the plastic insulating sheet back from the rear end of the door. Take care not to damage the sheet.
3   Working through the apertures in the door, disconnect the operating rods from the interior and exterior handles, and release the clips on the door, where applicable (photo).
4   Reach in through the lower door aperture and unclip the plastic shield from the lock.
5   On models with central locking, lower the window half way, then disconnect the battery negative lead, and working half way, then disconnect the battery negative lead, and working through the lower aperture in the door, disconnect the wiring plug from the central locking motor. Note that a clip must be depressed to release the wiring plug.
6   Unscrew the three Torx bolts securing the lock assembly to the rear edge of the door, then manipulate the lock assembly (complete with central locking motor, where applicable, and operating rods) around the window regulator mechanism and out through the lower door aperture (photo).
7   Refitting is a reversal of removal, but check the operation of the door lock, handle, and window regulator mechanisms before refitting the door trim panel, and refit the trim panel with reference to Section 17. If the lock operation is not satisfactory, note that the exterior handle operating rod can be adjusted by turning the knurled plastic adjuster wheel at the end of the rod (photo).

Rear door
8   Fully lower the window, then remove the door inner trim panel and the plastic insulating sheet, as described in Section 17.
9   Working through the apertures in the door, disconnect the operating rods from the interior and exterior handles, and from the lock button bellcrank.
10   Pull the weatherstrips from the rear edge of the window aperture, then unscrew the now-exposed window rear guide rail securing screw. Note that the screw is of the Torx type.
11   Unscrew the remaining window rear guide rail securing screw (Torx type), which is accessible through the inner door skin, then withdraw the guide rail from the door. The weatherstrip can be left attached to the guide rail, in which case position the guide rail to one side out of the way, taking care not to damage the vehicle paintwork.
12   Reach in through the aperture in the rear of the door, and unclip the plastic shield from the lock (photo).
13   On models with central locking, disconnect the battery negative

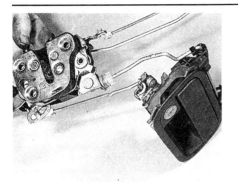

21.3 View of removed door lock and exterior handle assembly, showing operating rod attachments

21.6 Removing the lock assembly – model with central locking

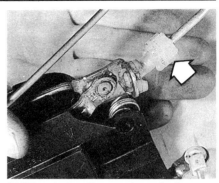

21.7 Exterior handle operating rod adjuster wheel (arrowed) at lock end of rod

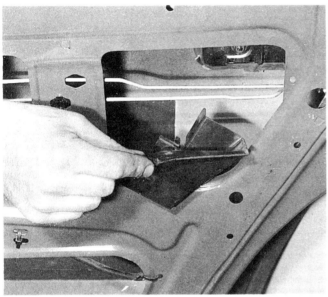

21.12 Unclip the plastic shield from the lock

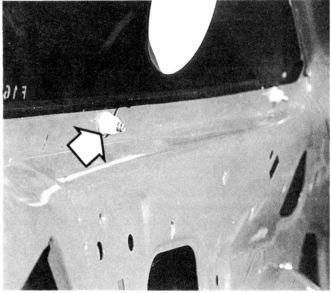

24.2 Upper rear quarter trim panel removed, exposing rear quarter window securing nut (arrowed)

lead (if not already done) and disconnect the wiring plug from the central locking motor. Note that a clip must be depressed to release the wiring plug.

14   Proceed as described in paragraphs 6 and 7.

22   Door check arm – removal and refitting

1   Open the door fully, then using a suitable punch, drive the roll pin from the door check arm pivot.
2   Remove the door inner trim panel, as described in Section 17.
3   Working at the front edge of the door, unscrew the two bolts securing the check arm to the door, then withdraw the check arm through the inside of the door.
4   Refitting is a reversal of removal, but use a new roll pin to secure the check arm to the pivot.

23   Windscreen and rear window – removal and refitting

1   With the exception of the rear quarter windows, all fixed glass is bonded in position, using a special adhesive.
2   Special tools, adhesives and expertise are required for successful removal and refitting of glass fixed by this method. Such work must therefore be entrusted to a Vauxhall dealer, a windscreen specialist or other competent professional.
3   The same remarks apply if sealing of the windscreen or other glass surround is necessary.

24   Rear quarter windows – removal and refitting

1   Remove the upper rear quarter trim panel, as described in Section 36.
2   Have an assistant support the quarter window from outside the vehicle, then unscrew the plastic securing nuts, and push the window from the body (photo).
3   Refitting is a reversal of removal, but ensure that the seal on the rear of the glass is seated correctly against the body as the window is fitted.

25   Door window – removal and refitting

Front door
1   Fully lower the window, then remove the door inner trim panel and the plastic insulating sheet, as described in Section 17.
2   Unscrew the window rear guide rail securing bolt from the rear edge of the door, then manipulate the guide rail out through the lower aperture in the door.
3   Pull the weatherstrips from the inside and outside lower edge of the window aperture.
4   Pull the plastic end stop from the window upper guide rail (photo).
5   Remove the two screws securing the lower guide rail to the door, and lower the guide rail (photo).
6   Manipulate the window regulator mechanism as necessary, and tilt the window glass forwards until it can be withdrawn from outside the door through the window aperture.

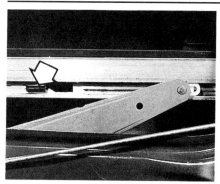

25.4 Window upper guide rail plastic end stop (arrowed)

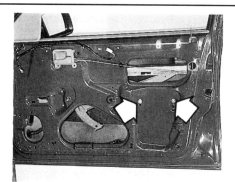

25.5 Window lower guide rail securing screws (arrowed)

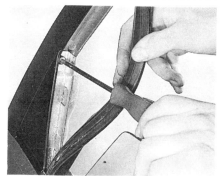

25.12 Unscrewing the window rear guide securing screw

25.13A Remove the remaining securing screw ...

25.13B ... then withdraw the guide rail from the door

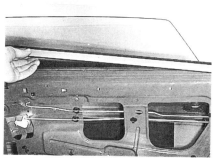

25.14 Pulling the inside weatherstrip from the window aperture

7   Refitting is a reversal of removal, but adjust the angle of the lower guide rail by means of the two securing screws until smooth operation of the window is achieved, and refit the door inner trim panel with reference to Section 17.

8   On models with electric windows, on completion, the electronic control system must be programmed as follows.

9   Close all the doors, and switch on the ignition.

10   Close each window in turn, using the relevant switch, and when each window has fully closed, continue to keep the switch depressed for at least two seconds.

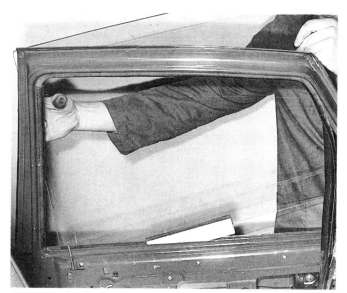

25.15 Withdrawing the window glass from the door

Rear door

11   Fully lower the window, then remove the door inner trim panel and the plastic insulating sheet, as described in Section 17.

12   Pull the weatherstrip from the rear edge of the window aperture, then unscrew the now exposed window rear guide rail securing screw (photo). Note that the screw is of the Torx type.

13   Unscrew the remaining window rear guide rail securing screw (Torx type), which is accessible through the inner door skin, then withdraw the guide rail from the door (photo). The weatherstrip can be left attached to the guide rail, in which case position the guide rail to one side out of the way, taking care not to damage the vehicle paintwork.

14   Pull the weatherstrips from the inside and outside lower edge of the window aperture (photo).

15   Manipulate the window regulator mechanism as necessary, and tilt the window glass forwards until it can be withdrawn from outside the door through the window aperture (photo).

16   Refitting is a reversal of removal, but refit the door inner trim panel with reference to Section 17.

17   On models with electric windows, on completion the electronic control system must be programmed, as described in paragraphs 9 and 10.

---

26   Door window regulator – removal and refitting

Front door

1   Lower the window halfway, then remove the door inner trim panel and the plastic insulating sheet, as described in Section 17.

2   Support the window in the half-open position by placing a wooden prop under it, ensuring that the prop is clear of the regulator mechanism.

3   Drill out the rivets securing the regulator mechanism to the door, using an 8.5 mm (0.34 in) diameter drill. Take care not to damage the door panel.

4   Pull the plastic end stop from the window upper guide rail.

5   Remove the two screws securing the lower guide rail to the door, and lower the guide rail.

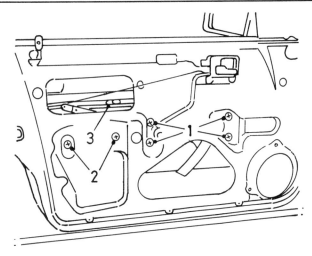

H. 19986

Fig. 10.4 Front door window regulator and guide components (Sec 26)

1	*Regulator mechanism securing rivets*	*2 Lower guide rail securing screws*
		3 Upper guide rail and stop

6   On models with electric windows, disconnect the battery negative lead (if not already done), then disconnect the wiring plug from the central locking motor.
7   Carefully manipulate the window regulator assembly out through the lower aperture in the door.
8   Refitting is a reversal of removal, bearing in mind the following points.
9   Ensure that the regulator arms are correctly positioned in the guide

rails before securing the regulator assembly to the door.
10   Secure the regulator assembly to the door, using new rivets.
11   Adjust the angle of the lower guide rail by means of the two securing screws, until smooth operation of the window is achieved.
12   Refit the door inner trim panel with reference to Section 17.
13   On models with electric windows, on completion, the electronic control system must be programmed, as described in Section 25, paragraphs 9 and 10.

Rear door

14   Proceed as described in paragraphs 1 to 3 inclusive, and paragraphs 6 and 7.
15   Refitting is a reversal of removal, bearing in mind the following points.
16   Ensure that the regulator arm is correctly positioned in the guide rail before securing the regulator assembly to the door.
17   Secure the regulator assembly to the door, using new rivets.
18   Check the regulator mechanism for satisfactory operation before refitting the door trim panel, then refit the panel with reference to Section 17.
19   On models with electric windows, on completion, the electronic control system must be programmed, as described in Section 25, paragraphs 9 and 10.

---

27   Door mirror – removal, overhaul and refitting

Glass renewal

1   If desired, the mirror glass can be removed for renewal without removing the mirror. On models with electric mirrors, disconnect the battery negative lead.
2   Carefully prise the glass from its balljoints using a screwdriver, and where applicable, disconnect the heater wires from the glass. Take care, as the glass is easily broken if forced (photo).
3   To refit, simply push the glass onto the balljoints, ensuring that the heater wires are connected (where applicable).

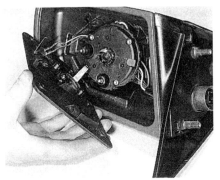

27.2 Removing the mirror glass – electric mirror (mirror removed)

27.6 Removing the mirror trim panel ...

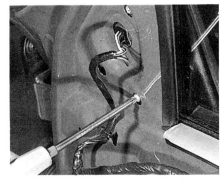

27.7A ... for access to the mirror securing screws

27.7B Withdraw the mirror and disconnect the wiring plug

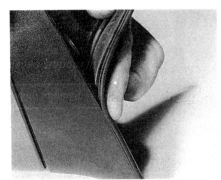

27.8 Locating the weather seal on the mirror housing

27.10 Mirror motor securing screws (arrowed)

Mirror – removal and refitting

4   On models with electric mirrors, disconnect the battery negative lead.

5   On models with manually-adjustable mirrors, pull off the interior adjuster lever.

6   Prise the mirror trim panel from the inside front edge of the door (photo).

7   Extract the three now-exposed securing screws, and withdraw the mirror assembly from the door. On models with electric mirrors, disconnect the wiring plug (photos).

8   Refitting is a reversal of removal, but ensure that the rubber weather seal is correctly located on the mirror housing (photo).

Electric motor – removal and refitting

9   Remove the mirror glass, as described previously in this Section.

10   Extract the three motor securing screws, and disconnect the wiring plug, then withdraw the motor (photo).

11   Refitting is a reversal of removal, but ensure that the wiring is routed behind the motor, to avoid interfering with the adjustment mechanism.

28 Bumpers – removal and refitting

Front bumper

1   Remove both headlamps, as described in Chapter 11, Section 38.

28.4 Unscrewing the right-hand front bumper securing bolt (air cleaner removed)

2   The bumper is removed as a complete assembly with the front trim panel, therefore on models with front foglamps, disconnect the foglamp wiring plugs.

3   The bumper is secured by a single bolt at each end, and by clips. It is possible to unscrew the right-hand securing bolt with the air cleaner assembly in place, using a suitable open-ended spanner, but if desired the air cleaner assembly can be removed for improved access, as described in Chapter 3, Section 5 or 31 as applicable.

4   Remove the left and right-hand bumper securing bolts from the body side panels behind the headlamp apertures (photo).

5   Release the bumper retaining clips from the body by pushing each end of the bumper towards the front of the vehicle, then pulling the end of the bumper out from the wing (photo).

6   Carefully withdraw the bumper from the vehicle.

7   Refitting is a reversal of removal.

Rear bumper

8   Remove the rear trim panel from the luggage compartment, to expose the two bumper securing nuts (photos).

9   Note that the bumper is removed as a complete assembly with the rear trim panel.

10   Disconnect the battery negative lead, then prise the number plate lamp from the bumper, and disconnect the wiring.

11   Unscrew the bumper securing nuts, and recover the washers.

12   Release the bumper retaining clips from the body by pushing each end of the bumper towards the rear of the vehicle, then pulling the end of the bumper out from the wing.

13   Carefully withdraw the bumper from the vehicle, taking care not to strain the number plate lamp wiring.

14   Refitting is a reversal of removal.

29 Radiator grille panel – removal and refitting

All models except GSi 2000

1   With the bonnet fully open and supported, pull the upper edge of the grille panel forwards and free the retaining clips using a screwdriver, then lift the panel to release the lower locating lugs from their grommets in the lower body front panel (photo).

2   Refitting is a reversal of removal, but ensure that the lower locating lugs seat correctly in their grommets, and take care not to push the grommets from their holes in the body front panel.

GSi 2000 models

3   Extract the three screws securing the grille panel to the body front panel, then lift the grille panel to release the lower locating lugs from their grommets in the lower body front panel.

4   Refitting is a reversal of removal, with reference to paragraph 2.

28.5 Front bumper retaining clips released from body

28.8A Remove the trim panel ...

28.8B ... to expose the bumper securing nuts

29.1 Freeing a radiator grille panel retaining clip using a scredriver

30 Windscreen cowl panel – removal and refitting

1   Remove the wiper arms, with reference to Chapter 11, Section 48 if necessary.
2   Disconnect the washer fluid hose from the reservoir, and feed it through the cowl panel, noting its routing as a guide to refitting. Be prepared for fluid spillage.
3   Where applicable, disconnect the battery negative lead, then disconnect the underbonnet lamp wiring plug and feed it through the cowl panel, noting its routing as a guide to refitting.
4   Working from one end of the cowl panel, carefully prise the panel from the body. Care must be taken, as the panel is easily damaged.
5   Refitting is a reversal of removal, ensuring that the panel is correctly seated along its length, and that the washer fluid hose, and where applicable the underbonnet lamp wiring, is correctly routed.

31 Wheel arch liners – removal and refitting

1   The plastic wheel arch liners are secured by a combination of self-tapping screws and plastic clips. Removal and refitting is self-explanatory, bearing in mind the following points (photo).

31.1 Removing a wheel arch liner

2   Some of the securing clips may be held in place using a central pin, which must be tapped out to release the clip.
3   The clips are easily broken during removal, and it is advisable to obtain a few spare clips for possible use when refitting.
4   Certain models may have additional underbody shields and splash-guards fitted, which may be attached to the wheel arch liners.

32 Engine undershield (GSi 2000 models) – removal and refitting

1   Apply the handbrake, then jack up the front of the vehicle, and support on axle stands.
2   Extract the two securing screws, and remove the oil filter access panel.
3   Working around the edges of the splash shield, remove the self-tapping screws which secure the shield to the body, noting that some of the screws also secure the wheel arch liners.
4   With the help of an assistant, pull the shield from the vehicle, and place it to one side to avoid damage.
5   Refitting is a reversal of removal.

33 Fuel filler flap – removal and refitting

1   Open the flap for access to the four screws securing the flap to the rear wing.
2   Remove the securing screws, and withdraw the flap.
3   Refitting is a reversal of removal.

34 Sunroof – removal and refitting

Note: *The sunroof is a complex piece of equipment, consisting of a large number of components. It is strongly recommended that the sunroof mechanism is not disturbed unless absolutely necessary. If the sunroof mechanism is faulty, or requires overhaul, consult a dealer for advice.*

Glass panel – removal and refitting
1   Push the sunshade fully rearwards, and open the glass panel halfway.
2   Extract the four securing screws from the front edge of the guide rail plastic surround, and withdraw the surround down through the sunroof aperture (photos).
3   Move the glass panel forward, and open it to its tilt position.
4   Prise the plastic trim strips from the guide rails, to expose the glass panel securing screws (photo).
5   Extract the three securing screws from each guide rail, and where applicable, recover the lockwashers (photo).
6   Carefully lift the glass panel from the roof aperture, taking care not to damage the vehicle paintwork (photo).
7   Refitting is a reversal of removal, bearing in mind the following points.
8   Before refitting the glass panel, measure the distance between the mounting flanges. Bend the flanges if necessary to achieve the desired dimension – see Fig. 10.5.
9   Where applicable, ensure that the glass panel securing screw lockwashers engage with the locating pins on the guide rails.
10   Before fully tightening the glass panel securing screws, close the panel, and adjust its position to give the dimensions shown in Fig. 10.6.
11   If a new glass panel has been fitted, peel off the protective foil on completion of adjustment.

Gutter – removal and refitting
12   Remove the glass panel, as described previously in this Section.
13   Extract the two securing screws (Allen or Torx type), then lift the gutter from the roof aperture.
14   Refit the gutter to the roof aperture at an angle, pushing it up to the stop on both sides until the retaining lugs engage with the gutter guides.
15   Refit and tighten the securing screws.
16   Refit and adjust the glass panel, as described previously in this Section.

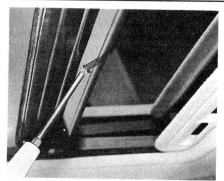

34.2A Extract the four securing screws ...

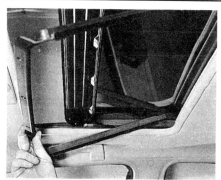

34.2B ... and withdraw the guide rail plastic surround

34.4 Prising a plastic trim strip from the guide rail

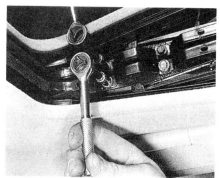

34.5 Loosening a glass panel securing screw

34.6 Lifting the glass panel from the roof aperture

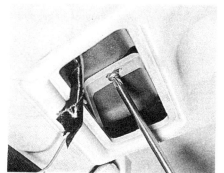

34.22A Extract the securing screws ...

34.22B ... then withdraw the trim panel from the roof ...

34.23 ... to expose the crank drive – securing screws arrowed

Sunshade – removal and refitting

17   Remove the glass panel and the gutter, as described previously in this Section.
18   Carefully prise the four sunshade spring clips out of the roof guides using a plastic or wooden implement to avoid damage, then withdraw the sunshade from the guides – see Fig. 10.7.
19   Refitting is a reversal of removal, but ensure that the spring clips engage correctly with the roof guides.

Crank drive – removal and refitting

20   Prise out the trim and unscrew the crank handle securing screw. Prise the crank from the drive spindle.
21   Disconnect the battery negative lead, then prise the courtesy lamp from the roof trim panel, and disconnect the wiring.

22   Remove the two trim panel securing screws, and withdraw the trim panel from the roof (photos).
23   Extract the two securing screws, and remove the crank drive assembly (photo).
24   Refitting is a reversal of removal, bearing in mind the following points.
25   Before finally refitting the crank handle, the crank drive must be adjusted as follows.
26   Temporarily refit the crank handle, and position it so that it faces forwards, then depress the locking button.
27   Remove the crank handle and turn the crank drive pinion anti-clockwise by hand as far as the stop.
28   Refit the crank handle so that it faces directly forwards, then tighten the securing screw and refit the trim.

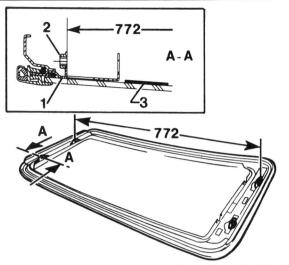

Fig. 10.5 Sunroof glass panel mounting flange dimension (Sec 34)

1	Mounting flange	3	Protective foil
2	Nut	A-A	Cross-section cutting point
	Dimensions in mm		

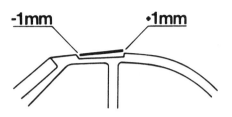

Fig. 10.6 Sunroof glass panel fitting position (Sec 34)

35 Interior trim panels – general

1   The various interior trim panels are secured by a variety of screws and plastic clips.
2   Where press-fit plastic fasteners are used, it is advisable to use a forked tool similar to that shown to remove them, in order to avoid damage to the clips and the trim panel (photo).
3   Removal and refitting of most of the trim panels is self-explanatory, but in all cases, care must be taken, as the panels are easily damaged by careless handling and the use of sharp instruments to release clips.

36 Interior trim panels – removal and refitting

Sill trim panel

1   When working on the passenger side of models fitted with ABS, extract the three securing screws and remove the cover from the ABS control module. Note that two of the screws are covered by plastic caps, which must be prised out to expose the screws.
2   The sill trim panel can be removed by simply prising it upwards to release the securing clips from the floor (photo).

Fig. 10.7 Sunshade spring clip locations (arrowed) (Sec 34)

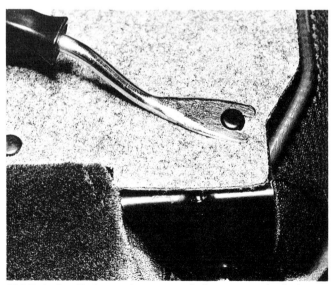

35.2 Forked tool being used to remove clip from rear seat back trim

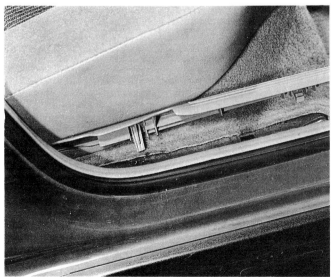

36.2 Sill trim panel removed to expose securing clips

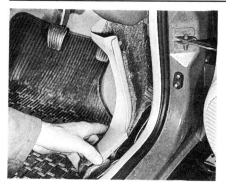

36.5 Removing the driver's footwell side trim panel

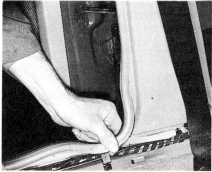

36.10 Pull the weatherstrip from the sides of the body pillar ...

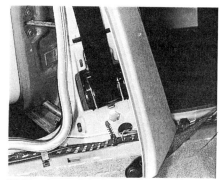

36.11 ... then pull the lower trim panel from the pillar

36.17 Withdrawing the upper rear quarter trim panel – Hatchback model

36.19A Removing the rubber stop from the seat catch

36.19B Withdrawing the lower rear quarter trim panel – Hatchback model

3   Refitting is a reversal of removal, but ensure that the panel is corrected seated with its top edge located under the sill weatherstrip.

Footwell side trim panel

4   Release the front end of the sill trim panel from the floor, as described previously in this Section.
5   Prise the footwell side trim panel from the footwell (photo). If necessary, pull the weatherstrip from the edge of the door aperture.
6   Refitting is a reversal of removal, but ensure that the trim panels are correctly seated under the weatherstrip.

Front body pillar trim panel

7   Prise the trim panel from the body pillar to release the six retaining clips. If necessary, pull the weatherstrip from the edge of the pillar.
8   Refitting is a reversal of removal, but ensure that the trim panel is correctly seated under the weatherstrip.

Centre body pillar trim panels

9   Remove the sill trim panel, as described previously in this Section.
10   Prise the weatherstrips from the sides of the body pillar (photo).
11   Pull the lower trim panel from the pillar to release the retaining clips (photo).
12   With the lower trim panel removed, the upper trim panel can be withdrawn in the same way after unbolting the upper seat belt mounting. Prise off the trim to expose the upper seat belt mounting bolt, then unscrew the bolt and recover the spacer.
13   Refitting is a reversal of removal, but ensure that the trim panels are seated correctly under the weatherstrips.

Rear quarter trim panels

14   Prise off the trim and unbolt the seat belt upper mounting from the body pillar. Recover the spacer.
15   Pull back the weatherstrip from the rear edge of the rear door aperture. On Hatchback models, remove the parcel shelf.
16   Remove the screws securing the upper rear quarter trim panel to the body. Note that all the screws are of the Torx type, and when working on the right-hand side of Hatchback models, it will be necess-

ary to open the first-aid kit/warning triangle cover flap in the luggage compartment for access to some of the screws.
17   Withdraw the upper seat quarter trim panel carefully, taking care not to damage surrounding panels (photo). Where applicable, disconnect the wiring from the loudspeaker.
18   With the upper rear quarter trim panel removed, the lower trim panel can be removed.
19   The lower rear quarter trim panel is secured by a variety of screws, nuts and clips, depending upon model. Removal and refitting of the panel is self-explanatory, bearing in mind the points made in Section 35. Note that the rubber stop must be removed from the seat catch before the trim panel can be withdrawn (photos).

Luggage compartment rear trim panel

20   Prise the trim panel from the rear of the luggage compartment to release the securing clips.
21   Refitting is a reversal of removal.

Tailgate trim panels (Hatchback models)

22   The tailgate trim panels are secured by screws, and removal and refitting are self-explanatory. Note that the lower side panel securing screws also secure the rear panel.

37   Facia panels – removal and refitting

Note: *Before removing any of the facia panels, the battery negative lead should be disconnected, as several permanently-live feed wires are routed behind the facia*

Footwell trim panels

1   The lower footwell trim panels on the driver's and passenger sides are secured by turnbuckle type plastic clips.
2   To remove a panel, use a screwdriver to turn the heads of the clips through 90° (photo), then withdraw the panel from the facia.
3   Refitting is a reversal of removal.

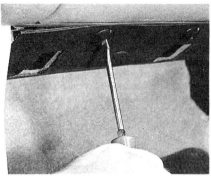

37.2 Releasing a footwell trim panel securing clip

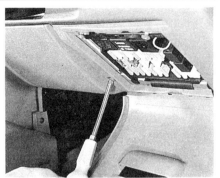

37.5A Remove the four securing screws from the fusebox aperture ...

37.5B ... then withdraw the lower facia panel

37.7 Removing the column adjuster lever

37.9A Prise out the covers ...

37.9B ... then remove the front column shroud securing screws (steering wheel removed)

37.10A Remove the three lower column shroud securing screws ...

37.10B ... then remove the lower ...

37.10C ... and upper shrouds (steering wheel removed)

Driver's side lower facia panel

4   Open the flap covering the fusebox to expose the four lower facia panel securing screws.

5   Remove the four screws, then lower the panel and pull it towards the driver's door to release the two securing clips. Withdraw the panel from the facia (photos).

6   Refitting is a reversal of removal.

Steering column shrouds

7   On models with an adjustable tilt steering column, move the column to its fully-raised position, then unscrew the adjuster lever (photo).

8   Turn the steering wheel as necessary to expose one of the front steering column shroud securing screw covers.

9   Prise out the cover, and remove the column shroud securing screw, then turn the steering wheel to enable the remaining cover and screw to be removed (photos).

10   Remove the three securing screws from the underside of the lower column shroud, then remove the lower and upper shrouds (photos).

11   Refitting is a reversal of removal, but make sure that the column switch gaiters engage in the cut-outs in the upper shroud.

Instrument panel lower trim panel

12   Remove the steering column shrouds, as described previously in this Section.

13   The panel is secured by clips at either end, which must be released by pulling the ends of the panel from the facia (photo). This is a tricky operation, as to release both ends, the panel must be bent slightly at its centre. Take great care, as the panel is easily broken.

14   Refitting is a reversal of removal.

Instrument panel upper trim panel

15   Remove the instrument panel lower trim panel, as described previously in this Section.

37.13 Removing the instrument panel lower trim panel

37.16 Unscrewing the left-hand instrument panel upper trim panel securing screw

37.17 Withdrawing the instrument panel upper trim panel

37.20 Removing the lower left-hand lighting switch panel securing screw

37.22 Disconnecting the wiring plugs from the lighting switches

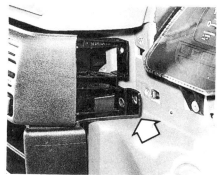

37.29A Radio/oddments tray right-hand securing lug (arrowed) resting behind heater control panel securing lug

37.29B Manipulating the radio/oddments tray from the facia

37.30A Slide the radio support tray from the facia ...

37.30B ... then disconnect the wiring and aerial plugs

16   Extract the two now-exposed lower trim panel securing screws, one from each end of the panel, noting that the left-hand screw also secures the heater control panel (photo).
17   Withdraw the panel from the facia (photo).
18   Refitting is a reversal of removal.

Lighting switch panel
19   Remove the instrument panel upper and lower trim panels, as described previously in this Section.
20   Remove the remaining securing screw from the left-hand side of the lighting switch panel (photo).
21   Pull the lighting switch panel from the facia, to release the securing clips at the right-hand end.
22   Ensure that the battery negative lead has been disconnected, then disconnect the wiring plugs from the switches, and withdraw the switch panel (photo).

23   Refitting is a reversal of removal.

Radio/oddments tray panel
24   Remove the radio, as described in Chapter 11, Section 61.
25   Remove the lower and upper instrument panel trim panels, as described previously in this Section.
26   Remove the lower securing screw from the right-hand side of the heater control panel.
27   Remove the clock or trip computer, as applicable, from the facia with reference to Chapter 11 if necessary.
28   Remove the two now-exposed heater control panel securing screws from the clock/trip computer aperture.
29   Carefully manipulate the heater control panel forwards within the limits of the control cable travel, then manipulate the radio/oddments tray out from the facia. This is a tricky operation, as the radio/oddments

37.32 Prise the side trim panels from the oddments tray ...

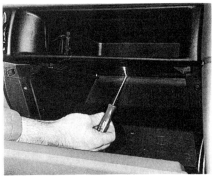

37.33A ... then release the lower retaining clips ....

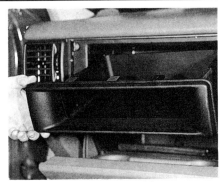

37.33B ... and withdraw the oddments tray

37.35A Extract the upper ...

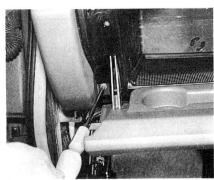

37.35B ... and lower glovebox securing screws ...

37.35C ... then withdraw the glovebox

tray securing lugs rest behind the heater control panel securing lugs (photos). Take care not to strain the heater control cables.

30   With the radio/oddments tray removed, the radio support tray can be removed if desired by unscrewing the two securing screws, then sliding the tray forwards to disconnect the wiring and aerial plugs (photos).

31   Refitting is a reversal of removal, taking care not to damage the heater control components as the radio/oddments tray is manipulated into position.

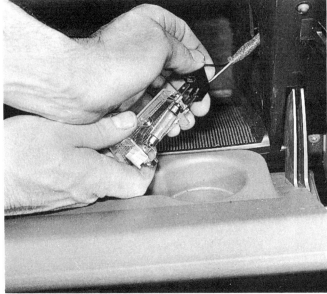

37.34 Prise out the glovebox lamp and disconnect the wiring

Glovebox assembly

32   Carefully prise the side trim panels from the passenger's oddments tray, using a screwdriver (photo).

33   Open the glovebox, then using a screwdriver, release the two lower retaining clips at the rear of the oddments tray, and withdraw the oddments tray from the facia (photos).

34   Where applicable, prise out the glovebox lamp, and disconnect the wiring (photo).

35   Extract the two upper and two lower securing screws, then withdraw the glovebox assembly from the facia (photos).

36   Refitting is a reversal of removal, but where applicable, feed the wiring through the glovebox lamp aperture as the assembly is offered into position.

38   Centre console – removal and refitting

Rear section

1   Prise the trim panel from the front of the rear centre console section to expose the front securing screw (photo).

2   Extract the front securing screw (photo).

3   Release the gaiter from the rear of the handbrake lever grip, then pull the grip from the front of the handbrake lever (photo).

4   Pull the cassette storage box or the rubber mat, as applicable, from the rear of the centre console to expose the rear securing screw (photo).

5   Extract the rear securing screw (photo), then withdraw the rear centre console section upwards, feeding the gaiter over the handbrake lever.

6   Where applicable, ensure that the battery negative lead has been disconnected, then disconnect the wiring plug(s) from the electric window and/or trip computer switches.

7   Refitting is a reversal of removal.

38.1 Prise the trim panel from the centre console ...

38.2 ... then extract the front securing screw

38.3 Pull the grip from the handbrake lever

38.4 Pull the cassette storage box from the console ...

38.5 ... then extract the rear securing screw

38.11 Disconnecting the wiring plugs from the cigarette lighter

38.12 Extract the two centre console-to-facia securing screws

38.13 Unscrewing a side centre console-to-facia securing screw

Front section

8   Remove the rear centre console section, as described previously in this Section.

9   Remove the gearchange lever, as described in Chapter 6, Section 5.

10   Disconnect the battery negative lead, if not already done.

11   Pull the ashtray assembly from the centre console, and disconnect the wiring plugs from the cigarette lighter (photo).

12   Extract the two now-exposed screw securing the centre console to the facia (photo).

13   Working at either side of the centre console, remove the two lower centre console-to-facia securing screws, and the two centre console-to-floor bracket securing screws (photo).

14   The front centre console section can now be withdrawn.

15   Refitting is a reversal of removal, but feed the cigarette lighter wiring through the aperture in the centre console as the centre console is offered into position.

39 Headlining – removal and refitting

1   Where applicable, remove the sunroof crank drive, as described in Section 34.

2   Remove the grab handles from the sides of the roof (photo).

3   Remove the sunvisors. On models with illuminated sunvisor vanity mirrors, disconnect the battery negative lead, then pull the lamp wiring from the roof as the sunvisor is withdrawn and disconnect the wiring plugs.

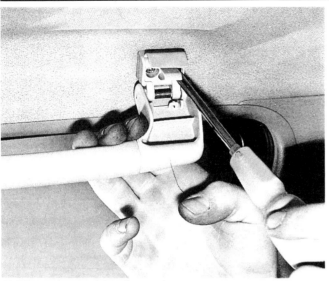

39.2 Removing a grab handle securing screw

4   On models without a sunroof, disconnect the battery negative lead (if not already done), then prise the courtesy lamp and its trim panel from the roof and disconnect the wiring.
5   Open the doors, and prise the weatherstrips from the tops of the door apertures.
6   Remove the front body pillar and centre body pillar trim panels, as described in Section 36.
7   Loosen the upper edge of the rear quarter trim panels, with reference to Section 36 if necessary.
8   On Hatchback models, open the tailgate, and prise the rear trim panel from the roof.

9   With the help of an assistant, lower the headlining from the roof, and withdraw it through the tailgate on Hatchback models or through one of the door apertures on Saloon models.
10   Refitting is a reversal of removal, but where applicable, refit the sunroof crank drive, as described in Section 34.

40   Seats – removal and refitting

Front seats
1   Remove the single securing screw from the front edge of the outer seat rail trim, then withdraw the trim (photo).
2   Unclip the trim from the rear edge of the inner seat rail (photo).
3   Remove the four bolts which secure the seat rails to the floor, then withdraw the seat, complete with rails. Recover the washers and backplates (photo).
4   If desired, the seat can be separated from the rails for attention to the adjustment mechanism.
5   Refitting is a reversal of removal. Note that the manufacturers recommend the use of new bolts to secure the seat rails to the floor.

Rear seat cushion (all models except GSi 2000)
6   Fold the seat cushion forwards, to expose the hinge pins at the front edge of the cushion.
7   To remove a hinge pin, extract the circlip from the end of the pin, and withdraw the pin from the hinge (photo).
8   With the hinge pins removed, the seat cushion can be withdrawn from the vehicle.
9   Refitting is a reversal of removal.

Rear seat cushion (GSi 2000 models)
10   Reach under the seat cushion, and pull the grab handles at either end to release the cushion from the catches on the vehicle floor.
11   Withdraw the complete cushion from the vehicle, through one of the rear doors.

40.1 Withdrawing the outer seat rail trim

40.2 Remove the trim from the rear edge of the inner seat rail

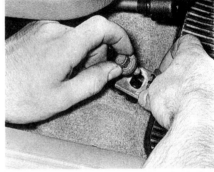

40.3 Removing a front seat rail securing bolt, washer and backplate

40.7 Removing a rear seat cushion hinge pin – all models except GSi 2000

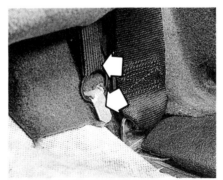

40.19 Seat back-to-body panel securing strap and lug (arrowed)

40.21 Extracting a hinge-to-seat back securing screw

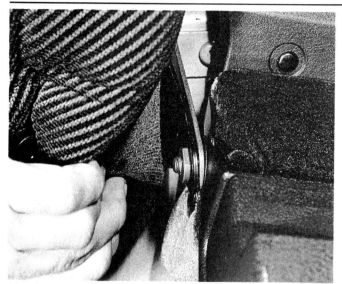

40.22 Rear seat cushion pulled back to expose seat back hinge nut and bolt – split type rear seat back

ing the hinges on the seat back.

16   Extract the screws securing the hinges to the seat back, then withdraw the seat back from the vehicle.

17   Refitting is a reversal of removal, but ensure that, where applicable, the rubber strap securing lugs are bent back against the body panel, to avoid fouling the seat cushion.

Rear seat back (split type)

18   Fold forwards or remove the rear seat cushion, as applicable.

19   Where applicable, bend up the lug on the body panel, and disconnect the rubber strap securing the relevant section of the seat back to the body panel (photo).

20   Carefully remove the securing clips, and pull back the trim covering the hinge on the seat back.

21   Extract the screws securing the hinge to the seat back (photo).

22   Working at the central pivot of the two seat back sections, prise back the seat cushions from the centre bracket, to expose the securing nut and bolt. Note that the bolt passes through both seat back sections (photo).

23   Unscrew and remove the nut and bolt, then carefully withdraw the seat back.

24   Refitting is a reversal of removal, but ensure that, where applicable, the rubber strap securing lugs are bent back against the body panel, to avoid fouling the seat cushion.

12   Refitting is a reversal of removal. Push the seat cushion into position until the securing catches lock.

Rear seat back (one-piece type)

13   Fold forwards or remove the rear seat cushion, as applicable, then fold down the seat back.

14   Where applicable, bend up the lugs on the body panel, and disconnect the two rubber straps securing the ends of the seat back to the body panel.

15   Carefully remove the securing clips, and pull back the trim cover-

---

41   Seat belts – removal and refitting

Front seat belt

1   Open both front and rear doors, and prise the weatherstrips from the edge of the centre body pillar.

2   Prise off the pillar lower trim panel to expose the inertia reel unit.

3   Unscrew the securing bolt, and tilt the inertia reel unit from the body pillar (photo).

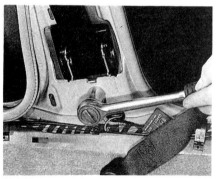

41.3 Unscrewing a front seat belt inertia reel securing bolt

41.8 Rear seat belt lower side mounting – Hatchback model

41.9 Removing a rear seat belt upper mounting from the body pillar – Hatchback model

41.13 Rear seat belt inertia reel unit location – Hatchback model

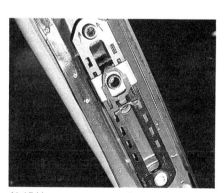

41.15 Upper rear quarter trim panel removed, to expose upper seat belt mounting height adjuster

42.4A Remove the two heater control panel securing screws from the clock/trip computer aperture ...

42.4B ... and the remaining screw from the right-hand end of the panel

42.5 Heater control cables disconnected, showing cable end securing clips

4   Prise off the trim and unbolt the seat belt upper mounting from the body pillar. Recover the spacer.

5   Similarly, unbolt the seat belt lower mounting, then withdraw the seat belt assembly from the vehicle.

6   If desired, the seat belt stalk can be unbolted from the seat frame, and the upper mounting height adjuster (where applicable) can be unbolted from the body pillar (Torx bolts), after prising off the pillar upper trim panel.

7   Refitting is a reversal of removal, but note that, when refitting the height adjuster, the arrows should be uppermost, pointing towards the vehicle roof. Ensure that the belt is fitted untwisted.

Rear seat belt

8   Fold the rear seat cushion forwards, or remove it, as applicable, for access to the seat belt lower mountings. Prise up the carpet to expose the mounting bolts, and unscrew the relevant bolt(s) from the floor (photos).

9   Prise off the trim, and unbolt the seat belt upper mounting from the body pillar. Recover the spacer (photo).

10   Open the relevant rear door, and pull back the weatherstrip from the rear of the door aperture.

11   On Hatchback models, remove the screws securing the upper rear quarter trim panel to the body. Note that all the screws are of the Torx type, and when working on the right-hand side, it will be necessary to open the first-aid kit/warning triangle cover flap in the luggage compartment for access to some of the screws. Withdraw the trim panel carefully, taking care not to damage surrounding panels.

12   Detach the front edge of the lower rear quarter trim panel from the body. The panel is secured by clips on Saloon models, and by screws on Hatchback models.

13   Pull the lower rear quarter trim panel away from the body sufficiently to gain access to the seat belt inertia reel unit (photo).

14   Unscrew the securing bolt, and lift the inertia reel unit from the body panel, then withdraw the seat belt assembly from the vehicle.

15   If desired, the upper seat belt mounting height adjuster can be unbolted from the body pillar (Torx bolts), after removing the upper rear quarter trim panel (photo).

16   Refitting is a reversal of removal, but note that, when refitting the height adjuster (where applicable), the arrows should be uppermost, pointing towards the vehicle roof. Ensure that the belt is fitted untwisted.

---

42   Heater control panel – removal and refitting

1   Disconnect the battery negative lead.

2   Remove the passenger side footwell trim, the steering column shrouds, and the instrument panel lower and upper trim panels, as described in Section 37.

3   Remove the clock or trip computer, as applicable, from the facia, with reference to Chapter 11 if necessary.

4   Remove the two heater control panel securing screws from the clock/trip computer aperture, and the remaining securing screw from the right-hand end of the panel (exposed by removing the instrument panel lower trim panel) (photos).

5   Working through the passenger footwell, reach up behind the facia, and disconnect the bowden cables from the control levers at the rear of the heater control panel. Note that each cable is secured by a plastic clip, and in some cases, by an additional metal clip, which must be released before the cable end can be disconnected from the control lever (photo). This is a tricky operation, and some patience will be required. Mark the cables to ensure that they are refitted in their original positions.

6   Withdraw the heater control panel from the facia, and disconnect the wiring plugs from the rear of the panel.

7   Refitting is a reversal of removal, but on completion, move all the control levers through their full extent of travel, and check the heater mechanism for correct operation.

---

43   Heater matrix – removal and refitting

1   Drain the cooling system, as described in Chapter 2, Section 3.

2   Working in the engine compartment, disconnect the coolant hoses from the heater matrix pipes at the bulkhead.

3   Working inside the vehicle, remove the front centre console section, as described in Section 38.

4   Extract the two front and two rear securing screws, and remove the plastic cover from under the heater matrix (photo).

5   Remove the two front retaining screws from the heater matrix securing straps, then lower the securing straps and withdraw the heater matrix from the facia (photo). Note that the pipes at the rear of the matrix

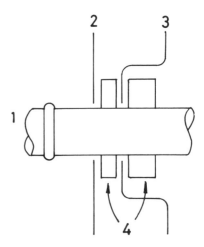

Fig. 10.8 Heater matrix coolant pipe grommet location (Sec 43)

1   Coolant pipe   3   Heater matrix housing
2   Engine compartment   4   Grommet
    bulkhead

43.4 Removing the plastic cover from the heater matrix

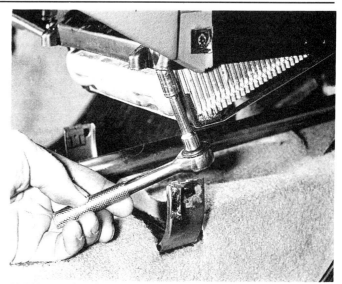

43.5 Unscrewing a heater matrix securing strap screw

must be fed through the bulkhead, and the grommets in the heater matrix housing may be displaced as the matrix is withdrawn. Where applicable, recover the grommets.

6   Refitting is a reversal of removal, bearing in mind the following points.

7   Ensure that the coolant pipe grommets are seated correctly in the heater matrix housing, as shown in Fig. 10.8.

8   Ensure that the rubber mounting strips are correctly seated between the mounting straps and the matrix.

9   On completion, refill the cooling system, as described in Chapter 2, Section 5.

44 Heater blower motor – removal and refitting

1   The heater blower motor is situated under the windscreen cowl panel.

2   Remove the windscreen cowl panel, as described in Section 30.

3   Remove the windscreen wiper motor and linkage, as described in Chapter 11, Section 50.

4   Unclip the cover from the top of the motor (photo).

5   Disconnect the motor wiring plug.

6   Remove the two clamp screws, then lift off the clamp and withdraw the motor assembly from its housing (photo).

7   It is possible to renew the motor resistor by pressing the retaining clips together to release the resistor bracket. Fit the new resistor, ensuring that the retaining clips lock it into position (photo).

8   No overhaul of the motor assembly is possible, and if faulty, the unit must be renewed.

9   Refitting is a reversal of removal, ensuring that the mounting rubber is correctly seated between the clamp and the motor.

45 Facia ventilation nozzles – removal and refitting

Centre facia ventilation nozzles

1   Using a screwdriver, carefully prise the cap from the hazard warning flasher switch.

2   Carefully prise the nozzle assembly from the facia, using a screwdriver with a piece of card under the blade, to avoid damage to the facia trim (photos).

3   If desired, the nozzle housing can be removed as follows.

4   Move the knurled airflow adjuster wheel to the 'O' position, then pull the actuating rod sideways from its carrier.

5   Release the two lower securing clips by levering with a screwdriver, and pull the housing from the facia.

6   Refitting is a reversal of removal, but note that if the housing has been removed, the airflow adjuster actuating rod must be pulled out to its stop, then pressed into its carrier with the adjuster wheel in the 'O' position.

Passenger side facia ventilation nozzle

7   Carefully prise the nozzle from the facia, using a screwdriver with a piece of card under the blade, to avoid damage to the facia trim.

8   If desired, the nozzle housing can be removed as follows.

9   Move the knurled airflow adjuster wheel to the 'O' position, then pull the actuating rod sideways from its carrier.

10   Extract the single screw securing the housing to the facia, then release the securing clips and pull the housing from the facia.

11   Refitting is a reversal of removal, with reference to paragraph 6.

44.4 Unclip the cover from the heater blower motor

44.6 Unscrewing a heater blower motor clamp screw

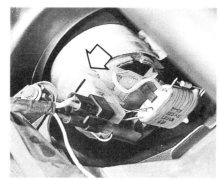

44.7 Heater blower motor resistor retaining clip (arrowed)

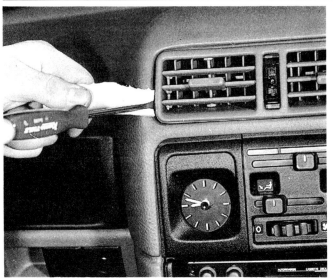

45.2A Using a screwdriver with protected blade ...

45.2B ... to release the centre facia ventilation nozzles

Driver's side facia ventilation nozzle

12   The procedure is as described for the passenger side nozzle, except that there is no screw securing the housing to the facia.

Side window demister nozzles

13   Simply prise the nozzle from the facia, taking care not to damage the facia trim.

14   To refit, push the nozzle into position until it locks.

Chapter 11 Electrical system

For modifications, and information applicable to later models, see Supplement at end of manual

Contents

Specifications

System type .... 12 volt, negative earth

Battery capacity .... 36, 44, 55 or 66 Ah

Alternator
Type .... Bosch or Delco-Remy
Output .... 55 or 70 A, depending upon model
Minimum brush length:
   Bosch type alternator .... 5.0 mm (0.20 in) protrusion
   Delco-Remy type alternator .... 11.0 mm (0.43 in) overall length

Wiper blades
Type .... Champion X-4803

Starter motor
Type .... Pre-engaged, Bosch or Delco-Remy
Minimum brush length:
   Bosch DF type starter motor .... 11.5 mm (0.45 in)
   Bosch DM type starter motor .... 3.0 mm (0.12 in)
   Bosch DW type starter motor .... 4.5 mm (0.18 in)
   Delco-Remy type starter motor .... 4.0 mm (0.16 in)

Fuses

Rating:

Red	10 A
Blue	15 A
Yellow	20 A
Green...	30 A

Torque wrench settings

	Nm	lbf ft
Alternator mounting bolts..	25	18
Starter motor mounting bracket-to-cylinder block bolt............................	25	18
Starter motor mounting bolts:		
1.4 and 1.6 litre models..	25	18
1.8 and 2.0 litre models:		
Engine side..	·45	33
Gearbox side..	75	55

1 General description

The electrical system is of the 12 volt negative earth type, and consists of a 12 volt battery, alternator with integral voltage regulator, starter motor, and related electrical accessories, components and wiring. The battery is of the maintenance-free 'sealed for life' type, and is charged by an alternator, which is belt-driven from the crankshaft pulley. The starter motor is of the pre-engaged type, incorporating an integral solenoid. On starting, the solenoid moves the drive pinion into engagement with the flywheel ring gear before the starter motor is energised. Once the engine has started, a one-way clutch prevents the motor armature being driven by the engine until the pinion disengages from the flywheel.

Further details of the electrical systems are given in the relevant Sections of this Chapter.

Caution: *Before carrying out any work on the vehicle electrical system, rear through the precautions given in the 'Safety first!' Section at the beginning of this manual, and in Section 2 of this Chapter.*

2 Electrical system – precautions

It is necessary to take extra care when working on the electrical system, to avoid damage to semi-conductor devices (diodes and transistors), and to avoid the risk of personal injury. In addition to the precautions given in the *'Safety first!'* Section at the beginning of this manual, take note of the following points when working on the system.

1   *Always remove rings, watches, etc before working on the electrical system.* Even with the battery disconnected, capacitive discharge could occur if a component live terminal is earthed through a metal object. This could cause a shock or nasty burn.
2   *Do not reverse the battery connections.* Components such as the alternator, or any other component having semi-conductor circuitry, could be irreparably damaged.
3   If the engine is being started using jump leads and a slave battery, connect the batteries *positive to positive* and *negative to negative.* This also applies when connecting a battery charger.
4   Never disconnect the battery terminals, or alternator multi-plug connector, when the engine is running.
5   The battery leads and alternator wiring must be disconnected before carrying out any electric welding on the vehicle.
6   Never use an ohmmeter of the type incorporating a hand-cranked generator for circuit or continuity testing.

3 Routine maintenance

1   At the intervals specified in the *'Routine maintenance'* Section at the beginning of this manual, carry out the following maintenance operations and checks.
2   Check the operation of all the electrical equipment, ie wipers, washers, lamps, direction indicators, horn etc. Refer to the appropriate

Sections of this Chapter if any components are found to be inoperative.
3   Visually check all accessible wiring connectors, harnesses and retaining clips for security, or any signs of chafing or damage. Rectify any problems encountered.
4   Check the alternator drivebelt for cracks, fraying or damage. Renew the belt if necessary or, if satisfactory, check and adjust the belt tension, as described in Section 7.
5   Check the condition of the wiper blades, and if they are cracked or show signs of deterioration, renew them, as described in Section 47. Check the operation of the windscreen and tailgate washers (where applicable). Adjust the nozzles using a pin, if necessary.
6   Check the battery terminals, and if these is any sign of corrosion, disconnect and clean them thoroughly. Smear the terminals and battery posts with petroleum jelly. If there is any corrosion on the battery tray, remove the battery, clean the deposits away, and treat the affected metal with an anti-rust preparation. Repaint the tray in the original colour after treatment.
7   The maintenance-free 'sealed for life' battery does not require topping-up. The only maintenance requirement with this battery type is to inspect the battery lead terminals for security and any sign of corrosion.
8   Check and if necessary top up the washer fluid reservoir, and check the security of the pump wires and water pipes.
9   It is advisable to have the headlamp aim checked, and if necessary adjusted, using optical beam setting equipment.
10   While carrying out a road test, check the operation of the direction indicator self-cancelling mechanism.

4 Battery – testing and charging

Note: *Refer to Section 2 before proceeding*

1   Topping-up and testing of the electrolyte in each cell is not possible. The condition of the battery can therefore only be tested by observing the battery condition indicator.
2   The battery condition indicator is fitted in the top of the battery casing, and indicates the condition of the battery from its colour. If the indicator shows green, then the battery is in a good state of charge. If the indicator turns darker, eventually to black, then the battery requires charging, as described later in this Section. If the indicator shows clear/yellow, then the electrolyte level in the battery is too low to allow further use, and the battery should be renewed. **Do not** attempt to charge, load or jump start a battery when the indicator shows clear/yellow.
3   If the battery is to be charged, remove it from the vehicle and charge it as follows.
4   The maintenance-free type battery takes considerably longer to fully recharge than the standard type, the time taken being dependent on the extent of discharge.
5   A constant-voltage type charger is required, to be set, when connected, to 13.9 to 14.9 volts with a charger current below 25 amps.
6   If the battery is to be charged from a fully-discharged state (less than 12.2 volts output), have it recharged by a Vauxhall dealer or a competent automotive electrician, as the charge rate is high, and constant supervision during charging is necessary.

5 Battery – removal and refitting

Note: *Refer to Section 2 before proceeding*

1 The battery is located at the left-hand front corner of the engine compartment.
2 Disconnect the lead(s) at the negative (earth) terminal by unscrewing the retaining nut and removing the terminal clamp.
3 Disconnect the positive terminal lead(s) in the same way.
4 Unscrew the clamp bolt sufficiently to enable the battery to be lifted from its location. Keep the battery in an upright position, to avoid spilling electrolyte on the bodywork.
5 Refitting is a reversal of removal, but smear petroleum jelly on the terminals when reconnecting the leads, and always connect the positive lead first and the negative lead last.

6 Alternator – description

1 A Delco-Remy or Bosch alternator may be fitted, depending on model and engine capacity. The maximum output of the alternator varies accordingly.
2 The alternator is belt-driven from the crankshaft pulley. Cooling is provided by a fan, mounted outside the casing on the end of the rotor shaft. An integral voltage regulator is incorporated, to control the output voltage.
3 The alternator provides a charge to the battery even at very low engine speed, and basically consists of a coil-wound stator in which a rotor rotates. The rotor shaft is supported in ball-bearings, and slip rings are used to conduct current to and from the field coils through the carbon brushes.
4 The alternator generates ac (alternating current), which is rectified by an internal diode circuit to dc (direct current) for supply to the battery.

7 Alternator drivebelt – removal, refitting and tensioning

1 Disconnect the air intake trunking from the air cleaner, and the air box or throttle body, as applicable, and remove it for improved access.
2 Correct tensioning of the drivebelt will ensure that it has a long life. Beware, however, of overtightening, as this can cause excessive wear in the alternator.
3 The belt should be inspected regularly, and if it is found to be worn, frayed or cracked, it should be renewed as a precaution against breakage in service. It is advisable to carry a spare drivebelt of the correct type in the vehicle at all times.

4 On 1.6 litre models with power steering, the alternator drivebelt also drives the power steering pump.
5 To remove the belt, on 1.8 and 2.0 litre models first remove the power steering pump drivebelt, as described in Chapter 9, Section 42.
6 Loosen the two alternator mounting nuts and bolts sufficiently to allow the alternator to be pivoted in towards the engine.
7 Slide the belt from the pulleys.
8 Fit the belt around the pulleys, ensuring that the belt is of the correct type if it is being renewed, and take up the slack in the belt by swinging the alternator away from the engine and lightly tightening the mounting nuts and bolts.
9 Although special tools are available for measuring the belt tension, a good approximation can be achieved if the belt is tensioned so that there is approximately 13.0 mm (0.5 in) of free movement under firm thumb pressure at the mid-point of the longest run between pulleys.
10 With the mounting bolts just holding the unit firm, lever the alternator away from the engine using a wooden lever at the mounting bracket end until the correct tension is achieved, then tighten the mounting nuts and bolts. **On no account** lever at the free end of the alternator, as serious internal damage could be caused.
11 On 1.8 and 2.0 litre models, refit and tension the power steering pump drivebelt, as described in Chapter 9, Section 42.
12 Refit the air intake trunking.
13 When a new belt has been fitted, it will probably stretch slightly when it is first run, and the tension should be rechecked and if necessary adjusted after approximately 250 miles (400 km) of running.

8 Alternator – removal and refitting

Note: *Refer to Section 2 before proceeding*

1 Disconnect the battery leads.
2 Disconnect the air trunking from the air cleaner, and the air box or throttle body, as applicable, and remove it for improved access.
3 Disconnect the wiring plug, or disconnect the wires from their terminals on the rear of the alternator, noting their locations (photo).
4 Remove the drivebelt, as described in Section 7.
5 Unscrew the two mounting bolts and nuts and recover any washers and insulating bushes, noting their locations. Note the earth strap attached to the top mounting bolt (photo).
6 Withdraw the alternator, taking care not to knock or drop it, as this can cause irreparable damage.
7 Refitting is a reversal of removal, bearing in mind the following points.
8 Ensure that the earth lead is in place on the top mounting bolt.
9 Refit and tension the drivebelt, as described in Section 7.

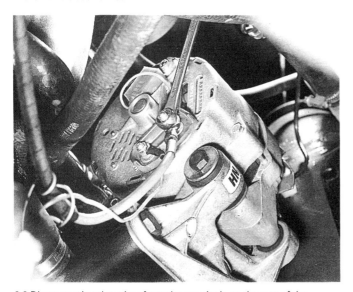

8.3 Disconnecting the wires from the terminals on the rear of the alternator – Delco-Remy alternator

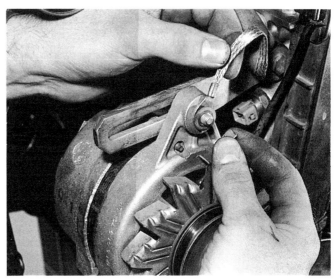

8.5 Disconnecting the earth lead from the top alternator mounting bolt

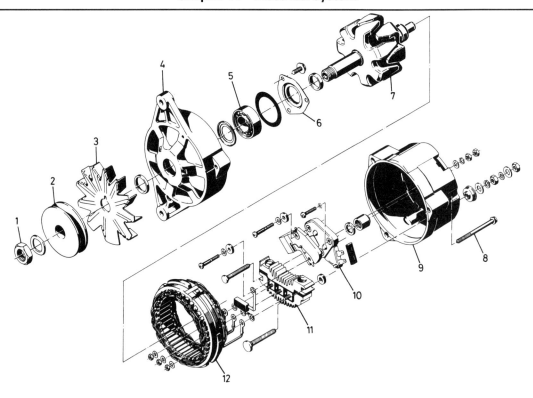

Fig. 11.1 Exploded view of Delco-Remy type alternator (Sec 10)

1	Pulley nut (not fitted to all models)	4	Drive end housing
2	Pulley	5	Bearing
3	Fan	6	Bearing retainer

7	Rotor	10	Brush holder/voltage regulator assembly
8	Through-bolt	11	Diode assembly
9	Slip ring end housing	12	Stator

9   Alternator – fault finding and testing

Due to the specialist knowledge and equipment required to test or service an alternator, it is recommended that if the performance is suspect, the vehicle is taken to a dealer or an automotive electrician, who will have the facilities to carry out such work. Because of this recommendation, information is limited to the inspection and renewal of the brushes. Should the alternator not charge, or the system be suspect, the following points may be checked before seeking further assistance:

(a)   Check the drivebelt tension, as described in Section 7
(b)   Check the condition of the battery and its connections – see Section 4
(c)   Inspect all electrical cables and connections for condition and security

Note that if the alternator is found to be faulty, it may prove more economical to purchase a factory-reconditioned unit, rather than having the existing unit overhauled.

10   Alternator brushes – removal, inspection and refitting

Delco-Remy type alternator

1   Remove the alternator, as described in Section 8.
2   Scribe a line across the drive end housing and the slip ring end housing, to ensure correct alignment when reassembling.
3   Unscrew the three through-bolts, and prise the drive end housing and rotor away from the slip ring end housing and stator (photo).
4   Check the condition of the slip rings, and if necessary clean with a rag or very fine glass paper (photo).
5   Remove the three nuts and washers securing the stator leads to the

10.3 Separating the drive end housing from the slip ring end housing – Delco-Remy alternator

10.4 Alternator slip rings (arrowed) – Delco-Remy alternator

10.5 Stator lead securing nuts (A) and brush holder/voltage regulator securing screws (B) – Delco-Remy alternator

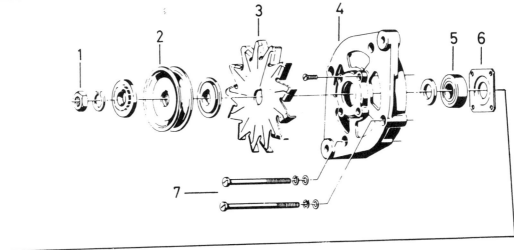

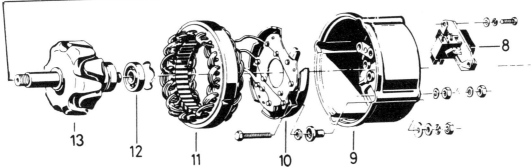

Fig. 11.2 Exploded view of Bosch type alternator (Sec 10)

1 Pulley nut	5 Bearing	8 Brush holder/voltage regulator assembly	10 Stator endplate
2 Pulley	6 Bearing retainer		11 Stator
3 Fan	7 Through-bolts	9 Slip ring end housing	12 Bearing
4 Drive end housing			13 Rotor

rectifier, and lift away the stator assembly (photo).
6 Remove the terminal screw and lift out the diode assembly.
7 Extract the two screws securing the brush holder and voltage regulator to the slip ring end housing, and remove the brush holder assembly. Note the insulation washers under the screw heads.
8 Check that the brushes move freely in their guides, and that the brush lengths are within the limits given in the Specifications. If any doubt exists regarding the condition of the brushes, the best policy is to renew them.
9 To fit new brushes, unsolder the old brush leads from the brush holder, and solder on the new leads in exactly the same place.
10 Check that the new brushes move freely in the guides.

Fig. 11.3 Alternator brush holder/voltage regulator securing screws – Bosch type alternator (Sec 10)

11 Before refitting the brush holder assembly, retain the brushes in the retracted position using a stiff piece of wire or a twist drill.
12 Refit the brush holder assembly so that the wire or drill protrudes through the slot in the slip ring end housing, and tighten the securing screws.
13 Refit the diode assembly and the stator assembly to the housing, ensuring that the stator leads are in their correct positions, and refit the terminal screw and nuts.
14 Assemble the drive end housing and rotor to the slip ring end housing, ensuring that the previously-made marks are aligned. Insert and tighten the three through-bolts.
15 Pull the wire or drill, as applicable, from the slot in the slip ring end housing so that the brushes rest on the rotor slip rings (photo).
16 Refit the alternator, as described in Section 8.

Bosch type alternator
17 Disconnect the air trunking from the air cleaner, and the air box or throttle body, as applicable, and remove it for improved access.
18 Disconnect the battery leads.
19 If desired, to improve access further, the alternator can be removed, as described in Section 8.
20 Remove the two securing screws, and withdraw the brush holder/voltage regulator assembly (photos).
21 Check that the brushes move freely in their guides, and that the brush lengths are within the limits given in the Specifications (photo). If any doubt exists regarding the condition of the brushes, the best policy is to renew them as follows.
22 Hold the brush wire with a suitable pair of pliers, and unsolder it from the brush holder. Lift away the brush. Repeat for the remaining brush.
23 Note that whenever new brushes are fitted, new brush springs should also be fitted.
24 With the new springs fitted to the brush holder, insert the new brushes, and check that they move freely in their guides. If they bind,

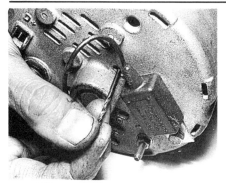

10.15 Withdrawing the twist drill used to retain the brushes – Delco- Remy alternator

10.20A Remove the securing screws ...

10.20B ... and withdraw the brush holder/voltage regulator assembly – Bosch alternator

10.21 Measuring the length of an alternator brush – Bosch alternator

10.26 Alternator slip rings (arrowed) – Bosch alternator

lightly polish with a very fine file or glass paper.

25   Solder the brush wire ends to the brush holder, taking care not to allow solder to pass to the stranded wire.

26   Check the condition of the slip rings, and if necessary clean with a rag or very fine glass paper (photo).

27   Refit the brush holder/voltage regulator assembly, and tighten the securing screws.

28   Where applicable, refit the alternator, as described in Section 8.

29   Reconnect the battery leads.

30   Refit the air trunking.

11   Starter motor – general description

The starter motor is mounted at the rear of the cylinder block, and may be of either Delco-Remy or Bosch manufacture. Both makes are of the pre-engaged type, ie the drive pinion is brought into mesh with the starter ring gear on the flywheel before the main current is applied.

When the starter switch is operated, current flows from the battery to the solenoid which is mounted on the starter body. The plunger in the solenoid moves inwards, so causing a centrally pivoted lever to push the drive pinion into mesh with the starter ring gear. When the solenoid plunger reaches the end of its travel, it closes an internal contact and full starting current flows to the starter field coils. The armature is then able to rotate the crankshaft, so starting the engine.

A special freewheel clutch is fitted to the starter driven pinion, so that as soon as the engine fires and starts to operate on its own it does not drive the starter motor.

When the starter switch is released, the solenoid is de-energised, and a spring moves the plunger back to its rest position. This operates the pivoted lever to the withdraw the drive pinion from engagement with the starter ring.

12   Starter motor – testing in the vehicle

Note: *Refer to Section 2 before proceeding*

1   If the starter motor fails to turn the engine when the switch is operated, assuming that engine seizure is not the problem, there are several other possible reasons:

(a)   The battery is faulty
(b)   The electrical connections between the switch, solenoid, battery and starter motor are somewhere failing to pass the necessary current from the battery through the starter to earth
(c)   The solenoid switch is faulty
(d)   The starter motor is mechanically or electrically defective
(e)   The starter motor pinion and/or flywheel ring gear is badly worn, and in need of replacement

2   To check the battery, switch on the headlamps. If they dim after a few seconds, then the battery is in a discharged state. If the lamps glow brightly, operate the starter switch and see what happens to the lamps. If they dim, then power is reaching the motor, but failing to turn it. If the starter turns slowly, proceed to the next check.

3   If, when the starter switch is operated, the lamps stay bright, then insufficient power is reaching the motor. Disconnect the battery and the starter/solenoid power connections, and the engine earth strap, then thoroughly clean them and refit them. Smear petroleum jelly around the battery connections to prevent corrosion. Corroded connections are the most frequent cause of electrical system malfunctions.

4   If the preceding checks and cleaning tasks have been carried out without success, a clicking noise will probably have been heard each time the starter switch was operated. This indicates that the solenoid switch was operating, but it does not necessarily follow that the main contacts were closing properly (if no clicking has been heard from the solenoid, it is certainly defective). The solenoid can be checked by connecting a voltmeter across the main cable connection on the solenoid and earth. When the switch is operated, these should be a reading on the voltmeter. If there is no reading, the solenoid unit is faulty, and should be renewed.

5   If the starter motor operates, but does not turn the engine, then it is likely that the starter pinion and/or flywheel ring gear are badly worn, in which case the starter motor will normally be noisy in operation.

6   Finally, if it is established that the solenoid is not faulty, and 12 volts are reaching the starter, then the motor itself is faulty, and should be removed for inspection.

13.4 Starter motor and solenoid viewed from underneath the vehicle. Solenoid wiring connections arrowed

13.5 Starter motor mounting bracket/exhaust bracket securing bolt (arrowed) – 1.6 litre model (engine removed)

13.6 Starter motor securing bolts (arrowed) – 1.6 litre model (engine removed)

13 Starter motor – removal and refitting

Note: *Refer to Section 2 before proceeding*

1 Disconnect the battery negative lead.
2 Apply the handbrake, then jack up the front of the vehicle, and support securely on axle stands positioned under the body side members.
3 On GSi 2000 models, remove the engine undershield, as described in Chapter 10.
4 Note the wiring connections on the solenoid, then disconnect them (photo).
5 Where applicable, unscrew the bolt securing the exhaust bracket and the starter motor mounting bracket to the cylinder block (photo).
6 Unscrew the two starter motor mounting bolts, noting that the top bolt on 1.8 and 2.0 litre models is fitted from the gearbox side, and also secures a wiring harness bracket (photo).
7 Withdraw the starter motor.
8 Refitting is a reversal of removal, but where applicable, ensure that the wiring harness bracket is in place on the top mounting bolt, and tighten all bolts to the specified torque.

14 Starter motor (Bosch) – overhaul

Note: *A two-legged puller, or suitable alternative tool, will be required to position the drive pinion thrust collar during reassembly*

DF and DM type starter motors
1 With the starter motor removed from the vehicle and cleaned, grip the unit in a vice fitted with soft jaw protectors.
2 Unscrew the nuts from the ends of the through-bolts, and remove the mounting bracket, where applicable.
3 Remove the nut and washer securing the field winding lead to the solenoid stud, and unhook the lead from the stud.
4 Remove the two screws securing the commutator end plate cap, then remove the cap and rubber seal.
5 Wipe any grease from the armature shaft, then remove the C-clip and shims from the end of the shaft.
6 Unscrew the two through-bolts, and lift off the commutator end plate.
7 Release the brush holders, complete with brushes, by pushing the brush holders towards the commutator and unclipping them from the brush plate. Withdraw the brush plate.
8 Separate the drive end housing and armature from the yoke by tapping apart with a soft-faced hammer.
9 Remove the three securing screws, and withdraw the solenoid yoke, then unhook the solenoid armature from the actuating arm and remove the armature.
10 Remove the rubber insert from the drive end housing, then unscrew the actuating arm pivot retaining nut and slide the pivot pin (bolt) from the housing.
11 Withdraw the armature assembly, complete with actuating arm, from the drive end housing. Unhook the actuating arm from the drive pinion flange.

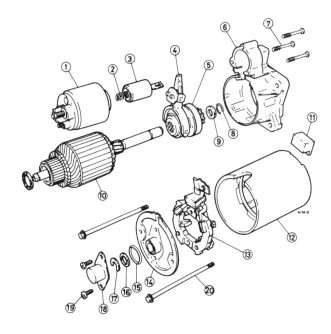

Fig. 11.4 Exploded view of Bosch DM type starter motor (Sec 14)

1 Solenoid yoke	11 Rubber insert
2 Solenoid return spring	12 Yoke
3 Solenoid armature	13 Brush plate
4 Actuating arm	14 Commutator end plate
5 Drive pinion and clutch assembly	15 Seal
6 Drive end housing	16 Shim
7 Solenoid securing screws	17 C-clip
8 C-clip	18 Commutator end housing cap
9 Thrust collar	19 Securing screw
10 Armature	20 Through-bolt

12 To remove the drive pinion from the armature shaft, drive the thrust collar down the shaft, using a suitable tube drift, to expose the C-clip. Remove the clip from its groove, and slide the thrust collar and drive pinion from the shaft. Do not grip the clutch assembly in a vice during this procedure, as damage will result.
13 Examine the components, and renew as necessary.
14 If the brushes have worn to less than the specified minimum length, renew them as a set. To renew the brushes, the leads must be unsoldered from the terminals on the brush plate, and the leads of the new brushes must be soldered to the terminals.
15 The commutator face should be clean and free from burnt spots. Where necessary, burnish with fine glass paper (**not** emery), and wipe with a fuel-moistured cloth. If the commutator is in very bad condition, it can be skimmed on a lathe, provided its diameter is not reduced excessively. If recutting the insulation slots, take care not to cut into the commutator metal.

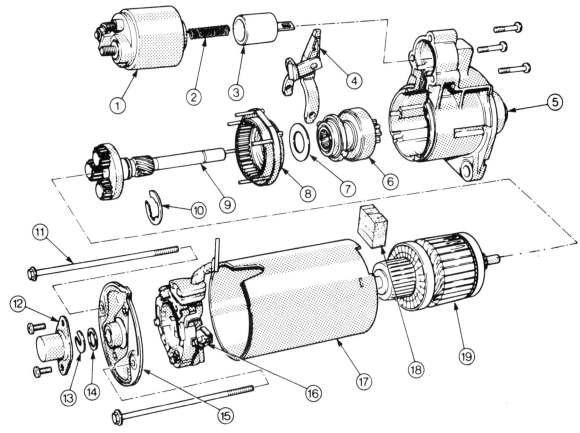

Fig. 11.5 Exploded view of Bosch DW type starter motor (Sec 14)

1	Solenoid yoke	6	Drive pinion and clutch	10	Circlip	15 Commutator end plate

1   Solenoid yoke
2   Solenoid return spring
3   Solenoid armature
4   Actuating arm
5   Drive end housing

6   Drive pinion and clutch
    assembly
7   Spacer
8   Ring gear and carrier
9   Output shaft and planet
    gear assembly

10 Circlip
11 Through-bolt
12 Commutator end plate
13 C-clip
14 Shim

15 Commutator end plate
16 Brush plate
17 Yoke
18 Rubber block
19 Armature

16   Renew the commutator end plate and drive end housing bushes, which are of the self-lubricating type, and should have been soaked in clean engine oil for at least twenty minutes before installation. Drive out the old bushes, whilst supporting the end plate/housing using a suitable drift.

17   Accurate checking of the armature, commutator and field coil windings and insulation requires the use of special test equipment. If the starter motor was inoperative when removed from the vehicle, and the previous checks have not highlighted the problem, then it can be assumed that there is a continuity or insulation fault, and the unit should be renewed.

18   Commence reassembly by sliding the driven pinion and thrust collar onto the armature shaft. Fit the C-clip into its groove, and then use a two-legged puller to draw the thrust collar over the clip.

19   Refit the actuating arm to the drive pinion flange, then refit the armature assembly and actuating arm to the drive end housing.

20   Refit the actuating arm pivot pin (bolt), and secure with the retaining nut. Fit the rubber insert into the drive end housing.

21   Apply a little lithium-based grease to the solenoid armature hook, then locate the hook over the actuating arm in the drive end housing. Ensure that the solenoid armature return spring is correctly positioned, then guide the solenoid yoke over the armature. Align the yoke with the drive end housing, and fit the three securing screws.

22   Guide the yoke over the armature and tap onto the drive end housing.

23   Position the brush plate over the end of the armature shaft, then assemble the brush holders, brushes and springs, ensuring that the brush holder clips are securely located. The brush plate will be positively located when the through-bolts are fitted.

24   Guide the commutator end plate into position, and fit the through-bolts.

25   Slide the armature into its bearings so that the shaft protrudes as far as possible at the commutator bearing end.

26   Fit sufficient shims to the end of the armature shaft to eliminate endfloat when the C-clip is fitted, then fit the clip.

27   Fit the rubber seal to the commutator end plate, then apply a little lithium-based grease to the end of the armature shaft and refit the end plate cap, securing with the two screws.

28   Reconnect the field winding lead to the solenoid stud, and secure with the nut and washer.

29   Refit the mounting bracket to the through-bolts, and secure with the two nuts, where applicable.

DW type starter motor

30   With the starter motor removed from the vehicle and cleaned, grip the unit in a vice fitted with soft jaw protectors.

31   Unscrew the nuts from the ends of the through-bolts, and remove the mounting bracket, where applicable.

32   Remove the two securing screws, and withdraw the armature shaft cover (photo).

33   Remove the C-clip and spacer from the end of the armature shaft (photos).

34   Unscrew the two through-bolts, and lift off the commutator end plate (photos).

35   Remove the securing nut, and disconnect the wiring from the solenoid terminal (photo).

36   Withdraw the complete yoke and armature assembly from the drive end housing (photo).

37   Retain the brushes in the brush holders using a large socket or metal tube, then remove the brush plate from the armature shaft (photos).

14.32 Removing an armature shaft cover screw – Bosch DW type starter motor

14.33A Remove the C-clip (arrowed) ...

14.33B ... and the spacer – Bosch DW type starter motor

14.34A Unscrew the two through-bolts ...

14.34B ... remove them ...

14.34C ... and lift off the commutator end plate – Bosch DW type starter motor

14.35 Disconnecting the wiring from the solenoid terminal – Bosch DW type starter motor

14.36 Withdraw the yoke and armature assembly – Bosch DW type starter motor

14.37A Place a large socket over the end of the armature ...

14.37B ... then slide the brushes onto it – Bosch DW type starter motor

14.37C Brushes retained in brush holders by socket – Bosch DW type starter motor

14.38 Withdraw the armature from the yoke – Bosch DW type starter motor

14.39A Extract the securing screws ...

14.39B ... and remove the solenoid yoke from the drive end housing ...

14.40A ... recover the spring ...

14.40B ... and unhook the solenoid armature – Bosch DW type starter motor

14.41 Withdrawing the pinion and clutch assembly – Bosch DW type starter motor

38   Withdraw the armature from the yoke (photo).
39   Extract the three securing screws, and remove the solenoid yoke from the drive end housing (photos).
40   Recover the spring, then unhook the solenoid armature from the actuating arm (photos).
41   Withdraw the complete pinion and clutch assembly from the drive end housing (photo).
42   To remove the drive pinion from the shaft, proceed as described in paragraph 12.
43   Examine the components, and renew as necessary.
44   To renew the brushes, the leads must be unsoldered from the terminals on the brush plate, and the leads of the new brushes must be soldered to the terminals.
45   Proceed as described in paragraphs 15 to 17 inclusive.
46   Commence reassembly by refitting the drive pinion to the shaft, as described in paragraph 18.
47   Refit the pinion and clutch assembly into the drive end housing, ensuring that the ring gear carrier and rubber block are correctly located.
48   Apply a little lithium-based grease to the end of the solenoid armature, and reconnect it to the actuating arm.
49   Ensure that the solenoid armature return spring is correctly positioned, then guide the solenoid yoke over the armature, and refit the three securing screws.
50   With brush components assembled to the brush plate, and the brushes retained in their holders using a socket or tube as during removal, position the brush plate over the end of the armature shaft, and withdraw the socket or tube.
51   Insert the armature into the yoke, making sure that the brush plate stays in place, and engage the rubber insulator with the cut-out in the yoke.
52   Refit the yoke and armature assembly to the drive end housing, aligning the sun gear with the planet gears.
53   Reconnect the wiring to the solenoid terminal, and fit the securing nut.
54   Refit the commutator end plate, and secure with the two through-bolts.

55   Refit the spacer and C-clip to the end of the armature shaft, then smear the end of the shaft with a little lithium-based grease.
56   Fit the armature shaft cover, and secure with the two screws.
57   Refit the mounting bracket to the through-bolts, and secure with the two nuts, where applicable.

15   Starter motor (Delco-Remy) – overhaul

Note: *A two-legged puller, or suitable alternative tool, will be required to position the drive pinion thrust collar during reassembly*

1   With the starter motor removed from the vehicle and cleaned, grip the unit in a vice fitted with soft jaw protectors.
2   Unscrew the nuts from the ends of the through-bolts, and remove the mounting bracket, where applicable.
3   Unscrew and remove the two through-bolts which hold the components of the starter motor assembly together (photo).
4   Extract the two small screws which secure the commutator end housing to the brush plate, then lift off the commutator end housing (photo).
5   Lift the brush retaining springs to remove the positive brushes from the brush holders, then lift the brush plate from the commutator (photo).
6   Remove the two securing screws, and withdraw the solenoid yoke and spring from the drive end housing (photo).
7   Extract the clip from the actuating arm pivot pin, then tap the pivot pin from the drive end housing (photos).
8   Remove the solenoid armature and the actuating arm, then unhook the actuating arm from the armature.
9   Separate the drive end housing and armature from the yoke by tapping them apart with a soft-faced hammer.
10   Proceed as described in Section 14, paragraphs 12 to 18 inclusive.
11   Hook the actuating arm onto the solenoid armature, then refit the

15.3 Unscrew the through-bolts ...

15.4 ... and extract the two small screws –
Delco-Remy type starter motor

15.5 Lift the brush plate from the
commutator – Delco-Remy type starter
motor

armature and actuating arm to the drive end housing.

12   Tap the actuating arm pivot pin into the drive end housing, and refit the retaining clip.

13   Refit the solenoid yoke and spring, and secure with the two screws.

14   Guide the yoke over the armature, and tap onto the drive end housing.

15   Refit the brushes to the brush holders, then position the brush plate on the commutator.

16   Fit the commutator end housing, and fit the two screws securing the end housing to the brush plate.

17   Refit the two through-bolts.

18   Where applicable, refit the mounting bracket, and secure with the two nuts.

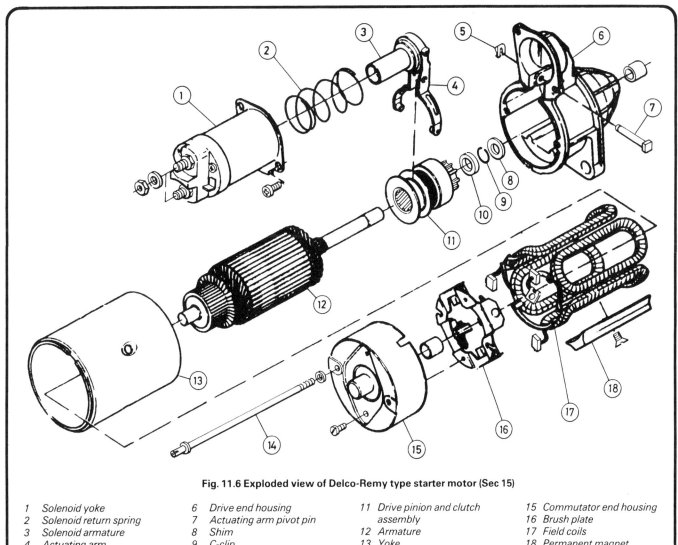

Fig. 11.6 Exploded view of Delco-Remy type starter motor (Sec 15)

1 Solenoid yoke	6 Drive end housing	11 Drive pinion and clutch	15 Commutator end housing
2 Solenoid return spring	7 Actuating arm pivot pin	assembly	16 Brush plate
3 Solenoid armature	8 Shim	12 Armature	17 Field coils
4 Actuating arm	9 C-clip	13 Yoke	18 Permanent magnet
5 Pivot pin clip	10 Thrust collar	14 Through-bolt	

15.6 Withdrawing the solenoid yoke and spring – Delco-Remy type starter motor

15.7A Extract the clip from the actuating arm pivot pin ...

15.7B ... then withdraw the pivot pin – Delco-Remy type starter motor

16.1 Main fuses and relays in facia panel – 2.0 litre SRi model shown

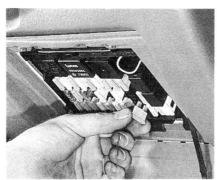

16.3 Removing a fuse – 2.0 litre model shown

16.5 Relays in engine compartment box – 2.0 litre SRi model shown

16   Fuses and relays – general

1   The main fuses and relays are located in a panel at the lower right-hand side of the facia, under a hinged cover (photo).
2   The circuits protected by the various fuses and relays are marked on the inside of the panel cover.
3   To remove a fuse or relay, open the cover and pull the relevant fuse or relay from the panel (photo). If desired, the lower end of the panel can be tilted forwards, after releasing the retaining clips to improve access.
4   Before renewing a blown fuse, trace and rectify the cause, and always use a fuse of the correct rating. Never substitute a fuse of a higher rating, or make temporary repairs using wire or metal foil, as more serious damage or even fire could result.
5   On certain models, additional relays are located in a box at the left-hand rear of the engine compartment (photo).

17   Ignition switch and lock cylinder – removal and refitting

1   Disconnect the battery negative lead.
2   Turn the steering wheel as necessary to expose the two front steering column shroud securing screws, which are covered by plastic caps. Prise out the caps and remove the screws.
3   Remove the three securing screws from the underside of the lower column shroud, then remove both the upper and lower shrouds.
4   To remove the lock cylinder, insert the ignition key and turn it to position '11'.
5   Insert a thin rod into the hole in the lock housing, then press the rod to release the detent spring, and pull out the lock cylinder using the key.
6   The ignition switch is secured to the steering lock housing by two grub screws. Disconnect the wiring plug, and remove the screws to extract the switch (photo). It is recommended that the switch and the

lock cylinder are not both removed at the same time, so that their mutual alignment is not lost.
7   Refitting is a reversal of removal.

18   Direction indicator/lighting switch – removal and refitting

1   Disconnect the battery negative lead.
2   Turn the steering wheel as necessary to expose the two front steering column shroud securing screws, which are covered by plastic

17.6 Removing an ignition switch securing screw

caps. Prise out the caps and remove the screws.
3   Remove the three securing screws from the underside of the lower column shroud, then remove both the upper and lower shrouds.
4   Disconnect the wiring plug from the switch.
5   Depress the switch retaining clip, and withdraw the switch from the housing.
6   Refitting is a reversal of removal.

19   Wash/wipe switch – removal and refitting

Proceed as described in Section 18.

20   Facia panel switches – removal and refitting

1   Disconnect the battery negative lead.

Lighting switch
2   Turn the switch to the 'dipped beam on' position, then insert a small screwdriver or suitable rod through the hole in the bottom of the switch knob to depress the knob retaining clip. Pull the knob from the switch (photo).
3   Press the two now-exposed switch securing clips towards the switch spindle, then pull the switch from the facia and disconnect the wiring plug (photos).
4   Note that the switch assembly cannot be dismantled, and if any part of the switch is faulty, the complete assembly must be renewed.
5   Refitting is a reversal of removal.

Pushbutton switches
6   First check beneath the switch, if there is a small hole in the facia, use a slim screwdriver or metal rod inserted into this hole to release the switch retaining spring clip by pressing it upwards against the switch, then remove the switch and disconnect its wiring. If there is no hole,

remove the switch by prising it out of the facia using a small screwdriver levering gently under the switch's lower edge (use adhesive tape or a piece of card to protect the facia's finish); disconnect the switch wiring plug and withdraw the switch (photo).
7   Refitting is a reversal of removal.

Headlamp aim adjustment switch
8   The procedure is as described for pushbutton switches.

Hazard warning flasher switch
9   Using a screwdriver, carefully prise the cap from the switch (photo).
10   Using a screwdriver with a piece of card under the blade to avoid damage to the facia trim, prise the ventilation nozzle from the facia.
11   Prise the switch from the facia and disconnect the wiring (photo).
12   Refitting is a reversal of removal.

Heater blower motor switch
13   Remove the heater control panel, as described in Chapter 10, Section 42.
14   Disconnect the wiring plug from the switch, if not already done.
15   Prise the switch out from the rear of the heater control panel.
16   Refitting is a reversal of removal, but refer to Chapter 10, Section 42 when refitting the heater control panel.

21   Electric door mirror switch – removal and refitting

1   Disconnect the battery negative lead.
2   Prise the plastic surround from the door interior handle.
3   Free the trim panel from the top edge of the door by releasing the securing clips. This can be done using a screwdriver, but it is preferable to use a forked tool, to minimise the possibility of damage to the trim panel and the clips.
4   Note the position of the mirror switch wiring connector in the bracket at the top of the door, then separate the two halves of the connector.

20.2 Using a thin rod to depress the lighting switch knob retaining clip

20.3A Press the switch securing clips towards the switch spindle ...

20.3B ... then pull the switch from the facia

20.6 Prising a pushbutton switch from the facia

20.9 Prising the cap from the hazard warning flasher switch

20.11 Withdrawing the hazard warning flasher switch from the facia

5   Prise the switch from the door trim panel, and feed the wiring through the panel.
6   Refitting is a reversal of removal, but ensure that the wiring is correctly routed, so as not to foul the door interior handle mechanism.

22   Sunroof operating switch – removal and refitting

1   Disconnect the battery negative lead.
2   Prise the courtesy lamp from the roof trim panel, and disconnect the wiring.
3   Remove the two trim panel securing screws, and withdraw the trim panel from the roof, disconnecting the wiring from the sunroof operating switch.
4   Release the securing clips, then pull the switch from the rear face of the trim panel.
5   Refitting is a reversal of removal.

23   Courtesy lamp switch – removal and refitting

1   Disconnect the battery negative lead.
2   Open the door and remove the switch securing screw.
3   Withdraw the switch from the door pillar, and pull the wiring out sufficiently to prevent it from springing back into the pillar.
4   Disconnect the wiring and remove the switch.
5   Refitting is a reversal of removal.

24   Luggage compartment lamp switch – removal and refitting

1   Disconnect the battery negative lead.
2   Open the boot lid or tailgate, as applicable, and remove the switch securing screw.
3   Withdraw the switch from the body panel, and pull the wiring out sufficiently to prevent it from springing back into the body.
4   Disconnect the wiring and remove the switch.
5   Refitting is a reversal of removal.

25   Brake lamp switch – removal and refitting

1   Disconnect the battery negative lead.
2   Remove the lower trim panel from the driver's footwell.

3   Disconnect the wiring plug from the brake lamp switch, then twist the switch anti-clockwise and remove it from its bracket.
4   Refitting is a reversal of removal.

26   Handbrake 'on' warning lamp switch – removal and refitting

For access to the switch, the handbrake lever must be removed. Removal and refitting of the switch is described as part of the handbrake lever removal and refitting procedure, in Chapter 8, Section 28.

27   Reversing lamp switch – removal and refitting

1   The reversing lamp switch is located at the front of the gearbox casing, and is accessible from the engine compartment.
2   To remove the switch, first disconnect the battery negative lead, then disconnect the wiring from the switch and unscrew the switch from the gearbox.
3   Refitting is a reversal of removal.

28   Oil pressure warning lamp switch – removal and refitting

1   Disconnect the battery negative lead.
2   The switch is screwed into the oil pump, on the inlet manifold side of the engine. On 1.4 and 1.6 litre models the switch projects at right-angles to the crankshaft axis, while on 1.8 and 2.0 litre models it is parallel to the crankshaft (photo).
3   In most cases the switch can be reached quite easily from above, but on some models access will be easier if the front of the vehicle is jacked up and supported on axle stands (ensure that the handbrake is securely applied) and the front right-hand roadwheel is removed.
4   Disconnect the switch wire and use a suitable spanner to unscrew the switch (photo). As you withdraw the switch, swifly plug the hole in the oil pump to minimise the loss of oil and to prevent the entry of dirt.
5   Refitting is the reverse of the removal procedure; tighten the switch securely but do not overtighten it, reconnect its wire, then check and if necessary top up the oil level, as described in Chapter 1. Wash off any spilt oil and check for leaks when the engine is restarted.

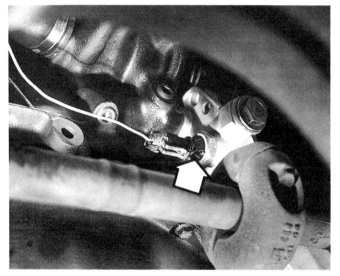

28.2 Oil pressure warning lamp switch (arrowed) viewed from underneath vehicle – 2.0 litre sohc model

28.4 Unscrewing the oil pressure warning lamp switch – 1.6 litre model (engine removed)

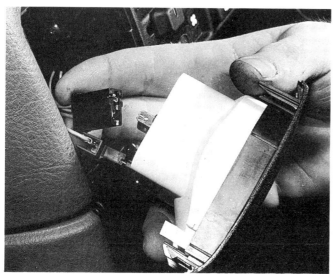

30.3 Disconnecting the wiring plugs from the clock

29 Cigarette lighter – removal and refitting

1 Disconnect the battery negative lead.
2 Slide the ashtray/cigarette lighter assembly from the facia, then disconnect the wiring and slide the illumination bulb from the cigarette lighter.
3 To remove the cigarette lighter assembly, simply pull it from the illumination ring assembly. If desired, the illumination ring assembly can be removed, by pulling it from the housing after depressing the retaining clips.
4 Refitting is a reversal of removal.

30 Clock – removal and refitting

1 Disconnect the battery negative lead.
2 Using a thin-bladed screwdriver, carefully prise the clock from the facia panel.
3 Disconnect the wiring plugs and withdraw the clock (photo).

31 Instrument panel – removal and refitting

1 Disconnect the battery negative lead.
2 Remove the steering wheel, as described in Chapter 9, Section 30.
3 Remove the steering column shrouds, and the instrument panel upper and lower trim panels, as described in Chapter 10, Section 37.
4 Remove the single upper, and two lower, instrument panel securing screws (photo).
5 Carefully withdraw the instrument panel, and disconnect the speedometer cable and the two wiring plugs. Note that the speedometer cable is retained by a clip, which must be pressed towards the speedometer to release the cable (photo).
6 If desired, the instrument panel can be dismantled, with reference to Section 32.
7 Refitting is a reversal of removal, but ensure that the speedometer cable is not kinked or twisted between the instrument panel and the bulkhead as the panel is refitted.

32 Instrument panel components – removal and refitting

1 With the instrument panel removed, as described in Section 31, proceed as follows.

Panel illumination and warning lamp bulbs
2 Twist the relevant bulbholder clockwise, and withdraw it from the printed circuit board on the rear of the instrument panel (photo).
3 The bulbs are integral with the bulbholders, and must be renewed as a unit.
4 Refitting is a reversal of removal.

Voltage stabiliser
5 Remove the single securing screw from the rear of the instrument panel, then pull the voltage stabiliser from the contacts on the printed circuit board (photo).
6 Refitting is a reversal of removal.

Fuel and temperature gauges – 'low series' models
7 Pull the trip meter reset pin from the front of the panel.
8 Release the two retaining clips at the top of the panel, and remove the panel shroud (photo).
9 Unscrew the two securing nuts, and withdraw the relevant gauge through the front of the instrument panel.
10 Refitting is a reversal of removal.

31.4 Unscrewing a lower instrument panel securing screw

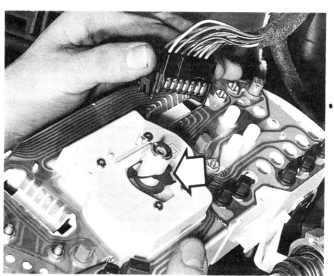

31.5 Disconnecting an instrument panel wiring plug. Note speedometer cable retaining clip (arrowed)

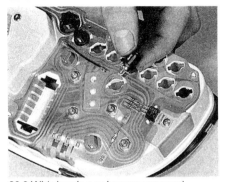

32.2 Withdrawing an instrument panel illumination lamp bulb

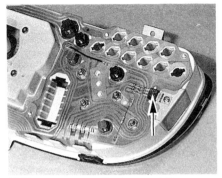

32.5 Instrument panel voltage stabiliser (arrowed)

32.8 Removing the instrument panel shroud

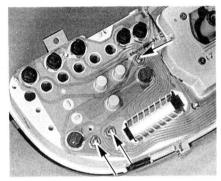

32.12 Tachometer securing nuts (arrowed)

32.14 Speedometer securing screws (arrowed)

Fuel and temperature gauge assembly – 'high series' models

11   The procedure is as described in paragraphs 7 to 10 inclusive, except that the gauge assembly is secured by four nuts.

Tachometer

12   The procedure is as described in paragraphs 7 to 10 inclusive, except that the tachometer is secured by three nuts (photo).

Speedometer

13   Proceed as described in paragraphs 7 and 8.
14   Extract the four securing screws from the rear of the panel (photo).
15   Refitting is a reversal of removal.

Printed circuit board

16   Remove all bulbs and instruments, and the voltage stabiliser, as described previously in this Section.
17   Carefully peel the printed circuit board from the instrument panel.
18   Refitting is a reversal of removal, but ensure that the printed circuit board is seated correctly on the rear of the instrument panel.

---

33   Trip computer components – removal and refitting

1   Disconnect the battery lead.

Display module

2   Using a thin-bladed screwdriver, carefully prise the module from the facia panel.
3   Disconnect the wiring plug and withdraw the module.
4   Refitting is a reversal of removal.

Display module illumination bulb

5   Remove the display module, as described previously in this Section.
6   Using a length of rubber sleeving of suitable diameter, or an alternator suitable tool, extract the bulb by inserting the tool through the

hole in the side of the display module – see Fig. 11.7.
7   Refitting is a reversal of removal.

Operating switch

8   Remove the rear section of the centre console, as described in Chapter 10, Section 38.
9   Release the wiring plug from the switch using a screwdriver.
10   Lift the switch, then pull it down and out from the centre console.
11   Refitting is a reversal of removal.

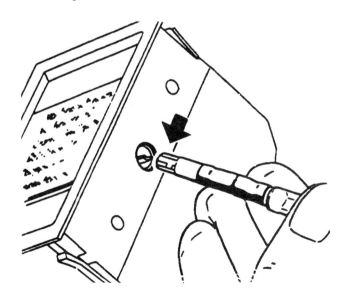

Fig. 11.7 Removing the trip computer display module illumination bulb (Sec 33)

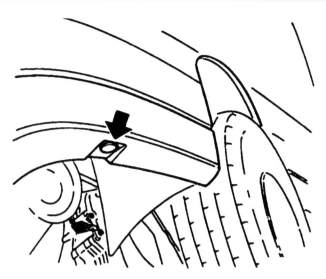

Fig. 11.8 Trip computer outside air temperature sensor location (arrowed) (Sec 33)

34.18 Engine oil level sensor – GSi 2000 model

Outside air temperature sensor

12   The sensor is located at the left-hand end of the front bumper.

13   Prise the cover cap from the bumper, then unclip the sensor, and disconnect the wiring plug.

14   Refitting is a reversal of removal.

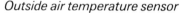

34   Check control system components – removal and refitting

1   Disconnect the battery negative lead.

Warning lamp bulbs

2   The warning lamp bulbs are located in the instrument panel, and removal and refitting are described in Section 32.

Control module

3   The control module is located behind the passenger side of the facia, above the glovebox.

4   Remove the glovebox assembly, as described in Chapter 10, Section 37.

5   Disconnect the control module wiring plug, then release the control module from its mounting and withdraw the unit.

6   Refitting is a reversal of removal.

Coolant level sensor

7   The coolant level sensor is integral with the coolant expansion tank cap.

8   Disconnect the wiring from the top of the cap, then unscrew the cap and withdraw it from the expansion tank.

9   If faulty, the complete cap assembly must be renewed.

10   Refitting is a reversal of removal.

Washer fluid level sensor

11   The sensor is mounted in the side of the fluid reservoir.

12   Disconnect the wiring from the sensor, then unscrew the sensor from the fluid reservoir. If the fluid level is above the level of the sensor, be prepared for fluid spillage.

13   Refitting is a reversal of removal.

Brake fluid level sensor

14   The procedure is as described for the coolant level sensor in paragraphs 7 to 10 inclusive.

Engine oil level sensor

15   Apply the handbrake, jack up the front of the vehicle, and support securely on axle stands positioned under the body side members.

16   On GSi 2000 models, remove the engine undershield, as described in Chapter 10, Section 32.

17   Disconnect the sensor wiring plug.

18   Unscrew the three or four sensor securing screws, as applicable, and withdraw the sensor, manipulating the float through the hole in the sump (photo). Recover the sealing ring. Be prepared for some oil spillage.

19   Examine the condition of the sealing ring, and renew if necessary.

20   Refitting is a reversal of removal. On completion, check, and if necessary top up, the engine oil level.

Bulb failure sensor

21   The bulb failure sensor is mounted behind the fuse/relay panel in the facia.

22   Release the retaining clips from the lower end of the fuse/relay panel, and tilt it forwards.

23   Reach up behind the fuse/relay panel, and pull the sensor from its socket.

24   Refitting is a reversal of removal.

35   Horn(s) – removal and refitting

1   On models with a single horn, the horn is located in front of the radiator. On models with twin horns, the horns are located beneath the washer fluid reservoir, at the left-hand end of the front bumper.

Single horn

2   Disconnect the battery negative lead.

3   Remove the radiator grille panel, with reference to Chapter 10, Section 29.

4   Disconnect the wiring from the rear of the horn.

5   Reach up behind the mounting bracket, and unscrew the single nut securing the horn to the bracket (photo). Withdraw the horn.

6   Refitting is a reversal of removal.

Twin horns

7   Disconnect the battery negative lead.

8   Apply the handbrake, then jack up the front of the vehicle, and support securely on axle stands positioned under the body side members.

9   Remove the securing screws, and withdraw the plastic cover (where fitted) from the bumper/front wing to expose the horns.

10   Remove the bolt securing the horn mounting bracket to the bracket below the washer fluid reservoir (photo).

11   Withdraw the horns and disconnect the wiring.

12   If desired, the horns can be unbolted from the bracket.

13   Refitting is a reversal of removal.

35.5 Horn viewed from behind with radiator removed – 1.6 litre model

35.10 Horn mounting bracket securing bolt (arrowed) – 2.0 litre model

2   Using a thin-bladed screwdriver, prise the lamp from its location and disconnect the wiring (photo).

3   Refitting is a reversal of removal.

37   Interior lamp bulbs – renewal

1   Disconnect the battery negative lead.

Courtesy lamp

2   Using a thin-bladed screwdriver, prise the lamp from its location and disconnect the wiring.

3   On models fitted with a courtesy lamp with integral map reading lamps, the lens must be levered from the housing for access to the bulbs.

4   Remove the courtesy lamp bulbs by carefully prising it from its location using a thin-bladed screwdriver. Where applicable, the map reading lamp bulbs are a push fit in the bulbholders.

5   Refitting is a reversal of removal.

Glovebox lamp

6   Using a thin-bladed screwdriver, prise the lamp from its location and disconnect the wiring.

7   Carefully prise the bulb from the lamp.

8   Refitting is a reversal of removal.

Luggage compartment lamp, underbonnet lamp and kerb lamps

9   Using a thin-bladed screwdriver, prise the lamp from its location and disconnect the wiring.

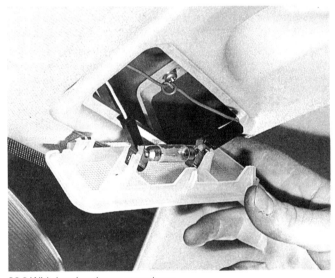

36.2 Withdrawing the courtesy lamp

36   Courtesy lamp, luggage compartment lamp, underbonnet lamp and kerb lamps – removal and refitting

1   Disconnect the battery negative lead.

37.10 Removing the underbonnet lamp bulb

37.16 Removing the clock illumination lamp bulbholder

37.20 Heater control panel illumination lamp bulbholder withdrawn

38.5A Unscrewing the lower headlamp securing screw

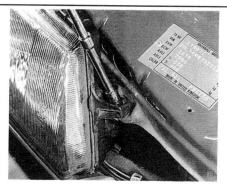

38.5B Unscrewing an upper headlamp securing screw

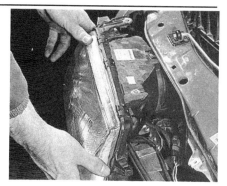

38.5C Withdrawing a headlamp unit

10   Carefully prise the bulb from the lamp (photo).
11   Refitting is a reversal of removal.

Cigarette lighter illumination lamp
12   Slide the ashtray/cigarette lighter assembly from the facia, then disconnect the wiring and pull the bulbholder from the rear of the cigarette lighter housing.
13   The bulb is a push fit in the bulbholder.
14   Refitting is a reversal of removal.

Clock illumination lamp
15   Remove the clock, as described in Section 30.
16   Twist the bulbholder and pull it from the rear of the clock (photo).
17   The bulb is a push fit in the bulbholder.

Trip computer display module illumination lamp
18   Refer to Section 33.

Heater control panel illumination lamp
19   Remove the heater control panel, as described in Chapter 10, Section 42.
20   Pull the bulbholder from the rear of the control panel (photo).
21   The bulb is a push fit in the bulbholder.
22   Refitting is a reversal of removal.

Facia panel switch illumination lamp
23   If a bulb fails in one of the facia panel switches, the complete switch assembly must be renewed, as described in Section 20, as no individual spare parts are available.

Vanity mirror illumination lamp
24   Lower the sunvisor and, using a thin-bladed screwdriver, prise out the mirror and diffuser assembly. Pull the bulb(s) from the spring contacts.

25   Refitting is a reversal of removal.

38   Headlamp unit – removal and refitting

1   Remove the radiator grille panel, as described in Chapter 10, Section 29.
2   Remove the front direction indicator lamp unit, as described in Section 41.
3   Remove the cover from the rear of the headlamp unit, and disconnect the wiring plugs from the bulbs.
4   Where applicable, disconnect the wiring plug from the headlamp aim adjustment motor.
5   Remove the three securing screws, and withdraw the headlamp unit (photos). Feed the wiring through the headlamp casing as it is removed.
6   If required, the headlamp lens can be removed by releasing the spring clips around its edge.
7   Refitting is a reversal of removal.
8   On completion, have the headlamp alignment checked, with reference to Section 40.

39   Headlamp aim adjustment motor – removal and refitting

1   Remove the headlamp, as described in Section 38.
2   Twist the motor clockwise to release it from the headlamp, then carefully disconnect the motor from the balljoint (photos).
3   Refitting is a reversal of removal, but ensure that the motor is correctly engaged with the balljoint.

39.2A Headlamp aim adjustment motor (headlamp removed)

39.2B Headlamp aim adjuster balljoint (arrowed)

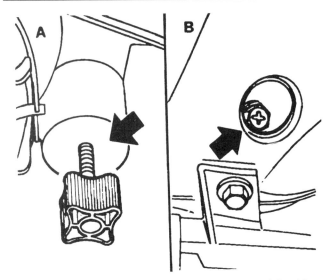

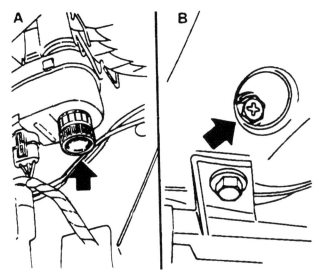

Fig. 11.9 Headlamp alignment adjustment screws – models without electric aim adjustment (Section 40)

A   Vertical adjustment screw   B   Horizontal adjustment screw

Fig. 11.10 Headlamp alignment adjustment screws – models with electric aim adjustment (Sec 40)

A   Vertical adjustment screw   B   Horizontal adjustment screw

40   Headlamps – alignment

1   Correct alignment of the headlamp beams is most important, not only to ensure good vision for the driver, but also to protect other drivers from being dazzled.
2   Accurate alignment should be carried out using optical beam setting equipment.
3   In an emergency, adjustments may be made by turning the adjustment screws shown in Fig. 11.9 or 11.10, as applicable. If an adjustment is made, the alignment should be checked using suitable beam setting equipment at the earliest opportunity.
4   Holts Amber Lamp is useful for temporarily changing the headlight colour to conform with the normal usage on Continental Europe.

41   Front direction indicator lamp unit – removal and refitting

1   Disconnect the battery negative lead.
2   Remove the single indicator lamp unit securing screw, which is accessible through the hole in the upper body panel (photo).

3   Pull the lamp unit forwards to release it from the body, then disconnect the wiring plug (photo).
4   Refitting is a reversal of removal.

42   Front direction indicator side repeater lamp – removal and refitting

1   Disconnect the battery negative lead.
2   Remove the wheel arch liner, as described in Chapter 10, Section 31.
3   Working in the engine compartment, disconnect the wiring plug, and detach the earth lead from the body panel.
4   Working under the wheel arch, depress the retaining tabs and manipulate the lamp through the outside of the wing, pulling the wiring and the grommet from the inner wing panel.
5   The lens can be removed from the lamp by twisting it to release the retaining clips.
6   Check the condition of the rubber sealing ring, and renew if necessary.
7   Refitting is a reversal of removal.

41.2 Unscrewing the front direction indicator lamp unit securing screw

41.3 Disconnecting the front direction indicator lamp unit wiring plug

43.7 Foglamp aim adjustment screw (arrowed)

43   Front foglamp – removal, refitting and adjustment

Removal and refitting

1   Disconnect the battery negative lead.
2   Removing (if necessary) the radiator grille panel, as described in Chapter 10, Section 29, disconnect the appropriate foglamp wiring plug.
3   Apply the handbrake, jack up the front of the vehicle and support it securely on axle stands positioned under the body side members.
4   If removing the driver's side foglamp, remove the securing screws and withdaw the plastic cover from the bumper/front wing to expose the lamp mountings.
5   Unscrew the three securing bolts and withdraw the lamp and wiring, the two bottom bolts are obvious, but the third is well-hidden at the top of the lamp.
6   Refitting is a reversal of removal, but on completion check the foglamp adjustment.

Adjustment

7   The vertical aim of the foglamps can be adjusted by turning the adjuster screw at the rear of the lamp in the required direction. It will be necessary to remove the plastic cover (driver's side only) from the bumper/front wing to expose the adjuster screw (photo).

44   Rear lamp unit – removal and refitting

1   Disconnect the battery negative lead.
2   Working in the luggage compartment, remove the cover from the rear of the lamp.

3   Release the top and bottom retaining clips, and pull the bulbholder from the lamp. Disconnect the wiring plug.
4   Remove the securing screws, and withdraw the lamp unit from outside the vehicle.
5   Note that the lens cannot be renewed separately, and if damaged, the complete lamp unit must be renewed.
6   Refitting is a reversal of removal.

45   Rear number plate lamp – removal and refitting

1   Disconnect the battery negative lead.
2   Using a thin-bladed screwdriver, carefully prise the lamp surround from the bumper.
3   Pull the lamp from the bumper, and disconnect the wiring.
4   Refitting is a reversal of removal.

46   Exterior lamp bulbs – renewal

Note: *The glass envelopes of the headlamp and foglamp bulbs must not be touched with the fingers. If the glass is accidentally touched, it should be washed with methylated spirits and dried with a soft cloth. Failure to observe this procedure may result in premature bulb failure*

1   Disconnect the battery negative lead.

Headlamps

2   Working in the engine compartment, release the retaining clip, and remove the cover from the rear of the headlamp (photo).
3   Pull the wiring plug from the base of the bulb, then release the spring clip, grasp the bulb by its contacts and carefully withdraw it (photos). Do not touch the bulb glass.
4   Refitting is a reversal of removal.

Sidelamps

5   Working in the engine compartment, release the retaining clip, and remove the cover from the rear of the headlamp.
6   Pull the wiring plug from the bulbholder, then pull the bulbholder from the headlamp (photo).
7   The bulb is a push fit in the bulbholder (photo).
8   Refitting is a reversal of removal.

Front direction indicator lamp

9   Working in the engine compartment, disconnect the wiring plug from the bulbholder.
10   Twist the bulbholder anti-clockwise, and pull it from the lamp unit (photo).
11   The bulb is a bayonet fit in the bulbholder (photo).
12   Refitting is a reversal of removal.

Front direction indicator side repeater lamp

13   Twist the lamp lens anti-clockwise, and pull it from the lamp.
14   The bulb is a push fit in the lamp (photo).
15   Refitting is a reversal of removal, but ensure that the rubber sealing ring is correctly seated between the lens and the body panel.

46.2 Removing the cover from the rear of the headlamp

46.3A Release the spring clip ...

46.3B ... and withdraw the headlamp bulb

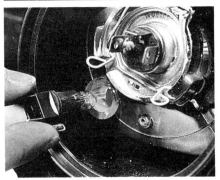

46.6 Pull the sidelamp bulbholder from the headlamp ...

46.7 ... then pull the bulb from the bulbholder

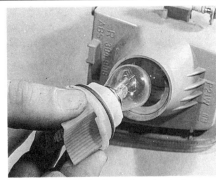

46.10 Withdraw the front direction indicator lamp bulbholder (lamp removed) ...

46.11 ... then remove the bulb

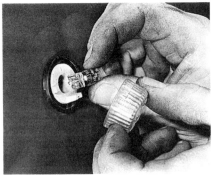

46.14 Removing a front direction indicator side repeater lamp bulb

46.18 Removing a front foglamp cover securing screw

46.19 Withdrawing a foglamp bulb

46.23 Release the rear lamp unit bulbholder retaining clips ...

46.24 ... then remove the relevant bulb

46.27 Unclip the lens from the rear number plate lamp ...

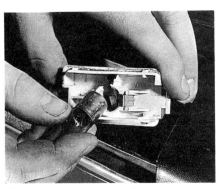

46.28 ... then remove the bulb

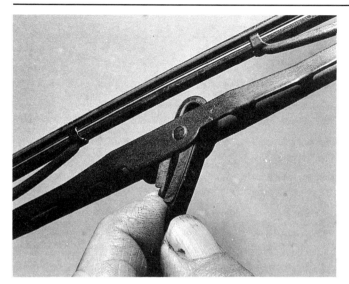

47.3 Removing a wiper blade

Front foglamp

16   To improve access, apply the handbrake, jack up the front of the vehicle, and support securely on axle stands positioned under the body side members.
17   Remove the securing screws, and withdraw the plastic cover (driver's side only) from the bumper/front wing to expose the foglamp.
18   Remove the security screw, and withdraw the cover from the base of the lamp (photo).
19   Release the spring clip, using a screwdriver if necessary, then grasp the bulb by its contacts and carefully withdraw it. Do not touch the bulb glass (photo).
20   Pull the wiring plug from the base of the bulb.
21   Refitting is a reversal of removal.

Rear lamp unit

22   Working in the luggage compartment, remove the cover from the rear of the lamp.
23   Release the top and bottom retaining clips, and pull the bulbholder from the lamp, taking care not to strain the wiring (photo).
24   The bulbs are a bayonet fit in the bulbholder (photo). Note that the brake/tail lamp bulb has offset bayonet pins so that it can only be fitted in one position; ensure that the correct type of replacement is obtained.
25   Refitting is a reversal of removal.

Rear number plate lamp

26   Using a thin-bladed screwdriver, carefully prise the lamp surround from the bumper.
27   Pull the lamp from the bumper, taking care not to strain the wiring, and unclip the lens (photo).
28   The bulb is a bayonet fit in the lamp (photo).
29   Refitting is a reversal of removal.

47   Wiper blades – renewal

1   The wiper blades should be renewed when they no longer clean the glass effectively.
2   Lift the wiper arm away from the glass. On some models it may be more convenient to do this with the bonnet open.
3   With the blade at 90° to the arm, depress the spring clip and slide the blade from the hook (photo).
4   If necessary, extract the two metal inserts and unhook the wiper rubber.
5   Refitting is a reversal of removal, but where applicable, make sure that the cut-outs in the metal inserts securing the rubber to the blade face each other.

48   Wiper arms – removal and refitting

Windscreen and rear window wipers

1   The wiper motor should be in its parked position before removing the wiper arm. Mark the position of the blade on the glass with adhesive tape as a guide to refitting.
2   Lift the hinged covers, and remove the nuts and washers securing the arms to the spindles.
3   Prise the arms from the spindles, using a screwdriver if necessary. Take care not to damage the paintwork.
4   Refitting is a reversal of removal. Note that the passenger side wiper arm is longer than that fitted to the driver's side; ensure that the arms are fitted to their correct locations, as incorrect installation can cause the blades to foul one another during operation of the wipers.

Headlamp wipers

5   The procedure is as described in paragraphs 1 to 4, but the washer hose must be disconnected from the stub on the body panel.

49   Washer nozzles – removal and refitting

1   To remove a nozzle, carefully prise it from its location using a thin-bladed screwdriver. Take care not to damage the paintwork.
2   Disconnect the washer hose and withdraw the nozzle.
3   To refit, reconnect the washer hose to the nozzle, and push the nozzle into its locating hole.
4   The nozzles can be adjusted by inserting a pin into the jet, and swivelling it to the required position.

50   Windscreen wiper motor and linkage – removal and refitting

1   Disconnect the battery negative lead.
2   Remove the wiper arms, as described in Section 48.
3   Remove the windscreen cowl panel, as described in Chapter 10, Section 30.

50.4 Disconnecting the windscreen wiper motor wiring plug

50.5A Unscrew the windscreen wiper motor/linkage assembly securing bolts ...

50.5B ... then withdraw the assembly

51.5 Tailgate wiper motor assembly. Note earth leads under heads of securing bolts

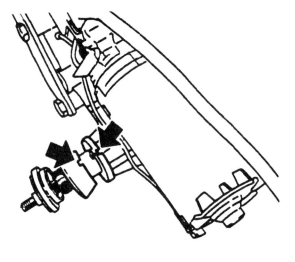

Fig. 11.11 Cut-out in tailgate wiper motor drive spindle rubber seal must engage with notch in drive spindle (Sec 51)

4   Disconnect the wiring plug from the motor (photo).
5   Unscrew the three bolts securing the motor/linkage assembly to the body, then withdraw the assembly (photos).
6   If desired, the motor can be removed from the linkage by unscrewing the three securing bolts. Do not attempt to dismantle the linkage.
7   Refitting is a reversal of removal.

51   Tailgate wiper motor – removal and refitting

1   Disconnect the battery negative lead.
2   Remove the wiper arm, as described in Section 48.
3   Extract the securing screws, and remove the rear tailgate trim panel.
4   Disconnect the motor wiring plug.
5   Unscrew the two motor securing bolts, noting the earth leads under the bolt heads (photo).
6   Manipulate the motor assembly from the tailgate.
7   Refitting is a reversal of removal, ensuring that the cut-out in the drive spindle rubber seal engages with the notch in the drive spindle – see Fig. 11.11.

52   Headlamp wiper motor – removal and refitting

1   Disconnect the battery negative lead.
2   Remove the wiper arm, as described in Section 48.
3   Remove the headlamp, as described in Section 38.
4   Disconnect the motor wiring plug.
5   Unscrew the two bolts securing the motor mounting bracket to the body panel, then withdraw the motor (photo).
6   Refitting is a reversal of removal.

53   Washer fluid reservoir – removal and refitting

1   Disconnect the battery negative lead.

Models without headlamp wash
2   Disconnect the wiring from the washer pump.
3   Disconnect the washer fluid hose from the pump. Be prepared for fluid spillage.
4   Remove the screw(s) securing the reservoir to the body, and withdraw the reservoir.

52.5A Unscrew the headlamp wiper motor securing bolts ...

52.5B ... and withdraw the motor

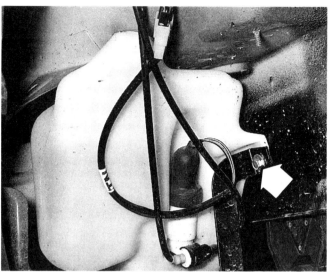

53.17 Horn/washer fluid reservoir support bracket securing bolt (arrowed) – model with headlamp wash

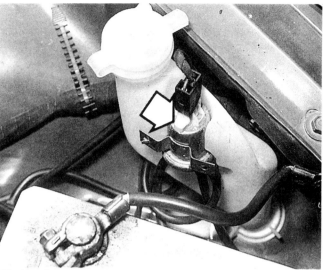

55.1 Headlamp washer fluid non-return valve (arrowed)

5   Refitting is a reversal of removal.

Models with headlamp wash

6   On models with headlamp wash, the reservoir is in two sections, the upper section, which can be removed from the engine compartment, and the lower section, which must be removed from under the wheel arch.
7   Disconnect the wiring from the headlamp wash non-return valve in the top of the reservoir.
8   Disconnect the washer fluid hoses from the non-return valve. Be prepared for fluid spillage.
9   Remove the screw securing the upper section of the reservoir to the wing panel.
10   Loosen the plastic collar securing the upper section of the reservoir to the lower section, then withdraw the upper section of the reservoir from the engine compartment.
11   To remove the lower section of the reservoir, proceed as follows.
12   Apply the handbrake, then jack up the front of the vehicle, and support on axle stands positioned under the body side members.
13   Remove the securing screws, and withdraw the plastic cover from the bumper/front wing to expose the lower section of the reservoir.
14   Remove the horns, as described in Section 35.
15   Remove the wheel arch liner, as described in Chapter 10, Section 31.
16   Disconnect the wiring and the fluid hoses from the washer pump. Be prepared for fluid spillage.
17   Unscrew the bolts securing the horn/reservoir support bracket and the reservoir to the body, then withdraw the bracket and the reservoir (photo).
18   Refitting is a reversal of removal.

54   Windscreen/tailgate/headlamp washer pump – removal and refitting

1   Disconnect the battery negative lead.

Models without headlamp wash

2   Disconnect the wiring and the fluid hose from the pump. Be prepared for fluid spillage.
3   Pull the pump from the reservoir, being prepared for fluid spillage if the reservoir still contains fluid.
4   Examine the condition of the sealing grommet, and renew if necessary, and clean the gauze filter at the end of the pump pick-up tube.
5   Refitting is a reversal of removal.

Models with headlamp wash

6   Apply the handbrake, then jack up the front of the vehicle, and support on axle stands positioned under the body side members.

7   Remove the securing screws, and withdraw the plastic cover from the bumper/front wing to expose the lower section of the fluid reservoir.
8   Remove the wheel arch liner, as described in Chapter 10, Section 31.
9   Proceed as described in paragraphs 2 to 5 inclusive.

55   Headlamp washer fluid non-return valve – removal and refitting

1   The valve is located on a bracket attached to the upper section of the washer fluid reservoir (photo).
2   Disconnect the battery negative lead.
3   Disconnect the wiring and the fluid hoses from the valve. Be prepared for fluid spillage.
4   Remove the screw securing the valve bracket to the reservoir, and withdraw the valve.
5   Refitting is a reversal of removal.

56   Electric window components – removal and refitting

Note: *Whenever any of the electric window components are removed, after refitting the components, the electric window controls must be programmed, as described in Section 57*

1   Disconnect the battery negative lead.

Rear door-mounted switches

2   Prise the plastic surround from the door interior handle.
3   Carefully prise the switch from its location, and disconnect the wiring plug.
4   Refitting is a reversal of removal, but make sure that the wiring is routed so that it does not foul the electric window or lock operating components.

Centre console-mounted switches

5   The switches must be removed as a complete assembly, and cannot be dismantled. If one of the switches is faulty, the complete assembly must be renewed.
6   Remove the rear section of the centre console, as described in Chapter 10, Section 38.
7   Release the securing clips, and withdraw the switch assembly through the top of the centre console.
8   Refitting is a reversal of removal.

Operating motors

9   Remove the door window regulator, as described in Chapter 10, Section 26.

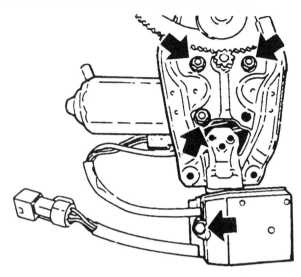

Fig. 11.12 Front door electric window motor securing nuts and pulse pick-up unit securing screw (arrowed) (Sec 56)

10   To remove the motor assembly from the front door window regulator, unscrew the three motor securing nuts, and the single screw securing the pulse pick-up unit to the regulator assembly. Withdraw the motor, complete with the pulse pick-up unit. Note that if the motor or pick-up unit is/are faulty, the two components must be renewed as an assembly, as no spare parts are available.

11   The motor assembly fitted to the rear door window regulator is an integral part of the regulator, and no attempt should be made at dismantling. If faulty, the complete motor/regulator assembly must be renewed, as no spares are available.

---

57   Electric window controls – programming

1   Whenever the battery is disconnected, or any of the electric window components are removed, on completion of work, the electric window controls must be programmed as follows.
2   Close all doors, and switch on the ignition.
3   Close one of the windows by pressing the relevant operating switch. Press and hold the switch for a further two seconds after the relevant window has fully closed.
4   Repeat the procedure for the remaining window(s).

---

58   Central door locking components – removal and refitting

1   Disconnect the battery negative lead.

Electronic control module
2   The module is mounted in the driver's footwell, behind the side trim panel.
3   Remove the driver's footwell side trim panel, as described in Chapter 10, Section 36.
4   Unscrew the two securing nuts, and lift the module from the body panel (photo).
5   Depress the retaining clip to release the wiring plug, then withdraw the module.
6   Refitting is a reversal of removal.

Operating switch
7   The operating switch takes the form of a microswitch, mounted inside the door at the rear of the exterior handle assembly.
8   Remove the door inner trim panel, as described in Chapter 10, Section 17.
9   Peel back the plastic insulating sheet sufficiently to gain access to the exterior handle.
10   Unclip the microswitch from the rear edge of the exterior handle assembly, and disconnect the switch wiring plug from the door wiring harness, then withdraw the switch (photo).
11   Refitting is a reversal of removal.

Door lock operating motor
12   Remove the door lock, as described in Chapter 10, Section 21.
13   Disconnect the lock operating rod from the motor.
14   Remove the two securing screws, and withdraw the motor from the lock assembly.
15   Refitting is a reversal of removal.

58.4 Unscrewing a central door locking control module securing nut

58.10 Central door locking operating microswitch (arrowed) in driver's door

58.18 Disconnecting the wiring plug from the tailgate lock operating motor – Hatchback model

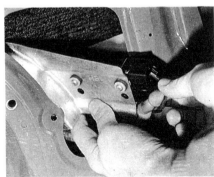

58.21 Disconnecting the wiring plug from the fuel filler flap operating motor – Hatchback model

59.3 Radio aerial earth lead securing screw (arrowed) – electric aerial

59.4A Unscrewing the radio aerial bracket securing screw – electric aerial

59.4B Disconnecting the aerial lead – electric aerial

Tailgate/boot lid lock operating motor

16   On Hatchback models, extract the securing screws and remove the rear tailgate trim panel.

17   Remove the two securing screws, and manipulate the motor to disconnect the lock operating rod.

18   Withdraw the motor and disconnect the wiring plug (photo).

19   Refitting is a reversal of removal.

Fuel filler flap lock operating motor

20   Remove the right-hand rear quarter trim panels, as described in Chapter 10, Section 36.

21   Disconnect the wiring plug from the rear of the motor (photo).

22   Unscrew the two screws securing the motor to the mounting bracket, then manipulate the motor to disconnect the lock operating rod. Withdraw the motor.

23   Refitting is a reversal of removal.

59   Radio aerial – removal and refitting

1   On models with an electric aerial, disconnect the battery negative lead.

2   Remove the left-hand rear quarter trim panel, as described in Chapter 10, Section 36.

3   Remove the screw securing the earth lead(s) to the body panel (photo).

4   Remove the screw securing the aerial bracket to the body panel, then ensure that the aerial is fully retracted, and pull it through the grommet in the bodywork into the luggage compartment. Disconnect

the wiring plug on models with an electric aerial, and disconnect the aerial lead (photos).

5   Refitting is a reversal of removal, but ensure that the rubber grommet is correctly seated in the bodywork.

60   Loudspeakers – removal and refitting

1   Disconnect the battery negative lead.

Facia-mounted loudspeaker

2   Using a thin-bladed screwdriver, carefully prise the loudspeaker from the top of the facia panel. Take care not to damage the facia trim (photo).

3   Disconnect the wiring and withdraw the loudspeaker. If desired, the plastic trim panel can be unclipped from the top of the loudspeaker.

4   Refitting is a reversal of removal.

Front door-mounted loudspeaker

5   Remove the door inner trim panel, as described in Chapter 10, Section 17.

6   Remove the three securing screws, and withdraw the loudspeaker from the door. Disconnect the wiring plug (photo).

7   Refitting is a reversal of removal, but note that the loudspeaker can only be fitted one way up, so that the lug on the bottom of the loudspeaker rim engages with the corresponding hole in the door skin.

Rear loudspeaker – Hatchback models

8   Remove the upper rear quarter trim panel, as described in Chapter 10, Section 36.

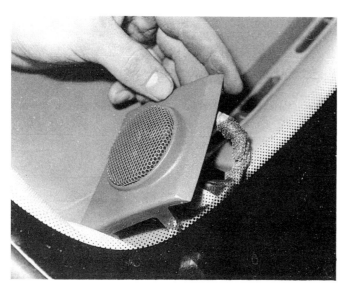

60.2 Removing a facia-mounted loudspeaker (viewed through windscreen)

60.6 Withdrawing a front door-mounted loudspeaker   wiring plug arrowed

61.3 Unscrew the grub screws ...

61.4 ... and withdraw the radio/cassette player using the special tools

9   Remove the four securing screws, and withdraw the loudspeaker.
10   Refitting is a reversal of removal.

Rear loudspeaker – Saloon models

11   Carefully prise the trim cover from the parcel shelf, to expose the loudspeaker.
12   Remove the four securing screws, withdraw the loudspeaker and disconnect the wiring.
13   Refitting is a reversal of removal.

61   Radio/cassette player – removal and refitting

1   All the radio/cassette players fitted to the Cavalier range have DIN standard fixings. Two special tools, obtainable from in-car entertainment specialists, are required for removal.
2   Disconnect the battery negative lead.
3   Unscrew the four grub screws from the corners of the radio/ cassette player, using a suitable Allen key or hexagon bit (photo).
4   Insert the tools into the holes exposed by removal of the grub screws, and push them until they snap into place. Pull the tools outwards to release the unit (photo).

5   Pull the unit forwards, and withdraw it from the facia.
6   To refit the radio/cassette player, simply push the unit into the facia until the retaining lugs snap into place, then refit the grub screws.

62   Sunroof motor – removal and refitting

1   Ensure that the sunroof is fully closed.
2   Disconnect the battery negative lead.
3   Prise the courtesy lamp from the roof trim panel, and disconnect the wiring.
4   Remove the two trim panel securing screws, and withdraw the trim panel from the roof, disconnecting the wiring from the sunroof operating switch.
5   Disconnect the wiring plugs from the motor.
6   Unscrew the securing nut, and withdraw the motor assembly.
7   Refitting is a reversal of removal.

63   Speedometer cable – removal and refitting

1   Remove the instrument panel, as described in Section 31.
2   Pull the cable through the bulkhead into the engine compartment, noting its routing.
3   Working in the engine compartment, unscrew the securing sleeve and disconnect the speedometer cable from the top of the gearbox (photo).
4   The cable can now be withdrawn from the vehicle, noting its routing so that it can be refitted in the same position.
5   Refitting is a reversal of removal, ensuring that the cable is correctly routed. Make sure that the cable is not kinked or twisted between the instrument panel and the bulkhead as the instrument panel is refitted. Note that the cable should be routed to the right of the steering column support bracket.

63.3 Speedometer cable securing sleeve (arrowed) at gearbox – 1.6 litre model

64   Anti-theft alarm – general

1   Certain models are fitted with an anti-theft alarm as standard equipment.
2   The alarm system is triggered by door, bonnet and boot lid/tailgate-mounted switches, and by ultrasonic sensors mounted inside the passenger compartment.
3   The alarm features a self-diagnostic function, and any faults should be referred to a Vauxhall dealer, who will have access to the necessary specialist diagnostic equipment.

65 Fault diagnosis – electrical system

Symptom	Reason(s)
Starter fails to turn engine	Battery discharged
	Battery defective internally
	Leads loose, or terminals corroded
	Loose connections at starter motor
	Engine earth strap loose, broken or missing
	Starter motor faulty or solenoid not functioning
	Starter motor brushes worn
	Commutator dirty or worn
	Starter motor armature faulty
	Field coils earthed
Starter turns engine very slowly	Battery in discharged condition
	Starter brushes badly worn, sticking or brush wires loose
	Loose wires in starter motor circuit
Starter spins but does not turn engine	Pinion or flywheel gear teeth broken or worn
Starter motor noisy or excessively rough engagement	Pinion or flywheel gear teeth broken or worn
	Starter motor retaining bolts loose
Battery will not hold charge for more than a few days	Battery defective, internally
	Electrolyte level too low or electrolyte too weak due to leakage
	Plate separators no longer fully effective
	Battery plates severely sulphated
	Alternator drivebelt slipping
	Battery terminal connections loose or corroded
	Alternator not charging
	Short-circuit causing continual battery drain
	Voltage regulator unit not working correctly
Ignition light fails to go out, battery runs flat in a few days	Alternator drivebelt loose and slipping or broken
	Alternator brushes worn, sticking, broken or dirty
	Alternator brush springs weak or broken
	Internal fault in alternator

Failure of individual electrical equipment to function correctly is dealt with under the headings listed below

Horn

Horn operates all the time	Horn push either earthed or stuck down
	Horn cable to horn push earthed
Horn fails to operate	Blown fuse
	Cable or cable connection loose, broken or disconnected
	Horn has an internal fault
Horn emits intermittent or unsatisfactory noise	Cable connections loose

Lamps

Lamps do not come on	If engine not running, battery discharged
	Wire connections loose, disconnected or broken
	Lamp switch shorting or otherwise faulty
	Lamp bulb filament burnt out or bulbs broken
Lamps give very poor illumination	Lamp glasses dirty
	Lamps badly out of adjustment
Lamps work erratically – flashing on and off, especially over bumps	Battery terminals or earth connection loose
	Lamps not earthing properly
	Contacts in lamp switch faulty

Wipers

Wiper motor fails to work	Blown fuse
	Wire connections loose, disconnected or broken
	Brushes badly worn
	Armature worn or faulty
	Field coils faulty
Wiper motor works very slowly and takes excessive current	Commutator dirty, greasy or burnt
	Armature bearings dirty or misaligned
	Armature badly worn or faulty

Symptom	Reason(s)
Wiper motor works slowly and takes little current	Brushes badly worn Commutator dirty, greasy or burnt Armature badly worn or faulty
Wiper motor works but wiper blades remain static	Wiper motor gearbox parts badly worn

Electrically operated windows*

Glass will only move in one direction	Defective switch
Glass slow to move	Stiff regulator or glass guide channels
Glass will not move: With motor running	Binding glass guide channels Faulty regulator
Motor not running	Faulty relay Blown fuse Fault in motor Broken or disconnected wire

*****Note:** *Whenever the battery has been disconnected, the electric window controls must be programmed, as described in Section 57. Confirm that this has been carried out before assuring that a fault exists*

Central door locking system

Complete failure	Blown fuse Faulty master switch Faulty relay Broken or disconnected wire
Latch locks but will not unlock, or unlocks but will not lock	Faulty master switch Poor contact in relay multi-plug Faulty relay
One motor will not operate	Poor circuit connections Broken wire Faulty motor Binding operating linkage Fault in lock

Instruments

Instrument readings increase with engine speed	Voltage stabilizer faulty
Fuel or temperature gauge gives no reading	Wiring open circuit Sender unit faulty Gauge faulty
Fuel or temperature gauge gives maximum reading all the time	Wiring short circuit Gauge faulty

Note: *This Section is not intended as an exhaustive guide to fault diagnosis, but summarises the more common faults which may be encountered during a vehicle life. Consult a dealer for more detailed advice.*

Chapter 12 Supplement:
Revisions and information on later models

Contents

1   Introduction

This Supplement contains information which is additional to, or a revision of, that contained in the preceding eleven Chapters of this manual. Since first publication of this manual the Cavalier range has undergone few significant changes or revisions apart from the introduction of fuel-injected, catalytic converter-equipped 1.6 and 1.8 litre models, and the fitting of catalytic converters (whether as an optional extra or as standard equipment) to all 2.0 litre models. Whilst primarily intended to cover models produced from late 1990 onwards, additional or revised information is included on earlier models. To use the Supplement to its best advantage, it is therefore recommended that it is always referred to before the main Chapters of this manual.

Definition of model years

Except for the one instance in Section 4, vehicles and changes are referred to at all times in this Supplement by their General Motors/Vauxhall model year, which is not necessarily the same as a vehicle's date of sale or registration; the manufacturer's model year begins in September of the preceding calendar year, so that a 1991-model Cavalier will have been built between September 1990 and August 1991, but may have been sold at any time from September 1990 onwards.

To identify a vehicle, note its VIN and engine numbers, including all prefixes, as stamped in the locations shown in *Buying spare parts and vehicle identification numbers* at the front of this manual (it is always a good idea to check that these numbers are correctly entered on the vehicle's registration document), and take them to a Vauxhall dealer who will have the information required to decode the numbers.

Project vehicles

The vehicle used in the preparation of this Supplement, and appearing in some of the photographic sequences, was a 1991-model Cavalier 1.6 L (C16 NZ engine); additional work was carried out and photographed on a 1992-model Cavalier 1.8 L (18 SV engine).

2   Specifications

The Specifications given below are revisions of, or supplementary to, those at the beginning of the preceding Chapters. Models with C16 NZ, C16 NZ2, X16 SZ or C18 NZ engines are the same as the earlier 1.6 or 1.8 litre models, except where noted below

General dimensions, weights and capacities
Weights
Kerb weight – Saloon models:

1.4 litre models	990 to 1013 kg (2183 to 2233 lb)
1.6 litre models – manual gearbox	1005 to 1041 kg (2216 to 2295 lb)
1.6 litre models – automatic transmission	1050 to 1081 kg (2315 to 2383 lb)
1.8 litre models – manual gearbox	1060 to 1111 kg (2336 to 2449 lb)
1.8 litre models – automatic transmission	1095 to 1146 kg (2414 to 2527 lb)
2.0 litre models – manual gearbox	1115 to 1155 kg (2458 to 2546 lb)
2.0 litre models – automatic transmission	1150 to 1179 kg (2535 to 2599 lb)

Kerb weight – Hatchback models:

1.4 litre models	1005 to 1028 kg (2216 to 2266 lb)
1.6 litre models – manual gearbox	1020 to 1056 kg (2249 to 2328 lb)
1.6 litre models – automatic transmission	1065 to 1096 kg (2348 to 2416 lb)
1.8 litre models – manual gearbox	1075 to 1126 kg (2370 to 2482 lb)
1.8 litre models – automatic transmission	1110 to 1161 kg (2447 to 2560 lb)
2.0 litre models – manual gearbox	1130 to 1170 kg (2491 to 2579 lb)
2.0 litre models – automatic transmission	1165 to 1194 kg (2568 to 2632 lb)

Capacities
Coolant capacity – models with automatic transmission:

1.6 litre models	5.6 litres (9.9 pints)
1.8 litre models	6.5 litres (11.4 pints)
2.0 litre models	7.0 litres (12.3 pints)
Automatic transmission (at fluid change)	3.0 to 3.5 litres (5.3 to 6.2 pints)

Engine
Manufacturer's engine codes (later models)
Single overhead camshaft (sohc) engines:

1.6 litre	C16 NZ, C16 NZ2, X16 SZ
1.8 litre	C18 NZ

Compression ratio

C16 NZ, C 16 NZ2	9.2:1
X16 SZ	10.0:1
C18 NZ	9.2:1

Underbonnet view of a 1991-model Cavalier 1.6 L

1	Air cleaner casing	6	Exhaust gas recirculation valve
2	Suspension strut top	7	Steering gear
3	Coolant expansion tank	8	Octane coding plug
4	Brake fluid reservoir	9	Washer fluid reservoir
5	Air box		

10	Battery	14	Engine oil level dipstick
11	Ignition coil	15	Engine oil filter
12	Distributor	16	Oxygen sensor
13	Cooling fan motor	17	Engine oil filler cap

Maximum power
C16 NZ, C16 NZ2 .... 55 kW (75 bhp) at 5200 rpm
X16 SZ .... 52 kW (71 bhp) at 5000 rpm
C18 NZ .... 66 kW (90 bhp) at 5400 rpm

Maximum torque
C16 NZ, C16 NZ2 .... 125 Nm (92 lbf ft) at 2800 rpm
X16 SZ .... 128 Nm (94 lbf ft) at 2800 rpm
C18 NZ .... 145 Nm (107 lbf ft) at 3000 rpm

Torque wrench settings

	Nm	lbf ft
Crankshaft pulley bolt – 1.4 and 1.6 litre models:		
23 mm thread length	55	40.5
30 mm thread length – 1st stage*	55	40.5
30 mm thread length – 2nd stage*	Angle-tighten a further 45° to 60°	Angle-tighten a further 45° to 60°
* *Always use new 30 mm thread length bolts*		
Flexplate bolts	60	44

Cooling system
Coolant capacity – automatic transmission
1.6 litre models .... 5.6 litres (9.9 pints)
1.8 litre models .... 6.5 litres (11.4 pints)
2.0 litre models .... 7.0 litres (12.3 pints)

Fuel and exhaust systems
Pierburg 2E3 carburettor – 1.6 litre (16 SV) and 1.8 litre (18 SV) models
Idle speed – automatic transmission .... 800 to 850 rpm
Fast idle gap .... 0.8 to 0.9 mm
Float level .... 28 to 30 mm
Float weight .... 5.75 to 5.95 g
Accelerator pump delivery quantity – per 10 strokes .... 10.5 to 13.5 cc
Fuel pump feed pressure .... 0.25 to 0.33 bars (3.6 to 4.8 lbf/in^2) @ 1950 rpm
                                                                       (return line disconnected)

Multec fuel injection system – 1.6 litre (C16 NZ, C16 NZ2, X16 SZ) and 1.8 litre (C18 NZ) models
Idle speed:
  1.6 litre models .... 720 to 880 rpm
  1.8 litre models .... 800 to 960 rpm
Idle mixture (CO content) .... 0.4% max
Injector resistance (approximate) – C18 NZ engine:
  @ 20°C (68°F) .... 1.5 ± 0.2 ohms
  Fully warmed up .... 1.8 ± 0.2 ohms
Fuel system pressure .... 0.76 bars (11.0 lbf/in^2)

Torque wrench settings

	Nm	lbf ft
Throttle body mounting nuts	20	15
Throttle body upper-to-lower section screws	6	4.5
Throttle potentiometer screws	2	1.5
Fuel injector retainer screw	3	2
Fuel pressure regulator screws	2.5	2
Idle air control stepper motor screws	2.5	2
Coolant temperature sensor	10	7.5
Oxygen sensor	38	28

Motronic fuel injection system – 2.0 litre (20 NE, C20 NE, 20 SEH, 20 XEJ, C20 XE) models
Idle mixture (CO content) – C20 NE engine .... 0.4% max
Fuel system pressure:
  C20 XE engine, 1991-on .... 3.0 bars (42.5 lbf/in^2)
  All other engines .... 2.5 bars (36.3 lbf/in^2)

Torque wrench settings

	Nm	lbf ft
Oxygen sensor – C20 NE and C20 XE engines	30	22

Ignition and engine management systems
Torque wrench settings

	Nm	lbf ft
DIS module retaining bolts	7	5
Camshaft phase sensor retaining bolts	15	11
Camshaft phase sensor disc retaining bolt	8	6

Automatic transmission

General

Type... Hydrodynamic torque converter with electrically-controlled mechanical lock-up system, two epicyclic gearsets giving four forward gears (including overdrive) and reverse, integral final drive; gearchanging under full electronic control, with three driving 'modes' selectable

Manufacturer... Aisin AW Co, Ltd
Model:
   1.6 litre models.. AF 14
   1.8 and 2.0 litre models.. AF 20

Lubrication

Recommended fluid.. Dexron II type ATF (Duckhams Uni-Matic)
Capacity – at fluid change.. 3.0 to 3.5 litres (5.3 to 6.2 pints)
Difference between dipstick MAX and MIN marks – approximate:
   + 20°C side.. 0.25 litre (0.4 pints)
   + 80°C side.. 0.40 litre (0.7 pints)

Torque wrench settings

	Nm	lbf ft
Fluid drain plug	45	33
Fluid cooler banjo union bolts	22	16
Dipstick/filler tube nut	20	15
Starter inhibitor switch/filler tube fastener to transmission	25	18.5
Starter inhibitor switch to selector lever shaft	8	6
Actuating lever to selector lever shaft	16	12
Selector cable clamp bolt	6	4.5
Selector console mounting bolts	10	7.5
Input/output sensor Torx screws	6	4.5
Fluid temperature sensor	25	18.5
Fluid temperature sensor cover bolts	25	18.5
Torque converter-to-flexplate bolts (using adaptor – see text)	50	37
Bellhousing cover plate bolts	7	5
Transmission-to-engine bolts	75	55
Engine/transmission left-hand mounting to subframe	65	48
Engine/transmission left-hand mounting to transmission	60	44

Driveshafts

Torque wrench settings

	Nm	lbf ft
Intermediate shaft support bearing:		
Bracket to cylinder block	55	40.5
Bearing flange to bracket	18	13

Braking system

Front discs – 1992-on models

Type – 1.4, 1.6 and 1.8 litre models.. Ventilated
Diameter – 1.8 litre models... 256.0 mm (10.1 in)
Minimum disc thickness after machining – 1.4, 1.6 and 1.8 litre models 18 mm (0.71 in)

Suspension and steering

Torque wrench settings

	Nm	lbf ft
Modified front suspension lower arm front (horizontal) mounting bolt:		
Stage 1	100	74
Stage 2	Angle-tighten a further 75°	Angle-tighten a further 75°
Stage 3	Angle-tighten a further 15°	Angle-tighten a further 15°
Rear hub unit (maintenance-free type) securing nuts:		
Stage 1	50	37
Stage 2	Angle-tighten a further 30°	Angle-tighten a further 30°
Stage 3	Angle-tighten a further 15°	Angle-tighten a further 15°

Bodywork

Torque wrench setting

	Nm	lbf ft
Front seat rails to floor	20	15

Electrical system

Torque wrench settings

	Nm	lbf ft
'Compact' series alternator upper mounting bolts	20	15
'Compact' series alternator lower mounting bolt	35	26

3   Routine maintenance

Models up to 1991
Timing belt inspection – models with sohc engines
1   Release the securing clips and remove the main outer timing belt cover, then unclip the smaller outer timing belt cover from the coolant pump.

2   Using a spanner applied to the crankshaft pulley/sprocket bolt, rotate the crankshaft so that the full length of the timing belt is checked. Check the belt carefully for any signs of uneven wear, splitting, cracks (especially at the roots of the belt teeth) or oil contamination. Renew it if there is the slightest doubt about its condition (see Chapter 1, Section 15).

3   If the belt is fit for further use, check its tension and adjust it, if necessary, as described in Chapter 1, Section 16.

Timing belt maintenance – models with automatic timing belt tensioners
4   Owners of later 1.4 or 1.6 litre models should note that the manufacturer no longer calls for routine checking of the timing belt. However, due to the importance of the timing belt to the engine's reliability, owners are advised to check the belt's condition, as described above (noting the differences mentioned in Section 4 of this Chapter), at the interval given in the *Routine maintenance* at the front of this manual. If the belt is found to be worn, damaged or in any way suspect, it must be renewed as soon as possible; refer to Section 4 of this Chapter and to Section 15 of Chapter 1 for details. Obviously, the belt's tension, once set on installation, does **not** require routine checking or adjustment.

Automatic transmission
5   Refer to Section 10 of this Chapter for details.

6   The fluid level must be checked every 12 months or 9000 miles (15 000 km), whichever occurs first.

7   For vehicles subjected to normal use, the fluid must be changed every 48 months or 36 000 miles (60 000 km), whichever occurs first. If a vehicle is used for heavy-duty work (eg taxi work, caravan/trailer towing, mostly short-distance, stop-start city driving) the fluid must be changed every 36 months or 27 000 miles (45 000 km), whichever occurs first.

1992-on models
General
8   A revised maintenance schedule has been introduced for all 1992-on models. As previously, it is based on the assumption of an average annual mileage of 9000 miles (15 000 km); the service is to be carried out annually or at this mileage, whichever occurs first. However the new schedule includes a high-mileage inspection for vehicles covering more than 18 000 miles (30 000 km) per year, and also provision for vehicles which cover very low mileages.

9   Essential points to note are as follows.

(a)   *The engine oil must be changed, and the oil filter renewed, at least annually or every 9000 miles (15 000 km), whichever occurs first. For vehicles which cover very low mileages, with frequent cold starts or predominantly short-distance, stop-start city driving, the oil and filter must be renewed each Spring and Autumn.*

(b)   *The remaining thickness of friction material on the disc brake pads (front and, where applicable, rear) and on the rear drum brake shoes must be checked at the interval given at the front of this manual. If any pad or shoe is worn to the specified minimum or less (Chapter 8), or if it is likely to be worn to this level before the next service interval, all four pads/shoes must be renewed (ie, as an axle set).*

(c)   *Ensure that the brake fluid is renewed annually, regardless of mileage.*

(d)   *The 'Exhaust Emissions test' brings together previously-separate operations such as the ignition timing check and adjustment, engine idle speed and mixture check/adjustment, crankcase ventilation system check, air cleaner intake air temperature control system check, and the general checks of the fuel and exhaust systems. These are combined with new operations such as a check of the emission control-related equipment performance, encompassing the catalytic converter and oxygen*

sensor, the evaporative emission control system and exhaust gas recirculation systems (where fitted). However all these tests are carried out using special test equipment and not all can be duplicated without it; owners may well be advised, therefore, to have much of this work carried out by a Vauxhall dealer.

(e)   *Lubrication of the throttle cable is no longer required.*

(f)   *The automatic transmission fluid need no longer be changed on vehicles subject to normal use. Only if a vehicle is subjected to strenuous use (eg taxi work) need the fluid be changed; this should be done every fourth interval (ie at 48 months or 36 000 miles/60 000 km, whichever is the sooner).*

(g)   *On engines fitted with an alternator/power steering pump drive-belt of the ribbed V-belt type, note that the belt should be inspected in the normal way, but retensioning is not required as this is catered for by the automatic tensioner.*

Basic service – every 1st, 3rd, 5th, 7th, etc, interval
10   This service is to be carried out after the first 12 months or 9000 miles (15 000 km), whichever is first, and every **other** interval after that. Carry out the following.

(a)   **Change the engine oil and renew the oil filter (Chapter 1).*

(b)   *Check the engine and transmission for leaks (Chapters 1 and 6, Sections 9 and 10 of this Chapter).*

(c)   *Check the coolant level, top up if necessary and check the cooling system for leaks (Chapter 2).*

(d)   *Exhaust Emissions Test (see note above).*

(e)   **Check the remaining thickness of friction material on the disc brake pads (front and, where applicable, rear), renewing them as a set if necessary (Chapter 8).*

(f)   *Renew the brake fluid (Chapter 8).*

(g)   *Check the condition of the braking system hoses and pipes (Chapter 8).*

(h)   **Check the tightening torque of the roadwheel bolts, check the tyre pressures and tread wear (including the spare). If uneven tread wear is evident, have the wheel alignment checked. On models so equipped, check the rear suspension level control system height (Chapter 9).*

(i)   **Check the condition and tension (adjusting it if necessary) of the power steering fluid pump drivebelt (Chapter 9 and Section 13 of this Chapter).*

(j)   *Check the bodywork for damage, and the underbody for signs of damage to its protective coating, or of actual corrosion (Chapter 10).*

(k)   **Check the condition and tension (adjusting it if necessary) of the alternator drivebelt (Chapter 11 and Section 15 of this Chapter).*

(l)   **Check the operation of all interior and exterior lamps, direction indicators/hazard warning lamps, brake lamps, headlamp flash and the horn (Chapter 11).*

(m)   *Have the headlamp alignment checked (Chapter 11).*

(n)   *Check the operation of the windscreen (and, where fitted, the rear window and headlamp) wipers and washers; renew the blades if worn and top up the washer fluid reservoir (Chapter 11).*

(o)   **Road test, checking for correct operation of all controls, warning lamps and switches, electric windows (if fitted), ventilation and heating systems, heated rear window, heated seats (if fitted), steering and brakes (including handbrake).*

Note: *All items above marked with an asterisk (*) are to be carried out as part of the additional high-mileage inspection (see above) where the vehicle covers 18 000 miles (30 000 km) annually, after the first 9000 miles (15 000 km).*

Full service – every 2nd, 4th, 6th, 8th, etc, interval
11   This service is to be carried out at the second 12 month/9000 mile (15 000 km) interval (ie at the first 24 months or 18 000 miles/30 000 km, whichever is the sooner), and every **other** interval after that. In addition to all those tasks listed for the basic service, carry out the following.

(a)   *On sohc engines only, at every 4th interval (ie, every 48 months or 36 000 miles/60 000 km, whichever is the sooner) check the condition of the timing belt and renew it if necessary (see paragraph 2 of this Section and Section 15 of Chapter 1). On early 1.4 and 1.6 engines, and all 1.8 and 2.0 (sohc) engines, if the belt is fit for further use, check its tension and adjust it if necessary (see Section 16 of Chapter 1).*

(b) On dohc engines only, at every 8th interval (ie, every 96 months or 72 000 miles/120 000 km, whichever is the sooner) renew the timing belt (see Chapter 1, Section 17).

(c) Renew the air cleaner element (Chapter 3).

(d) Renew the fuel filter (Chapter 3 or Section 6 of this Chapter).

(e) Renew the spark plugs (Chapter 4).

(f) Check, and adjust if necessary, the clutch cable (Chapter 5).

(g) Check the manual gearbox oil level and top up if necessary (Chapter 6).

(h) Check the automatic transmission fluid level and top up if necessary. Arrange for your Vauxhall dealer to check the electrical control system using special Vauxhall test equipment (Section 10 of this Chapter).

(i) Check for splits, lubricant leakage, wear or damage of the rubber gaiters or bellows on the driveshafts, steering and suspension components (Chapters 7 and 9).

(j) Check the remaining thickness of friction material on the rear drum brake shoes, renewing them as a set if necessary (Chapter 8).

(k) Where fitted, check the power steering fluid level and top up if necessary (Chapter 9).

(l) Check the operation of all door, bonnet and boot lid/tailgate locks and hinges; lubricate all moving parts as necessary (Chapter 10).

---

4   Engine

Engine identification codes – general

1   Before ordering spare parts, or carrying out any repair or overhaul operations on the engine, it is essential to identify the exact engine type being worked on. Later engines, although outwardly similar in appearance, often have significant differences in repair procedures, even though they may be of the same displacement and model year.

2   The following sub-Sections in this Chapter are mainly specific to engine type, as will be noted from the sub-Section headings. Check the engine identification code first, which is located on a horizontal surface on the exhaust manifold side of the cylinder block, at the distributor end or, on later engines, on the cylinder block-to-transmission flange, adjacent to the engine oil dipstick.

C16 NZ, C16 NZ2, X16 SZ (E-Drive) and C18 NZ engines – general

3   These engines, apart from minor modifications to the cylinder head, valve gear and camshaft drive, are virtually identical to the 1.6 and 1.8 litre carburettor engines described in the preceding Chapters of this manual.

Timing belt automatic tensioner – 14 NV and C16 NZ engines

General

4   Later 1.4 and 1.6 litre engines, identifiable by the squared-off top surfaces of the timing belt covers, are fitted with spring-loaded automatic timing belt tensioners to ensure correct belt tensioning on assembly and to eliminate the need for regular belt retensioning as part of the routine maintenance schedule.

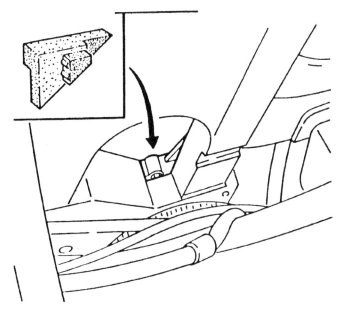

Fig. 12.1 Moulded sponge rubber insert for timing belt cover aperture (Sec 4)

Timing belt outer covers – removal and refitting

5   Refer to Chapter 1, Section 15, noting the following differences.

6   The timing belt main outer cover may be secured either by clips or by hexagon-headed screws to the rear cover; in some cases, a combination of clips and screws may be used.

7   Note the three screws securing the lower (small) outer cover to the rear cover; the fourth secures the tensioner (photo).

Timing belt/tensioner – removal and refitting

8   Remove the timing belt outer covers as described above.

9   To lock the tensioner in its slackest position for removal and refitting, move the tensioner indicator arm clockwise until the holes align in the baseplate and the arm, then insert a close-fitting pin, such as a drift, to retain them (photo). The tensioner can then be unbolted, or the belt can be removed.

10   On refitting, ensure that the tensioner baseplate lug engages with the hole in the oil pump housing, then tighten the tensioner bolt securely and remove the locking pin; the tensioner should be quite free to move.

11   Set the belt tension as described below.

Tensioner – examination

12   Check that the tensioner roller rotates smoothly and easily, with no noises or signs of free play, roughness or notchy movement. Check also that there is no sign of physical wear or damage. If the tensioner is faulty in any way, or if there is any reason to doubt the continued efficiency of its spring, the complete assembly must be renewed.

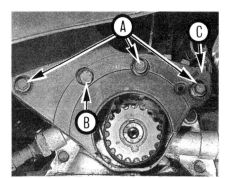

4.7 Timing belt lower (small) outer cover screws (A), tensioner screw (B), ignition timing fixed reference mark (C)

4.9 Using a close-fitting drift to lock the tensioner. Note baseplate lug engaged in oil pump housing (arrow)

4.15 Using a special spanner to adjust the timing belt by moving the coolant pump

4.16A Align punch mark (A) on crankshaft sprocket with timing belt rear cover notch (B) ...

4.16B ... and stamped line (A) on camshaft sprocket with timing belt rear cover notch (B)

4.19 Timing belt tension is correct when the tensioner indicator pointer aligns with the centre of the baseplate notch

Setting the timing belt tension

13   Whenever the timing belt is disturbed, whether during belt renewal or any other engine overhaul work, its tension must be set on assembly – note that this procedure must **only** be carried out on a **cold** engine.

14   It is assumed that the belt has been removed and refitted, ie that the crankshaft pulley and timing belt outer covers are removed, that the tensioner is unlocked (see above) and that No 1 cylinder is in its firing position (just before TDC on the compression stroke). Temporarily refit the crankshaft pulley bolt and remove the spark plugs so that the crankshaft can be rotated easily.

15   Note also that turning the coolant pump with the precision required is a great deal easier if a special spanner (Kent-Moore Part No KM-421-A) is used; proprietary alternatives are available from manufacturers such as Sykes-Pickavant (Part No 031300) (photo).

16   With the belt refitted and correctly routed (Chapter 1, Section 15), ensure that the punch mark on the crankshaft sprocket and the stamped line on the camshaft sprocket are aligned with their respective timing belt rear cover notches (photos).

17   Tighten the belt by slackening its three securing bolts, and turning the coolant pump clockwise until the holes align in the tensioner indicator arm and baseplate (the tensioner indicator arm will then have

moved fully clockwise to its stop). Lightly tighten the pump securing bolts, just sufficiently to prevent the pump from moving.

18   Using a spanner applied to the crankshaft pulley bolt, turn the crankshaft smoothly (and without jerking it or the belt may jump a tooth) through 2 complete revolutions (720°) clockwise, until the camshaft and crankshaft sprocket timing marks are once again aligned as described in paragraph 13; the position of the coolant pump must not alter.

19   Slacken the timing belt by turning the coolant pump anti-clockwise until the tensioner's indicator pointer is in the centre of its baseplate notch; the timing belt tension is then correct (photo). Tighten the coolant pump bolts to the specified torque wrench setting (see Chapter 2), then turn the crankshaft through two further turns clockwise and recheck the setting.

20   If the pointer and notch are not aligned, the operation must be repeated from paragraph 14. On completion, refit all components removed.

Timing belt cover aperture – 1.4 and 1.6 models

21   The rear timing belt cover fitted to 1991 and 1992 model year 1.4 and 1.6 litre engines, incorporates a small aperture just above the oil pump housing. In certain circumstances, it is possible for foreign objects, such as gravel, to penetrate through this aperture and cause the timing belt to jump a tooth on its sprockets. For this reason, it is desirable to cover the aperture to prevent the possibility of this occurrence. A modified cover without an aperture was introduced for 1993 models.

22   A piece of suitably moulded sponge rubber, part number 90 469 594, is available from Vauxhall dealers to enable the aperture to be covered. On models without power steering, the sponge rubber can be inserted into the cover aperture from above. If power steering is fitted, the sponge rubber is inserted into place from below. If access is difficult, particularly if the drivebelt is of the ribbed V-belt type, it may be easier to remove the alternator/power steering pump drivebelt as described in Chapter 11, Section 7, or Section 15 of this Chapter. Refit, and where applicable adjust, the belt tension on completion.

Timing belt automatic tensioner – C16 NZ2, C18NZ, 20NE, C20 NE and C20 XE engines, 1993-on
General

23   An alternative type of spring loaded automatic timing belt tensioner is fitted to C16 NZ2 engines, and all 1.8 and 2.0 litre sohc and dohc engines, from 1993 onward (Fig. 12.2). The tensioner assembly is similar to the arrangement described previously for 14 NV and C16 NZ engines, but the removal and refitting procedures vary considerably and are as follows.

Timing belt outer covers – removal and refitting

24   Refer to the appropriate Sections of Chapter 1, noting the following differences.

25   Where a ribbed V-belt is used to drive the alternator/power steering pump pulley, refer to Section 15 of this Chapter for removal and refitting procedures.

26   The timing belt main outer cover may be secured either by clips or by hexagon-headed screws to the rear cover; in some cases, a combination of clips and screws may be used.

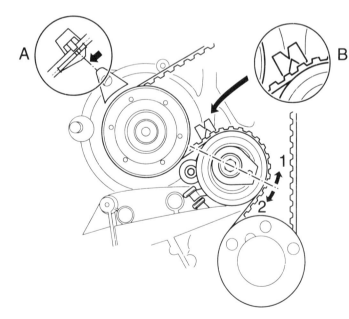

Fig. 12.2 Timing belt automatic tensioner details (alternative type) (Sec 4)

A   Alignment lugs on coolant pump and cylinder block
B   Tensioner pointer aligned with notch in tensioner bracket
1   Move the tensioner arm anticlockwise to release the belt tension
2   Move the tensioner arm clockwise to tension the belt

Timing belt (sohc engines) – removal, refitting and adjustment

27   The procedure for engines with a timing belt automatic tensioner

is essentially the same as described in Chapter 1, Sections 15 and 16, except that it is **not** necessary to slacken the coolant pump mounting bolts and move the pump to slacken and tension the belt. Instead, belt adjustment is catered for by means of the automatic tensioner as follows.

28   To release the belt tension prior to removal, unscrew the timing belt tensioner securing bolt slightly then, with a suitable tool inserted in the slot on the tensioner arm, turn the tensioner arm until the timing belt is slack. Tighten the securing bolt slightly to hold the tensioner in this position.

29   To refit the timing belt, first ensure that the coolant pump is correctly positioned by checking that the lug on the coolant pump flange is aligned with the corresponding lug on the cylinder block. If this is not the case, slacken the coolant pump mounting bolts slightly and move the pump accordingly. Tighten the bolts to the specified torque on completion (see Chapter 2).

30   Refit the timing belt as described in Chapter 1, Section 15, then tension it as follows.

31   Slacken the automatic tensioner securing bolt and move the tensioner arm anticlockwise, until the tensioner pointer lies at its stop. Tighten the tensioner securing bolt to hold the tensioner in this position.

32   Turn the crankshaft through two complete revolutions in the normal direction of rotation, and check that with the crankshaft pulley TDC mark aligned with the pointer on the rear timing belt cover, the TDC mark on the camshaft sprocket is still aligned with the notch in the timing belt rear cover.

33   Slacken the automatic tensioner securing bolt once again and move the tensioner arm clockwise, until the tensioner pointer is aligned with the notch in the tensioner bracket (Fig. 12.2). Tighten the tensioner securing bolt securely. Turn the crankshaft through one complete revolution, in the normal direction of rotation, and check that the crankshaft and camshaft timing marks still align, then refit the remainder of the components as described in Chapter 1, Section 15.

34   With the timing belt adjustment set in this way, correct tension will always be maintained by the automatic tensioner and no further checking or adjustment will be necessary.

Timing belt (dohc engines) – removal, refitting and adjustment

35   The operations are essentially the same as described in Chapter 1, Sections 17 and 18, except that the tensioner pulley incorporates an automatic adjuster which simplifies the procedure as follows.

36   To release the belt tension prior to removal, unscrew the timing belt tensioner pulley securing bolt slightly then, with a suitable tool inserted in the slot on the tensioner arm, turn the tensioner arm until the timing belt is slack. Tighten the securing bolt slightly to hold the tensioner in this position.

37   To refit the timing belt, first ensure that the coolant pump is correctly positioned by checking that the lug on the coolant pump flange is aligned with the corresponding lug on the cylinder block. If this is not the case, slacken the coolant pump mounting bolts slightly and move the pump accordingly. Tighten the bolts to the specified torque on completion (see Chapter 2).

38   Refit the timing belt as described in Chapter 1, Section 17, then tension it as follows.

39   Slacken the tensioner pulley securing bolt and move the tensioner arm anticlockwise, until the tensioner pointer lies at its stop. Tighten the tensioner pulley securing bolt to hold the tensioner in this position.

40   Turn the crankshaft through two complete revolutions in the normal direction of rotation and check that with the crankshaft pulley TDC mark aligned with the pointer on the rear timing belt cover, the TDC marks on the camshaft sprockets are still aligned with the notches in the camshaft cover.

41   Slacken the tensioner pulley securing bolt once again and move the tensioner arm clockwise, until the tensioner pointer is aligned with the notch in the tensioner bracket (Fig. 12.2). Tighten the tensioner pulley securing bolt securely. Turn the crankshaft through one complete revolution in the normal direction of rotation and check that the crankshaft and camshaft timing marks still align, then refit the remainder of the components as described in Chapter 1, Section 17.

42   With the timing belt adjustment set in this way, correct tension will always be maintained by the automatic tensioner and no further checking or adjustment will be necessary.

'Undersize' camshafts – all 1.8 and 2.0 litre sohc engines

43   The camshafts and camshaft housings for these engines are sorted on production into one of two size groups; standard and 0.10 mm

'undersize'. Note that this is not intended to provide replacements for worn engines, but is to allow for production tolerances; either may be fitted to new engines.

44   'Undersize' components are marked with a spot of violet-coloured paint, that on the camshaft housing being applied on top at the timing belt end.

45   Whenever the camshaft or its housing are to be renewed, check (by direct measurement, if necessary) whether they are standard or undersize and ensure that only matching items are obtained for re-assembly.

Hydraulic valve lifters – inspection

Sohc engines

46   On engines which have covered a high mileage, or for which the service history (particularly oil changes) is suspect, it is possible for the valve lifters to suffer internal contamination which, in extreme cases, may result in increased engine top end noise and wear. To minimise the possibility of problems occurring later in the life of the engine, it is advisable to dismantle and clean the hydraulic valve lifters as follows whenever the cylinder head is overhauled. Note that no spare parts are available for the valve lifters, and if any of the components are unser-viceable, the complete assembly must be renewed (photo).

47   With the cylinder head removed and dismantled as described in Chapter 1, first inspect the valve lifter bores in the cylinder head for wear. If excessive wear is evident, the cylinder head must be renewed. Also check the valve lifter oil holes in the cylinder head for obstructions.

48   Starting with number 1 valve lifter, carefully pull the collar from the top of the valve lifter cylinder. It should be possible to remove the collar by hand – if a tool is used, take care not to distort the collar.

49   Withdraw the plunger from the cylinder, and recover the spring.

50   Using a small screwdriver, carefully prise the cap from the base of the plunger. Recover the spring and ball from under the cap, taking care not to lose them as the cap is removed.

51   Carefully clean all the components using paraffin or a suitable solvent, paying particular attention to the machined surfaces of the cylinder (internal surfaces), and piston (external surfaces). Thoroughly dry all the components using a lint-free cloth. Carefully examine the springs for damage or distortion – the complete valve lifter must be renewed if the springs are not in perfect condition.

52   Lubricate the components sparingly with clean engine oil of the correct grade (see Chapter 1), then reassemble as follows.

53   Invert the plunger, and locate the ball on its seat in the base of the plunger (photo).

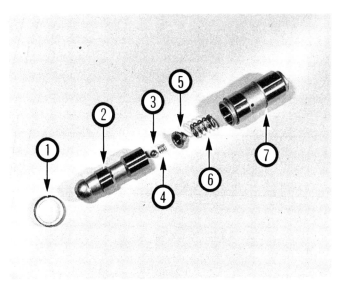

4.46 Hydraulic valve lifter components – sohc engines

1 Collar	5 Plunger cap
2 Plunger	6 Large spring
3 Ball	7 Cylinder
4 Small spring	

4.53 Locate the ball (1) on its seat (2) in the base of the plunger

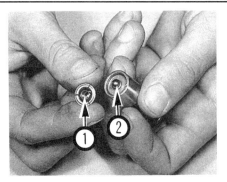

4.54A Spring (1) located in plunger cap, and ball (2) located on seat in plunger

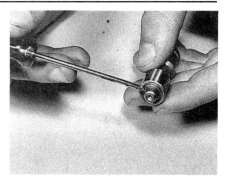

4.54B Locate the cap flange in the plunger groove

4.55A Locate the spring over the plunger cap ...

4.55B ... then slide the plunger and spring assembly into the cylinder

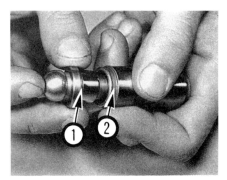

4.56 Slide the collar (1) over the top of the plunger and engage with the groove (2) in the cylinder

54   Locate the smaller spring on its seat in the plunger cap, then carefully refit the cap and spring, ensuring that the spring locates on the ball. Carefully press around the flange of the cap, using a small screwdriver if necessary, until the flange is securely located in the groove in the base of the plunger (photos).

55   Locate the larger spring over the plunger cap, ensuring that the spring is correctly seated, and slide the plunger and spring assembly into the cylinder (photos).

56   Slide the collar over the top of the plunger, and carefully compress the plunger by hand, until the collar can be pushed down to engage securely with the groove in the cylinder (photo).

57   Repeat the above procedures on the remaining valve lifters.

Dohc engines

58   Although the valve lifters on these engines cannot be dismantled, they should be carefully inspected for obvious signs of wear on the contact faces. Also check the valve lifter oil holes for obstructions and for any signs of oil sludge build-up. If excessive wear is evident (this is unlikely), all the valve lifters must be renewed as a set.

'Pot'-type flywheel – C18 NZ, C20 NE, C20 XE engines, 1992-on

59   These engines are fitted with a modified flywheel which has a deeply-recessed clutch friction disc contact surface.

60   Apart from its effect on clutch removal and refitting procedures, operations concerning the flywheel are unchanged from those given in Chapter 1.

Crankshaft pulley (automatic transmission) – removal and refitting

61   To lock the crankshaft so that the pulley bolt(s) can be unscrewed, the transmission bellhousing cover plate must be unbolted (three bolts) so that the flexplate ring gear teeth can be jammed using a suitable tool.

Flexplate (automatic transmission) – removal and refitting

62   Remove the transmission as described in Section 10 of this Chapter.

63   Prevent the flexplate from turning by jamming its ring gear teeth using a suitable tool.

64   Unbolt and remove the flexplate. Examine the bolts and renew them all as a set if there is the slightest doubt about their condition.

65   The ring gear can be checked, and renewed if necessary, as described in Chapter 1, Section 32.

66   Refitting is the reverse of the removal procedure. If the bolts are to be re-used, use a wire brush to clean their threads; apply a few drops of thread-locking compound (Vauxhall Part No 15 10 177, or equivalent) to the threads of each bolt on refitting. Tighten the bolts to the specified torque wrench setting.

67   Refit the transmission.

Engine – removal, leaving automatic transmission in vehicle

68   Refer to Chapter 1, Section 9, noting the following differences.

(a)   Disconnect the transmission fluid cooler hoses (Section 10 of this Chapter) when removing the radiator.

(b)   Disconnect the additional wiring, hoses, etc, from the carburettor (Section 6 of this Chapter).

(c)   Remove the bellhousing cover plate and unbolt the torque converter from the flexplate as described in Section 10 of this Chapter.

(d)   As the engine is removed, secure the torque converter as noted in Section 10 of this Chapter.

Engine – refitting (automatic transmission in vehicle)

69   Refitting is the reverse of the removal procedure, noting the remarks made in Section 10 of this Chapter.

Engine/automatic transmission – removal and separation

70   Refer to Chapter 1, Section 10, noting the following differences.

(a)   Disconnect the transmission fluid cooler hoses (Section 10 of this Chapter) when removing the radiator.

(b)   Disconnect the additional wiring, hoses, etc, from the carburettor (Section 6 of this Chapter).

(c)   Disconnect the transmission selector cable and wiring (Section 10 of this Chapter).

(d) Remove the bellhousing cover plate and unbolt the torque converter from the flexplate then, on separating the transmission from the engine, secure the torque converter as noted in Section 10 of this Chapter.

Engine/automatic transmission – reconnection and refitting

71   Refitting is the reverse of the removal procedure, noting the remarks made in Section 10 of this Chapter.

---

5   Cooling system

Hose clamps – later models

1   Note that later models may be fitted with self-tensioning spring clamps to secure the cooling system (including heater) hoses.
2   Maintenance is reduced to simply checking for signs of coolant leakage and for damage to the hoses; if a leak is found, check that the clamp is securely seated before renewing the hose.
3   These clamps can be released by squeezing together their free ends using a large pair of self-grip pliers or similar so that the clamp can be moved up the hose, clear of the union. Check that the clamp is securely seated, and check for leaks on reassembly.

Radiator (automatic transmission) – removal and refitting

4   On models with automatic transmission, the radiator left-hand side tank incorporates a heat exchanger to cool the transmission fluid. It is connected to the transmission by a pair of flexible hoses, with a metal pipe at each end.
5   When removing the radiator, either clamp the transmission fluid cooler flexible hoses, or slacken their clamps, work them off their unions and swiftly plug or cap each hose end and union to minimise the loss of fluid and to prevent the entry of dirt.
6   On refitting, reverse the removal procedure and do not forget to check the transmission fluid level, topping-up as necessary to replace the lost fluid, as described in Section 10 of this Chapter.

Coolant pump – refitting

7   Whenever the pump is removed, coat its sealing ring with silicone grease or petroleum jelly; similarly coat the mating surface in the cylinder block; this will prevent corrosion between the pump and block, thus easing future pump renewal or timing belt adjustment.
8   If the pump cannot be turned to adjust the timing belt tension, it can be freed by lightly striking it from below using a hammer and a long drift.

---

6   Fuel, exhaust and emission control systems

Pierburg 2E3 carburettor

Idle speed and mixture adjustment – models with automatic transmission

1   Always select position 'P' or 'N' (for safety's sake, preferably position 'P') before carrying out carburettor servicing work which involves running the engine.
2   Note that when position 'D' is selected (all electrical consumers switched off), the idle speed should not drop perceptibly; if it does, the vehicle should be taken to a Vauxhall dealer for the idle-up system to be checked using special Vauxhall test equipment.

Fuel filter – renewal

3   A small tubular filter gauze is fitted into the carburettor top cover's fuel inlet union to remove any particles of dirt from the fuel.
4   To ensure a clean fuel supply and to prevent the risk of misfiring, poor starting or other problems due to a restricted fuel supply, this filter must be cleaned and/or renewed at the interval specified in *Routine maintenance* at the beginning of this manual.
5   To reach the filter, remove the air cleaner or air box, as applicable, then disconnect and plug the hose from the fuel pump or vapour separator to the top cover union (Chapter 3).
6   Remove the filter by hooking it out with a small screwdriver, or by snaring it with a long thin screw (3 mm thread size, screwed approximately 5 mm into the filter).
7   If the filter is blocked or heavily fouled, or if it is torn, distorted or

6.8 Refitting the carburettor fuel filter

damaged in any way, it must be renewed. If it is fit for further use, clean it using a jet of compressed air or by brushing away particles of dirt with an old soft toothbrush, then flushing it in clean solvent of a suitable type, taking care not to allow any overspray to get into your eyes; if petrol is used, take care to prevent the risk of fire.
8   On refitting the filter, press it into the union until it catches (photo). The remainder of the reassembly procedure is the reverse of removal.

Float level – checking and adjustment

9   To check the float level, first remove the carburettor top cover and withdraw the gasket (Chapter 3, Section 17).
10   Hold the cover vertically, so that the float is hanging from its pivot, then tilt the cover until the float needle valve is just closed – the needle spring must not be compressed by the weight of the float.
11   Measure the distance (dimension x in Fig. 12.3) from the bottom of the float to the gasket surface on the top cover's underside. If the distance measured exceeds, or is less than, that specified, the float weight is incorrect and the float must be renewed.
12   When the float level is known to be correct, reassemble the carburettor, using a new top cover gasket. Check the idle speed and mixture settings as described in Chapter 3.

Vacuum unit – leak checking

13   If a vacuum source incorporating a gauge is available, apply approximately 300 mbars (9 in Hg) to the choke pull-down unit, at the hose nearest the carburettor body. Close off the vacuum source, and

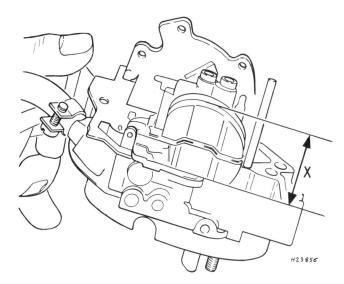

Fig. 12.3 Measuring the float level 'X' (Sec 6)

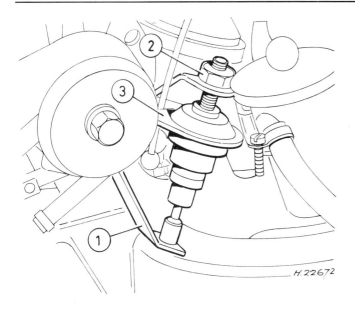

Fig. 12.4 Adjusting the throttle valve dashpot – models with
automatic transmission (Sec 6)

1   Lever   3   Dashpot
2   Locknut

check that the vacuum is held. If there is a leak, rectify or renew the
leaking component.
14   Similarly check the secondary throttle vacuum unit.
15   If a suitable vacuum source is not available, testing of a suspect
vacuum unit must be by the substitution of a known good item.

Throttle valve fast idle gap
16   Remove the carburettor.
17   Position the fast idle adjustment screw on the highest step of the
fast idle cam.
18   Use a gauge rod or twist drill of the specified diameter to measure
the opening of the primary throttle valve. Adjust if necessary at the fast
idle adjustment screw. Note that this is a preliminary adjustment; final
adjustment of the fast idle speed should take place with the engine
running.

Accelerator pump delivery
19   Remove the carburettor.
20   It will be necessary to feed the float chamber with fuel from a small
reservoir during this test. Take all necessary fire precautions when
dealing with fuel and fuel vapour.
21   Position the primary barrel over an accurate measuring glass. Fully
open and close the throttle ten times, taking approximately one second
for each opening, and pausing for three seconds after each return
stroke. Make sure that the fast idle cam is not restricting throttle travel at
either end.
22   Measure the quantity of fuel delivered, and compare this with the
specified value.
23   If adjustment is necessary, release the clamp screw and turn the
cam plate in the desired direction. Tighten the clamp screw, and recheck
the pump delivery (photo).

Throttle valve dashpot – adjustment
24   Remove the air cleaner or air box (Chapter 3, Section 15, paragraph 2).
25   Ensure that the lever (item 1 in Fig. 12.4) is in the idling position.
26   Slacken the locknut and unscrew the dashpot until a gap of 0.05
mm (0.002 in) exists between the lever and the dashpot tip, then screw
the dashpot downwards 2.5 full turns and tighten the locknut.
27   Refit all removed components.

Idle-up solenoid valve – models with automatic transmission
28   A solenoid valve may be fitted to maintain the idle speed at the
required level. No further information is available at the time of writing.

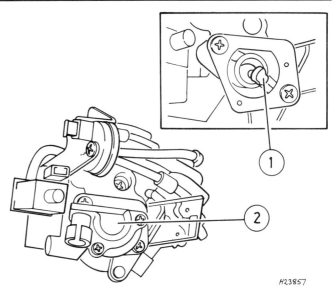

Fig. 12.5 Throttle position sensor – models with automatic
transmission (Sec 6)

1   Adaptor   2   Sensor

**Throttle position sensor – models with automatic transmission –
removal and refitting**
29   Disconnect the battery earth lead.
30   Disconnect the wiring plug from the sensor.
31   Either unscrew the two securing screws and withdraw the sensor
from its bracket, or unbolt the bracket.
32   Refitting is the reverse of the removal procedure, noting the
following points.

(a)   Install the sensor when the throttle valve is fully closed and
      ensure that the sensor adaptor (item 1, Fig. 12.5) seats correctly
      on the throttle valve spindle.
(b)   Tighten the screws carefully.

Removal and refitting – models with automatic transmission
33   In addition to the items mentioned in Chapter 3, Section 15,
disconnect the additional wiring, vacuum hoses, etc, as necessary to
release the carburettor from the manifold.

6.23 Accelerator pump delivery adjustment: ' + ' to increase, '–' to
reduce

Overhaul

34   With the carburettor removed from the vehicle, drain the fuel from the float chamber and vapour separator (where applicable). Clean the outside of the carburettor, then remove the top cover (Chapter 3, Section 17).

35   Blow through the jets and drillings with compressed air, or air from a foot pump – do not probe them with wire. If it is wished to remove the jets, unscrew them carefully with well-fitting tools.

36   Remove the fuel filter gauze from the inlet union (see above); Vauxhall recommend that it is renewed whenever the carburettor is cleaned.

37   Clean any foreign matter from the float chamber. Renew the float, the float needle valve and seat if wear is evident, or if the float is punctured or otherwise damaged; check that the needle valve closes completely before the float reaches the top of its movement. See the sub-Section above for details of float level checking.

38   Renew the diaphragms in the part-load enrichment valve and in the accelerator pump. If additional pump or valve parts are supplied in the overhaul kit, renew these parts also.

39   Further dismantling is not recommended. Pay particular attention to the throttle opening mechanism arrangement if it is decided to dismantle it; the interlocking arrangement is important.

40   Reassemble in the reverse order to dismantling. Use new gaskets and seals throughout; lubricate linkages with a smear or molybdenum-based grease.

Multec fuel injection system – C16 NZ, C16 NZ2, X16 SZ and C18 NZ engines

General description

41   The Multec system is essentially a simple method of air/fuel metering, replacing the carburettor with a single injector mounted in a throttle body; this type of system is therefore also known as Throttle Body Injection (TBi), Central Fuel Injection (CFi) or single- (or mono-) point injection. The whole system is best explained if considered as three sub-systems, these being fuel delivery, air metering and electrical control.

42   The fuel delivery system incorporates the fuel tank (with the electric fuel pump immersed inside it), the fuel filter, the fuel injector and pressure regulator (mounted in the throttle body), and the hoses and pipes connecting them. When the ignition is switched on (or when the engine is cranking, on X16 SZ engines) the pump is supplied with voltage, via the pump relay and fuse 11, under the control of the Electronic Control Unit (ECU); the pump feeds through the fuel filter to the injector. Fuel pressure is controlled by the pressure regulator, which lifts to allow excess fuel to return to the tank.

43   The air metering system includes the intake air temperature control system and the air cleaner, but its main components are in the throttle body assembly. This incorporates the injector, which sprays fuel onto the back of the throttle valve, the throttle potentiometer, which is linked to the throttle valve spindle and sends the ECU information on the rate of throttle opening by transmitting a varying voltage, and the idle air control stepper motor, which is controlled by the ECU to maintain the idle speed. **Note:** *There is no provision for the adjustment or alteration of the idle speed; if checking the idle speed, remember that it may vary constantly under ECU control.*

44   The electrical side of the fuel injection system consists of the electronic control unit (ECU) and all the sensors that provide it with information, plus the actuators by which it controls the whole system's operation. The basic method of operation is as follows; note that the ignition system is controlled by the same ECU, and is described in Section 7 of this Chapter.

45   The manifold absolute pressure sensor is connected by a hose to the inlet manifold; variations in manifold pressure are converted into graduated electrical signals which are used by the ECU to determine the load on the engine. The throttle valve potentiometer is explained above.

46   Information on engine speed and crankshaft position comes from the distributor on C16 NZ engines and from the crankshaft speed/position sensor on C16 NZ2, X16 SZ and C18 NZ engines.

47   An odometer frequency sensor provides the ECU with information on the vehicle's roadspeed, and the coolant temperature sensor provides it with the engine temperature. A knock sensor located in the cylinder block between cylinders 2 and 3 on the X16 SZ engine provides additional information to the ECU by detecting pre-ignition (detonation) during the combustion process.

48   All these signals are compared by the ECU with set values pre-programmed (mapped) into its memory; based on this information, the ECU selects the response appropriate to those values, and controls the ignition amplifier module (varying the ignition timing as required), the fuel injector (varying its pulse width – the length of time the injector is held open – to provide a richer or weaker mixture, as appropriate), the idle air control stepper motor (controlling the idle speed), the fuel pump relay (controlling the fuel delivery) and the oxygen sensor, accordingly. The mixture, idle speed and ignition timing are constantly varied by the ECU to provide the best settings for cranking, starting and engine warm-up (with either a hot or cold engine), idle, cruising and acceleration. The injector earth is also switched off on the overrun to improve fuel economy and reduce exhaust emissions. Additionally, on the X16 SZ engine, the ECU also controls the operation of the charcoal canister purge valve in the evaporative emission control system.

49   The oxygen sensor screwed into the exhaust manifold provides the ECU with a constant feedback signal which enables it to adjust the mixture (closed-loop control) to provide the best possible conditions for the catalytic converter to operate effectively.

50   Until the oxygen sensor is fully warmed up it gives no feedback so the ECU uses pre-programmed values (open-loop control) to determine the correct injector pulse width. When the sensor reaches its normal operating temperature, its tip (which is sensitive to oxygen) sends the ECU a varying voltage depending on the amount of oxygen in the exhaust gases; if the intake air/fuel mixture is too rich, the exhaust gases are low in oxygen so the sensor sends a low-voltage signal, the voltage rising as the mixture weakens and the amount of oxygen rises in the exhaust gases. Peak conversion efficiency of all major pollutants occurs if the intake air/fuel mixture is maintained at the chemically-correct ratio for the complete combustion of petrol of 14.7 parts (by weight) of air to 1 part of fuel (the 'stoichiometric' ratio). The sensor output voltage alters in a large step at this point, the ECU using the signal change as a reference point and correcting the intake air/fuel mixture accordingly by altering the fuel injector pulse width.

51   In addition, the ECU senses battery voltage, incorporates diagnostic capabilities, and can both receive and transmit information via the diagnostic connector, thus permitting engine diagnosis and tuning by Vauxhall test equipment.

Warning: *Many of the procedures in this sub-Section require the removal of fuel lines and connections which may result in some fuel spillage. Before carrying out any operation on the fuel system refer to the precautions given in Safety first! at the beginning of this Manual and follow them implicitly. Petrol is a highly dangerous and volatile liquid, and the precautions necessary when handling it cannot be overstressed.*

Depressurising the fuel system

Warning: *The following procedures will merely relieve the pressure in the fuel system. Remember that fuel will still be present in the system components, so take precautions before disconnecting any of them.*

52   The fuel system referred to in this sub-Section is defined as the tank-mounted fuel pump, the fuel filter, the fuel injector, the pressure regulator in the throttle body, and the metal pipes and flexible hoses of the fuel lines between these components. All these contain fuel which will be under pressure while the engine is running and/or while the ignition is switched on.

53   The pressure will remain for some time after the ignition has been switched off and must be relieved before any of these components is disturbed for servicing work.

54   Remove either the fuel pump fuse (number 11) or the fuel pump relay (whichever is convenient) and start the engine; allow the engine to idle until it cuts out. Turn the engine over once or twice on the starter to ensure that all pressure is released, then switch off the ignition; do not forget to refit the fuse or relay **when work is complete.**

Air cleaner element – renewal

55   Refer to Chapter 3, Section 4.

Air cleaner and air box – removal and refitting

56   Refer to Chapter 3, Section 5.

57   When removing the air box, which is secured by two screws to the top of the throttle body, take note of the routing and connections of the intake air temperature control system vacuum pipes (photo). Disconnect the engine breather hose from the air box and the vacuum pipe from the rearmost of the throttle body's three unions (A in photo 6.144). Do not lose the sealing ring as the air box is withdrawn.

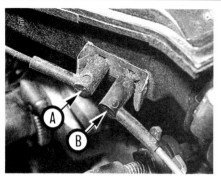

6.57 Vacuum pipe connections to air box –
(A) to throttle body, (B) to air cleaner

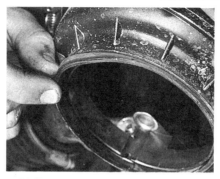

6.58A Ensure the sealing ring is located in the
air box groove

6.58B Do not overtighten the air box screws

58   On refitting, ensure that the sealing ring is seated correctly in the slot in the underside of the air box, tighten the screws, and reconnect the vacuum pipe and breather hose (photos).

Air cleaner intake air temperature control – description and testing
59   The system is controlled by a thermac switch mounted in the air box; when the engine is started from cold, the switch is closed to allow inlet manifold depression to act on the air temperature control valve in the air cleaner assembly. This uses a vacuum servo in the valve assembly to draw a flap valve across the cold air intake, thus allowing only (warmed) air from the exhaust manifold to enter the air cleaner.
60   As the temperature of the exhaust-warmed air in the air box rises, a bi-metallic strip in the thermac switch deforms and opens the switch to shut off the depression in the air temperature control valve; the flap is lowered gradually across the hot air intake until, when the engine is fully warmed up to normal operating temperature, only cold air from the front of the vehicle is entering the air cleaner.
61   To check the system, allow the engine to cool down completely, then remove the air cleaner cover; the flap valve should be securely seated across the hot air intake. Start the engine; the flap should immediately rise to close off the cold air intake and should then lower steadily as the engine warms up until it is eventually seated across the hot air intake again.
62   To check the thermac switch, disconnect the control valve vacuum pipe from the switch union (on the rear face of the air box) when the engine is running. With the engine cold, full inlet manifold depression should be felt sucking at the union; none at all should be felt when the engine is fully warmed up.
63   To check the air temperature control valve, remove the air cleaner cover; the flap valve should be securely seated across the hot air intake. Disconnect the control valve vacuum pipe from the switch union on the rear face of the air box and suck hard on its end; the flap should rise to shut off the cold air intake.
64   If either component is faulty, it must be renewed. This means renewing the air cleaner lower casing to obtain a new air temperature control valve, or renewing the air box in the case of the thermac switch.

Fuel pump – testing
65   Refer to Chapter 3, Section 33.

Fuel pump – removal and refitting
66   Depressurise the fuel system (see above), then remove and refit the fuel filler cap to ensure that the pressure is equalised inside and outside the tank.
67   Disconnect the battery negative terminal.
68   Fold forwards the rear seat cushion. Peel back the floor covering beneath it, then remove the cover plug from the vehicle floor to reach the pump mountings (photo).
69   Noting exactly how it is connected, and making your own marks or notes to ensure that it can be reconnected the same way round, disconnect the wiring plug from the pump.
70   Release the securing clip and disconnect the fuel hose from the pump. Clamp or plug the hose to prevent the loss of fuel and the entry of dirt.
71   Undo the pump mounting bracket screws, then withdraw the mounting bracket and pump assembly from the tank. Note the position

of the sealing ring and discard it, then cover the tank opening as a safety measure and to prevent the entry of dirt.
72   If the pump is to be renewed, first move it to a clean working area and carry out the following.
73   Prise off the filter at the base of the pump assembly, then release the securing clamp and disconnect the mounting bracket-to-pump fuel hose.
74   Making your own marks or notes to ensure that they can be reconnected the same way round, unsolder the wires connecting the pump to the mounting bracket.
75   Press the pump out of the rubber sleeve.
76   Reassembly and refitting are the reverse of the removal and dismantling procedures, noting the following points.

(a)   Ensure that the pump is seated correctly in the sleeve and that the hose is securely fastened.
(b)   Ensure that the wires are correctly reconnected and securely soldered.
(c)   Always renew the pump mounting bracket's sealing ring.
(d)   Apply a few drops of Vauxhall Sealing Compound (Part No 15 03 294) to the threads of the screws, then tighten them securely, but take care not to distort the sealing ring.

Fuel pump relay – renewal
77   The relay is mounted in the engine compartment relay box (Chapter 11); where more than one relay is fitted, the fuel pump relay is the one with the black base.

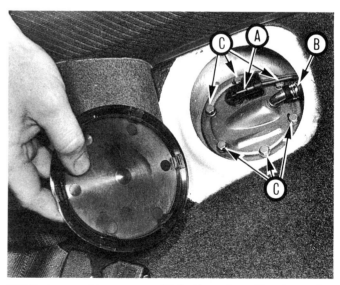

6.68 Fuel pump wiring connector (A), fuel hose clamp (B) and mounting bracket screws (C)

Fuel tank – removal and refitting

78   Proceed as described in Chapter 3, Section 9, noting the following.

(a) Depressurise the fuel system (see above).

(b) On models with C16 NZ and X16 SZ engines, disconnect the exhaust system from the manifold.

(c) When working on the fuel level sender unit, note that there is only one hose to be disconnected.

(d) Disconnect the fuel pump hose and wiring as described in paragraphs 68 to 70 above.

(e) When releasing the tank mounting straps, note that the fuel filter must either be moved aside or removed completely, whichever is most convenient.

(f) Refitting is the reverse of the removal procedure.

Fuel tank filler pipe – removal and refitting

79   Syphon out any remaining fuel in the tank into a clean container that is suitable for carrying petrol and is clearly marked as such.

80   Raise the bottom edge of the seal surrounding the filler neck and undo the single securing screw beneath.

81   Chock the front wheels, jack up the rear of the vehicle and support it securely on axle stands placed under the body side members (see Jacking, towing and wheel changing).

82   Unscrew the single filler pipe mounting bolt from the underbody, then work along the length of the pipe, cutting or releasing any clips or ties securing other pipes or hoses to it. Releasing their clips, disconnect the filler and vent hoses from the pipe's lower end and the small-bore vent hoses from the unions at its upper end.

83   Having ensured that all components have been removed or disconnected which might prevent its removal, manoeuvre the pipe away from the vehicle's underside.

84   To check the operation of the pipe's anti-leak valve, invert the filler pipe and fill the lower union (now uppermost) with petrol; if the valve is functioning correctly, no petrol will leak from the other union. If petrol leaks from the other union the valve is faulty and the complete filler pipe must be renewed.

85   Refitting is the reverse of the removal procedure, noting the following points (photo).

(a) Check the condition of all hoses and clips, renewing any components that are found to be worn or damaged.

(b) When reconnecting the small-bore vent hoses to the unions at the pipe's upper end, connect the hose from the charcoal canister to the uppermost union and the hose from the tank itself to the lower union.

(c) Replacing any that were cut on removal, use the clips or ties provided to secure any other pipes or hoses to the filler pipe.

(d) Check carefully for signs of leaks on refilling the tank; if any signs of leakage are detected, the problem must be rectified immediately.

Fuel level sender unit – removal and refitting

86   Refer to Chapter 3, Section 10, noting that there is only one hose connected to the sender unit, and that this must also be disconnected from the union on the inside of the unit before it can be withdrawn completely from the tank.

Fuel filter – renewal

87   Depressurise the fuel system (see above).

88   Chock the front wheels, jack up the rear of the vehicle and support it on axle stands placed under the body side members (see Jacking, towing and wheel changing). The fuel filter is located at the rear of the fuel tank, on the right-hand side.

89   Unclip the fuel hose from the filter mounting bracket.

90   Note carefully any markings on the fuel filter casing; there should be at least an arrow (showing the direction of fuel flow) pointing in the direction of the fuel supply hose leading to the engine compartment, and there may also be the words 'EIN' (in) and 'AUS' (out) embossed in the appropriate end of the casing.

91   Clamp the fuel filter hoses, then slacken the clips and disconnect the hoses.

92   Undo the single screw to release the mounting bracket, then open the clamp with a screwdriver to remove the fuel filter (photo).

93   Fit the new fuel filter using a reversal of the removal procedure, but ensure that the fuel flow direction arrow or markings point in the correct direction. Switch on the ignition and check carefully for leaks; if any signs of leakage are detected, the problem must be rectified before the engine is started.

Fuel pressure – check

94   Fuel pressure checking must be entrusted to a Vauxhall dealer, or other suitable specialist, who has the necessary special equipment.

Throttle pedal – removal and refitting

95   Refer to Chapter 3, Section 12.

Throttle cable – removal and refitting

96   Remove the air box (see above).

97   Where fitted, use a pair of needle-nosed pliers to extract the wire spring clip securing the cable end balljoint to the throttle linkage. Prise the cable end off the linkage.

98   Withdraw the clip and pull the cable outer seating grommet out of the cable bracket, then release the cable as far as the bulkhead.

99   Working inside the passenger compartment, remove the driver's footwell trim panel (Chapter 10, Section 37).

100   Release the end of the cable's inner wire from the 'keyhole' fitting at the top of the throttle pedal by easing back the spring and prising the cable end out of the slot.

101   Prise the grommet out of the bulkhead and tie a length of string to the cable.

6.85 Vent hose connections at fuel tank filler pipe – charcoal canister hose (A) and tank vent hose (B)

6.92 Fuel filter clamp screw (A) and hose clips (B)

6.113 Disconnecting the fuel injector wiring plug

6.114A Unscrewing the injector retainer Torx screw ...

6.114B ... to remove the injector – renew sealing rings (arrows)

102   Noting carefully its routing, withdraw the cable through the bulkhead into the engine compartment; untie the string, leaving it in place, as soon as the pedal end of the cable appears.
103   Refitting is the reverse of the removal procedure, noting the following points.

(a)   First ensure that the cable is correctly routed, then draw it through the bulkhead aperture using the string.
(b)   Ensure that the bulkhead grommet is correctly seated.
(c)   Connect the cable end to the throttle linkage, seat the cable outer grommet in the bracket and pull it through so that the cable inner wire is just taut when the throttle linkage is held fully closed. Fit the clip to secure the cable outer in that position.
(d)   Check the throttle operation and cable adjustment, as described below.

Throttle cable – adjustment

104   Remove the air box (see above).
105   First check that the pedal is at a convenient height for the driver. This setting can be adjusted by turning the pedal stop screw (it will be necessary to remove the footwell trim panel to reach the screw), but remember that the pedal must be left with enough travel for the throttle valve to open fully. Also check that the pedal pivot bushes are in good condition.
106   Returning to the engine compartment, check that the linkage pivots and balljoints are unworn and operate smoothly throughout their full travel. When the throttle valve is fully closed and the throttle pedal is released, there should be hardly any free play in the cable inner wire.
107   If adjustment is required, extract the clip securing the cable outer seating grommet in the cable bracket and replace it in the appropriate groove, so that the cable outer is repositioned correctly.
108   With an assistant operating the throttle pedal from the driver's seat, check that when the pedal is fully depressed, the throttle valve is fully open (if there is insufficient pedal travel to permit this, unscrew the pedal stop screw, then reset the cable at the throttle linkage).
109   When cable adjustment is correct, refit all disturbed components.

Fuel injector – removal and refitting

110   Depressurise the fuel system (see above).
111   Remove the air box (see above).
112   Disconnect the battery earth lead.
113   Disconnect the wiring plug from the fuel injector (photo).
114   Undo the Torx-type screw (size TX 20) securing the fuel injector retainer to the top of the throttle body, remove the retainer and lift out the injector (photos). Remove and discard the injector sealing rings.
115   Refitting is the reverse of the removal procedure, noting the following points.

(a)   Always renew both sealing rings; apply a smear of grease to each to ease injector refitting.
(b)   Refit the injector so that its wiring terminals point to the rear of the vehicle; locate the edge of the retainer securely in the groove at the top of the injector.
(c)   Apply a few drops of a suitable thread-locking compound to the screw threads, then tighten it carefully to the specified torque wrench setting.

(d)   Switch on the ignition and check carefully for signs of fuel leaks; if any signs of leakage are detected, the problem must be rectified before the engine is started.

Fuel injector – testing

116   A simple test of the injector's windings is possible for those who have a multi-meter of sufficient sensitivity. First disconnect the injector wiring plug as described in paragraphs 110 to 113 above, then connect the meter (set to the appropriate resistance scale) across the injector's terminals and note the reading obtained.
117   On C18 NZ engines, the reading should be within the specified tolerance; similar results can be expected on C16 NZ, C16 NZ2, and X16 SZ engines.
118   If the reading differs significantly from the specified value, indicating either shorted or open circuit windings, the injector must be renewed.
119   Note that this is only a test of the injector's electrical condition; it does not test its spray pattern or performance. If the injector is thought to be faulty it is always worth trying the effect of one of the proprietary injector-cleaning treatments such as Holts Redex Injector Treatment before renewing, perhaps unnecessarily, the injector. If this fails, the vehicle must be taken to a Vauxhall dealer for full testing on the correct test equipment.

Fuel pressure regulator – removal and refitting

120   Depressurise the fuel system (see above).
121   Remove the air box (see above).
122   Disconnect the battery earth lead.
123   Noting the dowels locating the cover, carefully unscrew the fuel pressure regulator cover Torx-type screws (size TX 15); ensure that the spring does not fly out as the cover is released. Remove the cover, spring seat, spring and diaphragm, noting how each is fitted (photo).
124   The diaphragm must be renewed whenever the cover is disturbed; if any of the regulator's other components are worn or damaged, they can be renewed only as part of the throttle body upper section assembly.
125   Refitting is the reverse of the removal procedure, noting the following points.

(a)   Fit the new diaphragm so that it locates in the throttle body groove.
(b)   Ensure that the spring and spring seat are correctly engaged with each other and with the diaphragm and regulator cover, then press the cover over its locating dowels and hold it in place while the screws are tightened.
(c)   Tighten the screws carefully to the specified torque wrench setting.
(d)   Switch on the ignition and check for signs of fuel leaks; if any signs of leakage are detected, the problem must be rectified before the engine is started.

Idle air control stepper motor – removal and refitting

126   Remove the air box (see above).
127   Disconnect the battery earth lead.
128   Disconnect the wiring plug from the stepper motor (photo).
129   Undo its two screws, then withdraw the stepper motor. Remove and discard the sealing ring (photos).

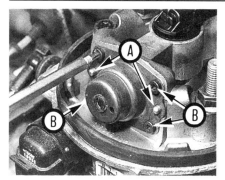

6.123 Fuel pressure regulator cover locating dowels (A) and mounting screws (B)

6.128 Disconnecting the idle air control stepper motor wiring plug

6.129A Unscrew retaining screws (second screw arrowed) ...

6.129B ... to remove the stepper motor – renew sealing ring (arrow)

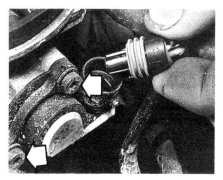

6.132 Disconnecting the throttle potentiometer wiring plug – note the mounting screws (arrows)

130 Refitting is the reverse of the removal procedure, noting the following points.

(a) Fit a new sealing ring, greasing it lightly to ease installation.

(b) To prevent the risk of damage, either to the throttle body or to the stepper motor, if the motor's plunger tip projects more than 28 mm (1.1 in) beyond the motor's mating surface, carefully press the plunger in until its stop is reached. The stepper motor will then be reset by the ECU as soon as the engine is restarted.

(c) Apply a few drops of a suitable thread-locking compound to their threads, then carefully tighten the screws to the specified torque wrench setting.

Throttle potentiometer – removal and refitting

131 Disconnect the battery negative lead.
132 Disconnect the wiring plug from the potentiometer (photo).
133 Unscrew the two Torx-type securing screws (size TX 25) and withdraw the potentiometer.
134 Refitting is the reverse of the removal procedure, noting the following points.

(a) Install the potentiometer when the throttle valve is fully closed, and ensure that its adaptor seats correctly on the throttle valve spindle.

(b) Tighten the screws carefully to the specified torque.

Throttle body – removal and refitting

135 Depressurise the fuel system (see above).
136 Remove the air box (see above).
137 Disconnect the battery negative lead.
138 Disconnect the wiring plugs from the fuel injector (pressing out the wiring rubber grommet), from the idle air control stepper motor and from the potentiometer.
139 Disconnect the fuel hoses from their unions and plug them to prevent loss of fuel and the entry of dirt; label them to ensure correct refitting. Be prepared for fuel spillage and take suitable safety precautions.
140 Disconnect the vacuum hoses and pipes from the body unions.

141 Disconnect the throttle valve operating linkage at the throttle body.
142 Undo the two nuts securing the throttle body to the inlet manifold and withdraw the body assembly; peel off and discard the gasket (photo).
143 If required, the throttle body's upper and lower sections may be separated by removing the two Torx-type securing screws; note that a new gasket must be fitted on reassembly. The fuel inlet and return unions may also be unscrewed, but note that new sealing rings must be fitted on reassembly, and the unions must be tightened securely.
144 Refitting is the reverse of the removal procedure, noting the following points (photo).

(a) Renew all gaskets and seals, and use suitable thread-locking compound where applicable.

(b) Check the throttle cable operation and adjustment (see above).

(c) When reconnecting the vacuum hoses and pipes, ensure that they are connected to the front unions as shown in the accompanying photograph.

(d) As no fuel vapour trap is fitted, it is essential that the manifold absolute pressure sensor vacuum hose is routed so that it falls steadily from the sensor to the throttle body. This precaution will prevent any fuel droplets being trapped in the sensor or hose and allowing them to drain into the inlet port.

(e) Ensure that the fuel hoses are correctly reconnected; the feed hose is on the injector end of the throttle body.

(f) Switch on the ignition and check for signs of fuel leaks from all disturbed unions; if any signs of leakage are detected, the problem must be rectified before the engine is started.

Electronic Control Unit (ECU) – removal and refitting

145 Disconnect the battery negative lead.
146 Remove the driver's footwell side trim panel (Chapter 10, Section 36).
147 Release the unit from its mountings and withdraw it until the wiring plugs' locking lugs can be released and the plugs can be disconnected (photo).

6.142 Throttle body mounting nuts (A) and upper-to-lower section Torx screws (B)

6.144 Intake air temperature control vacuum pipe (A), exhaust gas recirculation valve hose (B), charcoal canister control pipe (C) and fuel return hose (D)

6.147 Withdrawing the fuel injection/ignition system ECU

6.150 Oxygen sensor is screwed into exhaust manifold

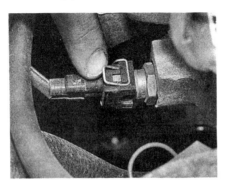

6.151 Disconnecting the coolant temperature sensor wiring plug

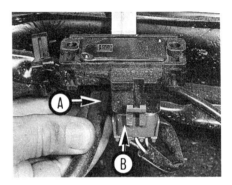

6.152 Manifold absolute pressure sensor vacuum hose (A) and wiring connector plug (B)

148   Note that the unit actually consists of two parts – the basic control unit and the Programmable Read-Only Memory (PROM). While it is possible to renew them separately, **do not** attempt to separate them; faults requiring this degree of attention can be diagnosed only by an experienced mechanic using the special Vauxhall test equipment and a previously-sound ECU could be seriously damaged by careless handling of the contacts between the two sub-units.

149   Refitting is a reversal of the removal procedure, ensuring that the wiring plugs are correctly reconnected and that the unit is located securely.

Oxygen sensor – removal and refitting

150   The procedure is as described in Chapter 3, Section 49, noting the following (photo). Trace the wiring from the sensor itself to the connector (either clipped to the radiator cooling fan shroud or behind the coolant expansion tank), release it from any clips or ties; disconnect the wiring before unscrewing the sensor.

Coolant temperature sensor – removal and refitting

151   Noting that the sensor is screwed horizontally into the rear of the inlet manifold, proceed as described in Chapter 2, Section 14 (photo). Tighten the sensor to its specified torque wrench setting on refitting.

Manifold absolute pressure sensor – removal and refitting

152   Proceed as described in Chapter 4, Section 13, paragraphs 1 to 6, noting the following differences (photo).

(a)   The sensor is located on the engine compartment bulkhead, under the left-hand end of the water-deflecting shield.

(b)   As no fuel vapour trap is fitted, it is essential that the sensor vacuum hose is routed so that it falls steadily from the sensor to the throttle body. This precaution prevents any fuel droplets being trapped in the sensor or hose, and allows them to drain into the inlet port.

Odometer frequency/roadspeed sensor – removal and refitting

153   At the time of writing, no information was available concerning the location of this component, or of removal/refitting and renewal.

Knock sensor and control module – removal and refitting

154   The knock sensor fitted to the X16 SZ engine is located on the cylinder block below the inlet manifold, between cylinders 2 and 3. To remove the sensor, disconnect the wiring and unscrew the unit from the block. To refit, tighten the unit securely and reconnect the wiring.

155   The knock sensor knock module and control unit are located on the left-hand side of the engine compartment behind the battery. Removal and refitting is simply a matter of disconnecting the wiring multiplug and removing the retaining screws or bolts.

156   Note that there is no provision for testing the knock sensor or control unit without dedicated Vauxhall test equipment.

Idle speed – checking and adjustment

157   The idle speed is controlled entirely by the ECU and there is no provision at all for any form of adjustment. Furthermore, accurate checking is not possible without the use of Vauxhall test equipment.

158   While it may be possible for owners with good quality tachometers to check the idle speed, the results should be regarded as no more than a rough guide. If the idle speed is thought to be incorrect, the vehicle should be taken to a Vauxhall dealer for checking; if the idle speed does prove to be incorrect, the system must be checked thoroughly by an experienced mechanic using the Vauxhall test equipment until the fault is eliminated and the defective component renewed.

Idle mixture – checking and adjustment

Note: *If the CO level reading is incorrect (or if any other symptom is encountered which causes you to suspect the presence of a fault) always check first that the air cleaner element is clean, that the spark plugs are in good condition and correctly gapped, that the engine breather and vacuum hoses are clear and undamaged, that there are no leaks in the air intake trunking, the throttle body or the manifolds and that the throttle cable is correctly adjusted (see above). If the engine is running very roughly, check the compression pressures (Chapter 1) and bear in mind the possibility that one of the hydraulic tappets might be faulty, producing an incorrect valve clearance. Check also that all wiring is in good condition, with securely-fastened connectors, that the fuel filter has been renewed at the recommended intervals and that the exhaust system is entirely free of air leaks which might upset the operation of the catalytic converter.*

Fig. 12.6 Motronic M2.8 fuel injection system modified component locations – C20 XE engines (Sec 6)

1 Intake air temperature sensor
2 Hot film mass airflow meter
3 Throttle valve potentiometer
4 Ignition amplifier module
5 Camshaft phase sensor
6 DIS module

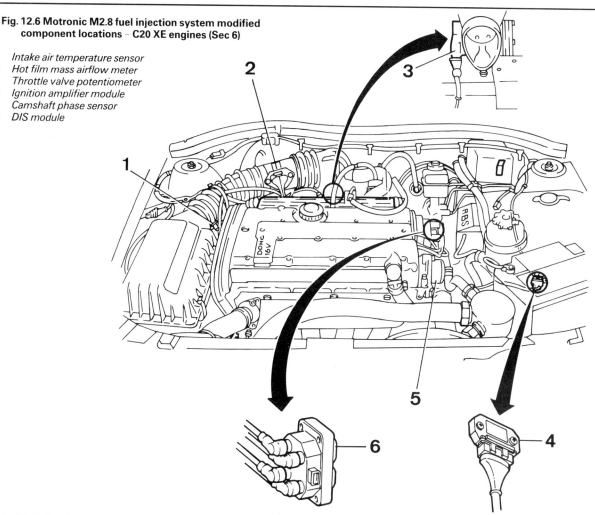

159 The idle mixture is controlled entirely by the ECU and there is no provision at all for any form of adjustment. Furthermore, accurate checking is not possible without the use of Vauxhall test equipment in conjunction with a good-quality, carefully-calibrated exhaust gas analyser.

160 While it may be possible for owners with access to such analysers to check the mixture, the results should be regarded as no more than a rough guide. If the mixture is thought to be incorrect, the vehicle should be taken to a Vauxhall dealer for checking; if the CO level exceeds the specified value the system must be checked thoroughly by an experienced mechanic using the Vauxhall test equipment until the fault is eliminated and the defective component renewed.

161 Note that the only test of the catalytic converter's efficiency is to check the level of CO in the exhaust gas, measured at the tailpipe with the engine running (with no load) at 3000 rpm. If the CO level exceeds the specified value, the Vauxhall test equipment must be used to check the entire fuel injection/ignition system. Assuming that the engine is mechanically sound, once the system has been eliminated, the fault must lie in the converter, which must be renewed.

System testing

162 Apart from basic electrical tests, there is nothing that can be done by the owner to test individual fuel system components.

163 If a fault arises, check first that it is not due to poor maintenance; check that the air cleaner filter element is clean, the spark plugs are in good condition and correctly gapped, that the engine breather hoses are clear and undamaged and that the throttle cable is correctly adjusted. If the engine is running very roughly, check the compression pressures (Chapter 1) and bear in mind the possibility that one of the hydraulic tappets might be faulty, producing an incorrect valve clearance.

164 If the fault is thought to be due to a dirty injector, it is worth trying one of the proprietary injector-cleaning treatments such as Holts Redex Injector Treatment before renewing, perhaps unnecessarily, the injector.

165 If the fault persists, check the ignition system components (as far as possible).

166 If the fault is still not eliminated, work methodically through the system, checking all fuses, wiring connectors and wiring, looking for any signs of poor connections, dampness, corrosion, dirt or other faults.

167 Once the system components have been checked for signs of obvious faults, take the vehicle to a Vauxhall dealer for the full system to be tested on the correct equipment if the fault has not been eliminated.

168 **Do not** attempt to 'test' any component, but particularly the ECU, with anything other than the correct test equipment, available at a Vauxhall dealer. If any of the wires to be checked lead to a component such as the ECU, always first unplug the relevant connector from the system components so that there is no risk of the component being damaged by the application of incorrect voltages from test equipment.

Inlet manifold – removal and refitting

169 Depressurise the fuel system (see above).

170 Remove the air box (see above).

171 Disconnect the battery negative lead.

172 Either remove the throttle body assembly (see above), or disconnect the throttle cable, wiring, fuel and vacuum hoses and pipes (see paragraphs 135 to 141 above) to allow the manifold to be removed with the throttle body.

173 Drain the cooling system (see Chapter 2).

174 Work as described in Chapter 3, Section 24, paragraph 4 onwards.

175 Refitting is the reverse of the removal procedure; renew all gaskets and seals disturbed.

Exhaust manifold – removal and refitting

176 Disconnect the battery negative lead and oxygen sensor wiring (see above), then proceed as described in Chapter 3, Section 25; take care not to damage the sensor.

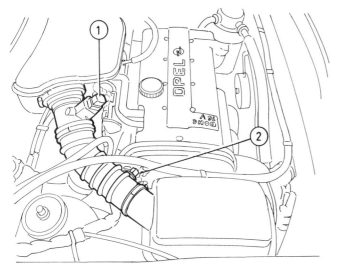

H.23993

Fig. 12.7 Hot film mass airflow meter attachments - Motronic M2.8 fuel injection system (Sec 6)

1   Hot film mass airflow meter wiring plug
2   Intake air temperature sensor wiring plug

Exhaust system and catalytic converter - checking, removal and refitting
177   Refer to Chapter 3, Section 52.

Motronic fuel injection system - all engines, 1993-on
Fuel pump - removal and refitting
178   All 1993-on Cavalier models equipped with Motronic fuel injection systems, have their fuel pump located inside the fuel tank. Removal and refitting procedures are the same as for engines with the Multec fuel injection system described previously in this Section.

Motronic M2.8 fuel injection system - C20 XE engines, 1993-on
General description
179   The Motronic M2.8 fuel injection system is a development of the M2.5 system described in detail in Chapter 3. The system is under the overall control of the Motronic engine management system (see Chapter 4, and Section 7 of this Chapter), which also controls the ignition system operation. The fuel injection side of the M2.8 system is basically the same as the earlier M2.5 system apart from the following.

(a)   *Hot Film Mass Airflow Meter - The hot wire type unit used previously is replaced on the M2.8 system by a hot film mass airflow meter. The operation is the same except that a thin, electrically heated plate rather than a wire is used. The plate is maintained at a constant temperature by electric current as the intake air mass passing over the plate trys to cool it. The current required to maintain the temperature of the plate is directly proportional to the mass flow rate of the intake air. The current is converted to a signal which is passed to the Motronic module.*
(b)   *Intake Air Temperature Sensor - The sensor is located in the hose between the hot film mass airflow meter and the air cleaner for precise monitoring of intake air temperature. Signals from the sensor are used in conjunction with other sensors to indicate the occurrence of a hot start condition. The Motronic module then interprets these signals to alter injector duration accordingly.*
(c)   *Throttle Valve Potentiometer - On the M2.8 system a throttle valve potentiometer replaces the throttle valve switch used previously.*

180   The component removal and refitting procedures that follow,

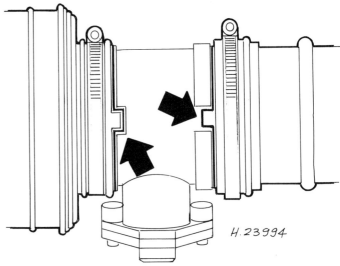

H.23994

Fig. 12.8 Correct attachment of air trunking to hot film mass airflow meter - Motronic M2.8 fuel injection system (Sec 6)

Arrows indicate air trunking to airflow meter alignment notches

relate to components that differ from the M2.5 fuel injection system. For all other fuel related procedures, refer to Chapter 3. For operations concerning the ignition side of the system, refer to Section 7 of this Chapter.

Hot film mass airflow meter - removal and refitting
181   Disconnect the battery negative lead.
182   Disconnect the wiring plug at the hot film mass airflow meter and at the intake air temperature sensor.
183   Remove the upper part of the air cleaner together with the intake air trunking and air flow meter.
184   Release the hose clamps and separate the airflow meter from the intake air trunking, noting the position of the trunking in relation to the air flow meter.
185   Refitting is a reversal of removal but ensure that the air trunking is connected to the airflow meter as shown in Fig. 12.8. Also ensure that the marks on the air trunking and air box are aligned as shown in Fig. 12.9.

Intake air temperature sensor - removal and refitting
186   Disconnect the battery negative lead.
187   Disconnect the wiring plug at the intake air temperature sensor.
188   Release the hose clips and remove the air trunking then remove the intake air temperature sensor from the trunking.
189   Refitting is a reversal of removal but ensure that the air trunking is connected to the airflow meter as shown in Fig.12.8.

Throttle valve potentiometer - removal and refitting
190   Disconnect the battery negative lead.
191   Disconnect the wiring plugs at the intake air temperature sensor and at the hot film mass airflow meter.
192   Undo and remove the bolts securing the air box to the throttle body. Remove the air box complete with air trunking.
193   Disconnect the wiring plug at the throttle valve potentiometer, then undo the two screws and withdraw the potentiometer from the throttle body.
194   Refitting is a reversal of removal.

Evaporative emissions control system - C16 NZ, C16 NZ2, X16 SZ and C18 NZ engines
195   An evaporative emissions control system is fitted to minimise the escape into the atmosphere of unburned hydrocarbons.
196   The fuel tank filler cap is sealed and a charcoal canister is mounted under the right-hand front wing to collect the petrol vapours generated in the tank when the vehicle is parked. It stores them until

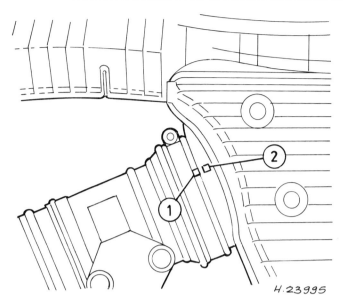

**Fig. 12.9 Air trunking and air box alignment marks (1 and 2) –
Motronic M2.8 fuel injection system (Sec 6)**

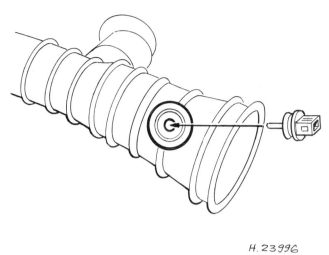

**Fig. 12.10 Removing the intake air temperature sensor from the air
trunking – Motronic M2.8 fuel injection system (Sec 6)**

they can be purged from the canister into the inlet tract to be burned by
the engine during normal combustion. The canister's control valve (on
the top of the canister) is opened by a vacuum pipe from the front of the
throttle body on C16 NZ, C16 NZ2 and C18 NZ engines, and by an
electronically activated purge valve, mounted on the camshaft housing,
on X16 SZ engines.

197   To reach the canister, remove the wheel arch liner (Chapter 10,
Section 31).

198   Note the hose and pipe connections to the canister, or label them,
to ensure that they are reconnected to their original unions, then
disconnect them (photo). Unscrew the two nuts securing the canister
mounting bracket to the vehicle body.

Evaporative emissions control system – C20 NE and C20 XE engines

199   The system is as described in the previous sub-Section, except
that the charcoal canister is purged under the control of the fuel
injection/ignition system module via the fuel tank vent valve. To ensure
that the engine runs correctly when it is cold and/or idling, and to protect
the catalytic converter from the effects of an over-rich mixture, the
valve is not opened by the module until the engine is under partial or full
load; the valve solenoid is then modulated on and off to allow the stored
vapour to pass into the inlet tract.

200   Canister removal and refitting is as described in the previous sub-
Section.

201   On C20 NE engines (all 2.0 litre models except GSi 2000), the vent
valve is mounted above the injectors for cylinders 2 and 3. To remove it,
disconnect the battery negative lead and the valve wiring plug, then
disconnect the two vent hoses having made note of their connections.
Either remove the valve from its mounting bracket, or unbolt the
bracket, as required.

202   On C20 XE engines (GSi 2000 models), the vent valve is mounted
on the left-hand end of the engine, underneath the end of the fuel
injector wiring harness housing (photo). Removal and refitting is as
described in the previous paragraph.

Exhaust gas recirculation (EGR) system – C16 NZ, C16 NZ2, X16 SZ and C18 NZ engines

203   The system reintroduces small amounts of exhaust gas into the
combustion cycle to reduce the generation of oxides of nitrogen (NOx).

204   On C16 NZ, C16 NZ2 and C18 NZ engines, the volume of exhaust
gas reintroduced is governed by manifold vacuum, through the EGR
valve mounted on the inlet manifold. When the valve is opened small
amounts of exhaust gas are allowed to enter the inlet tract, passing
through ports in the cylinder head.

205   On X16 SZ engines the EGR valve is operated by an EGR module,
mounted on the left-hand side of the engine compartment behind the

battery. This module amplifies signals received from the fuel system
ECU and operates the EGR valve electronically, providing precise control of exhaust gas recirculation under all engine conditions.

206   On C16 NZ, C16 NZ2 and C18 NZ engines, it is recommended that
the system is checked annually, by checking the movement of the
valve's diaphragm carrier plate as follows. Note that the carrier plate is
visible only through the apertures in the underside of the valve, so a
battery-operated torch and small mirror may be useful.

207   With the engine fully warmed up to normal operating temperature and idling, briefly open and close the throttle; the carrier plate
should move upwards as the manifold vacuum changes. When the
engine is idling smoothly again, press the carrier plate upwards (do this
very carefully, so that the plate is not distorted or the diaphragm
damaged); the idle speed should drop significantly (approximately 100
rpm).

208   If the valve does not respond as described, it must be cleaned.

209   Pull off the hose from the valve, then unbolt the valve and remove
it (photos). Clean away all carbon using a wire brush and a pointed tool,
but take care not to damage the valve seat. Renew the valve gasket to
prevent induction leaks.

210   Refit the valve and reconnect the hose, then recheck the system's
performance; if there is no improvement, the valve must be renewed.

211   On X16 SZ engines, Vauxhall test equipment is necessary to
check the EGR system.

Catalytic converters – general information and precautions

212   The exhaust gases from an internal combustion engine (however
efficient or well-tuned) which burns petrol consist largely (approximately 99%) of nitrogen (N_2), carbon dioxide (CO_2), oxygen (O_2), other
inert gases and water vapour (H_2O). The remaining 1% is made up of the
noxious materials which are currently seen (CO_2 apart) as the major
polluters of the environment; carbon monoxide (CO), unburned
hydrocarbons (HC), oxides of nitrogen (NOx) and some solid matter,
including a small lead content.

213   The device most commonly used to clean up vehicle exhausts is
the catalytic converter. It is fitted into the vehicle's exhaust system and
uses precious metals (platinum and palladium or rhodium) as catalysts
to speed up the reaction between the pollutants and the oxygen in the
exhaust gases, CO and HC being oxidised to form H_2O and CO_2 and (in
the three-way type of catalytic converter) NOx being reduced to N_2.
Note: *The catalytic converter is not a filter in the physical sense; its
function is to promote a chemical reaction, but it is not itself affected by
that reaction.*

214   The converter consists of an element (or 'substrate') of ceramic
honeycomb coated with a combination of precious metals in such a way
as to produce a vast surface area over which the exhaust gases must

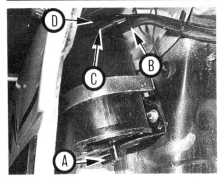

6.198 Charcoal canister – vent to atmosphere (A), vapour feed hose from filler pipe (B), vapour exhaust hose to inlet tract (C) and control valve vacuum pipe from throttle body (D)

6.202 Disconnecting the fuel tank vent valve wiring

6.209A Disconnecting the vacuum hose from the exhaust gas recirculation valve

6.209B Withdrawing the exhaust gas recirculation valve

6.215 The catalytic converter is protected by heat shields

flow. The three-way closed-loop type converter fitted to Cavalier models can remove over 90% of pollutants.

215   The catalytic converter is a reliable and simple device which needs no maintenance in itself, but there are some facts of which an owner should be aware if the converter is to function properly for its full service life (photo).

(a)   DO NOT use leaded petrol in a vehicle equipped with a catalytic converter. The lead will coat the precious metals, reducing their converting efficiency and will eventually destroy the converter.

(b)   Always keep the ignition and fuel systems well-maintained in accordance with the manufacturer's schedule (Routine maintenance and Section 3 of this Chapter). In particular, ensure that the air cleaner filter element, the fuel filter and the spark plugs are renewed at the correct interval. If the intake air/fuel mixture is allowed to become too rich due to neglect, the unburned surplus will enter and burn in the catalytic converter, overheating the element and eventually destroying the converter.

(c)   If the engine develops a misfire, do not drive the vehicle at all (or at least as little as possible) until the fault is cured. The misfire will allow unburned fuel to enter the converter, which will result in its overheating, as noted above.

(d)   The engine control indicator (the outline of an engine with a lightning symbol superimposed) will light when the ignition is switched on and the engine is started, then it will go out. While it may light briefly while the engine is running, provided it goes out again immediately and stays out, this is unimportant; if it lights and stays on while the engine is running, however, seek the advice of a Vauxhall dealer as soon as possible, since a fault has occurred in the fuel injection/ignition system which, apart from increasing fuel consumption and impairing the engine's performance, may damage the catalytic converter.

(e)   DO NOT push- or tow-start the vehicle. This will soak the catalytic converter in unburned fuel, causing it to overheat when the engine does start – see (b) above.

(f)   DO NOT switch off the ignition at high engine speeds. If the ignition is switched off at anything above idle speed, unburned

fuel will enter the (very hot) catalytic converter, with the possible risk of its igniting on the element and damaging the converter.

(g)   DO NOT use fuel or engine oil additives. These may contain substances harmful to the catalytic converter.

(h)   DO NOT continue to use the vehicle if the engine burns oil to the extent of leaving a visible trail of blue smoke. The unburned carbon deposits will clog the converter passages and reduce its efficiency; in severe cases the element will overheat.

(i)   Remember that the catalytic converter operates at very high temperatures – hence the heat shields on the vehicle's underbody – and the casing will become hot enough to ignite combustible materials which brush against it. DO NOT, therefore, park the vehicle in dry undergrowth, over long grass or over piles of dead leaves.

(j)   Remember that the catalytic converter is FRAGILE. Do not strike it with tools during servicing work, take great care when working on the exhaust system, ensure that the converter is well clear of any jacks or other lifting gear used to raise the vehicle, and do not drive the vehicle over rough ground, road humps, etc, in such a way as to 'ground' the exhaust system.

(k)   In some cases, particularly when the vehicle is new and/or is used for stop/start driving, a sulphurous smell (like that of rotten eggs) may be noticed from the exhaust. This is common to many catalytic converter-equipped vehicles and seems to be due to the small amount of sulphur found in some petrols reacting with hydrogen in the exhaust to produce hydrogen sulphide (H_2S) gas; while this gas is toxic, it is not produced in sufficient amounts to be a problem. Once the vehicle has covered a few thousand miles the problem should disappear. In the meanwhile a change of driving style or of the brand of petrol used may effect a solution.

(l)   The catalytic converter, used on a well-maintained and well-driven vehicle, should last for between 50 000 and 100 000 miles. From this point on, careful checks should be made at all specified service intervals of the CO level to ensure that the converter is still operating efficiently. If the converter is no longer effective it must be renewed.

7   Ignition and engine management systems

Testing 'Hall-effect' distributors – general

1   When testing any ignition system which uses a 'Hall-effect' generator in the distributor (models with 16 SV, 20 XE or C20 XE engines), note that such generators **cannot** be tested and no test equipment which uses its own power source (eg, an ohmmeter) may be connected to the distributor, or the 'Hall-effect' generator will be damaged.

Ignition amplifier module – 16 SV, 18 SV, 20 XE and C20 XE engines

2   With reference to Chapter 4, note that the MSTS and Motronic M2.5 systems also incorporate a separate ignition amplifier module which transmits amplified signals from the main system module to trigger the HT pulse from the ignition coil.

3   The module is mounted on the ignition coil's bracket/baseplate; removal and refitting is therefore as described in Chapter 4, Section 12, paragraphs 1 to 5.

Ignition coding plug – 20 XE and C20 XE engines

4   With reference to Chapter 4, Section 11 (paragraph 3 onwards), note that, on GSi 2000 models the ignition coding plug found in the location described is **not** an octane coding plug (although its method of operation is similar) and must **not** be altered from its factory setting. Its purpose is to ensure that the Motronic module uses the correct information, pre-programmed (or 'mapped') into its memory, to enable the vehicle to comply with the relevant national noise and exhaust emission legislation.

5   On these models, the knock sensor circuit allows the Motronic module to compensate for differences in the octane value of the petrol used, without the need for manual intervention. Remember, however, that all catalytic converter-equipped vehicles **must** use unleaded petrol **only**. This means that these models can use any grade of unleaded petrol on sale in the UK without the need for adjustment.

Checking ignition timing – 16 SV engine, 1990-on

6   The basic adjustment coding plug described in Chapter 4 is no longer fitted; for accurate checking, special Vauxhall test equipment must be used which causes the MSTS module to adopt its basic adjustment mode.

7   In the case of the private owner without access to such equipment, note that while it is possible to check and adjust the ignition timing (it may even be possible to arrive at a setting accurate enough for the engine to run smoothly), accurate results cannot be guaranteed. Owners are therefore advised to have this work carried out by a suitably-equipped Vauxhall dealer; at the very least, make the initial setting yourself and then have it checked as soon as possible.

8   If you do attempt to check the ignition timing yourself, note that the fixed reference mark is now an extended line embossed on the timing belt lower outer cover.

Ignition system – C16 NZ, C16 NZ2 and C18 NZ engines

Note: *Before starting work on any part of the ignition system, read carefully the notes and warnings given in Chapter 4.*

General description – C16 NZ and C16 NZ2 engines

9   The ignition system is fully electronic in operation and incorporates the Electronic Control Unit (ECU) mounted in the driver's footwell, a distributor (driven off the camshaft left-hand end and incorporating the amplifier module) as well as the octane coding plug, the spark plugs, HT leads, ignition HT coil and associated wiring.

10   The ECU controls both the ignition system and the fuel injection system, integrating the two in a complete engine management system; refer to Section 6 of this Chapter for information on any part of the system not given here.

11   As far as the ignition system is concerned, the ECU receives information in the form of electrical impulses or signals from the distributor (giving it the engine speed and crankshaft position), from the coolant temperature sensor (giving it the engine temperature) and from the manifold absolute pressure sensor (giving it the load on the engine). In addition, the ECU receives input from the octane coding plug (to provide ignition timing appropriate to the grade of fuel used) and from, where fitted, the automatic transmission control unit (to smooth gear-changing by retarding the ignition as changes are made).

12   All these signals are compared by the ECU with set values pre-programmed (mapped) into its memory; based on this information, the

ECU selects the ignition timing appropriate to those values and controls the ignition HT coil via the amplifier module accordingly.

13   The system is so sensitive that, at idle speed, the ignition timing may be constantly changing; this should be remembered if trying to check the ignition timing.

General description – C18 NZ engine

14   The system fitted to these engines is similar to that described above, except that the amplifier module is separate, and the ECU determines engine speed and crankshaft position using a sensor mounted in the right-hand front end of the engine's cylinder block; this registers with a 58-toothed disc mounted on the crankshaft so that the gap left by the missing two teeth provides a reference point, so enabling the ECU to recognise TDC.

15   Note that this simplifies the distributor's function, which is merely to distribute the HT pulse to the appropriate spark plug; it has no effect whatsoever on the ignition timing.

Spark plugs and HT leads – inspection and renewal

16   Refer to Chapter 4, Section 4.

Ignition coil – description and testing

17   Refer to Chapter 4, Section 5.

Ignition coil – removal and refitting

18   Refer to Chapter 4, Section 6.

Distributor cap and rotor arm – removal and refitting

19   Refer to Chapter 4, Section 7.

Distributor – removal and refitting

20   Refer to Chapter 4, Section 8 (photo).

Distributor – dismantling, inspection and reassembly – C16 NZ and C16 NZ2 engines

21   At the time of writing, no information was available concerning distributor overhaul and the availability of replacement parts; owners are advised to seek the advice of a Vauxhall dealer.

Checking ignition timing – C16 NZ and C16 NZ2 engines

22   As far as this procedure is concerned, these engines are the same as 1990-on 16 SV units (refer to paragraphs 6 to 8 above); owners are advised to have this work carried out by a suitably-equipped Vauxhall dealer. At the very least, make the initial setting yourself (Chapter 4, Section 10) and then have it checked as soon as possible.

Checking ignition timing – C18 NZ engine

23   The ignition timing is controlled by the ECU using the crankshaft speed/position sensor as reference; the timing can be checked only by a Vauxhall dealer on the special test equipment and no adjustment is possible.

7.20 Disconnecting the distributor wiring on the C16 NZ engine

7.27 Ignition amplifier module is part of distributor on the C16 NZ engine

Ignition timing – adjustment for use with unleaded petrol

24   In common with all other vehicles equipped with catalytic converters, Cavaliers fitted with C16 NZ, C16 NZ2 or C18 NZ engines **must use only** unleaded petrol.

25   These models are also fitted with the octane coding plugs described in Chapter 4 and are set at the factory for use with 95 RON fuel; this means the (Premium-grade) unleaded petrol most often found on sale in UK filling stations. No adjustment, therefore, is required to allow them to run on unleaded petrol. Super- or Superplus-grade unleaded petrol may also be used if required, with no ill-effects save that on the driver's wallet.

26   Note that, on these models, the octane coding plug's other setting is '91'; this is for use with 91 RON Regular or Normal-grade petrol not yet available in the UK. If you are taking the vehicle abroad, seek the advice of a Vauxhall dealer or of one of the motoring organisations to ensure that the coding plug is correctly set for the grades of petrol that you are likely to encounter.

Amplifier module – removal and refitting

27   On C16 NZ and C16 NZ2 engines, the amplifier module is mounted in the distributor; at the time of writing, it appears that the module can be renewed only as part of the distributor and no information is available concerning removal or refitting. Owners are advised to seek the advice of a Vauxhall dealer (photo).

28   On C18 NZ engines, the module is a separate unit mounted on the ignition coil's bracket/baseplate. Removal and refitting is as described in Chapter 4, Section 12, paragraphs 1 to 5.

Electronic Control Unit (ECU) – removal and refitting

29   See Section 6 of this Chapter.

Crankshaft speed/position sensor – removal and refitting – C18 NZ engine

30   Refer to Chapter 4, Section 13, paragraphs 13 to 19.

Ignition system – testing – general

Note: *Refer to the notes and warnings given in Chapter 4 before starting work. Always switch off the ignition before disconnecting or connecting any component and when using a multi-meter to check resistances. Any voltmeter or multi-meter used to test ignition system components must have an impedance of 10 meg ohms or greater.*

31   Electronic ignition system components are normally very reliable; most faults are far more likely to be due to loose or dirty connections, or to 'tracking' of HT voltage due to dirt, dampness or damaged insulation than to component failure. **Always** check all wiring thoroughly before condemning an electrical component and work methodically to eliminate all other possibilities before deciding that a particular component is faulty.

32   The old practice of checking for a spark by holding the live end of an HT lead a short distance away from the engine is not recommended;

not only is there a high risk of a powerful electric shock, but the ignition coil or amplifier module will be damaged. Similarly, **never** try to 'diagnose' misfires by pulling off one HT lead at a time. Note also that the ECU is at risk if the system is triggered with an open (ie, not properly earthed) HT circuit; ECUs are very expensive to replace, so take care!

33   If you are in any doubt as to your skill and ability to test an ignition system component or if you do not have the required equipment, take the vehicle to a suitably-equipped Vauxhall dealer; it is better to pay the labour charges involved in having the vehicle checked by an expert than to risk damage to the system or to yourself.

Testing – engine will not start

34   If the engine either will not turn over at all, or only turns very slowly, check the battery and starter motor. Connect a voltmeter across the battery terminals (meter positive probe to battery positive terminal), disconnect the ignition coil HT lead from the distributor cap and earth it, then note the voltage reading obtained while turning over the engine on the starter for (no more than) ten seconds. If the reading obtained is less than approximately 9.5 volts, check the battery, battery connections, starter motor and charging system (Chapter 11).

35   If the engine turns over at normal speed but will not start, check the HT circuit by connecting a timing light and turning the engine over on the starter motor; if the light flashes, voltage is reaching the spark plugs, so these should be checked first. If the light does not flash, check the HT leads themselves followed by the distributor cap, carbon brush and rotor arm (Chapter 4).

36   If there is a spark, check the fuel system for faults as far as possible (Section 6).

37   If there is still no spark, check the voltage at the ignition coil ' + ' or '15' terminal; it should be the same as the battery voltage (ie, at least 11.7 volts). If the voltage at the coil is more than 1 volt less than that at the battery, check the connections back through the ignition switch to the battery and its earth until the fault is found. Note, however, that the ECU controls the coil's feed; **do not** attempt to 'test' the ECU with anything other than the correct test equipment, which will be available only to a Vauxhall dealer. If any of the wires are to be checked which lead to the ECU, always first unplug the relevant connector from the ECU so that there is no risk of the ECU being damaged by the application of incorrect voltages from test equipment.

38   If the feed to the ignition coil is sound, check the coil's primary and secondary windings (Chapter 4, Section 5). Renew the coil if faulty, but check the condition of the LT connections themselves before doing so, to ensure that the fault is not due to dirty or poorly-fastened connectors.

39   If the ignition coil is in good condition, the fault may be within the amplifier module or the distributor on the C16 NZ and C16 NZ2 engines, or the amplifier or the crankshaft speed/position sensor on the C18 NZ engine. A quick check of these components can be made by connecting a low-wattage bulb across the ignition coil's (disconnected) LT terminals; if the bulb flickers or flashes when the engine is turned over, the amplifier and distributor (C16 NZ and C16 NZ2 engines), or amplifier and crankshaft speed/position sensor (C18 NZ engine), are sound.

40   If this is the case, the entire LT circuit is in good condition; the fault, if it lies in the ignition system, must be in the HT circuit components. These should be checked carefully, as outlined above.

41   If the indicator or bulb does not flash, the fault is in either the amplifier or the distributor (C16 NZ and C16 NZ2 engines), or the amplifier or crankshaft speed/position sensor (C18 NZ engine); owners should note, however, that by far the commonest cause of 'failure' of either of these is a poor connection, either between the components themselves or in the LT circuit wiring connections. If such a fault is suspected, the vehicle must be taken to a suitably-equipped Vauxhall dealer for testing; no information is available to eliminate these components by other means.

Testing – engine misfires

42   An irregular misfire suggests either a loose connection or intermittent fault on the primary circuit, or an HT fault on the coil side of the rotor arm.

43   With the ignition switched off, check carefully through the system ensuring that all connections are clean and securely fastened. If the equipment is available, check the LT circuit as described in paragraphs 37 to 41 above.

44   Check that the HT coil, the distributor cap and the HT leads are clean and dry. Check the leads themselves and the spark plugs (by substitution, if necessary), then check the distributor cap, carbon brush and rotor arm (Chapter 4).

45   Regular misfiring is almost certainly due to a fault in the distributor cap, HT leads or spark plugs. Use a timing light (paragraph 35 above) to check whether HT voltage is present at all leads.
46   If HT voltage is not present on any particular lead, the fault will be in that lead or in the distributor cap. If HT is present on all leads, the fault will be in the spark plugs; check and renew them if there is any doubt about their condition.
47   If no HT voltage is present, check the ignition coil; its secondary windings may be breaking down under load.
48   If all components have been checked for signs of obvious faults such as dirty or poorly-fastened connections, dampness, or 'tracking' and have been tested as far as is possible, but the system is still thought to be faulty, the vehicle must be taken to a Vauxhall dealer for testing on the correct equipment.

Ignition system – X16 SZ and C20 XE (1993-on) engines

49   On all X16 SZ engines, and on C20 XE (dohc) engines from 1993-on, a DIS (Direct Ignition System) module is used in place of the distributor and coil. On the X16 SZ engine the DIS module is attached to the camshaft housing in the position normally occupied by the distributor. On the C20 XE engine, a camshaft phase sensor is attached to the cylinder head at the non-driven end of the exhaust camshaft, in the position normally occupied by the distributor. The DIS module is attached, via a bracket, to the cylinder head at the non-driven end of the inlet camshaft.
50   The DIS module consists of two ignition coils and an electronic control module housed in a cast casing. Each ignition coil supplies two spark plugs with HT voltage: One spark is provided in a cylinder with its piston on the compression stroke, and one spark is provided to a cylinder with its piston on the exhaust stroke. This means that a 'wasted spark' is supplied to one cylinder during each ignition cycle, but this has no detrimental effect. This system has the advantage that there are no moving parts (therefore there is no wear), and the system is largely maintenance-free.
51   On X16 SZ engines the remainder of the ignition system functions as described earlier for the C18 NZ engine. The operation of the remainder of the ignition system on the C20 XE engine is as described for GSi 2000 models in Chapter 4.
52   The following procedures describe those operations which vary from procedures covered elsewhere in this manual.

Spark plugs and HT leads – inspection and renewal

53   Refer to Chapter 4, Section 4.

DIS module – removal and refitting

54   Disconnect the battery negative lead.
55   Disconnect the HT leads from the module terminals noting their locations to ensure correct refitting. Note that the HT lead cylinder numbers are stamped on the module, adjacent to each terminal, and similar numbers appear on each HT lead.

56   Disconnect the module wiring plug.
57   On X16 SZ engines, undo the three screws and remove the module from the camshaft housing. On C20 XE engines, undo the bolts securing the DIS module mounting bracket to the cylinder head and remove the module and bracket. Note the installed position of DIS module on its mounting bracket, undo the four securing screws and separate the module from the bracket.
58   Refitting is a reversal of removal.

Camshaft phase sensor – removal and refitting – C20 XE engine

59   The camshaft phase sensor is mounted on the end of the cylinder head in the position normally occupied by the distributor.
60   Disconnect the battery negative lead.
61   Disconnect the wiring plug then undo the phase sensor securing bolts.
62   Withdraw the phase sensor from the cylinder head, then undo the bolt and remove the phase sensor disc from the end of the camshaft.
63   Refitting is a reversal of removal.

Checking ignition timing

64   The ignition timing is controlled by the Multec or Motronic ECU using the crankshaft speed/position sensor as reference. The timing can only be checked by a Vauxhall dealer using special test equipment and no adjustment is possible.

Electronic control unit (ECU) – removal and refitting

65   Refer to Section 6 of this Chapter for X16 SZ engines, and to Chapter 4 for C20 XE engines.

Crankshaft speed/position sensor – removal and refitting

66   Refer to Chapter 4, Section 13, paragraphs 13 to 19.

Ignition system – testing – general

67   Due to the need for specialist test equipment and the delicate nature of some of the electronic circuitry, testing of the system must be left to a suitably equipped Vauxhall dealer.

---

8   Clutch

Removal and refitting – C18 NZ, C20 NE, C20 XE engines, 1992-on

Due to the size of the 'pot'-type flywheel fitted to these engines, the clutch components can no longer be overhauled with the gearbox in place in the vehicle. To renew the clutch, first remove the gearbox (Chapter 6), then proceed as described in Chapter 5; ignore all references to carrying out the task with the gearbox still in the vehicle.

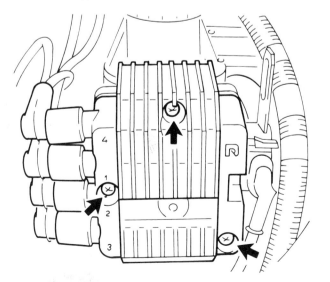

Fig. 12.11 DIS module retaining screw locations (arrowed) – X16 SZ engines (Sec 7)

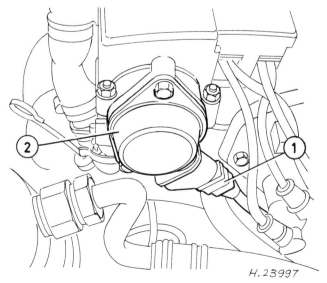

H.23997

Fig. 12.12 Camshaft phase sensor wiring plug (1) and phase sensor (2) – C20 XE engines (Sec 7)

9   Manual gearbox

Gear selector linkage – adjustment

1   On all 1.6, 1.8 and 2.0 litre models from 1993-on, the gear selector linkage adjustment procedure has been revised to enable a more precise setting to be achieved. The revised procedure is essentially the same as that described in Chapter 6, Section 3, but note the following.

2   The clamp securing the gear selector tube to the linkage has been repositioned slightly and is now more easily accessible from below the car.

3   With the gearchange lever in its correct position for adjustment (in neutral, in the 1st/2nd gear plane) a second 4.5 mm (0.18 in) diameter twist drill should be inserted into the holes in the gearchange lever and lever base provided for this purpose. This means that the lever can be positively locked for adjustment, and an assistant will not be required to hold the lever in the correct position.

4   The remainder of the procedure is unchanged but note that it is not necessary to check the lever free play, as described, between the lever hook and the lever base stop.

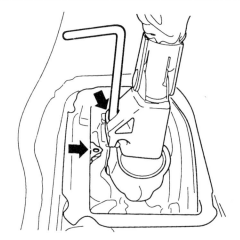

Fig. 12.13 Locking tool (twist drill) inserted in gear change lever and lever base alignment holes (arrowed) (Sec 9)

10   Automatic transmission

General description

1   The transmission comprises a hydrodynamic torque converter and a pair of epicyclic gearsets which are controlled hydraulically by multiplate clutches and a servo-assisted band brake to produce three forward ratios with an overdrive fourth, and reverse. The final drive differential is similar to that described in Chapter 6. Fluid temperature is controlled by a fluid cooler built into the radiator.

2   Gearchanging is electrically-controlled, with a mechanical lock-up on third and fourth gears, and three driving 'modes' selectable according to need or preference.

3   Gear shift points are varied, according to 'mode' and gear selected, after information concerning transmission fluid temperature and input-versus-output speed, throttle pedal and valve position, and engine coolant temperature has been fed, from various sensors, to the electronic control unit (located behind the glove compartment or behind the driver's footwell side trim panel).

4   The unit controls the transmission through four solenoids regulating hydraulic pressure to either select gears (solenoids 1 and 2), to control converter clutch lock-up (solenoid 3), or to control main fluid pressure according to throttle valve opening angle, thus altering shift quality (solenoid 4).

5   The control unit also retards the ignition timing during gearchanges to improve shift quality, has a self-diagnosis function which flashes a warning lamp in the event of system failure, and can institute a backup operation (using predetermined values which will enable the car to be driven for repair). It can also cut out the air conditioning (where fitted), depending on vehicle speed and the load on the engine, if air conditioning operation will affect the vehicle's driving performance.

6   Modes (selected from position 'D') are as follows:

7   'Economy' mode, switched on automatically when the engine is started (the facia warning lamp will light on switching on the ignition and starting, then go out), uses all four gears including overdrive/4th with gearchanges being made at low engine speeds for maximum smoothness and economy.

8   'Sport' mode, switched on by pressing the button 'S' in the top of the selector lever (the facia warning lamp will light), makes gearchanges at higher engine speeds and locks out (electrically) 4th gear. Switched off (to return to 'Economy') by pressing the button again, by switching the ignition on and off, by driving with the backup activated, or by switching to 'Winter' mode.

9   'Winter' mode (also known as the 'Starting-off Aid' or 'Start-Up Assistance'), switched on by pressing the button with a 'snowflake' symbol at the base of the selector lever, locks out 1st and 2nd gears so that the vehicle can start off smoothly (in 3rd gear) on slippery roads. Switched off (to return to 'Economy') by pressing the button again or by moving the selector lever to another position, by switching the ignition on and off or by holding the accelerator pedal fully depressed (to the kick-down position) for more than two seconds, by driving with the backup activated, or by exceeding 50 mph (80 km/h).

10   The transmission and its control system is complex but, if not abused, will prove reliable and durable. Repair and overhaul of the transmission itself are beyond the scope of many dealers, let alone the home mechanic, while the electrical control system can **only** be checked thoroughly using special Vauxhall test equipment. This Section is therefore restricted to those servicing procedures that can be carried out by the home mechanic. Any fault diagnosis, overhaul or repair work must be entrusted only to a suitably-equipped Vauxhall dealer or to an automatic transmission specialist who has the facilities and skill required to undertake such work.

Note: *If the vehicle has to be towed and the transmission is operational, it can be towed FORWARDS ONLY (transmission in position 'N') on all four wheels for a distance of no more than 62 miles (100 km), at speeds of no more than 50 mph (80 km/h). If the transmission is thought to be faulty, or if either the distance or the towing speed is likely to exceed the maximum stated, the vehicle MUST be towed with the front wheels off the ground. Refer also to 'Jacking, towing and wheel changing' at the front of this manual.*

Routine maintenance

11   At the intervals given in Section 3 of this Chapter, check the fluid level and change it (where necessary), as described in the relevant sub-Section below.

12   Carry out a thorough road test, ensuring that all gearchanges occur smoothly, without snatching and with no increase in engine speed between changes. Also check the operation of the kickdown. Check that all gear positions can be engaged at the appropriate movement of the selector lever and with the vehicle at rest, check that the operation of the parking pawl in position 'P' prevents it from being moved. Ensure that the starter motor will work only with the selector lever in positions 'P' or 'N', and that the reversing lamps light only when position 'R' is selected.

13   The manufacturer's schedule calls for a regular check of the electrical control system using the special Vauxhall test equipment; owners will have to have this check carried out by a Vauxhall dealer.

14   Periodically inspect the transmission casing, checking all joint surfaces and seals for signs of fluid leaks. If any are found, the fault must be rectified immediately.

15   Check also that the transmission breather hose (under the battery mounting bracket) is clear and not blocked, kinked or twisted.

Checking the fluid level

Note: *The transmission fluid level can be checked either when it is cold (only below 35°C (100°F) outside temperature) or when it is fully warmed up to normal operating temperature (after driving for a distance of approximately 12 miles/20 km). Since the fluid level must be checked with the engine running, ensure that the vehicle is parked on level ground with the handbrake firmly applied before leaving the driver's seat, and be careful to keep loose clothing, long hair, etc, well clear of hot or moving components when working under the bonnet.*

Transmission cold

16   Park the vehicle on level ground and apply the handbrake firmly. With the engine running at no more than idle speed and your foot firmly

Fig. 12.14 Cutaway through AF 14/20 automatic transmission (Sec 10)

1 Torque converter
2 Converter clutch
3 Fluid pump
4 Multi-plate brake B1
5 Multi-plate brake B2
6 Valve body assembly
7 Multi-plate brake B3
8 Multi-plate clutch C1
9 Multi-plate clutch C2
10 Free-wheel mechanism F1
11 Free-wheel mechanism F2
12 Free-wheel mechanism F3
13 Multi-plate clutch C3
14 Brake band B4
15 Final drive differential

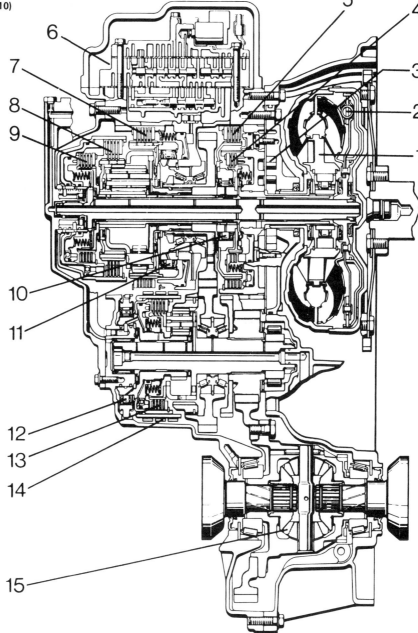

on the brake pedal, move the selector lever through all positions, ending in position 'P'. Allow the engine to idle for one minute, then check the level within two minutes.

17   With the engine still idling and position 'P' still selected, open the bonnet and withdraw the transmission dipstick from the filler tube located in the front of the transmission casing, at the left-hand end of the engine.

18   Note the fluid's condition (see below), then wipe clean the dipstick using a clean, non-fluffy rag, insert it fully back into the tube and withdraw it again.

19   The level should be up to the 'MAX' mark on the ' + 20°C' side of the dipstick.

20   If topping-up is required, switch off the ignition and add only good quality fluid of the specified type through the filler tube. If significant amounts of fluid are being lost (carefully note the amounts being added, and how often), check the transmission for leaks and either repair the fault or take the vehicle to a Vauxhall dealer for attention.

21   When the level is correct, ensure that the dipstick is pressed firmly into the filler tube.

Transmission fully warmed up
22   Work exactly as described above, but take the level reading from the ' + 80°C' side of the dipstick. In this case, the level must be between the dipstick 'MAX' and 'MIN' marks.

Checking the fluid's condition
23   Whenever the fluid level is checked, examine the condition of the fluid and compare its colour, smell and texture with that of new fluid.

24   If the fluid is dark, almost black, and smells burnt, it is possible that the transmission friction material is worn or disintegrating. The vehicle should be taken to a Vauxhall dealer or automatic transmission specialist for immediate attention.

25   If the fluid is milky, this is due to the presence of emulsified droplets of water. This may be caused either by condensation after a prolonged period of short journeys or by the entry of water through the dipstick/filler tube or breather. If the fluid does not revert to its normal appearance after a long journey it must be renewed or advice should be sought from a Vauxhall dealer or automatic transmission specialist.

26   If the fluid is varnish-like (ie light to dark brown and tacky) it has

**Fig. 12.15 Electrical control system of AF
14/20 automatic transmission – version with
Motronic fuel injection/ignition system
(Sec 10)**

1   *Distributor*
2   *Transmission fluid temperature sensor*
3   *Starter inhibitor switch*
4   *Connection for pressure-regulating
    solenoids*
5   *Transmission input speed sensor*
6   *Transmission output speed sensor*
7   *Speedometer cable connection*
8   *Throttle position sensor*
9   *Motronic module*
10 *Automatic transmission ECU*
11 *'Winter' mode button*
12 *'Economy/Sport' mode button*
13 *Kickdown switch*
14 *Brake lamp switch*

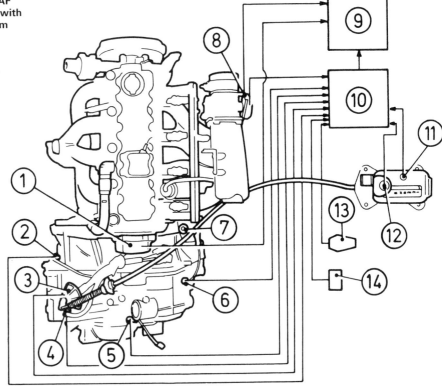

oxidised due to overheating or to over- or under-filling. If renewal of the fluid does not cure the problem, the vehicle should be taken to a Vauxhall dealer or automatic transmission specialist for immediate attention.

27   If at any time on checking the fluid level or on draining the fluid, particles of dirt, metal chips or other foreign matter are found in the fluid, the vehicle **must** be taken to a Vauxhall dealer or automatic transmission specialist for immediate attention; it may be necessary to strip, clean and reassemble at least the valve body, if not the complete transmission, to rectify any fault.

Changing the fluid
28   This operation is much quicker and more efficient if the vehicle is first taken on a journey of sufficient length to warm the engine/transmission up to normal operating temperature.
29   Park the vehicle on level ground, switch off the ignition, and apply the handbrake firmly. For improved access, jack up the front of the car and support it securely on axle stands (see *Jacking, towing and wheel changing*).
30   Withdraw the dipstick, then position a suitable container under the drain plug at the rear right-hand side of the transmission, below the driveshaft, and unscrew the plug.
31   Allow the fluid to drain completely into the container. If the fluid is hot, take precautions against scalding.
32   When the fluid has finished draining, clean the drain plug threads and those of the transmission casing, fit a new sealing washer and refit the drain plug, tightening it to the specified torque wrench setting. Where applicable, lower the vehicle to the ground.
33   Refill the transmission with the specified amount and type of fluid, then check the fluid level (see above).
34   Dispose of the old fluid safely; **do not** pour it down a drain.

Kickdown switch – adjustment
35   Remove the air box, air cleaner or intake ducting, as required, to see the throttle valve (Chapter 3, or Section 6 of this Chapter).
36   Have an assistant depress the throttle pedal until it contacts the switch on the vehicle's floor. Check that the throttle valve is fully open at this point, and that the pedal acts squarely on the centre of the switch button.
37   If the contact point requires adjustment, it must be made by

resetting the throttle pedal stop screw and then adjusting the cable (Chapter 3, or Section 6 of this Chapter) as required; if necessary, set the cable so that only the barest minimum of free play is left.
38   If the throttle pedal does not contact the switch button correctly, check that the pedal pivot bushes are in good condition and either reposition the switch on its retainer or bend the pedal carefully.

Kickdown switch – removal and refitting
39   Loosen the carpet retainer located under the throttle pedal and raise the carpet. Disconnect the switch wiring (the cable runs to the centre of the instrument panel) and unclip the switch from its retainer.
40   On refitting, guide the switch through the carpet aperture to reconnect the wiring; press the switch onto the retainer as far as the stop, then check its adjustment (see above).

Starter inhibitor switch – removal and refitting
41   With the handbrake firmly applied, select position 'N'.
42   Disconnect the battery negative lead.
43   Unscrew its retaining nut and withdraw the dipstick/filler tube.

**Fig. 12.16 When checking fluid level, ensure side of dipstick used
corresponds with fluid temperature – see text (Sec 10)**

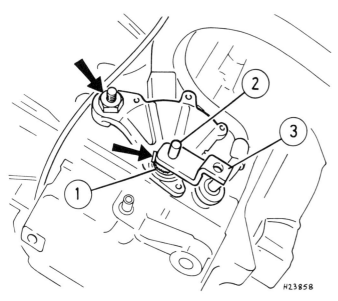

Fig. 12.17 Starter inhibitor switch details (Sec 10)

1   Large nut   3   Actuating lever
2   Selector lever shaft   Arrows indicate switch mountings

44   Prising off the retaining clamp and withdrawing the washer, disconnect the selector cable from the actuating lever on the transmission.
45   Disconnect the switch wiring at its connector plugs.
46   Using pliers to counterhold the shaft, unscrew the nut securing the actuating lever to the selector lever shaft; prise off the locking plate, and unscrew the large nut and washer securing the switch to the shaft.
47   Unscrew the fastener securing the switch to the transmission.
48   On refitting, ensure that the selector lever shaft is in position 'N' (the third detent from the front). Lower the switch onto the shaft and rotate it until the shaft's flattened surface is aligned with the outline on the switch housing, then secure the switch by tightening the switch/filler tube fastener to the specified torque wrench setting.
49   Next tighten (very carefully, noting its specified torque wrench setting) the large nut retaining the switch on the selector lever shaft; do not forget the washer. Refit the locking plate to secure the nut.
50   When tightening the actuating lever on the selector lever shaft, use pliers to counterhold the shaft; again tighten the nut to its specified torque wrench setting.
51   When refitting the dipstick/filler tube, always renew the sealing O-ring, greasing it to aid installation, and tighten the nut to its specified torque wrench setting.
52   Connect the switch wiring and the selector cable, then check the cable adjustment (see below).

Selector cable – adjustment
53   With an assistant operating the selector lever, check that the actuating lever on the transmission moves into the appropriate detent. Detent 'P' is at the front and marked, as is position 'N'; none of the other detents are marked. Check also that the parking pawl actually locks the roadwheels in this position.
54   If adjustment is required, check carefully that the selector lever is in position 'P', then unclip the cover (two clips on each side) from the top of the centre console and rotate it to one side. Using a box spanner through the aperture exposed, slacken the cable clamp bolt.
55   Returning to the engine compartment, press the transmission actuating lever fully forwards and to the right (ie, towards the battery holder), ensuring that it meets the stop.
56   Have the assistant hold the actuating lever in position while the cable clamp bolt is tightened, to its specified torque wrench setting.
57   Refit the cover and recheck the selector operation.

Selector cable – removal and refitting
58   With the handbrake firmly applied, select position 'P'.
59   Disconnect the battery negative lead.
60   Prising off the retaining clamp and withdrawing the washer,

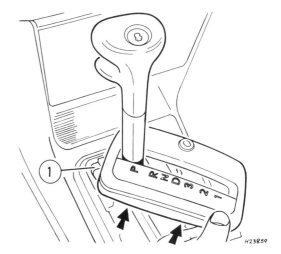

Fig. 12.18 Selector cable adjustment – release clips (arrows) to allow centre console top cover to be moved aside (Sec 10)

1   Box spanner can be inserted through aperture to slacken cable clamp bolt

disconnect the selector cable from the actuating lever on the transmission.
61   Unscrew the retaining nuts and withdraw the cable mounting bracket from the transmission.
62   Working in the passenger compartment, unclip the cover (two clips on each side) from the top of the centre console and remove the ashtray assembly, then withdraw the centre console rear section (Chapter 10, Section 38) until the selector lever cover can be removed. Check that the handbrake is still applied and move the selector lever to position '2'.
63   Slacken the cable clamp bolt and unscrew the cable locknut (items 1 and 2 in Fig. 12.19), then withdraw the cable from the centre console and pull it into the engine compartment, prising out the bulkhead grommet to do so.
64   Refitting is the reverse of the removal procedure; adjust the cable (see above) on completion.

Selector lever – removal and refitting
65   Disconnect the rear end (only) of the selector cable as described in paragraphs 58 to 59 and 62 to 63 above, then disconnect the wiring from the driving mode switches and unplug the illuminating bulb's socket from the panel.

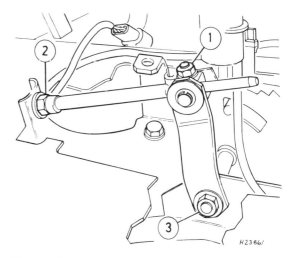

Fig. 12.19 Selector cable attachment at lever end (Sec 10)

1   Cable clamp bolt   3   Lever pivot nut
2   Cable locknut

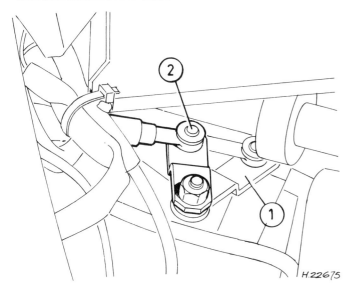

Fig. 12.20 Transmission actuating lever position 'P' (1) and position 'N' (2) (Sec 10)

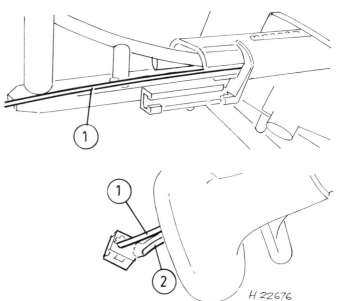

Fig. 12.21 Using welding rod (1) to press 'Economy/Sport' mode button out of selector lever – mark wires (2) before unsoldering, to ensure correct reconnection (Sec 10)

66   Unscrew the nut securing the lever to its pivot (item 3, Fig. 12.19) and withdraw the lever, manoeuvring it sideways to do so.
67   Refitting is the reverse of the removal procedure; adjust the cable (see above) on completion.

Selector lever console – removal and refitting
68   Remove the selector lever (see above).
69   Unscrew the four hexagon-headed screws securing the console to the floor panel and withdraw it.
70   Refitting is the reverse of the removal procedure; tighten the bolts to their specified torque wrench setting.

Driving 'mode' switches – removal and refitting
'Economy/Sport' mode button
71   Disconnect the battery negative lead.
72   Remove the selector lever (see above).
73   Using a length of welding rod or similar inserted into the lever's lower end, press out the switch.
74   Having made a careful note of the wiring connections, unsolder the wires from the switch.
75   On refitting, solder the wires onto the new switch's terminals, ensuring that they are correctly reconnected, then press the switch into the lever.
76   Refit the selector lever, as described above.

'Winter' mode button
77   Disconnect the battery negative lead.
78   Unclip the cover (two clips on each side) from the top of the centre console and move it to one side until the switch wiring plug can be disconnected.
79   Prise the switch out of the cover, taking care not to mark the finish.
80   Refitting is the reverse of the removal procedure.

Electronic Control Unit (ECU) – removal and refitting
81   The automatic transmission ECU is located either in the driver's footwell or behind the glovebox, depending on model and year.
82   Disconnect the battery negative lead.
83   To find the unit, first remove the driver's footwell side trim panel, and the lower facia and footwell trim panels (Chapter 10, Sections 36 and 37). If the unit cannot be seen, refit these panels and remove the glovebox assembly (Chapter 10, Section 37); the unit will be fastened to the underside of the facia top surface.
84   Release the unit from its mountings and withdraw it until the wiring plug's locking lugs can be released and the plug can be disconnected.
85   Refitting is a reversal of the removal procedure, ensuring that the wiring plug is correctly reconnected and that the unit is located securely.

Selector illumination bulb – renewal
86   Disconnect the battery negative lead.
87   Unclip the cover (two clips on each side) from the top of the centre console and move it to one side until the bulbholder can be unplugged.
88   The bulb is a push fit in the bulbholder.
89   Refitting is the reverse of the removal procedure.

Speedometer drive – removal and refitting
90   Tracing the speedometer cable down to the transmission, disconnect the cable (Chapter 1) and remove the drivegear as described in Chapter 6, Section 10, paragraph 3.
91   On refitting, always renew the sealing O-ring, and coat the splines with molybdenum disulphide grease. Tighten the retaining plate bolt to its specified torque wrench setting (Chapter 6).

Fluid cooler hoses and pipes – general
92   Check the hoses at regular intervals and renew them if there is the slightest doubt about their condition.
93   Always take note of the pipe and hose connections before disturbing them; also note the hose routing.
94   To minimise the loss of fluid, and to prevent the entry of dirt into the system, clamp (using self-locking pliers or proprietary hose-clamping tools) the hoses before disconnecting them, then slacken their securing clamps; work each hose in turn off its union and swiftly plug or cap the hose and union. If plugs are used, take care to remove them on refitting.
95   Discard the clamp(s) and fit new ones as a matter of course whenever a hose is disconnected.
96   Refit the hoses, ensuring that they are connected to their original unions and route them as noted on removal so that they are not kinked or twisted, and so that the movement of the engine on its mountings will not cause the hoses to stretch or rub against other components.
97   Align the new hose clamps so that they cannot foul any other component and tighten them securely.
98   Always renew the sealing washers if the banjo union bolts are disturbed, and tighten the bolts to their specified torque wrench setting. Be particularly careful when tightening the bolt or union into the plastic radiator/cooler body.

Differential bearing oil seals – renewal
99   Drain the transmission fluid (see above).
100   Work as described in Chapter 6, Section 7, using transmission fluid to lubricate the new seals on installation.
101   Refill the transmission with clean fluid and check the fluid level, as described above, on completion.

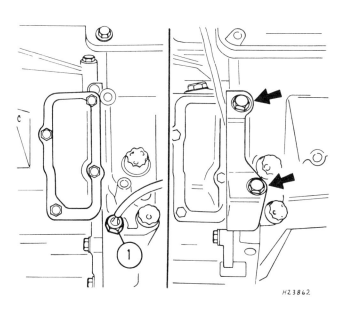

Fig. 12.22 Unbolt sensor cover (arrows) to unscrew fluid temperature sensor (1) (Sec 10)

Fluid temperature sensor – removal and refitting

102 Disconnect the battery negative lead.
103 Unbolt the sensor cover from the front of the transmission.
104 Disconnect the sensor wiring at its connector plug.
105 Unscrew the sensor; swiftly plug the aperture to prevent the loss of fluid and the entry of dirt.
106 Refitting is the reverse of the removal procedure. Always renew the sensor sealing ring; tighten the sensor (if possible) and the cover bolts to their specified torque wrench settings.

Input/output speed sensors – removal and refitting

107 The speed sensors are fitted into the transmission casing's upper surface. They are similar in appearance and can be identified by their wiring connectors; the input speed sensor is the unit closer to the transmission's left-hand end.
108 Disconnect the battery negative lead.
109 Disconnect the sensor wiring at its connector plug.
110 Unscrew the sensor's securing (Torx-type) screw and withdraw the sensor; swiftly plug the aperture to prevent the loss of fluid and the entry of dirt.
111 Refitting is the reverse of the removal procedure; always renew the sensor sealing ring and tighten the securing screw to its specified torque wrench setting.

Transmission – removal and refitting

Note: *If the transmission is being removed for repair, ensure first that the fault is genuinely in the transmission, rather than in the control system (see 'Fault diagnosis' below). The following procedure, being essentially the same as the removal/refitting of a manual gearbox, is based on that given in Chapter 6, Section 8; before starting work, read that Section as well as the following text, and ensure that you have all the tools and facilities required.*

112 Disconnect the battery negative lead.
113 Drain the transmission fluid (see above).
114 Disconnect the transmission wiring by unplugging the five connector plugs from the various switches, solenoids and sensors, then release the wiring from any clips or ties securing it to the vehicle.
115 Disconnect the selector cable from the transmission actuating lever, then either unbolt the cable bracket or release the cable from the bracket. Secure the cable clear of the transmission.
116 Releasing it from any clips or ties securing it, withdraw the transmission breather hose from under the battery bracket.
117 Disconnect the oxygen sensor wiring (where fitted).
118 Disconnect the speedometer drive cable.
119 Working as described above, disconnect the fluid cooler hoses (either at the transmission or at the radiator, as convenient).

120 Support the engine/transmission, remove the front suspension subframe and disconnect the driveshafts, working as described in Chapter 6, Section 8, paragraphs 7 to 10, referring where necessary to Chapters 7 and 9.
121 Unbolt the transmission bellhousing cover plate (three bolts), then use chalk or a felt-tip pen to mark the relationship of the torque converter to the flexplate before unbolting the torque converter. Applying a spanner to the crankshaft pulley/sprocket bolt, rotate the crankshaft until the first bolt appears, then use a screwdriver or similar to jam the flexplate ring gear teeth to prevent it from rotating as the bolt is unscrewed. Unscrew each of the three bolts in turn and discard them.
122 Working as described in Chapter 6, Section 8, paragraphs 17 to 21 (ignoring paragraph 19), remove the transmission. **Note:** *If the torque converter is removed (even partially) from the transmission, a considerable amount of the fluid inside it will leak out. To prevent this, when prising the transmission off its locating dowels and removing it, be careful to keep the torque converter pressed firmly into the transmission. If the transmission is to be removed for some time, retain the torque converter by bolting a strip of metal across the bellhousing mating surface.*
123 Refitting is the reverse of the removal procedure, noting the following points.

(a) *If any fluid was spilled from the torque converter, be careful to refill it as much as possible. Wipe clean the converter's spigot to prevent damage to the transmission's input shaft oil seal as the converter is installed, and ensure that the converter engages correctly on the fluid pump shaft.*

(b) *If the transmission has been renewed, be careful to flush clean the radiator fluid cooler passages. Vauxhall recommend the use of low-pressure compressed air, but this will require great care to avoid deforming the radiator.*

(c) *Be very careful to ensure that all components are scrupulously clean, to avoid the risk of dirt getting into the system.*

(d) *Use an M10 x 1.25 bottoming tap to clean the threads in the torque converter's threaded bosses and ensure that new bolts are available for reassembly.*

(e) *Check the threads of the engine/transmission left-hand mounting (Chapter 6, Section 8, paragraph 22) and ensure that new bolts are available for reassembly.*

(f) *Tighten all nuts and bolts to their specified torque wrench settings.*

(g) *When tightening the torque converter-to-flexplate bolts to their specified torque wrench settings, a commercially-available adaptor will be required (see Fig. 12.23).*

(h) *Adjust the selector cable on completion, and refill the transmission with fluid (see above).*

Fig. 12.23 Commercially-available torque wrench adaptor being used to tighten torque converter bolts (Sec 10)

Fault diagnosis – automatic transmission

124   In the event of a fault occurring in the transmission or its control system which cannot be cured by attention to the fluid level, or to any of the minor adjustments given in this Section, the vehicle must be taken to a Vauxhall dealer or automatic transmission specialist for checking.

125   **Do not** remove the transmission from the vehicle until professional fault diagnosis has been carried out.

---

11   Driveshafts

Intermediate shaft – all GSi 2000 models and all other 1991-on 2.0 litre models

Removal

1   First remove the right-hand outboard driveshaft as described in Chapter 7, Section 3.

2   Unbolt the support bearing's bracket from the cylinder block.

3   Placing a suitable container to catch the oil that will be released, pull the intermediate shaft out of the differential, and plug the aperture to minimise oil loss and to prevent the entry of dirt.

Overhaul

Note: *A press may be required to remove and refit the intermediate shaft support bearing.*

4   Turn the bearing by hand, feeling for signs of roughness, notchy movement or of free play. If there is any doubt about the condition of the bearing it must be renewed.

5   Unscrew the two bolts securing the flange to the bearing bracket; withdraw the bracket.

6   Remove the snap-ring from the intermediate shaft's outboard end, followed by the O-ring and the larger (bearing retaining) circlip.

7   Remove the bearing and flange from the shaft. If the bearing is a very tight fit, use a hydraulic puller or a press; be careful to support the bearing's inner race during removal if the bearing is to be re-used.

8   Support the flange on two wooden blocks placed on the work surface and drive out the bearing.

9   To fit the new bearing, heat it evenly if necessary using a hair dryer, paint-stripping heat gun or similar until it can be pressed onto the shaft. Using a hammer and a tubular drift which bears only on the bearing's inner race, tap the bearing fully onto the shaft until it seats against the shaft shoulder. Fit the flange over the other end of the shaft and onto the bearing outer race, then refit the retaining circlip, followed by a new O-ring and a new snap-ring.

10   Refit the bracket to the shaft assembly.

11   To ensure correct alignment, do not tighten the flange bolts until the shaft is refitted to the differential and the bearing bracket is correctly secured to the cylinder block (see below). When this has been done, apply a few drops of thread-locking compound (Vauxhall Part No 15 10

11.12 Right-hand driveshaft support bearing is bolted to the rear of the cylinder block

177, or equivalent) to their threads, and tighten the bolts to the specified torque wrench setting.

Refitting

12   Refitting is the reverse of the removal procedure, noting the following points (photo).

(a)   *Grease the shaft splines to prevent damage to the seal lip as the shaft is refitted.*

(b)   *Offer up the bracket to the cylinder block and tighten the bolt to its specified torque wrench setting.*

(c)   *If the support bearing assembly was dismantled, refit the flange to the bracket and tighten the two bolts (see above).*

(d)   *Refit the outboard driveshaft (Chapter 7, Section 3).*

---

12   Braking system

Front brakes – 1992-on 1.4, 1.6 and 1.8 models

1   These models are fitted with ventilated brake discs and the type of brake caliper described in Chapter 8 for 2.0 litre models. Ensure that the appropriate sub-Section of Chapter 8 is used when servicing the front brakes of one of these later models.

Rear drum brakes – 1992-on models

Brake shoe modification

2   The brake shoe lower anchorage has been modified so that it is now rectangular, necessitating modified brake shoes and a modified lower return spring; refer to Fig. 12.24 for details.

3   Overhaul procedures are as described in Chapter 8 (noting the different return spring routing), but note that the later type of shoes and return spring must not be used on earlier models with the original type of anchorage.

Wheel cylinder modification

4   The later wheel cylinders are fitted with L-shaped piston seals (see Fig. 12.25).

5   Ensure that the correct repair kit is obtained when overhauling a wheel cylinder, as the early and later components are not interchangeable.

6   Note that the later type of wheel cylinder can be used to replace the early type as a complete unit.

Brake pressure-proportioning valves – 1992-on models

7   The calibration of the valves has been altered to compensate for the other braking system modifications; if either is to be renewed, ensure that only the correct type (stamped on the valve body) is fitted.

Routing of braking system pipes

8   When checking the condition of the system's pipes and/or hoses, carefully check that they do not foul other components such as the power steering gear pipes (where applicable), so that there is no risk of the pipes chafing. If necessary use clips or ties to secure braking system pipes and hoses well clear of other components.

ABS-2EH system – 1992-on models

9   All models up to 1991 that were fitted with ABS used the ABS-2E system. From 1992 onwards an ABS-2EH was fitted, which can be identified by the location of the electronic control module; this is bolted to the hydraulic modulator.

10   The main differences between the two systems are in the electrical components and circuits, the most obvious of these being omission of the surge arrester relay on the 2EH system.

11   No further information is available at the time of writing; if the system is thought to be faulty the vehicle should be taken to a Vauxhall dealer for checking on special diagnostic equipment.

---

13   Suspension and steering

Front suspension lower arm – modifications

1   If any sign of damage or distortion of the front suspension lower arm in the region of the front pivot bolt is evident, a modified and strengthened arm is available from Vauxhall dealers.

2   The modified lower arm, which can be identified by the strengthen-

OLD   NEW

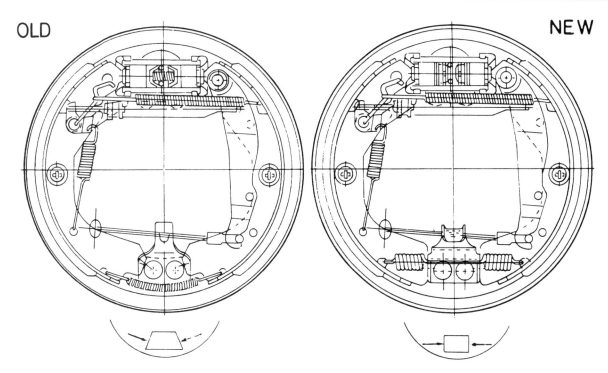

Fig. 12.24 Modified rear brake shoe lower anchorage – 1992-on models (Sec 12)

OLD   NEW

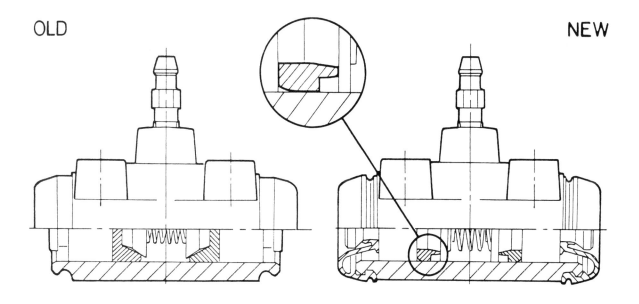

Fig. 12.25 Modified rear wheel cylinders – 1992-on models (Sec 12)

ing flange along the seam on the forward facing side of the arm, will be fitted in production from mid-1993 on.

3   The modified lower arm is fully interchangeable with the earlier version, but note that the torque wrench settings for the front mounting bolt have altered (see Specifications). Note also that if the modified arm is replacing an earlier version which incorporates a damper weight, the damper weight **should not** be fitted to the modified lower arm.

Rear hub and wheel bearings (later models equipped with ABS) – removal and refitting

Note: *The hub unit securing nuts must be renewed on refitting*

4   From 1993-on, all Cavalier models equipped with an Anti-lock Braking System (ABS) are fitted with a maintenance-free rear hub and wheel bearing assembly.

5   On these models, the stub axle, hub and wheel bearing are all one assembly. No adjustment is required as the bearing is sealed for life.

6   To remove the rear hub, remove the wheel trim, where applicable, then loosen the relevant rear roadwheel bolts and chock the front wheels. Jack up the rear of the vehicle and support on axle stands positioned under the body side members. Remove the roadwheel.

7   Remove the rear disc caliper as described in Chapter 8, Section 9. The caliper can be suspended out of the way, using wire or string, to avoid the need to disconnect the hydraulic fluid pipe.

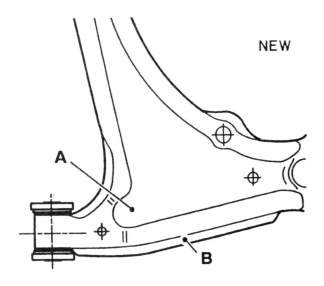

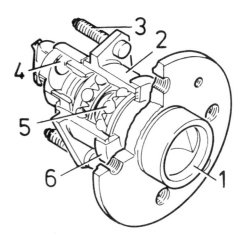

Fig. 12.27 Maintenance-free rear hub and wheel bearing assembly –
later models with ABS (Sec 13)

1	Hub	4	Dust cap with integral
2	Stub axle		ABS wheel speed sensor
3	Threaded bolt	5	Bearings
		6	Oil seal

Manual steering gear – overhaul

17   With reference to Chapter 9, Section 38 and Fig. 9.21, note that some steering gear assemblies have no provision for rack damper slipper adjustment. Specifically, items 8 and 9 (at least) have been replaced by a sealing plug that is peened in place (photo).
18   No further information was available at the time of writing; if steering gear overhaul appears to be necessary, seek the advice of a Vauxhall dealer. It may be that such assemblies have to be renewed if worn or faulty.

Power steering pump drivebelt (ribbed V-belt type) – removal, refitting and tensioning

19   Later models equipped with power steering are fitted with a single ribbed V-belt type drivebelt to drive both the alternator and power steering pump. Removal and refitting procedures are contained in Section 15 of this Chapter.

Steering column (air-bag equipped models) – precautions

20   When removing and refitting the steering column on models equipped with an air bag, read the contents of the following Sections carefully and follow the instructions implicitly.

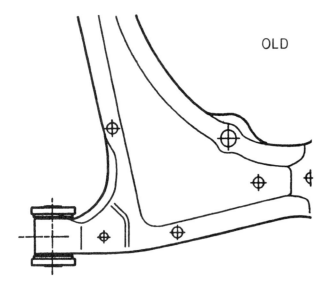

Fig. 12.26 Modified front suspension lower arm (Sec 13)

A   Modified inner   B   Strengthening flange along seam
    profile

8   Disconnect the return spring from the handbrake shoe lever and the brake backplate.
9   Undo the retaining screw and lift off the brake disc.
10   Disconnect the ABS sensor wiring plug at the rear of the hub assembly.
11   Unscrew the four securing nuts and withdraw the hub assembly complete with backplate. Detach the handbrake cable from the handbrake shoe lever as the hub assembly is withdrawn.
12   Refitting is a reversal of removal, bearing in mind the following points.
13   New hub assembly securing nuts must be used, and they must be tightened in the three stages given in the Specifications. Note that a socket extension and a universal joint may be required to enable the use of a torque angle gauge.
14   Make sure that the handbrake cable and return spring are correctly reconnected.
15   With the brake disc in place, refit the disc caliper as described in Chapter 8.
16   Before refitting the roadwheel and lowering the vehicle to the ground, check the handbrake cable adjustment as described in Chapter 8.

13.17 Steering gear rack damper slipper adjustment is replaced by sealing plug on some models

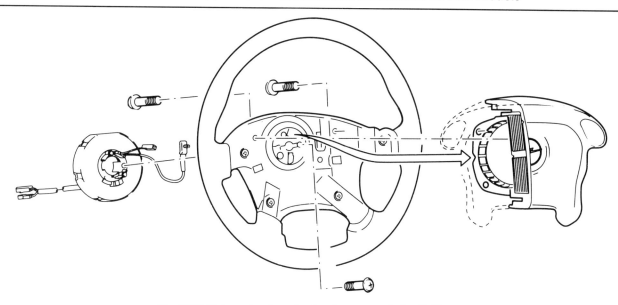

Fig. 12.28 Air bag, steering wheel and contact unit details (Sec 13)

21   The procedures for removing and refitting the steering column are as described in Chapter 9, but note that two additional bracing struts, to cater for the additional weight of the air bag assembly, are bolted between the column and centre floor tunnel.

Air bag – general
22   All 1993 Cavalier models are available with an air bag which is designed to prevent serious chest and head injuries to the driver during an accident. A similar bag for the front seat passenger is also available on certain models. Sensors in the centre of the car measure the vehicle deceleration rate and pass these signals to a microprocessor. This unit analyses the sensor data and compares the information with pre-programmed values stored in its memory, triggering the airbag if the deceleration is severe. The air bag is inflated in 50 milliseconds by a gas generator which forces the bag out of the module cover in the centre of the steering wheel.
23   No repairs are possible on the air bag unit or its associated parts. The contents of the following Sections are confined to removal and refitting of the air bag, purely for access to other non-related components.
24   Should a fault be suspected on the air bag unit, indicated by the warning light on the instrument panel, or if the car has been involved in an accident, however minor, consult a Vauxhall dealer immediately. **Do not** attempt to dismantle any of the air bag components or carry out any work whatsoever, other than the procedures described in the following Sections.
25   At the time of writing no information was available on the passenger's air bag, and the following instructions apply only to the unit as fitted to the driver's side.

Air bag unit – removal and refitting
Warning: *Handle the air bag unit with extreme care as a precaution against personal injury, and always hold it with the cover facing away from the body. If in doubt concerning any proposed work involving the air bag unit or its control circuitry, consult a Vauxhall dealer or other qualified specialist. On power steering models in particular, it will be advantageous to jack up the front of the car and support it on axle stands placed under the body side members, so that the steering wheel can be turned more easily.*

26   Disconnect the battery negative lead and cover the battery terminal to prevent accidental reconnection. **Warning**: *Before proceeding, wait a minimum of 15 minutes as a precaution against accidental firing of the air bag unit. This period ensures that any stored energy in the back-up capacitor is dissipated.*
27   With the steering wheel positioned in the straight-ahead position, turn it 90° clockwise so that the left-hand spoke is accessible from the rear.

28   Using a suitable Torx type socket, undo the first air bag retaining bolt from the rear of the steering wheel.
29   Turn the steering wheel 180° anticlockwise so that the right-hand spoke is accessible from the rear.
30   Undo the second retaining bolt from the rear of the steering wheel.
31   Return the steering wheel to the straight-ahead position then carefully lift up the air bag unit.
32   Disconnect the wiring plug and remove the air bag from the car. **Warning**: *Stand the unit with the cover uppermost and do not expose it to heat sources in excess of 100°C. Do not attempt to open or repair the air bag unit, or apply any voltage to it. Do not use any air bag unit which is visibly damaged or has been tampered with.*
33   Refitting is a reversal of removal.

Steering wheel (with air bag) – removal and refitting
Note: *A suitable two-legged puller will be required for this operation*

34   Remove the air bag unit as described previously.
35   Ensure that the steering wheel is in the straight-ahead position.
36   From the centre of the steering wheel unscrew the two screws securing the air bag contact unit.
37   Using a screwdriver, prise back the tabs on the lockwasher securing the steering wheel retaining nut.
38   Unscrew and remove the steering wheel retaining nut and the lockwasher.
39   Make alignment marks between the steering wheel and the end of the column shaft.
40   A suitably small two-legged puller must now be fitted to the steering wheel in order to pull it from the column shaft. Note that the steering wheel is a very tight fit on the shaft (see also Chapter 9 Section 30).
41   Once the steering wheel has been released from the column shaft, disconnect the horn wiring and remove the steering wheel.
42   Commence refitting by positioning the steering wheel on the column shaft, ensuring that the marks made on removal are aligned, and that the wheel correctly engages with the air bag contact unit. It may be necessary to tap the steering wheel fully home on the column shaft using a suitable metal tube and socket.
43   Reconnect the horn wiring.
44   Refit the lockwasher and the steering wheel retaining nut, and tighten the nut to the specified torque (see Chapter 9). Bend up the lockwasher to secure.
45   Refit the two screws securing the air bag contact unit.
46   Refit the air bag as described previously.

Air bag contact unit – removal and refitting
47   Remove the air bag and the steering wheel as described previously.

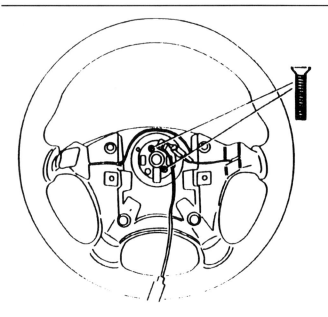

Fig. 12.29 Air bag contact unit retaining screws (Sec 13)

48   Remove the steering column upper and lower shrouds, referring to Chapter 9, Section 33 if necessary.
49   Disconnect the contact unit wiring plug below the steering column and withdraw the contact unit from the column, noting its fitted position as a guide to reassembly.
50   Before refitting the contact unit, ensure that the front wheels are in the straight-ahead position.
51   Place the contact unit on the column in the correct position as noted during removal.
52   Route the wiring harness under the steering column lock/ignition switch and connect the wiring plug.
53   Refit the steering column shrouds.
54   Refit the steering wheel and air bag as described previously.

Air bag control unit – removal and refitting
55   Disconnect the battery negative lead and cover the battery terminal to prevent accidental reconnection. **Warning:** *Before proceeding, wait a minimum of 15 minutes as a precaution against accidental firing of the air bag unit. This period ensures that any stored energy in the back-up capacitor is dissipated.*
56   Remove the centre console rear section as described in Chapter 10, Section 38.
57   Disconnect the control unit wiring plug, then undo the three nuts and remove the unit from the car.
58   Refitting is a reversal of removal.

---

14   Bodywork

Mechanical seat belt tensioners – general
1   All 1993-on Cavalier models are equipped with mechanical front seat belt tensioners which automatically tighten the front seat belts in the event of a head-on collision. The mechanically operated device ensures that the seat belt remains close to the body, thus preventing the wearer from sliding out, under the belt, during impact.
2   The tensioner system consists of a powerful preloaded spring, contained in a cylinder, which is released in the event of severe impact. The spring pulls back the seat belt by means of a bowden cable and fulcrum mechanism attached to the belt stalk, mounted on the seat frame.
3   The tensioner assembly, fitted to the underside of the front seat, is maintenance free and, once triggered, must be replaced as a complete unit.
4   Due to the specialist safety related nature of the seat belt tensioner system, replacement must be entrusted to a suitably equipped Vauxhall dealer.

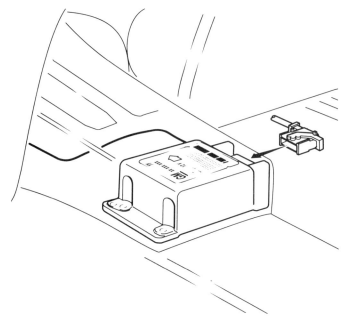

Fig. 12.30 Air bag control unit details (Sec 13)

Front seats (with seat belt tensioners) – removal and refitting

Warning: *The seat belt tensioners fitted to the front seat assemblies may cause injury if triggered inadvertently. Before carrying out any work on the front seats, the safety fork must be inserted into the seat belt tensioner cylinder, to prevent the possibility of the tensioner being triggered (see paragraphs 7 and 8 below). Seats should always be transported and installed with the safety fork in place. If a seat is to be*

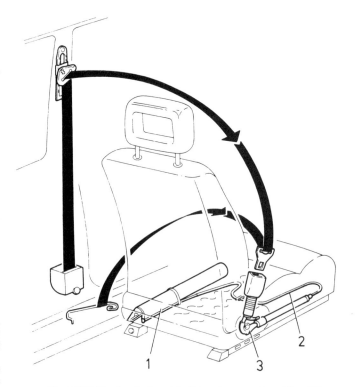

Fig. 12.31 Mechanical seat belt tensioner system (Sec 14)

1 *Spring*	3 *Fulcrum mechanism*
2 *Bowden cable*	

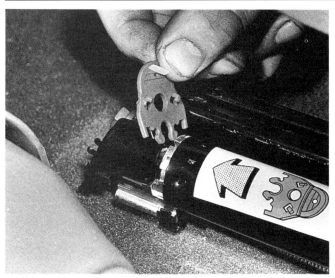

14.8 Inserting the safety fork into the aperture in the seat belt tensioner spring cylinder

14.9 Front outer seat rail securing bolt (1) – note seat belt tensioner safety fork (2) inserted in the spring cylinder

disposed of, the tensioner must be triggered before the seat is removed from the vehicle, by inserting the safety fork, and striking the tensioner cylinder sharply with a hammer. If the tensioner has been triggered due to a sudden impact or accident, the unit must be renewed, as it cannot be reset. Due to safety considerations, tensioner renewal should be entrusted to a Vauxhall dealer.

5   Remove the single securing screw from the front edge of the outer seat rail trim, release the rear retaining lug and remove the trim rearwards.
6   Unclip the trim from the rear edge of the inner seat rail.
7   Locate the plastic safety fork for the seat belt tensioner, which is usually taped to the outside of the tensioner spring cylinder.
8   Insert the fork into the aperture provided at the rear of the spring cylinder, ensuring that the fork engages securely (photo).
9   Remove the four bolts which secure the seat rails to the floor, then withdraw the seat complete with rails (photo). Recover the washers and backplates.
10   Seek the advice of a Vauxhall dealer if there is any doubt about the condition of the seat belt tensioner assembly.
11   Refitting is a reversal of removal. Note that the manufacturers recommend the use of new bolts to secure the seat rails to the floor. Tighten the bolts to the specified torque wrench settings (see Specifications) in the order – rear inner, front inner, rear outer, front outer.

Radiator grille panel (1993-on models) – removal and refitting
12   Later models are fitted with a modified radiator grille panel as part of the styling 'facelift' revisions.
13   The method of removal and refitting for all later models is as described in Chapter 10, Section 29, for the GSi 2000 models.

Bumpers (GSi 2000 models, and all 1993-on models) – removal and refitting
Front bumper
14   The procedures are basically the same as described in Chapter 10, Section 28, apart from the following additions.
15   Remove the radiator grille panel as described above.
16   Undo the retaining bolts or screws, and remove the water deflector.

Rear bumper
17   The procedures for rear bumper removal are also basically the same as described in Chapter 10, Section 28, apart from the following additions.
18   On GSi 2000 models, the bumper securing nuts are accessible from underneath the vehicle.
19   Where fitted, remove the special locking rivets, one each side, securing the bumper to the wheel arch.
20   Additional clips may be present on the underside of the bumper which must also be removed.

15   Electrical system

Routing of wiring harness – general
1   Whenever the occasion arises, carefully check the routing of the wiring harness, ensuring that it is correctly secured by the clips or ties provided so that it cannot chafe against other components. Carefully check points such as the clutch cable bracket, clutch housing and harness support bracket, the inlet manifold, the horn mounting bracket, the starter motor terminals, and the rear bumper and number plate lamp.
2   If evidence is found of the harness having chafed against other components, repair the damage and ensure that the harness is secured or protected so that the problem cannot occur again.

Automatic transmission switches – removal and refitting
3   Refer to Section 10 of this Chapter.

Heated front seats – general
4   Heating pads are fitted to the front seats of some models. Before attempting to remove a seat so equipped, disconnect the battery and the leads from the heating pad.

Windscreen washer nozzles – 1991-on models
5   The nozzles on all later models are fitted with twin jets.
6   On some later models, the nozzles are heated; the circuit is fed via fuse 29 and is live whenever the ignition is switched on. Current is regulated by a Positive Temperature Coefficient (PTC) resistor which takes outside temperature into account.

Windscreen wiper arms – 1992-on models
7   While these models are fitted with slightly modified windscreen wiper arms, removal and refitting procedures remain as described in Chapter 11 (photo).

Rear courtesy lamps
8   Some later models are fitted with courtesy lamps for the rear seat passengers. Bulb renewal, and the removal and refitting of the lamps and their switches, is as described in Chapter 11 for the front seat lamps.

Headlamp aim adjustment – general
9   All 1992-on models are fitted with the headlamp aim adjustment system, operated through the facia-mounted switch (photo).

Headlamp dim-dip system – general information
10   The system (where fitted) is governed by the dim-dip control unit mounted either behind and above the glovebox (early models), or behind the main fuse panel (later models).
11   The control unit uses the oil pressure warning lamp circuit to ensure that, when the engine is running and the sidelamps are switched

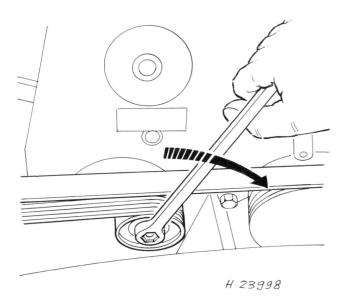

H·23998

Fig. 12.32 Releasing the ribbed V-belt type alternator drivebelt automatic tensioning roller (Sec 15)

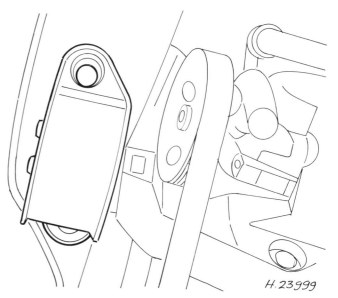

H·23999

Fig. 12.33 Right-hand engine mounting-to-body attachments (Sec 15)

on, reduced current is fed to the headlamp dipped-beam circuits; this lights the headlamps with approximately one-sixth of their normal power so that the vehicle cannot be driven using sidelamps alone.

12   To find the dim-dip control unit, open the main fuse panel covering flap and unclip it from its bottom and top mountings (Chapter 11, Section 16), then use a torch to see whether the unit is fastened to the plastic bracket behind the facia and fuse panel. The unit is usually rectangular, of black plastic, and can be identified by the colours of the five wires leading to it (see applicable wiring diagram).

13   If the unit can be seen, remove the driver's side lower facia and footwell trim panels (Chapter 10, Section 37), then unscrew the four retaining screws and lower the plastic bracket until the control unit can be detached.

14   If the unit cannot be seen, remove the glovebox assembly (Chapter 10); the unit will be fastened to the underside of the facia top surface.

15   Refitting is the reverse of the removal procedure.

Alternator drivebelt (ribbed V-belt type) – removal, refitting and tensioning

16   Later models equipped with power steering are fitted with a ribbed V-belt type drivebelt in conjunction with an automatic tensioning

roller. Once the belt is installed, no further adjustment is necessary as the correct tension is maintained by the automatic tensioning roller. Removal and refitting procedures are as follows.

17   For improved access, remove the air cleaner assembly and air intake trunking.

18   If the original drivebelt is to be refitted, mark the rotational direction on the belt with chalk.

19   Using a suitable spanner or socket on the automatic tensioning roller hexagon, turn the tensioning roller clockwise (as viewed from the right-hand side of the car) and hold it in this position. With the drivebelt tension released, slip the drivebelt off the pulleys, then allow the tensioner to return to its original position.

20   Support the engine under the sump with a suitable jack and interposed block of wood.

21   From under the car, unbolt the right-hand engine mounting block from the body.

22   Lower the engine support jack just sufficiently to allow the drivebelt to be withdrawn from between the mounting block and the body.

23   Slip the new drivebelt between the mounting block and body then raise the engine, by means of the jack, to its original position.

24   Clean the threads of the mounting block retaining bolts, apply

15.7 Windscreen wiper arms – 1992-on models

15.9 Removing the headlamp aim adjustment switch – 1992-on models

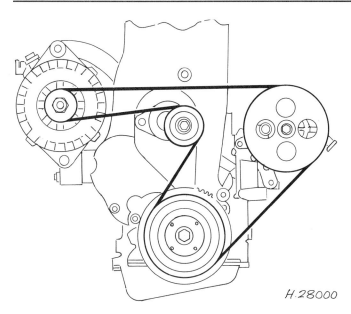

Fig. 12.34 Correct routing of the ribbed V-belt (Sec 15)

locking fluid, and refit the bolts. Tighten the bolts to the specified torque (see Chapter 1).

25   Rotate the automatic tensioner roller anticlockwise and route the drivebelt around the pulleys as shown in Fig. 12.34. With the belt correctly positioned, release the tensioner which will automatically apply the correct tension to the belt.

26   On completion, refit the air cleaner assembly and the air intake trunking.

Delco-Remy 'compact' series alternator – removal and refitting

27   In conjunction with the introduction of the ribbed V-belt type drivebelt with automatic tensioner, new 'compact' type alternators have been progressively introduced to the Cavalier range. Due to the revised method of drivebelt adjustment, these alternators are rigidly mounted to the engine; removal and refitting procedures are as follows.

28   Disconnect the battery negative lead.

29   Remove the air intake trunking and, if necessary for improved access, the air cleaner assembly.

30   Mark the rotational direction on the alternator drivebelt with chalk.

31   Using a suitable spanner or socket on the automatic tensioning roller hexagon, turn the tensioning roller clockwise (as viewed from the right-hand side of the car) and hold it in this position. With the drivebelt tension released, slip the drivebelt off the alternator pulley, then allow the tensioner to return to its original position.

32   Disconnect the electrical cable connections at the rear of the alternator.

33   Undo and remove the alternator lower mounting bolt, and slacken both upper bolts that secure the alternator mounting brackets to the engine.

34   Undo and remove both bolts that secure the alternator to its mounting brackets, noting the location of the different length bolts. Swing the brackets clear and remove the alternator from the engine.

35   Refitting is a reversal of removal. Tighten the mounting bolts to the specified torque, and refit the drivebelt as described earlier in this Section.

Fig. 12.35 Sectional view of the Delco-Remy 'compact' series alternator (Sec 15)

1   Drive end bracket
2   Stator
3   Rotor
4   Slip rings
5   Fan
6   Rectifier

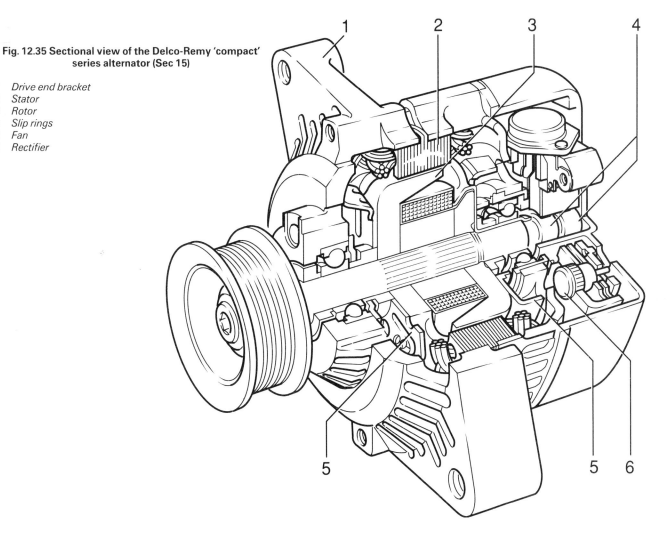

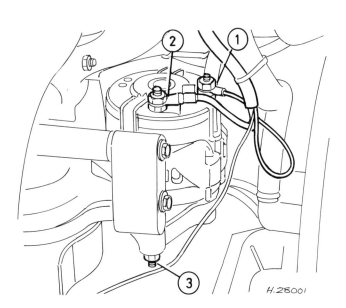

Fig. 12.36 Alternator lower attachments (Sec 15)

1   Cable connection   3   Lower mounting bolt
2   Cable connection

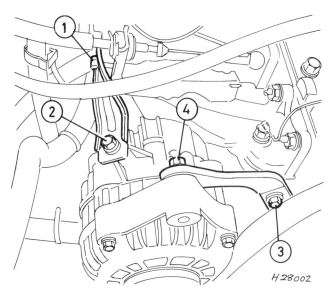

Fig. 12.37 Alternator upper attachments (Sec 15)

1   Side mounting bracket-   3   Front mounting bracket-
    to-engine retaining bolt   to-engine retaining bolt
2   Side mounting bracket-   4   Front mounting bracket-
    to-engine retaining bolt   to-alternator retaining bolt

Delco-Remy 'compact' series alternator brushes – removal, inspection and refitting

36   Remove the alternator as described previously.
37   Remove the plastic cover from the rear of the alternator.
38   Undo the two bolts securing the brush holder to the rear of the alternator, noting that one of the bolts also secures the suppression capacitor.
39   Remove the suppression capacitor then withdraw the brush holder, noting the flat plug on the side.
40   Check that the brushes move freely in their holder and that the brush lengths are within the limits given in the Specifications (see Chapter 11). If any doubt exists regarding the condition of the brushes, the best policy is to renew them.
41   Check the condition of the slip rings, and if necessary clean with a rag or very fine glass paper.
42   Refitting the brushes is a reversal of removal.

Anti-theft alarm system components – removal and refitting

Control unit
43   Disconnect the battery negative lead.
44   Remove the driver's side lower facia panel as described in Chapter 10, Section 37.
45   If necessary, remove the footwell side trim panel as described in Chapter 10, Section 36.
46   Undo the control unit retaining bolt, disconnect the wiring plug and remove the unit from its location.
47   Refitting is a reversal of removal.

Ultrasonic sensor
48   Disconnect the battery negative lead.
49   Remove the centre body pillar trim panel as described in Chapter 10, Section 36.
50   Carefully release the ultrasonic sensor trim panel and withdraw it downwards.
51   Release the ultrasonic sensor from its location, disconnect the wiring plug and remove the unit from the car.
52   Refitting is a reversal of removal.

Bonnet contact unit
53   Disconnect the battery negative lead.

54   Using a screwdriver, depress the catch at the base of the contact unit and withdraw the contact from its location.
55   Disconnect the contact wiring and remove the unit.
56   Refitting is a reversal of removal.

Horn
57   Disconnect the battery negative lead.
58   Disconnect the wiring from the horn, unscrew the securing nut and remove the horn.
59   Refitting is a reversal of removal.

Wiring diagrams – explanatory notes

60   The wiring diagrams are of the current flow type, each circuit being shown in the simplest possible fashion. Note that since the diagrams were originally written in German (to the DIN standard), all wire colours and abbreviations used on the diagrams themselves are in German;

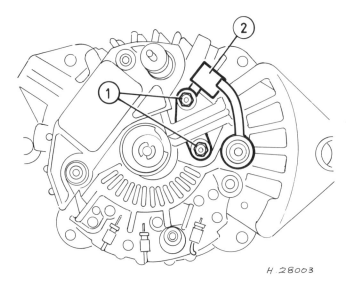

Fig. 12.38 Alternator brush holder retaining bolts (1) and suppression capacitor (2) (Sec 15)

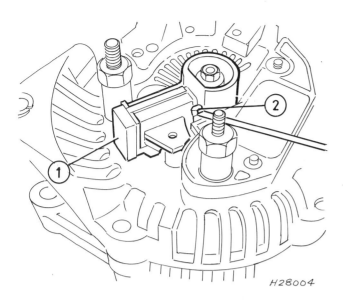

Fig. 12.39 Withdrawing the brush holder (1) by releasing the tag (2) (Sec 15)

refer to the information given on the diagram key or at the end of this Section for clarification.

61   The bottom line of the diagram represents the 'earth' or negative connection; the numbers below this line are track numbers, enabling circuits and components to be located using the key.

62   The lines at the top of the diagram represent 'live feed' or positive connection points. The line marked '30' is live at all times, that marked '15' is live only when the ignition is switched on.

63   Numbers on the diagram that are framed in square boxes at the end of a wire show the track reference number in which that wire is continued. At the point indicated will be another framed number referring back to the circuit just left.

64   As an example of how to use the diagrams, trace with the help of the following text the reversing lamp switch circuit located between

track reference numbers 496 and 498 on the 1991/2 model year diagram.

65   Starting at the top of track 497, the supply for the circuit comes from the line '15', showing that the circuit is fed only when the ignition is switched on, via fuse 22 (F22, rated at 10 amps). Note that this fuse can also protect the feed for several other circuits, some of which may not be applicable to the vehicle being worked on.

66   If the vehicle in question has a manual gearbox (MT), the circuit proceeds along a black wire of 0.75 mm cross-section (as shown by 'SW 0.75' in the wire path), via terminal 12 of connector X5 to the reversing lamp switch S7. From the switch the circuit continues along a white wire, with a black tracer and of 0.75 mm cross-section (WSSW 0.75), via terminal 2 of connector X5 and terminal 1 of connector X6, to the reversing lamp bulbs (E17 and E18). The circuit is completed by a brown wire from each bulbholder to earth; in this case the 'earth' wire simply attaches the component to the nearest piece of metal bodywork, but in other cases earthing is achieved by the component mounting and no wire is needed. The diagram shows, as simply as possible, that when the switch contacts (which are normally open) are closed by the driver selecting reverse gear, current is allowed to flow to earth via the switch and bulbs, causing the reversing lamps to light.

67   If the vehicle in question has automatic transmission (AT), the circuit differs in that the 'live feed' goes from fuse 22 to terminal 'F' of the transmission selector lever position switch connector X46 (track reference number 773). When position 'R' is selected, terminals 'F' and 'G' are connected so that the circuit feed continues (back to track reference number 496, the 'RFS/reversing lamp' circuit) along the same route described above for manual gearbox models.

Explanation of abbreviations used in wiring diagrams

ABS	Anti-lock braking system (ABS)
AC	Air conditioning
AZV	Trailer hitch
AT	Automatic transmission
ATC	Automatic temperature control
BR	Trip (on-board) computer
CC	Check control system
CRC	Cruise control
D	Diesel
DS	Theft protection
DT	Turbo Diesel
DWA	Anti-theft warning system

Fig. 12.40 Anti-theft alarm system component locations (Sec 15)

1   *Control unit*
2   *Ultrasonic sensor with LED*
3   *Ultrasonic sensor with probe*
4   *Radio contact*
5   *Bonnet contact unit*
6   *Horn*
7   *Relay*
    Calibra model shown – component locations identical on Cavalier

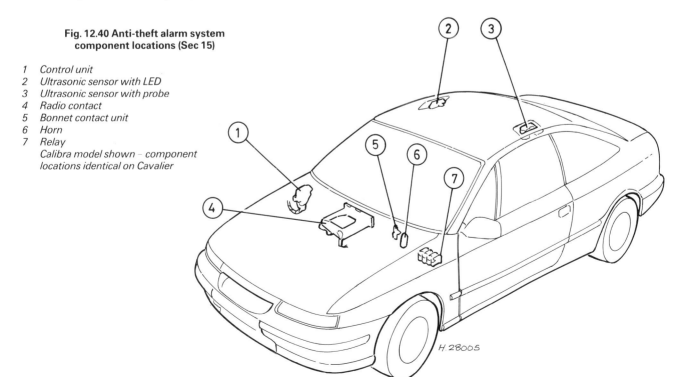

Explanation of abbreviations (continued)

DZM	Tachometer
EFC	Electric folding roof (Convertible)
EKS	Pinch guard (electric windows)
EMP	Radio
EUR	Euronorm (emission control standard) engine
EZ +	EI Plus ignition system (with self-diagnosis)
EZV	Ecotronic
FH	Electric windows
GB	Great Britain
HS	Heated rear window
HW	Rear window wiper
HZG	Heating
HRL	Luggage compartment lamp
INS	Instrument panel
IRL	Courtesy lamps
KAT	Catalytic converter
KBS	Wiring harness
KV	Contact breaker distributor
L3.1	Bosch L3.1 Jetronic fuel injection system
LCD	Liquid crystal display (LCD) instruments
LHD	Left-hand drive
4WD	Four-wheel-drive
LWR	Headlamp aim adjustment
M1.5	Bosch Motronic M1.5 engine management system
M2.5	Bosch Motronic M2.5 engine management system
MOT	Motronic (general)
MT	Manual gearbox

MUL	Multec fuel injection system
N	Norway
NS	Front foglamps
NSL	Rear foglamps
OEL	Oil level/pressure check system
OPT	Optional equipment
PBSL	Park and brake shift block (automatic transmission, selector lever in position 'P')
P/N	Park/neutral (automatic transmission)
POT	Potentiometer
RC	Rear suspension level control system
RFS	Reversing lamps
RHD	Right-hand drive
S	Sweden
SD	Sunroof
SH	Heated seats
SRA	Headlamp washers and wipers
TANK	Fuel level sender unit
TD	Turbo Diesel
TEMP	Temperature gauge
TFL	Daytime driving lamps
TKS	Courtesy lamp (door pillar) switches
TSZI	Transistorised ignition (inductive-triggered) system
VGS	Carburettor
WEG	Odometer frequency/roadspeed sensor
WHR	Rear suspension level control system
WS	Warning buzzer
ZV	Central locking
ZYL	Cylinder

Key to wiring diagram for 1989 models
Not all items fitted to all models

Refer to Chapter 12, Section 13 for details of diagram usage and abbreviations found

Wiring identification

Example: GE WS 1.5
GE – Basic colour
WS – Identification colour
1.5 – Section (mm²)

Colour code

BL	Blue	GN	Green
HBL	Light blue	RT	Red
BR	Brown	WS	White
GE	Yellow	SW	Black
GR	Grey	LI	Lilac
		VI	Violet

Circuit interconnections
A framed number, eg 180, refers to a grid reference at which the circuit is continued

No	Description	Track	No	Description	Track
E1	Side lamp – left	406	E39	Rear foglamp – right	455
E2	Tail lamp – left	302, 380, 407	E41	Courtesy lamp (with delay)	488 to 490
E3	Number plate lamp	413	E50	Kerb lamp – driver's door	635
E4	Side lamp – right	409	E51	Kerb lamp – passenger door	653
E5	Tail lamp – right	382, 410	F1 to	Fuse (in fusebox)	Various
E6	Engine compartment lamp	416	F30		
E7	Headlamp main beam – left	437	F32	Fuse – mixture preheating (not UK models)	232
E8	Headlamp main beam – right	438	F33	Fuse – electronic carburettor (not UK models)	201
E9	Headlamp dipped beam – left	384, 439	F34	Fuse (in relay box, engine compartment)	834
E10	Headlamp dipped beam – right	386, 440	F35	Voltage stabiliser	302
E11	Instrument illumination lamps	328 to 329	F36	Fuse – fuel filter heating (Diesel models)	866
E12	Gear selector lever illumination lamp (automatic transmission)	799	G1	Battery	101
E13	Luggage compartment lamp	485	G2	Alternator	110
E14	Courtesy lamp	487	G3	Battery – Diesel models	846
E15	Glovebox lamp	599	G6	Alternator – Diesel models	850 to 852
E16	Cigarette lighter illumination lamp	598	H2	Horn	591
E17	Reversing lamp – left	497	H3	Direction indicator warning lamp	318, 320
E18	Reversing lamp – right	498	H4	Oil pressure warning lamp	310
E19	Heated rear window	572	H5	Brake fluid level warning lamp	313
E20	Front foglamp – left	448	H6	Hazard warning flasher warning lamp	470
E21	Front foglamp – right	447	H7	Alternator charge warning lamp	310
E24	Rear foglamp – left	454	H8	Headlamp main beam warning lamp	322
E25	Seat heater – front left	575	H9	Brake lamp – left	388
E30	Seat heater – front right	579	H10	Brake lamp – right	390
E32	Clock illumination lamp	552	H11	Direction indicator lamp – front left	472
E38	Trip computer illumination lamp	539	H12	Direction indicator lamp – rear left	473
			H13	Direction indicator lamp – front right	481

No	Description	Track
H14	Direction indicator lamp – rear right	482
H16	Glow plug warning lamp (Diesel models)	323
H17	Trailer direction indicator warning lamp	321
H18	Horns (twin)	592, 593
H19	Headlamps-on warning buzzer	494, 495
H21	Handbrake-on warning lamp	315
H23	Radio/cassette player	585, 586
H25	Door mirror heater warning lamp	678
H26	ABS warning lamp	319
H30	Engine fault warning lamp	324
H33	Direction indicator side repeater lamp – left	476
H34	Direction indicator side repeater lamp – right	478
H42	Automatic transmission warning lamp	325
H45	Four-wheel-drive warning lamp	327
H46	Catalytic converter temperature warning lamp (not UK models)	329
K1	Relay – heated rear window	571 to 572
K5	Relay – front foglamps	448 to 450
K6	Relay – air conditioning (not UK models)	801 to 802
K7	Relay – air conditioning blower (not UK models)	808 to 809
K8	Relay – intermittent windscreen wipe	503 to 506
K9	Relay – headlamp wash	522 to 523
K10	Relay – direction indicator/hazard warning flashers	467 to 469
K20	HEI ignition control unit	122 to 124
K25	Relay – glow plugs (Diesel models)	856 to 859
K30	Relay – intermittent rear window wipe	515 to 517
K35	Relay – door mirror heater	683 to 685
K37	Central locking control unit	606 to 612
K45	Relay – mixture preheating (not UK models)	231 to 232
K47	Relay – surge arrester (ABS)	702 to 703
K50	ABS control unit	707 to 721
K51	Relay – cooling fan	830 to 831
K54	Electronic carburettor control unit (not UK models)	203 to 226
K55	Relay – electronic carburettor (not UK models)	203 to 206
K57	Fuel injection control unit (not UK models)	139 to 161
K58	Relay – fuel pump (not UK models)	162 to 163
K59	Relay – daytime running lamps (not UK models)	420 to 426
K61	Motronic M4.1 control unit	170 to 194
K62	Dim-dip control unit	428 to 432
K63	Relay – horn	593 to 594
K64	Relay – air conditioning blower (not UK models)	802 to 803
K67	Relay – cooling fan	827 to 828
K68	Relay – fuel injection system	294 to 299, 196 to 199
K69	Motronic M2.5 control unit	267 to 297
K71	Ride control unit (not UK models)	739 to 754
K80	Relay – fuel filter heater (Diesel models)	865 to 866
K82	Relay – engine revolution	862 to 863
K83	Four-wheel-drive control unit	725 to 731
K84	MSTS ignition control unit	247 to 256
K85	Automatic transmission control unit	771 to 797
K86	Check control unit	370 to 392
K87	Relay – auxiliary cooling fan	833 to 834
K88	Catalytic converter temperature control unit (not UK models)	760 to 762
K89	Relay – rear foglamps	444 to 447
K90	Relay – air conditioning compressor (not UK models)	820 to 821
K93	Relay – air conditioning compressor (not UK models)	821 to 822
L1	Ignition coil	121 to 122,133 to 134,174 to 175, 225 to 226,243 to 244,261 to 262
M1	Starter motor	105 to 106
M2	Windscreen wiper motor	501 to 504
M4	Cooling fan motor	113
M6	Headlamp wiper motor – left	525 to 527
M7	Headlamp wiper motor – right	529 to 531
M8	Rear window wiper motor	513 to 515
M13	Sunroof motor	692 to 694

No	Description	Track
M18	Central locking motor – driver's door	607 to 610
M19	Central locking motor – left rear door	622 to 624
M20	Central locking motor – right rear door	626 to 628
M21	Fuel pump	163,196,299
M26	Electric aerial motor	584 to 585
M30	Door mirror motor and heater – driver's door	674 to 676
M31	Door mirror motor and heater – passenger door	680 to 682
M32	Central locking motor – passenger door	614 to 617
M33	Idle speed adjuster	146 to 149, 183 to 184, 277 to 278
M37	Central locking motor – boot lid/tailgate	618 to 621
M39	Headlamp aim adjustment motor – left	557 to 560
M40	Headlamp aim adjustment motor – right	561 to 564
M41	Central locking motor – fuel filler flap	623 to 625
M43	Ride control actuator – front left (not UK models)	739 to 741
M44	Ride control actuator – front right (not UK models)	743 to 745
M45	Ride control actuator – rear left (not UK models)	747 to 749
M46	Ride control actuator – rear right (not UK models)	751 to 753
M47	Electric window motor – front left	636 to 640
M48	Electric window motor – front right	654 to 658
M49	Electric window motor – rear left	642 to 646
M50	Electric window motor – rear right	660 to 664
M55	Washer fluid pump	518 to 519
P1	Fuel gauge	304
P2	Coolant temperature gauge	306
P3	Clock	551
P4	Fuel level sender unit	304
P5	Coolant temperature sensor	306
P7	Tachometer	308
P8	Oil pressure gauge	341
P9	Voltmeter	339
P10	Oil pressure sensor	341
P11	Airflow meter (Motronic M4.1)	185 to 189
P12	Coolant temperature sensor	178, 272
P13	Trip computer outside air temperature sensor	542 to 543
P14	Distance sensor (not UK models)	336 to 337
P17	ABS wheel sensor – front left	707
P18	ABS wheel sensor – front right	710
P19	ABS wheel sensor – rear left	712
P20	ABS wheel sensor – rear right	714
P21	Speedometer frequency sensor (not UK models)	332
P23	Pressure sensor	249 to 250
P24	Oil temperature sensor	251
P24	Automatic transmission fluid temperature sensor	795
P27	Brake pad wear sensor – front left	375
P28	Brake pad wear sensor – front right	375
P29	Inlet manifold temperature sensor (not UK models)	207 to 208
P30	Coolant temperature sensor	209 to 210, 150
P31	Throttle position sensor (not UK models)	209 to 211
P32	Oxygen sensor – heated (not UK models)	193 to 194, 291 to 292
P33	Oxygen sensor	157
P34	Throttle position sensor	158 to 160, 780
P35	Crankshaft speed/position sensor	189 to 191, 223 to 225, 281 to 282
P39	Trailer bulb failure sensor	392 to 394
P43	Electronic speedometer	336
P44	Air mass meter (Motronic M2.5)	294 to 296
P45	Automatic transmission input speed sensor	787 to 788
P46	Knock sensor	284 to 285
P47	Distributor 'Hall-effect' sensor (Motronic M2.5)	287 to 288
P48	Automatic transmission distance sensor	785 to 786
P50	Catalytic converter temperature sensor (not UK models)	761 to 762
R2	Carburettor preheating	116, 228
R3	Cigarette lighter	596 to 597
R5	Glow plugs (Diesel models)	858 to 859

No	Description	Track
R7	Mixture preheating (not UK models)	232
R12	Automatic choke	117
R15	Mixture adjustment potentiometer (not UK models)	155 to 157
R19	Cooling fan-motor resistor	828, 848
S1	Ignition switch	102 to 106, 851 to 852
S2.1	Lighting switch	404 to 407
S2.2	Courtesy lamp switch	487
S2.3	Instrument illumination lamp dimmer	328
S3	Heater blower switch	837 to 844
S4	Heated rear window switch	570 to 571
S5.2	Dipped beam switch	438, 439
S5.3	Direction indicator switch	480 to 482
S5.4	Sidelamp switch	401 to 402
S7	Reversing lamp switch	497
S8	Brake lamp switch	462
S9.2	Windscreen wiper switch	501 to 504
S9.5	Rear window wash/wiper switch	516 to 518
S10	Automatic transmission switch	770 to 776
S11	Brake fluid level warning sensor	313
S13	Handbrake-on warning switch	315
S14	Oil pressure switch	310
S15	Luggage compartment lamp switch	485
S17	Passenger door courtesy lamp switch	490
S21	Front foglamp switch	450 to 452
S22	Rear foglamp switch	455 to 457
S27	Air conditioning compressor low-pressure switch (not UK models)	821
S28	Air conditioning compressor high-pressure switch (not UK models)	821
S29	Cooling fan switch	113
S30	Seat heater switch – front left	575 to 577
S31	Rear door courtesy lamp switch – left	491
S32	Rear door courtesy lamp switch – right	492
S35	Sunroof travel microswitch	692
S36	Sunroof travel microswitch	694
S37	Electric windows switch assembly	637 to 663
S37.1	Electric window switch – front left	637 to 639
S37.2	Electric window switch – front right	655 to 657
S37.3	Electric window switch – rear left	643 to 645
S37.4	Electric window switch – rear right	661 to 663
S37.5	Electric windows safety cut-out switch	641 to 642
S37.6	Electric windows anti-jam switch	659
S37.7	Electric windows automatic control	646 to 651
S39	Electric windows switch – rear left door	647 to 649
S40	Electric windows switch – rear right door	665 to 667
S41	Central locking switch – driver's door	601 to 603
S42	Central locking switch – passenger door	605
S44	Throttle position sensor	173 to 174, 278 to 279
S47	Driver's door courtesy lamp switch	493 to 494
S51	Cooling fan switch (not UK models)	825 to 827
S52	Hazard warning flasher switch	469 to 474
S55	Seat heater switch – front right	579 to 581
S57	Sunroof switch	690 to 696
S63.1	Trip computer function reset switch	543
S63.2	Trip computer clock hours adjustment switch	544
S63.3	Trip computer function select switch	545
S63.5	Trip computer clock minutes adjustment switch	546
S64	Horn switch	591 to 594
S68.1	Door mirror adjustment switch	672 to 677
S68.2	Door mirror heater switch	679 to 680
S68.3	Door mirror left/right selector switch	673 to 677
S76	Air conditioning compressor switch – high-pressure, cooling fan (not UK models)	832
S82	Washer pump switch	371
S91	Oil pressure switch (not UK models)	165 to 166
S93	Coolant level sensor	372
S95	Oil level sensor	373
S98	Headlamp aim adjustment switch	556 to 558

No	Description	Track
S99	Electric windows switch – driver's door	634
S100	Electric windows switch – passenger door	652
S104	Kickdown switch (automatic transmission)	792
S105	Start-up assistance switch (automatic transmission)	796 to 798
S106	Economy/power programme switch (automatic transmission)	791
S107	Throttle position sensor	771 to 776
S108	Cooling fan switch (Diesel models)	847 to 848
S109	Air conditioning compressor switch (not UK models)	817
S110	Ride control switch (not UK models)	738 to 743
S115	Automatic transmission fluid temperature sensor	793
S116	Brake lamp switch	464 to 465
S117	Four-wheel-drive hydraulic pressure switch	729
S118	Air conditioning refrigerant temperature switch (not UK models)	829
U2	Trip computer	538 to 548
U4	ABS hydraulic modulator assembly	705 to 718
U4.1	ABS hydraulic pump relay	706 to 709
U4.2	ABS solenoid valves relay	715 to 718
U4.3	ABS hydraulic pump	705
U4.4	ABS diode	717
U4.5	ABS solenoid valve – front left	710
U4.6	ABS solenoid valve – front right	711
U4.7	ABS solenoid valve – rear left	712
U4.8	ABS solenoid valve – rear right	713
U5.1	Check control tail lamp and dipped beam bulb failure warning lamp	362
U5.2	Check control brake lamp bulb failure warning lamp	363
U5.3	Check control coolant oil level warning lamp	360
U5.5	Check control brake pad wear warning lamp	364
U5.6	Check control washer fluid level warning lamp	359
U5.7	Check control coolant level warning lamp	361
U7	Air conditioning control unit (not UK models)	806 to 824
U7.6	Air conditioning blower switch (not UK models)	806 to 811
U7.8	Air conditioning switch (not UK models)	813 to 824
U12.1	Temperature switch (Diesel models)	865
U12.2	Fuel filter heater (Diesel models)	866
U13.1	Automatic transmission solenoid valve – shift 1	784
U13.2	Automatic transmission solenoid valve – shift 2	785
U13.3	Automatic transmission solenoid valve – lock-up control	786
U13.4	Automatic transmission solenoid valve – pressure control	787
V1	Brake fluid level warning lamp test diode (not UK models)	312
V8	Air conditioning compressor diode (not UK models)	820
X1	Trailer electrical socket	453, 458 to 460
X2	Accessory electrical connectors	587
X5 to X62	Wiring connectors	Various
Y1	Air conditioning compressor clutch (not UK models)	821
Y4	Headlamp washer solenoid valve	523
Y5	Fuel solenoid valve (Diesel models)	860
Y7	Fuel injectors	186 to 193, 280 to 287
Y10	Distributor (Hall-effect)	249 to 253
Y23	Distributor (Inductive discharge)	123 to 127
Y24	Distributor (Inductive discharge) (not UK models)	129 to 136
Y26	Throttle valve positioner (not UK models)	201 to 207
Y27	Pre-throttle valve (not UK models)	218 to 219
Y30	Cold start valve (Diesel models)	863
Y32	Fuel injector (not UK models)	140
Y33	Distributor	170, 262
Y34	Fuel tank ventilation valve (not UK models)	198, 292
Y43	Air conditioning vacuum control (not UK models)	815 to 818
Y44	Four-wheel-drive solenoid valve	731

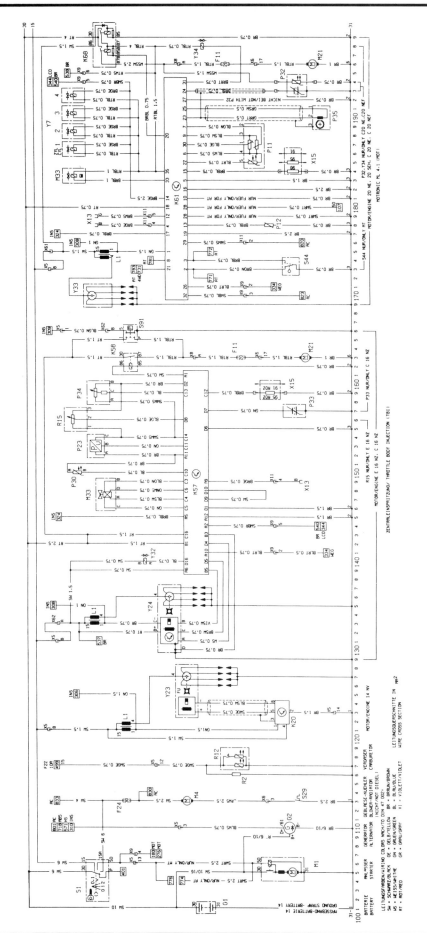

Wiring diagram for 1989 models

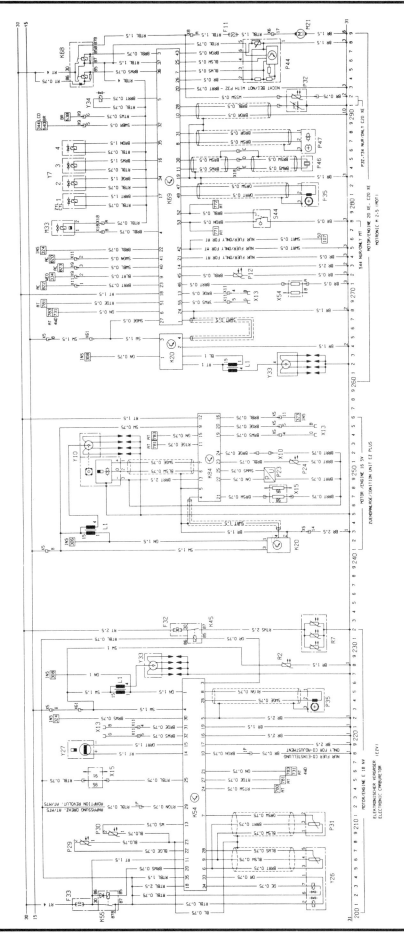

Wiring diagram for 1989 models (continued)

Wiring diagram for 1989 models (continued)

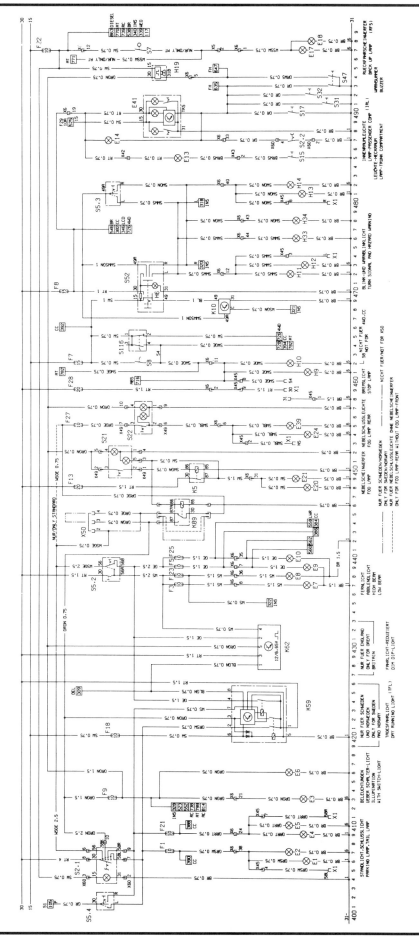

Wiring diagram for 1989 models (continued)

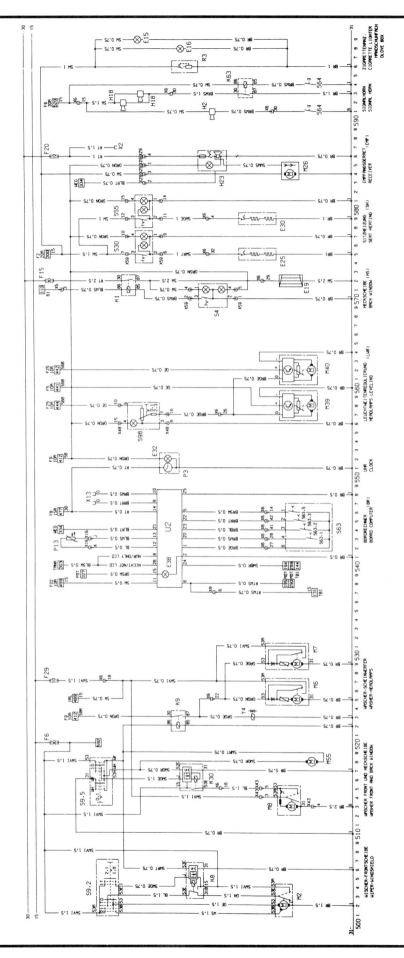

Wiring diagram for 1989 models (continued)

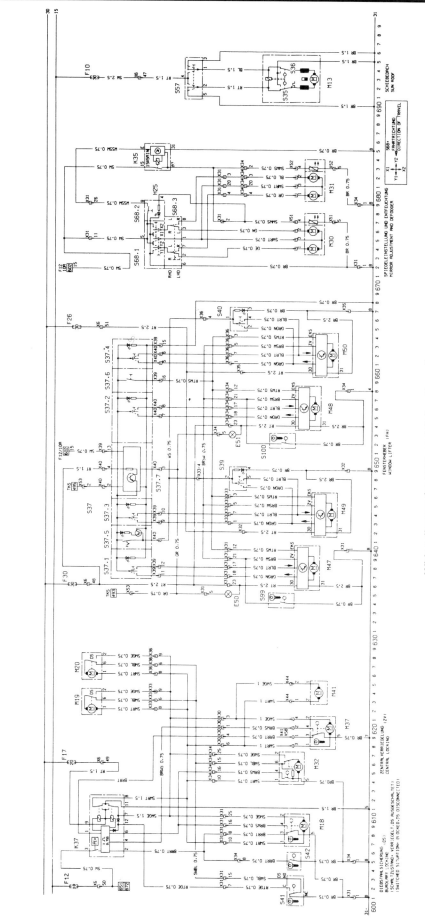

Wiring diagram for 1989 models (continued)

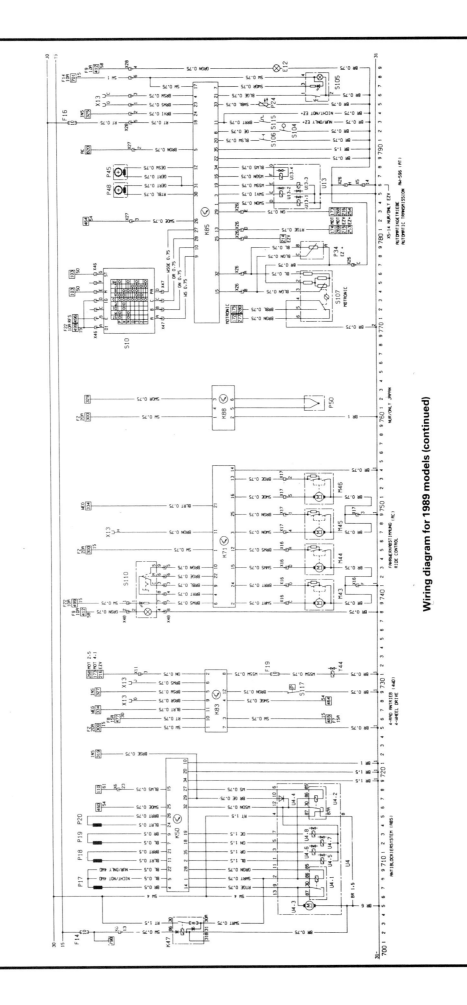

Wiring diagram for 1989 models (continued)

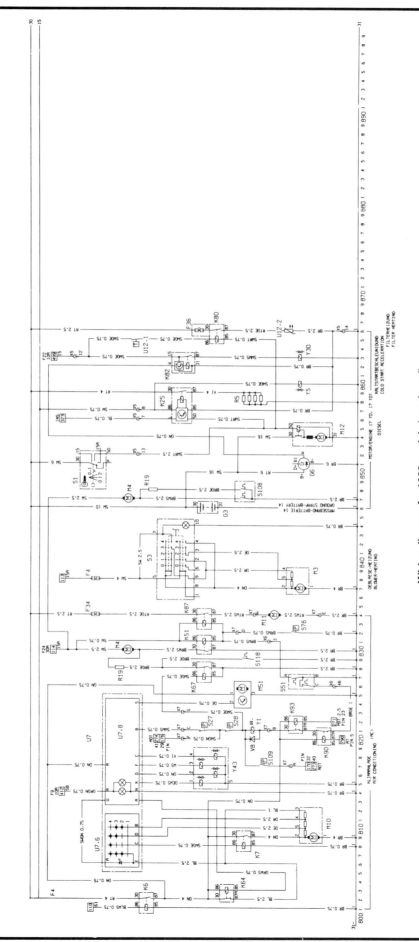

Wiring diagram for 1989 models (continued)

Key to wiring diagrams for 1990 models
Not all items fitted to all models

Refer to Chapter 12, Section 13, for details of diagram usage and abbreviations found

Wiring identification

Example: GE WS 1.5
GE – Basic colour
WS – Identification colour
1.5 – Section (mm²)

Colour code

BL	Blue	GN	Green
HBL	Light blue	RT	Red
BR	Brown	WS	White
GE	Yellow	SW	Black
GR	Grey	LI	Lilac
		VI	Violet

Circuit interconnections
A framed number, eg 180, refers to a grid reference at which the circuit is continued

No	Description	Track	No	Description	Track
E1	Side lamp – left	356, 406	E38	Trip computer illumination lamp	539
E2	Tail lamp – left	374, 407	E39	Rear foglamp – right	455
E3	Number plate lamp	413	E41	Courtesy lamp (with delay)	488 to 490
E4	Side lamp – right	358, 409	E50	Kerb lamp – driver's door	666
E5	Tail lamp – right	376, 410	E51	Kerb lamp – passenger door	684
E6	Engine compartment lamp	415	F1 to	Fuse (in fusebox)	Various
E7	Headlamp main beam – left	437	F30		
E8	Headlamp main beam – right	438	F32	Fuse – mixture preheating (not UK models)	232
E9	Headlamp dipped beam – left	360, 378	F33	Fuse – electronic carburettor (not UK models)	201
E10	Headlamp dipped beam – right	362, 380	F34	Fuse (in relay box, engine compartment)	834
E11	Instrument illumination lamps	328 to 329	F35	Voltage stabiliser	302
E12	Gear selector lever illumination lamp (automatic transmission)	799	F36	Fuse – fuel filter heating	866, 932
			F38	Fuse – anti-theft alarm	638
E13	Luggage compartment lamp	485	F39	Fuse – headlamp wash	532
E14	Courtesy lamp	487	F40	Fuse – radiator fan (Turbo Diesel models)	938
E15	Glovebox lamp	599	F41	Fuse – radiator fan (Turbo Diesel models)	942
E16	Cigarette lighter illumination lamp	598	G1	Battery	101
E17	Reversing lamp – left	497	G2	Alternator	111
E18	Reversing lamp – right	498	G3	Battery – Diesel models	846
E19	Heated rear window	576	G6	Alternator – Diesel models	850 to 852
E20	Front foglamp – left	448	H1	Radio/cassette player	589 to 590
E21	Front foglamp – right	447	H2	Horn	592
E24	Rear foglamp – left	454	H3	Direction indicator warning lamp	315 to 320
E25	Seat heater – front left	579	H4	Oil pressure warning lamp	310
E30	Seat heater – front right	583	H5	Brake fluid level warning lamp	313
E32	Clock illumination lamp	552	H6	Hazard warning flasher warning lamp	470

No	Description	Track
H7	Alternator charge warning lamp	310
H8	Headlamp main beam warning lamp	322
H9	Brake lamp – left	364, 382, 461
H10	Brake lamp – right	366, 384, 462
H11	Direction indicator lamp – front left	472
H12	Direction indicator lamp – rear left	473
H13	Direction indicator lamp – front right	461
H14	Direction indicator lamp – rear right	482
H16	Glow plug warning lamp (Diesel models)	323
H17	Trailer direction indicator warning lamp	321
H18	Horn	593
H19	Headlamps-on warning buzzer	494 to 495
H21	Handbrake-on warning lamp	315
H25	Door mirror heater warning lamp	656
H26	ABS warning lamp	319
H30	Engine fault warning lamp	324
H33	Direction indicator side repeater lamp – left	476
H34	Direction indicator side repeater lamp – right	478
H42	Automatic transmission warning lamp	325
H45	Four-wheel-drive warning lamp	327
H46	Catalytic converter temperature warning lamp (not UK models)	329
H47	Anti-theft alarm horn	638
H48	Horn	594
K1	Relay – heated rear window	575 to 576
K3	Relay – starter motor (anti-theft alarm)	109 to 110
K5	Relay – front foglamps	448 to 450
K6	Relay – air conditioning (not UK models)	801 to 802
K7	Relay – air conditioning blower (not UK models)	808 to 809
K8	Relay – intermittent windscreen wipe	503 to 506
K9	Relay – headlamp wash	519 to 520
K10	Relay – direction indicator/hazard warning flashers	467 to 469
K20	Ignition module	122 to 124, 236 to 237, 262 to 265
K25	Relay – glow plugs (Diesel models)	856 to 859
K30	Relay – intermittent rear window wipe	513 to 515
K35	Relay – door mirror heater	661 to 663
K37	Central locking control unit	606 to 612
K45	Relay – mixture preheating (not UK models)	231 to 232
K47	Relay – surge arrester (ABS)	702 to 703
K50	ABS control unit	707 to 721
K51	Relay – cooling fan	830 to 831, 838 to 839
K54	Electronic carburettor control unit (not UK models)	203 to 226
K55	Relay – electronic carburettor (not UK models)	203 to 226
K57	Fuel injection control unit (not UK models)	139 to 161
K58	Relay – fuel pump (not UK models)	162 to 163
K59	Relay – daytime running lamps (not UK models)	420 to 426
K62	Dim-dip control unit	427 to 431
K63	Relay – horn	
K64	Relay – air conditioning blower (not UK models)	802 to 803
K67	Relay – cooling fan	827 to 828
K68	Relay – fuel injection system	196 to 199, 294 to 299
K69	Motronic M2.5 control unit	267 to 297
K73	Relay – headlamp main beam (Calibra models)	432 to 433
K76	Glow plug control unit (Turbo Diesel models)	916 to 921
K77	Relay – glow plugs (Turbo Diesel models)	923 to 924
K78	Relay – preresistor (Turbo Diesel models)	926 to 927
K79	Alternator charge warning lamp relay	911 to 913
K80	Relay – fuel filter heater (Diesel models)	865 to 866, 931 to 932
K82	Relay – engine revolution	862 to 863
K83	Four-wheel-drive control unit	725 to 731
K84	MSTS ignition control unit	244 to 256
K85	Automatic transmission control unit	771 to 797
K86	Check control unit	347 to 368
K87	Relay – auxiliary cooling fan	833 to 834, 941 to 942
K88	Catalytic converter temperature control unit (not UK models)	758 to 760
K89	Relay – rear foglamps	444 to 447

No	Description	Track
K90	Relay – air conditioning compressor (not UK models)	820 to 821
K91	Motronic M1.5 control unit	170 to 194
K94	Anti-theft alarm control unit	633 to 647
K95	Relay – heated rear window time delay	569 to 571
K97	Relay – headlamp washer pump time delay	530 to 532
L1	Ignition coil	121 to 122, 133 to 134, 173 to 174, 225 to 226, 237 to 238, 261 to 262
M1	Starter motor	105 to 106
M2	Windscreen wiper motor	501 to 504
M3	Heater blower motor	837 to 841
M4	Cooling fan motor	114, 830, 847, 936
M6	Headlamp wiper motor – left	522 to 524
M7	Headlamp wiper motor – right	526 to 528
M8	Rear window wiper motor	511 to 513
M10	Air conditioning blower motor (not UK models)	809 to 812
M11	Cooling fan motor (not UK models)	834, 942
M12	Starter motor (Diesel models)	854 to 855, 905 to 906
M13	Sunroof motor assembly	873 to 876
M13.1	Sunroof motor	873 to 875
M13.2	Sunroof travel microswitch	873
M13.3	Sunroof travel microswitch	875
M18	Central locking motor – driver's door	607 to 610
M19	Central locking motor – left rear door	621 to 623
M20	Central locking motor – right rear door	625 to 627
M21	Fuel pump	163, 197, 229
M24	Headlamp washer pump	532
M26	Electric aerial motor	588 to 589
M30	Door mirror motor and heater – driver's door	652 to 655
M31	Door mirror motor and heater – passenger door	658 to 661
M32	Central locking motor – passenger door	613 to 616
M33	Idle speed adjuster	146 to 149, 185 to 186, 277 to 278
M37	Central locking motor – boot lid/tailgate	618 to 621
M39	Headlamp aim adjustment motor – left	557 to 560
M40	Headlamp aim adjustment motor – right	561 to 564
M47	Electric window motor – front left	667 to 671
M48	Electric window motor – front right	685 to 689
M49	Electric window motor – rear left	673 to 677
M50	Electric window motor – rear right	691 to 695
M51	Air conditioning air flap actuator (not UK models)	824 to 826
M55	Windscreen and rear window washer pump	516
M60	Central locking motor – tailgate (Calibra models)	627 to 628
M61	Sunroof motor assembly (Calibra models)	881 to 889
M61.1	Sunroof motor (Calibra models)	882 to 885
M61.2	Relay 1 – sunroof motor (Calibra models)	881 to 882
M61.3	Relay 2 – sunroof motor (Calibra models)	887 to 889
P1	Fuel gauge	304
P2	Coolant temperature gauge	306
P3	Clock	551
P4	Fuel level sender unit	304
P5	Coolant temperature sensor	306
P7	Tachometer	308
P8	Oil pressure gauge	341
P9	Voltmeter	339
P10	Oil pressure sensor	341
P11	Airflow meter (Motronic M1.5)	185 to 189
P12	Coolant temperature sensor	187, 272
P13	Trip computer outside air temperature sensor	542 to 543
P14	Distance sensor (not UK models)	336 to 337, 915 to 916
P17	ABS wheel sensor – front left	708, 740
P18	ABS wheel sensor – front right	710, 742
P19	ABS wheel sensor – rear left	712, 744
P20	ABS wheel sensor – rear right	714, 746
P21	Speedometer frequency sensor (not UK models)	332
P23	Pressure sensor	152 to 154, 249 to 250
P24	Oil temperature sensor	251
P24	Automatic transmission fluid temperature sensor	795
P25	Bulb failure sensor	373 to 386
P27	Brake pad wear sensor – front left	351, 396
P28	Brake pad wear sensor – front right	351, 396

No	Description	Track
P30	Coolant temperature sensor	150, 209 to 210
P31	Throttle position sensor (not UK models)	209 to 211
P32	Oxygen sensor – heated (not UK models)	194 to 195, 291 to 292
P33	Oxygen sensor	157
P34	Throttle position sensor	158 to 160,180 to 181,780
P35	Crankshaft speed/position sensor	189 to 191, 223 to 225,243 to 245,281 to 282
P39	Trailer bulb failure sensor	368 to 370,387 to 389
P43	Electronic speedometer	336
P44	Air mass meter (Motronic M2.5)	294 to 298
P45	Automatic transmission input speed sensor	787 to 788
P46	Knock sensor	284 to 285
P47	Distributor 'Hall-effect' sensor (Motronic M2.5)	287 to 288
P48	Automatic transmission distance sensor	785 to 786
P50	Catalytic converter temperature sensor (not UK models)	759 to 760
P53	Anti-theft alarm sensor – driver's side	639 to 642
P54	Anti-theft alarm sensor – passenger side	644 to 647
P55	Coolant temperature sensor – Turbo Diesel models	919
R2	Carburettor preheating	116, 228
R3	Cigarette lighter	597
R5	Glow plugs (Diesel models)	858 to 859,922 to 924
R7	Mixture preheating (not UK models)	232
R12	Automatic choke	117
R15	Mixture adjustment potentiometer (not UK models)	155 to 157
R19	Cooling fan motor resistor	828, 848, 936
R22	Glow plugs resistor (Turbo Diesel models)	927
S1	Ignition switch	105 to 106, 851 to 852
S2.1	Lighting switch	404 to 407
S2.2	Courtesy lamp switch	487
S2.3	Instrument illumination lamp dimmer	328
S3	Heater blower switch	837 to 844
S4	Heated rear window switch	574 to 575
S5.2	Dipped beam switch	438 to 439
S5.3	Direction indicator switch	480 to 482
S5.4	Sidelamp switch	401 to 402
S7	Reversing lamp switch	497
S8	Brake lamp switch	462
S9.2	Windscreen wiper switch	501 to 504
S9.5	Rear window wash/wipe switch	514 to 516
S10	Automatic transmission switch	770 to 776
S11	Brake fluid level warning sensor	313
S13	Handbrake-on warning switch	315
S14	Oil pressure switch	310
S15	Luggage compartment lamp switch	485
S17	Passenger door courtesy lamp switch	490
S21	Front foglamp switch	450 to 452
S22	Rear foglamp switch	455 to 457
S27	Air conditioning compressor low-pressure switch (not UK models)	821
S28	Air conditioning compressor high-pressure switch (not UK models)	821
S29	Cooling fan switch	114
S30	Seat heater switch – front left	579 to 581
S31	Rear door courtesy lamp switch – left	491
S32	Rear door courtesy lamp switch – right	492
S37	Electric windows switch assembly	668 to 694
S37.1	Electric window switch – front left	668 to 670
S37.2	Electric window switch – front right	686 to 688
S37.3	Electric window switch – rear left	674 to 676
S37.4	Electric window switch – rear right	692 to 694
S37.5	Electric windows safety cut-out switch	672 to 673
S37.6	Electric windows anti-jam switch	690
S37.7	Electric windows automatic control	677 to 682
S39	Electric windows switch – rear left door	678 to 680
S40	Electric windows switch – rear right door	696 to 698
S41	Central locking switch – driver's door	601 to 603
S42	Central locking switch – passenger door	605
S44	Throttle position sensor	278 to 279
S47	Driver's door courtesy lamp switch	493 to 494
S52	Hazard warning flasher switch	469 to 474

No	Description	Track
S55	Seat heater switch – front right	583 to 585
S57	Sunroof switch	871 to 876, 881 to 886
S63	Trip computer assembly	542 to 547
S63.1	Trip computer function reset switch	543
S63.2	Trip computer clock hours adjustment switch	544
S63.3	Trip computer function select switch	545
S63.5	Trip computer clock minutes adjustment switch	546
S64	Horn switch	592 to 595
S68.1	Door mirror adjustment switch	650 to 655
S68.2	Door mirror heater switch	656 to 657
S68.3	Door mirror left/right selector switch	650 to 655
S76	Air conditioning compressor switch – high-pressure, cooling fan (not UK models)	832
S82	Washer pump switch	347, 392
S88	Cooling fan switch	847 to 848, 936 to 938
S91	Oil pressure switch (not UK models)	165 to 166
S93	Coolant level sensor	348, 393
S95	Oil level sensor	349, 394
S98	Headlamp aim adjustment switch	556 to 558
S99	Electric windows switch – driver's door	665
S100	Electric windows switch – passenger door	683
S104	Kickdown switch (automatic transmission)	794
S105	Start-up assistance switch (automatic transmission)	796 to 798
S106	Economy/power programme switch (automatic transmission)	791
S109	Air conditioning compressor switch (not UK models)	817
S115	Automatic transmission fluid temperature sensor	788 to 789
S116	Brake lamp switch	464 to 465
S117	Four-wheel-drive hydraulic pressure switch	729
S120	Anti-theft alarm bonnet switch	635
S121	Heated rear window switch Calibra models)	568 to 570
S127	Central locking switch – tailgate (Calibra models)	630
S128	Air conditioning refrigerant temperature switch (not UK models)	826 to 827
U2	Trip computer	538 to 549
U4	ABS hydraulic modulator assembly	705 to 718, 738 to 751
U4.1	ABS hydraulic pump relay	706 to 709,739 to 742
U4.2	ABS solenoid valves relay	715 to 718,747 to 751
U4.3	ABS hydraulic pump	705, 738
U4.4	ABS diode	
U4.5	ABS solenoid valve – front left	710, 743
U4.6	ABS solenoid valve – front right	711, 744
U4.7	ABS solenoid valve – rear left	712, 745
U4.8	ABS solenoid valve – rear right	713, 745
U5	Check control display	346 to 353
U5.1	Check control washer fluid level warning lamp	352
U5.2	Check control oil level warning lamp	351
U5.3	Check control coolant level warning lamp	350
U5.4	Check control tail lamp and dipped beam bulb failure warning lamp	349
U5.5	Check control brake lamp bulb failure warning lamp	348
U5.6	Check control brake pad wear warning lamp	347
U6	LCD instruments (not UK models)	389 to 396
U6.1	Check control washer fluid level warning lamp (not UK models)	392
U6.2	Check control oil level warning lamp (not UK models)	394
U6.3	Check control coolant level warning lamp (not UK models)	393
U6.4	Check control tail lamp and dipped beam bulb failure warning lamp (not UK models)	391
U6.5	Check control brake lamp bulb failure warning lamp (not UK models)	395
U6.6	Check control brake pad wear warning lamp (not UK models)	396
U7	Air conditioning control unit (not UK models)	806 to 824
U7.6	Air conditioning blower switch (not UK models)	806 to 811
U7.8	Air conditioning switch (not UK models)	813 to 824
U12.1	Temperature switch (Diesel models)	865
U12.2	Fuel filter heater (Diesel models)	866
U13.1	Automatic transmission solenoid valve – shift 1	782

No	Description	Track
U13.2	Automatic transmission solenoid valve – shift 2	783
U13.3	Automatic transmission solenoid valve – lock-up control	784
U13.4	Automatic transmission solenoid valve – pressure control	785
V1	Brake fluid level warning lamp test diode (not UK models)	312
X1	Trailer electrical socket	405, 411
X2	Accessory electrical connectors	591
X5 to X79	Wiring connectors	Various
Y1	Air conditioning compressor clutch (not UK models)	821
Y4	Headlamp washer solenoid valve	520
Y5	Fuel solenoid valve (Diesel models)	860, 928

No	Description	Track
Y7	Fuel injectors	187 to 194, 280 to 287
Y10	Distributor (Hall-effect)	
Y23	Distributor (inductive discharge)	123 to 127
Y24	Distributor (inductive discharge) (not UK models)	129 to 136
Y26	Throttle valve positioner (not UK models)	201 to 207
Y27	Pre-throttle valve (not UK models)	218 to 219
Y30	Cold start valve (Diesel models)	863
Y32	Fuel injector (not UK models)	140
Y33	Distributor	170, 228, 262
Y34	Fuel tank ventilation valve (not UK models)	193, 292
Y43	Air conditioning vacuum control (not UK models)	815 to 818
Y44	Four-wheel-drive solenoid valve	731

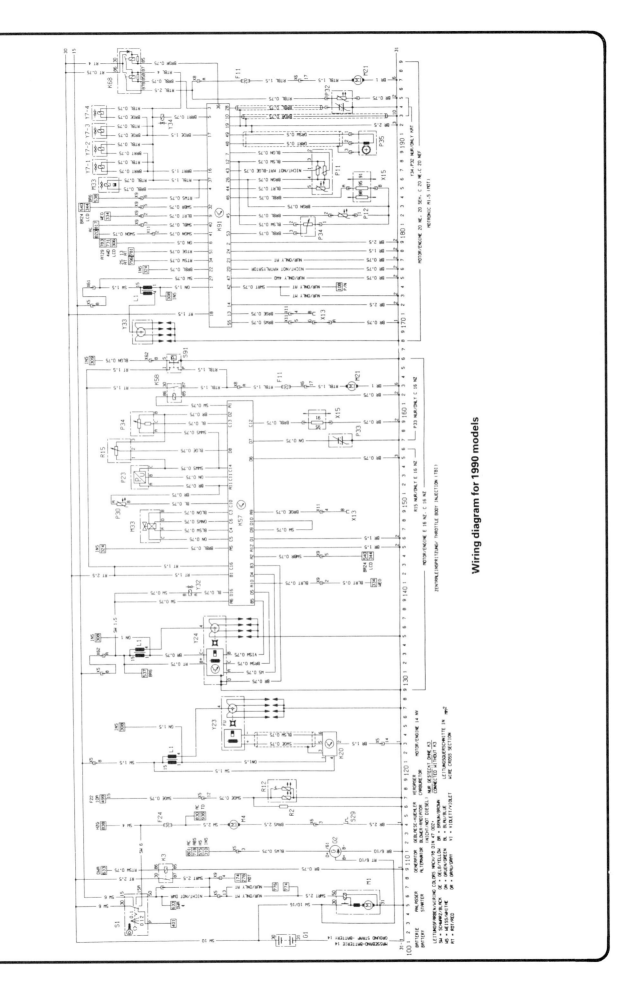

Wiring diagram for 1990 models

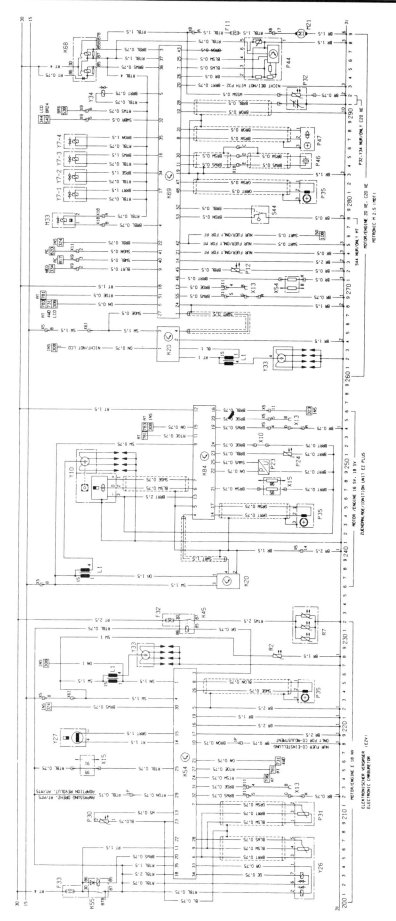

Wiring diagram for 1990 models (continued)

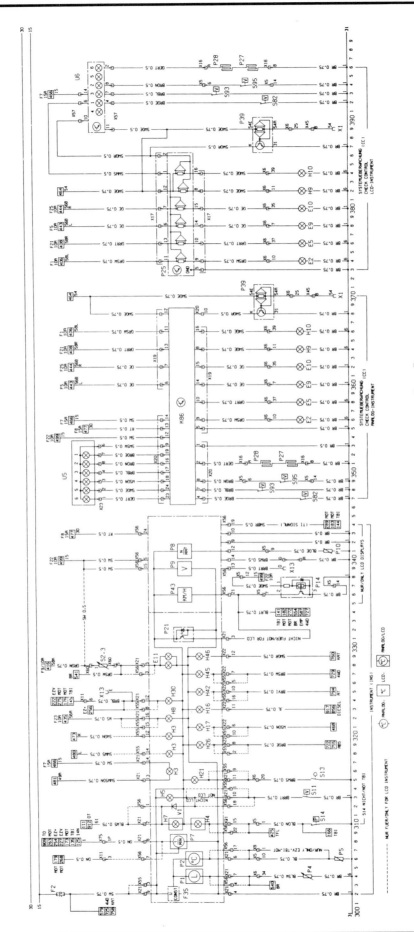

Wiring diagram for 1990 models (continued)

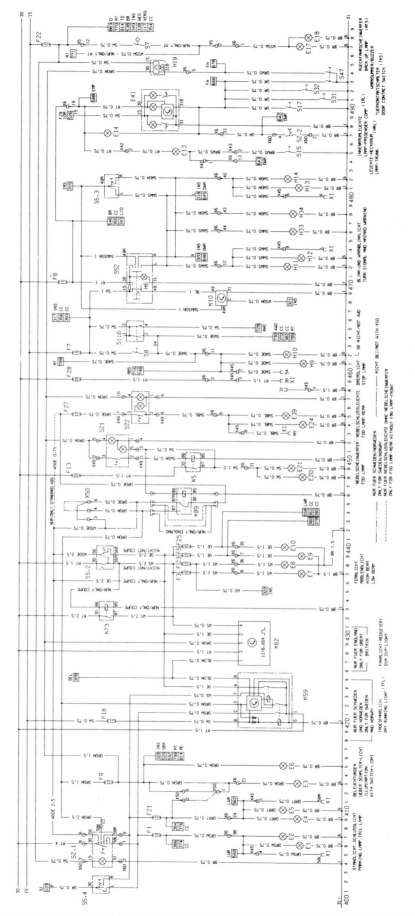

Wiring diagram for 1990 models (continued)

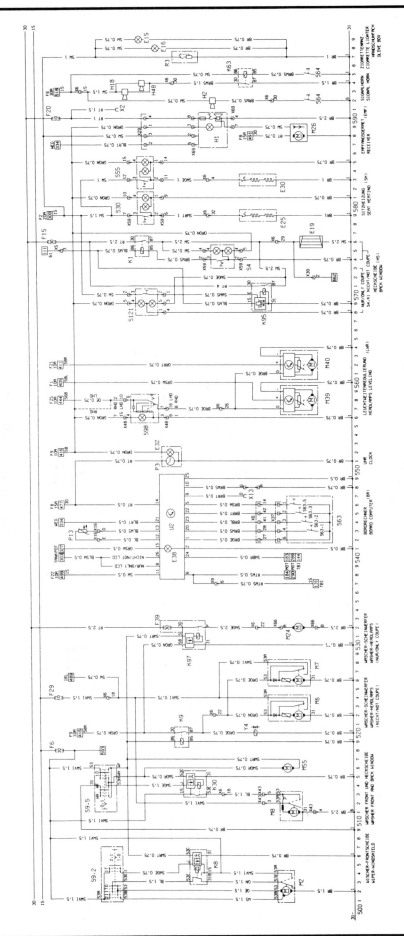

Wiring diagram for 1990 models (continued)

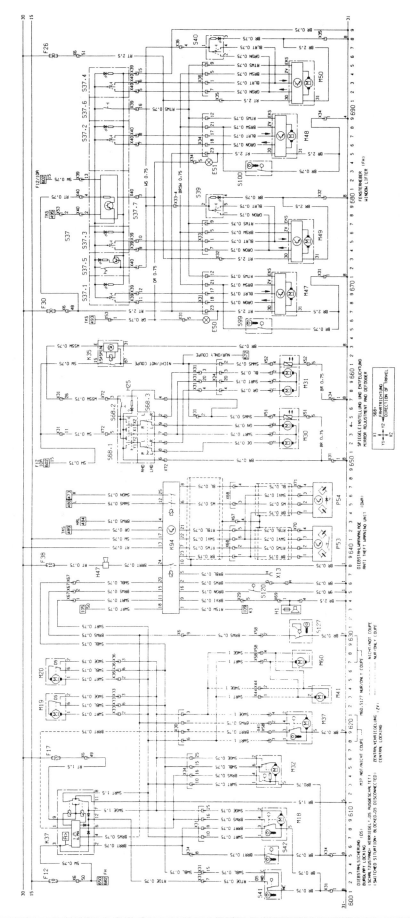

Wiring diagram for 1990 models (continued)

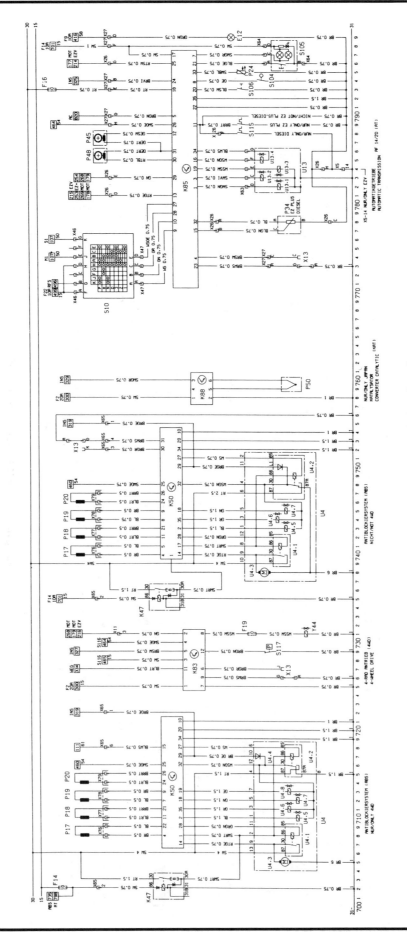

Wiring diagram for 1990 models (continued)

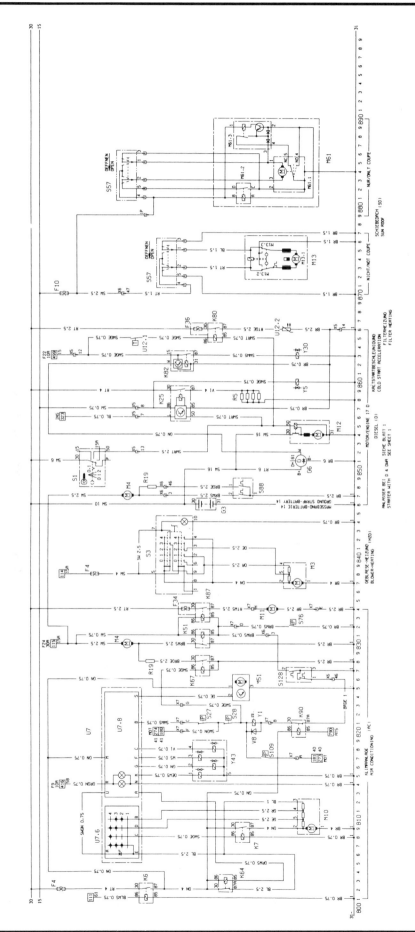

Wiring diagram for 1990 models (continued)

Wiring diagram for 1990 models (continued)

Key to wiring diagram for 1991 models
Not all items fitted to all models

Refer to Chapter 12, Section 15 for details of diagram usage and abbreviations found

Wiring identification

Example: GEWS 1.5
GE – Wire basic colour
WS – Wire tracer colour
1.5 – Wire cross-section in mm²

Colour code

BL	Blue	RT	Red
HBL	Light blue	WS	White
BR	Brown	SW	Black
GE	Yellow	LI	Lilac
GR	Grey	VI	Purple
GN	Green		

Location of (applicable) circuits	Track	Location of (applicable) circuits	Track
Air conditioning system	800 to 850	Glovebox lamp	599
Alternator	111	Headlamp aim adjustment system	758 to 766
Anti-lock braking system (ABS)	701 to 722	Headlamp dim-dip	427 to 431
Anti-theft alarm system	633 to 647	Headlamp washers	519 to 532
Automatic transmission control system	773 to 799	Headlamps	437 to 442
Battery	100	Headlamps 'ON' warning buzzer	493 to 495
Brake lamps	461 to 462	Heated front seats	560 to 566
Carburettor	118 to 121	Heated rear window	549 to 556
Central locking system	600 to 627	Heater blower motor	853 to 862
Check control system	347 to 371	Horn(s)	592 to 596
Cigarette lighter	597 to 598	Ignition (HEI) – 14 NV engine	121 to 128
Clock	661 to 663	Ignition (MSTS/EZ +) – 16 SV, 18 SV engines	236 to 256
Courtesy lamps – front	487 to 494	Instruments	301 to 344
Courtesy lamps – rear	569 to 573	Luggage compartment lamp	485
Direction indicator and hazard warning lamps	467 to 482	Radiator cooling fan	113, 115
Door mirrors	536 to 548	Radio/cassette player	586 to 591
Electric windows	665 to 699	Rear number plate lamp	413
Engine compartment lamp	415	Reversing lamps	496 to 498
Foglamps – front	444 to 452	Side and tail lamps	401 to 410
Foglamps – rear	444 to 457	Starter motor	102 to 110
Fuel injection and ignition (Multec) – C16 NZ engine	129 to 164	Sunroof	863 to 870
Fuel injection and ignition (Multec) – C18 NZ engine	972 to 997	Tailgate wiper	510 to 516
Fuel injection/ignition (Motronic M1.5) – 2.0 litre sohc engines	168 to 199	Trip computer	650 to 662
		Windscreen and tailgate washers	511 to 529
Fuel injection/ignition (Motronic M2.5) – 2.0 litre dohc engines	261 to 299	Windscreen wipers	501 to 506

No	Description	Track
E1	Side lamp – left	406
E2	Tail lamp – left	356, 374, 407
E3	Number plate lamp	413
E4	Sidelamp – right	409
E5	Tail lamp – right	358, 376, 410
E6	Engine compartment lamp	415
E7	Headlamp main beam – left	437
E8	Headlamp main beam – right	438
E9	Headlamp dipped beam – left	360, 378, 439
E10	Headlamp dipped beam – right	362, 380, 440
E11	Instrument illumination lamps	328 to 329
E12	Selector lever illumination lamp (automatic transmission)	799
E13	Luggage compartment lamp	485
E14	Courtesy lamp	487
E15	Glovebox lamp	599
E16	Cigarette lighter illumination lamp	596
E17	Reversing lamp – left	497
E18	Reversing lamp – right	498
E19	Heated rear window	552
E20	Front foglamp – left	448
E21	Front foglamp – right	447
E24	Rear foglamp – left	454
E25	Driver's seat heater	580
E27	Courtesy lamp – rear left	569 to 570
E28	Courtesy lamp – rear right	572 to 573
E30	Passenger front seat heater	564
E32	Clock illumination lamp	663
E38	Trip computer illumination lamp	654
E39	Rear foglamp – right	455
E41	Courtesy lamp (with delay)	488 to 490
E50	Kerb lamp – driver's door	666
E51	Kerb lamp – passenger door	684
F1 on	Fuses	Various
G1	Battery	101
G2	Alternator	111
G3	Battery (Diesel models)	882, 901
G6	Alternator (Diesel models)	884 to 886, 909 to 911
H1	Radio/cassette player	589 to 590, 634
H2	Horn	592
H3	Direction indicator warning lamp	315 to 320
H4	Oil pressure warning lamp	310
H5	Brake fluid level warning lamp	313
H6	Hazard warning flasher lamp	470
H7	Alternator charge warning lamp	310
H8	Headlamp main beam warning lamp	322
H9	Brake lamp – left	364, 382, 461
H10	Brake lamp – right	366, 384, 462
H11	Direction indicator lamp – front left	472
H12	Direction indicator lamp – rear left	473
H13	Direction indicator lamp – front right	461
H14	Direction indicator lamp – rear right	482
H15	Fuel level warning lamp	305
H16	Glow plug warning lamp (Diesel models)	323
H17	Trailer direction indicator warning lamp	321
H18	Horn	593
H19	Headlamps-on warning buzzer	494 to 495
H21	Handbrake-on warning lamp	315
H25	Door mirror warning lamp	542, 952
H26	ABS warning lamp	319
H30	Engine fault warning lamp	324
H33	Direction indicator side repeater lamp – left	476
H34	Direction indicator side repeater lamp – right	478
H42	Automatic transmission warning lamp	325
H45	Four-wheel-drive warning lamp	327
H46	Catalytic converter temperature warning lamp	329
H47	Anti-theft alarm horn	638
H48	Horn	594
K3	Relay – starter motor (anti-theft alarm)	109 to 110
K5	Relay – front foglamps	448 to 450
K6	Relay – air conditioning	801 to 802
K7	Relay – air conditioning blower	804 to 805
K8	Relay – intermittent windscreen wipe	503 to 506

No	Description	Track
K9	Relay – headlamp wash	519 to 520
K10	Relay – direction indicator/hazard warning flashers	467 to 469
K20	Ignition amplifier module	122 to 124, 236 to 237, 975 to 976
K25	Relay – glow plugs (Diesel models)	889 to 892
K30	Relay – intermittent rear window wipe	513 to 515
K35	Relay – door mirror heater	550 to 552
K37	Central locking control unit	606 to 612
K47	Relay – surge arrester (ABS)	702 to 703, 735 to 736
K50	ABS control unit	707 to 721, 740 to 754
K51	Relay – cooling fan	829 to 830, 842 to 843, 837 to 838
K57	Multec electronic control unit (ECU)	139 to 161
K58	Relay – fuel pump	163 to 164, 996 to 997
K59	Relay – daytime running lamps	420 to 426
K62	Dim-dip control unit	427 to 431
K63	Relay – horn	594 to 595
K64	Relay – air conditioning blower	802 to 803
K67	Relay – cooling fan	825 to 826, 849 to 850
K68	Relay – fuel injection system	196 to 199
K69	Motronic M2.5 module	267 to 297
K73	Relay – headlamp main beam relay (Calibra models)	432 to 433
K76	Glow plug control unit (Turbo diesel models)	916 to 921
K77	Relay – glow plugs (Turbo diesel models)	923 to 924
K78	Relay – preresistor (Turbo diesel models)	926 to 927
K79	Alternator charge warning lamp relay	911 to 913
K80	Relay – fuel filter heater (Diesel models)	898 to 899, 931 to 932
K82	Relay – engine revolution	895 to 896
K83	Four-wheel-drive control unit	725 to 731
K84	MSTS ignition module	242 to 256
K85	Automatic transmission control unit	774 to 797
K86	Check control unit	347 to 368
K87	Relay – auxiliary cooling fan	832 to 833, 839 to 840, 940 to 941
K88	Catalytic converter temperature control unit	758 to 760, 966 to 968
K89	Relay – rear foglamps	444 to 447
K90	Relay – air conditioning compressor	820 to 821
K91	Motronic M1.5 module	170 to 194
K94	Anti-theft alarm control unit	633 to 647
K97	Relay – headlamp washer pump time delay	530 to 532
K101	Relay – electric mirror parking position	961 to 964
K102	Parking brake control unit (automatic transmission)	769 to 771
K103	Relay – cooling fan	845 to 847
K107	Multec electronic control unit (ECU)	978 to 996
L1	Ignition coil	121 to 122, 133 to 134, 173, 174, 237 to 238, 974 to 975
M1	Starter motor	105 to 106
M2	Windscreen wiper motor	501 to 504
M3	Heater blower motor	854 to 856
M4	Radiator cooling fan motor	113, 115, 829, 847, 935
M6	Headlamp wiper motor – left	522 to 524
M7	Headlamp wiper motor – right	526 to 528
M8	Rear window wiper motor	511 to 513
M10	Air conditioning blower motor	805 to 808
M11	Cooling fan motor	840, 941
M12	Starter motor (Diesel models)	887 to 888, 905 to 906
M13	Sunroof motor assembly	865 to 869
M13.1	Sunroof motor	866 to 868
M13.2	Sunroof travel microswitch	866
M13.3	Sunroof travel microswitch	868
M18	Central locking motor – driver's door	607 to 610
M19	Central locking motor – left rear door	621 to 623
M20	Central locking motor – right rear door	625 to 627
M21	Fuel pump	164, 197, 229, 997
M24	Headlamp washer pump	532
M26	Electric aerial motor	588 to 589
M30	Door mirror motor and heater – driver's door	538 to 541
M31	Door mirror motor and heater – passenger door	544 to 547

No	Description	Track
M32	Central locking motor – passenger door	613 to 616
M33	Idle speed adjuster/idle air control stepper motor	146 to 149, 185 to 186, 277 to 278, 985 to 988
M39	Headlamp aim adjuster motor – driver's side	759 to 762
M40	Headlamp aim adjuster motor – passenger side	763 to 766
M41	Central locking motor – fuel filler	623 to 624
M47	Electric window motor – front left	667 to 671
M48	Electric window motor – front right	685 to 689
M49	Electric window motor – rear left	673 to 677
M50	Electric window motor – rear right	691 to 695
M55	Windscreen and rear window washer pump	516
M60	Central locking motor (Calibra models)	627 to 628
M61	Sunroof assembly (Calibra models)	872 to 880
M61.1	Sunroof motor (Calibra models)	873 to 876
M61.2	Relay 1 – sunroof motor (Calibra models)	872 to 873
M61.3	Relay 2 – sunroof motor (Calibra models)	878 to 880
M62	Door mirror motor – driver's door	947 to 953
M63	Door mirror motor – passenger door	956 to 962
P1	Fuel gauge	304
P2	Coolant temperature gauge	306
P3	Clock	662
P4	Fuel level sender unit	304
P5	Coolant temperature gauge sender	306
P7	Tachometer	308
P8	Oil pressure gauge	341
P9	Voltmeter	339
P10	Oil pressure sensor	341
P11	Airflow meter (Motronic M1.5)	185 to 189
P12	Coolant temperature sensor	182, 272
P13	Trip computer outside air temperature sensor	655 to 656
P14	Distance sensor	336 to 337, 915 to 916
P17	ABS wheel sensor – front left	707, 740
P18	ABS wheel sensor – front right	710, 742
P19	ABS wheel sensor – rear left	712, 744
P20	ABS wheel sensor – rear right	713, 746
P21	Speedometer frequency sensor	332
P23	Pressure sensor	152 to 154, 984 to 986
P24	Automatic transmission fluid temperature sensor	252, 795
P25	Bulb failure sensor	373 to 386
P27	Brake pad wear sensor – front left	351, 396
P28	Brake pad wear sensor – front right	351, 396
P30	Coolant temperature sensor	150, 982
P32	Oxygen sensor – heated	194 to 195, 291 to 292
P33	Oxygen sensor	157, 991
P34	Throttle position sensor/potentiometer	158 to 160, 180 to 181, 777 to 778, 987 to 989
P35	Crankshaft speed/position sensor	189 to 191, 281 to 282, 982 to 984
P39	Trailer bulb failure sensor	368 to 370, 387 to 389
P43	Electronic speedometer	336
P44	Air mass meter (Motronic M2.5)	294 to 298
P45	Automatic transmission input speed sensor	791 to 792
P46	Knock sensor	284 to 285
P47	Distributor 'Hall-effect' sensor (Motronic M2.5)	287 to 288
P48	Automatic transmission output speed sensor	789 to 790
P50	Catalytic converter temperature sensor	759 to 760, 977 to 978
P53	Anti-theft alarm sensor – driver's side	639 to 642
P54	Anti-theft alarm sensor – passenger side	644 to 647
P55	Coolant temperature sensor (Turbo diesel models)	919
R2	Carburettor preheating	121
R3	Cigarette lighter	597
R5	Glow plugs (Diesel models)	891 to 892, 922 to 924
R12	Automatic choke	118
R13	Heated windscreen washer nozzle – left	526
R14	Heated windscreen washer nozzle – right	528
R15	Mixture adjustment potentiometer	155 to 157
R19	Cooling fan motor resistor	115, 832, 935
R22	Glow plugs resistor (Turbo diesel models)	927
S1	Ignition switch	105 to 106, 885 to 886, 905 to 906
S1.2	Key contact switch	586
S2.1	Lighting switch	404 to 407

No	Description	Track
S2.2	Courtesy lamp switch	487
S2.3	Instrument illumination lamp dimmer	328
S3	Heater blower switch	853 to 860
S4	Heated rear window and mirror switch	554 to 556
S5.2	Dipped beam switch	438 to 439
S5.3	Direction indicator switch	480 to 482
S5.4	Sidelamp switch	401 to 402
S7	Reversing lamp switch	497
S8	Brake lamp switch	462
S9.2	Windscreen wiper interval switch	501 to 504
S9.5	Rear window washer/wiper switch	514 to 516
S10	Automatic transmission starter inhibitor switch	773 to 779
S11	Brake fluid level warning sensor	31
S13	Handbrake-on warning switch	315
S14	Oil pressure switch	310
S15	Luggage compartment lamp switch	485
S17	Passenger door courtesy lamp switch	490
S21	Front fog lamp switch	450 to 452
S22	Rear foglamp switch	455 to 457
S24	Air conditioning blower motor switch	804 to 811
S27	Air conditioning compressor low-pressure switch	821
S28	Air conditioning compressor high-pressure switch	821
S29	Cooling fan switch	113
S30	Driver's seat heater switch	560 to 562
S31	Rear door courtesy lamp switch – left	491
S32	Rear door courtesy lamp switch – right	491
S37	Driver's door electric window switch assembly	668 to 694
S37.1	Electric window switch – front left	668 to 670
S37.2	Electric window switch – front right	686 to 688
S37.3	Electric window switch – rear left	674 to 676
S37.4	Electric window switch – rear right	692 to 694
S37.5	Electric window safety cut-out switch	672 to 673
S37.6	Electric window anti-jam switch	690
S37.7	Electric window automatic control	677 to 682
S39	Electric window switch – rear left door	678 to 680
S40	Electric window switch – rear right door	696 to 698
S41	Central locking switch – driver's door	601 to 603
S42	Central locking switch – passenger door	605
S44	Throttle position sensor	278 to 279
S47	Driver's door courtesy lamp switch	493 to 494
S52	Hazard warning flasher switch	469 to 474
S55	Passenger seat heater switch	564 to 566
S57	Sunroof switch	864 to 869, 872 to 877
S63.1	Trip computer function reset switch	656
S63.2	Trip computer clock hours adjustment switch	657
S63.3	Trip computer function select switch	658
S63.5	Trip computer clock minutes adjustment switch	659
S64	Horn switch	592, 595
S68.1	Door mirror adjustment switch	538 to 540, 945 to 950
S68.3	Door mirror left/right selector switch	537 to 541, 946 to 950
S68.4	Door mirror parking position switch	952
S76	Air conditioning compressor switch – high-pressure cooling fan	827
S82	Washer pump switch	347, 392
S88	Cooling fan switch	115 to 116, 935 to 936
S93	Coolant level sensor	348, 393
S95	Oil level sensor	349, 394
S98	Headlamp aim adjustment switch	758 to 760
S99	Electric window switch – driver's door	685
S100	Electric window switch – passenger door	683
S101	Air conditioning compressor switch	822 to 824
S102	Air conditioning circulation switch	816 to 818
S104	Automatic transmission kickdown switch	794
S105	Automatic transmission 'Winter' mode button	796 to 798
S106	Automatic transmission 'Economy/Sport' mode button	793
S109	Air conditioning compressor switch	818
S115	Automatic transmission coolant temperature switch	788 to 789
S116	Brake lamp switch	464 to 465
S117	Four-wheel-drive hydraulic pressure switch	729

No	Description	Track
S119	Air conditioning refrigerant temperature switch	829, 843
S120	Anti-theft alarm bonnet switch	635
S127	Central locking switch – tailgate (Calibra models)	630
S128	Air conditioning refrigerant temperature cooling switch	825 to 826
S131	Air conditioning defroster lever limit switch	815
U2	Trip computer	651 to 662
U4	ABS hydraulic modulator assembly	705 to 718, 738 to 751
U4.1	ABS hydraulic pump relay	706 to 709, 739 to 742
U4.2	ABS solenoid valves relay	715 to 718, 747 to 751
U4.3	ABS hydraulic pump	705, 738
U4.4	ABS diode	717
U4.5	ABS solenoid valve – front left	710, 743
U4.6	ABS solenoid valve – front right	711, 744
U4.7	ABS solenoid valve – rear left	712, 745
U4.8	ABS solenoid valve – rear right	713
U5	Check control display	347 to 355
U5.1	Check control washer fluid level warning lamp	352
U5.2	Check control oil level warning lamp	351
U5.3	Check control coolant level warning lamp	350
U5.4	Check control tail lamp and dipped beam bulb failure warning lamp	349
U5.5	Check control brake lamp bulb failure warning lamp	348
U5.6	Check control brake wear warning lamp	347
U6	LCD instruments	
U6.1	Check control washer fluid level warning lamp	392
U6.2	Check control oil level warning lamp	394
U6.3	Check control coolant level warning lamp	393
U6.4	Check control tail lamp and dipped beam bulb failure warning lamp	391
U6.5	Check control brake lamp bulb failure warning lamp	395
U6.6	Check control brake pad wear warning lamp	396

No	Description	Track
U12.1	Temperature switch (Diesel models)	898, 931
U12.2	Fuel filter heater (Diesel models)	899, 932
U13	AF 14/20 automatic transmission	782 to 786
U13.1	Solenoid – 1/2 and 3/4 shift up	782
U13.2	Solenoid – 2/3 shift up	783
U13.3	Solenoid – converter lock-up control	784
U13.4	Solenoid – main fluid pressure control	785
V1	Brake fluid level warning lamp test diode	312
V8	Air conditioning compressor diode	820
Y1	Air conditioning compressor clutch	821
Y4	Headlamp washer solenoid valve	520
Y5	Fuel solenoid valve (Diesel models)	893, 928
Y7	Fuel injectors	187 to 194, 280 to 287
Y10	Distributor (Hall-effect)	246 to 251
Y23	Distributor (inductive discharge)	123 to 127
Y24	Distributor (inductive discharge)	129 to 136
Y25	Idle-up solenoid valve (automatic transmission)	242
Y30	Cold start valve (Diesel models)	896
Y32	Fuel injector	140, 979
Y33	Distributor	170, 262, 972 to 974
Y34	Fuel tank vent valve	193, 292
Y35	Air conditioning circulation solenoid valve	816
Y44	Four-wheel-drive solenoid valve	731
Y47	Parking brake lock lifting magnet (automatic transmission)	769
X13	Diagnostic equipment connector	149, 170 to 171, 254 to 255, 269 to 270, 325, 339 to 340, 752 to 753, 774 to 775, 992 to 993
X15	Octane coding plug	160, 184 to 185, 248 to 249, 990 to 991
X54	Ignition coding plug	270 to 271
X1 on	Wiring connectors	Various

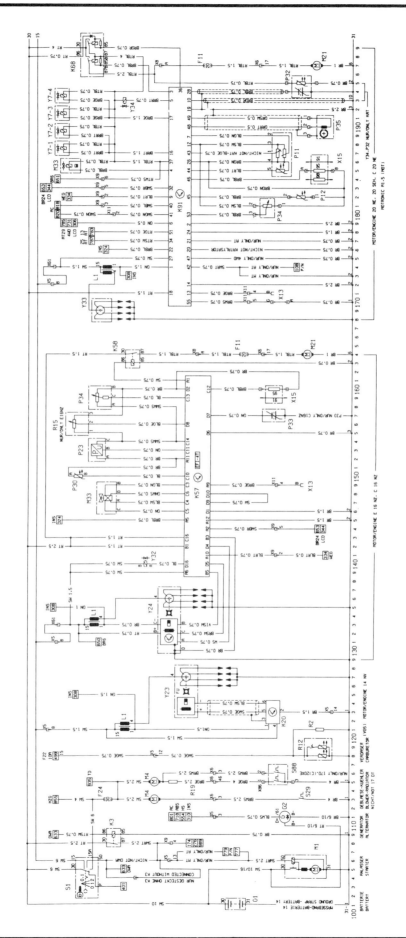

Wiring diagram for 1991 models

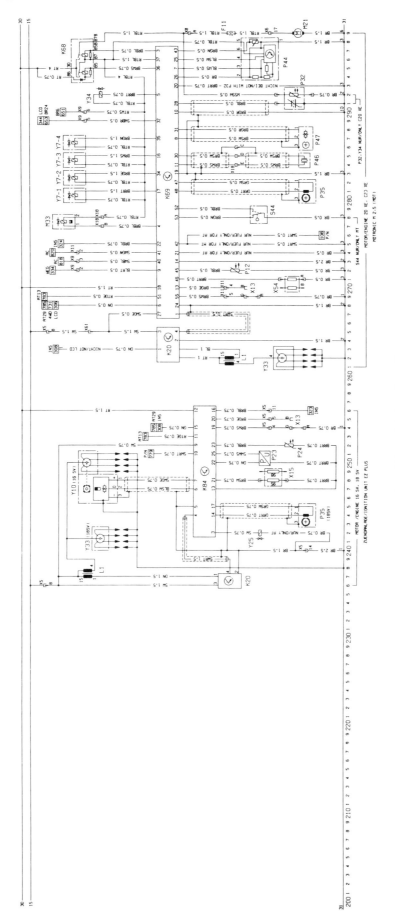

Wiring diagram for 1991 models (continued)

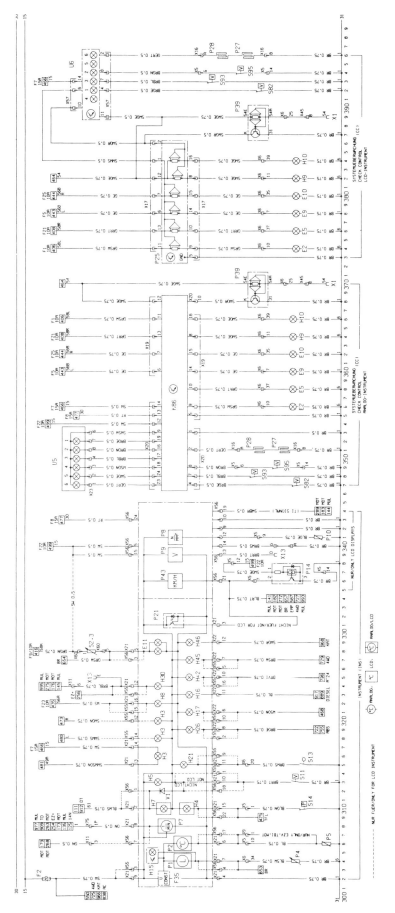

Wiring diagram for 1991 models (continued)

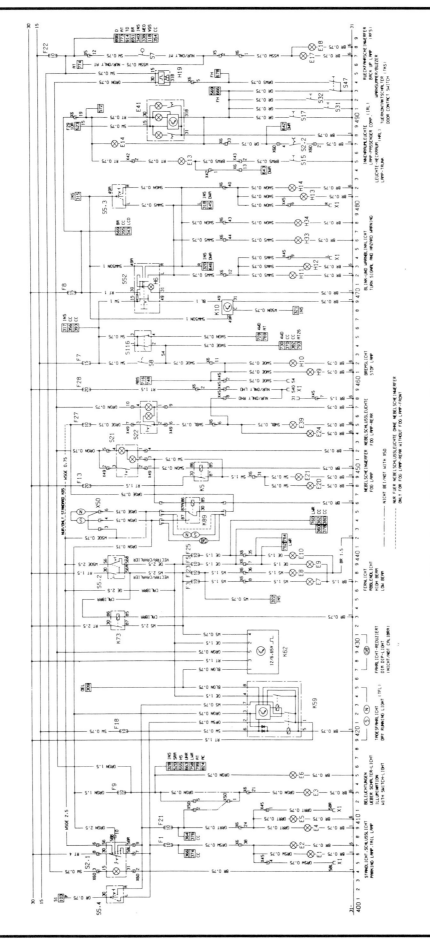

Wiring diagram for 1991 models (continued)

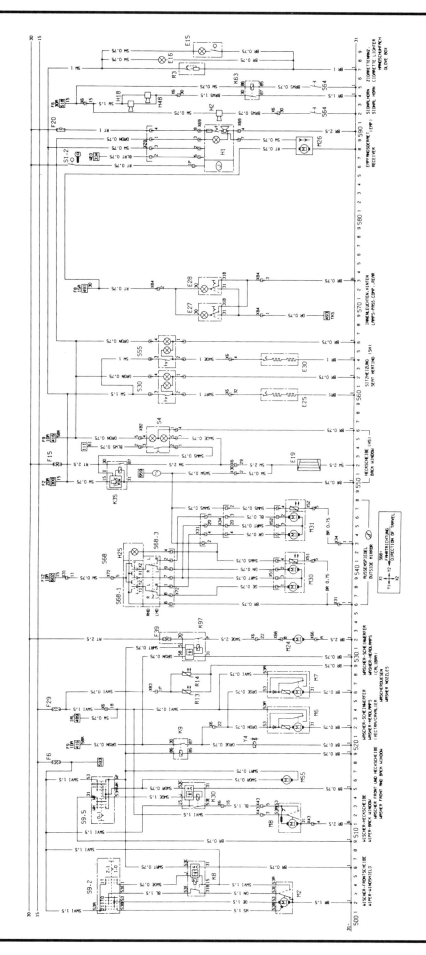

Wiring diagram for 1991 models (continued)

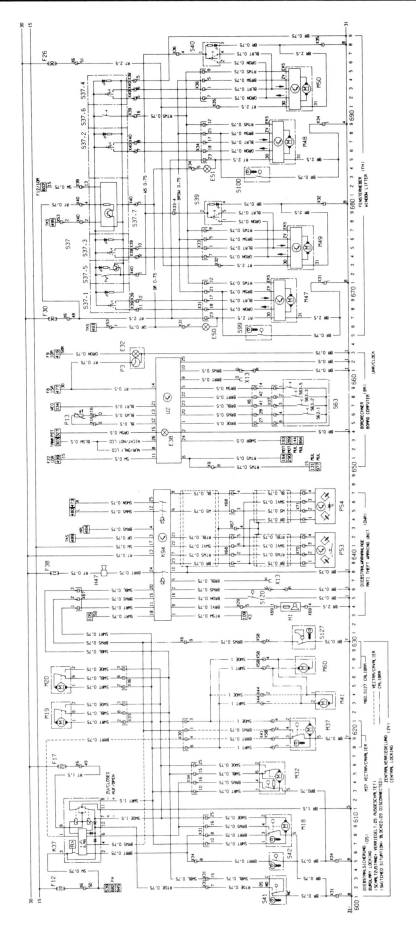

Wiring diagram for 1991 models (continued)

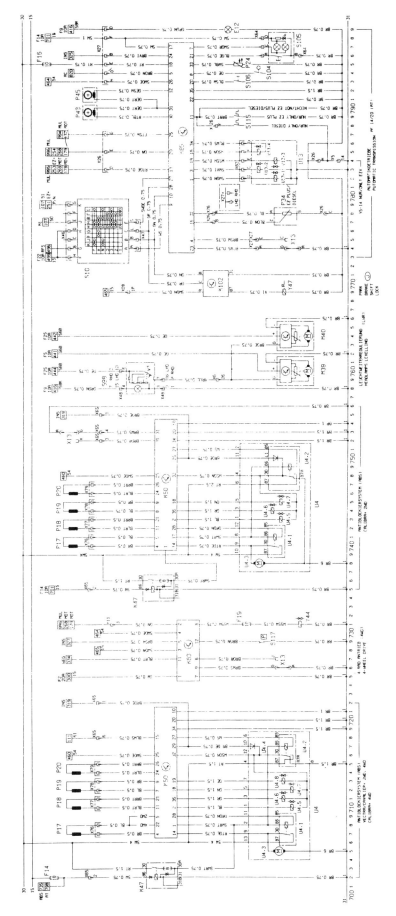

Wiring diagram for 1991 models (continued)

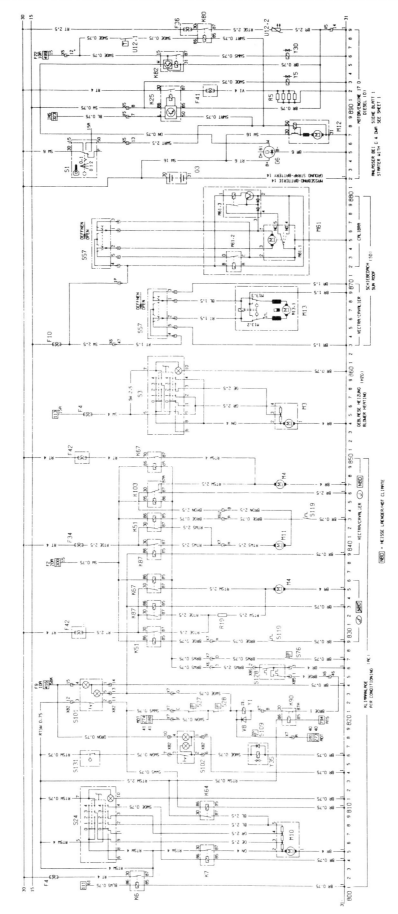

Wiring diagram for 1991 models (continued)

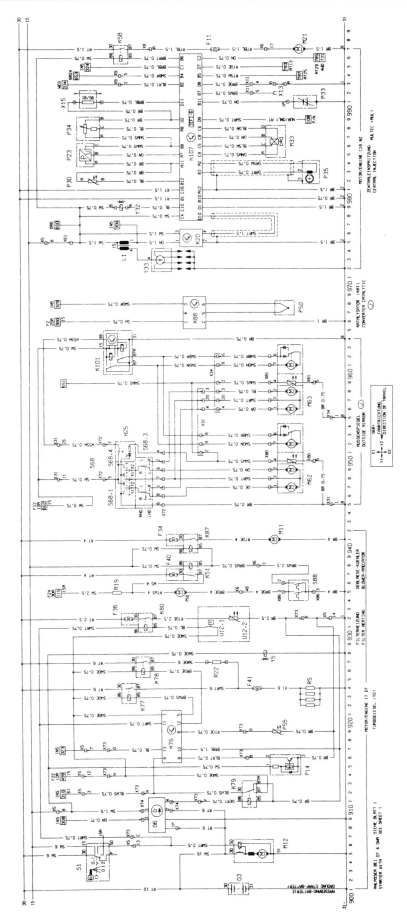

Wiring diagram for 1991 models (continued)

Key to wiring diagram for 1992-on models

Not all items fitted to all models

No	Description	
E1	Left parking lamp	506
E2	Left tail lamp	507, 745
E3	Licence plate lamp	513
E4	Right parking lamp	509
E5	Right tail lamp	510, 746
E6	Engine compartment lamp	515
E7	Left high beam	535
E8	Right high beam	536
E9	Left low beam	537, 747
E10	Right low beam	538, 748
E11	Instrument lights	728, 729
E12	Selector lever lamp	498, 499
E13	Boot lamp	585
E14	Passenger compartment lamp	587
E15	Glove box lamp	677
E16	Cigarette lighter lamp	676
E17	Left reversing lamp	597
E18	Right reversing lamp	598
E19	Heated back window	652
E20	Left fog lamp	553
E21	Right fog lamp	554
E24	Left rear fog lamp	548
E25	Left front heating mat	660
E27	Left rear reading lamp	680, 681
E28	Right rear reading lamp	683, 684
E30	Right front heating mat	664
E32	Clock lamp	863
E37	Left mirror make-up lamp	686
E38	Computer lamp	854
E39	Right rear foglamp	549
E40	Right mirror make-up lamp	688
E41	Passenger compartment delay lamp	588 to 590
E50	Driver door lamp	866
E51	Passenger door lamp	884
F1 on	Fuses	Various
F35	Voltage stabilizer	702
G1	Battery	101
G2	Alternator	114
G6	Diesel alternator	402 to 405
H1	Radio	784 to 798
H3	Turn signal lamp telltale	716, 718
H4	Oil pressure telltale	710
H5	Brake fluid telltale	712
H6	Telltale hazard warning system	570
H7	Charging indicator lamp	710
H8	High beam telltale	722
H9	Left stop lamp	561, 749
H10	Right stop lamp	562, 750
H11	Left front turn signal lamp	572
H12	Left rear turn signal lamp	573
H13	Right front turn signal lamp	581
H14	Right rear turn signal lamp	582

No	Description	
H15	Fuel telltale	705, 706
H16	Preheating time telltale	715
H17	Trailer turn signal lamp telltale	717
H18	Horn	670
H19	Headlamps on warning buzzer	594, 595
H21	Parking brake telltale	713
H23	Airbag telltale	719
H25	Heated back window & mirror telltale	642, 765
H26	ABS telltale	721
H27	Safety checking warning buzzer	996 to 998
H28	Seat belt warning telltale	723
H30	Engine telltale	724
H33	Left auxiliary turn signal lamp	576
H34	Right auxiliary turn signal lamp	578
H36	Additional stop lamp	563
H37	Left front loudspeaker	788 to 790
H38	Right front loudspeaker	794 to 796
H39	Left rear loudspeaker	788, 789
H40	Right rear loudspeaker	791, 792
H42	Automatic programme power telltale	725
H45	Four wheel drive telltale	727
H46	Catalytic converter temperature telltale	729
H47	Anti-theft warning unit horn	838
H48	Horn	671
H51	Traction control telltale	720
H52	Left front tweeter	787 to 791
H53	Right front tweeter	793 to 797
K3	Starter relay anti-theft warning unit	109, 110
K5	Fog lamps relay	554 to 555
K6	Air conditioning relay	901, 902
K7	Four stage air conditioning blower relay	904, 905
K8	Windshield wiper interval relay	603 to 606
K9	Headlamps washer unit relay	619, 620
K10	Flasher unit	567 to 569
K20	Ignition coil module	149, 150, 171, 172, 241, 242, 302 to 305, 361 to 364, 1001 to 1005, 1055 to 1061
K22	Coolant pump relay	133, 134, 969, 970
K25	Glow time relay	440 to 443
K26	Radiator blower relays	972 to 974
K27	Radiator blower relay	137 to 139
K30	Back window wiper interval relay	613 to 615
K31	Airbag control unit	1191 to 1198
K34	Radiator blower time delay relay	356 to 358, 956 to 958
K35	Heated back window & mirror time delay relay	650 to 652
K37	Central locking control unit	805 to 812
K51	Radiator blower relay	430, 431, 942, 943, 956, 957
K52	Radiator blower relay	145 to 147, 433, 435, 982 to 984, 960 to 962
K57	Multec unit control	211 to 230, 244 to 262

No	Description	
K58	Fuel pump relay	231, 232, 262, 263
K59	Running light relay	520 to 525
K60	Compressor relay	931, 932
K61	Motronic control unit	270 to 294, 307 to 337, 366 to 396, 1007 to 1037, 1063 to 1096
K63	Horn relay	671, 672
K64	1 stage air conditioning blower relay	913, 914
K67	Radiator blower relay	142, 143, 436, 437, 948, 949, 964, 965, 986, 987
K68	Fuel injection unit relay	295 to 299, 393 to 397, 334 to 338, 1093 to 1097, 1034 to 1038
K73	High beam relay (Calibra)	530, 531
K76	Glow time control unit	413 to 417
K77	Glow plugs relay	419, 420
K78	Preresistor relay (70A)	422, 423
K79	Charge indicator relay	406 to 408
K80	Filter heating relay	426, 427, 452, 453
K82	Engine revolution relay	447, 448
K83	Four wheel drive unit control	342 to 349
K84	EZ Plus control unit	155 to 166, 177 to 191
K85	Automatic transmission control unit	473 to 496
K86	Check control unit	736 to 752
K87	Radiator blower relay	945, 946, 953, 954, 977, 978
K88	Catalytic converter temperature control unit	462 to 464
K89	Rear fog lamp relay	543 to 545
K90	Compressor relay (automatic transmission only)	930, 931
K94	Anti-theft warning unit control unit	833 to 847
K95	Traction control ECU	1125 to 1140
K97	Headlamps washer pump time delay relay	630 to 632
K101	Parking position mirror relay	774 to 777
K102	Park brake shift lock control unit	469 to 471
L1	Ignition coil	150, 172, 205, 273, 241, 302, 361
L2	Ignition coil	1000 to 1004, 1054 to 1059
M1	Starter	105, 106
M2	Windshield wiper motor	601 to 604
M3	Heating blower motor	127 to 129
M4	Radiator blower motor	118, 120, 140, 356, 431, 948, 954, 980
M6	Left headlamp wiper motor	622 to 624
M7	Right headlamp wiper motor	626 to 628
M8	Back window wiper motor	611 to 613
M10	Air conditioning blower motor	905 to 908
M11	Radiator blower motor	136, 434, 962, 984
M13	Vectra/Cavalier sun roof motor	1172 to 1175
M13.1	Sun roof motor	1172, 1174
M13.2	Timing box microswitch	1172
M13.3	Timing box microswitch	1174
M18	Driver door central locking motor	807 to 810
M19	Left rear door central locking motor	821 to 823
M20	Right rear door central locking motor	825 to 827
M21	Fuel pump	232, 263, 297, 339, 399, 834, 1098, 1039
M23	Alternator blower motor	135, 974
M24	Headlamps washer pump	632
M26	Automatic antenna motor	798 to 799
M30	Driver side outside mirror	638 to 641
M31	Passenger side outside mirror	644 to 647
M32	Passenger door central locking motor	813 to 816
M33	Idle speed actuator	285, 286, 317, 318, 381, 382, 1019, 1020, 1075, 1076
M37	Tail gate/boot lid central locking motor	818 to 821
M39	Left headlamp levelling motor	692 to 695
M40	Right headlamp levelling motor	696 to 699
M41	Fuel filler door central locking motor	823, 824
M47	Driver door window lifter motor	867 to 871
M48	Passenger door window lifter motor	885 to 889
M49	Left rear window lifter motor	873 to 877
M50	Right rear window lifter motor	891 to 895
M55	Windshield and back window washer pump	617
M57	Coolant pump	134, 970
M60	Calibra tailgate central locking motor	827, 828
M61	Calibra sun roof motor	1178 to 1186
M61.1	Sun roof motor	1179 to 1182
M61.2	Relay 1	1178, 1179
M61.3	Relay 2	1184 to 1186
M62	Driver side outside mirror	760 to 767
M63	Passenger side outside mirror	769 to 776
M65	TC throttle valve actuator	1130 to 1134
M66	Idle air stepper motor	215 to 218, 250 to 253
P1	Fuel indicator	704
P2	Coolant temperature indicator	706
P3	Clock	862
P4	Fuel sensor	704
P5	Coolant temperature sensor	706
P7	Tachometer	708
P11	Airflow meter	285 to 289
P12	Coolant temperature sensor	282, 381
P13	Outside temperature sensor	856
P14	Distance sensor	412, 413
P17	Left front revolution sensor	1110, 1154
P18	Right front revolution sensor	1113, 1157
P19	Left rear revolution sensor	1116, 1160
P20	Right rear revolution sensor	1119, 1163
P21	Distance sensor	731
P23	Intake manifold absolute pressure sensor	160, 161, 185, 186, 217 to 219, 250 to 252
P24	Engine oil temperature sensor	162, 187
P27	Left front brake lining sensor	740
P28	Right front brake lining sensor	740
P29	Intake manifold temperature sensor	382, 1016, 1072
P30	Coolant temperature sensor	215, 248, 313, 1017, 1073
P32	Heated exhaust oxygen sensor	294, 295, 331, 332, 391, 392, 1034, 1035, 1093, 1094
P33	Exhaust oxygen sensor	229, 257
P34	Throttle valve potentiometer	221 to 223, 280, 281, 253 to 255, 383 to 385, 478, 479, 1018, 1019, 1074, 1075
P35	Crankshaft impulse sensor	178 to 180, 289 to 291, 248 to 250, 318 to 320, 373 to 375, 1025 to 1027, 1084 to 1086
P38	Transmission oil temperature sensor	494
P39	Trailer bulb test sensor	752 to 754
P43	Electronic speedometer	733
P44	Air mass meter	393 to 397, 334 to 338, 1037, 1038, 1096, 1097
P45	Transmission input revolution sensor	490, 491
P46	Knock control sensor	322, 323, 377, 378, 1022, 1023, 1078, 1079
P47	Cylinder identification hall sensor	325 to 327, 385 to 387, 1028 to 1030, 1087, 1089
P48	Automatic transmission distance sensor	488, 489
P50	Catalytic converter temperature sensor	463, 464
P53	Driver side anti-theft warning unit sensor	839 to 847
P54	Passenger side anti-theft warning unit sensor	839 to 847
P55	Engine coolant temperature sensor	415
P56	Knock control sensor II	1080, 1081
P57	Antenna	797
R3	Cigarette lighter	675
R5	Glow plugs	418 to 420, 441 to 443
R13	Left heated washer nozzle	626
R14	Right heated washer nozzle	628
R19	Radiator blower pre-resistor	120, 140, 945
R22	Glow plugs pre-resistor	423
R23	Driver airbag squib	1194
S1	Starter switch	103 to 106
S1.2	Key contact switch	783
S2	Light switch assembly	
S2.1	Light switch	504 to 507
S2.2	Passenger compartment lamp switch	587
S2.3	Instrument lights dimmer	728

No	Description	
S3	Heating blower switch	123 to 130
S4	Heated back window & mirror switch	654 to 657
S5	Turn signal switch assembly	
S5.2	Low beam switch	536, 537
S5.3	Turn signal switch	580 to 582
S5.4	Parking lamp switch	501, 502
S7	Reversing lamp switch	597, 599
S8	Stop lamp switch	562
S9	Wiper unit switch	
S9.2	Interval windshield wiper switch	601 to 604
S9.5	Back window and washer unit wiper switch	614 to 616
S10	Automatic transmission switch	472 to 478
S11	Brake fluid control switch	712
S13	Parking brake switch	713
S14	Oil pressure switch	710
S15	Boot lamp switch	585
S17	Passenger door contact switch	590
S20	Pressure switch	
S20.1	Low pressure compressor switch	925
S20.2	High pressure compressor switch	925
S20.3	High pressure blower compressor switch	939
S21	Fog lamps switch	555 to 557
S22	Rear fog lamp switch	549 to 551
S24	Air conditioning blower switch	904 to 911
S29	Coolant temperature switch	118, 137, 357, 942, 957, 972
S30	Left front heating mat switch	660 to 662
S31	Rear left door contact switch	591
S32	Rear right door contact switch	592
S33	Traction control switch	1130, 1131
S37	Window lifter switch	868 to 894
S37.1	Left window lifter switch	868 to 870
S37.2	Right window lifter switch	886 to 888
S37.3	Left rear window lifter switch	874 to 876
S37.4	Right rear window lifter switch	892 to 894
S37.5	Safety switch	872, 873
S37.6	Window anti-jam off switch	890
S37.7	Automatic window lifter control	877 to 882
S39	Left rear door window lifter switch	878 to 880
S40	Right rear door window lifter switch	896 to 898
S41	Driver door burglary locking switch	800 to 802
S42	Passenger door central locking switch	805
S44	Throttle valve switch	316, 317
S47	Driver door contact switch	593, 594
S52	Hazard warning switch	569 to 573
S53	First gear identification switch	372
S55	Right front heating mat switch	664 to 666
S57	Sun roof switch	1170 to 1183
S63	Computer switch	
S63.1	Function reset switch	856
S63.2	Clock hours adjustment switch	857
S63.3	Function select switch	858
S63.4	Clock minute adjustment switch	859
S64	Horn switch	672
S68	Outside mirror switch assembly	
S68.1	Outside mirror adjustment switch	638 to 640, 758 to 762
S68.3	Left/right outside mirror switch	637 to 641, 759 to 763
S68.4	Parking position switch	765
S82	Washer fluid minimum capacity control switch	736
S88	2 stage coolant temperature switch	120, 121, 137, 138, 430, 431
S89	Seat belt switch	998
S93	Coolant minimum capacity control switch	737
S95	Engine oil minuimum capacity control switch	738
S98	Headlamps levelling switch	691 to 693
S99	ZV driver door window lifter switch	865
S100	ZV passenger door window lifter switch	883
S101	Compressor switch	926 to 928
S102	Circulation switch	918 to 920
S103	Transmission temperature switch	350
S104	Kickdown switch	493
S105	Start-up assistance switch	495 to 497
S106	Economy power programme switch	492

No	Description	
S109	Acceleration revolution pressure switch	921
S115	Coolant temperature switch	487, 488
S116	Stop lamp switch	564, 565
S117	Hydraulic pressure switch	346
S120	Engine compartment hood (anti-theft warning unit) switch	835
S127	Calibra tail gate central locking switch	831
S128	Coolant temperature switch	936, 937
S131	Defroster lever limit switch	918
U2	Computer	851 to 862
U4	ABS hydroaggregate	1102 to 1122, 1146 to 1164
U4.1	Pump motor relay	1102, 1103, 1146, 1147
U4.2	Solenoid valves relay	1104, 1105, 1148, 1149
U4.3	Pump motor	1102, 1146
U4.4	Diode	1105, 1149
U4.5	Left front solenoid valve	1109, 1153
U4.6	Right front solenoid valve	1111, 1155
U4.7	Rear axle solenoid valve	1113, 1157
U4.8	ABS control unit	1106 to 1122, 1150 to 1164
U4.9	Solenoid valves plug	1109 to 1113, 1153 to 1157
U5	Check control display	
U5.1	Washer fluid minimum capacity telltale	741
U5.2	Oil minimum capacity telltale	740
U5.3	Coolant minimum capacity telltale	739
U5.4	Tail light & low beam telltale	738
U5.5	Stop light failure telltale	737
U5.6	Front brake lining telltale	736
U12	Filter heater	
U12.1	Temperature switch	426, 452
U12.2	Filter heater	427, 453
U13	Automatic transmission	
U13.1	Solenoid valve (shift 1)	481
U13.2	Solenoid valve (shift 2)	482
U13.3	Solenoid valve (lock up control)	483
U13.4	Solenoid valve (pressure control)	484
U17	Roof antenna amplifier	795
V1	Brake fluid test bulb diode	712
V8	Air conditioning compressor diode	926
X1 on	Wiring connectors	Various
X10	Anti theft warning unit code	837
X13	Diagnostic link	164, 165, 189, 190, 226, 270, 271, 258, 259, 309, 310, 370, 371, 343, 344, 473, 474, 573, 725, 836, 837, 860, 861, 1012, 1013, 1069, 1070, 1118, 1119, 1136, 1162, 1163
X15	Octane number plug	157, 158, 182, 183, 225, 226, 257, 258, 284, 285
X54	Ignition coding plug	310, 311, 1014, 1070, 1071
Y1	Air conditioning compressor clutch	925
Y4	Headlamps washer solenoid valve	620
Y5	Fuel solenoid valve	410, 445
Y7	Fuel injection valves	287 to 294, 320 to 327, 384 to 391, 1025 to 1032, 1078 to 1089
Y10	Hall sensor ignition distributor	153 to 158
Y11	Hot start solenoid valve	375, 376
Y12	Charging pressure control changeover valve	377, 378
Y18	Exhaust gas recirculation valve	1093
Y23	Inductive sensor distributor	201 to 208
Y24	Distributor (inductive discharge)	
Y25	Acceleration revolution solenoid valve	155, 177
Y30	Cold start acceleration solenoid valve	448
Y32	Fuel injection valve	212, 245
Y33	Ignition distributor	175 to 177, 268 to 270, 238 to 240, 301 to 303, 360 to 362
Y34	Tank ventilation valve	293, 331, 332, 379, 380, 1092, 1016, 1017,
Y35	Circulation solenoid valve	918
Y44	Four wheel drive solenoid valve	350
Y47	Park brake shift lock lifting magnet	469

Wiring diagram for 1992-on models

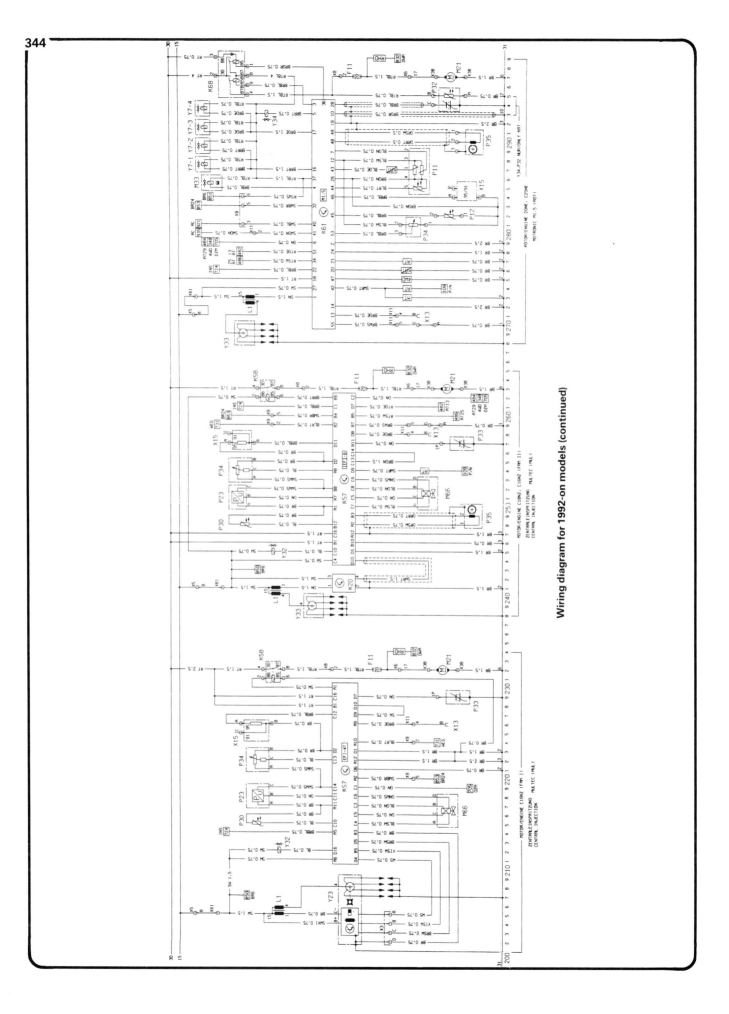

Wiring diagram for 1992-on models (continued)

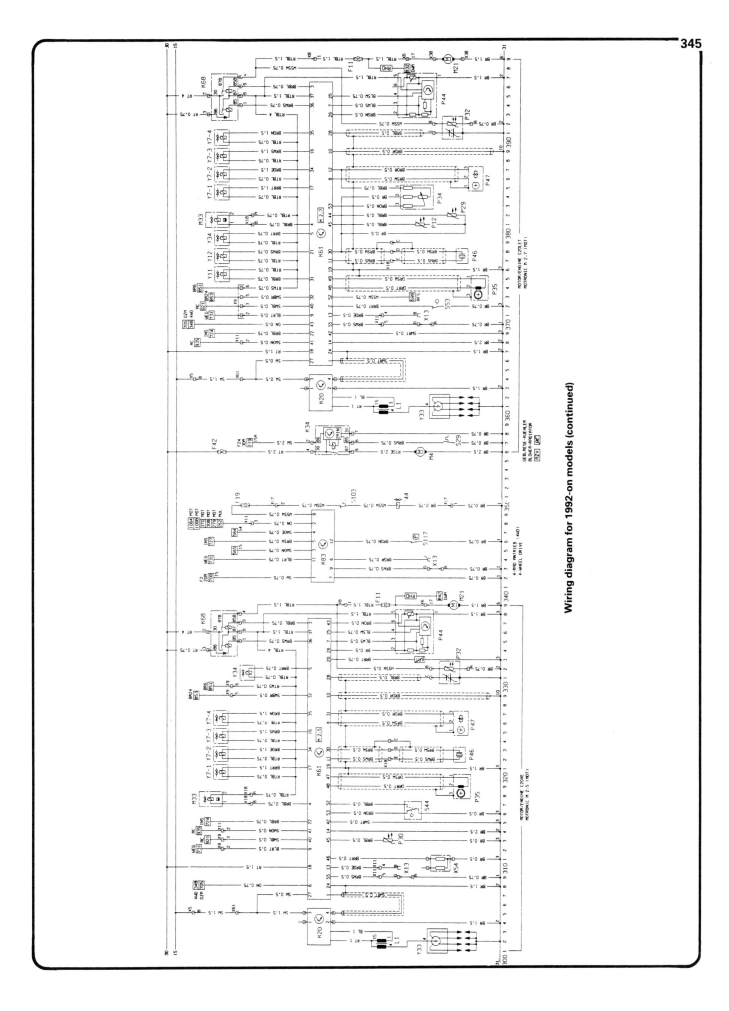

Wiring diagram for 1992-on models (continued)

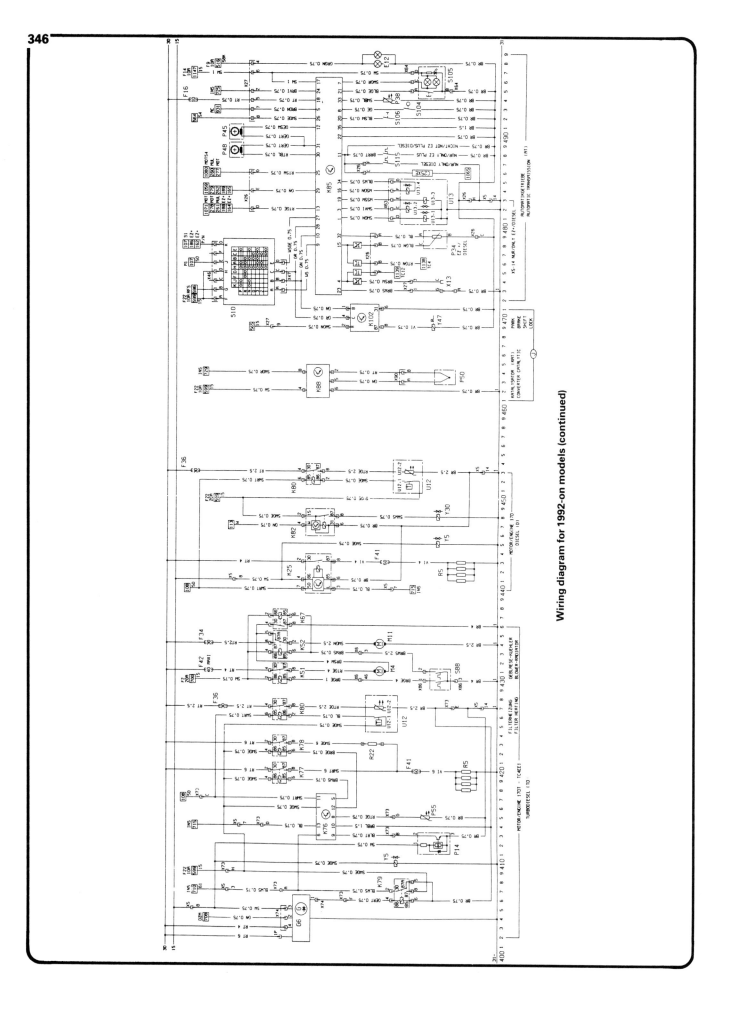

Wiring diagram for 1992-on models (continued)

Wiring diagram for 1992-on models (continued)

Wiring diagram for 1992-on models (continued)

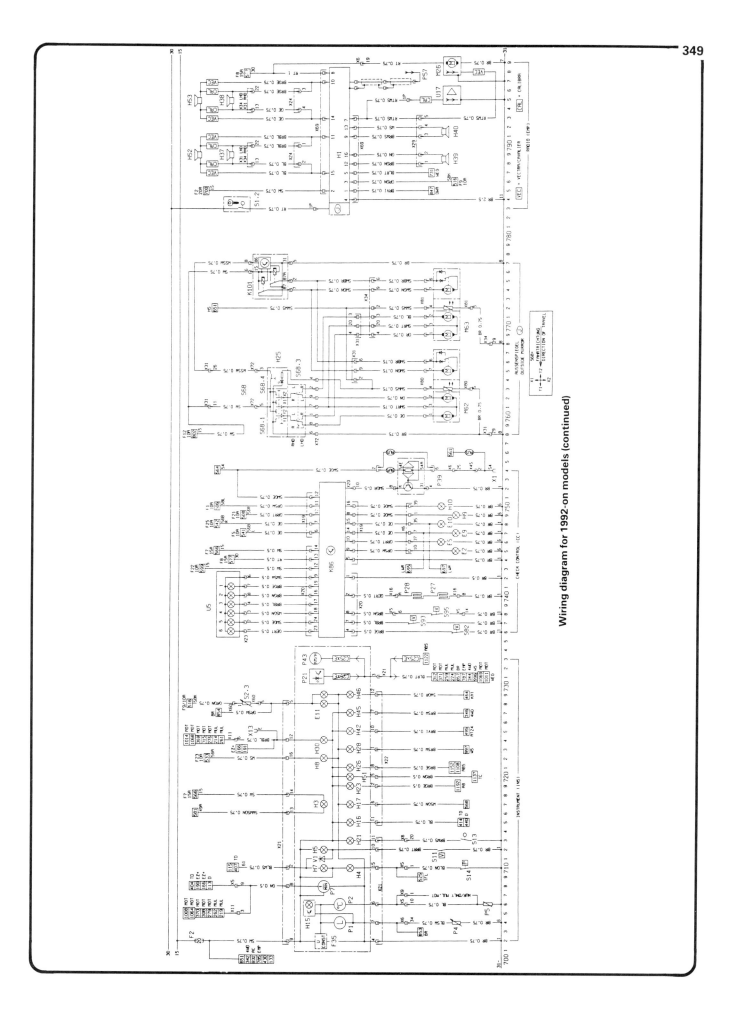

Wiring diagram for 1992-on models (continued)

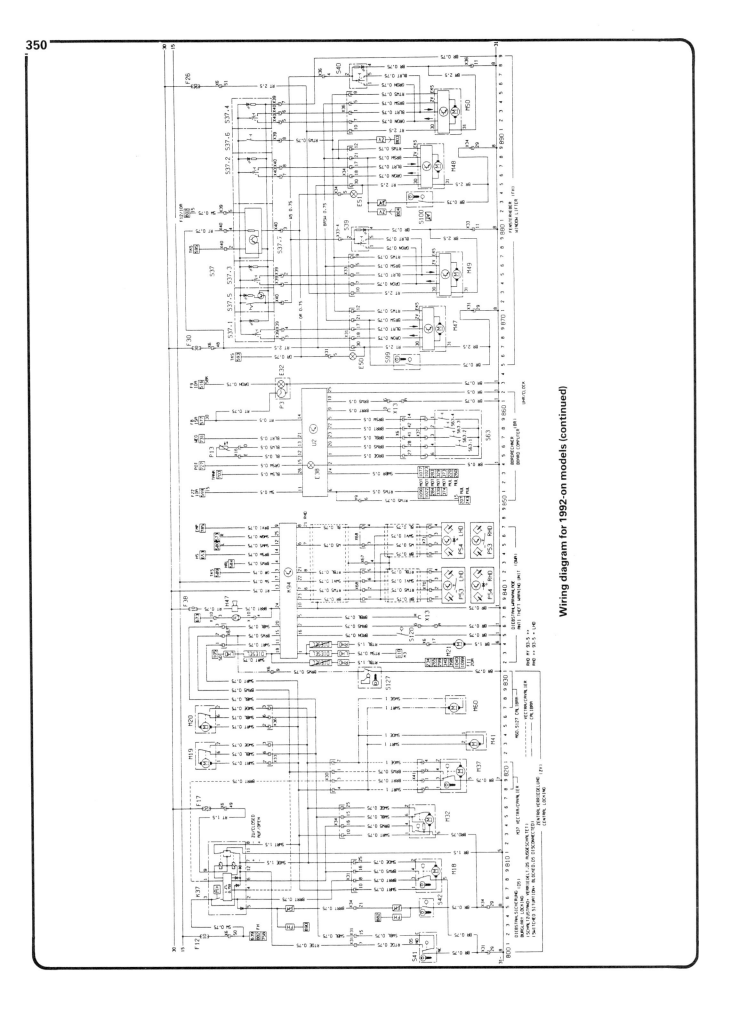

Wiring diagram for 1992-on models (continued)

Wiring diagram for 1992-on models (continued)

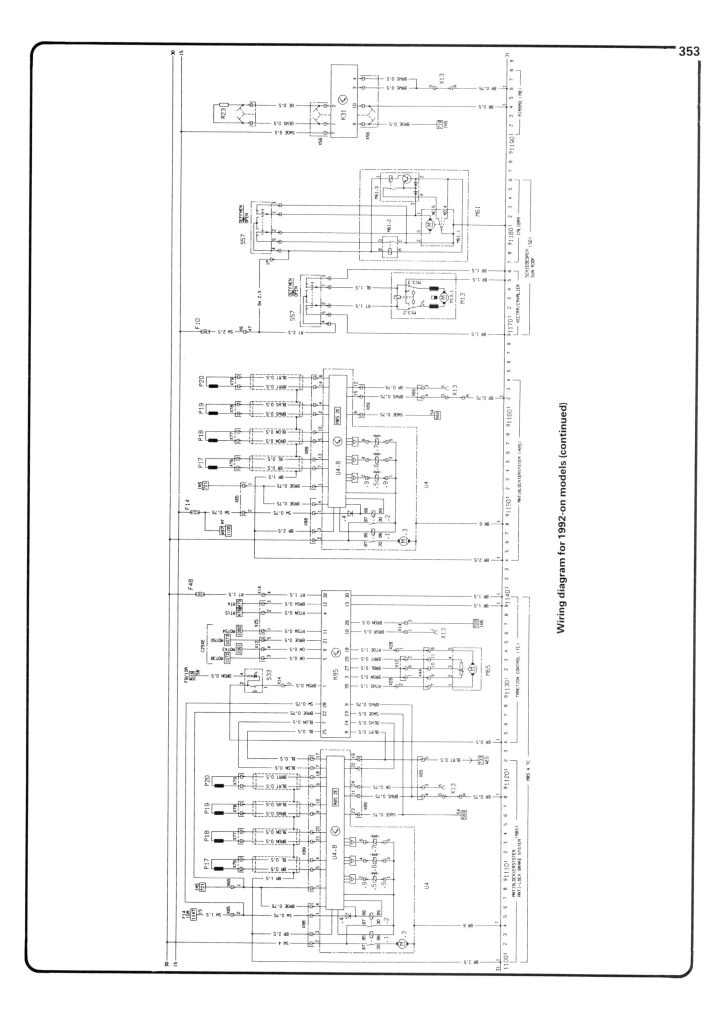

Wiring diagram for 1992-on models (continued)

Index